DOS® 6 Developer's Guide

DOS® 6 Developer's Guide

Jim Kyle

SAMS PUBLISHING

A Division of Prentice Hall Computer Publishing
11711 North College, Carmel, Indiana 46032 USA

FIRST EDITION

International Standard Book Number: 0-672-30291-8

Library of Congress Catalog Card Number: 93-83879

96 95 94 93 4 3 2 1

Interpretation of the printing code: the rightmost double-digit number is the year of the book's printing; the rightmost single-digit, the number of the book's printing. For example, a printing code of 93-1 shows that the first printing of the book occurred in 1993.

Trademarks

All terms mentioned in this book that are known to be trademarks or service marks have been appropriately capitalized. Sams Publishing cannot attest to the accuracy of this information. Use of a term in this book should not be regarded as affecting the validity of any trademark or service mark. DOS is a registered trademark of Microsoft Corporation.

Composed in AGaramond and MCPdigital
by Prentice Hall Computer Publishing

Printed in the United States of America

Publisher

Richard K. Swadley

Associate Publisher

Jordan Gold

Acquisitions Manager

Stacy Hiquet

Acquisitions Editor

Gregory S. Croy

Development Editor

Phillip W. Paxton

Managing Editor

Grant Fairchild

Production Editor

Jill Bond

Editorial Coordinators

Bill Whitmer
James R. Welter II

Editorial Assistants

Sharon Cox
Molly Carmody

Technical Reviewer

Greg Guntle

Marketing Manager

Greg Wiegand

Director of Production and Manufacturing

Jeff Valler

Cover Designer

Dan Armstrong

Imprint Manager

Kelli Widdifield

Book Designer

Michele Laseau

Production Analyst

Mary Beth Wakefield

Proofreading/Indexing Coordinator

Joelynn Gifford

Graphics Image Specialists

Tim Montgomery, Dennis Sheehan
Sue VandeWalle

Production

Claudia Bell, Lisa Daugherty, Terri Edwards, Mitzi Gianakos, Dennis Clay Hager, Carla Hall, Jay Lesandrini, Mike Mucha, Linda Quigley, Michelle Self, Tonya Simpson, Amy Steed, Suzanne Tully, Dennis Wesner, Donna Winter, Lillian Yates, Alyssa Yesh

Indexers

Michael Hughes, Suzanne Snyder, Johnna VanHoose

OVERVIEW

Contents

Part II Your Tools

Part III The Techniques

Part IV Reference Manual

PREFACE

This book is intended for anyone interested in developing software to run under MS-DOS Version 6, regardless of previous experience. A reader who does not already have some knowledge of the tools described in Chapter 3, "Languages, Compilers, Assemblers, and the Like," however, should gain familiarity with them before attempting to apply this material, because full tutorial information about any one of the several tools described would require an entire book in itself.

The word *developer,* as used in this book, means something a bit different from either a *programmer* or an *analyst.* A developer is a person who takes an idea, and develops it into a complete program or application. As such, the developer must first apply all the tools of analysis and design in order to understand the essentials of the idea, and then must change to a programming mindset in order to create the program or application itself. As you shall see, the developer's attention must continually cycle between both these points of view. Neither can be neglected in favor of the other; both are essential to the developer's success.

In many ways, software development is much like the music profession. In music, as in software development, the successful practitioner brings to the performance both originality and technique. Either, alone, isn't enough; both are necessary. Without a solid foundation of skilled technique, the most original ideas fall short of acceptance.

The aim of this book is to show you how to build that foundation of software development technique and to provide you with information on many of the tools you'll use most frequently when developing applications to run under MS-DOS Version 6. The emphasis on tools and techniques, in contrast to the much easier approach of simply listing all MS-DOS and BIOS functions, is what I hope will distinguish this book from the many others available on the shelves.

While mine is the only name appearing on the cover or the title page, this book is actually a collection of ideas picked up over the past 25 years from far too many folk, to name in this space. That's the essence of learning: to collect good ideas wherever they appear, and to retain the best. However, a number of the people I've exchanged techniques with over those years have provided so many ideas, and provoked so many avenues of experimentation, that I want to single them out for special thanks. They include Chris Dunford, author of *PCED* and many other great utilities and one of the forum administrators for the IBMNET group of forums on CompuServe; Dave Angel, whose intimate knowledge of the internals of MS-DOS is matched by few other people; and virtually the entire membership of the *Computer Language Magazine* forum on CompuServe, where I've been the primary forum administrator since 1985.

Also, a special word of thanks to Andy Thomas and Eric Straub of Microsoft, who helped me obtain information in a timely manner about the new MRCI features, to Greg Croy for thinking of me when the subject of a book like this came up, and to the editorial and production staff at Sams.

While all of these people have helped the book come into existence, full responsibility for any errors or omissions in it remains strictly my own; and if you find any, I'd like to know about them so that I can correct them in future editions. Similarly, if you find additional information necessary, drop me a note; that may improve any future versions also. You can reach me on CompuServe at UserID 76703,762 via Cmail, or via the Internet as 76703,762@compuserve.com.

Jim Kyle
Oklahoma City, OK
May, 1993

Section 1: Planning for Success

The starting point for any software developer is to know exactly what is to be developed, and gaining that knowledge requires at least some analysis of the situation.

The two chapters of this section, "Before You Begin" and "Analysis and Design: The Endless Circle," are intended to provide an introduction to the skills needed to perform a useful analysis and to get started on the design of a project in an organized fashion. These two areas appear to be the ones that are the least emphasized in most books on programming, yet without some sort of plan, it's simply impossible to bring any project to successful completion.

Chapter 1, "Before You Begin," deals mainly with the preliminary planning necessary to establish a firm foundation for any project. Chapter 2, "Analysis and Design: The Endless Circle," then concentrates on the activities necessary at the start of any specific project.

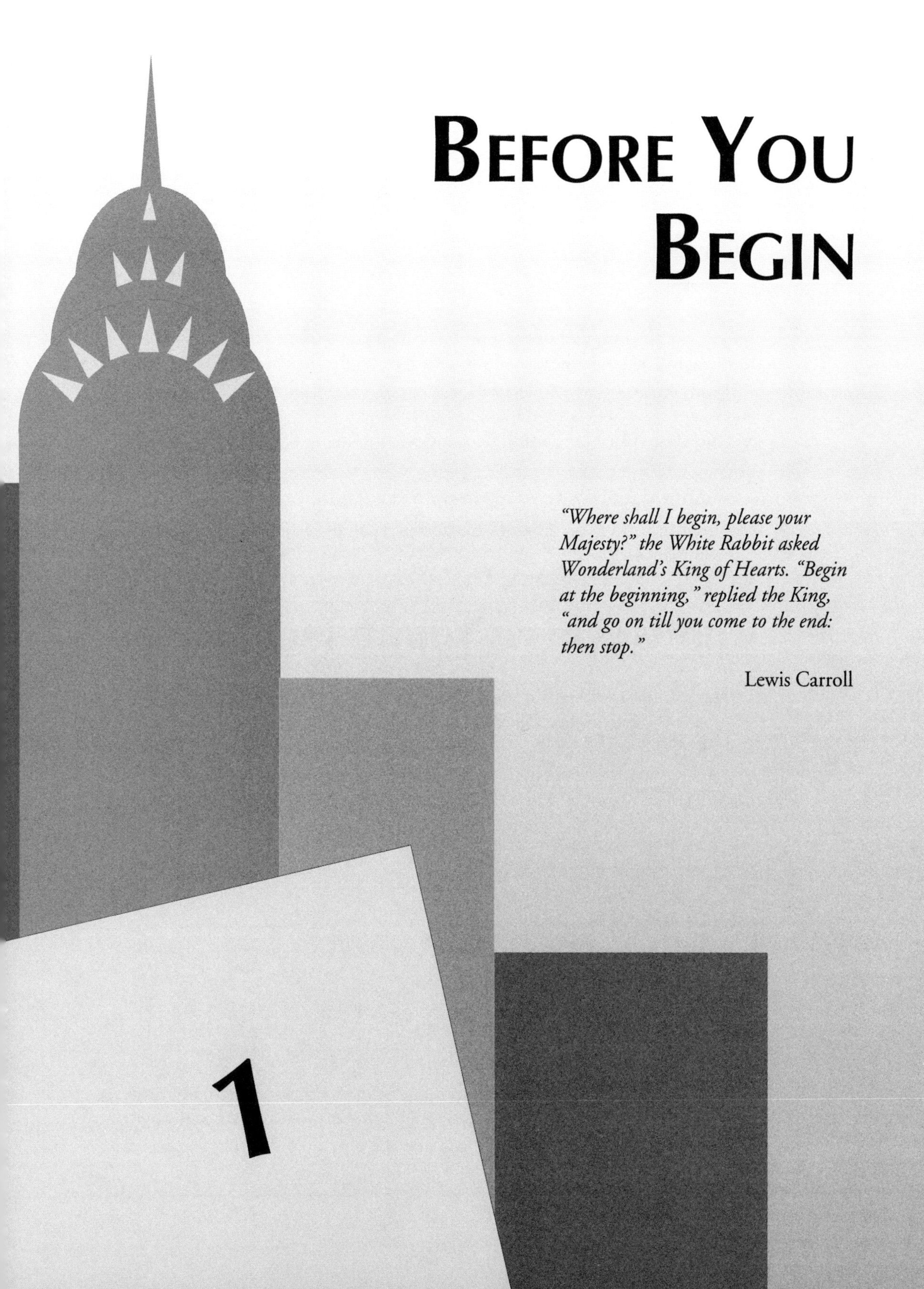

Before You Begin

"Where shall I begin, please your Majesty?" the White Rabbit asked Wonderland's King of Hearts. "Begin at the beginning," replied the King, "and go on till you come to the end: then stop."

Lewis Carroll

1

Lewis Carroll made many contributions to the science of symbolic logic, which was one of the most direct ancestors of our computer industry, but I doubt that any was more relevant than this. Nevertheless, many, if not most, software projects seem never to have a real starting place; far too many of them "hit the ground running" and careen in all directions at once, with no hint of control.

One of the purposes of this book is to help you develop software in a professional manner, whether you do it for fun or for profit. One of the first rules for doing this is to always start each project at a real beginning. This chapter and Chapter 2, "Analysis and Design: The Endless Circle," deal exclusively with techniques for planning your project and establishing exactly what you want it to accomplish.

In this chapter, you learn about the preliminary planning considerations you need to handle, even before any formal analysis of project requirements can commence.

Know Where You're Headed

You can ask any assortment of professional software developers "What's the most important thing to do first?" and you probably will get a different answer from each developer in the group. If, however, you ask them to list the five most important things without ranking just which is which, most of the time "Knowing where you're going" will be in each developer's list.

The reason is simple enough. One of the better expressions of it was set down by the Latin philosopher Seneca: "Our plans miscarry because they have no aim. When a man does not know what harbor he is making for, no wind is the right wind."

Lewis Carroll's Cheshire Cat was more succinct but had the same message when Alice admitted that she didn't care much where she got to: "Then it doesn't matter which way you go." Without a target, you have nothing to guide your development efforts and they will founder like a ship that has lost its rudder. And, like such a ship, they are quite likely to run aground or be lost.

Deciding where you want a project to go sounds simple enough, but most beginning developers, and far too many established professionals, simply ignore the need and charge blindly ahead into the unknown, trusting to instinct to lead them to success. It's much safer to spend a little time drawing out a map so that you can chart your path. The first step of this map-making is to set a single strategic goal for the project. You then can estimate how long it will take you to get there, and can get a preliminary list of the things you are most likely to encounter along the way.

Establishing the Strategic Goal

When you start any project, no matter how small, it's essential to have a clear idea of just why you are doing it: decide what your efforts are to accomplish. Far too many of us tend to have the attitude of "Let's play around a little and see what comes out." I have even succumbed to this temptation myself.

There's nothing wrong with play in itself, and it's a great way to learn the limits of both your knowledge and your tools. When you're "playing" in this respect, however, you're actually working towards the goal of "learning something new" or "having fun" or maybe even "passing time until a client responds," and in all these cases, you really do have a goal for your activity. Knowing what it is cannot hurt, and may help you.

After all, if the goal is "to learn something new," then it's only logical to avoid doing things by the methods you know and use for a short-deadline mission-critical project. Using the old techniques doesn't exercise new methods, and thus does nothing for achieving the goal.

Similarly, if the goal really is to deliver a working accounting system by the end of this month, then you will not want to lose any time trying new tricks. A target of this sort, especially if your groceries depend on hitting the target on schedule, calls for tried-and-true methods you know are going to work first time.

So how do you determine the goal for a project? The first step may seem obvious; however, often it's overlooked. You need to ask yourself, or the person assigning you the task, "Why does this need to be done at all?"

When you ask this question, try to be completely honest in your reply. "Because I need a new program to sell" is a perfectly valid strategic goal, although it says nothing about what that new program should be or do. What it *does* tell you is that you don't really care what the program does, as long as it can be sold, and this in turn dictates that your next actions be directed to finding out what type of program can be sold most easily.

That simple answer has converted your current project from one of developing a program into one of market research to determine what type of program to develop. This puts it outside the scope of this book; however, after you do your homework and decide on a program, you will have both a new project and a strategic goal, and will be back at this same point in the development cycle.

Establishing the strategic goal for a project is the first step of analysis, which is covered in greater detail in Chapter 2, "Analysis and Design: The Endless Circle." Analysis, in itself, is at least as time-consuming a part of software development as is design or implementation, and too often overlooked in the haste to create.

A number of excellent books have been written about this analysis and it's becoming more widely accepted. This book, however, does not explore it in any significant depth.

The immediate concern is that you have a goal for even the smallest task; otherwise, you have no way to determine when you finish it. This goal may change as the task develops, and may spawn sub-tasks and sub-goals along the way, but without it, you're not "developing" a thing. You're just spinning wheels in hopes of getting somewhere.

Scoping Out the Job

After you firmly define a strategic goal for your project, the next step is to scope out the job: you need to determine how large the project is likely to be. Total precision isn't required at this stage of your planning; however, you need to have some idea whether it's a one-person, two-hour task, or a job that will keep half a dozen teams of program designers busy for the next three years.

Granted, the preceding examples are extreme: it makes little sense to spend two days planning out a two-hour task, and if you're working alone, the chances of your taking on a multi-team project are very small. When a potential customer asks if you can perform a particular task, however, you must determine very early (before replying) whether it's within your capabilities. And in this situation, "capabilities" includes the size of the effort.

Constant practice in estimating the complexity of each task you encounter is necessary to become (or remain) a software developer at the professional level. It's similar to being a professional musician: daily practice is necessary to make the performance appear effortless. After you form the habit of scoping out every task, you will be able to give quick estimates more accurately. This in itself gives you a competitive edge.

So how do you go about gaining this skill in estimating project scope? It's done in much the same way that a concert pianist develops skill in fingering rapid arpeggios: by constant, painstaking attention to tedious details.

The starting point is to form the habit of estimating how long each task is going to take you—before you start. Keep notes while you work so that when you complete the job, you actually can see how long it took, and you can compare this with your original estimate.

If you're working for someone else, you may already be doing this for payroll purposes, but in most shops, the "time logs" turned in to the payroll office bear little resemblance to the actual time spent on a project. In addition, the account numbers in which you log time against may cover many tasks rather than single tasks.

Because of this, you probably will find it necessary to keep your own private log, whether you work for yourself or for someone else. The idea is to find out how long your typical tasks actually take.

At first, you may be amazed, and somewhat disappointed, to discover that most tasks really require anywhere between 4 and 20 times as long as you estimated at the outset. This, however, is not unusual. In the software business, it is commonplace for time estimates to be as much as 100 percent in error. MS-DOS Version 6.0 was scheduled originally for release at the end of summer 1992. Version 5.0 was almost 6 months later reaching the shelves than its last published "revised" schedule promised. Inability to accurately estimate how long the job will actually take nearly is universal in this industry, so if you're in a 50 percent margin of error in your initial attempts, you're far better than average.

Identifying Sub-Tasks and Sub-Goals

For any project other than the very simplest ones, you probably will find that identifying the strategic goal for the job still leaves plenty of questions yet to be answered about how to get to that goal. This is because all but the most simple of tasks are built up of many sub-tasks, each of which has its own goal to be reached, and those sub-tasks in turn have their own building blocks.

If this sounds as if the job of goal identification will never be done, thus making it impossible to ever start a project, you're beginning to get the idea. A couple thousand years ago a Greek philosopher named Xeno realized that motion involved a progression through successive points in order to reach a destination, and posed a puzzle that some folk cite to this day in an effort to prove that motion is not logically possible.

Briefly, the point of Xeno's argument was that because one first had to cross half of the distance to the goal, then cross half of the remaining distance, and so on, proved that there would always be some infinite distance remaining. It's not possible to reduce a value to zero by continually cutting it in half, no matter how long you try, because half of "something" is still "something" and can never be reduced to "nothing" regardless of how tiny it might eventually become.

Xeno's paradox, however, simply proved that he was looking at the situation from the wrong point of view, not that it's impossible to get anywhere. Similarly, the need to identify sub-tasks in the process of pinning down your strategic goal doesn't require that you spend an infinite amount of time trying to identify every separate action needed to finish the job.

What this does mean is that you should note down any bits and pieces, (that is, the sub-tasks in their raw forms) as they occur to you during the process of spotting the real strategic goal.

Identifying the goal makes it possible for you to know when you reach it, and thus complete the task. Identifying the sub-tasks along the way gives you valuable pointers to progressing toward the final target. Collecting the random ideas that spring into your head as you study the situation enable you to identify those sub-tasks a bit easier.

It is important to note that, in practice, putting this description down on paper makes it seem much more formal than it really needs to be; thus, after you identify the strategic goal, you actually can brainstorm to collect information that can be useful along the development path. Your notes need be nothing more elaborate than memory joggers scribbled on index cards or yellow post-it notes. (I frequently sketch out ideas on scrap sheets of fanfold paper ripped from program listings that are always in abundant supply on my desk.)

After you identify a strategic goal, a preliminary estimate of the time it will take to get there, and a sheaf of ideas about what the sub-tasks are likely to be, you should have a pretty good idea where the task is going. Now you're ready to address the second major part of your initial planning, and learn why you're taking the trip.

Know Why You're Going

To succeed in your project, regardless of what it might be, you must be aware of everything that can influence the way you view the task ahead. This means that you must look at your own motivations, at the way the project will affect the rest of your time, and at everything else that might have any effect. Remember that this study is not judgmental in that there is no best or worst facet; you just need to be aware of all significant factors so that you can come by all decisions along the path honestly.

Three major questions can help you know why you're doing this. First, ask yourself what is the major motivation both for the project, and for your part in it if that might be different. With that established, ask how the priorities of the project are set and how they may interact with your non-project activities. Finally, ask how the future is likely to bring change to the project, if it is anything more than a rapid one-time task.

What's the Motivation?

Knowing the motivation for a project is essential whether it's your own personal idea being done for fun, or a mission-critical task on which your employer's future might depend. In fact, it's not too strong a statement to say that without honest, strong motivation, no project can possibly succeed.

In many cases, the project's motivation and your own personal reason for being part of it may be identical. When you're developing one of your own ideas as a solo effort, the two are almost always the same. The only time the motivations are likely to be different is when you're working for someone else, and are assigned a task you did not originate or suggest.

In order to handle the situations when the two motivations do differ, however, the following discussion assumes that they are different. If only one set applies to your situation, it's up to you to blend the differences together.

The total motivation for the project usually is established by the person or entity putting up the capital to finance it, whether it be the employer or the client. It can be as simple and direct as "let's do something that can be profitable" or as idealistic as "we can really advance the state of the art with this one."

You probably will find it impossible, however, to get your management or clients to enunciate the motivation that clearly. In many cases, you will need to ask many diplomatic questions to uncover the real reasons for the project's existence.

Other times, motivation is much easier to uncover. If your client's data storage system has just gone over the hill and the backup disks have turned out to be unreadable, motivation for the project of deciphering the format used by those backup disks and recovering the data is fairly obvious. Don't waste your time looking for hidden reasons when the obvious explanation is perfectly adequate.

The second motivation about which you need to be fully informed concerns your own reasons for being involved. This can be as simple and blunt as "keeping my job" or as emotion-laden and driving as "to salvage my last week's work."

Whatever your reasons, the idea is to be fully honest with yourself about why you're doing what you are doing so you are not led astray by false assumptions. You do not need to put these factors on paper or to tell anyone else about them; they're totally for your own guidance as a developer.

The reason for emphasizing such introspective points as "motivation" is that you will find it absolutely necessary to "buy into" the main motivator for the job in order to do your best work. If you find serious conflict between the project's driving force and your own personal motivating factors, you will be far better off not getting involved in the first place.

Establishing Priorities

With motivation established, the next step is to determine the sequence in which the sub-tasks identified earlier can be tackled. It is pointless, for example, to wrestle with the details of program output routines until you determine the type of output devices to be supported; however, traps of this sort often capture unwary developers eager to "get to work" and start producing code.

Before setting priorities within the project, you should determine if any non-project conflicts exist. If they do, they can be project-killers.

Non-Project Conflicts

If you are developing software as an independent programmer-for-hire and have at least partial control over your assignments, it's important that your initial project plans recognize and deal with non-project priorities. Even though they may be intensely personal in nature, they're going to have significant impact on your professional performance, and honesty demands that you account for this in your planning from the very start of any project. It's equally important, of course, even if you cannot control your assignments, but it's less likely that you will be able to do as much about them.

While in every case, you have to reach your own personal resolution of conflict situations and then proceed as you see fit, you first must be aware of its existence in order to factor it into your project plan. In order for your plan to be realistic, every non-project conflict must be factored in, and if possible resolved, before setting any schedules.

Project Priorities

The first priority, after you establish a goal and resolve any potential conflicts it may involve, is to sit down and think about it for a while. Avoid the ever-present temptation to dive right in and get to work writing code.

No one is immune to this tendency. Even though more than 25 years of experience in programming mainframes, minicomputers, and micro systems have taught me this, occasionally I still tend to fall victim to this temptation, especially for a "quick and dirty" project. Every time I do, however, I find myself forced to fall back, regroup my thoughts, and figure out an approach that's likely to work.

Now you must evaluate your progress. You know you have a strategic goal and that no unresolved non-project conflicts exist; however, many other important factors still remain to be discovered, such as the following:

- What do the end users of the program want it to do?
- What are the major cost constraints?
- What type of equipment will the program run on?
- How much time will it take to complete the project?

Before you actually can begin a design, you must answer these questions. Chapter 2, "Analysis and Design: The Endless Circle," discusses this in deeper detail. For now, however, you need to establish the most basic priorities for the project.

You first must determine what the end users actually need the program to do, without being overly concerned about how to solve those problems.

After you make a first-pass analysis of requirements, you can sketch out a preliminary design that suggests possible solutions. Before moving ahead to actually writing any code, however, it's best to obtain opinions of the users to verify the accuracy of the analysis, and the adequacy of the proposed design.

You may spend nearly as much time analyzing as you do writing code; however, every false start you eliminate during this step represents that much code you will not have to throw away later. Planning is much less work than coding.

The fourth priority is the actual writing of code from the semi-final design. Even though you put forth your best efforts in the design stage, you're still likely to find that some redesign is necessary while coding the program; however, because of your planning, the redesign time should be much less.

Finally, you must verify that the completed program meets all the identified requirements. If it does, your initial version will be complete; however, it's a rare application that fails to undergo significant change in requirements between the original analysis and the final testing. Because this happens so often, you will be safest to allow as much time as possible for the test-and-rework activity before you schedule first deliveries.

Creating a Route Map

After you identify your project's original list of priorities, you can create your first route map and assign estimated dates to each step. This serves the same purpose as using a road map when traveling: it helps you decide where you are now, and where you want to go from here.

The biggest advantage of the route map at this point is that it enables you to assign times to specific sub-tasks. As you identify the various sub-tasks involved in the "analysis" area, for example, you can add them to your map, and assign tentative start and finish dates to each.

While these target dates on the schedule often are called "milestones" by managers, especially those who believe that project management can be mechanized rather than being an art, you will get more good out of them if you make them small and close together on the calendar so that you can think of them as "inch-pebbles." Make the measurement points so close together that you cannot go far astray between them, and so small that little time is necessary to verify that they have been reached. If every inch-pebble is met satisfactorily, so will all the major milestones.

Preserving the Plan for Posterity

After you create your route map, with specific inch-pebbles of action noted so that you can keep track of your progress as you proceed, take a little time to make a permanent record of it. To do this, you can create a project-plan file on your development system, where it will be easily available for reference as your project continues.

If you have a word processing program with outlining capability, use it to create the draft plan. If you don't have outline capability, get a word processing program that contains one. It's possibly the most valuable tool you can own in the early stages of program development.

Outlining capability is valuable because as your planning continues, matures into analysis, and finally becomes the design of your application, you frequently will need to move chunks of the effort from their original positions in the sequence to some other position in the plan.

Outlining tools make this shuffling of items extremely simple. Any other technique is cumbersome, at best, and the details of accomplishing the move may get in the way and prevent you from concentrating on the really important question: where should this item go?

How About the Future?

Before looking at such implementation details as the platforms to be supported or the tools to be used, you should consider what the project's future is likely to involve. What potential exists for upgrading the project after your initial delivery is complete? Will this program be a one-shot quick-and-dirty effort, or will it become the cornerstone of your work for years to come?

Future upgrading refers to possible ways to use the current project as a foundation for future growth on they same types of systems rather than moving the package to alternate platforms.

Even if the initial plan indicates no need for, or desirability of, ever upgrading the application, it's a subject you should examine. Most programs, like most automobile models, undergo annual revisions, even if it's no more than a change in the location of the chrome trim. For commercial developers, it can be the basis for continued ongoing cash flow.

Even though upgrades have become, in the eyes of many folk, a marketing tool, they actually serve useful purposes. When user requirements change too late in the schedule for the new ones to make it into your program, for example, the necessary new functions can be added via the upgrade route.

Similarly, time or budget constraints that prevent total solutions to the problem in the first version can be overcome by implementing only the most essential parts of the solution at the original release, and then issuing upgrades to bring in those parts left out initially.

And of course, as technical advances continue to make improved system performance possible on an almost daily timetable, you're quite likely to find that periodic upgrades of your program are necessary just to keep pace with the new performance possibilities as they become available.

Consider all these factors before ruling out upgrade potential for your program. Even if it turns out that no upgrade is expected to be necessary, it doesn't hurt to put things together in such a manner that it will not be difficult to add features, should this decision ever change.

If it's definite that no upgrade will ever be done, then you also must take much greater care in everything you do while developing the application, because you will be, in effect, walking the high wire with no net to catch you in case of a misstep. Don't ever believe it when the user, or the boss, insists that this is only a quick-and-dirty one-time thing that will not ever be used again. Those programs are the ones that remain in use the longest!

Know What You're Taking Along

Choose a platform, anticipate the inevitability of constant change, and then choose the weapons with which you will battle the monsters of unwritten programs. Those three things are all that remain between you and the real beginning of your project. The following sections look at each a bit more closely.

Defining the Platform

Multi-platform programming tends to be a buzzword this year, presumably meaning that developers are expected to create programs capable of equal performance on such diverse platforms as regular MS-DOS, Windows, OS/2, and possibly UNIX. Unfortunately, that "equal" performance often turns out, in practice, to mean that all versions of the program perform equally poorly.

While this book focuses exclusively on the development of software for use with MS-DOS, and concentrates on the use of DOS Version 6.0, that doesn't mean that your design is restricted to only this system. After you put in the necessary effort to analyze your users' requirements and work out solutions to their problems, you don't need to go through it all again when the fickle users decide to move to a different system.

The essential things that permit you to keep most of your programming intact should a move be required are to (a) anticipate the possibility of migration (moving the application to some other system, such as OS/2, the Macintosh, or UNIX, for example) from the very beginning of your planning, and (b) concentrate on restricting to the smallest part of the program any possible effects that might result from a system change. Then, should the application ever move to another platform, only that small part will need modification.

To anticipate the possibility of migration, you need to identify every part of the problem that might be dependent in any way on the specific system in use. Your users, for example, may want to include interactive use of drag-and-drop mouse features as part of the application. Doing so, however, will rule out moving the program to any system that does not include hardware support for pointing devices.

Similarly, it's impossible to take an application that depends on all-points-addressable graphics displays that are widely available in the MS-DOS environment, such as everyday computer graphics displays like the VGA, and move it to a system that uses only "dumb terminals" with no graphics capability for user interfacing.

Portability doesn't always involve moving the entire system. Sometimes only a part of the hardware needs changing. The original color displays available to

MS-DOS machines, for example, provided only 16 cartoon-like colors. Later video subsystems extended this to 256 colors, and now newer systems with more than 32,000 hues or even 16 million colors are making their appearance.

In these cases, too, keeping all hardware-dependent parts of your package "quarantined" into the smallest possible area will ease the impact when you find it necessary to support different equipment. To accomplish this, however, you must never lose sight of the problems portability implies.

In order not to miss any critical details, this is something you need to fix firmly in mind from the very start of each project. Each aspect of every requirement must be examined for the possibility that it may affect portability. When the time comes that a move is necessary (and such a time will come eventually if your program gains any degree of success) you will be very happy you did this.

Check Your Crystal Ball

"The only constant," someone once observed, "is change itself." Nowhere is this quite so true, I suspect, as in the craft of software development. Every developer should invest in a top-grade crystal ball as the first working requirement, but so far I have yet to find one that has enough accuracy to be effective in preventing me from getting unpleasant surprises nearly every day.

So I've become resigned to the fact that constant change is simply unavoidable, and turned my attention to finding ways to deal with it adequately and at the same time minimizing its disruption of my carefully prepared plans.

The most effective rule for dealing with this situation that I have discovered yet is never to paint myself into a corner. I try to make all my decisions leaving the maximum amount of freedom possible for dealing with any change that might happen in the future.

I try to keep all lists of features open-ended, so that new ones can be added when it becomes necessary. Similarly, I try to make all routines include "none of the above" default options, even when they actually don't do anything, to permit expansion in directions that nobody anticipated in advance. And I try to make each and every module I design as reusable as possible, so that I can easily grab a feature from an existing program and add it to the latest one.

I still don't know how to predict the changes the future is certain to bring my way, but by building safety pads into all my existing material, I've made it much easier to deal with it when it does arrive. I highly recommend that you do the same in your own development. The payoff is much greater than the original cost, which is small because programs that follow this approach also are much easier to produce and have a better chance of working right with minimum rework.

Experience indicates that after you develop an item and release it to its users, the users will invent ways of using it that you, as the developer, find unbelievable. If your design encourages this, you're more likely to have a successful product. And if you design your applications with an eye to keeping out of trouble, most of the time, you will get just such a design as a by-product.

Deciding on Your Tools

Chapter 3, "Languages, Compilers, Assemblers, and the Like," discusses your tools and how to decide which of them to use. When you get to the bottom line, however, after all the discussion, one fact should be clear: the tool you need to use is dependent on the project requirements, and vice versa.

The more tools you know how to use, the more choices will be open to you for any specific task. And the more different types of tasks you take on, the more tools you need to become familiar with. A developer who restricts all efforts to the construction and maintenance of databases may spend an entire career without ever using any tool other than a versatile database management system, but one who deals with a variety of projects will find it worthwhile to become familiar with an equally wide assortment of tools.

The *Turing principle*, proved as an exercise in logical thinking by computer pioneer Alan Turing long before computers were invented, indicates that any system which meets certain primitive requirements can do anything that can be done with any other system meeting those same requirements, although the time necessary to do so may vary widely between the two systems. The requirements are so few, too, that virtually every computer in existence today meets them.

That means, for example, that you can do anything that's possible on a Cray supercomputer, using only your palmtop portable. It may take the small machine a few thousand years to accomplish what the big one would do in a few milliseconds, but in theory at least, it's *possible*.

The same principle applies to most language tools. Our hypothetical database specialist could, if necessary, write an entire operating system using only the DBMS tools already known; however, it may take many years to do so, and it may perform with agonizing lack of speed when completed. While just about anything may be *possible* in this business, that doesn't mean it's always *practical* also.

If I leave you only one clear thought from this discussion, it should be this: If you want to become a well-rounded developer, don't fall into the common trap that when you have only a hammer, everything looks like a nail. There's no single "best" tool, not even for a single kind of task. We have only tools for a job that are more suitable rather than less suitable; thus, a developer needs to have a variety of available tools.

The early "mountain men" survived fierce winters with few tools other than an axe and a knife. Today's handyman may own a small assortment of carpentry and plumbing tools to help him cope with the complexities of modern living. A master cabinetmaker, for example, will collect a shop filled with highly specialized tools, each of which may do only one thing, but does that one thing to near perfection.

In all these examples, each individual has all the tools needed to deal with the tasks at hand. Your programming progress can follow these models.

- If you need programming tools only to survive in the wilderness of some other career, you can emulate the mountain man and carry the least amount of luggage that's necessary to meet your goal.
- If you aspire to be a journeyman developer, which is in itself adequate to put you near the top of the programming ranks, you need only a small set of tools.
- If, however, your professional goal is to become a programming virtuoso, you will never stop collecting tools, nor will you begrudge the time you spend practicing with them constantly as you seek to master every aspect of each one. A lifetime is too short to reach this goal, but the pursuit is, in and of itself, well worth undertaking.

Chapter 2 deals with techniques for analyzing the problems the project presents, and for designing a workable solution based on the outcome of your analysis.

2

Analysis and Design: The Endless Circle

I used to have a cast-metal trivet hanging on the wall over my desk that proclaimed: "Blessed are they who go around in circles, for they shall be known as The Big Wheels." I always felt it was appropriate, because I seem to spend a large part of my development hours going around in circles.

That's not entirely due to confusion on my part, either, although I must admit that things aren't always as clear as they might be (or as I try to make them look in these pages).

A large part of the reason for my circular journey through the development jungle is that two of the most essential and time-consuming parts of the whole process, *analysis* and *design,* actually form a repeated sequence similar to the mathematical technique known as *successive approximation.*

The repeated-sequence approximation method isn't unique to mathematics or to software design. The idea is quite basic: start with your best guess, and then see how far it misses the mark. The actual distance isn't important, but the direction of the miss is. Then you try a correction that's guaranteed to miss again, but on the other side.

From there, you fall into the sequence; however, each time you cut the size of the correction factor in half. Even if you miss by a mile with the first shot, it takes only half a dozen corrections to bring you within a hundred feet of the target, which is usually close enough to do the job.

It works the same way when doing program design. First, you use all the tools and techniques you know to get the best handle you can on the problem to be tackled. Next, you create a preliminary design based on your understanding of the problem.

Before doing any coding, however, bring your preliminary design back to the people who will use your product, and ask them to tell you how close you have come to the real target: their needs.

Most of the time, you will find that your initial attempt is far from the bull's eye, unless you happen to be dealing with a problem you have already worked with in the past (in which case this isn't really a first-pass design, but a rework based on everything you learned from previous problems). That's okay, because the real reason for the review at this stage is to find out how far your first try missed, and in what direction.

Getting the answers to those two questions takes you out of design and back to the analysis phase, but you now have better information as to what the real problem is. It hardly ever bears much resemblance to the way the users originally described it to you; however, because you now know where the differences are, you can analyze the needs that much more accurately. Then come up with a revised design, based on the new, more accurate, analysis, and return for another review by the users.

The process can go on forever because in the time it takes you to do the analysis and create your revised design, at least some of the user requirements will change again. Fortunately, it seldom takes more than three or four times around the circle to finalize a design at least enough so that you can really start coding from that design.

As you code and test your program, requirements will continue to change, so you will find yourself putting your analysis cap back on time and time again as the project continues. If you don't, you will have major problems at delivery time.

Because analysis, to some degree, must continue throughout the life of a project, many would-be developers want to ignore it and get "right to work" generating code. "Why waste time?" they ask. "Especially because we'll do it over and over again anyway?"

The answer, simply enough, is that going through enough preliminary analysis and design to ensure that you're solving the real problem is never a waste of time. By stopping you from charging off in the wrong direction, it actually saves you time in the long run. And this is true even if you, yourself, will be the only user of the program you are designing.

A Place to Start: What's the Problem?

One place to start in the endless circle of analysis and design is to simply ask (either yourself, or a typical user of the program-to-be) "What is the problem this package is going to solve?" This approach assumes that you or the user actually knows the real problem at hand. In practice, this assumption is seldom valid and is never safe.

Even if the assumption is valid, assumptions always are dangerous to build foundations on. It is much better practice to verify every assumption before spending much effort building a design based on them.

In the case of program development, you can test the assumption by repeatedly asking the question of different potential users, and comparing their answers. If you find a high level of similarity between the responses, this indicates increased probability that the replies really are valid.

It's still possible, however, even with a large number of similar responses, to discover down the way that you have been working on the wrong problem after all, simply because none of the people you interviewed up front really understood the full situation.

A Factory Management System That Failed

A major manufacturer of computer peripherals, where I spent nearly 25 years of my career, controlled its entire manufacturing process for many years with a home-grown management information system running on a huge mainframe. Over this period, however, the system had grown cumbersome as new requirements were patched in piecemeal.

The plant manager eventually decided that it was time for a modern manufacturing control system. To avoid past problems, he decreed that the new system would be an off-the-shelf commercial product, capable of running on a minicomputer system located within the factory building rather than at a remote site as was the original mainframe.

In order to select the right system from the dozen or so that were available off the shelf, he formed a task force of senior staff personnel. Most of them were managers who had little day-to-day contact with the existing system other than to scan over the thousand-page reports it produced every Monday morning.

After a year of study, the task force narrowed the field down to two candidates. Both firms promised to create reports of equal or greater detail, and both allowed for a large number of terminals to be connected so that even better tracking could be performed. In addition, one of them promised to integrate all order entry, inventory control, shipping, and accounting activities. And the costs for the two finalists were approximately the same.

The task force unanimously recommended purchase of the most elaborate of the finalists. One of the deciding factors, in addition to the extra bells and whistles available, was its capability to generate custom reports on demand that could show virtually anything a manager wanted to see.

No one, however, thought to ask certain critical questions about the system's processing capabilities. Not until all the hardware was in place, all the records were converted to the new system, and we were far past the point of no return, did anyone discover that the fancy new system took more than 24 hours of continuous (and exclusive) processing to create a single work order for a new assembly to start down the production line, although our business requirements demanded that at least a dozen new assemblies start down each of three production lines each and every working day.

Similarly, the reports that looked so beautiful to the task force required an entire weekend of processing to generate. The new system, quite simply, didn't have the horsepower for the job.

It turned out that all the successes cited by the vendor had been much smaller companies, with far fewer parts in each assembly built and much less variety in their product lines. Had the task force asked the right questions, to verify that the data they saw actually applied to an operation of our size, they might have avoided the disaster. But most of their questions dealt only with report generation capabilities.

By the time I was transferred to the project to try to keep it running, it was beyond salvation. In order to maintain the production schedule, the floor managers had been "working around" the system, keeping records on scraps of paper with hopes of somehow making the books come out right in the end.

As a result, replacement supplies were not getting ordered on time, so delays of up to a week waiting for new parts to be shipped in by air from distant suppliers at premium charges became common. And because nothing could be shipped or billed in the absence of a valid work order, the accountants also were forced to fake it by hand. The books were out of balance by millions of dollars.

At that point, corporate management stepped in. Nearly every member of the task force was booted out the door. Most of the managers who had kept production going by cheating the system were fired. Drastic reductions in force cost many others (including me) their jobs. Finally, the plant manager suddenly found himself unemployed. A new study began, and as of this writing, a replacement system (this time based on networked PCs) is being implemented to save the business.

So what does this sad story have to do with developing software for PC applications? Simply this: no matter what the experience of the people you get information from, be wary of their responses. You don't have to be openly skeptical, but be sure to always cut the cards after the shuffle and before the deal.

Now, the Positive Side of the Story

Despite the preceding example, it is always necessary to try to find a valid answer to the question "What's the problem?" Without at least a hazy understanding of the precise problem with which you are dealing, you have no way to know whether you have solved it.

Another way of saying the same thing is "If you don't know where you're going, you can't tell when you get there." Failure to stop when the job is finished is one of the endemic ailments among software developers, both amateur and professional. So, despite the dangers of placing too much trust in the answer, you must always try to state the problem before you try to solve it.

To balance the previous gloomy picture, following is an example to show how this approach can be helpful.

When this book was in its earliest planning stages, all of us (writer, editor, and publisher) agreed that each chapter dealing with actual program techniques must include at least one interesting, meaningful example program to illustrate the major points addressed in that chapter. These programs can be found on the companion diskette that accompanies the book.

That requirement, in itself, seems clear enough; however, for each chapter involved it created a separate problem to be solved by the example program of that chapter: How can these techniques be clearly illustrated and at the same time have an interesting and useful program?

Because each chapter deals with separate groups of techniques in both BIOS and DOS, each chapter has its own detailed problem. This illustration concentrates on just one chapter's sample. Chapter 7, "Console I/O," which deals with Console Input and Output, is the first one that actually requires a sample program.

First you examine the general requirements that apply to all the chapter examples. Only then do you look at those requirements that are specific to the techniques to be illustrated for a specific chapter.

General Requirements

For a first cut at discovering the *general requirements*, that is to say, the primary purpose for the program's existence in the first place, break the phrase "interesting, meaningful example program" apart into single items:

1. *Interesting.* In context, this requirement says that our samples must, as a minimum, avoid boring you as you read them, but it doesn't go to the other extreme and demand that they have the suspense of a Tom Clancy action novel either.

2. *Meaningful.* This requirement says that each sample program must have at least some real-world utility. Without an actual purpose to be served, no program can be considered to be meaningful. To define *meaningful* by contrast, the classic `Hello, World` program that appears in so many language tutorials is the absolute antithesis of "meaningful" because its only reason for existence is to illustrate a few programming techniques. A meaningful program, on the other hand, exists to solve a real problem although it may actually have been written to demonstrate techniques.

3. *Example.* This requirement means that the sample program should illustrate all major items discussed in its chapter or sub-chapter. While it's possible that some chapters may cover such diverse topics that no single program could illustrate them all and still meet the requirements that it be meaningful and interesting, if I do my organizational tasks properly and select topics so that they are coherent, the possibility should never actually occur.

   Only those three general requirements existed in the initial task definition, but in fact a fourth requirement exists, dictated by the details of how we humans learn things.

4. No sample should use any techniques that have not already been discussed, so far as this is possible. Attempting to adhere totally to this requirement would make it impossible to meet the other three, because meaningful and interesting subjects aren't always as clearly organized as the outline of a manuscript, but no example should depend totally on things that are still mysteries when you first encounter it.

Specific Requirements

Now that you have a list of four general requirements that may apply to each of the sample programs to be developed, look ahead to Chapter 7 and see how each of these four might translate into more specific needs.

Because Chapter 7 covers the basic techniques for keyboard input and CRT display, any sample program for it needs to exercise all the various input methods and display routines described. In accordance with the fourth general requirement, the example cannot do very much else that requires the use of functions described only in later chapters, such as writing output to disk or examining files.

With such severe restrictions on just what the sample program will be permitted to do, it might seem nearly impossible to create one that also is interesting and meaningful while meeting the third general requirement. I feel safe in assuming that this was the reason the `Hello World` example was initially introduced, and also why it became so popular that it is now a tradition.

The problem, however, is not impossible to solve. Throughout your career as a developer, for example, you're likely to keep referring to tables of ASCII codes. Because of this, a program to display the ASCII code corresponding to any key that was pressed would definitely be meaningful and might even be made interesting.

The only problem with a simple table-display program of this type is that it might not be capable of meeting the third general requirement because it would use only a few of the many techniques described in Chapter 7.

Because you now know at least one way to meet each of the other requirements, ask again, "What's the problem?" With the problem now reduced to that of meeting the third general requirement, the next step is to list the techniques that this third requirement demands be illustrated:

1. Keyboard input, waiting for a keystroke and then echoing it to the CRT.
2. Keyboard input, waiting for a keystroke but not echoing it to the CRT.
3. Keyboard input, waiting, no echo, not checking for Control-C.
4. Keyboard input, without waiting if no key is pressed.
5. Keyboard input of an entire string of characters terminated by enter, with function-key editing controls.
6. Keyboard input of an entire string, without any editing capability.
7. Checking keyboard status without reading any keystrokes.
8. Emptying keyboard buffer, and then performing one of the other input-with-wait actions.
9. BIOS equivalents for many of the preceding eight DOS functions.

10. CRT display of single characters via DOS functions with checking for Control-C and automatic translation of tab characters and CR/LF action.
11. CRT display of single characters via DOS functions without checking or translation.
12. CRT display of entire strings of characters via DOS (two functions available for this, both equivalent in actions but one cannot display a dollar sign).
13. CRT cursor control via DOS and ANSI.SYS.
14. CRT color control via DOS and ANSI.SYS.
15. CRT display of single characters via BIOS functions.
16. CRT cursor control via BIOS.
17. CRT color control via BIOS.
18. Control-C and Control-Break checking.
19. The IOCTL capabilities of character devices.
20. Single-character input from the AUX device (usually COM1 serial port).
21. Single-character output to the AUX device.
22. Single-character output to the printer.

Of these 22 techniques, only the first 12 could be demonstrated and illustrated adequately by the keycode table-lookup program already suggested. Making this list, however, leads to some other ideas, discussed later in this chapter.

Finding the Answer

In the case of the programs for this book, I found that asking myself questions proved to be adequate to specify my initial targets. No end-user feedback was possible or required. Later in this chapter, we return to the Chapter 7 example and see how a better (though still not totally complete) solution evolved. But first, look at an alternate technique, which can help you start planning when you cannot determine an acceptable target just by asking.

Another Starting Place: Inputs and Outputs

All too often, those who eventually will be using your program simply aren't available for extensive questioning, or don't want to "waste time" trying to tell you their requirements. Many users consider it part of the developer's duties to determine the requirement details; they just want to give you a rough outline of their problem, and have you take it from there to a successful solution.

While it's difficult, if not impossible, to reach a completely successful solution to any problem if you cannot get timely feedback from the people who really know the problem's details, there's a fairly simple trick you can use to get started toward a solution. Just collect two lists, one that tells you all available input data, and the other that specifies all the outputs the users want to obtain.

If you have a whiteboard handy, use it for your lists, because you will be wiping away many false starts as you get things moving. Otherwise, get an ample supply of scratch paper and a couple of soft pencils. There's no need to try to make things neat while exploring. You can polish everything after you get an accurate handle on probable requirements.

Arrange your list in two columns; one for *inputs* that your program can count on having, and the other holding *outputs* that your program will need to generate. Don't be concerned about matching up inputs and outputs. That comes a bit later.

After you list everything of which you're personally aware, try to get a few of your eventual users to look over the lists to see whether you missed anything significant. It's certain that as your efforts proceed, you will find that you did indeed leave out major details, but the more complete you can make the lists at this stage, the closer to adequate your resulting plan will become.

After you complete the two lists, look at the output column one item at a time and draw lines from that item to each item in the input list that contributes to the creation of the output item. At this point, you will find it helpful to color-code the connecting lines, with a different shade for each output item's connections.

If, while doing this, you find that you need something that doesn't appear in the list of inputs, add the new requirement to a new list of "intermediate items" and connect it to the associated output entry. If the new requirement actually is an available input you failed to think of originally, just add it to the list of input items rather than to the intermediate list.

After you connect all the output items to their associated input items and to any added intermediate entries, repeat the previous step for the list of intermediate items. Again, if you cannot reasonably obtain the intermediate entry from any of the existing inputs, add the data required to do so to another, new, second-level list of intermediates.

Do this until all the outputs and all the intermediate items as well are connected to input data. What you have as a result is a first draft of your project plan in terms of required outputs and available inputs.

If you find that you have any unconnected input items at this point, take it as a possible danger signal that may be warning you that the output list isn't really complete. It may also simply mean, however, that some of the items identified as potential inputs really don't provide anything to help generate your necessary output. If this is the case, just erase them from the list; however, first make absolutely certain that you're not erasing an early warning signal.

Before trying to translate the spiderweb of list items and colored connecting lines into a program design, take the time to group related things together in a new, cleaned-up layout.

You probably will find that some input items connect to many different output requirements. If you move all those output items to adjacent positions in your tables, you will find it easier to see the connections.

Similarly, you probably found it necessary to add several intermediate columns off to the side (because the original pair of lists didn't leave room between the columns for any additions). Again, it will be easier to see relationships if you put these columns in between the input-items column and the output column.

And again, if at all possible, ask your end users or clients to review your list before you move ahead. It's much less difficult to fix problems at this point in development than it will ever be again on the current project. Without accurate feedback as you go, your chances of success are slim, and none.

Getting from Here to There

The next step is to learn how to convert input and output information into an outline of your program or system by building bridges out of programs. Such bridges form the bedrock beneath the much-hyped *HIPO* (hierarchical input processing output) design method that some consider to be the epitome of structured programming and design. Those who hold this belief, however, often tend to be unaware that design and programming are significantly different parts of the development process.

To see how this bridge-building technique works, look at a simple example that really has nothing to do with DOS software development. Most modern automobiles, especially those that feature computer-controlled systems, provide a handy "distance till empty" or "DTE" display in addition to the usual fuel gauge on the instrument panel. This display simply tells you how far you can expect to go, based on your present driving techniques and the remaining amount of gas in the tank.

To see how the dual-list approach works, create a first-draft design outline for such a display. First, list the available inputs:

1. Amount of fuel in tank.
2. Distance traveled.

   Next, list the outputs desired. In this example, there's only one:

   Number of miles remaining until running dry.

3. Connect outputs with the associated inputs, introducing intermediate items if necessary:

```
INPUTS                          INTERMEDIATE                      OUTPUT

1. Amount of fuel in tank. -------------------------------   1. DTE display
                                                                in miles to go.
                                                                      |
2. Distance travelled. ----  ---------|                               |
                                                                      |
                                a. Fuel consumption in                |
                                   miles per gallon. -------  --------|

3. Amount of fuel used per                |
   mile traveled. ------------------------|
```

To determine how much distance remains before running out, it might seem that you simply could use the known tank capacity and the distance traveled because it was full; however, what if the driver parks by the side of the road and leaves the engine running for an hour or two? No distance at all is being covered, but fuel is being consumed.

That implies that in order to approach an accurate prediction, you must maintain a running calculation of current fuel consumption expressed as miles per gallon. The computer then can multiply this figure by the number of gallons remaining in the tank to show a good estimate of the remaining available distance, based on the assumption that the MPG figure doesn't change.

When the car is left parked with the motor running, MPG rapidly drops to zero, and so does the DTE display. If nothing happens to change things, it won't move an inch before emptying the tank. And that's reasonable.

On the other hand, if you're really going somewhere and the DTE display tells you that there is not enough fuel left to reach the next station, you can try to conserve what you have by lightening your accelerator pressure, keeping as constant a speed as possible, and so on. As soon as these changes produce a better MPG reading, the DTE display will show you how you're doing and may make it possible for you to coast to the pump without having to take a walk.

I won't go any further with this example. As I said, it has little to do with software development; however, it does illustrate how listing inputs and outputs can focus in on the real requirements of the problem. Now it's time to see some ways of solving the problems, after the requirements are known.

Each of the connection groups on your final input-output table may form a program module. Logically, then, you can specify one module for each such group, listing for it the inputs it requires and the outputs that it produces. This is the basis of the HIPO methodology, but it does not in itself guarantee that you will come up with the best design you can achieve.

The quality of your design depends on you, and there's no magic tool that can create perfect programs for you with no effort on your part. If you make effective use of modularity, cohesion, and coupling, however, you're much more likely to wind up with simple, effective designs. The following sections discuss each of these, and then explain when to stop work at this stage of a project and move on to the next.

Achieving Modularity

Program *modules* have been described as "logical groupings of code" (by William H. Roetzheim, in *Structured Computer Project Management*) and this is by far the clearest definition I have encountered. Some examples of program modules may include subroutines, subprograms, program units, functions, and procedures. A program module also may consist of several such submodules, grouped into a logical unit.

While every subroutine, function, or procedure is a program module, not all program modules are designed to be modular. *Modularity* refers to a module's capability for easy comprehension and its potential for reuse, among other things, and can be measured by attributes such as the module's structure, its coupling to other modules, its cohesion, its scope, and far from least, its maintainability after the project has been delivered initially.

In a modularized design, each module can be a *control* module or a *terminal* module. Control modules act as dispatchers while terminal modules do most of the real work, such as changing data, writing files, and so on. In a truly modular application, each terminal module does only one thing, but it does that one thing without needing to call on any other terminal module for help.

The top-level executable module should always be a control module, which sorts out any information supplied by the user to specify what is to be done when the program runs. Between this top-level control module, and the lowest-level terminal modules that do the actual work, you can have whatever other control modules turn out to be needed by your specific application.

Here's a sample, based on an image-format-conversion program I was recently asked to create. The project goal was to convert several thousand scanned document images that had been stored in one file format to a second, new file format so that they could be viewed on Sun SPARC workstations rather than on MS-DOS equipment.

The available inputs were the image files themselves; each file contained within itself adequate information to permit the needed conversion from a proprietary abbreviated format. Required outputs were the converted files, in standard TIF format. The client didn't care whether the conversion was done under MS-DOS or on the Sun workstations, so I coded the application in standard C to enable him to run it in either environment.

The following shows a block diagram of the modular structure I created for the program. The top-level module represents the actual C `main()` procedure; it simply verifies that two parameters, presumed to be filenames, are passed in on the command line.

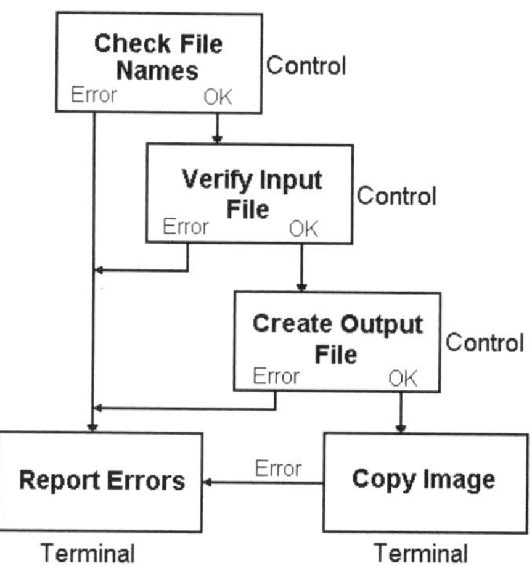

Figure 2.1. A block diagram of the modular structure.

If two parameters exist, both are passed along to the next control module. If less than two values are passed in, the `Error` route is taken out of the top level and a usage message appears, instructing the user of what input the program expects to receive. Such a usage message always is welcomed by users because it keeps them from having to remember all the details of every program they use.

If the input-file module cannot open the specified file, it takes the error exit and displays a message telling what went wrong. If it can open the file, it reads the file header into a data structure that is available to all modules of the program, and then passes the input file pointer and the output filename on to the third-level control module.

This module attempts to create the output file. If it can do so, it then copies the information from the input file header to the output file header, and writes the header to the newly created TIF file. After doing so, it calls the `copy image` terminal module to do the actual copy operation.

If the output file cannot be created, or if the TIF-header write fails, again the error exit is taken and a report shown to the user. If all is right, however, the copy-image module performs the copy as requested, reporting any error that might occur during the process.

The preceding program does not show how the various levels actually nest within each other to ensure that any file opened gets closed, and that all allocated memory is released before leaving the program. All that appears is the logical structure involved.

So far as its structure is concerned, this program exhibits a high degree of modularity. The only processing that takes place within any control module is almost incidental: the reading of the original header in one module, and the writing of the new header in another.

As you will see in the next section, the cohesion factor for this program also is quite high. A purist may raise questions about the degree of coupling used here, however. This is discussed in more detail, and you will see why I chose to take the route I did, after you explore cohesion and its importance.

Maximizing Cohesion

Before examining ways of improving a program module's cohesiveness, you need to learn just what that term means.

My pocket dictionary says that *to cohere* means "to stick together" and adds that "cohesive" is the adjective form of this verb. So when we say that a module is cohesive, or has a high degree of cohesion, we're just saying that the module "sticks to the point" rather than wandering off doing everything simultaneously.

In other words, a *cohesive module* is one that has only one primary purpose, and does little if anything else. The more secondary jobs the module tries to perform, the less cohesive it will be. The preceding program, for example, assigns the purpose "Check Filenames" to its highest-level module. When I actually wrote the code for this program, that module translated into the usual C-language `main()` function. In the following program, the `main()` module for the program consists of only these four lines. It's difficult to create a module more cohesive than this one.

```
/*****************************************************************
*     Function   :   void main(   int argc,   char  **  argv    )
*      Purpose   :   convert named file to TIF output file
*  Last change   :   02/17/93  -  jk  created function
*****************************************************************/
void main (   int argc, char  **  argv    )
{ if(    argc  <  3  )
    usage( );
  else
    openin(   argv[1], argv[2]   );
}
```

As you can see, the preceding module consists of only four lines, and one of those four is the single keyword `else`. The test for presence of two parameters on the command line is done by the first line, and if it fails, a module named `usage()` is called. Otherwise (that is, if the test succeeds), a module named `openin()` is called, with both parameters being passed to this lower-level module. That module, in turn, sees that all the rest of the program's actions are performed.

One of the best tests to determine whether a proposed module will have good cohesion simply is to try to describe its purpose. If the description takes over one sentence or two at the most, the module probably is trying to do too much.

While most modules that have high cohesion also tend to be rather short because it seldom takes huge amounts of code to do just one job, the often-quoted rule that a module should "be complete on a single screen" really has no more universal truth than does any other such glittering generality.

Short modules tend to be easier to deal with than long ones because the shorter modules tend to be more cohesive, and when only one job is being performed, it's always much easier to keep track of what is going on.

When the job isn't that simple, you usually will find it advisable to divide it into subtasks, and assign each of these to a single cohesive module. Breaking up a function into chunks of arbitrary size to comply with some silly single-screen rule, however, not only fails to add cohesion, but actually reduces it. The chopping-up leaves no function that performs the complete task, or any identifiable subtask within it. What's even worse, the short noncohesive modules are tightly coupled to each other, because none really is complete.

The more tightly modules are coupled one to another, the more difficult it becomes to debug and maintain them. In fact, should a situation ever arise in which you must choose between keeping cohesiveness, and eliminating tight coupling, you will find that cohesion should usually give ground first. When excessive coupling exists, the entire program becomes a nightmare, and changes become nearly impossible to introduce with any hope of success.

Minimizing Coupling

Coupling exists between two modules when either of them is affected significantly by things the other one does. All modules within any program are coupled to some degree; otherwise the program would fit the World War II aviation mechanic's description of the Flying Fortress bomber: "a collection of spare parts flying in close formation."

If there's too much coupling, however, any change you make within one module may require significant change to many other modules, too. One way of generating excessive coupling was built into many early development tools, that allowed only "global" storage for data.

That made it easy for one module to write a variable for another module to use, and this technique became standard operating procedure for many people. I've worked, for example, with FORTRAN programs composed of dozens of individual modules, each of which included 10 pages of `named COMMON` data declarations used to pass information around.

That's excessive coupling, and the reason should be apparent: When you want to know what caused the variable your module uses to be holding the value in it, you need to examine, and what's worse, understand each of the dozens of other modules involved. You never have any guarantee that someone else isn't changing one or more of them, at the same time that you're trying to learn what's going on.

Nevertheless, even today you can run into programs and entire applications that still suffer from excess coupling. Once it's built into a program, it's almost impossible to eliminate; however, you can keep it from getting a foothold in your work by putting the principles of single-point control and information hiding to work.

Single-point control means that for each variable in an application, there should be a single point in a single module that writes that variable. Any other module that needs to change the value should do so by calling the single control point. Similarly, modules that need to read the value should call the control point to find out what's in it.

When this rule is adopted, you immediately have the freedom to make any change you need to in the way that variable actually is stored, secure in the knowledge that it's coupled only to your single control point for it.

Even if you need to convert the storage from signed integer format to double-precision floating point, no harm can be done to any other modules because only your own routines can be affected by the change.

Strictly speaking, however, even if you provide single-point control, nothing but good programming prevents any other module from barging in and wresting control away from you. This especially is likely to happen on large team-based projects, but also can bite you on a one-person program, if you need to introduce a change several months after the original module was written.

Such ill-mannered aggressiveness is what information hiding was invented to control. The secret to *information hiding* is that the hidden information is not made globally available to all and sundry. Instead, it's concealed from meddlers, within its control module, and no functions other than those in this module itself are even aware of the actual variable's existence. This effectively prevents any other module or program from tampering with the data, thus enforcing the idea of single point control.

When these two concepts are carried to an ultimate conclusion, you wind up with something similar to (or possibly identical with) object-oriented programs. The process is not carried that far in this book. You will find, however, that by simply reducing the coupling between modules, you can obtain many of the benefits claimed for OOP techniques.

Coupling isn't always evil. By allowing modules that deal with large data structures to share global access to them, you can avoid passing the structures around from module to module like a serving dish at a family dinner. The little conversion program first shown in Figure 2.1 is a case in point.

In this program, the input file has a fixed-format header, and the output file must have a different format (Tagged Image File format, abbreviated TIF) header on it. Some of the information necessary to build the TIF header is available only from the header of the input file and may vary from one file to the next. Other TIF-header material remains constant for all files.

Rather than allocate space for these file headers within the module that made most use of them, or better yet in a separate module intended only to provide single-point control, I made both headers global and enabled them to be accessed by all modules of the program.

While this increased the possibility of excessive coupling between my modules, and did in fact allow me to couple the `Read Input` and `Create Output` modules by way of common access to the input file header, I don't consider this undesirable for a program of this size and function.

The size of the TIF header in this program is 266 bytes. If it were allocated as local storage, additional code would be necessary to set up its unchanging values. By making this structure global and defining it in the source program, most of the required constant content can be compiled into the program and thus requires no setup code.

The proprietary header, which is only six bytes long, was made global to hold down the number of arguments needed to pass between various modules. Because this entire program has only five modules and occupies only a couple of hundred lines (even counting the comments), there's little danger that the presence of these global structures will introduce harm.

The question of data coupling between modules in this example is trivial because the only data elements accessed by more than one module are the image height and width values read from the proprietary header and plugged into the converted TIF header. These values are both intimately associated with the image itself, and will vary from one file to another but in no case will vary between the input file and the output file.

Not all projects are so tolerant of tight coupling between modules as this example, however. It's still the best practice, in general, to minimize coupling by every practical means. When this brings you to the choice between passing dozens of parameters between modules as opposed to having a few global data items, however, think long and hard before making your choicc.

Knowing When Your Modules Are Right

Now that you have examined ways to achieve modularity, maximize cohesion, and minimize coupling, and you have seen how all these are goals to strive towards, it might seem that a perfect module would be totally cohesive and completely decoupled from everything else.

In practice, however, such a module would be absolutely useless because no way would exist to get any information into it for processing, or out of it after the processing was complete. It would be a closed system, and nothing would be able to pass through the system boundary.

So these goals, although worth aiming for, cannot in themselves guarantee that you will create good program designs. Is there anything that can give you such a guarantee?

The answer to this question, sadly enough, is no. There's no magic potion or silver bullet than can ensure that you will come up with excellent designs. There's not even a foolproof way to measure your design to assign a figure of merit to it. At this point, the software industry simply does not know what constitutes an excellent program, nor do we know how to prove we have one even when we recognize its existence.

What we do have is many years of experience that have taught us a few things that appear to have a cause-and-effect relationship: if we do things one way, the results are better than if we follow some other route. How much better, we can only estimate, and even then it may be a matter of opinion: one person's values, compared to another's.

That is why software development remains an art and a craft, best learned (like a musical instrument) by practice and example, rather than being a science or a manufacturing technology where you simply follow an established formula to achieve a predictable result.

Because what we're dealing with is an art, it's not possible to set down ironclad rules to tell you when your modules are organized correctly and it's time to stop the preliminaries and get on with program development. The best I can suggest is that this time has arrived after you deal with all the connection groups you listed, and your modules seem about the right size to work with.

Don't be overly concerned that you might be moving on too early. After all, you will find yourself coming back to this part of the process several times as the iterative process of program development continues, and each time you do, you will have a better idea of where you are, and where you want to wind up.

Making Sure Everything Works

One last point remains to be made, and then you can get that look I promised you at how I met the requirement of a sample program for Chapter 7. This point, however, is especially important, and may even spell the difference between success and failure for any project you develop. It's this: Above all, you must come up with ways to make sure that everything works as intended, and, if possible, to demonstrate on demand that it does so.

You can get a head start towards this generic requirement by always using defensive design techniques, sometimes called "belt-and-suspenders" programming. Don't depend on a single safety check; verify it by independent means whenever you can at an acceptable cost in complexity, space, or time.

The 19th-century politician "Boss" Tweed is reputed to have said, "It's impossible to underestimate the intelligence of the average voter." That sentiment is open to question, but it certainly is impossible to overestimate the amount of trouble your program can get into if it unquestioningly accepts input data its users provide and acts on it without checking.

The problems caused by bad user input can range from simple annoyances to downright disasters, but users won't blame themselves no matter what happens. Instead, they will blame your application for letting them hurt themselves, and the blame will be justified.

Input from a user should undergo some type of sanity check before you act on it. If any irrevocable action might result, such as accidentally reformatting the user's hard disk, the input should be questioned explicitly and the user warned of the potential consequences. Even this may not always be adequate to prevent problems, but it certainly beats having no protection at all.

These recommended "sanity checks" often can be incorporated as part of the program's normal activity. The format-conversion program used in several previous examples, for instance, only verifies that two parameters are passed to it on the command line before deciding to proceed. It's quite possible that either or both of these parameters may not be valid as a filename, or that the first of them might not name an actual valid file.

If the first parameter is not a valid filename, however, when the `openin()` module attempts to open that file to read in its header, the `fopen()` library call will fail rather than be successful. Thus, the check for validity of the name, and also for existence of the file, is included inside the normal action of opening the file for input.

If the file exists but is not an image file, however, it will not be detected by this program. If the file actually is a word processing document, for example, its first six bytes will be read, and these will be treated as if they were a valid image file header block. The program then will pass its second parameter to the `create output` module. If that parameter is acceptable to use as a filename, a TIF file will be created with the invalid image size information embedded in its header, and the rest of the document file copied in as the image content. The conversion program will never detect an error of this sort.

When the user invokes a TIF-format viewer program to look at the image, however, the error will surface. When the viewer attempts to load the file into RAM, using the information in the TIF header, the view program will not be able to do so and will display an error message, usually to the effect that the TIF file is damaged.

For the specific user who needed this program, no more error checking was needed. The user looks up input filenames in an existing database of images, and the names can therefore be assumed to be valid. If the program was intended to be used by a more casual or less experienced person than the database administrator, additional error-checking would be necessary.

Reasonable estimates for both the minimum and maximum image sizes are known, so when the program reads the size data from the input file header, those values can be checked against limits and if not within the expected range, an error can be reported. Similarly, the fifth byte of the 6-byte header is always `1` and the sixth byte is `0` for a valid image input file, giving one more test that can be applied.

You can apply this same philosophy to any input provided by a user, whether it arrives by way of a command-line argument or through a specific dialog box built into your application. If you have dealt with database management systems, you're probably familiar with the term *input validation* which means that the DBMS will test inputs when you supply it with information that tells it what kinds of tests to perform.

The only difference between DBMS input validation and the kind of testing I'm suggesting is that when you develop at the DOS level, you have to devise the tests yourself rather than just specifying the kind of testing.

Discussed next are some special cases of defensive design techniques.

Bulletproofing Your Programs

Developers often talk about making an application *bulletproof*. By this phrase, they mean that the program has been made resistant both to bad input received from users and to system errors, no matter what their cause. The analogy is to a police officer's donning a bulletproof vest when going into a dangerous situation for a bit of added protection against anticipated danger.

Just as no bulletproof vest can hope to resist every kind of weapon brought to bear on it, similarly bulletproofing a program cannot possibly deal with every danger you anticipate.

If the computer loses all its electrical power, for example, nothing you can do within your program can prevent the information still in RAM and that has never been written to disk from evaporating without trace. But you *can* minimize the loss caused by such unavoidable situations. To avoid losing much data, you can write results to disk more frequently, and you can flush the buffers to force DOS to do the physical write immediately rather than waiting until it's more convenient.

Taking this defensive attitude of preventing problems when possible, and minimizing the damage when prevention proves impossible is what the bulletproofing process boils down to. In general, you must deal with two general types of problem situations: those caused by system errors or failures, and those caused by user mistakes.

The next section discusses system errors and failures. For now, concentrate on user mistakes.

User Mistakes

I define *user mistakes* as honest mistakes made by the user, whether from impatience or from inadequate knowledge of the effects of an action.

I don't consider deliberate entry of bad data as a mistake; while bulletproofing can deal with mistakes, it cannot deal with sabotage, so I consider it a waste of effort to try. No matter what test I can devise, a determined saboteur can always find a way around it.

Fortunately, that's a situation that doesn't arise frequently. Most bad input received from users falls into the "mistake" category. Simple input validation techniques, such as making certain that telephone-number fields contain only numeric digits or certain punctuation marks such as the hyphen, will catch many of these and should be used when possible.

The situation that really requires you to be on your guard is that in which a user mistake can result in an irreversible action, such as overwriting a critical data file or leaving your program without saving the results of several hours of work.

One of the most useful tricks I know for preventing such mistakes from actually resulting in damage is what I call the "Mother, May I?" approach. The name stems from a bit of doggerel that's been circulating for years:

```
Mother, may I go out to swim?
     Yes, my darling daughter.
Hang your clothes on a hik'ry limb
     but don't go near the water.
          —"Origin dubious" per "The Shorter Bartlett's
              Familiar Quotations" 1953 edition.
```

A `Mother, May I?` routine is one that intercepts the user's potentially damaging directive before anything actually happens, and asks the user for confirmation. If the user fails to confirm the action is to be performed, nothing happens and control returns to the program. Only after confirmation explicitly is given will any irreversible event occur.

Assume that you have a program that performs all manner of wonderful computations, getting instructions through interactive input from the user. When the user tells the program to `quit and return to DOS` but the program still has results in memory that have not been saved for future reference, a `Mother, May I?` message should appear and advise the user that such unsaved results exist and will be lost if not saved.

This message should offer, as a minimum, options to continue (thus losing the data) or to cancel (thus returning to the program's user-input parser and giving the user a chance to save the data). It also could offer to save the data automatically, as a third choice.

If no unsaved data exists, however, there's no irreversible action to prevent because nothing will be lost, and in this case the `Mother, May I?` should remain on the sidelines, inactive. If your program asks the user's permission each and every time the `return to DOS` command is given, virtually all users will quickly learn to ignore the question and just choose "continue" automatically.

They will not, however, take the blame when this reflex action your program taught them was necessary causes them to actually lose hours worth of work, the exact situation that the `Mother, May I?` was intended to prevent. Instead, they will berate you for giving them a constant annoyance. And they will be correct to do so. Remember the fable of The Boy Who Cried Wolf, and apply it to all your "Mother, May I?" situations.

Overuse of the "Mother, May I?" questions, in fact, has become an inside joke in some development circles. At least one commercial developer often has threatened to create a special program to be submitted to magazines for review, which upon entry pops up a `Mother, May I?` that asks `Are you certain that you want to run this program?`

When the reviewer responds with "yes" or "continue," a second `Mother, May I?` would then appear with the question "Are you absolutely certain?"

An affirmative response to this one would simply generate a third `Mother, May I?`, and the process would continue until the reviewer ran out of patience and chose a "no" or "cancel" option. At that point, the program would announce primly "I didn't think you had the intelligence to be able to run this" and quietly return to the command line prompt.

To the best of my knowledge, no such program has actually been written, but far too many applications in common use do misuse the technique by forcing users to choose an option when the results are of absolutely no consequence. When used correctly, the "Mother, May I?" is one of the most valuable techniques you can employ. Overused, it becomes a worthless annoyance.

For the most effective presentation of the `Mother, May I?` dialog, you may need to use a display library that provides you with message-box capability.

It also can be done, however, without any special display tricks, just by asking the question and showing your user the acceptable input choices.

Catching Problems Early

Even if you religiously test every input value provided by a user, and take great care to anticipate any possible error that might result from bad input, your program still can be driven crazy if a system error should occur and you don't discover it in time.

If you attempt to allocate memory space, for example, but there's not enough available to fill your request, you may corrupt vital system storage areas if you simply assume the allocation request succeeded and proceed then to build data structures.

Similarly, if your program tries to open a non-existent file for input, and fails to catch the error indication that DOS gives in such a case, it may try to read data from out of nowhere.

This, too, usually generates still another error condition, but it's possible that your read request could actually turn out to be valid although not for the file you expect to be reading. If your program then acts on the assumption that the information "read in" after such a sequence of errors actually is meaningful, the results are impossible to predict but are not likely to be good.

Fortunately, MS-DOS provides extensive error-detection and trapping capabilities. If your programs make effective use of these capabilities, they're not likely to be driven off the deep end by system failures (unless the failure is something massive, such as a total loss of power).

To make effective use of them, however, really isn't as simple as it might sound. You need to test for error conditions after calling any DOS or BIOS function that has the capability of returning an error signal, because if you don't catch the problem immediately after it happens, you may not catch it at all. If you do catch it later by chance, you're likely to get a wrong diagnosis of its cause that can cause you hours of wasted effort looking in the wrong place for the trouble.

Just testing for errors, while necessary, isn't enough. You need to define to your program exactly what it should do for every distinct error it can detect. It is best if you also define what it should do for any remaining errors, such as a situation in which DOS indicates an error but the error code returned is not a defined value. This usually indicates that something other than what you're being told actually is wrong; it's never safe to ignore a situation of this sort.

After you detect a specific error, you must provide code to deal with it properly. Sometimes it's safe to give the user a message suggesting a cure, and then let the program try the routine that went wrong one more time. This is, for example, the best way to deal with the discovery that the floppy disk drive the program has been told to read data from doesn't have any diskette in it: display an informational message `Please insert the diskette in Drive A and press Enter to continue`, wait for the keystroke and try again to read the data.

Your program, however, should perform enough analysis of what's wrong to prevent it from displaying that same message when an attempt to read fixed drive C: fails, because even the rankest beginner among your users will be frustrated when told to `Insert the diskette in Drive C...` and is quite likely to distrust your entire program once this happens.

When discussing the techniques for development of software to run with MS-DOS Version 6 in Chapters 7 through 12, you will study the details of the various ways that DOS functions help you deal with error trapping, analysis, and reporting. For now, we will stick with the bigger picture and general rules to keep in mind.

One point to remember when devising your general strategy for dealing with errors, both those caused by user mistakes and those due to system failures of one sort or another, is that every test you put into your program during the design and debugging phases should be left in place for the final release versions of your application.

It's fairly common to lace a package liberally with error traps during its development, and then excise them all just before final release in the belief that doing so is essential to reducing program size, complexity, and execution time.

It should, however, be obvious that making any change to a program after it has been tested and before it goes to production means that you will be producing a program that has *not* been tested, because removing those tests changes the program into something very different from the one that passed its final inspection. The modified program may work; however, it also may not. The risk is not worth assuming, nor is the effort required to remove the tests well spent.

In the next section of this chapter, you learn about tracing tools you can use during system development to find out what's really happening in your code. Comments about not removing error-testing routines don't apply to these tracing tools, which are never part of your actual program design any more than the doctor's stethoscope is part of your body. Such tools simply provide you with a way to peer inside the program's operation; after you no longer need such code stethoscopes you can, and should, remove them.

Actually, eliminating all error checks may reduce a program's size slightly, but it's not likely to have any significant effect on its complexity or its running time. In the absence of errors, the error-analysis and reporting routines are never invoked, so they will contribute nothing to either category.

And when (not if) something does go wrong after the program is in the user's hands, it's very nice to have full reports available to help you find and fix the problem. In fact, many minor errors are cured on-site by the users themselves, if your program gives them accurate and adequate information. If a disk has filled, for example, they can provide more room, and so on.

In this general look at "error reporting," one special technique deserves mention. That's the `usage()` feature that apparently originated with UNIX at Bell Telephone Labs in the early 1970s but really should be a part of every program that runs from the DOS command line.

You can see an example of a call to `usage()` in the first sample program; if the user fails to provide at least two parameters on the command line, the routine is called rather than the actual program function being performed. The program then returns to the command line so that the user can try again.

The following program shows the code called from the previous program. These three lines tell the user exactly what types of parameters the program is prepared to receive. The `exit(1)` line is not necessary, because as the first program shows, the `main()` module does nothing else if `usage()` is invoked. The following is a typical terminal module that does nothing except display three message lines, and then exit from the program completely.

```
/***********************************************************
*      Function   :   void usage( void )
*       Purpose   :   tell how to use the program
*    Last change   :   02/17/93  -  jk  created function
**********************************************************/
void usage(  void  )
{  puts(  "  USAGE:  MAKETIF infilename outfilename"  )
   puts(  "          <infilename> is full name of NDI file to➥
convert"  );
   puts   "          <outfilename> is full name for TIF file to be➥
created" );
   exit( 1 );
}
```

When you can, include a similar module in your applications, and make it easy for your users to display it. MS-DOS uses the special option switch `/?` on all its external commands (since Version 4, where some commands had the feature; with Version 6 it has been extended to all of them) to generate such a usage display.

My own preference, for programs that normally require one or more command line parameters, is to detect the situation of too few parameters and respond with the usage display. Users quickly grasp the idea that just typing the program name brings up the reminder of how to use it.

Tools for Tracing Trouble

As you develop your programs, you frequently will wish you had some way to look inside the machine and see exactly what it's doing. This wish can grow to become an absolute necessity when trouble arises and its cause is not obvious.

Fortunately, you can use a simple technique to trace exactly what is happening in your program. This technique works equally well with all high level languages. It's a trifle more difficult to implement if you write in assembly language, but it's not impossible to use. I call it *program tracing,* and the tool I use becomes my tracing tool.

I first learned to use this technique when I was programming in BASIC many years ago, and have carried it along with me, unchanged, as I moved through FORTRAN, Algol, and a number of other languages. I use it today in C and C++ for looking at what's going on inside both my DOS applications and my Windows programs. It's a truly universal tool.

The tracing tool itself, however, is so simple that you may tend to discount how effective it can be. All it consists of is a print statement at a strategic point within the program module being debugged, that will report `At line 219` within the module or possibly `Entering ReadFile routine` at the entry point and `Leaving ReadFile` at the end.

As you run the program after adding such tracing tools, you get a continual flow of reports on-screen. For really complicated tracing, I sometimes modify the print statement to send the message to my printer rather than to the screen; this slows down the program significantly, but gives me a permanent record of what's actually happening, which I then can compare to a program listing line-by-line to see if reality matches what I thought I was telling the program to do.

The very first run of the program, after adding tracing tools, often reveals the exact thing that's causing my problem. Even if I'm not quite that lucky, seeing where the actual performance departs from what I had intended usually gives me a better idea of where to look next.

For Windows programs, I do the same thing, but I use the `MessageBox` function rather than using the simple print statement I use for DOS.

The technique is so effective that I hardly ever find any need to resort to more powerful debugging techniques. On the few occasions I'm forced to resort to single-stepping through the program at the individual-opcode level, earlier use of the tracing tools shows me the exact area that needs examination.

Tracing tools, unlike program error-trapping routines, should be removed after they serve their purpose. These are your tools, not part of your program even though they're being used there and at first glance are not distinguishable from ordinary program code.

If you don't remove the tracing tools before you begin quality assurance testing, you can wind up testing something that's not exactly what you will give your customers. If you leave them in and something does go wrong for an end user, the sudden appearance of your cryptic debugging message is certainly going to lower that user's confidence in your professionalism.

If you program in C or C++, you easily can handle a form of tracing by using the ASSERT macro. It's part of the now-standardized C library, but has been defined in header file `assert.h` in every MS-DOS C compiler I have used. The following definition is adapted from the one supplied with Microsoft C Version 4.0:

```
#ifndef NDEBUG
#define assert(exp){                                           \
if (!(exp)) {                                                  \
  fprintf(stderr, "Assertion failed: file %s, line %d\n",     \
          __FILE__, __LINE__);                                 \
  exit(1);                                                     \
  }                                                            \
}
#else
#define assert(exp)
#endif /* NDEBUG */
```

After you include `assert.h` in your source file, you can insert tracing tools where you suspect trouble might occur quite easily. To verify that file pointer `fp` refers to a file that was opened successfully, for example, you can follow the call `fp = fopen( filename, "r" );` with the line `assert fp!=NULL;`.

The macro would expand into code that would verify that `fp` was indeed not equal to `NULL`, and if the assertion failed (that is, `fp` was equal to `NULL`) it would display the `Assertion failed` message together with the filename and line number telling you where in your source code the macro appears.

This expansion, however, takes place only if the macro `NDEBUG` is undefined. If such a macro is defined, even though it has no content, the `assert` macro doesn't expand into any code; thus, the tracing tool is removed from your program's production version automatically.

I personally dislike the standard `ASSERT` macro because it's a continual temptation to use it for "normal" error checks that really must remain in the production version of a program. I prefer the following variation:

```
#ifndef NDEBUG
#define TRACE {                                                \
  fprintf(stderr, "TRACE: in file %s at line %d\n"            \
          __FILE__, __LINE__);                                 \
     }
#else
#define TRACE
#endif /* NDEBUG */
```

To direct the trace reports to the printer rather than to the screen, just change `stderr` to `stdprn` (`_stdprn` in some ANSI-compliant compilers). This version shares the advantage of automatic removal or insertion depending on the flag macro `NDEBUG`, but removes the temptation to use it rather than normal error analysis routines.

Back to the Drawing Board

Now that you have seen more of the analysis and design process, we return to the need for an example program to include in Chapter 7 and see how I found ways to meet most of the requirements.

First, rather than addressing the actual requirements directly, I tried to specify what would be required for each of several possible sample applications. When I tried this for "a system to control colors on-screen," I found that not one, but two programs would be necessary. One of them actually sets the colors to be used and saves the result in a file, while the other is only a module that can be included inside any application and can read that configuration file and establish display colors accordingly.

That meets the requirements that the sample be both meaningful and interesting. Let's see how it does at illustrating all or most of the 22 functions described in the chapter.

If the configuration setup program shows all possible color combinations and enables the user to navigate by means of the arrow keys, it can illustrate nearly all the BIOS-level display control functions, and the keyboard input function also. It also can show how use of BIOS removes any need to worry about Control-C keystrokes.

By making the color control module use DOS functions for display rather than BIOS functions, most of the remaining items can be illustrated. A few items, such as string output, are missed, and it's necessary to use some disk I/O calls to save and read back the configuration information, but these shortcomings are more than made up for by the real utility of the finished package.

The actual color control is accomplished via ANSI.SYS control sequences that amply illustrate those functions. Having selected this system as the sample program, following is the requirement list for the configuration setup program I drew up for each half of the system:

- Allow simple selection of colors by the end user.
- Provide automatic instant previewing of the effect of each color pair selected.
- Allow the user to start over without needing to get out of the program, so that any number of things can be viewed to help "get it right" before finally writing the configuration file to disk.

Following are the requirements for the color-control module to be added to application programs:

- Must be compatible with all high-level languages although this can be done through standard OBJ-format files.
- Must not generate "garbage" in the application's output if it is redirected to a disk file or to the printer.
- Must have minimum impact on the operation of the application in which it's included.

Because each of the two halves of the system had different requirements, they were designed independently. The two halves are coupled to each other by the format of the color configuration file that is written by one to be read by the other. No other coupling between them exists, however, and it's not even necessary to have ANSI.SYS installed in order to run the setup program (although it is a requirement when the control module is used).

Both modules exhibit high cohesion and a good safety factor. Even if the configuration program has never run and thus no configuration file exists, the control module will behave sanely and will not harm the operation of any application that contains it. And the ANSI sequences will not be sent if output is redirected away from the screen.

For more detail of this design, see Chapter 7, "Console I/O." It's not perfect by any means, but it's adequate for the purpose. Most of the time, that's about the best you can hope to achieve. And if you achieve it most of the time, you will be doing far better than the majority of would-be developers manage.

Knowing When You're Finished

Now you are at the end of this chapter, but the task of analysis and design is far from being complete. It will continue through the life of your project, and you may even carry some of the material from the current project into the next one you tackle, as well.

That's not a bad thing to do. By carrying along those things you have found to work best, you will continue to grow as a software developer. Nevertheless, it's essential that you also know when to stop planning and start actual coding.

One good indication that your current phase of analysis may be nearing completion is that you find less new material. When you have to dig twice as deep to find half as much information, you're approaching the point of diminishing returns. That is the time to get into the design phase and start putting your findings to work.

Trying to get that last little dollop of information is always tempting, but it can cause you to miss your schedule, and if that happens, the information you worked so hard to dig out will become useless.

More than one project has missed its window of opportunity because its leaders were unable to take advantage of the moment. Many a mediocre product has become a market leader because it had a champion who recognized the right time to make a move and wasn't afraid to do so.

One thing to always keep in mind is that if you really left out something important, your users will let you know about it when they review your preliminary design, or when you get into product test. Analysis, design, implementation, and testing form a closed ring of activity: each leads inexorably to the next.

Even though an application may occasionally emerge and go into production, that's almost accidental and doesn't break the endless circle. It just changes the name, from "development" to "maintenance" of the application, and the big wheel keeps on turning.

Chapter 3 covers the most popular languages, examines the leading versions of each, and then looks at other tools. These other tools, though not so widely known as are compilers and assemblers, are equally necessary for real software development.

Section 2: Your Tools

The four chapters in Section 2 examine the tools required to develop applications for MS-DOS, including those tools that are available as callable functions from both BIOS and MS-DOS.

Chapter 3, "Languages, Compilers, Assemblers, and the Like," discusses (as its title clearly states) languages, compilers, assemblers, and other utility programs that are useful in the development process. Features of the four most widely-used language families (BASIC, Pascal, C/C++, and assemblers) are compared. Then the emphasis turns to such other utilities as linkers, library managers, MAKE and its relatives, and configuration control systems.

The remaining chapters describe (at introductory level) the actual software tools available in MS-DOS and the BIOS code. Chapter 4, "DOS Itself: Interrupt 21h," describes the Interrupt 21h MS-DOS interface, with special emphasis on its data structures. Chapter 5, "Other DOS Interrupts," discusses the other Interrupt services that are documented as being dedicated to DOS, and finally Chapter 6, "BIOS When We Must," examines the BIOS interface for those times when nothing else will do the necessary job.

Languages, Compilers, Assemblers, and the Like

To develop applications for MS-DOS 6.0 (or any older versions for that matter) you must not only analyze the requirements involved and design a solution that meets those requirements, you must continue and turn that design into an executable program.

3

To convert your design into a program, you need tools that can do the job properly, and need to know how to use those tools to best advantage. The main purpose of this book is to help you learn the techniques of using your tools; however, first you need to choose the tools you will be learning to use.

This chapter presents a concise overview of some tools favored by many developers for turning their designs into finished programs. These include compilers for the three or four most popular programming languages for MS-DOS, assemblers, linkers, library managers (librarian programs), and a potpourri of support tools such as program dependency trackers and version control systems.

The languages explored include: BASIC, Pascal, and finally C and C++ (discussed together because the current crop of compilers combine support for both languages in a single tool kit). The majority of all MS-DOS applications are written in one of these high-level languages or in assembly language.

The first high-level language discussed in this chapter is BASIC. While many believe that BASIC cannot be called a professional development language, a respectable number of serious applications still are being created and maintained in it. Among the major software language publishers, only Microsoft remains a leading producer of BASIC packages. The language is far from dead, and Microsoft seems determined to keep it alive forever. Their current line includes QuickBasic, the Professional Development System, and Visual Basic for DOS. All three products are explored in some detail.

Pascal is discussed next. In this area, one name stands out from all the rest. Borland's products essentially have defined the language so far as the MS-DOS world is concerned, although it doesn't conform closely to the ISO standard. Borland currently offers two separate packages of Pascal development systems, which are both examined.

Because Microsoft and Borland dominate the C/C++ compiler market, this chapter concentrates on their offerings when discussing these languages; however, this chapter also looks briefly at such high-end products as those from Watcom and JPI/TopSpeed, as well as a low-priced but surprisingly capable compiler from Mix, Power-C.

While many other languages, such as FORTRAN, COBOL, Forth, Lisp, Prolog, AWK, Modula-2, and Ada, exist and have strong followings, none of them has yet cracked into the "preferred" group for microcomputer program development. The language that seems closest to doing so, Ada, is required by law for Department of Defense projects, however, only recently have reasonably priced development systems for the Ada language become available in the MS-DOS world.

To deal with MS-DOS at its own level, however, none of the high-level languages are really up to the job. To make the most effective use of the techniques the operating system makes available to you, you need to get right down to the viewpoint of the machine. This calls for assembly language.

As you study the subsequent chapters, so that you can combine the best of both worlds and have the power of assembly language while retaining the simpler control capabilities of high-level languages, you will learn how to create small snippets of assembly language code into routines that the higher-level languages then can deal with.

In order for these snippets of assembly language to make sense so that you can put them to best use, you probably will find it necessary to invest in an assembler even if you never plan to use it to write a full program. The similarities and differences among Microsoft's MASM and ML, Borland's TASM, and the super-speedy OptAsm from SLR Systems, Inc. also are examined.

If you're using any language other than Pascal, you will find it necessary to "link" your final program after you compile or assemble it. While virtually all language tool kits include a linking tool as part of the package, significant differences still exist among linker programs, and you may find it helpful to mix and match some selections. This discussion will help you decide. Librarian programs that enable you to manage libraries of precompiled routines, share the characteristic of being freely furnished yet significantly different one from another, also are discussed in the same section of this chapter.

Finally, you will learn about the "general support" group of tools. These include such things as MAKE utilities, Version Control Systems, and archival storage systems.

Getting Down to Basics

BASIC came into existence in 1964, some 11 years before the first widely-publicized microcomputer system became available, at Dartmouth College in Hanover, New Hampshire. It was the creation of the late John Kemeny and Thomas Kurtz, who anticipated that computer literacy would become essential to their graduates.

To ensure that literacy, the Dartmouth administration wanted to make computers available to every student rather than just to the math and engineering majors. At that time, however, "computing" involved punched cards, massive mainframe computing centers, and extensive special training in programming. That was not something that every student could be required to study.

The General Electric Company also had a vision for the future, and cooperated with the college in setting up a pioneering *timesharing* service (the prototype of today's G-E Information Services Network) on campus. The school made terminals available in every campus building. All that remained was to develop a language that would be easy for the students, none of whom had been exposed to computers except in science-fiction films before, to learn and use.

Kemeny and Kurtz used the just-published ALGOL language as a base, and stripped out everything but the most essential functions. They discarded all distinctions of data types and string-handling capability, keeping only single-precision floating-point variables. When they were finished, they had a miniature language with only 15 keywords, and they called it the *Beginner's Algebraic Symbolic Instruction Compiler* or *BASIC.*

A quick learner, even with no prior knowledge of computing or programming, could become fluent in the language in less than an hour's study. The goal had been met.

As time passed, improvements were added to the language until, by 1969 or so, it had passed FORTRAN in general capability. In addition to G-E, which promoted the language worldwide, it was adopted by Honeywell, Digital Equipment Corporation, Hewlett-Packard, NCR, Sperry/Univac (now Unisys), Xerox, Control Data, Wang, Digital Research, and even IBM.

Its use was not restricted to students, either. By 1971, parts of some DEC operating systems were written in an advanced dialect of BASIC called Basic Plus (which later evolved into Basic Plus 2 and in turn to VAX Basic).

When microcomputing burst onto the scene in 1975, BASIC was quite possibly the best known of all computer languages, and remained true to its origins in that it was easy for a beginner to learn. With all the improvements made over time, the name had changed to *Beginner's All-purpose Symbolic Instruction Code* but its role remained essentially the same: bringing computing power to the mass of untrained end users.

It was only natural that someone would bring BASIC into the world of microcomputers. The young student who did so, Bill Gates, used the DEC Basic

Plus dialect as his prototype rather than the original Dartmouth/G-E branch of the by-then-crowded BASIC family tree. With his high school friend, Paul Allen, he built an empire on that foundation, naming it Microsoft.

To this day, Microsoft, under Gates' leadership, continues to find new uses for the language. The most recent is as a *scripting language* for interprocess communication (a scripting language differs from a programming language only in that it's meant to be used by people who don't write programs; Word for Windows, for example, uses WordBasic for its internal macros). But it's still very much alive as an application development language, too.

One reason for its continued popularity is that BASIC has always provided powerful tools for dealing with the specific things that people seem to do most frequently with small computers, such as displaying text and graphics, accepting data from the keyboard, and working with files of data.

The original Dartmouth BASIC was, contrary to popular legend, a compiled language. It, however, required huge amounts of computing power in order to provide the near-instant response that has been its trademark for nearly 30 years. When it moved to the microcomputer world, it made its debut as an interpreted language.

The difference between *interpreting* and *compiling* is that a compiler translates the language into machine code only once, and the system then retains the translated version for all future use. An interpreter, on the other hand, translates each line of the language as it's encountered, and then performs the specified actions and immediately forgets the translation. Because it must translate everything every time the program runs, it's usually much slower (but does start producing results with no delay, even after you make program changes).

For program development, only compiled languages are acceptable. Fortunately, BASIC compilers have been available for quite some time, even longer than MS-DOS itself.

One characteristic shared by all the Microsoft versions of BASIC stems from the historical fact that the original version (Altair/Microsoft 4K Basic, 1975) was designed to run with no operating system at all, and therefore had to provide all DOS services for itself.

This common characteristic is that they tend to take over the hardware from the usual DOS drivers, and don't always preserve the characteristics you already set up in BIOS or DOS. This can become irksome, but it's the price you pay if you choose to use today's BASIC systems for your application development.

Experienced BASIC developers simply accept this as the "normal" operating condition and see nothing amiss. Because most applications they develop are for vertical-market use, which means that their customers seldom use any other programs, the users don't seem to find anything wrong with the situation either. If you are just now selecting the language you plan to use, however, because it might affect your decision, it's something you need to know.

Because of the many problems involved in making BASIC programs operate in any way other than those anticipated by the language implementors, none of the examples in this book are presented in BASIC. You can interface OBJ modules written in assembly language with most versions of BASIC when you want special DOS actions, by following the instructions on *mixed-language programming* that come with your compiler.

QuickBASIC

QuickBASIC first appeared on the scene around 1985; however, the initial version bore more resemblance to a stripped-down version of the older BASCOM compiler for the language than it did to the product sold today.

When Version 2.0 appeared in 1986, the major sales points emphasized on the box were "a complete programming environment" and its capability to create "structured and modular programs that can be updated and maintained effortlessly."

Somehow, the nearly 600-page manual that came with the package tended to belie the accuracy of "effortlessly" but despite that small point, the product rapidly gained wide popularity. Even its use of special QuickLib libraries and its inability to chain to programs developed using Version 1.0 didn't slow it down.

The success encouraged Borland to enter the competition with Turbo Basic, and the race was on. By 1987 Microsoft had responded with QuickBASIC 3.0, adding a competent debugging capability and the capability to link in OBJ files created by QuickBASIC or by separate assembly language files and still keeping the price at an entry-level $99 figure.

The requirement for special QuickLib format library files still hampered the use of QuickBASIC for serious program development; however, it went away with the introduction of QuickBASIC 4.0. At that point, QuickBASIC became a fully competent development system. The current version, 4.5, is widely-used by professional developers who have stuck with BASIC from the beginning; many use it in preference to its big brother, the Professional Development System.

Figure 3.1 shows what a QuickBASIC screen looks like, although this actually is a view of the screen from BCX.EXE, a part of the PDS that emulates QuickBASIC actions and appearance.

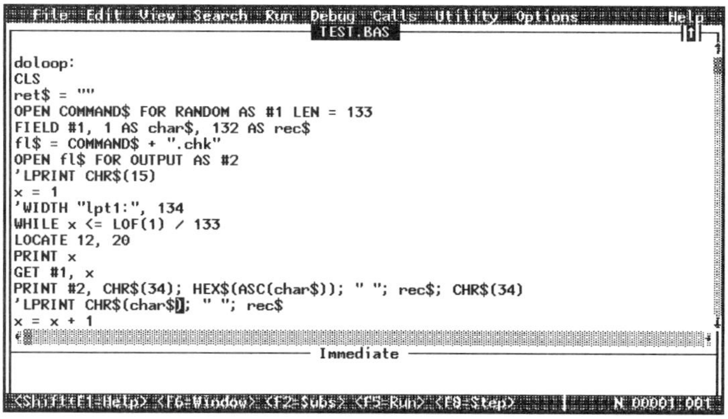

```
File Edit View Search Run Debug Calls Utility Options          Help
                              TEST.BAS
doloop:
CLS
ret$ = ""
OPEN COMMAND$ FOR RANDOM AS #1 LEN = 133
FIELD #1, 1 AS char$, 132 AS rec$
fl$ = COMMAND$ + ".chk"
OPEN fl$ FOR OUTPUT AS #2
'LPRINT CHR$(15)
x = 1
'WIDTH "lpt1:", 134
WHILE x <= LOF(1) / 133
LOCATE 12, 20
PRINT x
GET #1, x
PRINT #2, CHR$(34); HEX$(ASC(char$)); " "; rec$; CHR$(34)
'LPRINT CHR$(char$); " "; rec$
x = x + 1
                              Immediate

<Shift+F1=Help> <F6=Window> <F2=Subs> <F5=Run> <F8=Step>     N 00001:001
```

Figure 3.1. This screen appearance is typical for all versions of QuickBASIC, although it actually shows the QB component (BCX.EXE) of one of the PDS packages.

One of the biggest problems users of QuickBASIC have faced through the years is that no two versions have been fully compatible with each other. That lack of compatibility caused some developers to stay with Version 3.0, which was fully compatible with the PDS line when 4.0 appeared. This is not likely to be a problem in the future; no significant upgrades to QuickBASIC have appeared for several years, and none are anticipated in the foreseeable future.

Professional Development System

Even before MS-DOS came into existence, Microsoft developed a compiler for its CP/M version of the BASIC interpreters known as *BASCOM.* One of the first tools converted from the CP/M environment to work with MS-DOS, back in Version 1.0, was BASCOM itself. The compiler, in turn, helped convert many other programs.

Over the years, BASCOM evolved into the "Microsoft BASIC Professional Development System" and the current version (7.1) first appeared in 1989 as Version 7.0. While the more-recently-designed QuickBasic package put most of its emphasis on ease of use, the PDS packages have gone all out for fully professional programming capabilities. They feature *ISAM* (indexed sequential access method; a mainframe standard) support routines as part of the compiler libraries, for example. They also allow access to RAM beyond the 64K limit that ordinary BASIC imposes.

Figure 3.2 shows the command-line options that BASIC PDS 7.1 makes available to you as a programmer. If BASIC is your language of choice and you want an absolute minimum of restrictions on what you can do with it, this is the version for you.

```
Microsoft (R) BASIC Compiler Version 7.10
Copyright (C) Microsoft Corporation 1982-1990. All rights reserved.

Usage: BC sourcefile [objectfile] [listingfile] [optionlist] [;]
Options:

/?     Display BC options              /Ii:n Set number of ISAM indexes
/A     Generate assembly listing       /Lp   OS/2 protected mode
/Ah    Enable huge dynamic arrays      /Lr   DOS or OS/2 real mode
/C:n   Set default COM buffer size     /MBF  Support MS binary format numbers
/D     Run-time error checking         /O    Compile stand-alone EXE
/E     Enable ON ERROR checking        /Ot   Quick call optimization
/Es    Enable EMS sharing              /R    Store arrays in row-major order
/FBr   Restricted Browse info          /S    Disable string compression
/FBx   Extended Browse info            /T    Terse: no compiler warnings
/FPa   Alternate math pack             /V    ON EVENT check each statement
/FPi   80x87 or emulator math pack     /W    ON EVENT check each label
/Fs    Enable far-string support       /X    Enable RESUME NEXT support
/G2    Code generation for 286         /Z    PWB-style error messages
/Help  Display help on BC              /Zd   Limited CodeView information
/Ib:n  Set number of ISAM buffers      /Zi   Full CodeView information
/Ie:n  Reserve non-ISAM EMS

 2:23:31p, Fri  Feb 12, 1993
F:\>
```

Figure 3.2. This help screen lists the command-line options available with PDS Version 7.1. Note the addition of built-in ISAM support.

Like all versions of BASIC, however, you do not have as much freedom to exploit all DOS' capabilities as you can enjoy under either Pascal or C. While it's possible to write assembly-language routines to be used by any of the three major languages, BASIC is much more likely to step in and cancel the effects of your routines with its own built-in hardware interfacing.

Visual Basic for DOS

One of the largest changes in program development technology to occur in the past several years was the introduction of *Visual Basic for Windows.* This package offered a different way to create programs, by dragging *controls* into position on a display *form* and then writing code to handle the *events* specified for each control. This was enthusiastically accepted by those who were struggling with the intricate details of programming for Windows use.

With the introduction of Visual Basic for DOS, Microsoft brought that same capability to DOS developers. Available in two editions, *Standard* and *Professional,* this package enables you to design your user interface by selecting standard controls and positioning them on one or more forms, and then write only the code necessary to service the events for those controls to which you want to respond.

This programming technique is significantly different from the methods used with other languages; some find it easier and others find it more difficult. As Figure 3.3 shows, however, it's totally unlike more familiar programming.

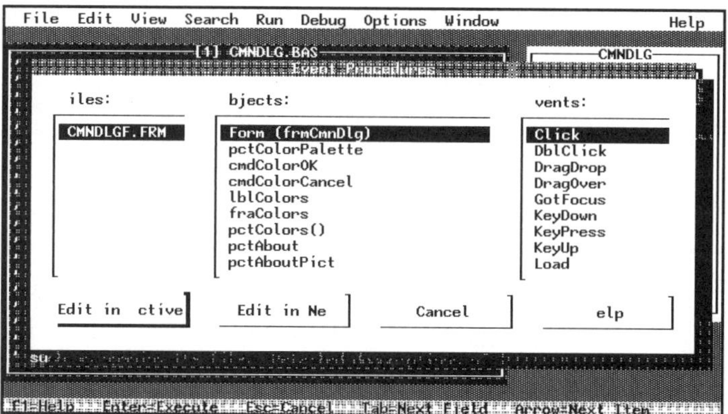

Figure 3.3. The Visual Basic for DOS screen attempts to emulate its Windows-based counterpart and bears little resemblance to the QuickBasic environment.

After you design your interface and write the code associated with each event, you can test your application from the VB design screens directly, or you can compile it for stand-alone testing.

VBDOS also provides a command-line interface so that programs designed using the on-screen techniques of Visual Basic can be maintained by more conventional methods such as makefiles. Figure 3.4 shows the options available for this version.

```
Microsoft (R) Visual Basic (TM) for MS-DOS (R)
Compiler - Professional Edition Version 1.00
Copyright (C) 1982-1992 Microsoft Corporation. All rights reserved.

BC [optionlist] sourcefile [objectfile] [listfile] [;]

Option List:
 /?     Display command-line options        /Ii:n Set number of ISAM indexes
 /A     Generate assembly listing           /MBF  Support MS binary format numbers
 /Ah    Enable huge dynamic arrays          /O    Compile stand-alone EXE
 /C:n   Set default COM buffer size         /R    Store arrays in row-major order
 /D     Run-time error checking             /S    Disable string compression
 /E     Enable ON ERROR checking            /T    Terse: no compiler warnings
 /Es    Enable EMS sharing                  /V    ON EVENT check each statement
 /FPa   Alternate math pack                 /W    ON EVENT check each label
 /G2    Code generation for 286             /X    Enable RESUME NEXT support
 /G3    Code generation for 386             /Zd   Limited CodeView information.
 /Ib:n  Set number of ISAM buffers                Requires ASCII format sourcefile
 /Ie:n  Reserve non-ISAM EMS                /Zi   Full CodeView information.
                                                  Requires ASCII format sourcefile

 2:24:16p, Fri  Feb 12, 1993
F:\>
```

Figure 3.4. Visual Basic for DOS can be compiled from the command line. Actual program development, however, virtually requires use of the special environment to lay out screens and assign properties to the various controls involved.

To use DOS features not provided as part of the Visual Basic language, you need to create your own custom controls or Quick Libraries. The manuals that come with the Professional edition contain full instructions for doing so, and also contain instructions for converting conventional programs to the Visual Basic environment.

Pascal Compilers

Pascal (named for mathematician Blaise Pascal, who invented one of the first machines capable of performing arithmetic) was developed in the late 1960s by Professor Niklaus Wirth. Wirth had two principal aims, as set forth by him in the second edition of the *Pascal User Manual and Report.* The first was "to make available a language suitable to teach programming as a systematic discipline" and the second "to develop implementations ... which are both reliable and efficient."

Until the International Standards Organization established its specification many years later, the *Pascal User Manual and Report*, co-authored by Kathleen Jensen and Professor Wirth (Springer-Verlag, New York, 1974), was the primary definition of the language. While the language aroused intense interest in the academic community, commercial reaction was almost nil.

A number of industry leaders, however, saw promise in Pascal. In the December 1977 issue of *Byte Magazine*, editor Carl T. Helmers, Jr. devoted his editorial column to the idea that Pascal replace BASIC as the main programming language for the personal computing field, and promised full support for such a movement. Shortly thereafter, he published a major tutorial on the language, and within a few months, his magazine had published an implementation of *Tiny Pascal* for micros.

Acceptance of the language, however, despite Helmers' support for it, was slow in coming about. Not until the introduction of Turbo Pascal Version 1.0 in 1983, only a couple of years after the birth of MS-DOS itself, did the language enter the mainstream of microcomputing.

Since that time, however, Turbo Pascal and its publisher, Borland International, have essentially defined the language despite significant differences from other, older, and more official standards. Borland claims to have sold more than two million copies (counting all versions) which would make it the world's most popular compiler for microcomputer use.

Borland now offers three separate packages: *Turbo Pascal 7.0*, intended as an entry-level system; *Turbo Pascal for Windows 1.5*, a similar entry-level product for Windows use only; and *Borland Pascal with Objects 7.0*, the complete professional-level development system.

Turbo Pascal 7.0: A De Facto Standard

When it was introduced in 1983, Turbo Pascal had only two claims to fame: it was fast—far faster than any competing product—and it was inexpensive, selling through mail order for $49. Borland CEO Philippe Kahn has recounted in print several times the story of how he came to the USA from his native France on a tourist visa, set up shop in a loft above a garage, and convinced *Byte Magazine* to sell him an ad on credit to first offer his product to the market.

Because a similar-sounding product had been highly touted in the programming press only a few months earlier, it definitely was not the best time to offer a $49 Pascal compiler; those who sent in their money in response to the earlier promotion had been left holding the bag when that company evaporated.

Nevertheless, Kahn charged ahead, and because his product was not only delivered as promised but performed even better than he had claimed, he soon had a runaway success to deal with. In the ensuing decade, Borland claims to have shipped more than two million copies of Turbo Pascal in its various versions, making it the world's most popular compiler. It was one of the first, if not the first, programming language to provide a fully *Integrated Development Environment* (*IDE* in Borland's list of acronyms) that combined editor, compiler, linker, and debugging all into a single program.

In the early days, Turbo Pascal competed primarily with Microsoft and IBM versions of Pascal, and with early C compilers, such as Aztec and CI's C-86. Because Pascal was much easier to learn than C, and Turbo Pascal was much faster in all respects than the competing versions, Borland rapidly took over the market for entry level program development systems.

By 1987, however, Turbo Pascal (then at Version 3.0) was beginning to lose ground to C packages. Where Pascal had been developed with emphasis on easy learning and solid protection against typical beginner's mistakes, C was the product of highly competent systems programmers trying to escape some of the complexity of assembly language coding and emphasized raw power with no safety mechanisms that might get in the designer's way.

As microcomputer applications grew more ambitious, developers who built such systems as Turbo Tax and Generic CADD with the Borland product began drifting away into the C camp. Borland's response was to introduce some radical changes into Turbo Pascal at Version 4.0. This version relaxed many safeguards (but only if specifically requested to do so by the programmer) and added many power features that had heretofore distinguished C from Pascal. By doing so, it enticed at least some die-hard C programmers (your author was one of them) into the Borland fold.

The trend has continued ever since. Version 5.0 added automatic overlays, and Version 5.5 brought object-oriented programming to Turbo Pascal even before an inexpensive C++ compiler was available from any source. Version 6.0 improved the integration of the new object keywords and techniques, and Version 7.0 added a capability for compiling even the largest applications without leaving the IDE. In fact, Version 7.0 provides two different IDE choices, and three separate compilers. The compilers are TURBO.EXE, the real-mode

IDE; TPX.EXE, the high-capacity protected-mode IDE for DOS; and TPC.EXE, the real-mode command-line compiler.

Other features of Turbo Pascal 7.0 include the following:

- More flexible scope rules
- New optimization that improves already amazing speed
- An *Object Browser* feature for navigating through source code
- Color syntax highlighting
- Unlimited undo and redo capability in the editor
- Open-ended capability for adding custom tools and help to the IDE (see Figure 3.5)

The package includes Turbo Vision, a DOS application framework that provides Windows-like treatment of menus, dialogs boxes, and mouse action, and over a megabyte of on-line help files.

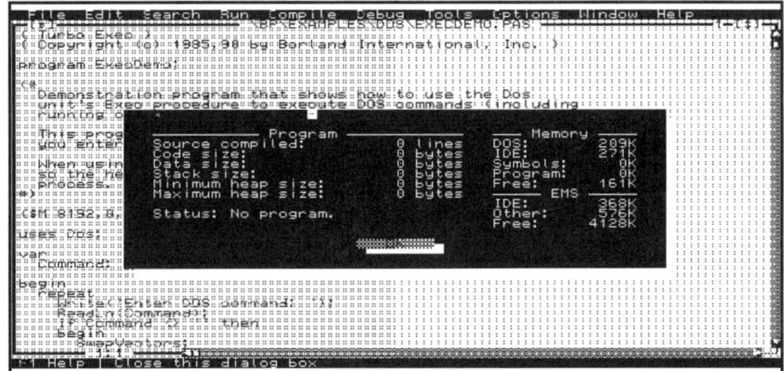

Figure 3.5. The information box that Turbo Pascal 7.0 makes available in its IDE tells you more than you may want to know about the status of both your program and your system.

To install Version 7.0 of Turbo Pascal, you will need at least 512K of RAM, and dual floppy disks or a hard disk. To use its protected-mode features, you need at least an 80286 processor in your system, together with a hard disk and a minimum of 2Mb of RAM.

Turbo Pascal for Windows 1.5

Turbo Pascal for Windows 1.5, in essence, is the previous version of Turbo Pascal for DOS; however, its IDE is a standard Windows application rather than being a DOS program, and this version creates only Windows applications (see Figure 3.6).

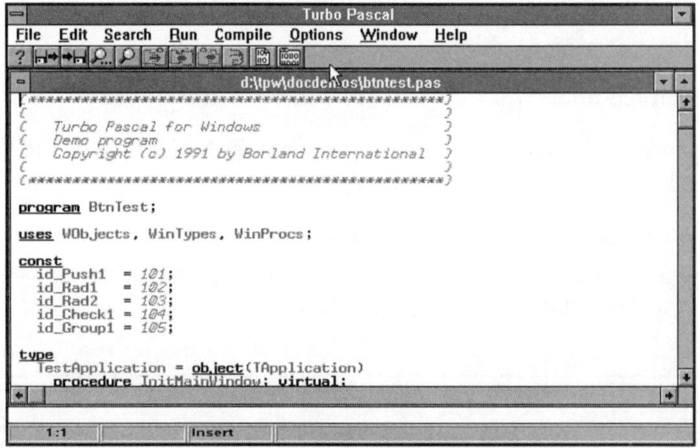

Figure 3.6. One handy feature introduced with Turbo Pascal for Windows 1.5 was the color-coding of various syntax elements to help you rapidly spot keywords, variable names, and comments. This feature also is now available for the other Borland products.

The TPW 1.5 package includes the ObjectWindows application framework; however, does not include its source files. This package has been a favorite with Windows developers seeking a programming language capable of generating high-quality dynamic link libraries (DLLs) for Windows use, however, free of the complications associated with C and the Software Development Kit.

Borland Pascal with Objects 7.0

While the original Turbo Pascal Professional product line was renamed to Borland Pascal with the release of Version 7.0 of the compiler, the new BP offers more than just a name change. This package includes not one, but three

Integrated Development Environments, five compilers, the TASM assembler, TLINK linker, TLIB library manager, assorted miscellaneous utilities, and both, with full source code to them, the Turbo Vision and ObjectWindows Library application frameworks (see Figure 3.7).

Because of its protected-mode features, this package requires an 80286 or higher processor and a minimum of 2Mb of RAM.

The three IDEs you can choose from include two for DOS and one for Windows. The DOS versions provide one, BP.EXE, that runs in protected mode, enabling you to create huge applications for DOS protected-mode or Windows use in addition to conventional DOS real-mode applications. The other DOS IDE, TURBO.EXE, is the familiar DOS real-mode package that creates only DOS real-mode applications but does so with speed unmatched by any other language processor.

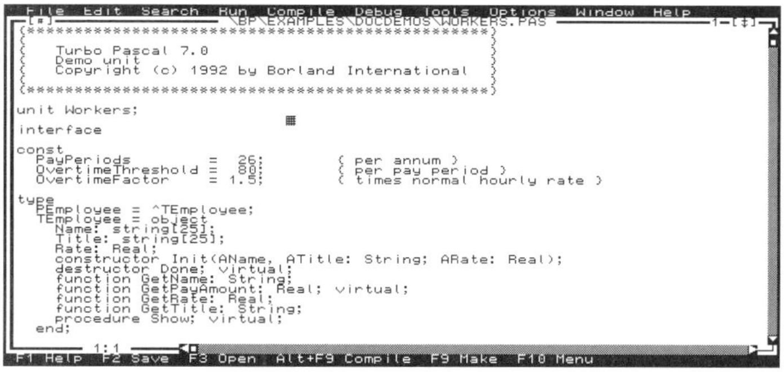

Figure 3.7. Borland Pascal 7.0 provides two IDEs for use in DOS text-mode. One is identical to that for TP 7.0 and the other is shown here. In addition, a similar desktop is available for Windows use.

The Windows compiler, BPW.EXE, like the DOS protected-mode version, can create applications for Windows, DOS real-mode use, or DOS protected mode. This is a significant change from previous versions of the Borland product line, which were limited to only one type of application. Those that ran under Windows created Windows applications, and those that ran under DOS created applications that could run only under DOS. This package is the first from Borland to include the capability of creating programs to run in protected mode, although earlier products could run in protected mode themselves.

The remaining two compilers, BPC.EXE and TPC.EXE, operate from the command line. BPC operates in protected mode and has all the features of BP.EXE and BPW.EXE, while TPC operates only in real mode and is essentially identical to the compiler in Turbo Pascal 7.0.

In addition to the full array of compilers and support utilities, Borland Pascal also includes both Application Frameworks libraries: *TurboVision* and *ObjectWindows*. Like all Borland's Pascal compilers since Turbo Pascal Version 5.5, Borland Pascal with Objects 7.0 supports object-oriented programming techniques but does not require you to use them.

A significant capability added to Borland Pascal was that of creating, and using, runtime *Dynamic Link Libraries* for DOS programs. While the use of DLLs has been standard for Windows and OS/2 development for years, DOS programmers have not been able to take advantage of them.

Borland's DLL interface makes it possible to access any Windows or OS/2 DLL at runtime, as long as the DLL does not require any of the special features of the graphics interfaces. The capability to create DLLs also makes it possible for you to put all parts of your application except the actual user interfaces into a common DLL that can be called from your DOS program, from a Windows-based variant, or from OS/2.

These new capabilities did not destroy compatibility with code that was written earlier for Turbo Pascal (the DOS version) or Turbo Pascal for Windows. This means that you can still use any older libraries you might with the new compiler, although most of them may need to be recompiled because of certain internal changes in the generated TPU files.

Like all its contemporaries, Borland Pascal With Objects Version 7.0 is hungry for disk space, though its appetite seems small in comparison to the C and C++ gluttons discussed next. After installation, it occupies more than 20Mb of fixed disk space (although this figure includes all its supporting utilities in addition to the three IDEs and five compilers). Installing it, however, requires you to have 27Mb free so that the temporary files it uses can be accommodated.

The C Language (and C++)

The C language and its descendant, C++, are quite probably the most widely-used languages for development of microprocessor software today.

The C programming language was designed and built by Dennis Ritchie at Bell Laboratories in the early 1970s. Originally intended as the implementation language for the UNIX operating system, C combined the power of assembly language and the structural simplicity of high-level languages. As a result, it moved rapidly into the realm of general application programming.

C++, also from the Bell Labs heritage, was created by Bjarne Shoustrop in order to add some of the elements of object-oriented programming to C. While doing so, however, he also created a "better C" that solved problems some developers found to be critical.

The languages are similar in their syntax but not identical. Their differences are not so large that one compiler cannot deal with both, and today, most microcomputer compilers for one language also process the other.

For approximately the first 15 years of its existence, C was defined primarily by the book on it written by Ritchie and Brian Kernighan. A number of variants came into use, however, and the original description turned out to contain a few ambiguities. After several years of discussion, an ANSI standard for the language was established, and the same standard was subsequently adopted as the international standard by the ISO. Today's compilers virtually are all ANSI-compliant, meaning that they comply in all particulars with the standard.

ANSI C and the older versions, collectively known as *K&R C*, vary in a number of areas. One of the most significant is that ANSI C requires that any function that does not return the default *int* data type be either *declared* or *defined* prior to its use; K&R C permitted this, however, did not require it. Programs written to K&R standards that did not follow this practice may require minor modification in order to be compiled with an ANSI-compliant version.

The distinction between the declaration of a function and its definition is that the definition provides the actual code for the function, while the declaration (also known as the function prototype) simply tells the compiler the type and number of arguments the function expects, and the type of value (if any) returned. The K&R standard omitted the argument list from declarations.

In the sample programs that appear in this book, you will notice that I prefer to define functions prior to use, rather than including declarations of them at the top of a source file and defining them later. This is purely a matter of personal style and you're free to do as you like.

In the definition itself, the K&R standard permitted the types of the arguments to be specified immediately after the function's name and argument list, and before the body of the definition. The ANSI standard includes the type of each argument within the argument list, and omits the separate listing.

Following, for example, is the conventional `main()` function in K&R format:

```
main( argc, argv )
int argc;
char *argv[];
{
   ...body of function...
}
```

Following, the same function in ANSI format, is defined as:

```
main( int argc, char *argv[] )
{
   ...body of function...
}
```

An ANSI-compliant compiler accepts the K&R style declarations and definitions; however, it does not check such functions for proper parameter type passing, nor does it apply its newer type conversion rules when calling them.

Some vendors have interpreted the ANSI standard to require addition of a leading underscore to many of the older "standard" names such as `stdprn` or `stdaux`, in addition to some library functions, and have made such changes to their support files.

In order to maintain compatibility with older programs, these vendors also supply an object module OLDNAMES.OBJ that simply translates the older name to its new form.

If you find a program generating large numbers of `undefined external reference` errors, just after you upgrade your C compiler, try adding OLDNAMES.OBJ to the linker's file list. It probably will cure the problem.

Microsoft's C/C++ Compilers

Microsoft's line of C compilers stretches back almost a decade, although the first compiler sold as "Microsoft C" actually was the Lattice product, marketed under license until Microsoft's language developers could perfect their own version. When introduced as Microsoft C Version 4.0, it quickly set the industry standard for performance.

In early 1987, Borland entered the C compiler market with Turbo C. Not long afterward, an entry-level compiler from Microsoft, Quick C, appeared, becoming a direct competitor with Borland's product.

Both Quick C and its big brother have undergone a number of upgrades since their introduction. The current version of Quick C is 2.5, while at this writing Microsoft C is at Version 7 and was just replaced in the product line by Visual C++.

Quick C 2.5 (for DOS)

Since its introduction, Quick C has provided essentially the same compiling engine as its big brother, however, without the optimization and multiplatform features. Leaving these out kept the package simpler and easier for its intended user, a beginning developer, to learn.

In line with its easy-to-use features, the development environment was kept as simple as possible without omitting anything essential. As you can see from the screen shown in Figure 3.8, there is recognizable similarity to the IDE introduced by Turbo Pascal, although the Quick environment was kept even simpler than the one Borland offered.

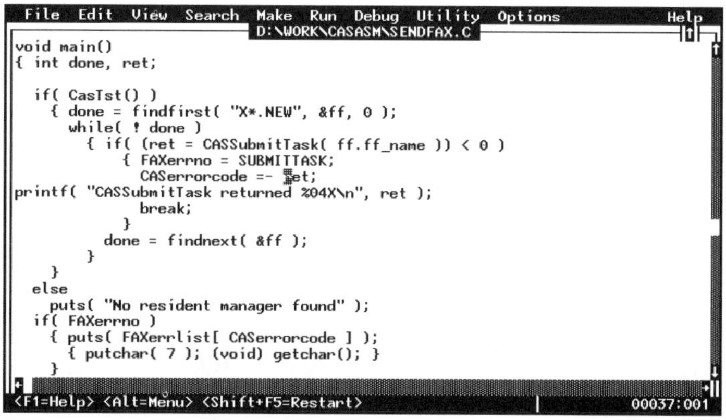

```
 File  Edit  View  Search  Make  Run  Debug  Utility  Options          Help
                           D:\WORK\CASASM\SENDFAX.C
void main()
{ int done, ret;

  if( CasTst() )
    { done = findfirst( "X*.NEW", &ff, 0 );
      while( ! done )
        { if( (ret = CASSubmitTask( ff.ff_name )) < 0 )
            { FAXerrno = SUBMITTASK;
              CASerrorcode =- ret;
printf( "CASSubmitTask returned %04X\n", ret );
              break;
            }
          done = findnext( &ff );
        }
    }
  else
    puts( "No resident manager found" );
  if( FAXerrno )
    { puts( FAXerrlist[ CASerrorcode ] );
      { putchar( 7 ); (void) getchar(); }
    }
<F1=Help> <Alt=Menu> <Shift+F5=Restart>                          00037:001
```

Figure 3.8. The Quick-C 2.5 development environment gives you all that's needed to edit and compile your application but does not provide menu entries that might confuse a beginning developer.

While Quick C was intended as an introductory tool, developers rapidly discovered that it was every bit as powerful as the full-blown compiler, and much less costly. QC 2.0 duplicated the functions of Microsoft C 5.0, and QC 2.5 duplicates the capability of MSC 6.0.

You also may encounter versions numbered 2.01 and 2.51; these include, in addition to the C compiler, the Basic Assembler which is an entry-level version of MASM 5.1 and can be used within the IDE.

Microsoft C/C++ 7.0

By the time Microsoft's top-of-the-line C compiler reached Version 6.0, it had gone about as far as the C language itself could be taken. Arch-competitor Borland, however, soon thereafter came onto the scene with a professional grade C++ compiler, and industry watchers knew another new package from Redmond could not be far behind.

That package, when it appeared, was labeled as Microsoft C/C++ 7.0 and included, as a bonus, the Software Development Kit for Windows Version 3.1. It also contained nearly 40 pounds of documentation, making up for a tactical error at the release of MSC 6.0, when reference manuals turned out to be an extra-cost item.

The inclusion of C++ capability was the major change introduced at Version 7.0; however, three other significant improvements were added at the same time. The compiler (actually, the preprocessor) was made capable of working with precompiled header files for quicker compilation, support for `p-code` (a semi-interpretive technique) was included to reduce program size, and support for remote debugging was made available.

The package grew also, and not only in weight. To install Version 7.0 you need an 80386 or later processor, 4Mb of available RAM, at least 8Mb of free disk space on your hard drive (27Mb to install all the bells and whistles), and run Microsoft Windows 3.0 or above, or another DPMI server. This version works only in protected mode.

Despite requiring Windows (or some alternate DPMI server) to be present on the system and running, MSC 7.0 remains a DOS text-based application, as you can see from Figure 3.9.

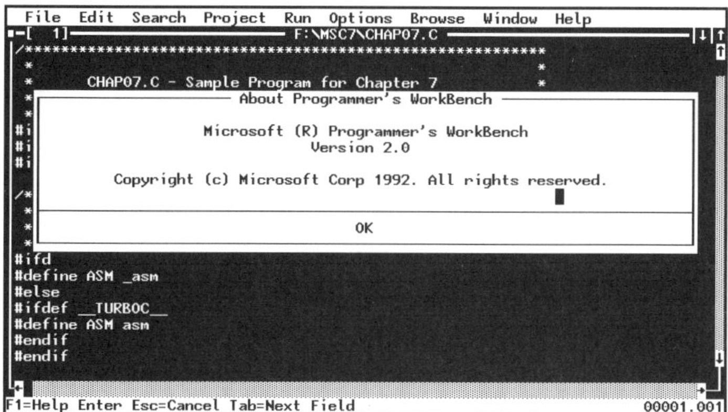

Figure 3.9. The Programmer's Workbench, Microsoft's IDE supplied with Microsoft C/C++ 7.0, is a DOS text-mode application like that used by Quick-C; however, it is expanded to provide access to many more needed tools.

If you are familiar with C and install MSC 7.0 or some other C++ compiler, it's not difficult to convert your C code to C++ by taking advantage of the "better C" aspects of the C++ language. You usually can convert existing C programs to C++ by simply following these steps:

1. Rename the source files from *.C to *.CPP.
2. Supply function prototypes for all functions.
3. Make sure that all declarations follow correct form and are consistent with the matching definitions.
4. Supply a typecast whenever you make use of a pointer passed as a `(void *)` data type.
5. Define external symbols once and once only. C permits multiple definitions and ignores them unless they conflict; C++ does not permit them.

You also may find it necessary, if you use any libraries that were created in C rather than C++, to bracket the declarations of the associated header files with an `extern "C"` declaration, to defeat the C++ "decoration" of symbols that enforces type safety.

> **Note:** This technique by no means provides all the advantages possible from the use of C++; all it does is enable you to start. The rest can come later.

Visual C++

The newest C/C++ development system from Microsoft, a tightly-integrated visual development system to streamline development of C++ applications, is *Visual C++* development system Version 1.0 for Windows.

Visual C++ comes in both Standard and Professional Editions. The Standard Edition replaces QuickC for Windows, and the Professional Edition succeeds Microsoft C/C++ Version 7.0.

Unlike C/C++ Version 7.0, Visual C++ is completely Windows hosted and optimized to boost programmer productivity throughout the development cycle. Visual C++ is fully-compatible with applications developed in Version 7.0.

Visual C++ development system includes the following new features:

- Visual WorkBench
- AppStudio
- AppWizard
- ClassWizard
- Microsoft Foundation Class Library Version 2.0

Visual WorkBench, shown in Figure 3.10, is the Windows-hosted development environment. Using it, you can edit, build, debug, and browse C or C++ code. While Visual C++ is intended primarily for Windows development tasks, it's also capable of creating conventional DOS programs.

With all the added features, Visual C++ is not small. It comes on 21 high-density 3.5-inch diskettes and requires a whopping 45.6Mb of your hard disk to install everything. The saving virtue is that you don't need much more to have a complete development system, if C and C++ are your languages of choice.

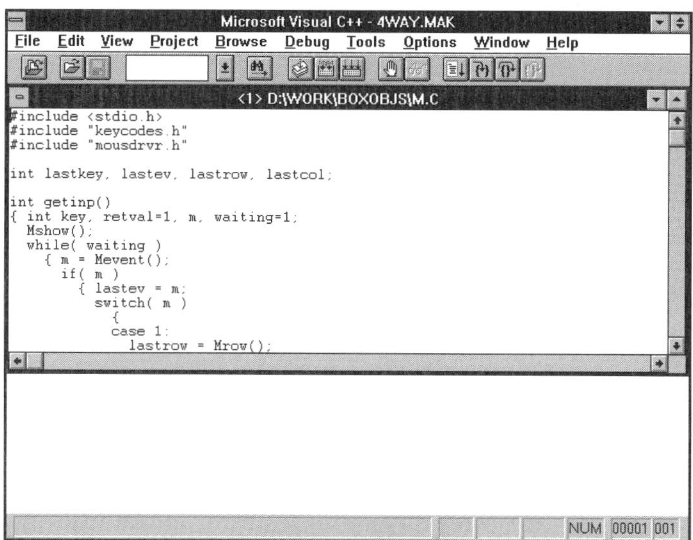

Figure 3.10. Visual C++ is a full development system that provides access to all needed development tools from the Windows desktop. Although you can use the command-line compiler, its IDE does not operate at all under DOS itself.

Borland and Turbo Versions

In the third annual C-language feature roundup published by *Computer Language* magazine, in February 1987, glowing praise was heaped on a new C compiler from an unknown developer, "Wizard C," that carried a $450 price tag (right in line with Microsoft and other established compilers). The review, however, ended on an ominous note: the developer's phone messages were being forwarded from the Massachusetts number listed in the manual, to a number in California, but were not returned. "I hope their new location doesn't mean that Wizard's excellent support has changed," the reviewer wrote.

The very next issue of that same magazine featured a full-page ad on the back cover for a new product from Borland known as Turbo C and priced at $99.95.

No one associated the two events immediately; however, as time passed and Turbo C rapidly became a strong competitor not to the others in its price range (of which there were several) but to the top-of-the-line systems, Wizard Systems quietly vanished from the scene and the word spread that Turbo C was actually the next generation of Wizard.

In the years since that beginning, Turbo C has evolved from Version 1.0 to become Turbo C++ 3 (because TC 2's next upgrade became TC++ 1.0 and there also were a couple of minor version steps while it was still TC, that's five major version steps all together). Along the way, it picked up a Standard and Professional packaging option, and at Version 3, the Turbo C++ Professional package was renamed to "Borland C++ Version 3.0."

Borland currently offers three products for C and C++ enthusiasts: TC++ comes in separate DOS and Windows versions, while BC++ provides both in a single package, together with an assortment of utilities to assist in development chores.

At this writing, the two TC++ versions are both at 3.0 while BC++ is at 3.1; however, because neither Borland nor Microsoft ever lets the other get very far ahead in this race, an upgrade may have appeared by the time you read this.

Turbo C++ for DOS

Since the appearance of Version 1.0 in March of 1987, Turbo C and now TC++ has concentrated on high performance, with compact executable code and the Borland trademark IDE that permits all editing, building, and debugging to take place without ever leaving the development environment.

Figure 3.11 shows the screen from TC++ Version 2.1, with an empty message window below the edit window, and a help window over both of them.

From the beginning, Turbo C has been positioned to be not so much as an "entry level" product as it has a "trailblazer" item. Borland's initial C++ compiler, for example, appeared here. TC had one of the first fully capable graphics libraries available in the MS-DOS arena. Only with the advent of the separate Borland line of professional-grade compilers did Turbo fall back to a supporting role. It still, despite the entry-level classification, provides you large amounts of bang-for-the-buck, not to mention being one of the very few development packages still available that can fit into a 20Mb disk system.

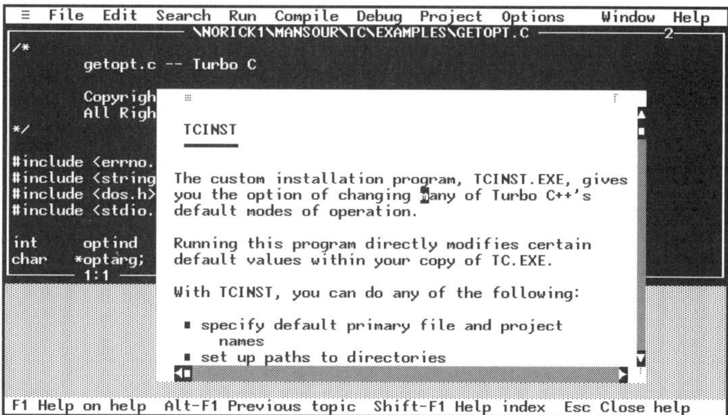

Figure 3.11. The Turbo C++ IDE looks much like that for QuickBasic or for Turbo Pascal, and serves much the same purposes. You can edit, build, and debug a program without ever getting out of the IDE.

Turbo C++ for Windows

Unlike TC++ for DOS, which is restricted by performance constraints to use text-mode displays for the IDE, TCW++ can provide a full user interface with toolbars and a browsing capability (see Figure 3.12).

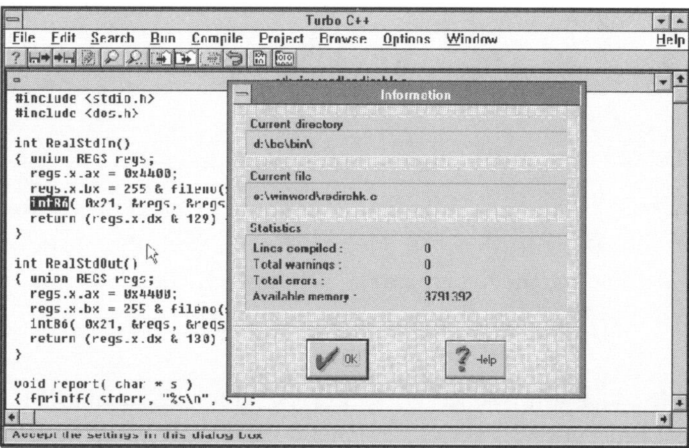

Figure 3.12. Turbo C++ for Windows provides an integrated view of your application, on the Windows desktop, and access to all development features you might need.

TCW++, unlike its big brother BC++, is intended for generating Windows programs only and cannot be used to develop applications to run in DOS text mode. For that reason it is not examined in any depth.

Borland C++

Borland C++ provides capabilities for dealing with virtually any need. Its ANSI-C language processor accepts conventional C-language programs, and its C++ compiler (conforming to AT&T's Version 2.0) allows full use of the object-oriented features of that language.

Prior to Version 3.1, BC++ was restricted to text-mode operation although it was fully capable of creating Windows applications. Figure 3.13 shows the IDE for Version 3.0. As of Version 3.1, this environment has been transported to the standard Windows desktop look and feel, greatly resembling the TCW++ screen shown in Figure 3.12.

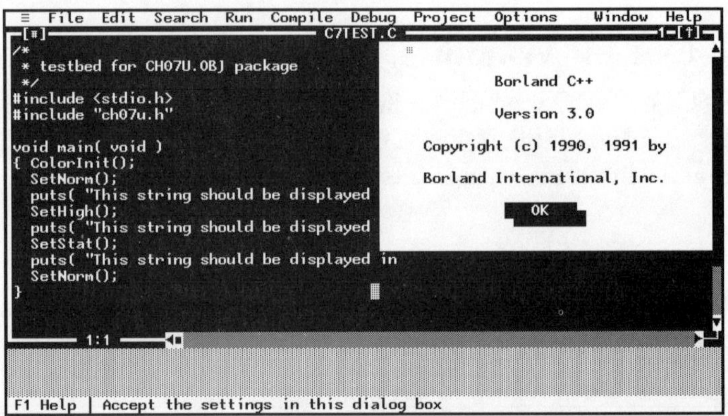

Figure 3.13. Like Microsoft's MSC7 Programmer's WorkBench, Borland's C++ Version 3.0 is a DOS text-mode application. With the release of Version 3.1 (an upgrade for support of Windows 3.1 development), this was duplicated as a Windows-desktop package.

All the added features necessary to support both DOS and Windows development had a price, however. Version 3.0 required 31Mb of fixed disk space for a less-than-complete installation, and Version 3.1 requires nearly one-third again more room.

Because BC++ comes with a full set of class libraries and separate Application Frameworks for DOS and Windows use, as does Borland Pascal with Objects, compensating for this is the fact that you may need few, if any, third-party support libraries with this package.

Other C Systems

While Microsoft and Borland tend to dominate the market for C and C++ compilers, by no means are they the only games in town. A number of other firms offer competition; some of these concentrate on higher performance, while others concentrate on lower price. Several of these offerings are discussed briefly, with the caveat that this is only a sampling of what is available. Because the C and C++ compiler market is a rapidly changing field, check the latest issues of programming magazines to keep up.

Watcom's Compilers

Since the earliest days of compiler design, long before microcomputing came onto the scene, the University of Waterloo (located in Canada) has been a leader in the art. It's not very surprising that one of the most highly-respected C compilers for micro use comes from that area, produced by Watcom Systems, Waterloo, Ontario.

This package definitely is for the full-time professional user. The full system occupies 19 directories, nested as deep as 4 levels, on your fixed disks, and you will not get any appreciable change from a thousand-dollar bill when you buy it. For that investment, however, you wind up with full development capabilities for DOS, Windows, and OS/2, and if you get the latest version, you also get 32-bit capability for all three platforms and a royalty-free DOS extender from Rational Systems.

The current version of Watcom C is 9.0. Earlier versions were used to develop such widely known products as FoxPro 2.0, AutoDesk, and Novell's network support utilities. In fact, a version of Watcom C is sold by Novell for development of network-capable applications, such as Network C for NLM's Software Development Kit.

TopSpeed Systems

Another advanced-level development system is the TopSpeed family of languages from Jensen & Partners International, that includes C, C++, Modula-2, and Pascal. The distinguishing feature of this system is that different modules within your application can be written in different languages within the system, or (as with Microsoft and Borland products) in assembly language, and melded together at linktime into a single unified package.

Another distinction held by the TopSpeed family, up until the advent of Borland Pascal 7.0, was that it was the only system that permitted the use of dynamic link libraries in the standard DOS environment. Unfortunately, the TopSpeed DOS DLLs, unlike those of BP7, were not compatible with the existing Windows DLL formats, so applications which made use of them required modification in order to move into the Windows world subsequently.

In order to provide full compatibility among the various language parsers used, TopSpeed's products use their own non-standard parameter passing techniques, which tends to make them somewhat less than compatible with many third-party support libraries. That, and the drastically different way in which project organization is handled under the TopSpeed system, may be why they have not become a larger force in the compiler wars.

The TopSpeed C compiler claims full ANSI compliance, and the system provides support tools equivalent to those supplied with the Microsoft and Borland professional-level packages. Cost is roughly comparable, as well.

Power C from Mix

Both Watcom and JPI set out to produce the most powerful development systems they could create and accepted the need for a high price tag on the resulting products. Mix Software, on the other hand, reversed the process when they created Power C: they aimed to keep the user's cost low, and even so, came up with a high-performance package that belies its low price.

Power C provides support for the ANSI C standard, the UNIX System V functions, and the common features of most other C compilers, which makes it fairly easy to import existing C programs from just about anywhere.

It's also, for the same reasons, an excellent tool for learning the language. Its only major disadvantage is that, unlike most other systems, Power C does not generate standard OBJ-format output files that work with conventional linker programs and third-party libraries. Instead, it creates output files in its own unique format (*.MIX files) that then must be linked by the Power C Linker (PCL.EXE). This restriction blocks you from access to any library that is not supplied in source-code format.

The package includes a conversion utility that translates standard OBJ files into the MIX format; however, attempting to perform such a conversion on a large support library is an exercise in frustration.

A secondary disadvantage of the unique file format is if you eventually move on to some other C compiler, you will find it necessary to rebuild all your object files. Because most developers rebuild object files fairly frequently for other reasons anyway, this is not a serious flaw.

The need for access to third-party libraries is somewhat mitigated by the fact that the Power C function library supplies approximately 400 different functions, including direct access to DOS and to the hardware. Support for the entire range of video cards also is part of this library.

And if that's not enough, Mix also offers source-code tool kits priced just as low as the compiler itself. This system definitely is worth investigating if you want to try the C language without investing a hundred dollars or more to find out if you like it.

The Lowest Level: Assemblers

No matter how you slice and dice it, the fact remains that all computer programs ultimately become reduced to plain binary machine-language *operation codes* (*opcodes*) in order to make them executable. The closest language to this pure binary code that even begins to make sense to human programmers is known as *assembly language* and the programs that convert assembly language code into the binary machine format are known as *assemblers*.

You may find several assemblers available for use with MS-DOS; however, three are discussed in the following sections.

MASM, the Unofficial Standard

MASM, Microsoft's Macro Assembler language, has been the unofficial standard for ASM language since Version 1.0 of PC-DOS. Originally distributed under the name "IBM Personal Computer Assembler 1.0," in 1981, as part of the standard set of DOS diskettes, it supported only the 8086 and 8088 processors at the start, and later added the 80286 used in the PC-AT systems.

When Tandy entered the MS-DOS marketplace with a system using the 80186 processor, however, MASM was ready for it. MASM 2 was released in 1983, Version 3 a year later, followed by Version 4 in 1985.

Those first four versions had more similarities than differences; however, when Version 5.0 came out in 1987, significant additions appeared. The program then supported the 80386 processor in addition to all the older versions, and added a full-screen debugging utility, CODEVIEW.EXE.

The most significant change, however, was the introduction of *simplified segment directives* to ease the task of assigning segment-register equivalencies, possibly the most arcane activity involved in the creation of assembly language programs with the older versions.

Not long after Version 5.0 appeared, a maintenance release (5.10) replaced it, and until the appearance of MASM 6 (actually renamed to reflect the major changes that were introduced) that was the program that set the standard for the industry.

The current version, 6.1, requires protected-mode hardware that rules it out unless you have at least an 80286 system. Although, like most developers, I do use a protected-mode system for speed, I continue to use Version 5.10a, which runs on any system that can use MS-DOS, and provides full capability for all my professional needs.

MASM 5.1 includes an ample selection of option switches that enable you to tailor its output to your needs. The list is available from the command line when you need to refresh your memory (see Figure 3.14). While the illustration shows some options in uppercase and others in lowercase, they are not case-sensitive and you can use either. This is not always true of the option switches for other development tools, however, particularly C compilers.

The original set of rules for creating assembly language programs in MASM required you to specify program segments by means of a `SEGMENT` directive, and use another directive called `ASSUME` to inform the assembler of the actual segment address expected to be in each of the four segment registers.

```
Usage: masm /options source(.asm),[out(.obj)],[list(.lst)],[cref(.crf)][;]

/a                  Alphabetize segments
/c                  Generate cross-reference
/d                  Generate pass 1 listing
/D<sym>[=<val>]     Define symbol
/e                  Emulate floating point instructions and IEEE format
/I<path>            Search directory for include files
/l[a]               Generate listing, a-list all
/M{lxu}             Preserve case of labels: l-All, x-Globals, u-Uppercase Globals
/n                  Suppress symbol tables in listing
/p                  Check for pure code
/s                  Order segments sequentially
/t                  Suppress messages for successful assembly
/v                  Display extra source statistics
/w{012}             Set warning level: 0-None, 1-Serious, 2-Advisory
/X                  List false conditionals
/z                  Display source line for each error message
/Zi                 Generate symbolic information for CodeView
/Zd                 Generate line-number information
```

Figure 3.14. To obtain this list of the available options for MASM Version 5.1, just type **MASM /HELP** at the command prompt.

To generate a typical EXE file, for example, you needed a source file that looked something like this:

```
DATASEG   SEGMENT   WORD PUBLIC 'DATA'
; data definitions here
DATASEG   ENDS

STACKSEG  SEGMENT   STACK
     db   2048 dup(?)    ; for 2K stack
STACKSEG  ENDS

CODESEG   SEGMENT   BYTE PUBLIC 'CODE'
ASSUME    CS:CODESEG
ASSUME    DS:DATASEG
ASSUME    SS:STACKSEG
ASSUME    ES:NOTHING
start:    mov  ax,DATASEG
     mov  ds,ax
     mov  ax,4C00h
     int  21h
CODESCEG   ENDS

     END  start
```

Any time the content of a segment register could change, it was necessary to plug another ASSUME into the code to keep the assembler up-to-date. This information was required so that the assembler could avoid adding segment override prefixes to each generated instruction; however, it caused much grief for many programmers while doing so.

With the advent of Version 5.0, MASM made available a set of *simplified segment directives* that greatly reduced the complexity of writing assembly language programmers for those of us who were willing to live within the constraints of a few simple conventions. That same do-nothing example, rewritten using the simplified directives, looks like this:

```
.MODEL    SMALL
     .DATA
; data definitions here

     .STACK    2048 ; for 2K stack
     .CODE
start     PROC
     mov  ax,@data  ; name changed
     mov  ds,ax
     mov  ax,4C00h
     int  21h
start     ENDP

     END  start
```

These simplified segment directives make life much easier for developers working at both high and low levels. By eliminating the arcane complexity of the SEGMENT and ASSUMES statements in most cases, they enable you to concentrate on the structure required by the application rather than on the framework around it that the assembler might need. The price paid is simply acceptance of the Microsoft standard naming conventions, which are not all that onerous (especially because they remain invisible and out-of-mind most of the time).

Additional benefits beyond the increased simplicity accrue, too, when these directives are used. The .MODEL statement, which is required in order to initialize the assembler for simplified segment processing, enables you to specify either a SMALL, COMPACT, MEDIUM, LARGE, or HUGE memory model for your program. This especially is important when you write assembly language modules intended to interface with programs in a high-level language. In that case, your .MODEL statement should match the memory model required by your HLL program. The specifier keyword and the resulting data-segment and code-segment address conventions are as follows:

Keyword	Code Segments	Data Segments
SMALL	Single, near addressing	Single, near addressing
COMPACT	Shared, near addressing	Multiple, far addressing
MEDIUM	Multiple, far addressing	Single, near addressing
LARGE	Multiple, far addressing	Multiple, far addressing
HUGE	Multiple, far addressing	Multiple, far addressing

The `SMALL` memory model puts all code into one 64K-maximum-size segment, and all data into another, allowing a maximum program size of 128K. Both the `CS` and `DS` segment registers remain constant throughout the program and all addressing is *near mode*, by offset only.

The `MEDIUM` model provides a separate code segment for each procedure but retains a single shared segment for all data. Thus, jumps and calls require *far* addressing, however, data references remain *near* and the DS register normally holds the same value as the SS register because the Stack segment is included within the data group. This is the most popular model for many developers, and is the standard model used in most Windows programs.

The `COMPACT` model reverses the situation from that in the `MEDIUM` model; this model provides a single-shared code segment for all procedures but the total amount of data may exceed the 64K limitation. This is not widely-used.

The `LARGE` model provides multiple segments for both code and data, and is the choice for large programs. No single data structure in this model, however, can be larger than 64K.

The `HUGE` model is the same as the `LARGE` model, except that the 64K limit on each data structure is eliminated. The cost of removing this limit is the requirement for significant additional calculations when addressing the oversized data structures, so this model should be used only if necessary.

In Version 5.1, MASM's simplified segment directives added automatic support for high-level languages, obtained by adding an optional language specifier to the `.MODEL` statement following the model keyword.

MASM then provides the appropriate prologue and epilogue code to each `PROC` definition to generate procedures fully-compatible with the specified language's standards, and in some cases, modifies all symbols to comply with the language's naming conventions. All procedures also are made `PUBLIC` so that they are visible to the linker when the programs are finally put together into a single EXE file.

The language specifiers accepted are C, PASCAL, FORTRAN, or BASIC. If C is specified (`.MODEL MEDIUM, C`), then all public symbols have a single underscore placed in front of them to conform to the C compiler's conventions, and parameter definitions follow the right-to-left convention used by the compiler when pushing their values onto the stack to pass them to functions.

Borland's TASM

Borland's assembler, *TASM*, can emulate MASM 5.1 (including its quirks that are more often called *bugs*), but also offers a significantly different operating mode called IDEAL Mode whch has a more consistent syntax many developers prefer (see Figure 3.15).

```
C:\> tasm /help
Turbo Assembler  Copyright (c) 1988, 1992 Borland International
Syntax:  TASM [options] source [,object] [,listing] [,xref]
/a,/s            Alphabetic or Source-code segment ordering
/c               Generate cross-reference in listing
/dSYM[=VAL]      Define symbol SYM = 0, or = value VAL
/e,/r            Emulated or Real floating-point instructions
/h,/?            Display this help screen
/iPATH           Search PATH for include files
/jCMD            Jam in an assembler directive CMD (eg. /jIDEAL)
/kh#             Hash table capacity # symbols
/l,/la           Generate listing: l=normal listing, la=expanded listing
/ml,/mx,/mu      Case sensitivity on symbols: ml=all, mx=globals, mu=none
/mv#             Set maximum valid length for symbols
/m#              Allow # multiple passes to resolve forward references
/n               Suppress symbol tables in listing
/os,/o,/op,/oiObject code: standard, standard w/overlays, Phar Lap, or IBM
/p               Check for code segment overrides in protected mode
/q               Suppress OBJ records not needed for linking
/t               Suppress messages if successful assembly
/uxxxx           Set version emulation, version xxxx
/w0,/w1,/w2      Set warning level: w0=none, w1=w2=warnings on
/w-xxx,/w+xxx Disable (-) or enable (+) warning xxx
/x               Include false conditionals in listing
/z               Display source line with error message
/zi,/zd,/zn      Debug info: zi=full, zd=line numbers only, zn=none
```

Figure 3.15. This is the help screen for the version of TASM shipped as part of the Borland Pascal with Objects 7.0 package.

TASM is a multi-pass assembler with forward-reference resolution and high-assembly speed, featuring full 80386 support, improved syntax type-checking, local labels, and far from least, the optional `IDEAL` mode syntax.

Unlike MASM, which (through Version 5.1) processed all files using two passes or phases of assembly, TASM can perform as many passes as necessary to resolve all references. You enable this feature and specify a limit to the number of passes attempted with a command-line option switch. This feature helps remove MASM's ubiquitous phase error failure that was the bane of an assembly language programmer's life. If the option switch is not used, TASM is a single-pass assembler, and will not resolve such errors.

Like MASM, TASM sports the simplified segment directives and support for high-level languages; however, in addition to the five memory models and four languages supported by MASM, TASM adds two more models and two more languages, plus extending the directive to optionally allow a *model modifier*, a *language modifier*, or both.

In addition, TASM permits you to specify the language, using the same set of keywords as in the `.MODEL` directive, as part of virtually all its directives that refer to symbols, such as `PUBLIC`, `EXTRN`, `CALL`, and so on.

The added models are TINY, that specifies the COM-file format in which all code and data together fit into a single 64K segment, and all segment registers contain the same value, TCHUGE, a modification of HUGE to provide compatibility with the huge memory model of Borland's C++ products.

The added languages are PROLOG and NOLANGUAGE. Both have the same effect as C except that no leading underscore characters are added to public symbol names.

The model modifiers allowed are NEARSTACK or FARSTACK. This controls whether SS will be assumed equal to DS (NEARSTACK) or not equal (FARSTACK), which becomes important when working with Windows programs.

The language modifiers are WINDOWS, ODDNEAR, ODDFAR, or NORMAL. These control automatic generation of code for stack setup and cleanup in Windows procedures, operation of overlays, and conventional entry and exit code.

The IDEAL mode, offered only by TASM, finds favor with many programmers who never need to switch to other assembly languages; however, as a professional called upon to deal with several different languages in the course of a single week, I believe that it's too confusing to be usable. If you don't need to stay fluent in multiple dialects of assembly language, however, it will definitely be worth looking at.

With the advent of TASM Version 3.1, Borland also added support for object-oriented programming. Like IDEAL mode, however, this feature presently is unique to TASM.

OPTASM: Greased Lightning

OPTASM, a product of SLR Systems, Inc., is by far the fastest assembler program available for MS-DOS; however, as of this writing, it has not been upgraded since 1988 and consequently fails to include features introduced to MASM and TASM since MASM's Version 5.0.

As a result, it cannot handle the special 386-and-above machine opcodes as can both MASM and TASM, nor does it support the high-level language features introduced in MASM 5.1 and in TASM 1.0. It does provide the original simplified segment directives. What it does have, and has had since its introduction, is absolutely breathtaking speed in action.

SLR Systems, Inc., is a small firm in Butler, Pennsylvania, that first came on the scene in CP/M days with an assembler and linker package that could create programs far faster than any product from the "big name" software houses.

As the CP/M market evaporated and gave way to MS-DOS, founder and guiding genius Steve Russell applied his skills to doing the same thing for the 80x86 line of processors, and the result was OPTASM, described at its introduction as "the only plug-compatible assembler that supports the incompatibilities between MASM Versions 3, 4, and 5."

> **Note:** Since 1989, I have written virtually all of SLR's software manuals, so my feelings about their products may not be totally impartial. I have made, however, every effort to eliminate bias, and any possible conflict of interest, in these overviews and comparisons of features.

Where TASM quotes a figure of 48,000 lines per minute, the speed of OPTASM is listed at 75,000 lines per minute (MASM does not quote such figures but Version 5.0 was measured at approximately 17,000 lines per minute). In the absence of rigidly controlled tests, however, such figures have little meaning; disk access-time variations from one system to another can introduce wide variations.

OPTASM was the first assembler to totally do away with the phase-error situation by running as many passes as necessary to eliminate all such problems. This also did away with `NOP padding` that was common for forward jump instructions in MASM.

Because most users of assembly language had discovered that tracking down MASM's frequent phase errors (the result of forward references that caused inadequate space to be reserved for one or more machine opcodes and thus made the addresses change between the two passes or "phases" of the assembly process) took the lion's share of their development efforts, this feature alone prompted many to adopt OPTASM.

Possibly the greatest advantage of OPTASM, other than its speed and freedom from phase errors, is its inclusion of *make* and *cross-reference* utilities as integral parts of the assembler rather than as add-on utilities. This permits applications that use multiple source files to be managed more easily.

Another major advantage introduced with OPTASM and now included in all products from SLR Systems, Inc., is the capability to customize your copy of the tool to automatically default to the options you use most frequently. This eliminates the need for complicated sets of option switches each time you assemble an application or program module.

All SLR products, from the beginning, have been directed primarily toward the professional developer and have concentrated on features that reduce total product development time. As a result, they have become the tools of choice for many programmers, both at the professional level and in the class of serious amateurs.

These users have chosen to surrender some of the more advanced features in newer products to retain the speed and convenience of OPTASM but continue to request that it be upgraded without losing the advantages it still provides.

Linkers and Librarians

While the language translator itself (the BASIC, Pascal, C, or C++ compiler or the assembler) is the most obvious tool in your development kit, it seldom stands alone. Most language translators produce only OBJ-format files as their output, and these files are not yet ready to execute. They must be made so by running a linker that will resolve any address references, and usually, add reusable code stored in system libraries.

While system libraries always are supplied as part of the compiler packages, and also are available from third-party publishers, you find as you proceed that you reuse many of your own routines from one project to the next, and it would be nice to build your own custom libraries of such modules. That's what library manager programs, often called librarians, do for you.

Linkers: The Final Step

The primary purpose of the *linker* is to resolve all address references correctly, in order to generate an executable program file. For a single-module COM file, virtually no such resolution is required and the linker's task becomes almost trivial; however, when multiple modules and external libraries become involved, the amount of work necessary takes a steep climb.

All common linkers for MS-DOS development take input from files in Object Module Format (OMF). This format was originally specified by Intel, well before MS-DOS was created but has since been modified extensively by Microsoft, Borland, and other publishers of linker programs.

Microsoft published an application note that documents nearly all the currently used features of OMF files, including many that previously were considered proprietary. This document (*SS0288: Relocatable Object Module Format*) is available to the developer community through Microsoft's "Developer Network."

Most of the time, however, you will not find this information necessary unless you intend to write a disassembler for object files, or an equally arcane task.

The OMF modules that form the linker's input may be in OBJ files generated by your compiler or assembler, or in LIB files created by a library manager program, or both. The linker's job is to combine the modules you specify into a single executable file, resolving all symbol references first from the OBJ files you furnish, and then looking up any remaining ones in the LIB files.

Most development languages provide accompanying linkers as part of the package, and in addition a number of third-party products are available. Some third-party linkers provide special features, such as support for automatic program overlays. Others are capable of faster operation than the "standard" versions.

In general, the linker that comes with your language package is the best one to use, unless you need the special features available only with some other product. The following discussion looks briefly at a cross-section of the available linker programs and compares the features available in MS LINK, Borland's TLINK, SLR's OptLink family, and several less well-known products.

LINK from Microsoft

The original Microsoft Linkage Editor program, universally known simply as *LINK*, was provided as an integral part of Version 1.0 of MS-DOS. Since that time, it has undergone many revisions and incremental changes. Today's LINK offers overlay support, the capability to create both normal MS-DOS executable files and the Segmented-EXE files required by both Windows and OS/2, and a large number of options as shown in Figure 3.16.

```
C:\>link /?

Microsoft (R) Segmented Executable Linker  Version 5.30
Copyright (C) Microsoft Corp 1984-1992.  All rights reserved.

Usage:

LINK
LINK @<response file>
LINK <objs>,<exefile>,<mapfile>,<libs>,<deffile>

Valid options are:
  /?                              /ALIGNMENT
  /BATCH                          /CODEVIEW
  /CPARMAXALLOC                   /DOSSEG
  /DSALLOCATE                     /DYNAMIC
  /EXEPACK                        /FARCALLTRANSLATION
  /HELP                           /HIGH
  /INFORMATION                    /LINENUMBERS
  /MAP                            /NODEFAULTLIBRARYSEARCH
  /NOEXTDICTIONARY                /NOFARCALLTRANSLATION
  /NOGROUPASSOCIATION             /NOIGNORECASE
  /NOLOGO                         /NONULLSDOSSEG
  /NOPACKCODE                     /NOPACKFUNCTIONS
  /OLDOVERLAY                     /ONERROR
  /OVERLAYINTERRUPT               /PACKCODE
  /PACKDATA                       /PACKFUNCTIONS
  /PAUSE                          /PCODE
  /PMTYPE                         /QUICKLIBRARY
  /r                              /SEGMENTS
  /STACK                          /TINY
  /WARNFIXUP
```

Figure 3.16. These options are available to you from Microsoft's LINK program Version 5.3, by typing the command line shown. Older versions of LINK may omit several of the option switches.

The Borland Version: TLINK

Originally, Borland's flagship product, Turbo Pascal, had no need of a linker, and none was provided. When Turbo C appeared in 1987, however, it required a linker, and the Borland tradition of speed demanded that the one supplied be as fast as possible. The result was *TLINK*, a compact linker with far fewer bells and whistles than were available from LINK, but much higher speed.

As Borland's product line expanded, so did the number of options available for TLINK; however, it's still a much shorter list than the corresponding one for LINK. TLINK. Nevertheless, it has adequate capability for most, if not all, purposes. It can even create COM files, which is something that LINK has never done directly.

In addition, TLINK can support overlays, and generate both normal and segmented EXE files. Like LINK, TLINK ignores the case of symbols by default, but provides an option to restore case-sensitivity. Figure 3.17 shows the options available with the latest version of TLINK in my collection.

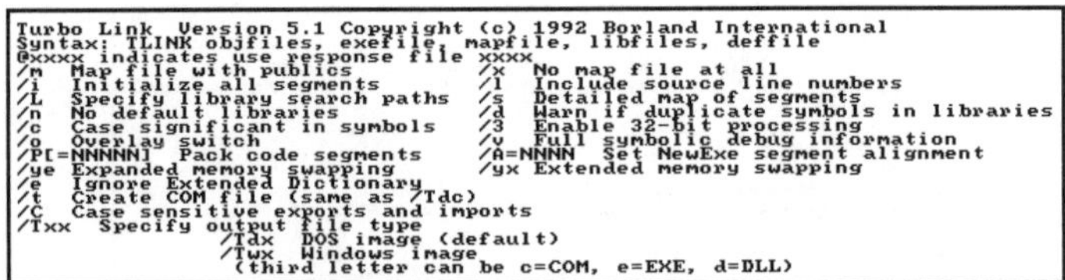

```
Turbo Link  Version 5.1 Copyright (c) 1992 Borland International
Syntax: TLINK objfiles, exefile, mapfile, libfiles, deffile
@xxxx indicates use response file xxxx
/m  Map file with publics           /x  No map file at all
/i  Initialize all segments         /l  Include source line numbers
/L  Specify library search paths    /s  Detailed map of segments
/n  No default libraries            /d  Warn if duplicate symbols in libraries
/c  Case significant in symbols     /3  Enable 32-bit processing
/o  Overlay switch                  /v  Full symbolic debug information
/P[=NNNNN]  Pack code segments      /A=NNNN  Set NewExe segment alignment
/ye Expanded memory swapping        /yx Extended memory swapping
/e  Ignore Extended Dictionary
/t  Create COM file (same as /Tdc)
/C  Case sensitive exports and imports
/Txx  Specify output file type
          /Tdx  DOS image (default)
          /Twx  Windows image
           (third letter can be c=COM, e=EXE, d=DLL)
```

Figure 3.17. Borland's TLINK includes options for dealing with both conventional DOS executable files, segmented executables required by Windows, and Dynamic Link Libraries (DLLs) that can be used both in DOS and in Windows programs.

OPTLINK from SLR Systems, Inc.

OPTLINK, the "new-generation-of-technology" based product from SLR Systems, Inc. that competes with both LINK and TLINK, has evolved by a circuitous route from its beginning simply as a super-fast linking program. First, an advanced compression capability was added to provide significantly better file shrinkage than LINK's *exepack* option could generate, and later an overlay manager version was offered.

Today's product, however, sold as OPTLINK for Windows, Version 2.5, gives primary billing to the speed with which it can create segmented EXE files, in comparison to the products from both Microsoft and Borland.

Despite the emphasis on creation of segmented EXE files, this product still includes full support for building conventional MS-DOS executable programs, and as Figure 3.18 shows, offers a larger number of options than do any of its competitors.

Other Linkers

In addition to OPTLINK, a number of other third-party linkers are in wide use. One of these is *Plink86+*, the latest version of the original overlay linker for MS-DOS use. Originally created by Phoenix Software Associates, the program has been through a number of owners since then. The most recent appears to be Lifeboat Software of Shrewsbury, New Jersey.

Plink86+, like all other MS-DOS linkers, combines object modules created by compilers and looked up in library files to form an executable output file. Its major feature, however, is that it provides a mechanism by which you can build and run programs far too big to fit into the 640K memory space available to MS-DOS at one time.

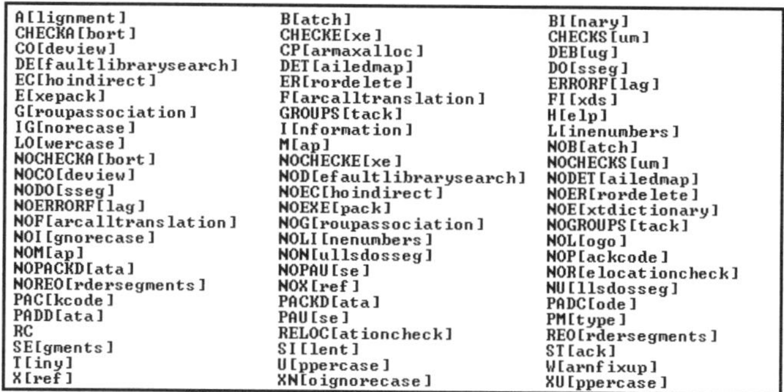

```
A[lignment]                 B[atch]                      BI[nary]
CHECKA[bort]                CHECKE[xe]                   CHECKS[um]
CO[deview]                  CP[armaxalloc]               DEB[ug]
DE[faultlibrarysearch]      DET[ailedmap]                DO[sseg]
EC[hoindirect]              ER[rordelete]                ERRORF[lag]
E[xepack]                   F[arcalltranslation]         FI[xds]
G[roupassociation]          GROUPS[tack]                 H[elp]
IG[norecase]                I[nformation]                L[inenumbers]
LO[wercase]                 M[ap]                        NOB[atch]
NOCHECKA[bort]              NOCHECKE[xe]                 NOCHECKS[um]
NOCO[deview]                NOD[efaultlibrarysearch]     NODET[ailedmap]
NODO[sseg]                  NOEC[hoindirect]             NOER[rordelete]
NOERRORF[lag]               NOEXE[pack]                  NOE[xtdictionary]
NOF[arcalltranslation]      NOG[roupassociation]         NOGROUPS[tack]
NOI[gnorecase]              NOLI[nenumbers]              NOL[ogo]
NOM[ap]                     NON[ullsdosseg]              NOP[ackcode]
NOPACKD[ata]                NOPAU[se]                    NOR[elocationcheck]
NOREO[rdersegments]         NOX[ref]                     NU[llsdosseg]
PAC[kcode]                  PACKD[ata]                   PADC[ode]
PADD[ata]                   PAU[se]                      PM[type]
RC                          RELOC[ationcheck]            REO[rdersegments]
SE[gments]                  SI[lent]                     ST[ack]
T[iny]                      U[ppercase]                  W[arnfixup]
X[ref]                      XN[oignorecase]              XU[ppercase]
```

Figure 3.18. OPTLINK Version 2.5, designed to support the segmented EXE file format used by Windows and OS/2 but also capable of generating normal MS-DOS executable files, provides these 72 option switches to control its actions. Many of them are not available from any other linker.

Plink86+ does this by breaking the oversized program into overlays. Overlays simply are sections of a program that don't need to be in RAM at the same time. You can, therefore, assign them to the same memory area and add automatic controls that determine which overlay is in RAM, which enables you to bring in another from the disk when it is needed.

For a number of years, Plink86+ was the only widely-available overlay manager and many developers became familiar with it. The complex planning necessary to obtain the best results from its overlay features, however, became a driving force that led a number of toolmakers to seek simpler solutions to the problems of RAM cram. One of the first such solutions to reach the market was *WarpLink.*

WarpLink, from hyperkinetix, inc. in Orange, California, is a linker that conforms fully to Microsoft specifications. It has been tested with all popular compilers, reads extended library information in LIB format, and accepts the `LIB`, `OBJ`, and `TMP` environment variables.

The advantages claimed by hyperkinetix (the lack of capitalization is part of their corporate identity) for WarpLink are that it will speed your development time with faster linking, and will support full dynamic overlays by eliminating costly static-overlay design time.

The first overlay linker designs (such as Plink86+) required you to plan all overlays carefully, and then you had to arrange their sequence at compile time. WarpLink provides dynamic overlays that enable your program to configure itself at runtime to make best use of available memory. Some overlay managers also allow only one level of overlay for your program to use. This means that some overlay routines cannot call others. WarpLink permits nesting to any level that allows any code to call any other code, regardless of the overlay structure.

OPTLINK, Plink86, and WarpLink are by no means the only third-party linkers available. *Blinker*, from Blink Inc., is another, as is *.RTLink* from Pocket Soft in Houston, Texas. The linker field is one area in which toolmakers still compete to find new techniques, and new products appear continually. To keep up with what's available, check the ad pages of your favorite programming magazine.

Library Managers

Microsoft, Borland, and SLR Systems offer *librarian programs*. The Microsoft and Borland products are supplied as part of the language packages when you buy a compiler or a complete development kit. SLR provides full compatibility with both other products, together with added features that simplify the creation and maintenance of your libraries.

LIB: The Microsoft Standard

The Microsoft Library Manager, *LIB*, has (like LINK) been available since the earliest days of MS-DOS. The latest version, supplied with Visual C++, is 3.30. LIB creates, organizes, and maintains standard libraries. These libraries resolve references to external routines and data during the linking process.

Standard libraries provide a common set of useful routines and data; some libraries are furnished with your compiler, others are published by tool makers, and you can create your own if you want. After you link a program to a library, that program can use a routine or data item as if it was included in the program.

LIB enables you to create a library file, add modules to a library, and delete or replace them. You can combine libraries, or copy or move a module to a separate object file. You also can produce a listing of all public symbols in the library modules. You can provide input to LIB in three ways, separately, or in combination: (a) by specifying input on the command line, (b) by responding interactively to prompts that LIB displays if you provide no option switches or command line input, or (c) by giving the program the name of a response file that contains the expected input.

To see the syntax that LIB requires, just type **LIB /?** on the command line (see Figure 3.19). This lists the seven option switches the program can accept, and the five commands to which it responds. If you type **LIB /HELP** instead, the program uses the QuickHelp system to display its option list. You then can browse through its subjects for additional information. This two-level help system is available for all components of the Programmer's WorkBench package distributed with MSC/C++ 7.0.

```
C:\>lib /?

Microsoft (R) Library Manager  Version 3.20
Copyright (C) Microsoft Corp 1983-1992.  All rights reserved.

Usage: LIB library [options] [commands] [,listfile [,newlibrary]]
Options:

    /?                     : display LIB options
    /HELP                  : display help on LIB
    /IGNORECASE            : ignore case on names
    /NOEXTDICTIONARY       : do not build extended dictionary
    /NOIGNORECASE          : do not ignore case on names
    /NOLOGO                : do not display signon banner
    /PAGESIZE:n            : set library page size to n
Commands:
    +name                  : add object file
    -name                  : delete object file
    -+name                 : replace object file
    *name                  : copy (extract) object file
    -*name                 : move (delete and extract) object file
```

Figure 3.19. When you type **LIB /?** at a command prompt, this full-screen display appears.

TLIB from Borland

The librarian supplied with Borland languages is named *TLIB,* in keeping with Borland's tradition of using the "T" initial letter. Unfortunately, in this case, it conflicts with the name of another popular program discussed later in this chapter—the TLIB version control package from Burton Systems.

Borland's TLIB is based on the same principles that guided development of TLINK: make the program small and fast by eliminating all unnecessary bells and whistles. As Figure 3.20 shows, the same five commands used by LIB are accepted; however, only three options are available. Unlike LIB and OPTLIB, TLIB provides no capability for interactive use; you must provide all information on the command line, or create a directive file to provide the input it needs.

```
C:\>tlib
TLIB 3.02 Copyright (c) 1991 Borland International
Syntax: TLIB libname [/C] [/E] [/P] commands, listfile
    libname      library file pathname
    commands     sequence of operations to be performed (optional)
    listfile     file name for listing file (optional)

A command is of the form: <symbol>modulename, where <symbol> is:
    +            add modulename to the library
    -            remove modulename from the library
    *            extract modulename without removing it
    -+ or +-     replace modulename in library
    -* or *-     extract modulename and remove it

    /C           case-sensitive library
    /E           create extended dictionary
    /PSIZE       set the library page size to SIZE

Use @filepath to continue from file "filepath".
Use '&' at end of a line to continue onto the next line.
```

Figure 3.20. Unlike the Microsoft or SLR librarians, no `/help` option is required by Borland's TLIB. Just typing the single word **TLIB** produces this display.

OPTLIB from SLR Systems, Inc.

The *OPTLIB* library manager from SLR Systems, Inc., now at Version 3.0, provides many more options than do the Microsoft or Borland programs (see Figure 3.21). Some of these, such as `extrnrename` and `publicrename`, control features that neither of the compiler-furnished products provide. Others simply enable you to have more control over the reports created if you ask for a listing.

```
OPTLIB Copyright (C) SLR Systems 1988-92
All rights reserved.
A[co]               B[maximum]          CHECKA[bort]
CHECKS[um]          EC[hoin]            EX[trnrename]
F[illblock]         H[elp]              I[ndex]
M[ap]               NOCHECKA[bort]      NOCHECKS[um]
NOE[choin]          NOF[illblock]       NOI[ndex]
NOM[ap]             NOO[kmultidef]      NOS[tats]
NOU[pdatetime]      NOV[erbose]         NOX[ref]
O[kmultidef]        P[agesize]          PU[blicrename]
PW[idth]            S[tats]             T[co]
U[pdatetime]        V[erbose]           X[ref]
```

Figure 3.21. The option switch list shown by SLR's OPTLIB library manager indicates by case differences how you can abbreviate the option name.

Like LIB, OPTLIB accepts input from the command line, interactively, or from a response file. Unlike either LIB or TLIB, it enables you to use conventional MS-DOS wild-card characters (* and ?) in the names of the object modules to be acted on, and also provides additional commands to permit time-based replacement of modules in the LIB file.

These differences can save you much work. The single OPTLIB command `OPTLIB mylib, ~ *;`, for example, causes every module in file MYLIB.LIB for which a newer OBJ file exists to be updated.

Achieving the same result with LIB or TLIB requires you to issue a separate command for each module to be replaced. If MYLIB has a large number of modules, the difference in effort can be significant.

Other Development Tools

In addition to the translators, linkers, and library managers, you will encounter many more specialized development tools. Following are some of the more useful members of this group.

The discussion begins with utilities that simplify the actual building of your project each time a change is required, and then moves on to examine ways of keeping the various versions of your program under control, and how you can maintain archives of your past work for safety.

MAKE and Its Relatives

A program maintenance utility, often called a *makefile*, although strictly speaking, that name applies only to the description file that tells the utility what to do, works by comparing the time stamps of a target file to those of its dependent files.

A *time stamp* is the time and date the file was last modified, and is assigned by MS-DOS when the file is stored. A *target file* usually is a file you want to create, such as an executable file. A *dependent file* usually is a file from which a target is created, such as a program module source file. A target typically has more than one dependent; however, this is not required.

A *description file* or *makefile* you supply defines the relationships between target and dependent files, and provides instructions for building your project.

A target is out-of-date if any of its dependents contain a later time stamp than the target, or if the target does not exist. When a target is determined to be out-of-date, to bring it up to date, its dependents are processed using the commands you associated with the dependency.

It Started at Bell Labs

In mid-1978, S. I. Feldman of Bell Laboratories in Murray Hill, New Jersey, the birthplace of UNIX, described the very first such program maintenance utility. The title of his paper was *MAKE: A Program for Maintaining Computer Programs* and it set forth the technique that has been followed ever since for such utilities.

The basic operation of MAKE, Feldman wrote in his paper, was to find the name of a needed target in the description file, ensure that all files on which it depended existed and were up-to-date, and then create a new version of the target if the existing version had not been modified since the files on which it depended were.

MAKE was actually an implementation of the principles of graph theory. Because a final target file might involve many levels of dependency, the description file actually defines a graph of dependencies. The program then does a depth-first search of this graph to determine what work is really necessary, and does only that much.

Compiler-Supplied Versions

Both Microsoft and Borland supply MAKE-based maintenance utilities as parts of their compiler packages. All these utilities, in general, follow Feldman's original rules; however, a few differences of detail exist. If you work with products from both vendors, it's perfectly safe to choose one of these utilities and use it for all your work, even with the competing compiler. By doing so, you will not need to remember these details where they differ.

Microsoft's Program Maintenance Utility (*NMAKE*) follows the original UNIX conventions, unlike its ancestor MAKE.EXE that Microsoft shipped with some older development systems. The current version of NMAKE, Version 1.30 (supplied with Visual C++), is a 32-bit MS-DOS-extended program and requires an 80386 or higher system, running in protected mode.

NMAKE provides built-in definitions for a number of "macro" strings, together with automatic dependency rules for the most common development situations. These all are based on Microsoft languages. If you want to use NMAKE with compilers from other vendors, however, you can redefine any of these items in your makefiles.

Older versions of NMAKE were capable of being used in all MS-DOS systems. If you do not require the larger capacity made possible by protected mode operation, you may want to retain an older version, such as 1.20 (see Figure 3.22).

```
C:\>nmake /?

Microsoft (R) Program Maintenance Utility   Version 1.20
Copyright (c) Microsoft Corp 1988-92. All rights reserved.

Usage:  NMAKE @commandfile
        NMAKE [options] [/f makefile] [/x stderrfile] [macrodefs] [targets]

Options:

/A Build all evaluated targets          /B Build if time stamps are equal
/C Suppress output messages             /D Display build information
/E Override env-var macros              /HELP Display online help
/I Ignore exit codes from commands      /K Build unrelated targets on error
/M Ignore extended/expanded memory      /N Display commands but do not execute
/NOLOGO Suppress copyright message      /P Display NMAKE information
/Q Check time stamps but do not build   /R Ignore predefined rules/macros
/S Suppress executed-commands display   /T Change time stamps but do not build
/V Inherit macros during recursion
/? Display brief usage message
```

Figure 3.22. These 18 options are recognized by NMAKE on its command line.

Both NMAKE and Borland's corresponding utility, MAKE, allow something that many other versions of MAKE do not: conditional directives similar to those allowed for their compilers. You can use these directives to include other makefiles, to make the rules and commands conditional, to print out error messages, and to undefine macros.

Directives in a makefile begin with an exclamation point (!). Following is the list of Borland MAKE directives (NMAKE also recognizes a few others):

```
!include
!if
!else
!elif
!endif
!error
!undef
```

Figure 3.23 shows the list of options available from the most recent version of the Borland MAKE utility.

```
MAKE Version 3.6  Copyright (c) 1991 Borland International
Syntax: MAKE [options ...] target[s]
    -B                  Builds all targets regardless of dependency dates
    -Dsymbol            Defines symbol
    -Dsymbol=string     Defines symbol to string
    -Idirectory         Names an include directory
    -K                  Keeps (does not erase) temporary files created by MAKE
    -N                  Increases MAKE's compatibility with NMAKE
    -S                  Swaps MAKE out of memory to execute commands.
    -W                  Writes all non-string options back to the .EXE file
    -Usymbol            Undefine symbol
    -ffilename          Uses filename as the MAKEFILE
    -dswapdir           Writes MAKE's swap file to swapdir
    -a                  Performs auto-dependency checks for include files
    -e                  Ignores redefinition of environment variable macros
    -i                  Ignores errors returned by commands
    -m                  Displays the date and time stamp of each file
    -n                  Prints commands but does not do them
    -p                  Displays all macro definitions and implicit rules
    -q                  Returns zero if target is up-to-date and nonzero
                        if it is not (for use in batch files)
    -r                  Ignores rules and macros defined in BUILTINS.MAK
    -s                  Silent, does not print commands before doing them
    -? or -h            Prints this message
      Options marked with '+' are on by default. To turn off a default
      option follow it by a '-', for example: -a-
```

Figure 3.23. The most recent version of Borland's MAKE utility includes an option switch for increased compatibility with NMAKE.

Configuration Control

As long as your development activity is confined entirely to the creation of programs for your own personal use, you really don't have any pressing requirement for a form of configuration control, also known as *version control* and *source code control.* Even in this limiting case, however, you may find it useful. If your work is distributed to others, whether as a free giveaway program, a shareware package, or commercially, you will discover that configuration control becomes absolutely necessary.

The purpose of configuration or version control is to simplify your work by capturing a permanent copy of all files that go into the creation of your applications, each time a new version is released. This makes it possible for you to maintain older versions, even though several years may have elapsed since you last dealt with that specific revision of the program.

The following section examines only a few such programs; many others are available in the marketplace, however.

The UNIX Source Code Control System

Version control first was reduced to a formal system, apparently, at Bell Laboratories as a part of the UNIX development effort. The original *Source Code Control System* (*SCCS*) was simply a "shell script" that used a number of standard system utilities, such as DIFF (a text-file comparison program) and SED (a stream editor) to capture differences from a "baseline" copy of each source file at each release level.

This set of preserved difference files permitted later reconstruction of any desired revision level, by making a fresh copy of the file and then performing edits that would introduce all the captured differences into this new copy.

Although the technique sounds primitive, it was effective and gained wide acceptance. Several variations of the basic technique have been available as freeware and shareware for MS-DOS users since as early as 1985.

As more developers began using the SCCS techniques, however, toolmakers saw an opportunity, and created single programs that did the work for you. The basic principle involved remained the same, however. Rather than using a shell script, you just invoke the version control utility and instruct it to update your archived version files with the latest revision, or extract from the archives the specific revision with which you need to work.

A number of such utilities are available at prices ranging from less than $200 to over $1,000. Each developer seems to have a personal favorite. Rather than attempt to describe them all, I will concentrate on the one I use: TLIB from Burton Systems Software in Cary, North Carolina.

TLIB From Burton

Burton's *TLIB* package is, unfortunately, often confused with Borland's library manager package, although the two have nothing in common with the name (Dave Burton was using this name for quite some time before Borland chose it for their product). On my own systems, I renamed both programs to avoid confusing my command interpreter. If you use only one of the programs, however, it's not a significant situation.

Now in Version 5.0, TLIB offers a wide range of custom capabilities. It enables you to embed version information automatically in both your source files and (indirectly) in the executable programs. It also permits unlimited comments that describe the reason for each revision. If you work with others and find it necessary to prevent another programmer's changes from undoing the ones you just made, you will welcome the check-in and check-out features and the capability to merge two different sets of changes into a common, non-conflicting file.

One of the things you will like most about TLIB is that it's near the bottom of the price range for version-control packages.

The capability to roll back to any prior version of a program, without losing track of the current source file, is essential to anyone who must maintain programs over a long period of time. Now that I have used TLIB for several years, I am amazed that so many developers try to get along without such a tool.

Figure 3.24 shows the original TLIB menu from Version 4.12, while the menu display available from the newer Version 5.00 is shown in Figure 3.25.

The `W<ho` prompt shown in Figure 3.24 results from the fact that I originally configured the system to provide check-in and check-out services for use by multiple developers. In Figure 3.25, you can see how the multiple-letter commands allow added flexibility. I configured this version to provide only single-programmer support, without check-in or check-out, to illustrate how each user's choices modify the displayed menu automatically.

```
C:\>tlib
TLIB 4.12h one-user version. Copr. 1985-90 D. Burton, all rights reserved.

TLIB> N<ew-lib  U<pdate  E<xtract  R<egress4browse  L<ist  P<ath-lib  T<est
      W<ho  F<ast  K<eep  B<rowse  X<regress4modify  I<n  O<ut  Q<uit  ?<help
      A<dd-branch  M<ake-branch/keep
```

Figure 3.24. This is the customized display screen shown by the version of Burton's TLIB I have used for the past three years.

```
C:\>tlib
TLIB 5.00e one-user version. Copr. 1985-92 D. Burton, all rights reserved.

 TLIB Version Control
                      E=Extract source              U=Update library
 C=Configure F=Filter ES=R=X=Specify version#       UF=Freshen
 CP=P=library Path                                  US=Specify branch#
                      N=New library
 L=list  S=Snapshot   NS=Specify starting#          Q=quit  ?=help
```

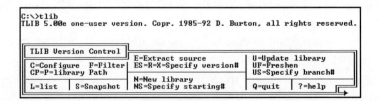

Figure 3.25. Contrast this menu, from the newest version of TLIB, with Figure 3.24.

This winds up the look at development tools you may find useful. Next, in Chapter 4, "DOS Itself: Interrupt 21h," comes an overview of the techniques involved in using MS-DOS itself, with special emphasis on the structures involved.

DOS Itself: Interrupt 21h

Now that you have a grasp of the development tools available, it's time to look at the tools that MS-DOS itself provides. These include the 109 functions for Interrupt 21h, plus additional functions available through the other 15 interrupt services reserved for use by DOS. Also, although they are not provided by MS-DOS itself, ROM-BIOS functions (Interrupts 10h through 1Ch) are available on most current systems that run MS-DOS.

This chapter concentrates on Interrupt 21h itself, which is the primary method used to obtain services from the DOS kernel code. Most of this chapter is devoted to explanation of the major data structures associated with these services. Later, in Chapters 7 through 12, you learn how to use these structures in connection with specific techniques.

All but 1 of the 15 other Interrupt services are much less complex than Interrupt 21h. The exception, Multiplex interrupt 2Fh, allows unlimited extension of DOS services and has become approximately equal to Interrupt 21h in complication. Chapter 5, "Other DOS Interrupts," discusses all 15 services.

The BIOS services, while more varied than those of the operating system, also are more constrained because all must conform rather closely to the limitations designed into the original IBM BIOS code in 1981. In general, no significant extensions have taken place since the introduction of the PS/2 line, and even those were confined primarily to the video services. Chapter 6, "BIOS When We Must," provides an overview of the BIOS.

Why Interrupt 21h?

Before looking in detail at the essential data structures used by the Interrupt 21h functions, this chapter explores just why such an arcane interface is used at all between application programs and the operating system's kernel code. Before getting an answer to the question, "Why Interrupt 21h?," the explanation begins with a quick look at the way in which MS-DOS evolved, and then at the interrupt features of the Intel family of 80x86 processor chips.

A Short History of MS-DOS

What subsequently evolved into MS-DOS was originally written by Tim Paterson, of Seattle Computer Products, in 1980, who started in April and finished the task in August. The system was known initially as 86-DOS and was sold with SCP's proprietary computer line. This original version, compared to Version 6.0, was almost primitive.

86-DOS was designed with a primary goal of making it as easy as possible to import applications from Digital Research's CP/M, the most widely-used microcomputer operating system of that era. The basic structures for file control blocks and functions were deliberately kept identical to those of CPM, to permit automatic translation of programs into 86-DOS. Even some function codes required by CP/M but not used in 86-DOS were retained, and for years, were documented mysteriously as "reserved." (They actually were explained in 86-DOS itself; the mystery was added later because IBM did not want to publicize a competing system.)

In a marketplace ruled by Z-80 and 8080 processor chips and CP/M, few knew that the 8086 or 86-DOS existed until IBM started quietly seeking a system to control its new Personal Computer line. Microsoft licensed 86-DOS in the last quarter of 1980 to fill that need, and, in July 1981, bought all rights to the system.

When IBM released the PC, Microsoft was ready with MS-DOS 1.0 (PC-DOS, for IBM machines, although subsequently Digital Research registered "PC-DOS" as a trademark and the latest IBM versions are identified simply as "DOS"). Because IBM released most of its own software to operate with PC-DOS, although two other competing systems also were available, developers rapidly flocked to it also, and before long it had become the "official" standard of the PC industry.

In the years that have followed, a number of versions have evolved. Prior to Version 3.1, the original equipment manufacturers to whom Microsoft licensed the system were free to make major changes to it, and those older versions tended to vary widely from one OEM to the next, even though version numbers did not change. With the introduction of network support in Version 3.1, it became necessary to stabilize the system significantly. Since that time, most versions at the same number level are almost totally interchangeable with each other. Following is the list of major version changes, with the release date for each and the major change involved:

Version	Date	Major Change Involved
86-DOS	August 1980	Seattle Computer Products' version
1.0	August 1981	Original PC, single-sided floppy disk
1.1	May 1982	Double-sided floppy disk
2.0	March 1983	PC XT system, including hard disk, subdirectories, and handles
2.1	October 1983	IBM PCjr and Portable PC

Version	Date	Major Change Involved
3.0	August 1984	PC AT system, including high-capacity disk
3.1	March 1985	Networking
3.2	December 1985	Enhanced support for new media
3.3	April 1987	Support for PS/2 product line
4.0	June 1988	Support for disk drives larger than 32Mb; integration of EMS memory capability
5.0	August 1990	Upper-memory blocks and High Memory Area
6.0	March 1993	Microsoft Realtime Compression Interface (MRCI)

Using Software Interrupts

A feature of the Intel 80x86 line of processor chips is the capability to execute a *software interrupt* in response to the assembly-language instruction `INT` *nn* where *nn* is a numeric value in the range 0 through 255 (0FFh). This allows for any of the 256 possible interrupt vectors to be called from within a program. The same vectors are used for hardware interrupts, which means that a program is capable of emulating an interrupt from hardware at any time; however, this is not the major usage of the Interrupt instruction.

The CPU design reserves the first 1024 memory locations for a table of 256 4-byte interrupt vectors, each of which is a memory address in far-pointer format. Upon responding to a hardware interrupt or to a software interrupt, the processor pushes its flags register to whatever stack is in use at the time. To disable additional interrupt service, it then (for hardware interrupts only) clears its IF and TF flags. These flags are not changed if a software interrupt is being serviced. Whether the interrupt is requested by hardware or by software, though, the processor pushes its CS register onto the stack after the flags register.

After pushing the existing CS register value onto the stack, the processor loads the CS register from the upper two bytes of the interrupt vector identified by the interrupt number, then pushes the IP register onto the stack and loads IP from the lower two bytes of the vector. This automatically performs a jump to the byte pointed at by the vector, which is always presumed to contain valid code. If it does not, you have a *wild interrupt.* Because interrupt service is disabled at this point and the keyboard cannot respond to a warm-boot request, the only way to regain control of the machine is to power it down and reboot.

In the PC architecture originated by IBM and since standardized through generations of clones, only a handful of true hardware interrupts exist. The most significant are the eight served by the IRQ lines that provide the realtime clock timer, fast keyboard response, video display status, serial-port communications, some hard disk and floppy disk drive services, and printer notification capabilities. In addition, Interrupt 02h is the non-maskable interrupt that can be used for a *panic switch* if an appropriate driver is provided, and Interrupts 00h through 07h normally are reserved for the CPU, although not all CPU chips generate all eight conditions.

The software interrupt list usually starts with Interrupt 10h, the BIOS video service. BIOS usage continues through Interrupt 1Fh, however, not all the vectors actually point to code. Two of them point to data tables, which should never be invoked unless you want to experience a wild pointer lockup.

The vectors for Interrupt 20h through 2Fh are reserved by MS-DOS for system use. Chapter 5, "Other DOS Interrupts," discusses them all except Interrupt 21h. Those for Interrupt 30h and 31h again are not valid; you will see why later in this chapter. Interrupt 33h is used by mouse drivers, while 60h through 67h were originally set aside to be defined by users. Interrupt 67h later was adopted for the Expanded Memory (EMS) interface.

Other interrupts have been defined, and virtually every one of the 252 usable vectors has at least one application that depends on it. When you need to know what any one of them is used for, get a recent copy of *The Interrupts List,* a multi-megabyte file maintained on Internet, Compuserve, and many BBS systems by Ralf Brown; it's updated approximately four times each year, and grows by a couple of hundred applications each time.

Software interrupts operate in much the same way as ordinary subroutine calls; however, they have one significant advantage that is especially helpful when the routines that provide the requested services, and the applications that call them, are created by different groups. That is the fact that the table lookup to translate an interrupt number to a specific machine address is built into the processor chip, making it impossible for the users to change. At the same time, a new function can readily be substituted for an existing one by a program that replaces the address in the vector table (for the interrupt that provides that function) with the address of the new routine.

When MS-DOS starts up, for example, each time you boot your system, it fills the vectors for Interrupts 20h through 2Fh with the appropriate addresses for your own system, calculated on the spot. If you load DOS=HIGH rather than leave it in low RAM, these addresses will be different and may change significantly if you add more device drivers to your system. You don't, however, need to worry about this because the Interrupt 21h vector always stays right at address 0000:0084 (00084h in 20-bit address-line format) which is where each call to the DOS kernel code will look for the actual address of the dispatch routine.

The Central API

Now that you know what this software interrupt business is all about, you are ready to answer the question, "Why Interrupt 21h?" The simple answer is that using a single software interrupt for the interface provides a consistent, uniform way of connecting applications to the operating system, without requiring applications themselves to be aware of more than that single interrupt number for all system functions.

Such a single connection point, together with the specifications for all functions that make use of it, usually is referred to as an *Applications Program Interface* (*API*). The central MS-DOS API represented by Interrupt 21h and the functions reached through it is the primary subject matter of this book.

It was absolutely arbitrary to choose Interrupt 21h for this single connection point; any other vector could have been chosen back in 1980. Because the CP/M system that 86-DOS was designed to emulate did not have the automatic interrupt-vector feature, it was limited to only 64K total of RAM, but still used a single hook to reach its "Basic DOS" or "BDOS" dispatcher. (Location 0005 contained a jump to the start of BDOS, so all applications set up the CPU registers as required, and then executed a CALL 5 command.)

That interface survives, even in MS-DOS Version 6. At offset 5 of the PSP data structure, you will find a far call to an address that turns out to be the Interrupt 30h vector if you run DOS in low RAM, or a corresponding address in the HMA if you run DOS there. At either of these points, you will find a far jump to a special routine in the DOS dispatcher that shuffles registers to convert the CP/M convention to MS-DOS standards, and then drops into the normal routines reached via Interrupt 21.

That's how it's intended to work. Unfortunately, back in Version 2.0 someone miscalculated the address and the actual address is two bytes short of the far jump. That error is still present in Version 6.0 despite having been publicized for years.

What's New in MS-DOS Version 6?

Every time a new version of MS-DOS appears, developers everywhere clamor to ask "What's new this time?"

As you have seen, virtually every major version change in the past has introduced new *functions* to the MS-DOS interface, and also most have added significant new *features.* The actual "look and feel" of the MS-DOS command line, the *face* of MS-DOS, however, hasn't undergone significant change from Version 1.0. Until now.

New Functions

The description of new lowest-level functions of interest to developers is very short—there aren't any. MS-DOS Version 6.0 contains exactly the same list of functions available via Interrupt 21h that was present in Version 5.0, and none of them has undergone a significant change. The modifications that changed the version number had nothing to do with actual DOS functions.

New Features

Unlike the major changes introduced in Version 4 and in Version 5, Version 6.0 of MS-DOS added only one new capability for developers—the *Microsoft Real-Time Compression Interface* (*MRCI*). MRCI, pronounced *merci,* permits a single Compression Server, implemented in software or hardware, to provide compression for disk storage, backup files, or any other purpose.

Version 6.0 makes available several applications that use MRCI, including the new *DoubleSpace* disk compression utility that promises to nearly double your available disk capacity, the new *Backup* programs for normal DOS use and for Windows, and a *Flash Card* support package for some laptop systems.

While Microsoft has designed MRCI to permit its implementation with hardware, none were announced at the time this was written. Several, however, may appear by the time this book reaches you.

The structures associated with MRCI are described later in this chapter, and its operation is explored in more detail in Chapter 9, "Disk Storage and the File System."

A New Face

Unlike previous upgrades of MS-DOS, the major emphasis in Version 6.0 is to simplify use of the system by the end user. To this end, the DoubleSpace utility already mentioned has been added, and the memory management capabilities of the existing drivers (HIMEM.SYS and EMM386.SYS) are enhanced. *MemMaker*, a new memory optimization program, has been created to improve organization of system drivers, TSRs, and other utilities automatically.

The `MEM` command was enhanced to give more information about your system's setup, and the `LOADHIGH` and the `DEVICEHIGH` commands gained additional power to enable MemMaker to more accurately use existing RAM space.

For data security, an anti-virus program now is included, as is an *undelete* system that provides three levels of protection. Two new commands, `MOVE` and `DELTREE`, help you organize your disk storage.

Finally, a multiple-boot configuration system has been added to CONFIG.SYS and AUTOEXEC.BAT so that you can select your system's options from a menu each time you power up rather than editing these startup files or using a third-party utility. The changes in this area also make it possible for you to bypass both files entirely, if necessary, so that you can still reboot your system without a boot diskette, even if you make a mistake while editing one or another of the files.

The Essential Structures of MS-DOS

Much of the operation of MS-DOS is controlled by a small number of tightly-defined data structures. Before getting to the actual techniques for using the MS-DOS functions, the following sections discuss these essential structures and explain the layout and organization.

To accommodate the differences that exist between the ways data structures are declared in the major development languages, each structure is shown in three different ways: first, as it would be declared for use by a MASM, TASM, or OPTASM assembly language program, next in the form of a BASIC TYPE declaration, and finally as a C/C++ `struct` definition.

Following these presentations, each element of the structure being shown is fully described. Because each of the three presentations uses the same names for each element, these descriptions apply to all three formats.

The structure definitions for each language also appear in files on the companion diskette so that you do not need to type in anything to make use of them. All definitions for one language are grouped into a single file; if you don't need all the definitions for a program, worry not. Unused definitions don't take up any space in your final application. They just instruct the assembler or compiler how to deal with the data.

If you're not already familiar with the MS-DOS functions, note that most of these structures may not make much sense at this stage. By discussing them now before dealing with the details of any specific uses for them, however, we can establish a uniform starting point and provide a ready reference for later use.

Internal Framing Structures

This section describes structures used by MS-DOS to maintain control of its internal resources. They include Memory Control Blocks, device driver headers, and device driver command packets.

The Memory Control Block (MCB) Structure

One *Memory Control Block* (MCB) structure precedes each block of RAM in the system at all times after system startup. These blocks form a linked list, known as the *memory arena,* that permits MS-DOS to keep track of RAM and parcel it on request. For more information about the functions that perform this task, see Chapter 8, "Managing Time and Space."

Following is the format for the MCB structure in assembly language:

```
MCB STRUC
TAG DB  'M' ; OR 'Z' FOR LAST BLOCK
OWNER   DW  ?
SIZE DW  ?
FILL DB  3 DUP (?)
NAME DB  8 DUP (?)
MCB ENDS
```

Following is the MCB layout defined as a record for BASIC:

```
TYPE MCB
   TAG AS STRING*1   ' M OR Z
   OWNER   AS INTEGER
   SIZE AS INTEGER
   FILL AS STRING*3
   NAME AS STRING*8
END TYPE ' MCB
```

Finally, here's the data layout for the MCB structure as a C-language declaration:

```
struct MCB {
   char Tag; /* M or Z   */
   int Owner;
   int Size;
   char fill[3];
   char Name[8];
};
```

The fields within the 16-byte MCB structure have the following significance:

Tag. This 1-byte field identifies the MCB structure and indicates whether this is the last MCB in the chain. All MCB's except the last contain "M" in this field; the final MCB contains "Z". Any other value indicates a corrupted memory arena, and renders further use of the system impossible until a reboot is performed.

Owner. This 2-byte field contains the Process Identifier (PID) of the process to which this block of memory was originally allocated, or zero to indicate that the controlled block of RAM is available for allocation. The indicated process may, however, no longer exist in the system (this is the normal case for RAM allocated during startup).

Size. This 2-byte field indicates the size of the memory block in 16-byte paragraphs, not counting the paragraph occupied by the MCB itself.

Fill. This 3-byte field normally is not used, although some third-party memory manager programs make special use of it for upper-memory-block control.

Name. This 8-byte field contains the filename, less extension, from which the process was loaded, if the RAM controlled by this MCB contains an executable program, and is not used otherwise.

The Device Driver Header (DD_HDR) Structure

One of the features that gives MS-DOS its extreme flexibility and enables it to be used for a wide range of needs is its capability to accept installable Device Drivers. To add to your system a new kind of hardware, such as a CD-ROM player or an image scanner, simply copy its device driver to your boot disk, add one line to CONFIG.SYS to direct MS-DOS to install the driver, and you're up and running as soon as you reboot.

The secrets to this flexibility are the Device Driver's fixed-format header and command structures that freeze the interface so far as MS-DOS is concerned, yet allow the driver's creator to do whatever must be done to support the hardware involved.

Following is the format for the `DD_HDR` structure in assembly language:

```
DD_HDR   STRUC
LINK DD  0FFFFFFFFH    ; NEXT DEVICE => NONE
ATTR DW  8000H       ; ATTRIBUTE BITS (CHAR)
```

```
STRAT   DW  STRATEGY ; STRATEGY ENTRY POINT
INTER   DW  INTERRUPT ; INTERRUPT ENTRY POINT
NAME DB  'DVC_NAME'   ; DEVICE NAME
DD_HDR   ENDS
```

While it's essentially impossible to write a device driver using BASIC, you might need to interpret the device driver header from within a BASIC program. Following is the `DD_HDR` layout defined as a record for BASIC:

```
TYPE DD_HDR
     LINK AS LONG
     ATTR AS INTEGER
     STRAT AS INTEGER
     INTER AS INTEGER
     NAME AS STRING*8
END TYPE ' DD_HDR
```

Finally, here's the data layout for the `DD_HDR` structure as a C-language declaration:

```
struct DD_HDR {
     void far *link; /* must be 0xFFFFFFFF  */
     unsigned attr; /* attribute bits */
     unsigned strat; /* strategy entry point */
     unsigned inter; /* interrupt entry point   */
     char name[8];  /* device name   */
};
```

The fields within the 18-byte `DD_HDR` structure have the following significance:

link. This 4-byte field is initialized to 0000FFFFh in the disk copy of a device driver, and is updated to maintain the link to the next driver in the chain when MS-DOS installs the driver.

attr. This 2-byte field contains attribute bits that define the device driver's characteristics. The bits of this field have significance determined by the most significant bit.

Bit Values	Meaning
8000h	Indicates that device is character oriented (CON, PRN, COM1, and so on) rather than block oriented (disk unit). If this bit is zero, the driver is for a block device.

(For a character device, the remaining bits of this field have the following significance (any bits not defined here are reserved and should be zero):

Bit Values	Meaning
4000h	Supports the IOCTL Read and IOCTL Write functions.
2000h	Supports Output Till Busy operation.
0800h	Supports the `Open Device` and `Close Device` functions.
0040h	Supports IOCTL Query.
0020h	Supports Generic IOCTL operation.
0010h	Services undocumented fast-output Interrupt 29h for direct screen output, bypassing redirection.
0008h	Default CLOCK$ unit.
0004h	Default NUL unit.
0002h	Default STDOUT unit.
0001h	Default STDIN unit.

(For a block device, the remaining bits of this field have the following significance. Any bits not defined here are reserved and should be zero):

Bit Values	Meaning
4000h	Supports the IOCTL Read and IOCTL Write functions.
2000h	Requires MS-DOS to supply the first sector of the first File Allocation Table (FAT) when driver function 2 (Build BPB) is invoked.
0800h	Supports the `Open Device`, `Close Device`, and `Removable Media` functions.
0040h	Supports IOCTL Query.
0020h	Supports Logical Drive Mapping or Generic IOCTL operation, or both.
0002h	Processes 32-bit sector addresses.

strat. This 2-byte field identifies the entry point to the strategy routine for the driver as an offset in bytes from the first byte of the link field.

inter. This 2-byte field identifies the entry point to the interrupt routine for the driver, as an offset in bytes from the first byte of the link field.

name. This 8-byte field contains the driver name in ASCII characters if the driver is for a character device. Any unused positions must contain blanks (20h). If the driver is for a block device, the first byte of this field may supply the number of units the driver supports, however, this information is not required. MS-DOS fills the byte with the actual number of units installed after initializing the driver when it is loaded.

The Device Driver Command Packet (DD_PKT) Structure

Each of the 21 functions that a device driver may be called on to execute contains its own specific command packet structure; however, all share a common header format that provides the information needed to distinguish the functions from each other. That common packet header structure is identified here as the `DD_PKT` structure.

Following is the format for the `DD_PKT` structure in assembly language:

```
DD_PKT  STRUC
     RHLENGTH DB  ?  ; LENGTH IN BYTES OF ENTIRE PACKET
     RHUNIT  DB  ?  ; UNIT NUMBER (FOR BLOCK DEVICE ONLY)
     RHFUNCTION   DB  ?  ; FUNCTION NUMBER
     RHSTATUS DW  ?  ; STATUS RETURNED BY DRIVER
     RHRESERVED   DB  8 DUP(?) ; NOT USED
DD_PKT   ENDS
```

Following is the `DD_HDR` layout defined as a record for BASIC:

```
TYPE DD_PKT
     RHLENGTH AS STRING*1
     RHUNIT  AS STRING*1
     RHFUNCTION   AS STRING*1
     RHSTATUS AS INTEGER
     RHRESERVED   AS STRING*8
END TYPE ' DD_PKT
```

Finally, here's the data layout for the DD_PKT structure as a C-language declaration:

```
struct DD_PKT {
     char rhLength; /* length in bytes of entire packet   */
     char rhUnit;  /* unit number (for block device only) */
     char rhFunction;   /* function number */
     int rhStatus; /* status returned by driver */
     char rhReserved[8]; /* not used  */
};
```

The fields within the DD_PKT structure have the following significance:

rhLength. This 1-byte field contains the length in bytes of the entire packet, including the function-specific portion.

rhUnit. This 1-byte field identifies the specific driver unit to which the command packet is addressed. Only block devices support multiple-unit operation.

rhFunction. This 1-byte field contains the number of the function requested. The values in this field have the following significance:

Value	Function Requested
00h	Driver initialization (all devices).
01h	Media Check (block devices only).
02h	Build BIOS Parameter Block (BPB) (block devices only).
03h	IOCTL Read (all devices).
04h	Read (all devices).
05h	Nondestructive read (character devices only).
06h	Input status (character devices only.)
07h	Input flush (character devices only).
08h	Write (all devices).
09h	Write with verify (all devices).
0Ah	Output status (character devices only).

Value	Function Requested
0Bh	Output flush (character devices only).
0Ch	IOCTL Write (all devices).
0Dh	Open Device (all devices).
0Eh	Close Device (all devices).
0Fh	Removable media (block devices only).
10h	Output until busy (character devices only).
13h	Generic IOCTL (all devices).
17h	Get logical device (block devices only).
18h	Set logical device (block devices only).
19h	IOCTL Query (all devices).

rhStatus. This 16-bit field contains the status returned by the driver. The bits of this field have the following significance:

Bits	Meaning
0-7	Error code, but only if Bit 15 is set. The error value can be any of the following values:

Error	Meaning
00h	Write-protect violation was attempted.
01h	Unknown unit was specified.
02h	Drive not ready.
03h	Unknown function code specified.
04h	CRC error was detected.
05h	Incorrect length was specified for command packet structure.
06h	Seek error occurred.

	Error	Meaning
	07h	Unknown media.
	08h	Sector not found.
	09h	Printer out of paper.
	0Ah	Write fault.
	0Bh	Read fault.
	0Ch	General failure. Returned when more specific analysis cannot be performed for any reason.
	0Dh	Reserved, not used.
	0Eh	Reserved, not used.
	0Fh	Invalid disk change.
8	Operation has completed. Until this bit is set, the requested operation is not finished.	
9	If this bit is set, the device is busy.	
15	Error has occurred and Bits 0-7 contain error code.	

rhReserved. This 8-byte field is not used and serves only to separate the common header from the function-specific portion of the command packet.

File System Structures

The structures described in this section deal with the file structure of MS-DOS, and include such things as identifying the volume serial number and label, searching directories for a file or directory, and two types of file control block.

The Media Identification (MID) Structure

The *Media Identification* (MID) structure, used by IOCTL function 440Dh minor codes 66h (Get Media ID) and 46h (Set Media ID), contains information that uniquely identifies a disk or other storage medium.

Following is the format for the MID structure in assembly language:

```
MID STRUC
MIDINFOLEVEL  DW 0
MIDSERIALNUM  DD ?
MIDVOLLABEL  DB 11 DUP (?)
MIDFILESYSTYPE DB 8 DUP
MID ENDS
```

Following is the MID layout defined as a record for BASIC:

```
TYPE MID
     MIDINFOLEVEL  AS INTEGER
     MIDSERIALNUM  AS LONG
     MIDVOLLABEL  AS STRING*11
     MIDFILESYSTYPE AS STRING*8
END TYPE ' MID
```

Finally, here's the data layout for the MID structure as a C-language declaration:

```
struct MID {
     int midInfoLevel;
     long midSerialNum;
     char midVolLabel[11];
     char midFileSysType[8];
};
```

The fields within the MID structure have the following significance:

midInfoLevel. This 2-byte field must be zero.

midSerialNum. This 4-byte field contains the serial number for the medium, in binary form.

midVolLabel. This 11-byte field contains the volume label. If the label contains fewer than 11 characters, space characters (ASCII 20h) fill the remaining bytes.

midFileSysType. This 8-byte field contains the type of file system as an 8-byte blank-padded ASCII string that can have either of the following values:

Name	Meaning
FAT12	12-bit file allocation table (FAT)
FAT16	16-bit FAT

The Directory Search (FILEINFO) Structure

The `FILEINFO` structure is used by the `FindFirst` and `FindNext` functions of Interrupt 21h to search for files that match a search mask. The structure contains information about a file or directory name, access attributes, date, and time. Some of the fields within this structure are not documented officially; these fields control where the `FindNext` function will resume its search, and should never be modified by an application.

Following is the format for the `FILEINFO` structure in assembly language:

```
FILEINFO    STRUC
FIRESERVED    DB   21 DUP (?)
FIATTRIBUTE   DB   ?
FIFILETIME    DW   ?
FIFILEDATE    DW   ?
FISIZE        DD   ?
FIFILENAME    DB   13 DUP (?)
FILEINFO ENDS
```

Following is the `FILEINFO` layout defined as a record for BASIC:

```
TYPE FILEINFO
     FIRESERVED    AS STRING*21
     FIATTRIBUTE   AS STRING*1
     FIFILETIME    AS INTEGER
     FIFILEDATE    AS INTEGER
     FISIZE        AS LONG
     FIFILENAME    AS STRING*13
END TYPE ' FILEINFO
```

Finally, here's the data layout for the `FILEINFO` structure as a C-language declaration:

```
struct FILEINFO {
     char fiReserved[21];
     char fiAttribute;
     unsigned fiFileTime;
     unsigned fiFileDate;
     long fiSize;
     char fiFileName[13];
};
```

The fields within the `FILEINFO` structure have the following significance:

fiReserved. This 21-byte field is reserved for use by MS-DOS and should not be modified in any way. These bytes are initialized by the `FindFirst` function, and contain information that the `FindNext` function uses to resume its directory search.

fiAttribute. This 1-byte field contains the attributes of the file or directory in bit-mapped form. If no attribute bits are set, the file is a normal file (ATTR-NORMAL). The bits of this field have the following significance:

Value	Meaning
`ATTR-READONLY` (01h)	Read-only file.
`ATTR-HIDDEN` (02h)	Hidden file or directory.
`ATTR-SYSTEM` (04h)	System file or directory.
`ATTR-VOLUME` (08h)	Volume label. The entry contains no other usable information (except for date and time of creation) and can occur only in the root directory. Only one such entry should appear.
`ATTR-DIRECTORY` (10h)	Directory.
`ATTR-ARCHIVE` (20h)	Modified file.

fiFileTime. This 2-byte field contains the time at which the file was created or last updated. The bits of this field have the following significance:

Bits	Meaning
0-4	Specifies two-second intervals, in the range 0 through 29.
5-10	Specifies minutes, in the range 0 through 59.
11-15	Specifies hours, in the range 0 through 23.

fiFileDate. This 2-byte field contains the date on which the file was last written. The bits of this field have the following significance:

Bits	Meaning
0-4	Specifies day, in the range 1 through 31.
5-8	Specifies month, in the range 1 through 12.
9-15	Specifies year, relative to 1980.

fiSize. This 4-byte field contains the size in bytes of the file.

fiFileName. This 13-byte field contains the name and extension of the file or directory, in ASCIIZ format (C-style terminating byte of all zero bits) with a . (period) separating the two if an extension exists.

The File Control Block (FCB) Structure

The *File Control Block* structure (FCB) contains a file control block, which was the original method of controlling access to files under CP/M and MS-DOS Version 1.0. Because the FCB makes no provision for subdirectories, it is generally considered to be obsolete. Certain operations involving directory names and volume labels, however, still require its use.

Following is the format for the FCB structure in assembly language:

```
FCB STRUC
FCBDRIVELD   DB  ?
FCBFILENAME  DB  8 DUP(?)
FCBEXTENT DB  3 DUP(?)
FCBCURBLOCKNO DW  ?
FCBRECSIZE   DW  ?
FCBFILESIZE  DD  ?
FCBFILEDATE  DW  ?
```

```
FCBFILETIME   DW  ?
FCBRESERVED   DB  8 DUP(?)
FCBCURRECNO   DB  ?
FCBRANDOMRECNO DD  ?
FCB ENDS
```

Following is the FCB layout defined as a record for BASIC:

```
TYPE FCB
     FCBDRIVELD    AS STRING*1
     FCBFILENAME   AS STRING*8
     FCBEXTENT AS STRING*3
     FCBCURBLOCKNO AS INTEGER
     FCBRECSIZE    AS INTEGER
     FCBFILESIZE   AS LONG
     FCBFILEDATE   AS INTEGER
     FCBFILETIME   AS INTEGER
     FCBRESERVED   AS STRING*8
     FCBCURRECNO   AS STRING*1
     FCBRANDOMRECNO AS LONG
END TYPE ' FCB
```

Finally, here's the data layout for the FCB structure as a C-language declaration:

```
struct FCB {
     char fcbDrivelD;
     char fcbFileName[8];
     char fcbExtent[3];
     int fcbCurBlockNo;
     int fcbRecSize;
     long fcbFileSize;
     int fcbFileDate;
     int fcbFileTime;
     char fcbReserved[8];
     char fcbCurRecNo;
     long fcbRandomRecNo;
};
```

The fields within the FCB structure have the following significance:

fcbDriveID. This 1-byte field specifies which drive contains the file (0 = default, 1 = A, 2 = B, and so on).

fcbFileName. This 8-byte field contains the name of the file. The filename must be padded with space characters (ASCII 20h) if it has fewer than eight characters.

fcbExtent. This 3-byte field contains the extension. The extension must be padded with space characters (ASCII 20h) if it has fewer than three characters.

fcbCurBlockNo. This 2-byte field contains the current block number, which points to the block that contains the current record. A block is a group of 128 records. This field and the `fcbCurRecNo` field together constitute the record pointer used by obsolete FCB-oriented operations. When opening the file, MS-DOS sets this field to zero.

fcbRecSize. This 2-byte field contains in bytes the size of a logical record. MS-DOS sets this field to 128. Any program that uses a different record size must set this field *after* opening the file.

fcbFileSize. This 4-byte field contains in bytes the size of the file. When opening an existing file, MS-DOS initializes this field from the file's directory entry.

fcbFileDate. This 2-byte field contains the date on which the file was last written. When an existing file is opened, MS-DOS initializes this field from the directory. The bits of this field have the following significance:

Bits	Meaning
0-4	Specifies day, in the range 1 through 31.
5-8	Specifies month, in the range 1 through 12.
9-15	Specifies year, relative to 1980.

fcbFileTime. This 2-byte field contains the time at which the file was created or last updated. MS-DOS initializes this field from the directory entry when opening an existing file. The bits of this field have the following significance:

Bits	Meaning
0-4	Specifies two-second intervals, in the range 0 through 29.
5-10	Specifies minutes, in the range 0 through 59.
11-15	Specifies hours, in the range 0 through 23.

fcbReserved. This 8-byte field is reserved for use by MS-DOS, although no indication exists that it has ever been used or will be in the future. It is a heritage from the older CP/M system retained for compatibility.

fcbCurRecNo. This 2-byte field contains the current record number, which points to one of 128 records in the current block. This field and the `fcbCurBlockNo` field together constitute the record pointer used by obsolete `FCB`-oriented operations. This field is maintained by MS-DOS, but is not initialized when opening the file. The calling program must set it before performing a sequential read or write operation.

fcbRandomRecNo. This 4-byte field contains the relative record number for obsolete `FCB`-oriented random file access. This field specifies the index of the currently selected record, counting from the beginning of the file. If the record size is less than 64 bytes, all 4 bytes of this field are used. Otherwise, only the first 3 bytes are used. MS-DOS does not initialize this field when opening the file. The calling program must set it before performing a random read or write operation.

The Extended File Control Block (XFCB) Structure

The *Extended File Control Block* (`XFCB`) structure contains a file control block (`FCB`) preceded by 7 additional bytes, including an attribute byte.

Following is the format for the `XFCB` structure in assembly language:

```
XFCB  STRUC
EXTSIGNATURE  DB  0FFH
EXTRESERVED  DB  5 DUP(0)
EXTATTRIBUTE  DB  ?
EXTDRIVELD  DB  ?
EXTFILENAME  DB  8 DUP(?)
EXTEXTENT DB  3 DUP(?)
EXTCURBLOCKNO DW  ?
EXTRECSIZE  DW  ?
EXTFILESIZE  DD  ?
EXTFILEDATE  DW  ?
EXTFILETIME  DW  ?
EXTRESERVED  DB  8 DUP(?)
EXTCURRECNO  DB  ?
EXTRANDOMRECNO DD  ?
XFCB  ENDS
```

Following is the XFCB layout defined as a record for BASIC:

```
TYPE XFCB
     EXTSIGNATURE  AS STRING*1
     EXTRESERVED  AS STRING*5
     EXTATTRIBUTE  AS STRING*1
     EXTDRIVELD   AS STRING*1
     EXTFILENAME  AS STRING*8
     EXTEXTENT AS STRING*3
     EXTCURBLOCKNO AS INTEGER
     EXTRECSIZE   AS INTEGER
     EXTFILESIZE   AS LONG
     EXTFILEDATE  AS INTEGER
     EXTFILETIME  AS INTEGER
     EXTRESERVED  AS STRING*8
     EXTCURRECNO  AS STRING*1
     EXTRANDOMRECNO AS LONG
END TYPE ' XFCB
```

Finally, here's the data layout for the XFCB structure as a C-language declaration:

```
struct XFCB {
     char extSignature;
     char extReserved[5];
     char extAttribute;
     char extDrivelD;
     char extFileName[8];
     char extExtent[3];
     int extCurBlockNo;
     int extRecSize;
     long extFileSize;
     int extFileDate;
     int extFileTime;
     char extReserved[8];
     char extCurRecNo;
     long extRandomRecNo;
};
```

The fields within the XFCB structure have the following significance:

extSignature. This 1-byte field contains 0FFh, the extended FCB signature.

extReserved. This 5-byte field is specified as `reserved; must be zero`. Its only known use is to separate the signature and attribute bytes.

extAttribute. This 1-byte field contains the attributes of the file or directory in bit-mapped form. If no attribute bits are set, the file is a normal file (ATTR-NORMAL). The bits of this field have the following significance:

Value	Meaning
`ATTR-READONLY` (01h)	A read-only file.
`ATTR-HIDDEN` (02h)	A hidden file or directory.
`ATTR-SYSTEM` (04h)	A system file or directory.
`ATTR-VOLUME` (08h)	A volume label. The entry contains no other usable information (except for date and time of creation) and can occur only in the root directory. Only one such entry should appear.
`ATTR-DIRECTORY` (10h)	A directory.
`ATTR-ARCHIVE` (20h)	A modified file.

extDriveID. This 1-byte field specifies which drive contains the file (0 = default, 1 = A, 2 = B, and so on).

extFileName. This 8-byte field contains the name of the file. The filename must be padded with space characters (ASCII 20h) if it has fewer than 8 characters.

extExtent. This 3-byte field contains the extension. The extension must be padded with space characters (ASCII 20h) if it has fewer than three characters.

extCurBlockNo. This 2-byte field contains the current block number, which points to the block that contains the current record. A block is a group of 128 records. This field and the `fcbCurRecNo` field together constitute the record pointer used by obsolete `FCB`-oriented operations. When opening the file, MS-DOS sets this field to zero.

extRecSize. This 2-byte field contains the size of a logical record, in bytes. MS-DOS sets this field to 128. Any program that uses a different record size must set this field *after* opening the file.

extFileSize. This 4-byte field contains the size of the file in bytes. When opening an existing file, MS-DOS initializes this field from the file's directory entry.

extFileDate. This 2-byte field contains the date on which the file was last written. When an existing file is opened, MS-DOS initializes this field from the directory. The bits of this field have the following significance:

Bits	Meaning
0-4	Specifies day, in the range 1 through 31.
5-8	Specifies month, in the range 1 through 12.
9-15	Specifies year, relative to 1980.

extFileTime. This 2-byte field contains the time at which the file was created or last updated. MS-DOS initializes this field from the directory entry when opening an existing file. The bits of this field have the following significance:

Bits	Meaning
0-4	Specifies two-second intervals, in the range 0 through 29.
5-10	Specifies minutes, in the range 0 through 59.
11-15	Specifies hours, in the range 0 through 23.

extReserved. This 8-byte field is reserved for use by MS-DOS; however, no indication exists that it has ever been used or will be in the future. It is a heritage from the older CP/M system retained for compatibility.

extCurRecNo. This 2-byte field contains the current record number, which points to one of 128 records in the current block. This field and the `fcbCurBlockNo` field together constitute the record pointer used by obsolete `FCB`-oriented operations. This field is maintained by MS-DOS, however, is not initialized when opening the file. The calling program must set it before performing a sequential read or write operation.

extRandomRecNo. This 4-byte field contains the relative record number for obsolete FCB-oriented random file access. This field specifies the index of the currently selected record, counting from the beginning of the file. If the record size is less than 64 bytes, all 4 bytes of this field are used. Otherwise, only the first 3 bytes are used. MS-DOS does not initialize this field when opening the file. The calling program must set it before performing a random read or write operation.

Process Control Structures

The structures described in this section are used for *process control.* That is, they control program loading and execution. They include the control block used by the MS-DOS program loading function, the structure for the EXE file header, and the Program Segment Prefix (PSP).

The Loader Control Block (LOAD_CB) Structure

The *Loader Control Block* (LOAD_CB) structure, used by the Load and Exec functions, contains addresses of the environment block, the command tail to be copied into the PSP area, and default FCB's to be used by the spawned process. Only the first four fields of this structure are used by the Exec function. Additional fields, used only by the Load function, enable the function to return program initialization information to the parent process. For more details of these functions, see Chapter 11, "Process Management."

Following is format for the LOAD_CB structure in assembly language:

```
LOAD_CB  STRUC
    LDENVIRONMENT DW  ?
    LDCOMMANDTAIL DD  ?
    LDFCB_1  DD  ?
    LDFCB_2  DD  ?
    LDCSIP   DD  ?  ; USED ONLY BY LOAD
    LDSSSP   DD  ?  ; USED ONLY BY LOAD
LOAD_CB  ENDS
```

Following is the `LOAD_CB` layout defined as a record for BASIC:

```
TYPE LOAD_CB
     LDENVIRONMENT AS INTEGER
     LDCOMMANDTAIL AS LONG
     LDFCB_1  AS LONG
     LDFCB_2  AS LONG
     LDCSIP  AS LONG
     LDSSSP  AS LONG
END TYPE ' LOAD_CB
```

Finally, here's the data layout for the `LOAD_CB` structure as a C-language declaration:

```
struct LOAD_CB {
     unsigned ldEnvironment;
     char far *   ldCommandTail;
     char far *   ldFCB_1;
     char far *   ldFCB_2;
     void far *   ldCSIP;
     void far *   ldSSSP;
};
```

The fields within the `LOAD_CB` structure have the following significance:

ldEnvironment. This 2-byte field contains the segment address of an environment block to be passed to the spawned process. If it contains zero, MS-DOS will create a copy of the parent's environment and pass it to the spawned process.

ldCommandTail. This 4-byte field contains a far pointer to a command tail, including its leading count byte and terminated by a Carriage Return (0Dh) byte, which will be copied to offset 80h of the `PSP` created for the spawned process.

ldFCB_1. This 4-byte field contains a far pointer to a default `FCB1` which will be copied to offset 5Ch of the `PSP` created for the spawned process.

ldFCB_2. This 4-byte field contains a far pointer to a default `FCB2` which will be copied to offset 6Ch of the `PSP` created for the spawned process.

ldCSIP. This 4-byte field, used only by `LOAD`, is filled in with the CS:IP address (in far pointer form) derived from the file that was loaded, for use by the parent on return from the `LOAD` function.

ldSSSP. This 4-byte field, used only by LOAD, is filled in with the SS:SP address (in far pointer form) derived from the file that was loaded, for use by the parent upon return from the LOAD function.

The EXE Header (EXE) Structure

The *EXE* header (EXE) structure controls the loading process for all normal MS-DOS EXE files. This structure defines the necessary relocation information, memory requirements, and program start address required to prepare the process for execution.

Following is the format for the EXE structure, in assembly language:

```
EXE STRUC
     EXESIG  DW  ?
     EXELEFTOVER  DW  ?
     EXEPAGES DW  ?
     EXEITEMS DW  ?
     EXEHDRSIZ DW  ?
     EXEREQSIZ DW  ?
     EXEDESSIZ DW  ?
     EXEINITSS DW  ?
     EXEINITSP DW  ?
     EXECHKSUM DW  ?
     EXEINITIP DW  ?
     EXEINITCS DW  ?
     EXEFIRSTRELOITEM  DW  ?
     EXEOLAYNBR  DW  ?
     EXERESERVED  DW  16 DUP(?)
     EXENEWEXE DD  ?
EXE ENDS
```

Following is the EXE layout defined as a record for BASIC:

```
TYPE EXE
     EXESIG  AS INTEGER
     EXELEFTOVER   AS INTEGER
     EXEPAGES   AS INTEGER
     EXEITEMS AS INTEGER
     EXEHDRSIZ AS INTEGER
     EXEREQSIZN AS INTEGER
     EXEDESSIZ AS INTEGER
```

```
     EXEINITSS AS INTEGER
     EXEINITSP AS INTEGER
     EXECHKSUM AS INTEGER
     EXEINITIP AS INTEGER
     EXEINITCS AS INTEGER
     EXEFIRSTRELOITEM  AS INTEGER
     EXEOLAYNBR   AS INTEGER
     EXERESERVED  AS STRING*32
     EXENEWEXE AS LONG
END TYPE ' EXE
```

Finally, here's the data layout for the EXE structure as a C-language declaration:

```
struct EXE {
     unsigned exeSig;
     unsigned exeLeftOver;
     unsigned exePages;
     unsigned exeItems;
     unsigned exeHdrSiz;
     unsigned exeReqSiz;
     unsigned exeDesSiz;
     unsigned exeInitSS;
     unsigned exeInitSP;
     unsigned exeChkSum;
     unsigned exeInitIP;
     unsigned exeInitCS;
     unsigned exeFirstReloItem;
     unsigned exeOlayNbr;
     unsigned exeReserved[16];
     unsigned long exeNewExe;
};
```

The fields within the EXE structure have the following significance:

exeSig. This 2-byte field always contains the EXE-file signature, 0x5A4D, 'MZ'.

exeLeftOver. This 2-byte field contains the number of bytes actually used on the last 512-byte page of the file.

exePages. This 2-byte field contains the number of 512 byte pages in the file.

exeItems. This 2-byte field contains the number of Relocation Table items in the file.

exeHdrSiz. This 2-byte field contains the size, in 16-byte paragraphs, of the header.

exeReqSiz. This 2-byte field contains the size, in 16-byte paragraphs, of the minimum RAM necessary for loading of the file.

exeDesSiz. This 2-byte field contains the size, in 16-byte paragraphs, of the amount of RAM desired to be allocated for the file. It usually is 0FFFFh, causing all remaining RAM to be allocated when the file loads.

exeInitSS. This 2-byte field contains the offset, in 16-byte paragraphs, of the initial value for the SS register, relative to the load point of the file. MS-DOS relocates this when the program is loaded.

exeInitSP. This 2-byte field contains the initial value for the SP register.

exeChkSum. This 2-byte field contains the one's complement (inverse) of the sum of all other bytes of the file, treated as 16-bit values, so that when all (including this field) are added together, the sum will be zero. Not all languages or linkers create this field properly.

exeInitIP. This 2-byte field contains the initial value for the IP register.

exeInitCS. This 2-byte field contains the offset, in 16-byte paragraphs, of the initial value for the CS register, relative to the load point of the file. MS-DOS relocates this when the program is loaded.

exeFirstReloItem. This 2-byte field contains the offset, in bytes from the front of the file, to the first item in the Relocation Table.

exeOlayNbr. This 2-byte field contains the overlay number if the file is an overlay, or is zero if this is a main program file.

exeReserved. This 16-byte area is not used.

exeNewExe. This 2-byte field contains the offset, in bytes from the front of the file, to the start of the Segmented EXE header if one is present, and is zero for a normal EXE file.

The Program Segment Prefix (PSP)

Each time MS-DOS loads a program for execution, it creates a *Program Segment Prefix* (PSP) structure for that program. The PSP serves a number of purposes: it provides a usually-unique identifier for the program the DOS kernel can use to keep track of resource assignments (under Windows, however, the PSP does not always identify a process uniquely), and it furnishes storage space where DOS can build certain tables required to deal with the program's input/output needs. Last, but certainly not least, it keeps track of just where control should return to when the program finishes its operation.

The PSP always is 256 bytes in length, and always starts on a paragraph boundary (that is, an offset address in which all four low bits are zero). Thus, the first address available to a program to begin its execution is offset 0100h within the program segment.

The size of the PSP is a heritage from the older CP/M operating system, and much of the layout of the PSP also is based on how CP/M's first 256 bytes of program area were used. There's historical reason for this: MS-DOS is descended directly from a system that was sold by Seattle Computer Products for quite some time before Microsoft purchased it, and one of the major features of the SCP operating system was that it had been designed to make it easy for CP/M users to transfer their programs into the 16-bit world of the 8086 processor, without redesigning.

The PSP, therefore, was deliberately laid out to duplicate the first 256 bytes of the CP/M system's transient program area so that all program functions could use addresses identical to those used by the older CP/M versions. Then, as features were added to MS-DOS in Version 2.0 and later, they were incorporated into the PSP wherever they could be made to fit.

Following is the format for the PSP structure in assembly language:

```
PSP STRUC
     TERM   DW ?
     MEMSIZ     DW ?
     SKIP1     DB ?
     CPMCALL  DB 5 DUP (?)
     SAVI22     DD ?
     SAVI23     DD ?
     SAVI24     DD ?
     PARENT     DW ?
```

```
     HANDLES  DB 20 DUP (?)
     ENVSEG     DW ?
     SAVSTK     DD ?
     NUMHDL     DW ?
     HTABLE     DD ?
     SHARECHAIN    DD ?
     SKIP2     DB ?
     TNAMEFLAG DB ?
     SKIP3     DB 10 DUP (?)
     WOLDAPP  DB ?
     SKIP4     DB 7 DUP (?)
     NIXDISP  DB 3 DUP (?)
     SKIP5     DB 2 DUP (?)
     EXTFCB     DB 7 DUP (?)
     FCB1   DB 16 DUP (?)
     FCB2   DB 20 DUP (?)
     TAILCOUNT DB ?
     TAIL   DB 127 DUP (?)
PSP ENDS
```

Following is the PSP layout defined as a record for BASIC:

```
TYPE PSP
     TERM   AS INTEGER
     MEMSIZ     AS INTEGER
     SKIP1     AS STRING*1
     CPMCALL  AS STRING*5
     SAVI22     AS LONG
     SAVI23     AS LONG
     SAVI24     AS LONG
     PARENT     AS INTEGER
     HANDLES  AS STRING*20
     ENVSEG     AS INTEGER
     SAVSTK     AS LONG
     NUMHDL     AS INTEGER
     HTABLE     AS LONG
     SHARECHAIN    AS LONG
     SKIP2     AS STRING*1
     TNAMEFLAG AS STRING*1
     SKIP3     AS STRING*10
     WOLDAPP  AS STRING*1
     SKIP4     AS STRING*7
     NIXDISP  AS STRING*3
```

```
    SKIP5     AS STRING*2
    EXTFCB     AS STRING*7
    FCB1   AS STRING*16
    FCB2   AS STRING*20
    TAILCOUNT AS STRING*1
    TAIL   AS STRING*127
END TYPE ' PSP
```

Finally, here's the data layout for the PSP structure as a C-language declaration:

```
struct PSP {
    int     Term;
    int     MemSiz;
    char    Skip1;
    char    CPMCall[5];
    void far *   SavI22;
    void far *   SavI23;
    void far *   SavI24;
    int     Parent;
    char    Handles[20];
    int     EnvSeg;
    void far *   SavStk;
    int     NumHdl;
    void far *   HTable;
    void far *   ShareChain;
    char    Skip2;
    char    TNameFlag;
    char    Skip3[10];
    char    OldApp;
    char    Skip4[7];
    char    NixDisp[3];
    char    Skip5[2];
    char    ExtFCB[7];
    char    FCB1[16];
    char    FCB2[20];
    char    TailCount;
    char    Tail[127];
};
```

The fields within the PSP structure have the following significance:

Term. This 2-byte field contains the hexadecimal values CD followed by 20, the binary opcode for the Interrupt 20 instruction that can be used to terminate operation of the process.

MemSiz. This 2-byte field contains the address of the first RAM segment past the end of the RAM allocated to the program. The size of the program can be determined by subtracting the segment address of the PSP from the value in this field.

Skip1. This 1-byte field serves as a filler to align the next field at offset 5.

CPMCall. This 5-byte field contains a far CALL to the MS-DOS dispatcher, permitting programs to emulate the CP/M convention CALL 5 for accessing the operating system functions rather than using Interrupt 21. It is preserved for compatibility's sake; few, if any, applications actually use it.

SavI22. This 4-byte field contains the address to which control should return when the current process terminates, as a far pointer. The loader copies the value of the Interrupt 22h vector into this field initially, but the field may be changed to direct control elsewhere if desired for special purposes. Methods for using this field are not well documented.

SavI23. This 4-byte field contains, as a far pointer, the value of the Interrupt 23h (Control-C handler) vector in effect when the process was loaded.

SavI24. This 4-byte field contains, as a far pointer, the value of the Interrupt 24h (Critical Error handler) vector in effect when the process was loaded.

Parent. This 2-byte field contains the Process ID (PSP segment address) of the process from which the current process was loaded. Command interpreters, such as COMMAND.COM, are their own parents.

Handles. This 20-byte field contains indices into an undocumented system structure. The handles used by most file and device I/O as described in Chapters 7 and 9 actually are index values into this table.

EnvSeg. This 2-byte field contains the segment portion of the address for the environment strings associated with this process.

SavStk. This 4-byte field contains the saved value of SS:SP at the last invocation of Interrupt 21h, stored as a far pointer.

NumHdl. This 2-byte field contains the number of handles available to this process.

HTable. This 4-byte field contains a far pointer to the handle table for this process, usually located at offset 0018h of the `PSP` structure (handles).

ShareChain. This 4-byte field contains a far pointer to `SHARE`'s closing chain if SHARE.EXE is loaded; otherwise, all 32 bits are set to 1.

Skip2. The purpose of this 1-byte field is unknown.

TNameFlag. This 1-byte field contains APPEND's `TrueName` flag.

Skip3. The purpose of this 10-byte field is unknown.

WOldApp. This 1-byte field contains the Windows `OldApp` flag.

Skip4. The purpose of this 7-byte field is unknown.

NixDisp. This 3-byte field contains machine instructions to call Interrupt 21, and then performs a far return. This field was intended to supply a UNIX-like dispatcher capability. It is virtually never used.

Skip5. The purpose of this 2-byte field is unknown.

ExtFCB. This 7-byte field provides an extended `FCB1` should the process need it.

FCB1. This 16-byte field contains an `FCB` created from the first parameter on the command line.

FCB2. This 20-byte field contains an `FCB` created from the second parameter on the command line.

TailCount. This 1-byte field contains the number of characters contained in the `Tail` field.

Tail. This 127-byte field contains the actual command line passed in from the parent process. The 128-byte area starting at `TailCount` also is used as the default Disk Transfer Address (DTA) unless a program explicitly changes the DTA, and will be overwritten whenever an `FCB`-based read and write operation takes place, or when a handle-based `FindFirst` call is executed.

MRCI Structures

The *Microsoft Real-Time Compression Interface*, MRCI, defines two new structures not present in previous versions of MS-DOS. This section describes them both.

The MRCINFO Structure

The `MRCINFO` structure, one of the two DOS structures that's new in Version 6.0, contains information concerning the MRCI server and its capabilities, if such a server is present in the system. A pointer to such a structure is returned by the `MRCQuery` function of the MRCI API, and is sent on `MRCNotifyLoad`.

Following is the format for the 18-byte `MRCINFO` structure in assembly language:

```
MRCINFO STRUC
MI_LVENDOR      DD  ?
MI_WVENDORVERSION      DW  ?
MI_WMRCIVERSION   DW  ?
MI_PFNOPERATE DD  ?
MI_FLCAPABILITY   DW  ?
MI_FLHWASSIST DW  ?
MI_CBMAX     DW  ?
MRCINFO ENDS
```

Following is the `MRCINFO` layout defined as a record for BASIC:

```
TYPE MRCINFO
     MI_LVENDOR     AS STRING*4
     MI_WVENDORVERSION  AS INTEGER
     MI_WMRCIVERSION   AS INTEGER
     MI_PFNOPERATE AS LONG
     MI_FLCAPABILITY   AS INTEGER
     MI_FLHWASSIST AS INTEGER
     MI_CBMAX    AS INTEGER
END TYPE ' MRCINFO
```

Finally, here's the data layout for the `MRCINFO` structure as a C-language declaration:

```
struct MRCINFO {
     char  mi_lVendor[4];
     int   mi_wVendorVersion;
     int   mi_wMRCIVersion;
     void far *mi_pfnOperate; /* func ptr */
     unsigned mi_flCapability;
     unsigned mi_flHWAssist;
     int   mi_cbMax;
};
```

The fields within the `MRCINFO` structure have the following significance:

mi_lVendor. This 4-byte field identifies the creator of the MRCI server by means of a 4-letter alphanumeric code. Microsoft's code is `MSFT`.

mi_wVendorVersion. This 2-byte field provides the version number of the MRCI server. Its high byte is the major version number, and the low byte is the minor version. Version 3.20 of a server returns `0314h` in this field, for example, while version 10.01 returns `0A01h`.

mi_wMRCIVersion. This 2-byte field provides the MRCI version number that is supported by this server.

mi_pfnOperate. This 4-byte field contains a far pointer to the server's compression entry point.

mi_flCapability. This 2-byte field indicates the server's capabilities in bit-mapped form. The bits of this field have the following significance:

Bit	Meaning
0	Standard compression supported.
1	Standard decompression supported.
2	Update supported.
3	Reserved, do not use.
4	Reserved, do not use.
5	Incremental decompression supported.
6-14	Unused, must be zero.
15	`MRCINFO` structure is read-only.
All Set	If all bits are set at input, the Server is directed to deinstall itself and suspend all service.

mi_flHWAssis. This 2-byte field indicates hardware assisted server capabilities in bit-mapped form. The bits have the same significance as the `mi_flCapability` bits. A bit set in this field indicates the corresponding capability is hardware assisted.

mi_cbMax. This 2-byte field indicates the maximum number of bytes the server can compress or decompress on a single call. Requests to compress or decompress buffers in excess of this length will fail. All MRCI servers are required, by specification, to support blocks up to at least 8,192 bytes (8K) as a minimum.

The MRCREQUEST Structure

The `MRCREQUEST` structure, the other new DOS structure in version 6.0, is used to pass information between the MRCI server and its clients for all compression and decompression actions.

Following is the format for the `MRCREQUEST` structure in assembly language:

```
MRCREQUEST    STRUC
MR_PBSRC     DD ? ; PTR TO SOURCE BUFFER
MR_CBSRC     DW ? ; SIZE IN BYTES
MR_OFFUPDATE     DW ?
MR_PBDST     DD ? ; PTR TO DEST BUFFER
MR_CBDST     DW ? ; SIZE IN BYTES
MR_CBCHUNK      DW ?
MR_DWINCDECOMP DD ?
MRCREQUEST    ENDS
```

Following is the `MRCREQUEST` layout defined as a record for BASIC:

```
TYPE MRCREQUEST
     MR_PBSRC AS LONG
     MR_CBSRC AS INTEGER
     MR_OFFUPDATE  AS INTEGER
     MR_PBDST AS LONG
     MR_CBDST AS INTEGER
     MR_CBCHUNK   AS INTEGER
     MR_DWINCDECOMP AS LONG
END TYPE   ' MRCREQUEST
```

Finally, here's the data layout for the MRCREQUEST structure as a C-language declaration:

```
struct MRCREQUEST {
     char far *   mr_pbSrc;
     int mr_cbSrc;
     unsigned int  mr_offUpdate;
     char far *   mr_pbDst;
     int mr_cbDst;
     int mr_cbChunk;
     long mr_dwIncDecomp;
};
```

The fields within the MRCREQUEST structure have the following significance:

mr_pbSrc. This 4-byte field contains a far pointer to a source buffer. The content of the buffer pointed to by this field depends on the type of operation being requested from the MRCI server.

If the requested operation is compress, the buffer contains uncompressed data. If the requested operation is update, the buffer contains valid, uncompressed data starting at the offset specified by the `mr_offUpdate` field. Other content, from the start of the buffer to the byte just prior to this offset, is ignored.

If the requested operation is decompress, the buffer contains compressed data. If the requested operation is incremental decompress, this field points to the next section of compressed data to be uncompressed. The server updates the offset portion of this address after each incremental decompress call. Your application should not modify this address between incremental decompress calls on the same block of compressed data.

The buffer defined by `mr_pbSrc` and `mr_cbSrc`, and the one defined by `mr_pbDst` and `mr_cbDst`, must not be allowed to overlap. The safest practice is to make `mr_cbSrc` and `mr_cbDst` identical.

mr_cbSrc. This 2-byte field contains the size of the source buffer. If the requested operation is compress, this is the amount of data to be compressed. This value is ignored for a decompress operation. The amount of data to be decompressed is specified by the `mr_offUpdate` field.

mr_offUpdate. This 2-byte field is used only for update operations, and has different significance at the start and finish of an operation. On input (start of an operation), this is the offset (within the same segment specified by `mr_pbSrc`) in the source buffer where the changed uncompressed data begins. On output (finish of an operation), this is the offset (same segment as `mr_pbDst`) in the destination buffer where the changed compressed data starts.

mr_pbDst. This 4-byte field contains a far pointer to a destination buffer. The content of the buffer pointed to by this field depends on the type of operation being requested from the MRCI server.

If the requested operation is compress, the buffer receives the compressed data. If the requested operation is update, the buffer must contain the original (non-updated) compressed representation of the uncompressed data in the source buffer. When the operation completes, the buffer receives the compressed result.

If the requested operation is decompress, the buffer receives the uncompressed result of the operation. If the requested operation is incremental decompress, this field points to the next location in the destination buffer where uncompressed data is to be stored. The server will update the offset portion of this address after each incremental decompress call, and the application should not modify this address between incremental decompress calls on the same block of compressed data.

The buffer defined by `mr_pbSrc` and `mr_cbSrc`, and the one defined by `mr_pbDst` and `mr_cbDst`, must not be allowed to overlap. The safest practice is to make `mr_cbSrc` and `mr_cbDst` identical.

`mr_cbDst`. The value of this 2-byte field at the start of an operation depends on the type of operation requested from the MRCI server. If the requested operation is compress, the value is the size of the destination buffer. If the compressed data would overflow this length, the operation fails and the server returns the error `MRCI_ERROR_BUFFER_OVERFLOW`.

If the requested operation is decompress, the value must be the exact number of bytes to be decompressed. The MRCI server uses this value to stop decompressing. If the requested operation is incremental decompress, the value is the number of bytes to be uncompressed at this time. This typically will be less than the original uncompressed size of the compressed block.

A single compressed block can be uncompressed in steps, by making multiple incremental decompress calls for smaller sized blocks. To process an entire compressed block in this way, however, the individual `mr_cbDst` values must total to exactly the number of bytes originally compressed so that the MRCI server can determine when to stop. The value of this field, provided by the server at the end of an operation, is always the actual size of the resulting compressed or uncompressed data.

mr_cbChunk. This 2-byte field contains information that enables the Server compression routines to complete their tasks as rapidly as possible. It specifies a threshold. If compression cannot save at least that many bytes, no action need be attempted.

Valid threshold values range from 1 (indicating that the client wants compression if even 1 byte will be saved) up to 32767, which prevents compression unless the savings amount to 32K. The DbleSpace driver uses a value of 512 for this threshold, and the Flash File System passes a value of 1.

Use of this field is most easily explained with an actual example: DblSpace allocates storage in 512-byte increments (the usual disk sector size) and, therefore, sets this field to 512 because smaller savings would have no effect on space usage.

The compression server then can use this information for either of the following optimizations:

- If the Server cannot compress the uncompressed data enough to save at least 512 bytes, then no compression is attempted, even if doing so could save a smaller amount of space.
- When compressing, if the remaining uncompressed data can be encoded simply (that is, by run length rather than a more complicated algorithm) without crossing a 512 byte boundary, then the Server is permitted to do the simpler encoding.

  These optimizations often may be hard to perform rapidly in software-only servers, but hardware may be able to do them with little or no loss of performance.

  mr_dwIncDecomp. This 4-byte field is used only for incremental decompression. For the first such call on a compressed block, the field's value must be set to zero. Upon return, the field contains state information for use on the next incremental decompress call, and must not be modified between subsequent incremental decompress calls on the same compressed block.

DoubleSpace Structures

This section describes the layout of a *DoubleSpace Compressed Volume File* (`CVF`), and the data structures associated with this utility. If the DoubleSpace server is present on a system, you can use it as a generic MRCI driver in addition to its normal functions.

CVF Layout

A DoubleSpace `CVF` consists of the following regions that occur in the order listed. Offset and size are in sectors rather than bytes.

Name	Offset	Size	Description
`MDBPB`	0	1	The `MDBPB` contains fields that describe the rest of the `CVF`.
`BitFAT`	1	Varies	The `BitFAT` has a bit for each sector in the Sector Heap (see later in list). A bit is 1 if the corresponding sector is in use, and is 0 if the corresponding sector is free. The space allocated for the `BitFAT` is a function of the `MaximumCapacity` of the CVF. For the largest `MaxCap` (512Mb), the `BitFAT` occupies 128K. The actual space in use varies, depending on the current size of the Sector Heap. The `BitFAT` tracks which sectors in the Sector Heap are in use. Each word of the `BitFAT` maps 16 sectors in the Sector Heap. The high bit (bit 15) of the word corresponds to the

Name	Offset	Size	Description
			first sector of the 16 sectors, bit 14 corresponds to the second sector, and so on, and bit 0 corresponds to the 16th sector. To ensure that the `BitFAT` is correct, it is rebuilt (by scanning the `MDFAT`) each time the CVF is mounted.
`Reserved1`	Varies	1	Reserved for future use by DoubleSpace.
`MDFAT`	Varies	Varies	A table of 4 byte entries that maps FAT clusters to sectors in the Sector Heap that contain the (usually compressed) data for a cluster.
`Reserved2`	Varies	31	This region is reserved for future use by DoubleSpace.
`Boot`	Varies	1	The boot sector for the DoubleSpace drive. This is not used for booting, even if the DoubleSpace drive is mounted as drive C. When MS-DOS reads sector 0 from the compressed volume, this is the sector that is returned. This structure is a standard MS-DOS boot sector. This is present for compatibility, but is not used for booting the system, even if the C drive is compressed.
`Reserved3`	Varies	Varies	This region is reserved for future use by DoubleSpace. This exists to position the FAT at a desired sector-multiple offset in the CVF. The first 4 bytes of this region contain the first DoubleSpace signature stamp (`F8,'D','R',0`).

Name	Offset	Size	Description
FAT	Varies	Varies	FAT for the DoubleSpace drive. This is a normal MS-DOS File Allocation Table. DoubleSpace drives only contain a single FAT in the CVF, but DBLSPACE.BIN virtualizes this as two FATs, to be compatible with software that does not expect a hard drive to have a single FAT. Writes to the virtual 2nd FAT are ignored, and reads from the virtual 2nd FAT are mapped to reads from the true 1st FAT.
Root Dir	Varies	32	The root directory for the DoubleSpace drive. Standard MS-DOS root directory (512 entries of 32 bytes each).
Reserved4	Varies	2	Reserved for future use by DoubleSpace.
Sect Heap	Varies	60	Sectors that store the (usually compressed) data for clusters. This region forms the majority of all space used by the CVF.
2nd Stamp	Varies	1+	Starts at the last full sector of the CVF, and contains the second DoubleSpace signature stamp ('M','D','R',0).

The MDBPB Structure

The *MDBPB* structure appears in the first sector of a Compressed Volume File, and contains information that describes the size and location of the remaining parts of the CVF. This structure defines virtually all characteristics of the CVF and establishes the size of its other regions.

Following is for the MDBPB structure in assembly language:

```
MDBPB    STRUC
     JMPBOOT  DB  3 DUP(?)
     ACHOEMNAME   DB  8 DUP(?)
     CBPERSEC DW  ?
     CSECPERCLU   DB  ?
     CSECRESERVED  DW  ?
     CFATS   DB  ?
     CROOTDIRENTRIES   DW  ?
     CSECTOTALWORD DW  ?
     BMEDIA  DB  ?
     CSECFAT  DW  ?
     CSECPERTRACK  DW  ?
     CHEADS  DW  ?
     CSECHIDDEN   DD  ?
     CSECTOTALDWORD DD  ?
     SECMDFATSTART DW  ?
     NLOG2CBPERSEC DB  ?
     CSECMDRESERVED DW  ?
     SECROOTDIRSTART   DW  ?
     SECHEAPSTART  DW  ?
     CLUFIRSTDATA  DW  ?
     CPAGEBITFAT  DB  ?
     RESERVED1 DW  ?
     NLOG2CSECPERCLU   DB  ?
     RESERVED2 DW  ?
     RESERVED3 DD  ?
     RESERVED4 DD  ?
     F12BITFAT DB  ?
     CMBCVFMAX DW  ?
MDBPB ENDS
```

Following is the MDBPB layout defined as a record for BASIC:

```
TYPE MDBPB
     JMPBOOT  AS STRING*3
     ACHOEMNAME   AS STRING*8
     CBPERSEC AS INTEGER
     CSECPERCLU   AS STRING*1
```

```
    CSECRESERVED  AS INTEGER
    CFATS   AS STRING*1
    CROOTDIRENTRIES   AS INTEGER
    CSECTOTALWORD AS INTEGER
    BMEDIA  AS STRING*1
    CSECFAT  AS INTEGER
    CSECPERTRACK  AS INTEGER
    CHEADS  AS INTEGER
    CSECHIDDEN   AS LONG
    CSECTOTALDWORD AS LONG
    SECMDFATSTART AS INTEGER
    NLOG2CBPERSEC AS STRING*1
    CSECMDRESERVED AS INTEGER
    SECROOTDIRSTART   AS INTEGER
    SECHEAPSTART  AS INTEGER
    CLUFIRSTDATA  AS INTEGER
    CPAGEBITFAT  AS STRING*1
    RESERVED1 AS INTEGER
    NLOG2CSECPERCLU   AS STRING*1
    RESERVED2 AS INTEGER
    RESERVED3 AS LONG
    RESERVED4 AS LONG
    F12BITFAT AS STRING*1
    CMBCVFMAX AS INTEGER
END TYPE ' MDBPB
```

Finally, here's the data layout for the MDBPB structure as a C-language declaration:

```
struct MDBPB {
    BYTE jmpBOOT[3];
    char achOEMName[8];
    WORD cbPerSec;
    BYTE csecPerClu;
    WORD csecReserved;
    BYTE cFATs;
    WORD cRootDirEntries;
    WORD csecTotalWORD;
    BYTE bMedia;
    WORD csecFAT;
    WORD csecPerTrack;
```

```
    WORD cHeads;
    DWORD   csecHidden;
    DWORD   csecTotalDWORD;
    WORD secMDFATStart;
    BYTE nLog2cbPerSec;
    WORD secMDReserved;
    WORD secRootDirStart;
    WORD secHeapStart;
    WORD cluFirstData;
    BYTE cpageBitFAT;
    WORD RESERVED1;
    BYTE nLog2csecPerClu;
    WORD RESERVED2;
    DWORD   RESERVED3;
    DWORD   RESERVED4;
    BYTE f12BitFAT;
    WORD cmbCVFMax;
};
```

The fields within the `MDBPB` structure have the following significance:

jmpBOOT. This 3-byte field contains machine code for a jump to the bootstrap routine, just as a normal MS-DOS drive's boot sector begins.

achOEMName. This 8-byte field contains the OEM name like a normal boot sector's start. All DoubleSpace `CVF`'s contain the string `MSDBL6.0` in this position.

cbPerSec. This 2-byte field contains the count of bytes per sector, which always is 512 for a DoubleSpace `CVF`. This field through the `csecTotalDWORD` field is a clone of a standard MS-DOS BIOS Parameter Block.

csecPerClu. This 1-byte field contains the count of sectors per cluster, which is always 16 for a DoubleSpace `CVF`.

csecReserved. This 2-byte field contains the count of reserved sectors.

cFATs. This 1-byte field contains the count of FATs, which always is one for a DoubleSpace `CVF`. Even though only one FAT is stored on-disk, when the drive is mounted, the DoubleSpace driver simulates two FATs because many programs use the number of FATs to distinguish between RAM drives and physical disks.

cRootDirEntries. This 2-byte field contains the count of root directory entries, which is always 512 for a DoubleSpace CVF.

csecTotalWORD. This 2-byte field contains the count of total sectors if that count does not exceed 65,535. If the count is larger, this field contains zero, and the count is contained in the csecTotalDWORD field.

bMedia. This 1-byte field contains the Media Code byte, which is always 0F8h (hard disk) for a DoubleSpace CVF.

csecFAT. This 2-byte field contains the count of sectors occupied by the FAT.

csecPerTrack. This 2-byte field contains the count of sectors-per-track. Although present for structure compatibility, this field is ignored by DoubleSpace and its content may, therefore, have any value.

cHeads. This 2-byte field contains the count of heads. Although present for structure compatibility, this field is ignored by DoubleSpace and its content may, therefore, have any value.

csecHidden. This 4-byte field contains the count of hidden sectors.

csecTotalDWORD. This 4-byte field contains the count of total sectors, if the csecTotalDWORD field's value is zero. This is the final field of a standard MS-DOS BPB. The fields that follow have meaning only to DoubleSpace.

secMDFATStart. This 2-byte field contains the number of the first logical sector of the MDFAT region. This field and all that follow are DoubleSpace extensions.

nLog2cbPerSec. This 1-byte field contains the log (base 2) of the cbPerSec field that indicates the number of shifts required during calculations. Because cbPerSec is always 512, the value of nLog2cbPerSec always is 9 in a DoubleSpace CVF.

csecMDReserved. This 2-byte field contains the number of sectors that precede the DOS boot sector region of the CVF.

secRootDirStart. This 2-byte field contains the number of the first logical sector of the Root Directory region of the CVF.

secHeapStart. This 2-byte field contains the number of the first logical sector of the Sector Heap region of the CVF.

cluFirstData. This 2-byte field contains the total number of MDFAT entries (clusters) occupied by the DOS boot sector, reserved area, and root directory regions of the CVF.

cpageBitFAT. This 1-byte field contains the count of 2K pages in the BitFAT region of the CVF.

RESERVED1. This 2-byte field is not used.

nLog2csecPerClu. This 1-byte field contains the log (base 2) of the csecPerClu field that indicates the number of shifts required during calculations. Because csecPerClu always is 16, the value of nLog2csecPerClu always is 4 in a DoubleSpace CVF.

RESERVED2. This 2-byte field is not used.

RESERVED3. This 4-byte field is not used.

RESERVED4. This 4-byte field is not used.

f12BitFAT. This 1-byte field indicates the size of FAT entries. It contains 1 if the CVF uses a 12-bit FAT, or 0 if the CVF uses a 16-bit FAT.

cmbCVFMax. This 2-byte field contains the maximum CVF size, in megabytes (1024*1024). This field is important particularly because it determines the maximum possible size of the CVF (the maximum amount of uncompressed data that can be stored in the CVF).

DBLSPACE.EXE establishes the maximum capacity of a CVF at the time the CVF is created, and bases the value on the size of the host drive rather than on the initial size requested for the compressed volume. In particular, the BitFAT, MDFAT, and FAT regions of the CVF are sized to support this maximum capacity, even though the CVF's actual size may not require use of the complete BitFAT, MDFAT, and FAT regions. This preallocation permits the CVF to grow (and shrink) rapidly because the only actions required are to (1) change the CVF size itself (to adjust the Sector Heap size), and (2) change a few fields in the MDBPB.

The MDFAT Structure

The *MDFAT* region of a CVF is a table containing 4-byte MDFAT-structure entries, one for each cluster on the compressed drive. The size of this table is determined by the maximum capacity of the CVF as defined by the MDBPB structure field cmbCVFMax. For the largest possible CVF (512Mb), the MDFAT occupies 256K.

Each entry in the MDFAT of a CVF consists of 32 bits. The entry points to the location in the Sector Heap where the data for the cluster is stored, and contains flags that indicate whether the data is compressed and if the cluster is in use. It also shows the compressed and uncompressed length of the cluster. This structure is unusual among MS-DOS data because it is bit-aligned rather than being aligned on byte boundaries. Because of this unusual alignment, the structure descriptions cannot be provided in any portable fashion.

The bit fields of each 32-bit MDFAT structure have the following significance (bit offset is indicated from the least significant bit of a doubleword rather than from left to right within the MDFAT):

Offset	Size (bits)	Name	Description
0	22	secStart	22-bit sector number of the first sector in the Sector Heap used to store the data for this sector. All sectors for a cluster are contiguous. Add one to this number to get the CVF sector number.
22	4	csecCoded	4-bit count of the number of sectors (minus 1) used to store this cluster. If csecPlain is less than 15, it is possible for csecCoded to be larger than csecPlain.
26	4	csecPlain	4-bit count of the number of sectors required to store this cluster in uncompressed format.

Offset	Size (bits)	Name	Description
30	1	`fUncoded`	Flag bit indicating whether data for this cluster is stored compressed (0) or uncompressed (1). Data is stored uncompressed when Double Space cannot compress it, to avoid taking more space than uncompressed data requires.
31	1	`fUsed`	Flag bit indicating that this `MDFAT` entry is in use (1) or unused (0). This bit is used by the DoubleSpace Server in part to support undelete operations.

The Sector Heap

The sectors for each cluster are stored contiguously in the Sector Heap region of the `CVF`. When this space is all used, no more free space on the partition exists (even though MS-DOS may report that there is because free clusters exist in the FAT).

The sectors in the Sector Heap are controlled by the `BitFAT` structure, which is an array of 16-bit values, in which each 16-bit entry records the state of 16 clusters. Within each entry, the structure uses one bit for each sector in the heap. Each time DoubleSpace needs disk space to store data on the compressed volume, it gets a free sector from the sector heap, and sets the corresponding bit in the `BitFAT` to indicate the sector is in use. Each time a sector is released, the corresponding bit in the `BitFAT` is cleared.

Each compressed cluster begins with a 4-byte tag that indicates how its data is compressed:

4D 44 00 00 Indicates the data is StandardCompressed

Uncompressed clusters have no leading tag field.

The DS_PKT Structure

The DS_PKT structure is used to pass commands to flush ('F') or invalidate ('I') the buffers associated with a specific disk volume compressed by means of the DoubleSpace utility provided with DOS Version 6.0. A pointer to such a structure is passed to the DoubleSpace server, normally DBLSPACE.BIN, via the IOCTL write-to-block-device function of MS-DOS, as described in Chapter 9, "Disk Storage and the File System." The server returns information within this structure to indicate whether the request succeeded or failed.

Following is the format for the DS_PKT structure in assembly language:

```
DS_PKT  STRUC
DSPSTAMP DW ?
DSPCOMMAND   DB ?
DSPRESULT DW ?
DSPPADDING   DB 5 DUP(?)
DS_PKT  ENDS
```

Following is the DS_PKT layout defined as a record for BASIC:

```
TYPE DS_PKT
     DSPSTAMP AS STRING*2
     DSPCOMMAND   AS STRING*1
     DSPRESULT AS STRING*2
     DSPPADDING   AS STRING*5
END TYPE ' DS_PKT
```

Finally, here's the data layout for the DS_PKT structure as a C-language declaration:

```
struct DS_PKT {
     char dspStamp[2];
     char dspCommand;
     char dspResult[2];
     char dspPadding[5];
};
```

The fields within the 10-byte DS_PKT structure have the following significance:

dspStamp. This 2-byte field confirms that the packet is a DoubleSpace command packet, and must contain the value 'DM'.

dspCommand. This 1-byte field contains the command (`'F'` or `'I'`) to be performed.

dspResult. This 2-byte field, set to zero when the packet is sent via the IOCTL function, contains the result code returned by DBLSPACE.BIN. Upon return, it contains the characters `'OK'` if no error occurred; any error causes it to remain unchanged.

dspPadding. This 5-byte field is not used currently but must be provided in the structure.

The Master Boot Record (MBR) Structure

The *Master Boot Record* (`MBR`) structure specifies the size and the starting and ending sectors of a partition on a disk that can be partitioned. This structure, although used by MS-DOS, also is defined for many other operating systems and permits different systems to coexist on the same fixed disk.

Following is the format for the `MBR` structure in assembly language:

```
MBR STRUC
PEBOOTABLE    DB  ?
PEBEGINHEAD   DB  ?
PEBEGINSECTOR DB  ?
PEBEGINCYLINDER   DB  ?
PEFILESYSTEM  DB  ?
PEENDHEAD DB  ?
PEENDSECTOR  DB  ?
PEENDCYLINDER DB  ?
PESTARTSECTOR DD  ?
PESECTORS DD  ?
MBR ENDS
```

Following is the `MBR` layout defined as a record for BASIC:

```
TYPE MBR
     PEBOOTABLE   AS STRING*1
     PEBEGINHEAD  AS STRING*1
     PEBEGINSECTOR AS STRING*1
```

```
     PEBEGINCYLINDER   AS STRING*1
     PEFILESYSTEM  AS STRING*1
     PEENDHEAD AS STRING*1
     PEENDSECTOR  AS STRING*1
     PEENDCYLINDER AS STRING*1
     PESTARTSECTOR AS LONG
     PESECTORS AS LONG
END TYPE ' MBR
```

Finally, here's the data layout for the `MBR` structure as a C-language declaration:

```
struct MBR {
     char peBootable;
     char peBeginHead;
     char peBeginSector;
     char peBeginCylinder;
     char peFilesystem;
     char peEndHead;
     char peEndSector;
     char peEndCylinder;
     long peStartSector;
     long peSectors;
};
```

The fields in the `MBR` structure have the following significance:

peBootable. This 1-byte field indicates whether the partition is bootable. If this field is 80h, the partition is bootable; if the field is 00h, the partition is not bootable. All other values are undefined and indicate a corrupted structure.

peBeginHead. This 1-byte field contains the head number used, together with `peBeginCylinder`, to determine the first track in the partition.

peBeginSector. This 1-byte field contains the number of the first sector in the partition, relative to the partition's first track.

peBeginCylinder. This 1-byte field contains the cylinder number used, together with `peBeginHead`, to determine the first track in the partition.

peFileSystem. This 1-byte field indicates what type of file system is present in the partition, and can be one of the following values. (Although other values are possible, MS-DOS recognizes only those given.)

Value	Meaning
00h	Unknown type
01h	12-bit file allocation table (FAT); partition smaller than 10Mb
04h	16-bit FAT; partition smaller than 32Mb
05h	Extended DOS partition
06h	16-bit FAT; partition larger than or equal to 32Mb

peEndHead. This 1-byte field contains the head number used, together with `peEndCylinder`, to determine the last track in the partition.

peEndSector. This 1-byte field contains the number of the last sector in the partition, relative to the partition's first track.

peEndCylinder. This 1-byte field contains the cylinder number used, together with `peEndHead`, to determine the last track in the partition.

peStartSector. This 4-byte field contains the number of the first sector in the partition, relative to the beginning of the disk.

peSectors. This 4-byte field contains the number of sectors in the partition.

Summing Up

In this chapter, you learned the answer to the question "Why Interrupt 21h?" and then examined what's new in Version 6, compared to previous versions of MS-DOS. You then learned about the essential structures that the Interrupt 21h functions use extensively, the internal framing, the file system, process control, the new MRCI and DoubleSpace details, and finally the partition entry or Master Boot Record.

You can find the structure declaration files containing all the examples from this chapter, in the CHAP04 subdirectory on the companion diskette.

In Chapter 5, "Other DOS Interrupts," you learn about the other 15 interrupts reserved for use by MS-DOS.

Other DOS Interrupts

5

Although a total of 256 interrupt numbers are allowed by the architecture of the Intel 80x86 family of processor chips, a number of these are reserved for use by the hardware and still others have been taken over by the ROM-BIOS writers. MS-DOS uses but a fraction of the total number available.

Originally, Microsoft claimed only the 16 vectors in the range 20h through 2Fh for use by the operating system. In the official *MS-DOS Programmer's Reference* for Version 5.0, however, the list of interrupts "reserved for MS-DOS" had grown to 32, with the highest number advancing to 3Fh. The reserved numbers, and the names of the corresponding services, are as follows:

INT Number	Interrupt Name
20h	Terminate Process
21h	Main DOS Kernel
22h	Termination Return Address
23h	User Signal (Ctrl-C) Handler
24h	Critical Error Handler
25h	Absolute Disk Read
26h	Absolute Disk Write
27h	Terminate and Stay Resident
28h	Idle Time
29h	Fast CRT Output
2Ah	Network Redirector
2Bh-2Dh	Not used
2Eh	COMMAND.COM Hook
2Fh	Multiplexing
30h-31h	CP/M Dispatch Jump
32h	Not used
33h	Mouse driver
34h-3Fh	Not used

Interrupts, in general, can be used for two purposes. They can provide a simplified *interface* for widely-used system services by furnishing a single connection point available to all programs, as described in Chapter 4, "DOS Itself: Interrupt 21h," for Interrupt 21h, or they can be used to trap and respond to *exception* conditions no matter when they may occur.

Exceptions frequently are confused with *errors*, but the two kinds of conditions are fundamentally different in nature.

An exception is a condition that creates significant impact on a program's capability to continue operation, or on the desirability of permitting it to do so.

An error, on the other hand, may (and usually does) impact the accuracy of the results created by a program, but normally has no effect on the program's capability to continue after the error is detected.

Attempting to take a directory listing from Drive A when there's no diskette mounted in the drive, for example, creates an exception, as shown in Figure 5.1.

```
C:\>dir a:


Not ready reading drive A
Abort, Retry, Fail?f
Volume in drive A has no label

Not ready reading drive A
Abort, Retry, Fail?f
Fail on INT 24
```

Figure 5.1. The default exception handler for critical errors that is supplied by COMMAND.COM generates succinct, but not always extremely informative, advisory messages to users.

This exception was passed to the default Critical Error handler contained in COMMAND.COM, which first reported its inability to read the drive after trying to read the volume label.

Because the user told the system to `fail` rather than `abort` or *retry* after this initial error, the DIR internal command again attempted to read the nonexistent diskette, and generated a second exception. Not until the second attempt failed also did the program end and return to the prompt.

Not all exception handlers are as cryptic, or as dim-witted, as the default model. Performing the exact same sequence of events under the alternate command interpreter 4DOS, with its slightly smarter Critical Error handler, for example, produces the single report shown in Figure 5.2.

```
C:\>dir a:
Drive not ready--close door
R(etry), I(gnore), F(ail), or A(bort)? f
Invalid drive "A:"
```

Figure 5.2. Exception handlers need not be cryptic, however, as this response from the 4DOS.COM default Critical Error handler shows.

Rather than reporting only an inability to read the drive, the 4DOS handler digs into drive status deeply enough to discover that the door is open. After the user instructs it to fail, the handler concluded that additional attempts to read would be useless. It therefore reported that the drive letter is not valid, and returned to the prompt.

An error, on the other hand, simply may cause the program to report its existence, and continue operating, as Figure 5.3 shows. In this case, one byte of the header information of a PK-ZIP archive file was changed deliberately, and then a listing of archive contents was attempted.

```
C:\>pkunzip -t langmod

PKUNZIP (R)    FAST!    Extract Utility    Version 1.1    03-15-90
Copr. 1989-1990 PKWARE Inc. All Rights Reserved. PKUNZIP/h for help
PKUNZIP Reg. U.S. Pat. and Tm. Off.

Searching ZIP: LANGMOD.ZIP
Testing: RDMSG.AWK      OK
Testing: UNMSG.AWK      OK
Testing: AWK.DOC        OK
PKUNZIP: Warning! inconsistent local header for file: MKMSG.AWK
Testing: MKMSG.AWK      PKUNZIP: Warning! file fails CRC check
Testing: AWK.EXE        OK
Testing: AWK.MAN        OK

LANGMOD.ZIP has errors!
```

Figure 5.3. Unlike an exception, an error in a file simply causes the program to take corrective action and continue. In this case, the corrective action is nothing more than notifying the user that an error is detected.

Of the 13 interrupts actually used by MS-DOS, out of the 32 vectors to which it lays claim, all but two provide simplified single-point interfaces. The two interrupts that deal with exceptions are the *User Signal Interrupt* (23h) and the *Critical Error Interrupt* (24h).

Because the designers of MS-DOS expected both exception handlers to be replaced frequently by handlers more suitable for any specific application, the vectors for both of them are saved in the PSP automatically each time a new process is launched, and on termination of the process, both are restored automatically from the values that were saved previously.

No other interrupt handler addresses receive this automatic save-and-restore treatment, so if your application installs handlers for any other interrupts it must take care to explicitly save the original vector content and restore it before terminating. You can, however, replace either or both of the default DOS exception handlers without worrying about it.

Interrupt 20h: Terminate Process

Terminate Process (Interrupt 20h), like Terminate Program (Interrupt 21h Function 00h) and End Program (Interrupt 21h Function 4Ch), ends operation of the current program, and returns control to MS-DOS. MS-DOS then frees all resources owned by the program, such as allocated memory, stack space, open files, and standard devices.

Interrupt 20h was the original method of terminating a program's operation. In the older CP/M system, the standard method to terminate a program was to jump to location 0, and at offset 0 in each program's PSP, the two-byte machine code sequence for INT 20h appears to transfer control from there to the DOS kernel.

In Version 2.0, when a major enhancement of MS-DOS capabilities (including handles and subdirectories) was implemented, the idea of an *exit code* for each program was introduced as part of the upgrade. The simple JMP 0 or INT 20h procedure that had sufficed, however, didn't provide any way to pass such an exit code back to the parent process, so the End Program function (Interrupt 21h Function 4Ch) was introduced to replace the older techniques.

For backwards compatibility, the older techniques were left in place, and some programs continue to use them. All three of the older procedures force the exit code returned to be zero, which renders the ERRORLEVEL feature of COMMAND.COM and most other command interpreters useless unless the End Program function is used for termination.

This interrupt is not recommended for new programs. It has been labeled "superseded" in Microsoft's official documentation.

Interrupt 22h: Termination Address Storage

The *Termination Address,* stored in the vector for Interrupt 22h, is the address within the current program's parent process to which control should return. Because this address is not actually an interrupt service routine, Interrupt 22h should never be invoked by a program.

All five of the process termination operations—Terminate Program (Interrupt 20h), Terminate Program (Interrupt 21h Function 00h), Keep Program (Interrupt 21h Function 31h), End Program (Interrupt 21h Function 4Ch), or Terminate and Stay Resident (Interrupt 27h)—use this vector as a far pointer in order to return control to the parent.

As the last step in completing any of the termination functions, MS-DOS performs a far jump to the address stored in this vector. Changing the vector from inside your program does nothing. The functions always restore the vector-table entry from the current PSP before making the jump, so all changes the program makes directly to the vector-table entry itself are ignored.

Before jumping to the restored termination address, MS-DOS returns its focus to the parent program's stack and PSP. In addition, if a program does not remain resident by using one of the two TSR functions, MS-DOS will free all resources that were allocated to the program, such as memory, stack space, open files, and standard devices.

However, no automatic removal of any special interrupt handlers or error traps the program might have installed is done, and such handlers or traps will virtually guarantee a system crash if left in place after an abnormal termination of your program. You can use the termination address to make sure that such additions are removed no matter how your program terminates.

Even though MS-DOS ignores any changes you make to the Interrupt 22h vector directly, you still can control what happens when your program ends. If the program, for example, adds a special handler for the serial port and you want to be certain it is removed before the memory that contains the handler is released for re-use, you can create a special routine to be performed when your program terminates.

Some languages, such as ANSI C, provide hooks to tie such routines into the program using the keyword `atexit`, but even those may not suffice if your program ends because of a detected critical error through Interrupt 24h (discussed later in this chapter). By modifying the program's Termination Address, however, you can ensure that your cleanup code always is called.

To do this, you must modify the saved Termination Address pointer stored at offset 0Ah in your PSP, so that it points to your cleanup code rather than to the saved address. When you do this, be sure to preserve the original pointer's value within your cleanup code, and jump through that saved pointer to the original Termination Address after performing your special processing.

Interrupt 23h: User Signal Handler

The *User Signal Handler* (Interrupt 23h) is called automatically by MS-DOS if the Control-C character (ASCII 03h) is detected while processing certain system functions. When the handler returns to the system, MS-DOS restarts the system function or terminates the current program.

Although the exact details may vary depending on the specific brand of BIOS chip involved, in most computers, a Ctrl-C character is stuffed in at the head of the keyboard buffer when you press the Ctrl-Break key combination. This makes the Ctrl-Break combination appear to act the same as Ctrl-C although the actual detection methods are totally different, and permits a single User Signal handler to process both signals.

The User Signal interrupt is invoked from only a few locations within the MS-DOS kernel code, and should never be called by a user program because of its special requirements in regard to entry conditions.

The primary purpose of the User Signal interrupt, and also of the BIOS Control-Break Signal interrupt, is to enable you to escape from a runaway program. This sometimes is called *bailing out* of the program, by analogy to a pilot's taking leave of a fatally stricken aircraft.

Like the pilot's escape from the impending crash, however, any exit from a complicated program must be done in an orderly manner to ensure that all file buffers are written to disk properly, directory entries are updated, any special interrupt handlers are removed from the system before memory is released, and so on. Because the default versions supplied with MS-DOS don't do all of these things, achieving this orderly exit requires you to create a custom handler.

When you press Ctrl-C, MS-DOS does not issue Interrupt 23h immediately. Instead, the system places the resulting character (ASCII 03h) in the keyboard buffer. When the character finally reaches the front of the buffer, MS-DOS detects it while carrying out a system function.

If the I/O mode for the keyboard (or input device) is set to ASCII or COOKED, MS-DOS checks the keyboard buffer for the Ctrl-C character while executing most of the character I/O functions (Interrupt 21h Functions 0lh through 0Ch). If the Ctrl-C check flag is set, the check also is performed during other system functions. The Ctrl-C check flag can be controlled from CONFIG.SYS by `BREAK=ON` or `BREAK=OFF` lines, or from your program by Interrupt 21h Function 3301h.

If the I/O mode for the keyboard (or input device) is set to BINARY or RAW, the system disables Ctrl-C character processing while a program uses Read File or Device (Interrupt 21h Function 3Fh) and the Ctrl-C character is processed simply as normal input.

When a Ctrl-C character is detected, MS-DOS does the following things to prepare for any eventuality before issuing Interrupt 23h:

1. All registers are restored to the values they had when the interrupted system function was called initially.
2. The program's stack is made the current stack. When the handler receives control, the program's stack will contain the following data (starting from the top of the stack):
   a. The return address (CS:IP) and flags needed for the `iret` instruction back to the system
   b. The return address (CS:IP) and flags needed for the `iret` instruction back to the program
3. Any internal system variables, such as the `ErrorMode` and `InDOS` flags, are cleared to zero, to permit the handler to use system functions or even to return directly to the program with no disruption of system operations.

Because of these precautions, a User Signal handler can call any system function, even though it actually is called from within the MS-DOS kernel.

On return to MS-DOS from Interrupt 23h, the method of return determines what action will be taken.

If the handler returns to MS-DOS by using the `iret` instruction, or by clearing the carry flag and using the `retf` instruction, the system repeats the system function from the beginning. To permit this to succeed, the handler must preserve all registers at entry and restore them before returning to the system.

If the handler sets the carry flag and uses the `retf` instruction to return, MS-DOS terminates the program by calling End Program (Interrupt 21h Function 4Ch) and passing an exit code of zero.

COMMAND.COM provides a default handler that terminates the current program unless a batch file is running. Any files opened using handles will be closed; however, FCB-based files will not nor will any other cleanup be performed. This can cause data in buffers to be lost, and if the program has installed special interrupt handlers, this even can leave invalid addresses in the interrupt vectors. If you want more complete control of what happens in such a situation, you need to provide a custom handler rather than simply using the default version.

If a batch file is being executed, the default handler prompts the user to determine whether to continue. Because this action suspends execution of the program until the user responds, the default handler should be replaced for any programs that lock resources (especially if the program may be used through a network), in order to ensure that other programs can gain access to needed resources at all times.

Providing a custom exception handler for Interrupt 23h is not as complicated as you might imagine. All that's really required is that you (a) prevent MS-DOS from doing its own interpretation, and (b) signal your program that the user wants to get out. You can do this simply by providing a global flag that your program checks at strategic points during its operation.

If the flag is found to be set, your program then can clean up and stop its operation in an orderly manner. The flag is cleared initially when your program starts, and can be set only by your custom Interrupt 23h handler, which consists of the following two instructions:

```
NewI23:     inc     QuitFlag
            iret
```

The `iret` causes MS-DOS to repeat the system function in process when the user pressed Ctrl-C or Ctrl-Break. This, however, normally does not cause problems, especially if your program tests `QuitFlag` after every request for keyboard input, and ignores that input if an exit has been requested.

Interrupt 24h: Critical Error Handler

MS-DOS issues *Critical Error Interrupt* (24h) when a critical error (that is, any error that prevents an I/O operation from completing satisfactorily) is detected while MS-DOS is attempting to read from or write to a device or a file.

A handler to service this interrupt must respond to such errors, and then return to the system to ignore the error, try the function again, terminate the function, or terminate the program.

When starting each program, MS-DOS establishes a default critical-error handler for it by copying the parent program's handler address to the vector for Interrupt 24h, and to offset 12h in the new PSP.

COMMAND.COM includes a default handler that displays a message (not always in the most informative terms) about the error, then prompts the user for a response such as `Abort, Retry, Fail, or Ignore?`, and when the user replies, returns an appropriate action code to the system. If your program does not define its own handler and install it, this handler will be used.

Just like the User Signal Handler for Interrupt 23h, the Critical Error Handler should be replaced by your own custom version any time your application needs to maintain complete control of system actions. Unlike the User Signal Handler, however, you must keep your Critical Error Handler within strict limits to avoid problems within MS-DOS itself. This comes about because the handler is only half of the error handling procedure. The other half is inside MS-DOS, in the routine that sets things up before calling your handler, and then responds to the action code that your handler returns.

Note that although any program can freely change its vector as necessary to install a new handler, it must never change the address saved in its PSP because MS-DOS uses this address to restore the handler for the parent program.

When a critical error condition is detected, MS-DOS automatically retries the operation several times (the exact number of attempts can be set by the user, but defaults to 5 if not changed) before calling Critical Error Interrupt 24h. Before making the interrupt call, MS-DOS does the following to prepare for error analysis and reporting and to prevent repeated errors from causing a system lock-up:

1. The AX, DI, BP, and SI registers are loaded with error information, such as the error value, error location, type of operation, and type of device.

2. The program's stack is made current. When the handler receives control, the stack contains the following data (from the top):

    a. The return address (CS:IP) and flags for the `iret` instruction back to the system.

b. The program registers that were passed to the failed function, in the order AX, BX, CX, DX, SI, DI, BP, DS, and ES.

c. The return address (CS:IP) and flags for the `iret` instruction back to the program.

The stack's layout at entry to the handler, therefore, looks like the following (keep in mind that the stack grows downward, so that the lowest address is the top of the stack; that's why the layout may seem to be reversed):

Register	Description
Flags	From original Int 21h call (at highest address)
CS	From program's original Int 21h call
IP	From program's original Int 21h call
ES	Value that was pushed on entry to Int 21h
DS	Value that was pushed on entry to Int 21h
BP	Value that was pushed on entry to Int 21h
DI	Value that was pushed on entry to Int 21h
SI	Value that was pushed on entry to Int 21h
DX	Value that was pushed on entry to Int 21h
CX	Value that was pushed on entry to Int 21h
BX	Value that was pushed on entry to Int 21h
AX	Value that was pushed on entry to Int 21h
Flags	From Int 24h call
CS	From Int 24h call
IP	From Int 24h call (at lowest address, SS:SP at entry)

3. Internal system variables, such as those for `InDOS` and `ErrorMode`, are set. `InDOS` is set to zero to permit the handler to call system functions. `ErrorMode` is set to 1 to prevent the system from issuing another

Interrupt 24h before the handler returns. MS-DOS can deal with only one Interrupt 24h at a time. More create an infinite loop.

MS-DOS passes error information to the handler in four registers, as follows:

Register	Description
AH	Specifies when and where the error occurred, and how the handler is permitted to respond. The bits of this register can have the following values:

Bit	Meaning
0	Specifies operation causing the error. If this bit is 0, the error occurred during a read. Otherwise, the error occurred during a write.
1, 2	Specifies location of the error if the error occurred on a block device. These bits can have the following values: 00-Error in reserved sector (MS-DOS area) 01-Error in file allocation table (FAT) 10-Error in directory 11-Error in data area These bits are not used for character devices.

4. Specifies whether handler is permitted to terminate the function. If this bit is 1, the handler is permitted to terminate the function. Otherwise, it cannot attempt to do so.
5. Specifies whether handler is permitted to retry the function. If this bit is 1, the handler is permitted to retry the function. Otherwise, it cannot attempt to do so.
6. Specifies whether handler is permitted to ignore the error. If this bit is 1, the handler is permitted to ignore the error. Otherwise, it cannot attempt to do so.
7. Reserved. This bit is not used and remains 0.

8. Specifies the type of device on which error occurred. If this bit is 0, the error occurred on a block device. If this bit is 1, the error occurred on a character device or in the memory image of the FAT, and the handler must check bit 15 in the word at offset 04h of the Device Driver Header structure to determine which. If bit 15 is set, the error occurred on a character device. Otherwise, the error occurred in the memory image of the FAT.

Register	Description
AL	If the error occurred on a block device, specifies drive number (0 = A, 1 = B, 2 = C, and so on). Not used for errors on character devices.
DI	Error value. The upper byte of the DI register is undefined. The value, in the lower byte only, can be one of the following:

Value	Meaning
00h	Attempt to write on write-protected disk
0lh	Unknown unit
02h	Drive not ready
03h	Unknown command
04h	CRC error in data
05h	Incorrect length of drive-request structure
06h	Seek error
07h	Unknown media type (non-MS-DOS disk)
08h	Sector not found
09h	Printer out of paper
0Ah	Write fault
0Bh	Read fault
0Ch	General failure
0Fh	Invalid disk change

Register	Description
BP:SI	Points to the Device Driver Header structure (described in Chapter 4) for the device on which the error occurred. The handler must not change the contents of this structure.

Any critical error handler must determine what should be done in response to the error, and then take the appropriate actions. The default handler, for example, displays brief (and sometimes cryptic) information about the error, and then asks the user how to proceed, as was shown in Figure 5.1 earlier in this chapter.

The critical error handler is permitted to use only these functions of Interrupt 21h:

Character I/O (Functions 01h through 0Ch)
Get CTRL-C Check Flag (Function 3300h)
Set CTRL-C Check Flag (Function 3301h)
Get Startup Drive (Function 3305h)
Get MS-DOS Version (Function 3306h)
Set PSP Address (Function 50h)
Get PSP Address (Functions 51h and 62h)
Get Extended Error (Function 59h)

Get Extended Error (Function 59h) is especially useful for handlers that need as much information as possible about the error because this function retrieves detailed error information.

The critical-error handler returns to the system by using the `iret` instruction. The handler must preserve the BX, CX, DX, DS, ES, SS, and SP registers, and restore their values before returning. The handler also must set the AL register to specify the action the system should take. Depending on the actions allowed (specified by bits 3, 4, and 5 of the AH register), AL can contain one of the following action code values:

Value	MS-DOS Response if Code is Allowed
00h	Ignore error. The failing function returns to the program as if it had completed successfully.
0lh	Retry operation. The failing function is called again. The handler must preserve and restore all registers before returning.

Value	MS-DOS Response if Code is Allowed
02h	Terminate program. The system sets the termination type to be EXIT-CRITICAL-ERROR (02h) and carries out the same actions as Interrupt 21h Function 4Ch.
03h	Terminate function. The failing function returns to the program with an error indication.

MS-DOS checks the action code returned by the handler to verify that it is one of those allowed. If values `00h` or `01h` are returned when not allowed, MS-DOS terminates the function. If value `03h` is returned when not allowed, MS-DOS terminates the program.

You can write a custom handler that returns directly to your program; however, if you do this, your handler must clean up the stack by removing all but the last three words before it issues an `iret` instruction.

When you perform this direct return, the handler returns to the statement directly after the I/O function that caused the error, and MS-DOS is in an "unstable" condition until some Int 21h function greater than 0Ch is called.

Specifically, the `ErrorMode` flag MS-DOS set before calling the handler remains set when you return directly. This creates potential problems for the internal stacks within the MS-DOS kernel. Your handler can overcome this problem by getting the flag's address and clearing it explicitly, but such modification of normal DOS actions definitely is not recommended. If your handler can possibly do so, its best action is to return to the calling program through DOS rather than attempting to do this directly.

Note that Extended File Open (Interrupt 21h, Function 6Ch), added to DOS in Version 4.0, enables you to specify that the default Critical Error handler not be allowed to produce visible output for a file. If, when the file is opened, you set the bit that requests this action, then any critical error detected when dealing with that file will result in automatic `action code 3` return, with no message.

Each time control returns to COMMAND.COM, the default Critical Error Handler is restored to Interrupt 24h. This means that it is not possible to provide a single system-wide replacement handler that installs as a TSR. Each program that requires custom handling of critical errors must install its own handler when the program begins operation.

Interrupts 25h and 26h: Absolute Disk Read and Write

Absolute Disk Read (Interrupt 25h), and *Absolute Disk Write* (Interrupt 26h) have been part of MS-DOS from its beginning. These services provide direct linkage to the BIOS disk services from within MS-DOS, allowing access to data not contained within normal MS-DOS files.

Neither of these services, however, have enjoyed wide use. Both are now officially listed in the MS-DOS Programmer's Reference for Version 5.0 as having been superseded by generic IOCTL functions described in Chapter 9, "Disk Storage and the File System."

Absolute Disk Read: Interrupt 25h

Absolute Disk Read (Interrupt 25h) reads data from the disk into memory by directly accessing the desired logical sector, without using the MS-DOS directory structure.

Because it does bypass all the MS-DOS internal safeguards, this type of access must be handled with extreme care to avoid causing irreparable damage to the file system and possibly losing all data stored there. For such tasks as reading root directories themselves, or other parts of the file system that are not themselves files, however, this (or an equivalent service) is your only option.

This interrupt (together with Absolute Disk Write Interrupt 26h) now is officially listed in the MS-DOS Programmer's Reference for Version 5.0 as having been superseded by generic `IOCTL` functions described in Chapter 9.

The Absolute Disk Read Interrupt addresses the data it will read by means of a *Logical Sector Number* (LSN) that uniquely identifies a specific sector within a single logical disk or partition. The LSN, however, applies only within a partition that is known to MS-DOS and is not a hidden sector.

In particular, the Absolute Disk Read Interrupt cannot be used to read the Master Boot Record from a hard disk that contains multiple partitions. For that task, you must go to BIOS or to the `IOCTL` function, which have the capability to address the disk using physical head, cylinder, and sector numbering.

Logical sectors, unlike physical sector numbers, are zero-based and are numbered sequentially beginning with track 0, head 0. The first sector on this track is LSN 0.

After the final sector on this first track, the sequence continues to the next head, and then the next track, and so on. Logical sector numbers correspond to the sequence of sector numbers stored magnetically on the disk itself and often will not correspond to the physical sector sequence. By specifying interleaving factors, physical separation can be introduced between consecutive logical sectors on the disk. This often is done to improve the disk's access efficiency.

A number of popular disk utilities, such as SpinRite from Gibson Research, enable you to measure and optionally to modify the interleaving factor in use, without losing any data from the disk. Such utilities usually use either Absolute Disk Read Interrupt 25h or the BIOS disk interface to read the sectors into memory, and then rearrange the physical sequence, and write the entire track back out via BIOS.

This function is difficult to use directly from high-level languages because when the function returns, the word containing the CPU flags, pushed onto the stack originally by the INT 25h call's execution, is still there. This confuses all subsequent code, because all `push` operations are expected to have corresponding `pop` actions to clean up after them.

To restore the stack to its expected condition, you can use `popf` to remove the value from the stack, or you can do an `add sp,2` to increment the stack pointer past the unwanted flag word.

Because high-level languages don't include direct facilities for this kind of operation, this interrupt must be called from assembly language to prevent failure of the system. The call can, however, be done by means of embedded assembly language as you will see in Chapter 9.

In Version 4.0 of MS-DOS, the possible size of a logical sector number grew to 32 bits. To take care of this larger value, an extended format was invented for Interrupts 25h and 26h. The newer extended format must be used when reading from any volume greater than 32Mb in size, even though the actual sector number may be capable of being expressed in only 16 bits. Thus, extended format is required by most modern systems that run Version 5 or 6 of MS-DOS with large-capacity hard disks.

To show that the extended format is in use, set CX to FFFFh (-1). The DS:BX register pair then is interpreted as pointing to a `DISKIO` structure rather than to the buffer to read data into.

Following is the format for the `DISKIO` structure in assembly language:

```
DISKIO              STRUC
    DISTARTSECTOR   DD ?    ; LSN TO START AT
    DISECTORS       DW ?    ; NBR SECTORS TO TRANSFER
    DIBUFFER        DD ?    ; FAR POINTER TO BUFFER
DISKIO              ENDS
```

Following is the `DISKIO` layout defined as a record for BASIC:

```
TYPE DISKIO
    DISTARTSECTOR   AS LONG
    DISECTORS       AS INTEGER
    DIBUFFER        AS LONG
END TYPE            ' DISKIO
```

Finally, here's the data layout for the `DISKIO` structure as a C-language declaration:

```
struct DISKIO {
    long         diStartSector;
    int          diSectors;
    char far *   diBuffer;
};
```

The fields within the `DISKIO` structure have the following significance:

diStartSector. This 4-byte field is the Logical Sector Number at which the reading should begin.

diSectors. This 2-byte field contains the number of sectors to transfer.

diBuffer. This 4-byte field is a far pointer to the buffer to receive the data.

Absolute Disk Write: Interrupt 26h

Absolute Disk Write (Interrupt 26h) writes data from memory to the disk by directly accessing the desired logical sector, without using the MS-DOS directory structure.

Because it does bypass all of the MS-DOS internal safeguards, this type of access must be handled with extreme care to avoid causing irreparable damage to the file system and possibly losing all data stored there. For such tasks as rewriting root directories, however, should changes be necessary, this (or an equivalent service) is your only option.

This interrupt (together with Absolute Disk Read Interrupt 25h) now is officially listed in the MS-DOS Programmer's Reference for Version 5.0 as having been superseded by generic `IOCTL` functions described in Chapter 9.

The Absolute Disk Write Interrupt, like its Absolute Disk Read sibling, addresses the disk area it will write by means of a Logical Sector Number (LSN). This LSN is determined in exactly the same fashion described for Absolute Disk Read actions.

Like Absolute Disk Read, this function is difficult to use directly from high-level languages for the same reason. The same restrictions apply.

The extended format introduced with MS-DOS Version 4.0 applies to this service also. To show that the extended format is in use, set `CX` to FFFFh (-1). The DS:BX register pair then is interpreted as pointing to a DISKIO structure rather than to the buffer to read data into. Formats for this structure are described in the preceding subsection of this chapter.

Interrupt 27h: Terminate and Stay Resident

The *Terminate and Stay Resident* (Interrupt 27h) ends operation of the program that calls it, but preserves the memory area and all resources assigned to the program so that operation can be resumed later.

The original purpose of this service, available since the initial release of MS-DOS, was to permit installation of special device drivers and system-wide interrupt service routines. It has since been superseded by Keep Program Function 31h of Interrupt 21h, described in Chapter 11, "Process Management."

Interrupt 27h suffers two serious limitations. First, the CS register must be set to the program's PSP when Interrupt 27h is called. This was no problem for the single-segment COM programs that were standard when Interrupt 27h was introduced; however, this will hardly ever be the case for today's EXE programs unless you set the register explicitly.

More significantly, the TSR program's size is limited to a single segment's maximum, 64K bytes. While most TSRs attempt to stay smaller than this, in order to leave as much space as possible for user programs, it can be a fatal barrier for some.

When called, the procedure for Interrupt 27h restores the vectors for Interrupt 22h (Terminate Address), Interrupt 23h (User Signal Handler), and Interrupt 24h (Critical Error Handler) from data saved in the calling program's PSP. The routine then jumps to the termination address via the vector for Interrupt 22h, enabling the calling program to retain all resources assigned to it.

Unlike the three "normal" Terminate procedures, this interrupt does not close any open files or devices. If you want them closed, you must explicitly do so before calling this interrupt.

This point is especially important in TSR design because users may redirect output messages to the NUL device when they install your TSR program. Because that device, unless you close it, remains open after the TSR goes resident, one of the limited number of file handles available to the system (established by the `FILES=` line in CONFIG.SYS) is kept in use as a result. To prevent this waste of resources, your program should always explicitly close all handles (0 through 255) except those for files or devices that must stay open, before calling Interrupt 27h to go resident.

Interrupt 28h: The Idle Handler

In order to enable background printing while other processes continue to operate in the foreground, MS-DOS has included an *Idle Time* hook since its initial release.

This hook, Interrupt 28h, is called by MS-DOS from several locations in its internal console-input-polling loops where it is safe to perform file system operations (or many other DOS functions) while waiting for the user to press a key.

Normally, the vector for Interrupt 28h points to a single `iret` instruction. This `iret` does nothing, serving merely as a stub.

Each handler that hooks this vector is expected to preserve the previous vector content as a far pointer, and to perform an indirect jump through that saved far pointer when ready to return to MS-DOS. This preserves the chain so that all processes in it can get a chance to run.

Any handler you install should always chain to the next handler in line by following the chain rather than returning to MS-DOS. By enabling the original default `iret` to take care of returning to the system, you ensure that all processes that depend on Interrupt 28h get their turns to run while MS-DOS is waiting for input at a command-line prompt.

This Idle Handler is closely related to a documented service for the Multiplex Interrupt known as the Idle Call; however, where this handler is called when a device waits for console input, the Idle Call to the Multiplex interface is intended to release the time slice assigned to the waiting process, in a multitasking environment such as Windows.

If you develop TSRs that may be used in such environments, including keyboard-input waiting loops, good practice indicates that you should always include two calls inside any such loop: the first of them should be to Interrupt 28h to allow any process that depends on it being invoked frequently to get a time slice, and the other, immediately afterward, should be to the Multiplex interrupt's Idle Call to release the current time slice and give all other tasks in the system a chance to run.

Interrupt 29h: Fast Console Output

Fast Console Output (Interrupt 29h) is called by a number of MS-DOS output routines if the output is directed to a device. The device driver's attribute word contains bit 3 set to 1, thus, indicating that it supports this fast-output service.

This interrupt originated when device drivers and ANSI.SYS were introduced to MS-DOS in Version 2.0, but documentation for it was dropped from the manuals at the next major revision of the system. From Version 3.0 until Version 5.0, Interrupt 29h was not documented as being supported. It, nevertheless, was the output method used by ANSI.SYS in all of the intervening versions.

All versions of ANSI.SYS include handlers for this service. In addition, because much of the internal MS-DOS kernel code uses it for displaying output, the default CON device driver that is part of the IO.SYS hidden file also contains a handler, which merely passes each character to the BIOS video service for output, using default attributes of light gray characters on a black background.

The purpose of Interrupt 29h is to achieve speed in the display. The original versions used direct calls to the BIOS video services to replace the slower MS-DOS character output functions. In some third-party replacements for ANSI.SYS, the BIOS calls are replaced by direct writes to video RAM.

Interrupt 2Ah: The Critical-Section Hook

The *Critical-Section Hook* (Interrupt 2Ah) was introduced in Version 3.1 of MS-DOS to provide protection against interference among multiple users on a networked system. Calls to this interrupt appear frequently within the internal code of MS-DOS itself.

In the absence of network software, the routines that call Interrupt 2Ah are disabled; when a network package that is aware of this service is installed, the disabling code is patched out automatically. The interrupt then can control access to critical regions of code. It is not for use in applications programs at any time.

Interrupts 2Bh Through 2Dh: Not Now Used

These interrupts, though reserved for use by MS-DOS since its initial release, have never actually been used in any released version of the operating system. They all are normally vectored to the same `iret` instruction, and are not called by any standard MS-DOS internal routines.

Interrupt 2Eh: COMMAND.COM's Entry

Interrupt 2Eh, sometimes called *the back door to COMMAND.COM,* is undocumented and is not meant for general use. This service, used in the processing of batch files under COMMAND.COM, provides a direct entry point to reach the command interpreter's main input and parsing procedures, so that the batch file processor can operate just as if input were coming from the keyboard rather than from a batch file.

Although this service's existence appears to offer great promise for enhancing system operations, the only really useful application of it outside of the MS-DOS and COMMAND.COM internal code is to gain access to the *master* copy of the system's *environment block* associated with the primary command shell. Because this interrupt goes to that primary shell, regardless of how subsequent processes may be nested, it allows access to the master environment automatically.

Some networking systems, especially Novell's NetWare, make special use of this vector for their own undocumented purposes, and may fail to operate properly if Interrupt 2Eh is hooked or otherwise modified.

Interrupt 2Fh: The Multiplex Interrupt

Multiplex (Interrupt 2Fh) provides an open-ended capability for adding extensions to MS-DOS in a well-organized fashion. Many third-party toolmakers have taken advantage of it. When this feature was created originally, it served only the PRINT.COM print spooler program; however, the potential became obvious almost immediately and Program ID codes were assigned to make it possible to share the interface.

The Program ID code, found in the AH register at entry to the service and which may have any value from 01h through FFh, identifies the specific one, of the many possible clients, to which any call to this service is addressed.

Every program that hooks the Multiplex Interrupt is expected to test for presence of its own Program ID code, and if the test fails, to pass the call unmodified on to the next program in the chain. The chain, like that for Idle Handler 28h, eventually ends in an `iret` instruction that returns control to the original caller if the intended addressee is not found along the way. If the Program ID code test matches, the program will grab the call, process it, and return without passing the call any further.

At first, Program ID codes 00h through 7Fh were reserved for use by MS-DOS, leaving 80h through FFh available for user programs.

In Version 3.3 of MS-DOS, however, Program ID code B7h was taken by the MS-DOS function APPEND. Since that time, ID codes 00h through BFh have been reserved for use by MS-DOS, while C0h through FFh are documented as available to user programs.

Despite the published rules, however, a number of non-MS-DOS programs use Program ID codes below C0h. At least one third-party utility searches the Interrupt 2Fh chain looking for any available code, and uses the first free one that appears.

A complete listing of all possible services that use INT 2Fh is impossible to compile because new applications are being added virtually every day of the year. The most accurate list available is maintained by Ralf Brown and is available at no charge through Internet, or can be downloaded from Compuserve and from many BBSes systems worldwide. In the most recent copy of this list available when this text was written, 97 of the 256 possible Program ID codes are shown as being in use, and a number of them are used by several different programs.

Ralf updates this list, known simply as *The Interrupts List,* approximately four times each year, and the most recent compilation showed some 4,500 entries (this, however, covers all interrupts, not just those hooking up to INT 2Fh).

MS-DOS documents 13 different Program ID codes it uses, but actually implements many more. The following list of INT 2F functions used by MS-DOS itself was compiled using DEBUG to trace all tests made by INT 2Fh, first on a bare system with no device drivers or TSR programs, and then on my usual MS-DOS 6.0 setup with HIMEM, EMM386, DBLSPACE, MOUSE, and SMARTDRV drivers and TSRs in place.

This list also includes the 13 documented hooks shown for INT 2Fh in the MS-DOS Programmer's Reference, Version 5.0, from Microsoft. Those found during the trace, but not listed in the manual, are indicated as not documented, although some of these are described in connection with the associated drivers, in the reference section of this book (Chapter 14, "Other DOS Interrupts").

Program ID	Documented	Program Name/Description
01h	Yes	PRINT.EXE
06h	Yes	ASSIGN.COM
08h	No	DRIVER.SYS
10h	Yes	SHARE.EXE
11h	Yes	Network Redirector
12h	No	MS-DOS Internals
13h	No	Cleanup for ReBooting
14h	Yes	NLSFUNC.SYS
16h	Partially	Windows Hooks
1Ah	Yes	ANSI.SYS
43h	Yes	Extended Memory Manager
46h	No	Memory Swapping?
48h	Yes	DOSKEY.COM
4Ah	No	More MS-DOS Internals
4Bh	Yes	Task Switcher
53	No	MOUSE.COM TSR
55	No	COMMAND.COM Internals
0ADh	Yes	KEYB.COM
0B0h	Yes	GRAFTABL.COM
0B7h	Yes	APPEND.EXE

The reservation by MS-DOS of all Program ID codes below C0h for its own use is honored more in the breach than in the observance, as the following list of non-MS-DOS programs that use codes in the reserved range reveals. This table was extracted from the most recent copy of The Interrupts List available at the time of writing, and omits multiple uses of a single code.

Program ID	Program Name/Description
02	PC LAN Program
0C	AD-DOS
23	DR-DOS 5.0 GRAFTABL
27	DR-DOS 6.0 TaskMAX
2A	Gammafax DOS Dispatcher
39	Kingswood TSR Interface
41	LAN Manager 2.0 DOS Enhanced NETPOPUP.EXE
42	LAN Manager 2.0 DOS Enhanced MSRV.EXE
45	Microsoft Profiler (PROF.COM/VPROD.386)
62	PC Tools V7.0+ VDEFEND, DATAMON
64	SCRNSAV2.COM
70	License Service API
72	SRDISK V1.30
7A	Novell NetWare—Low-Level API (IPX)
80	FaxBIOS Interface
81	Nanosoft, Inc. TurboNET Redirector
82	RESPLAY
89	WHOA!.COM
90	RAID
92	Couriers LAN E-Mail—API
93	InnerMission V1.7+

Program ID	Program Name/Description
9C	Couriers LAN E-Mail OPERATOR.EXE—API
A1	Ergo DOS Extenders
A4	Futurus Team
A9	METZTSR.COM
AA	VIDCLOCK.COM
AB	Btrieve Multi-User
B4	IBM PC3270 Emulation Program, Version 3
B9	PC Network RECEIVER.COM
BE	REDVIEW
BF	PC LAN Program REDIRIFS.EXE Internal

Following are a few of the Program ID codes in the user-program area that are used by some of the better-known clients of the Multiplex Interrupt. This table also was compiled from The Interrupts List.

Program ID	Program Name/Description
C0	Novell ODI Link Support Layer (LSL.COM)
CB	Intel's Communicating Applications Specification
CC	Qualitas Qcache
CD	Intel Image Processing Interface
D0	Lotus CD/Networker
D2	Quarterdeck—QEMM/QRAM/VIDRAM/ MANIFEST
D4	4DOS.COM
D7	BANYAN VINES
D8	Novell NetWare Lite
DF	HyperDisk
E3	ANARKEY.COM

Program ID	Program Name/Description
E4	NDOS—API
ED	Phar Lap DOS Extenders
FB	Borland's DPMILOAD.EXE
FE	Norton Utilities TSRs
FF	Topware Network Operating System

A primary reason for TSR programs to use the Multiplex Interrupt chain is to determine whether they already are resident and thus prevent multiple installations, which only waste scarce resources. To simplify such tests, the subfunction 00h (the content of the AL register at entry) of all functions was officially reserved for test use and named the *get installed status* operation.

Any well-behaved Multiplex Interrupt client is expected to return its installation status in the AL register in response to a get installed status request addressed to its Program ID code. This installation status may be any of three distinct values: 00h indicates that the function is not yet present, but may be installed; 01h indicates that the function is not installed and may not be; and FFh indicates that the function is already in place.

It may appear a bit ridiculous to expect a function that has not yet been installed to report anything, but as it happens, this occurs automatically. The 00h *not installed* status response is, by design, identical to the 00h get installation status request. If the Program ID code never matches anything in the chain, then when the query returns by way of the `iret` at the end of the line without any change ever having been made to the AL register along the way, the 00h status will result automatically.

By following this convention, you can avoid multiple installations of the same resident package. Unfortunately, not every function that uses Interrupt 2Fh follows this standard, but most of them seem to do so.

The following sections discuss some of the functions for the Multiplex Interrupt, as documented in the MS-DOS Programmer's Reference for Version 5.0.

PRINT.EXE: Program ID Code 01h

Print spooling, available since the earliest days of MS-DOS, has become a normal method of operation for many PC users. Program ID code 01h gives a program access to *PRINT.EXE* (or PRINT.COM in some versions), the printer spooler furnished with MS-DOS. This function provides six documented subfunctions that enable you to add or remove files from the queue to be printed, and permits status checking to be performed.

Subfunction 00h enables a program to determine whether the spooler is installed. Subfunction 01 enables you to specify a file to be printed. The spooler takes over and prints the file automatically, unless you intervene. Subfunction 02 enables you to remove pending files from the print queue. It accepts wildcard characters (* and ?) in the file specification, allowing multiple terminations from a single call.

Subfunction 04 returns a pointer to the print queue, a series of buffers containing filenames. The first buffer in the list is the name of the file presently being printed. The last entry has a zero length file-name string. This subfunction also halts the spooler's action so that no information can become obsolete before the caller can act upon it. Subfunction 05 cancels the HOLD status established by Subfunction 04 and allows print spooling action to resume. Subfunction 06 indicates whether or not the queue is empty, and returns a pointer to the device driver for the currently active printer.

ASSIGN.COM: Program ID Code 06h

ASSIGN.COM was a TSR supplied as part of MS-DOS prior to Version 6.0, which altered the letters assigned to various drives. In particular, it was useful when dealing with programs that insisted on calling the floppy drive "A:" when it is necessary to install from the drive normally known as "B:". Because the same function can be performed by the SUBST command, ASSIGN (and its relative, JOIN) were dropped from MS-DOS in Version 6.0.

Although ASSIGN.COM is no longer part of MS-DOS, as of Version 6.0, if it was on your fixed disk when you installed Version 6, it will remain in place and also is available as one of many discontinued utilities on a supplemental disk. Therefore, the support for it documented in the official MS-DOS Programmer's Reference for Version 5.0 remains intact in Version 6.

Multiplex Interrupt Program ID Code 06h, with one documented and one undocumented subfunction, communicates with the ASSIGN TSR. Documented subfunction 00h tests for presence of the TSR, while undocumented subfunction 01h returns the segment address at which the TSR is installed, giving full access to its internal data.

DRIVER.SYS: Program ID Code 08h

DRIVER.SYS is a device driver that, after being loaded into memory by a DEVICE or DEVICEHIGH command in your CONFIG.SYS file, creates a logical drive that you can use to refer to a physical floppy disk drive. A logical drive is a pointer to an actual physical disk drive within your system, but has a drive letter that may differ from the one assigned to that same drive by MS-DOS. This driver enables you to specify different sets of operating conditions for a single disk drive, if needed in your system.

Multiplex Interrupt Program ID Code 08h, with four undocumented subfunctions, communicates with the DRIVER.SYS driver to modify the normal actions of MS-DOS. Subfunction 00h is the conventional test, subfunction 01h adds a new block device to the internal drive data table list maintained by MS-DOS, subfunction 02h passes a command to the driver for action, and subfunction 03h gets a pointer to the head of the MS-DOS drive data table list.

SHARE.EXE: Program ID Code 10h

The *SHARE* command, when executed from your AUTOEXEC.BAT file or from an `INSTALL=` line in CONFIG.SYS, installs the SHARE TSR into your system. SHARE provides file-sharing and locking capabilities to your disks and network drives. It often is used when running Windows, even in non-networked systems, to permit multiple applications to access the same files, with no danger of one application writing over the data stored by another program.

Multiplex Interrupt Program ID Code 10h, with one documented and two undocumented subfunctions, communicates with the SHARE TSR to modify the normal actions of MS-DOS. Documented subfunction 00h is the usual test, while undocumented subfunction 80h disabled sharing (in Version 4 only) and undocumented subfunction 81h enabled sharing (also in Version 4 only). The undocumented subfunctions were removed in Version 5.0.

Network Redirector: Program ID Code 11h

Multiplex Interrupt Program ID Code 11h, with one documented and 51 undocumented subfunctions, communicates with the Network Redirector to modify the normal actions of MS-DOS. This Program ID Code also has been assigned, by Microsoft, to the MSCDEX CD-ROM interface program. To distinguish between the two programs, MSCDEX places a word containing the value 0DADAh on the top of the stack when calling Interrupt 2Fh.

The redirector, introduced to MS-DOS in Version 3.1, essentially duplicates normal file system operations, but at the remote device rather than on local drives.

The documented subfunction, 00h, is the usual presence test, while the undocumented functions provide the duplicated capabilities such as creating, changing, or destroying directories, opening, reading from, writing to, or closing files, and all other actions that deal with data storage and retrieval.

NLSFUNC.SYS: Program ID Code 14h

You can use `NLSFUNC` from the command line, or from CONFIG.SYS, to load country-specific information for national language support (NLS) and character set (code page) switching. Do not, however, use the NLSFUNC command while running Windows. Your computer might stop responding.

Multiplex Interrupt Program ID Code 14h, with one documented and four undocumented subfunctions, communicates with the NLSFUNC driver. This Program ID Code also has been assigned, by Microsoft, to their (never sold in the United States) European MS-DOS Version 4's POPUP capability, which contains three undocumented subfunctions in addition to the usual test for presence.

The documented subfunction, 00h, is the same in both cases and is the usual presence test. The undocumented NLSFUNC subfunctions are change code page (01h), get country information (02h), set country information (03h), and get country information (04h). The undocumented subfunctions for European MS-DOS Version 4's POPUP are open or close popup screen (01h), save popup screen (02h), and restore screen (03h).

Windows Hooks: Program ID Code 16h

Multiplex Interrupt Program ID Code 16h, with 26 documented and two undocumented subfunctions, communicates with the *Windows Hooks*. Only one of the 28 subfunctions is documented in the official MS-DOS Programmer's Reference for Version 5.0, but the remaining 25 are described in the Windows Software Developer's Kit information.

The single subfunction documented for MS-DOS itself is 80h, the Idle Call, which releases the time slice assigned to the current process when it is called. TSR programs that might operate under Windows should include this call within any keyboard-input waiting loop to enable other applications to share system resources.

ANSI.SYS: Program ID Code 1Ah

The *ANSI.SYS* device driver, introduced to MS-DOS in Version 2.0, must be loaded by a `DEVICE` or `DEVICEHIGH` command in your CONFIG.SYS file. As described in Chapter 7, "Console I/O," this driver defines escape sequences to control your system's screen and keyboard.

An ANSI escape sequence is a sequence of ASCII characters, the first two of which are the escape character (1Bh) and the left-bracket character (5Bh). The character(s) following the escape and left-bracket characters specify an alphanumeric code that controls a keyboard or display function. ANSI escape sequences distinguish between uppercase and lowercase letters; for example, "A" and "a" have completely different meanings.

Prior to MS-DOS Version 4.0, no standard method existed for a program to determine whether ANSI.SYS was present in a system. In Version 4.0, Program ID Code 1Ah was assigned for this purpose. It now provides one documented and two undocumented subfunctions.

Many replacements for the original ANSI.SYS driver have been created, and most of the newer ones also support this Multiplex Program ID code in the same manner as ANSI.SYS itself. Some of these replacements install as TSR programs rather than as device drivers, and have greatly extended the number of subfunctions for this Program ID Code. AVATAR.SYS, for example, adds 15 new subfunctions to the list.

Extended Memory Managers: Program ID Code 43h

Extended Memory Specification (XMS) Version 3.0, dated January, 1991, is a joint effort of Microsoft Corporation, Lotus Development Corporation, Intel Corporation, and AST Research, Inc. The purpose of XMS is to allow DOS programs to use additional memory found in Intel's 80x86 based machines in a consistent, machine independent manner.

With some restrictions, XMS adds almost 64K to the memory space that DOS programs can access directly in real mode operation. XMS also provides DOS programs a standard method for storing and managing data in extended memory (above the area that can be reached in real mode). Depending on the hardware available, XMS may provide even more memory to DOS programs.

HIMEM.SYS is an extended memory manager program written to conform to the XMS specification Version 3.0 that coordinates the use of your computer's extended memory, including the high memory area (HMA), so that no two applications or device drivers use the same memory simultaneously. The version of HIMEM.SYS supplied with MS-DOS Version 6.0 is 3.09; the version shipped with Windows 3.1 was 3.07, while that shipped with MS-DOS Version 5.0 was 2.70. Always use the latest available version of this driver.

You install `HIMEM` by adding a `DEVICE` command for HIMEM.SYS to your CONFIG.SYS file. This HIMEM.SYS command line must come before any other commands that might start applications or install device drivers that use extended memory. The HIMEM.SYS line, for example, must come before the EMM386.EXE command line.

Multiplex Interrupt Program ID Code 43h, with two documented subfunctions plus two additional undocumented subfunctions, communicates with the Extended Memory Manager. The two documented subfunctions are 00h, which is a non-standard test that returns the specific value 80h if an XMS3 driver exists in the system, and 10h, which returns a far pointer to the driver's API entry point. All other communication with the driver is intended to be performed through the far pointer returned by subfunction 10h.

The undocumented functions, added to HIMEM.SYS in Version 2.77, are 08h, which returns information about the A20-line handler currently in use, and 30h, which permits an external program to provide an A20 handler for support of hardware that HIMEM.SYS itself does not support. Neither of them is useful except to manufacturers of non-standard hardware.

DOSKEY.COM: Program ID Code 48h

The *DOSKEY* TSR program provides a "command history" feature that enables you to recall MS-DOS commands, edit command lines, and create and run macros. When installed, DOSKEY occupies about 3K of resident memory.

Multiplex Interrupt Program ID Code 48h, with two documented subfunctions, communicates with the DOSKEY TSR to modify the normal actions of MS-DOS. The first, 00h, tests for presence of the service but does not return the usual status values. Instead, it returns a non-zero value in AL if the service is present, and zero if it's missing.

The other subfunction, 10h, requires that you provide a far pointer to a buffer that will receive a command line in the same format required by Interrupt 21h Function 0Ah, and invokes the TSR to enable you to browse through the history queue or invoke a macro.

Task Switcher: Program ID Code 4Bh

The Task Switcher service, consisting of eight notification functions and seven service functions, was introduced to MS-DOS some time prior to being documented in the official MS-DOS Programmer's Reference for Version 5.0. While designed primarily to support the MS-DOS Shell Task Swapper, this interface was made general enough to enable its use with other swappers, and can even permit multiple swappers to be in a system at the same time.

Multiplex Interrupt Program ID Code 4Bh, with six documented subfunctions, communicates with the Task Switcher notification and service functions.

The service of the Multiplex Interrupt and the associated notification and service functions are of interest primarily to developers of operating-system enhancements. Individual applications have no need of the services provided here, and any attempt to make use of them is quite likely to interfere with proper system operation.

KEYB.COM: Program ID Code ADh

KEYB.COM is one of six separate parts of the National Language Support capability, and all six parts must be invoked in the correct sequence in order for the result to be satisfactory.

The KEYB program, which configures a keyboard for a specific language, is the last of the six parts to be invoked at system boot time. This program configures the keyboard for a language other than United States English. In addition to *us* for the United States English layout, the program recognizes 22 other country abbreviations, all of which are listed in the chapter titled "Customizing for International Use" in the MS-DOS 6 User's Guide.

The other five parts of the NLS system are COUNTRY.SYS and DISPLAY.SYS, which must be installed in CONFIG.SYS, and `NLSFUNC`, `MODE CON CP PREP`, and `CHCP`, which are called (in that sequence) within AUTOEXEC.BAT before `KEYB` can be invoked.

Multiplex Interrupt Program ID Code ADh, with four documented and six undocumented subfunctions, communicates with the DISPLAY.SYS device driver and the KEYB TSR to modify the normal actions of MS-DOS.

The four documented subfunctions all communicate with the `KEYB` TSR. They are 80h, which obtains the `KEYB` version number, 81h, which sets the active code page for the `KEYB` routines, 82h, which sets the country flag, and 83h, which gets the country flag's current value.

The six undocumented functions all communicate with DISPLAY.SYS. They are 00h, the usual Multiplex service presence test, 01h, which sets the active code page for the DISPLAY driver, 02h, which gets the current value of the DISPLAY driver's active code page, 03h, which obtains a variety of code page information, and two other subfunctions of unknown purpose, 04h and 10h.

GRAFTABL.COM: Program ID Code B0h

GRAFTABL.COM was a TSR supplied as part of MS-DOS prior to Version 6.0, which could change the way in which the extended ASCII characters in the range 128 through 255 appeared. When installed, it used about 1K of memory. Most systems did not require its use in order to display these characters, but a few needed it.

Although GRAFTABL.COM is no longer part of MS-DOS as of Version 6.0, if it was on your fixed disk when you installed Version 6, it will remain in place. It also is available as one of many discontinued utilities on a supplemental disk. Therefore, the support for it that was documented in the official MS-DOS Programmer's Reference for Version 5.0 remains intact in Version 6.

Multiplex Interrupt Program ID Code B0h, with two documented subfunctions, communicates with the GRAFTABL TSR to modify the normal actions of MS-DOS. Subfunction 00h is the usual test for presence of the TSR, and subfunction 01h obtains a far pointer to the graphics font table that this TSR uses to display all extended ASCII characters.

APPEND.EXE: Program ID Code B7h

The *APPEND.EXE* TSR furnished with MS-DOS enables programs to open data files in specified directories as if the files were in the current directory. The specified directories are called *appended* directories because, for the sake of opening data files, they can be found as if they were appended to the current directory. Multiplex Interrupt Program ID Code B7h, with six documented and three undocumented subfunctions, communicates with the APPEND TSR to modify the normal actions of MS-DOS. Unless otherwise indicated, the functions described in the following paragraphs are fully documented in the MS-DOS Programmer's Reference manual for Version 5.0, and appear to remain unchanged for Version 6.0 as well.

Subfunction 00h determines whether APPEND has been installed. Because networking software is not well standardized, some networks fail to respond correctly to this query.

The action of subfunction 01h, the first of the undocumented trio, is difficult to ascertain; its use should be avoided.

Subfunction 02h determines whether all features of APPEND (many of which were added in Version 4.0 of MS-DOS) are available. Subfunction 00h returns `installed` if any version of APPEND is present; subfunction 02h establishes that the version is the most recent full-featured one, or at least contains all of the features.

Subfunction 03h, the second of the undocumented subfunctions, toggles a flag used internally by APPEND and should not be used because this may disrupt normal actions of the APPEND functionality.

Subfunction 04h gets a far pointer to the active APPEND path list, subfunction 06h reads the current value of the internal Modes flag of APPEND, and subfunction 07h is used to set a new value into the Modes flag.

The last of the undocumented subfunctions is 10h, which not only reads the Modes flag in the same way as 06h, but also returns the major and minor version numbers for APPEND. This function may be useful if you write programs that need such information, but because it is not officially documented should be approached with extreme caution.

Finally, subfunction 11h causes APPEND to modify the action of Functions 3Dh, 43h, and 6Ch of Interrupt 21h. When this subfunction is executed, a flag is set in the PSP, so that the next time you call any of the listed functions, the fully qualified filename returns in the same buffer used to pass the original filename to the function.

If you use this capability, be sure the buffer has enough room (67 bytes minimum) to accept any possible return value.

After a fully expanded filename returns, the flag set by this function is cleared automatically, and operation of the Interrupt 21h functions returns to normal. Thus, each use of this APPEND subfunction affects only one call to an Interrupt 21h function.

Interrupts 30h and 31h: CP/M Dispatcher Jump

As described in the "Short History of MS-DOS" section of Chapter 4, one of the critical requirements in the original design of the operating system that evolved into MS-DOS Version 6.0 was that it be simple to translate programs originally written for the CP/M system automatically so that they could run on the new system.

Since all CP/M programs used address 0005 for the same purpose that MS-DOS uses Interrupt 21h, MS-DOS had to be able to deal with the `CALL 5` instructions that permeated CP/M programs. To deal with this, a far call to the dispatch code for MS-DOS was designed into the PSP, at location CS:0005. This eliminated any need to change that part of the application programs during automatic translation.

To maintain the freedom for relocation that can be achieved by using interrupt vectors, however, the instruction put into offset 0005h of the PSP did not attempt to go directly from the PSP to the INT 21h dispatch code. Instead, it detours by way of another instruction placed in the vectors for INT 30h and INT 31h when MS-DOS initializes, each time you boot your system.

No one has made a public explanation of the reason it was done, so far as I can determine; however, the method chosen for getting to the INT 30h vector was almost Byzantine in its obscurity, and has since led to some strange situations. Rather than simply making a direct far CALL to location 0000:00C0, the INT 30h vector address, the instruction placed into offset 5 of the PSP was a far call to an address that was outside the range of the original PC and its 20-bit address bus, at 100C0h.

With only 20 bits physically present, the system ignored the 21st bit at the high end, making the effective address 0000:00C0. That's the INT 30h vector, and it contains the actual far jump to the dispatcher code.

When the 80286 processor made its appearance in IBM's PC-AT line, however, more address lines were added to allow it to access extended memory, and then the extra bit could no longer be ignored.

To preserve proper operation of not only this, but many other areas of MS-DOS that depended on *address wraparound* from FFFF:FFFF to 0000:0000, the system architects found it necessary to add a hardware circuit to *gate* address lines A20 through A23 (the new ones just added to the design).

When the A20 gate is turned off, the newer machines exhibit address wraparound just as did the original systems. When the gate is turned on, the full range of extended memory can be addressed; however, features that now depend on wraparound will no longer work.

To preserve the operation of the *location 5* CP/M interface and maintain backward compatibility, even though few programs that actually used the feature remained in service, it became necessary to duplicate the far jump located in the vectors for INT 30h and INT 31h at the corresponding location of the High Memory area, which is the one actually addressed from PSP offset 5: F01D:FEF0.

Or, more correctly, that is the location that *should* be addressed, but for some reason during the introduction of MS-DOS Version 2.0 a two-byte error was introduced into the calculations, and that error persists right into Version 6.0. Rather than using F01D:FEF0, the system actually calls F01D:FEEE as shown in this sequence of instructions captured using DEBUG under Version 6.0:

```
-U CS:0005 L5
1D4E:0005 9AEEFE1DF0      CALL   F01D:FEEE
-U F01D:FEEE L7
```

```
F01D:FEEE 0000           ADD   [BX+SI],AL
F01D:FEF0 EAD0101601     JMP   0116:10D0
-U 0000:00C0 L5
0000:00C0 EAD0101601     JMP   0116:10D0
```

The first `JMP` shown is the jump in the HMA, and in this case, the error doesn't keep control from getting to the dispatcher; however, it does cause possible random changes to memory content by adding whatever is in AL at the time to the byte that is addressed through DS:BX+SI. This undoubtedly would cause strange symptoms if anyone actually tried to use the CP/M interface.

For the `JMP` actually located in the vector table, the situation is worse. The two-byte error changes the machine instruction totally, from a `JMP` to some other code determined by the high byte of the segment address of the current Multiplex Interrupt hook pointer, and would send the system on an immediate trip to never-never land.

Given that this feature has been essentially useless (and potentially dangerous) through the last five major versions of MS-DOS, the major question is why Microsoft has even tried to preserve it. The answer to that, however, remains undocumented.

Even more amazing is the fact that the *DOS Protected Mode Interface* (DPMI), a joint development of Borland, Eclipse, IGC, Intel, Locus, Lotus Development, Microsoft, Phar Lap, Phoenix Technologies, Quarterdeck, and Rational Systems, took over Interrupt 31h, thus destroying the backward compatibility anyway.

The DPMI specification, which is discussed in more detail in Chapter 8, "Managing Time and Space," defines a standard that enables extended DOS applications to exploit the capabilities of protected mode for 80x86-based personal computers. It provides at least 77 major functions, several of them boasting many subfunctions each.

The standard interface DPMI defines enables extended DOS applications to be multitasked reliably under many multitasking operating environments, including those supporting system-wide virtual memory. It is noted previously that the most recent C/C++ compilers from both Microsoft and Borland require DPMI in order to operate. As the trend continues, and the original real-mode-only processors gradually lose all significance to most developers, you can expect to see the CP/M Dispatch "feature" eventually disappear from MS-DOS. It's still there, however, and still is incorrect in Version 6.0.

Interrupts 32h through 3Fh: Not Now Used

These 14 interrupt vectors, although reserved for use by MS-DOS since the release of Version 5.0, actually are not used by the operating system itself. They all are normally vectored to the same `iret` instruction, and are not called by any standard MS-DOS internal routines.

Interrupt 33h, however, has been defined as the "standard" interface point for communication with the mouse driver since the introduction of Microsoft's original mouse. Interrupt 3Fh is the default vector used by Microsoft's overlay manager which controls replacement of code segments when executable files use overlays, and also is used by similar functions created by other linker programs.

For both Interrupt 33h and Interrupt 3Fh, pointers to the code contained in the mouse driver or the executable program replace those to the `iret` instruction that MS-DOS installs. In the case of Interrupt 33h, the driver usually remains resident until you reboot your system. The vector for Interrupt 3Fh normally is restored when any program that installed its own overlay manager returns control to MS-DOS; otherwise, the vector's address would no longer point to valid code for execution.

The New MRCI Rendezvous Interrupt Services

One of the few truly new features added to MS-DOS Version 6.0 was the *Microsoft RealTime Compression Interface* (MRCI). This capability is described more fully in Chapter 9, but it did define two brand new *rendezvous* interrupt services that applications can use to ensure full compatibility with existing MS-DOS software.

While one of the new features simply is a new call added to an existing Multiplex Interrupt Program ID code that handles several internal MS-DOS functions, they are discussed together here in this section because in practice, they should be used as a matched pair.

One call detects a software-based MRCI server while the other checks for a hardware-based server. An application (a potential MRCI client) that wants to make use of the MRCI features may need to use both calls to determine whether an MRCI server is present in a system.

The two services are a call (AX=4A12h) added to Multiplex Interrupt 2Fh to enable an MRCI client to detect a RAM-based (presumably software-based) MRCI server, and a call (AX=B001h) added to BIOS-service Interrupt 1Ah to enable the first RAM-based MRCI server installed, or the client, to detect a ROM BIOS (presumably hardware-based) MRCI server.

Potential MRCI clients check first for the presence of an existing MRCI server by issuing the `INT 2Fh` call. If that fails, then they should issue the `INT 1Ah` call. If that fails, no MRCI server is present in the system. If no server is present, the application has the choice of installing one, using other features instead, or simply refusing to run. MRCI servers, when initializing themselves after installation, should perform these same checks.

If a software-based MRCI server installs over an existing hardware-based MRCI server, or a MRCI client is to remain resident (either as an MS-DOS device driver or TSR program), then it must hook INT 2Fh and create a RAM copy of the MRCINFO structure. This procedure allows subsequent programs to supersede the MRCI server, without cutting the initial resident program out.

The Software-Based Server's Rendezvous

To call the software-based server *rendezvous* interrupt, just load `4A12h` into the AX register, the ASCII character pair `MR` into the CX register, another character pair `CI` into DX, and then invoke `INT 2Fh`.

Upon return, if `CX` now contains `IC` and `DX` contains `RM` (that is, if the 32-bit string representing MRCI has been reversed to read ICRM), then you have a software-based MRCI server present in the system, and ES:DI contains a far pointer to its `MRCINFO` structure which in turn points to the actual server. They should be saved for all additional communication with the server.

If `CX` and `DX` contain anything else, including the values with which they started, then no software-based MRCI server is present and your application should check for presence of a hardware-based server.

The following code, adapted from an example provided in the MRCI specification, shows one way of meeting all the requirements. It also brings up a couple of interesting additional points.

```
;*  Check intMRCI vector
     XOR  AX,AX     ; interrupt vector table
     MOV  DS,AX
     LDS  SI,DS:[2Fh*4]
;*  Test if vector is plausible
     MOV  AX,DS
     OR   AX,AX     ; Vector non-NULL?
     JZ   MDR       ;   NO, check hardware
;*  Try to call the MPX server
     MOV  CX,'MR'   ; Signatures
     MOV  DX,'CI'
     MOV  AX,04A12h ; Query Function, s/w
     INT  2Fh       ; Try to call MPX server
;*  Check the signature returned
     CMP  CX,'IC'   ; Signature match?
     JNE  MDR       ;   NO, check hardware
     CMP  DX,'RM'   ; Signature match?
     JE   MDP       ;   YES, have server
;*   fall through to hardware server check
```

For the most part, this code fragment is completely straightforward. You may wonder, however, just why the first three lines use direct addressing of the interrupt vector for Interrupt 2Fh, at address 0000:00BC (calculated by the assembler from the `2Fh * 4` source expression), rather than following the usual rules and calling Interrupt 21h Function 35h to obtain the vector's content.

And, for that matter, you might question why it is necessary to verify that the vector contains a non-zero address, because MS-DOS always puts at least a minimum `iret` instruction there.

Because this query may, itself, be called from inside of the MS-DOS kernel code, the `standard` MS-DOS function cannot be used here to get the interrupt vector content. It may, for example, occur in the initialization routine for an installable device driver, and that routine is called by MS-DOS as part of the installation process. If this routine attempted to use the standard function, then the system could easily tie itself into an endless loop. By using the direct addressing technique, potential problems are neatly avoided.

A cost, however, exists. The system must be in real mode to execute this code correctly; in protected mode, there is no guarantee that all the appropriate descriptor tables are properly set up to access the actual interrupt vector table. Because MS-DOS always assumes real-mode operation, this is not really a problem; however, you need to be aware of the possibilities in case you try to adapt these examples to operate in protected mode.

Now for the reason to verify a non-zero vector: This code may be executed when CONFIG.SYS is processed, before MS-DOS has fully set up all the vectors. It also may be called from a non-MS-DOS system that has not initialized the Multiplex Interrupt vector before the MRCI server initialization takes place. Given these possibilities, it's a good idea to verify that the content of the interrupt vector is not all zeroes, which is never a valid destination for a transfer of control. It still can fail, but the chances of this happening are greatly reduced by making this test.

Although this sample code fragment doesn't show it, the content of ES:DI on return from the call will be a far pointer to the MRCINFO structure for the server and should be saved by your application. Your application then can use this for all subsequent MRCI communications.

The Hardware-Based Server's Rendezvous

If no software-based server is found by the call to its rendezvous, then a similar check for presence of a hardware-based MRCI server is needed. This is done by the same method. Only the value in AX and the interrupt number are different. Following is adapted from the example in the MRCI specification:

```
;*  Check intMRCIROM vector
mdr:  XOR   AX,AX                ; test INT1A vector
      MOV   DS,AX
      LDS   SI,DS:[1Ah*4]
;*  Test if vector is plausible
      MOV   AX,DS
      OR    AX,AX                ; Vector non-NULL?
      JZ    MDE                  ;   NO, search failed
;*  Try to call the ROM server
      MOV   CX,'MR'              ; Signatures
      MOV   DX,'CI'
      MOV   AX,0B001h            ; Query Function, h/w
      INT   1Ah                  ; Try to call server
```

```
;*  Check the signature returned
      CMP   CX,'IC'             ; Signature match?
      JNE   MDE                 ;   NO, search failed
      CMP   DX,'RM'             ; Signature match?
      JNE   MDE                 ;   No, search failed
;*   Fall through to code for server found
MDP:
```

Just as in the software-based-server check, the interrupt vector is obtained via direct addressing rather than by use of MS-DOS function 35h. It also is tested for an all-zero content in case no valid service for Interrupt 1Ah at the time of the call exists. Because the interrupt is present in every BIOS that claims IBM compatibility, however, this second possibility is extremely remote. Interrupt 1Ah is used by BIOS for date and time services, and most of MS-DOS would be severely crippled in its absence.

Also, like the software-based server rendezvous service, ES:DI contains a far pointer to the server's MRCINFO structure if the call is successful. In fact, one of the strong points of the MRCI specification is that the software- and hardware-based interfaces essentially are identical. After your application obtains a valid pointer to an MRCINFO structure, it never again needs to distinguish between the two classes of server because any function supported by one works the same way for the other.

At this writing, no hardware-based MRCI servers have been identified. It is unlikely, however, that they will be delayed for very long once MRCI comes into widespread use. The potential gain of using hardware rather than software for the computation-intensive compression actions has long been known, but in the absence of an industry-wide standard for interfacing, it has not been worth pursuing. MRCI is expected to change this situation significantly.

Other Interrupts DOS Changes/Modifies/ Affects/Does Things To

In addition to setting up services for the interrupt vectors to which it stakes its own private claim, MS-DOS modifies certain other vectors that are not, nominally, under its sole control. It does so primarily to create known default conditions. These default conditions may be changed as required by your applications, and in some cases, are modified dynamically as programs execute.

The four major categories of vectors affected in this way are debug hooks, the vectors associated with hardware interrupts, vectors involved when a system reboot is required, and finally a pair of miscellaneous entries.

Debug Hooks

Because of direct hardware interaction that is involved, the three vectors for Interrupts 01h, 03h, and 04h provide hooks that can be used for debugging programs.

If the chip's trap flag is set, Interrupt 01h is invoked automatically by the processor chip after the execution of each individual instruction. This provides a debugger the opportunity to single-step through a program.

Interrupt 03h is unique in that it can be invoked by means of a single-byte machine instruction, 0CCh, in addition to the usual two-byte INT 03 sequence. This enables it to set breakpoints on top of any executable instruction by replacing the first byte of the instruction, and then restoring that byte when the Interrupt 03h service is entered.

If Interrupt 04h was enabled beforehand, it can be called by executing the `into` (Interrupt on Overflow) instruction after performing an arithmetic operation. To enable the instruction, the Overflow Bit (bit 11) in the flag register must be set before the arithmetic instruction (such as `mul` or `imul`) is executed. Because the 80x86 family of CPU chips includes the Jump if Overflow and Jump if Not Overflow instructions, this interrupt is hardly ever used.

All three of these interrupt vectors are set by MS-DOS to point to an `iret` instruction so that if called, they will return immediately without performing any action.

When you run a debugger, such as `DEBUG` furnished with MS-DOS, it installs its own custom handlers for Interrupts 01h and 03h, and will, upon termination, restore the address of the original `iret` instruction. This means that while developing programs you can embed `INT 03h` or `DB 0CCh` instructions within them at locations where you may want a debugging breakpoint. If no debugger is active, such instructions may waste a few microseconds of execution time but have no other effect. By invoking `DEBUG` for your program, typing **G**, and then pressing Enter, however, causes your program to halt automatically when it reaches your breakpoint.

If you use this trick, you then need to step the Instruction Pointer (IP) register over the interrupt manually because the debugger does not remove it automatically as it does its own breakpoint traps.

Because these three interrupts are invoked automatically by the processor chip itself, they should never be called explicitly from a program except for the purpose described in the preceding paragraphs.

If you write your own debugger, you must take special care with the STI (Set Interrupt Flag) instruction to keep from trapping your own interrupt handler. When you enter your handler, interrupts are disabled and the trap flag is set. The first thing you should do when your handler gains control is to disable the trap flag, and then re-enable interrupts safely. If, however, you re-enable interrupts before turning off the trap flag, your interrupt handler will begin single stepping and you will need to reboot in order to regain control of the system.

Stack Handlers

At least 14 interrupt handlers within any MS-DOS system respond to hardware interrupt requests that may occur at any time. When a request comes in, the handler must use the stack area that happens to be in effect. It is quite possible that this area will not have enough space to hold all the information the interrupt handler must save.

If the handler charges blindly ahead and saves the information anyway, other vital data may be overwritten, which can cause the system to crash at some unpredictable later time.

MS-DOS now includes the capability, absent from its original versions, to switch stacks before responding to one of the unpredictable hardware interrupts. It accomplishes this by hooking each of the interrupt vectors involved, and switching to one of several special internal stacks allocated especially for the purpose before passing control to the actual handler. After the interrupt is processed, the handler returns control to the MS-DOS Stack Manager code, which marks the stack space as being free to use again.

The specific interrupt vectors that MS-DOS modifies to route all calls through its Stack Manager are 02h (the Non-Maskable Interrupt usually used to detect RAM failures), 08h through 0Eh (the BIOS IRQ-response services), 70h, 72h through 74h, 76h, and 77h. The last six of these are extended IRQ vectors used in systems that contain more than eight possible hardware interrupt requests.

Whether MS-DOS installs the Stack Manager can be controlled by the `STACKS=` line in CONFIG.SYS. If this line is not present or if one that reads `STACKS=9,256` is found, MS-DOS installs during the boot-up process its Stack Manager with nine stacks of 256 bytes each, and modifies the 14 listed vectors to route their calls through the Stack Manager.

If fewer than nine stacks are requested, the Stack Manager is not installed and no changes to the listed vectors are made. Because early versions of the Stack Manager tended to be rather error-prone, many applications advise you to include `STACKS=0,0` in CONFIG.SYS to disable this feature. In MS-DOS Versions 5 and 6, however, the Stack Manager has become reliable and there is no need to disable it.

Following is more information concerning the most common of the 14 services affected by the Stack Manager modifications:

- Interrupt 02h, the Non-Maskable Interrupt (NMI), is called by the CPU when a memory parity error or other major system failure is detected. When an NMI occurs, you probably will have no time to recover.
- Interrupt 08h, the System Timer, is tied to channel 0 of the system timer chip and is called approximately 18.2 times per second (65,536 times per hour).
- Interrupt 08h calls Interrupt 1Ch (Timer Tick) before the Interrupt 08h handler completes its processing. Because of this, all actions performed in a handler for Interrupt 1Ch take precedence over any other hardware interrupt requests.
- Interrupt 09h, the Keyboard Interrupt, occurs when you press or release a keyboard key. The handler for this interrupt reads the key information, processes it into character and scan code information, and then stores it in a keyboard buffer. Rather than accessing the keyboard directly, the BIOS input routines access this keyboard buffer, thereby, allowing type-ahead and flexibility in keyboard handling.
- Interrupt 0Bh provides COM1 and COM3 interrupt service for the original IBM PC and the PC XT, COM2, and COM4 interrupt service for the Personal Computer AT and industry-standard compatible systems, and is listed as reserved for the PS/2 systems. This service is called when serial port hardware issues an interrupt on the IRQ3 interrupt request line.

Communications programs generally replace this vector. All standard methods of accessing the serial port simply are too slow to handle speeds greater than 1,200 bps. By installing a carefully programmed custom interrupt handler, the application can handle speeds up to the capacity of the machine.

- Interrupt 0Ch, called when serial port hardware issues an interrupt on the IRQ4 interrupt request line, handles COM ports not handled by Interrupt 0Bh.
- Interrupt 0Dh is the Hard Disk (Disk Controller) Management Interrupt for the PC XT, provides control of LPT2 for the Personal Computer AT and industry-standard compatible designs, and is listed as reserved for the PS/2 product line. It is called by the designated hardware controllers, using hardware interrupt request line IRQ5.
- Interrupt 0Eh provides Floppy Disk Management services and is called by the floppy disk controller to detect disk transfer completions using hardware request line IRQ6.

Reboot Control Hooks

Because the processor chips themselves cannot ensure that all memory is properly initialized when you reboot a system, MS-DOS installs hooks into three BIOS interrupt vectors to trap reboot requests and ensure that all vectors are properly set up before enabling the actual reboot process.

The vectors trapped are 13h, 15h, and 19h. Interrupt 13h, the generic disk I/O service, is trapped only if a cache program is present, to make certain that the cache is properly flushed to disk. Interrupt 15h is trapped to detect the combination of Ctrl, Alt, and Delete keys in order to properly turn loose of resources. Interrupt 19h, the reboot service itself, deals with remaining eventualities.

The action taken for Interrupt 13h actually simply is to obtain the address of the original handler so that it can be used to force all buffers and cache contents to be physically written to disk when a reboot is requested. More detailed control than this is left to the discretion of the individual cache program; some of them intercept such requests and clean themselves out before MS-DOS can, however, this action is not universal.

By hooking Interrupt 15h Function 4Fh, MS-DOS can check every keystroke before BIOS key input routine INT 09h is allowed to service it. This enables detection of the classic "three-fingered salute" using Ctrl, Alt, and Delete to request warm-boot of the system so that any necessary corrective action can be taken.

Finally, the hook at Interrupt 19h enables MS-DOS to determine when any application attempts to initiate a boot sequence. The normal action of Interrupt 19h is to reboot the computer without losing the present status of memory. By installing the hook, MS-DOS can modify this action if required by the specific system configuration in use.

Other Overrides

Other interrupt handlers that MS-DOS replaces are those for Interrupt 00h (Divide by Zero exception) and Interrupt 1Bh (BIOS Control-Break Signal).

The Divide by Zero exception normally is generated automatically by the processor chip when a divide operation's internal shift counter overflows and thereby signals the operation can never finish. This happens if division by zero, an illegal operation in arithmetic, is attempted.

At start-up, Interrupt 00h is set to point to an `iret` instruction. MS-DOS later changes the vector. The handler installed by MS-DOS to deal with a Divide by Zero exception reports that such a forbidden arithmetic operation was attempted, and then terminates the program and returns control to the parent process (see Figure 5.4).

```
Microsoft(R) MS-DOS(R) Version 6
             (C)Copyright Microsoft Corp 1981-1993.

D:\WIN31>debug
-a
1E10:0100 idiv bx
1E10:0102
-p

Divide overflow
```

Figure 5.4. The default error message from Interrupt 00h, after MS-DOS installs its handler, is `Divide overflow`.

As shown in Figure 5.4, the single `IDIV BX` operation from within `DEBUG` served to force such an error, because at entry to `DEBUG`, all of the CPU registers except for the segment registers, `SP`, and `IP` are set to zero automatically.

This is handled at the DOS level because a corresponding handler does not exist at the BIOS level. A divide-by-zero error can leave the operating system unstable, resulting in other errors. If a divide-by-zero error occurs, the best course is to restart the system manually or to create a better handler, such as the one for DOS Int 24h.

This exception also can be raised by other arithmetic underflow situations that use the internal shift counter, however, such as a quotient becoming too large to fit into the register designated for it. This sometimes occurs when the user is unaware that arithmetic is being attempted and leads the user to utter confusion.

One situation that can cause such bewilderment involves attempting to access a file that contains a damaged directory entry. While MS-DOS is attempting to convert the faulty information from the directory into a form that can be passed to the disk subsystem, an Interrupt 00h can occur and frequently does.

If you are writing a program in which user input likely is to cause this kind of error, replace the interrupt with your own routine. It always is good practice to screen user inputs and attempt to anticipate this, and all other types of errors. Sometimes, however, your program can reach the divide by zero handler in ways that may never occur to you as being possible.

The BIOS Control-Break Signal (Interrupt 1Bh) is generated when the handler for Interrupt 09h detects that the Break key is pressed at the same time as either of the two Ctrl keys. If so, that key combination is not stored in the keyboard buffer. Instead, the Interrupt 09h handler invokes Interrupt 1Bh to process it.

The default handler MS-DOS installs to deal with Interrupt 1Bh fakes a User Signal exception by forcing a Control-C character (ASCII 03h) into the first position of the keyboard buffer where it is found by the next console read operation.

Even if you replace the User Signal Handler, the default handler for Interrupt 1Bh can cause problems because of placing the character into the keyboard buffer. You can prevent any action by making this vector point to a single `iret` instruction.

If you select an `iret` located in the MS-DOS kernel (such as the one used normally by Interrupt 2Bh, 2Ch, or 2Dh), or one located in the ROM-BIOS area, you do not need to remove the handler unless you want the Control-Break Signal action to come back into effect.

On to BIOS

In this chapter we've seen the interrupts that MS-DOS takes over and those which it modifies although not claiming exclusive ownership. Chapter 6, "BIOS When We Must," provides an overview of the BIOS services found in most systems.

BIOS When We Must

Between the 5 interrupt vectors used by the CPU for things such as signaling fatal error conditions and controlling debugging, and the 32 vectors reserved by MS-DOS, lie 27 vectors that actually include the gateway to the computer's Basic Input-Output System or BIOS services.

6

Not all 27 vectors are used by BIOS. Only 11, Interrupts 10h through 1Ah, reach standard service routines. The 5 vectors above this range include 2 that allow your code to be called from inside certain BIOS procedures. 3 vectors simply are far pointers to data rather than reach any code. Of the 11 located below 10h, 8 provide service for hardware interrupts (Interrupt 08h through 0Fh, corresponding to request lines IRQ0 through IRQ7 respectively), 1 responds when the PrintScrn key is pressed, and 2 are not used in most systems.

The 11 true BIOS services range from highly specialized things such as Interrupt 18h to the multi-purpose conglomerates. Interrupt 15h, which controls your mouse if you use a PS/2, reads cassette tapes if you have an original 1981 model PC, or accesses extended memory, as well as many other things.

When most developers think about "Going to the BIOS" to get something accomplished, however, they are looking at only a few of the BIOS services: those that deal with video, keyboard, printer, serial ports, and possibly the disk system. In these areas, especially the first three, use of BIOS services almost is as widespread as the use of MS-DOS functions.

Considering that the BIOS functions lack many of the newer bells and whistles, such as the capability to redirect input or output, their widespread use poses an interesting puzzle: why should this be so?

A number of years ago, Peter Norton wrote a regular column for *PC Magazine.* In one of those columns, he presented a penetrating analysis of the tradeoffs involved when choosing from the following three different methods of handling keyboard input and screen output.

- Rely strictly on MS-DOS functions.
- Use only BIOS services.
- Ignore both sets of pre-written services and go directly to the hardware itself.

His conclusions were that programs written to use only MS-DOS functions would be the most portable from one MS-DOS system to another but would be the slowest in operation. (Keep in mind that this analysis appeared in the days when at least half the available systems were not compatible with the PBM BIOS conventions.) Those written to use BIOS services would be significantly faster in operation, thus, far more attractive to their users. That, however, would shut out half the market that was not BIOS-compatible. Finally, those written to work directly at the hardware level were by far the snappiest in their response, but would fail to run unless the hardware itself was totally compatible with the IBM designs.

As a result of the analysis, he wrote, he was positioning his products to have the capability to configure to any one of the three methods. If the right-to-the-metal approach could be used, he would have highest performance, and the assurance that no competitor's product would be likely to outrun his own.

If that approach failed, however, then the user would be able to fall back to BIOS capability and lose only a modicum of speed. For the half of the possible market that was unable to use this middle ground, the final retreat to strict MS-DOS compliance still provided a usable (although slower) system.

Because before another year had passed, much of the argument had become moot; I can't say for sure whether his three-level approach ever made it to the marketplace. The systems without at least BIOS-level compatibility were disappearing from view and now have followed the dodo bird into extinction. Any advantages gained by writing direct to the hardware rapidly vanished as the enhanced keyboard with its added keys, and the PGA, EGA, and later VGA video systems made their appearance.

The result was that the choice dwindled to two options: go with BIOS for speed's sake, or stick with MS-DOS functions for the best portability. Those major market-makers that persisted in trying to stay with hardware-level interfaces saw their profits vanish and losses skyrocket as they were unable to bring new versions to market, while other less stubborn firms adapted to BIOS and won away the customers.

It remains true that BIOS services are often faster than the most widely-used MS-DOS functions; however, it's no longer an automatic conclusion. The continued popularity of the BIOS interfaces seems to be based on tradition and myth as much as on real technical differences. One proof of this assertion is the fact that MS-DOS Function 06h, Direct Console I/O, amounts to little more than a direct BIOS interface built into MS-DOS, yet this function goes almost unused while its BIOS equivalents, Interrupts 10h and 16h, can be found almost anywhere.

When developing your applications, the best rule to follow is to try to do everything using DOS functions. Only when those functions are too slow, or if they are incapable of doing what you need, should you consider using BIOS.

Before concluding that standard MS-DOS functions aren't speedy enough, be sure to try all the available options. The speed for both keyboard input and for CRT output, for example, can be increased significantly by using the `IOCTL` functions to set the `CON` device into `RAW` mode (this is described in detail, with sample code, in Chapter 7). Tricks of this nature frequently add enough speed to the standard functions to make any alternatives unnecessary.

Sometimes, however, MS-DOS functions do not provide what you may need. When this is the case, you have little choice other than going to BIOS, or to the actual hardware. When these are your only choices, it's best to use BIOS.

Video Services: Interrupt 10h

Interrupt 10h provides basic video services at the BIOS level. In addition to the 23 functions described in Chapter 15, a number of private functions have been grafted into this area for enhanced operation with various types of super VGA systems.

The first 16 functions, 00h through 0Fh, are available on all MS-DOS systems that feature IBM BIOS compatibility. Higher-numbered functions are not necessarily present on all systems. While most of these first 16 functions have MS-DOS equivalents, a few do not.

Significant among the cases that sometimes require you to use BIOS services is the need to control size, visibility, or placement of the text cursor. Another exception that requires the use of BIOS is when you need to clear the screen or scroll all or part of it up or down.

For that matter, if your application finds it necessary to switch between text and graphics modes, you will have to go to BIOS to do so, because MS-DOS recognizes the existence of only text mode and provides no graphics operations.

Because BIOS's dot-at-a-time approach is glacially slow, even it will not be much help if you're dealing with graphics output. When graphics displays are involved under MS-DOS (as opposed to under Windows), you really have no choice other than going directly to the hardware, despite the extreme limitations.

You're not required to avoid BIOS for every aspect of graphics operation, however. The only place it's necessary is the actual painting of images on-screen. However, much of the setup and housekeeping can be done through BIOS services. Function 10h controls many aspects of EGA and VGA operation, for both graphics and text modes. Function 11h modifies fonts and display sizes for text, in both text and graphics modes, for EGA, MCGA, or VGA video systems. Function 12h deals with miscellaneous video functions, using subfunctions specified in the BL register. Subfunctions 30h through 36h are for VGA only.

Other BIOS functions, such as Function 13h are near-duplicates of MS-DOS capabilities. The four subfunctions of Function 13h (CR, LF, BELL, and BS) differ only in the manner in which attributes are determined for each character in the string, and whether the cursor position is to be on the first character after the string at the end of the operation.

For dealing with systems that may include multiple video cards or monitors, and for additional advanced video manipulation, you may find BIOS necessary. Function 1Ah, available with VGA cards only, gets or sets type codes that indicate types of displays operating in the system. Function 1Bh provides access to additional details about the current video state for VGA-equipped systems. Finally, Function 1Ch saves or restores the video state.

Hardware Information: Interrupt 11h

You use BIOS to obtain information about the hardware of a system. BIOS *Interrupt 11h* returns a bitmap indicating the hardware configuration, as determined during the most recent *Power On Self Test* (POST). The POST is performed each time the system is cold-booted.

Memory Size: Interrupt 12h

Another item of information obtainable only from BIOS services is the amount of contiguous low memory installed in the system. (You can, however, determine this value indirectly via MS-DOS Function 48h.) BIOS *Interrupt 12h* returns in kilobytes in the AX register the amount of contiguous low memory available in the system.

This service actually reports the value stored at 0040h:0013h that, in PC and XT models, is set from switches on the motherboard and may be incorrect. In later models, the value is counted during POST operations and is more reliable.

Disk Services: Interrupt 13h

Although not as widely-used as the keyboard, video, and printer services, the direct disk services available through *Interrupt 13h* are used by many programs that bypass the MS-DOS file system to access absolute disk sectors directly.

The functions provided by this BIOS service apply to both floppy and fixed (hard) disks. Many functions can be achieved equally well by using the Generic `IOCTL I/O` commands for block devices. The Interrupt 13h services, however, still are widely-used and many programs continue to rely on them because of familiarity.

Even though your application may never need the services available through Interrupt 13h, as a developer, you need to be aware of them. This service provides a loophole through which many viruses attempt to crawl in and infect systems. Fortunately, many virus-detection packages are aware of this capability and place traps in their path.

Serial Communications: Interrupt 14h

Because the BIOS serial communications services provided through Interrupt 14h do not include support for hardware interrupts to transfer data from the modem or UART chip into the system's memory, they are almost useless for today's high-speed modems. Instead, the serial communication services use the polling technique, which prevents the system from doing anything else while waiting for a character to arrive. You cannot even test the keyboard to look for operator input.

That's bad enough but when it becomes necessary to scroll up the display a line, or to write incoming data to disk, several characters will be lost from the incoming stream unless interrupt-driven buffering is available. Even at 1200 BPS, considered slow in these days of 14,400-BPS modems, a minimum of 3 characters vanish in the time it takes BIOS to scroll up the screen by one line.

Because of the serious limitations built into the BIOS functions for this service, most practical applications that use serial communications provide their own interrupt-driven I/O functions rather than using the polled interface built into the BIOS. BIOS functions, however, still prove useful for initializing the port.

System Interfacing: Interrupt 15h

Interrupt 15h is the catch-all of BIOS services. Originally assigned to the cassette tape interface of the original IBM PC in 1981, the service saw little use. As diskette storage grew in popularity, Interrupt 15h became virtually obsolete.

When it became necessary to find vectors for features not anticipated in the original PC design, this one was a logical choice. One of the first official functions added was TopView, IBM's original effort at providing multitasking capability for the PC line. While TopView never became popular, third-party equivalents have kept the TopView assignments alive.

The next major official functions were added when the PC-AT model 339 and its successors appeared on the scene. They provided a method for programs to hook into BIOS code for Keyboard Interrupt 09h, and to prevent the normal code from processing desired keystrokes. Finally, with the introduction of the PS/2 line, another major group of functions to determine model type and control system configuration was assigned to this service.

The result today is that Interrupt 15h serves a host of disparate purposes. Most of its functionality is unavailable through standard MS-DOS interfaces. This is one BIOS service for which you have no real alternatives: if you need the information it provides, it's the only game in town. Fortunately, for the portability of most applications, the majority of programs never need these functions.

Keyboard Services: Interrupt 16h

BIOS keyboard services provided by *Interrupt 16h* are widely-used, even though MS-DOS makes available similar services (for more information about keyboard services, see Chapters 7 and 13). One possible reason is that BIOS provides access to the added functions available with the 101-key enhanced keyboard, while MS-DOS does not.

Although BIOS chips created before the introduction of the enhanced keyboard often fail to provide support for any of its functions, by using the BIOS, developers have the opportunity to test for presence of such a keyboard and to use its functions if one is present.

Nevertheless, that is not a very valid reason for abandoning the possibility of accepting input using redirection from files or other programs. The only time direct use of BIOS keyboard input is defensible is for real-time response to the arrow keys for cursor or menu control. Even this use can be handled by MS-DOS by way of Function 06h Subfunction 0FFh; however, using MS-DOS in this situation opens the door for problems that occur in the BIOS-to-DOS interfacing, which are described in detail in Chapter 7.

The upshot is that, in general, MS-DOS functions are preferred for keyboard input, except when your application makes intensive use of Alt-key combinations, function keys, and other special non-ASCII characters. In that case, the BIOS keyboard service is more reliable.

Printer Service: Interrupt 17h

The three functions of *Interrupt 17h* often are used to send output to the printer. Note, however, that these functions bypass many printer control features made available by MS-DOS.

ROM-BASIC Interface: Interrupt 18h

Only genuine IBM PCs contain BASIC in ROM, so the action of this interrupt is unpredictable for non-IBM equipment. It sometimes reboots the system, but frequently has no effect at all.

System Reboot: Interrupt 19h

Interrupt 19h is intended to reboot the system without clearing memory or restoring interrupt vectors. Because interrupt vectors are not changed and may point into RAM that is no longer valid, this interrupt usually causes a system hang if TSRs have been installed, particularly those that hook into Timer Interrupt 08h.

In many systems, Interrupt 19h fails to do its task properly and alternate methods are necessary to allow the program to reboot itself or the system. To perform a warm boot equivalent to Ctrl-Alt-Del, store 1234h at location 0040h:0072h, and then jump to FFFFh:0000h. For a cold boot equivalent to a reset, store 0000h at 0040h:0072h before jumping. The high-RAM address is valid for all members of the Intel 80x86 CPU family, and performs a full reset of the processor chip. It may not, however, do the same for adapter boards; modems frequently require physical powering down to achieve reset.

Time Services: Interrupt 1Ah

Interrupt 1Ah provides time and date services, both from the BIOS-maintained real-time clock counter derived from the CPU's clock signal, and from the hardware-maintained clock-calendar provided in 80286 and later systems.

Calling these services from applications, however, bypasses a basic design constraint of MS-DOS, and results in the missing midnight problem often described as a bug. The actual problem is that these BIOS services do not communicate with each other, and so using the get time call clears the flag which shows that midnight went by, without updating the day-counter data. Thus the clock continues to show correct time, but the calendar has lost a day.

This can be avoided by using MS-DOS services provided by Interrupt 21h (see Chapter 8, "Managing Time and Space"), or by using the `CLOCK$` device driver interface. Both are careful to maintain proper synchronicity of the calendar and clock. Unfortunately, so many commercial applications violate good practice and go direct to BIOS for time information that your best efforts may still be in vain.

Interrupt Vectors 1Bh Through 1Fh

Interrupts 1Bh and *1Ch* normally execute an `iret` instruction only, unless some application hooks them. The entire purpose of these two vectors is to enable user processes to hook into system operation at critical points. When a Ctrl-Break keystroke combination is detected, Interrupt 1Bh is called from the service routine for Interrupt 09h. Interrupt 1Ch is called from the service routine for Interrupt 08h, during the processing of each timer tick.

Interrupts 1Dh, 1Eh, and 1Fh do not point to executable code. The first two interrupts point to tables of parameters used by other BIOS services, and the last contains the address of the font patterns used when displaying extended ASCII characters while in certain graphics modes.

The RAM Structures BIOS Uses

BIOS makes use of a reserved 256-byte area near the start of conventional RAM, located at absolute address 00400, to maintain all sorts of information that may be useful to your applications. However, this area usually is addressed as 0040:0000. When possible, you should use defined BIOS or MS-DOS services to retrieve the information rather than directly accessing this BIOS scratchpad area. In many cases, however, the information can be obtained only by going to where it's stored.

As in Chapters 4 and 5, following are structure definitions in assembly language Basic, and C, for the BIOS RAM structures.

Because the area divides logically into a number of substructures, each of them is defined separately. Unlike many other structures defined in earlier chapters, however, these are at a fixed location. If you need to maintain your own copies, perform block transfer from the true location (0040:0000 through 0040:00FF) to a copy in your own workspace. Keep in mind, however, that none of the information in your private copy will be updated by BIOS.

The BIOSRAM Structure

Following is the format for the `BIOSRAM` structure in assembly language:

```
BIOSRAM   struc
  COM_port        dw    4  dup  (?)     ;  RS-232 port addresses
  LPT_port        dw    3  dup  (?)     ;  Printer port addresses
```

```
    EBIOS_seg       dw    ?                ;  Extended BIOS data
                                              (PS/2)or printer
                                           ;  Printer 4 (PC,XT,AT &
                                              compatibles
    equip_bits      dw    ?                ;  Equipment installed info
                                              bits
    test_flag       db    ?                ;  Initialization test
    main_ram_sz     dw    ?                ;  Base memory size 0-1Meg,
                                              1K steps
    chan_io_sz      dw    ?                ;  Channel i/o size
    kbstruc      KB_DATA         <>        ;  keyboard data structure
    fdkstruc     FDK_DATA        <>        ;  floppy disk data struc
                                              ture
    vidstruc     VID_DATA        <>        ;  video data structure
    genstruc     GEN_DATA        <>        ;  general data structure
    hdkstruc     HDK_DATA        <>        ;  hard disk data structure
    tmrstruc     TMR_DATA        <>        ;  timer data structure
    advidstruc   ADVID_DATA      <>        ;  advanced video data struc
                                              ture
    dskstruc     DSK_DATA        <>        ;  misc disk data structure
    akbstruc     AKB_DATA        <>        ;  advanced keyboard data
                                              structure
    rtcstruc     RTC_DATA        <>        ;  Real Time Clock data
                                              structure
    video_sav_tbls  dd    ?                ;  Pointer to a save table
                                              of more video info
BIOSRAM   ends
```

Following is the `BIOSRAM` layout defined as a record for BASIC:

```
Type BIOSRAM
     COM_port       as integer(4)
     LPT_port       as integer(3)
     EBIOS_seg      as integer
     equip_bits     as integer
     test_flag      as string*1
     main_ram_sz    as integer
     chan_io_sz     as integer
     kbstruc        as KB_DATA
     fdkstruc       as FDK_DATA
     vidstruc       as VID_DATA
     genstruc       as GEN_DATA
```

```
     hdkstruc       as HDK_DATA
     tmrstruc       as TMR_DATA
     advidstruc     as ADVID_DATA
     dskstruc       as DSK_DATA
     akbstruc       as AKB_DATA
     rtcstruc       as RTC_DATA
     video_sav_tbls as long
End Type              ' BIOSRAM
```

Finally, here's the data layout for the `BIOSRAM` structure as a C-language declaration:

```
typedef struct {
     int           COM_port[4];
     int           LPT_port[3];
     int           EBIOS_seg;
     int           equip_bits;
     char          test_flag;
     int           main_ram_sz;
     int           chan_io_sz;
     KB_DATA       kbstruc;
     FDK_DATA      fdkstruc;
     VID_DATA      vidstruc;
     GEN_DATA      genstruc;
     HDK_DATA      hdkstruc;
     TMR_DATA      tmrstruc;
     ADVID_DATA    advidstruc;
     DSK_DATA      dskstruc;
     AKB_DATA      akbstruc;
     RTC_DATA      rtcstruc;
     void far *    video_sav_tbls;
} BIOSRAM;
```

The fields within the `BIOSRAM` structure have the following significance:

COM_port. This 8-byte field at 0040:0000 contains port addresses for COM1 through COM4, as an array of four 16-bit words.

LPT_port. This 6-byte field at 0040:0008 contains port addresses for LPT1 through LPT3, as an array of three 16-bit words.

EBIOS_seg. This 2-byte field at 0040:000E contains the segment address for Extended BIOS data in the PS/2 line, or the port address for LPT4 in PC, XT, AT and compatible systems.

equip_bits. This 2-byte field at 0040:0010 contains a bitmap that indicates the equipment installed in the system. Its value is returned by Interrupt 11h.

test_flag. This 1-byte field at 0040:0012 is used during initialization tests.

main_ram_sz. This 2-byte field at 0040:0013 contains the base memory size (contiguous RAM below 1 megabyte) in 1,024-byte units. Its value is returned by Interrupt 12h. A value of 280h indicates a full 640K of RAM.

chan_io_sz. This 2-byte field at 0040:0015 contains the amount of expansion memory contained on cards plugged into the I/O Channel, as distinct from that plugged into the system's motherboard. This value is not often used by applications because it provides no information concerning the total amount of RAM available.

SubStructures. The 10 substructures listed in BIOSRAM are described in detail on the following pages. All are present always; the presentation is intended merely to group them for emphasis on their related usage.

video_sav_tbls. This 4-byte field at 0040:00A8 is a far pointer to a save table of more video information. For more information about the table, see Chapter 15, "BIOS Services."

The KB_DATA Structure

Following is the format for the KB_DATA structure in assembly language beginning at location 0040:0017:

```
KB_DATA     struc
     flags_1     db ?            ; Keyboard flag bits
     flags_2     db ?            ; Keyboard flag bits
     alt_num     db ?            ; Alt & digit pad number buffr area
     headptr     dw ?            ; Head ptr of circular key queue
     tailptr     dw ?            ; Tail ptr of circular key queue
     kbuffer     dw 16 dup (?)   ; 15 key queue for keyboard
KB_DATA     ends
```

Following is the KB_DATA layout defined as a record for BASIC:

```
Type KB_DATA
     flags_1     as string*1
     flags_2     as string*1
```

```
     alt_num     as string*1
     headptr     as integer
     tailptr     as integer
     kbuffer     as integer(16)
End Type         ' KB_DATA
```

Finally, here's the data layout for the KB_DATA structure as a C-language declaration:

```
typedef struct {
     char        flags_1;
     char        flags_2;
     char        alt_num;
     unsigned    headptr;
     unsigned    tailptr;
     unsigned    kbuffer[16];
} KB_DATA;
```

The fields within the KB_DATA structure have the following significance:

flags_1. This 1-byte field contains flag bits indicating the state of the keyboard's Shift, Alt, and Ctrl keys.

flags_2. This 1-byte field contains flag bits similar to those contained in `flags_1`.

alt_num. This 1-byte field is used as a buffer area when creating input characters using the Alt key and the numeric keypad.

headptr. This 2-byte field contains a near pointer (offset) to the head of the circular keyboard buffer.

tailptr. This 2-byte field contains a near pointer (offset) to the tail of the circular keyboard buffer.

kbuffer. This array of 16 2-byte fields provides a 15-keystroke buffer for keyboard input. The 16th position can never be used because when both the head and tail pointers have the same value, the buffer is treated as being full when entering keystrokes or empty when removing keystrokes.

The FDK_DATA Structure

Following is the format in assembly language for the FDK_DATA structure which begins at location 0040:003E:

```
FDK_DATA   struc
     recal_stat     db   ?
     motor_stat     db   ?
     motor_tmr      db   ?
     ret_code       db   ?
     dstatus        db   7 dup (?)
FDK_DATA   ends
```

Following is the FDK_DATA layout defined as a record for BASIC:

```
Type FDK_DATA
     recal_stat     as string*1
     motor_stat     as string*1
     motor_tmr      as string*1
     ret_code       as string*1
     dstatus        as string*7
End Type           ' FDK_DATA
```

Finally, here's the data layout for the FDK_DATA structure as a C-language declaration:

```
typedef struct {
     char       recal_stat;
     char       motor_stat;
     char       motor_tmr;
     char       ret_code;
     char       dstatus[7];
} FDK_DATA;
```

The fields within the FDK_DATA structure have the following significance:

recal_stat. This 1-byte field contains the bit pattern for the command used to recalibrate the floppy drive.

motor_stat. This 1-byte field contains motor-running status and disk-write information.

motor_tmr. This 1-byte field contains the motor timer (downcounted at each timer tick; at 0, the motor is turned off).

ret_code. This 1-byte field contains the status code returned by the floppy disk controller.

dstatus. This 7-byte field contains status bytes returned by the floppy disk controller.

The VID_DATA Structure

Following is the format for the VID_DATA structure, in assembly language, that begins at location 0040:0049:

```
VID_DATA   struc
     vid_mode       db  ?
     columns        dw  ?
     buf_siz        dw  ?
     segment        dw  ?
     curs_pos0      dw  ?
     curs_pos1      dw  ?
     curs_pos2      dw  ?
     curs_pos3      dw  ?
     curs_pos4      dw  ?
     curs_pos5      dw  ?
     curs_pos6      dw  ?
     curs_pos7      dw  ?
     curs_mode      dw  ?
     vid_page       db  ?
     video_port     dw  ?
     mode_reg       db  ?
     color_reg      db  ?
VID_DATA    ends
```

Following is the VID_DATA layout defined as a record for BASIC:

```
Type VID_DATA
     vid_mode      as string*1
     columns       as integer
     buf_siz       as integer
     segment       as integer
     curs_pos0     as integer
     curs_pos1     as integer
     curs_pos2     as integer
     curs_pos3     as integer
     curs_pos4     as integer
     curs_pos5     as integer
     curs_pos6     as integer
     curs_pos7     as integer
     curs_mode     as integer
     vid_page      as string*1
```

```
    video_port    as integer
    mode_reg      as string*1
    color_reg     as string*1
End Type          ' VID_DATA
```

Finally, here's the data layout for the `VID_DATA` structure as a C-language declaration:

```
typedef struct {
    char        vid_mode;
    unsigned    columns;
    unsigned    buf_siz;
    unsigned    segment;
    unsigned    curs_pos0;
    unsigned    curs_pos1;
    unsigned    curs_pos2;
    unsigned    curs_pos3;
    unsigned    curs_pos4;
    unsigned    curs_pos5;
    unsigned    curs_pos6;
    unsigned    curs_pos7;
    unsigned    curs_mode;
    char        vid_page;
    unsigned    video_port;
    char        mode_reg;
    char        color_reg;
} VID_DATA;
```

The fields within the `VID_DATA` structure have the following significance:

vid_mode. This 1-byte field contains the current video display mode.

columns. This 2-byte field contains the number of columns within one display line.

buf_siz. This 2-byte field contains the video buffer size in bytes, rounded to the next higher multiple of 2048.

segment. This 2-byte field contains the segment address of the active video memory.

curs_pos0. This 2-byte field contains the cursor position for video page 0, with the row in the first byte and the column in the second.

curs_pos1. This 2-byte field contains the cursor position for video page 1, with the row in the first byte and the column in the second.

curs_pos2. This 2-byte field contains the cursor position for video page 2, with the row in the first byte and the column in the second.

curs_pos3. This 2-byte field contains the cursor position for video page 3, with the row in the first byte and the column in the second.

curs_pos4. This 2-byte field contains the cursor position for video page 4, with the row in the first byte and the column in the second.

curs_pos5. This 2-byte field contains the cursor position for video page 5, with the row in the first byte and the column in the second.

curs_pos6. This 2-byte field contains the cursor position for video page 6, with the row in the first byte and the column in the second.

curs_pos7. This 2-byte field contains the cursor position for video page 7, with the row in the first byte and the column in the second.

curs_mode. This 2-byte field contains the values for cursor start and end scanlines, defining the shape and visibility of the cursor for all eight possible video pages.

vid_page. This 1-byte field tells which video page is currently active.

video_port. This 2-byte field contains the Video controller base I/O address.

mode_reg. This 1-byte field contains the bit pattern last sent to the Hardware mode register.

color_reg. This 1-byte field contains the bit pattern last sent to the Hardware Color set register in CGA modes.

The GEN_DATA Structure

Following is the format for the `GEN_DATA` structure in assembly that begins at location 0040:0067:

```
GEN_DATA  struc
    gen_io_ptr     dw ?
    gen_io_seg     dw ?
    int_occured    db ?
    timer_low      dw ?
    timer_hi       dw ?
```

```
    timer_rolled    db ?
    keybd_break     db ?
    boot_flag       dw ?
GEN_DATA  ends
```

Following is the GEN_DATA layout defined as a record for BASIC:

```
Type GEN_DATA
     gen_io_ptr      as integer
     gen_io_seg      as integer
     int_occured     as string*1
     timer_low       as integer
     timer_hi        as integer
     timer_rolled    as string*1
     keybd_break     as string*1
     boot_flag       as integer
End Type             ' GEN_DATA
```

Finally, here's the data layout for the GEN_DATA structure as a C-language declaration:

```
typedef struct {
     unsigned    gen_io_ptr;
     unsigned    gen_io_seg;
     char        int_occured;
     unsigned    timer_low;
     unsigned    timer_hi;
     char        timer_rolled;
     char        keybd_break;
     unsigned    boot_flag;
} GEN_DATA;
```

The fields within the GEN_DATA structure have the following significance:

gen_io_ptr. This 2-byte field contains the ROM initialization pointer.

gen_io_seg. This 2-byte field contains the ROM I/O segment address.

int_occured. This 1-byte field flags an unused interrupt.

timer_low. This 2-byte field contains the low word of the Timer, which advances every 55 msec in response to Timer Interrupt 08h.

timer_hi. This 2-byte field contains the high word of the Timer and is an approximate indicator of the hour on a 24-hour clock.

timer_rolled. This 1-byte field is set to 1 when the Timer reaches midnight (1800B0h), and is cleared by the next invocation of Interrupt 1Ah Function 00h.

keybd_break. This 1-byte field contains a keyboard-break flag. Bit 7 is set if the Break key is pressed.

boot_flag. This 2-byte field contains a value that controls the boot process. If it contains 0000h, a full POST boot is performed. If the value in this field is 1234h, a warm-boot is performed.

The HDK_DATA Structure

Following is the format for the HDK_DATA structure in assembly language which begins at location 0040:0074:

```
HDK_DATA    struc
     status_1      db ?
     n_h_drvs      db ?
     head_ctrl     db ?
     ctrl_port     db ?
HDK_DATA    ends
```

Following is the HDK_DATA layout defined as a record for BASIC:

```
Type HDK_DATA
     status_1      as string*1
     n_h_drvs      as string*1
     head_ctrl     as string*1
     ctrl_port     as string*1
End Type            ' HDK_DATA
```

Finally, here's the data layout for the HDK_DATA structure as a C-language declaration:

```
typedef struct {
     char         status_1;
     char         n_h_drvs;
     char         head_ctrl;
     char         ctrl_port;
} HDK_DATA;
```

The fields within the HDK_DATA structure have the following significance:

status_1. This 1-byte field contains hard disk status information.

n_h_drvs. This 1-byte field contains the number of hard disk drives.

head_ctrl. This 1-byte field contains head control information (XT only).

ctrl_port. This 1-byte field contains hard disk control port information (XT only).

The TMR_DATA Structure

Following is the format for the TMR_DATA structure in assembly language which begins at location 0040:0078:

```
TMR_DATA            struc
     prn_timeout_1  db ?
     prn_timeout_2  db ?
     prn_timeout_3  db ?
     prn_timeout_4  db ?
     com_timeout_1  db ?
     com_timeout_2  db ?
     com_timeout_3  db ?
     com_timeout_4  db ?
     keybd_begin    dw ?
     keybd_end      dw ?
TMR_DATA   ends
```

Following is the TMR_DATA layout defined as a record for BASIC:

```
Type TMR_DATA
     prn_timeout_1   as string*1
     prn_timeout_2   as string*1
     prn_timeout_3   as string*1
     prn_timeout_4   as string*1
     com_timeout_1   as string*1
     com_timeout_2   as string*1
     com_timeout_3   as string*1
     com_timeout_4   as string*1
     keybd_begin     as integer
     keybd_end       as integer
End Type             ' TMR_DATA
```

Finally, here's the data layout for the TMR_DATA structure as a C-language declaration:

```
typedef struct {
     prn_timeout_1;
     prn_timeout_2;
     prn_timeout_3;
     prn_timeout_4;
     com_timeout_1;
     com_timeout_2;
     com_timeout_3;
     com_timeout_4;
     keybd_begin;
     keybd_end;
} TMR_DATA;
```

The fields within the TMR_DATA structure have the following significance:

prn_timeout_1. This 1-byte field contains the number of timer ticks (normally 20) the system will wait for response from printer 1.

prn_timeout_2. This 1-byte field contains the number of timer ticks (normally 20) the system will wait for response from printer 2.

prn_timeout_3. This 1-byte field contains the number of timer ticks (normally 20) the system will wait for response from printer 3.

prn_timeout_4. This 1-byte field contains the number of timer ticks (normally 20) the system will wait for response from printer 4.

com_timeout_1. This 1-byte field contains the number of timer ticks (normally 1) the system will wait for response from COM1.

com_timeout_2. This 1-byte field contains the number of timer ticks (normally 1) the system will wait for response from COM2.

com_timeout_3. This 1-byte field contains the number of timer ticks (normally 1) the system will wait for response from COM3.

com_timeout_4. This 1-byte field contains the number of timer ticks (normally 1) the system will wait for response from COM4.

keybd_begin. This 2-byte field contains a near pointer to the beginning of the keyboard buffer.

keybd_end. This 2-byte field contains a near pointer to the end of the keyboard buffer.

The ADVID_DATA Structure

Following is the format for the ADVID_DATA structure in assembly language which begins at location 0040:0084:

```
ADVID_DATA struc
     scrn_rows     db ?
     chr_pixels    dw ?
     options       db ?
     switches      db ?
     reservd_1     db ?
     reservd_2     db ?
ADVID_DATA ends
```

Following is the ADVID_DATA layout defined as a record for BASIC:

```
Type ADVID_DATA
     scrn_rows     as string*1
     chr_pixels    as integer
     options       as string*1
     switches      as string*1
     reservd_1     as string*1
     reservd_2     as string*1
End Type           ' ADVID_DATA
```

Finally, here's the data layout for the ADVID_DATA structure as a C-language declaration:

```
typedef struct {
     dcharscrn_rows;
     unsigned     chr_pixels;
     char         options;
     char         switches;
     char         reservd_1;
     char         reservd_2;
} ADVID_DATA;
```

The fields within the ADVID_DATA structure have the following significance:

scrn_rows. This 1-byte field contains the number of text rows of characters (minus one) available on-screen.

chr_pixels. This 2-byte field contains the number of pixels-per-character in the current font.

options. This 1-byte field contains display adapter options; values vary depending on the adapter.

switches. This 1-byte field contains the switch setting bits from the video adapter's switches.

reservd_1. This 1-byte field is used for EGA/VGA control purposes.

reservd_2. This 1-byte field is reserved for use by the video system.

The DSK_DATA Structure

Following is the format for the `DSK_DATA` structure in assembly language, which begins at location 0040:008B:

```
DSK_DATA   struc
     dsk_data_rate     db ?
     hdsk_status_2     db ?
     hdsk_error        db ?
     hdsk_int_flags    db ?
     hdsk_options      db ?
     hdsk0_media_st    db ?
     hdsk1_media_st    db ?
     hdsk0_start_st    db ?
     hdsk1_start_st    db ?
     hdsk0_cylinder    db ?
     hdsk1_cylinder    db ?
DSK_DATA   ends
```

Following is the `DSK_DATA` layout defined as a record for BASIC:

```
Type DSK_DATA
     dsk_data_rate     as string*1
     hdsk_status_2     as string*1
     hdsk_error        as string*1
     hdsk_int_flags    as string*1
     hdsk_options      as string*1
     hdsk0_media_st    as string*1
     hdsk1_media_st    as string*1
     hdsk0_start_st    as string*1
     hdsk1_start_st    as string*1
     hdsk0_cylinder    as string*1
     hdsk1_cylinder    as string*1
End Type              ' DSK_DATA
```

Finally, here's the data layout for the DSK_DATA structure as a C-language declaration:

```
typedef struct {
     char        dsk_data_rate;
     char        hdsk_status_2;
     char        hdsk_error;
     char        hdsk_int_flags;
     char        hdsk_options;
     char        hdsk0_media_st;
     char        hdsk1_media_st;
     char        hdsk0_start_st;
     char        hdsk1_start_st;
     char        hdsk0_cylinder;
     char        hdsk1_cylinder;
} DSK_DATA;
```

The fields within the DSK_DATA structure have the following significance:

dsk_data_rate. This 1-byte field contains the last data rate sent to a diskette.

hdsk_status_2. This 1-byte field contains additional hard disk status information.

hdsk_error. This 1-byte field contains the most recent hard disk error code.

hdsk_int_flags. This 1-byte field contains the hard disk interrupt flag.

hdsk_options. This 1-byte field indicates controller options. Bit 0 is set to 1 when using a single controller for both hard disk and floppy drives.

hdsk0_media_st. This 1-byte field contains the media state for drive 0.

hdsk1_media_st. This 1-byte field contains the media state for drive 1.

hdsk0_start_st. This 1-byte field contains the start state for drive 0.

hdsk1_start_st. This 1-byte field contains the start state for drive 1.

hdsk0_cylinder. This 1-byte field contains the track number for drive 0.

hdsk1_cylinder. This 1-byte field contains the track number for drive 1.

The AKB_DATA Structure

Following is the format for the AKB_DATA structure in assembly language which begins at location 0040:0096:

```
AKB_DATA   struc
     flags_3     db ?
     flags_4     db ?
AKB_DATA   ends
```

Following is the AKB_DATA layout defined as a record for BASIC:

```
Type AKB_DATA
     flags_3   as string*1
     flags_4   as string*1
End Type        ' AKB_DATA
```

Finally, here's the data layout for the AKB_DATA structure as a C-language declaration:

```
typedef struct {
     char        flags_3;
     char        flags_4;
} AKB_DATA;
```

The fields within the AKB_DATA structure have the following significance:

flags_3. This 1-byte field contains special keyboard type and mode information.

flags_4. This 1-byte field contains advanced keyboard flag information in bitmap form.

The RTC_DATA Structure

Following is the format for the RTC_DATA structure in assembly language which begins at location 0040:0098:

```
RTC_DATA   struc
     timer_wait     dd ?
     timer_clk      dd ?
     timer_clk_flag db ?
     lan_bytes      db 7 dup (?)
RTC_DATA     ends
```

Following is the RTC_DATA layout defined as a record for BASIC:

```
Type RTC_DATA
     timer_wait      as long
     timer_clk       as long
     timer_clk_flag  as string*1
     lan_bytes       as string*7
End Type             ' RTC_DATA
```

Finally, here's the data layout for the RTC_DATA structure as a C-language declaration:

```
typedef struct {
     char far *timer_wait;
     long        timer_clk;
     char        timer_clk_flag;
     char        lan_bytes[7];
} RTC_DATA;
```

The fields within the RTC_DATA structure have the following significance:

timer_wait. This 4-byte field is a far pointer to a flag used by the timed wait function of Interrupt 15h.

timer_clk. This 4-byte field is a 32-bit counter for the 1-microsecond realtime clock used by BIOS timers, which are controlled through functions of Interrupt 15h.

timer_clk_flag. This 1-byte field contains a timer communication flag. It is set to 80h when the timer is posted, 1 when busy, and 0 to acknowledge the timer posting.

lan_bytes. This 7-byte field is used by LAN software when required.

The Toolbox Closes

This marks the end of Section 2, "Your Tools." The four chapters of this section have provided an overview of all the tools, both in the form of programs to use and in the form of MS-DOS and BIOS services available, that are available to developers.

The six chapters of Section 3, "The Techniques," show how to put these tools to work in applications and programs. Chapter 7, "Console I/O," describes how to communicate with the CRT and the keyboard.

Section 3: The Techniques

The six chapters in this section provide detailed techniques for using the MS-DOS and BIOS tools introduced in Section 2, "Your Tools."

Chapter 7, "Console I/O," covers all the standard methods for dealing with keyboard input and CRT output, concluding with a pair of sample programs that allow user configuration of screen colors.

Chapter 8, "Managing Time and Space," deals with the clock-calendar capabilities, and memory management. It provides a collection of utility libraries to help manage these areas in all applications.

Chapter 9, "Disk Storage and the File System," discusses all aspects of disk storage, culminating with a sample program that illustrates many of the described techniques.

Chapter 10, "Serial Communications," shows why the standard MS-DOS and BIOS features are inadequate to cope with modern needs. The example program for this chapter illustrates how the standard features can be employed for simplicity when their capability is enough for the job at hand.

Chapter 11, "Process Management," deals with the techniques for launching additional processes within an application, shows how TSR programs work, and then introduces a simpler alternative to the TSR technology.

Chapter 12, "Miscellaneous Functions and Structures," explains how to determine system configuration details, explores the little-publicized functions available to support international applications and discusses some rules that can simplify the conversion of programs from domestic-only to international use. Finally, Chapter 12 deals with some unusual uses for installable device drivers. This chapter contains two sample device driver programs, one of which is a troubleshooting tool and the other of which expands the BIOS keyboard buffer to more than eight times its original size.

CONSOLE I/O

7

This chapter begins with the DOS (and BIOS) functions concerned primarily with Console I/O actions. In addition to being the lowest-numbered functions in the entire list, these also are fundamental to all applications that require communication with the usual user. By gaining full understanding of them at the outset, you can use them with confidence while extending your horizons in subsequent chapters.

Historically, back before the earliest days of "computers for ordinary people," the usual operator interface to a computer system was a card punch and reader, or a bank of switches and lights. It didn't take long, however, for the pioneers to discover that even a trained operator could communicate with the system more easily by way of a specialized typewriter that contained a keyboard and printer.

The earliest units actually punched paper tape and communicated with the computer only indirectly. By the mid-1960s when the first mainframe-based commercial computer networks began operating, however, teleprinter devices popularly known as teletype machines had become standard.

When personal computers first appeared about a decade later, the TTY (Teletype's trademark) had become accepted as the standard user interface to computers, and so the operating systems for all PC's were TTY machines, or emulated them via TV monitors and keyboards.

DOS is no exception. All the basic Console I/O services covered in this chapter are based on the TTY model. The newer functions, however, have modified it somewhat to provide a feature called *device independence* which treats input and output as separate streams of data. The streams, however, are still implicitly assumed to connect with a TTY-like device, and the name itself survives in the little-used DOS command CTTY which switches the streams from the standard CON device to another standard device AUX in order to permit an actual TTY or its equivalent to be connected via a serial port or modem.

This chapter first examines the critical factors involved in choosing between DOS functions and the lower-level BIOS capabilities for dealing with Console I/O. Then the original DOS functions in this area plus the newer handle-based functions which may replace the older ones are covered. In this part of the chapter, you see why some of the Microsoft recommendations in this respect are being ignored by most market-aware developers.

Discussed next are the unpredictable interruptions from the user, the `IOCTL` interface as it applies to the Console and all other character devices, the functions that deal with Device I/O other than that meant for the console, and finally a sample program that makes full use of most of the techniques.

BIOS, Standard Handles, and Redirection

In the earliest days of MS-DOS, developers had to choose from three different methods of dealing with keyboard input and display output.

The first method was to use DOS itself, which was notoriously slow but was guaranteed to work on any system that was actually MS-DOS compatible. The second method was to bypass DOS and use the BIOS functions of the IBM PC, which gave significant improvements in performance but would work only with PC-compatible systems (many of which were not). The third method was to go directly to the hardware itself, which gave highest performance but required a much greater degree of IBM compatibility.

Most of the early commercial programs took the third route, although everyone agreed that this was not a good thing to do. Only Peter Norton's original utilities, among the leading success stories of the day, offered users the choice of all three methods for handling I/O chores.

When systems had only three or four possible arrangements of keyboard and video hardware, the direct-to-hardware approach was feasible. Today, with Super VGA systems more the rule than the exception, and every different make of system being somewhat different from all its competitors, going directly to the hardware isn't really a practical technique for any design that aspires to widespread use. The choice now narrows down to BIOS or DOS.

The question of compatibility, however, no longer has much applicability. Virtually all current systems provide near-total BIOS-level compatibility with the standards originally set by IBM but now considered to be industry standards, thus, your choice between the two should be based primarily on the question of performance requirements. Today, that doesn't really mean "Which is faster?" as it once did.

Because DOS itself is still based on the concept of data streams of bytes as might just as well be handled by a TTY system, it cannot easily deal with some requirements of full-screen displays. Among the things it isn't designed to control are such vital needs as placing the cursor where you want it on-screen, the colors used on the display, or even whether the blinking cursor is visible.

When you need these facilities not provided as an integral part of the DOS set of functions, your choices narrow down to using BIOS functions to handle them, or using DOS add-on helpers, such as the ANSI.SYS device driver.

One of the major differences between using DOS functions for keyboard input and display output, and using their BIOS equivalent functions, is that most the DOS functions deal with predefined standard handles for five separate data streams automatically and invisibly, and permit redirection of two of these five (which is normally done by COMMAND.COM or an equivalent command processor before your program is executed). Neither the standard handles nor the redirection capability are available to the BIOS functions. Following is a quick overview of what the DOS functions offer.

The five predefined standard handles in assembly language are known as `STDIN`, `STDOUT`, `STDERR`, `STDAUX`, and `STDPRN`; they are predefined by the command processor to be File Handles 0 through 4, in that same sequence: `STDIN` is handle 0 and `STDPRN` is handle 4. You do not need to open or close these handles, but can read from `STDIN`, `STDAUX`, and `STDPRN`, or write to any of them except STDIN, just as if you had opened them like any other data streams.

In C language programs, these five predefined handles are usually mapped to equivalent file pointer values that behave exactly the same way, but have names that are written in all-lower-case characters. Only `stdin`, `stdout`, and `stderr` are defined by the ANSI standards for the language and its standard library. Most compilers for use with MS-DOS, however, also supply `stdaux` and `stdprn` although some recent versions add a leading underscore to the names of these two.

While redirection of the standard handles is usually done by the command processor before your program is loaded for execution, you also can do it yourself. To make it happen, however, you must use some advanced file-system functions that we have not yet discussed, so I'll defer the details until we meet these advanced functions in a later chapter.

Console Input Functions

The functions described in this section deal with obtaining input from the operator via the console keyboard, or, more specifically, from the standard input device (in the case of the DOS functions). If redirection is in effect for input, the actual data may come from a file, or from some device other than the keyboard.

Note that most of these functions were declared to be superseded by Microsoft when Version 5.0 of MS-DOS was documented. Only one technique (that of using Function 3Fh to read from an input handle) still carries an official blessing.

The recommended technique, however, sacrifices many capabilities that the users of MS-DOS have come to expect, such as the capability to input keystrokes without having them appear on the display instantly, or to enter a single keystroke and have the system act on it immediately.

In fact, if you slavishly follow the technique that Microsoft officially suggests, you will find that your users will not be able to move the cursor around the screen with the arrow keys! No matter how many times a user presses a key, your program can see no input until the user presses Enter. Then, but not before, your program will receive the accumulated flood of strokes entered by your frustrated soon-to-be-ex-user.

For these reasons, and a host of others, most professional developers have chosen to ignore Microsoft's recommendations in this area and to continue using the superseded DOS functions that best fit their needs for each specific task to be performed in their programs. It's an attitude you will do well to emulate.

Function 01h: Read Keyboard with Echo

You might guess from its low function number that this is one of the oldest functions of all those contained in the MS-DOS arsenal, and you would be correct. It was originally inherited intact from the CP/M operating system, and the only significant change made to the function in all the time that's passed since then was to add the `STDIN` redirection capability to it when handle-based file structures came into existence in Version 2.0.

Function 01h reads a single character from the predefined or redirected `STDIN` handle, waiting for a keystroke if none is already available when the function is called. When a character is available, it is checked to determine whether it is a Control-C. If it is, DOS flushes both the `STDIN` and `STDOUT` handles automatically, and then invokes a Control-C handler which usually terminates your program. Similarly, if the character is Control-P, a flag internal to DOS that causes all `STDOUT` output to also go to `STDPRN` is toggled.

If the character is not one of the DOS control characters, however, it is echoed to the `STDOUT` handle (for display on the screen in the usual case) and also is returned to the caller in the AL register.

Function 01h takes no parameters when called, and returns no error indications. Its only action is to bring a keystroke into your program.

If the user's keystroke is one of the extended ASCII characters, such as a function key or one of the arrow keys, Function 01h initially returns 00h in AL. This signals you that a second call to the function is required in order to obtain the `scancode` and determine which key was pressed.

Unfortunately, all versions of MS-DOS from 1.0 through 6.0 have a nasty bug in their implementation of this function: the check for DOS control characters is carried out on every call to Function 01h even if an extended ASCII character is involved.

This means that if the `scancode` for an extended ASCII character happens to match one of the DOS control characters, such as Control-C or Control-P, the system may perform the associated control action rather than returning the `scancode` to you as it should.

The misinterpretation doesn't happen in every possible case. In my own system using DOS Version 6.0, for example, I find that Alt-Q toggles the echo-to-printer action just as if I had pressed Control-P (both involve the 10h code being interpreted by DOS), but Alt-R (with a `scancode` of 13h, the same as the ASCII code for Control-S) has no effect on the display although Control-S toggles a pause action. Apparently in some cases, the control is done by DOS, while in others it's a BIOS function; the Function 01h bug affects only those cases that are controlled by DOS. Control-2, however, has the same effect as Control-C even though Control-C seems to be at least partially a BIOS control feature.

No total workaround is known; a partial solution to the problem is to use some other function for keyboard input, instead.

The calling sequence, in assembly language, for this function is:

```
mov ah,01h  ; Function 01h
int 21h     ; call MS-DOS
mov chr,al  ; keystroke returns in AL
```

Function 08h: Read Keyboard Without Echo

Sometimes you need to accept input from the keyboard without echoing it back to the display or to STDOUT. You may, for example want to replace a simple y or n response with the words Yes or No on the display. Alternatively, you might just want to read cursor keys in order to move a menu bar up, down, left, or right. When you have this requirement, use DOS *Function 08h.*

Function 08h is identical to Function 01h in every respect, including the misinterpretation bug, except that it does not echo the character that it reads back to the STDOUT handle. All control checks, however, are performed.

In the innermost heart of DOS, Function 01h is actually implemented as a call to Function 08h's internal routine, followed by another call to the internal routine for Function 02h to echo the character, so it's only to be expected that these two functions would share all their characteristics except for the echo.

Function 08h takes no parameters when called, and returns no error indications. Its only action is to bring a keystroke into your program.

The calling sequence, in assembly language, for this function is:

```
mov ah,08h   ; Function 08h
int 21h     ; call MS-DOS
mov chr,al   ; keystroke returns in AL
```

Function 07h: Direct Console Input (Wait For Key)

Still a third possible requirement you might encounter would be a way to read input from the keyboard without either echoing it to STDOUT or performing any of the usual control checks such as Control-C or Control-P. This requirement arises when you want your program to deal with such control characters itself, rather than letting DOS intercept them and apply its standard reactions.

Meeting this requirement is the purpose of *Function 07h.* When called, this function waits indefinitely until a keystroke is available, then returns the keystroke to the caller.

Function 07h takes no parameters when called, and returns no error indications. Its only action is to bring a keystroke into your program.

Like the previous two functions, it returns `00h` as the first response if an extended ASCII key is pressed and must be called a second time to obtain the `scancode`. And like its predecessors, this function is subject to the misinterpretation bug.

Just as Function 01h is made up of a sort of sandwich (of Function 08h to get a key and Function 02h to echo it), Function 08h itself is implemented as a call to the internal routine for Function 07h, followed by the necessary tests for control characters.

The calling sequence, in assembly language, for this function is:

```
mov ah,07h  ; Function 07h
int 21h     ; call MS-DOS
mov chr,al  ; keystroke returns in AL
```

Function 06FFh: Direct Console Input (No Waiting)

All three of the keyboard input functions we have examined so far in this chapter share one characteristic: they wait for a keystroke to become available, if none is waiting in the keyboard buffer when the function is called.

Usually, this is a convenient feature to have, because most of the time the major reason for getting keyboard input is to give the human user a chance to tell the computer what to do next. By having the wait-for-a-key action built right into the function, you don't have to explicitly code a loop to hold things up while waiting.

But sometimes you don't want to wait. A wait, in fact, might even keep your program from working at all. Consider a modem program that enables you to communicate with an on-line service.

A communications program of this sort must accept the characters that you type at the keyboard and send them to the modem, but it must also, at the same time, receive each character as it arrives from the communications line, and display it on-screen. If such a program is forced to wait, doing nothing, for each key that you type, then it will miss many incoming characters each time you pause to decide what you will say next.

Another example might be an installation program that copies several megabytes of files from diskettes to your hard disk drive. You might want to enable the user to cancel the installation in mid-stream by pressing Control-C or perhaps by pressing Esc. Having a function that can read the keyboard without forcing any wait makes it possible for your copy loop to check the panic button frequently enough to respond rapidly if it's pressed, without losing any time waiting if it's not.

One way of dealing with this "keyboard strobing" need is to use BIOS, and we will examine that just a little later. But there's a special function available in DOS itself that is only a hair removed from the BIOS level of flexibility, called *Direct Console I/O* in the official documentation.

Function 06h, as its official name implies, deals with both output and input. To use it for input, you must load the DL register with `0FFh` to signal DOS that input is desired. Any other byte in DL is assumed to be for output.

Like all the previous functions, Function 06h returns `00h` as its first response if an extended ASCII key is pressed, and must then be called a second time to obtain the scancode. And like its predecessors, this function is subject to the misinterpretation bug. In fact, these two characteristics are the only essential differences between Function 06h and its BIOS-level counterpart, and are the reason that many developers use BIOS when this type of action is required.

The calling sequence, in assembly language, for this function is:

```
mov ah,06h  ; Function 06h
mov dl,0FFh  ; Input subfunction
int 21h    ; call MS-DOS
jz  NoChar  ; Z flag set if no char
mov chr,al  ; else char returns in AL
```

Function 0Ah: Buffered Keyboard Input

The functions we have looked at thus far all deal with getting a single character from the keyboard. To get a whole string of characters, such as a complete filename or a line of text, you would have to call one of them within a loop, store the received byte in a buffer set aside in your application, and continue until the input string was complete (usually signaled by the Enter character, with ASCII value 13 decimal).

If you wanted to enable the user of your application to correct spelling errors or do other kinds of editing on the string being input, you would also have to define the appropriate keys to signal the user's intention to your string-receiving loop, detect each such key when pressed, and provide code to execute each editing action.

Because so many programs, including COMMAND.COM itself, require this capability, DOS has included a single function to provide the whole thing. It's Function 0Ah. While Microsoft officially labeled this function as "superseded" in the MS-DOS Version 5.0 Programmer's Reference Manual, many developers continue to use it for reasons we will examine later.

Provide this function the address of a buffer within your program, then just call it. DOS will handle the loop and all the editing for you, and will not return to your own program from the call until the user presses Enter.

If the user presses either Control-C or Control-Break, the corresponding error handler will get control. In the usual case, this terminates your application and returns control to the program that launched your application. If you provide a special handler, it will get control instead, and may be able to return to your program. This, of course, depends on how you write the special handler, and that's not part of Function 0Ah.

The special editing keys recognized by Function 0Ah, and their corresponding actions, are listed in the accompanying table. These editing keystrokes have been part of MS-DOS because Version 1.0, and have been documented in the User's Guide supplied with each copy of MS-DOS through Version 5.0 (the Version 5 User's Guide devotes pages 166 through 169 to their actions, with examples).

While the descriptions of these keys have been dropped from the MS-DOS 6.0 User's Guide and are not discussed in the on-line help files that are supposed to replace most of the older User-Guide functionality, they are still available in Version 6. Presumably the expected flood of third-party books telling users how to operate MS-DOS 6.0 will include descriptions of these actions.

Note that the table makes continual reference to an *edit template* where the last-input command line is stored, but (like the descriptions in the older User's Guides) never explains anything about the location or format of this template. Actually, the "edit template" is simply the user buffer that you provide to the function, and DOS operates on the assumption that you have not modified this buffer in any way since your previous call to Function 0Ah because this is the way that Microsoft's own programs such as COMMAND.COM use it.

The *input area* mentioned repeatedly is a special buffer area within DOS' own data region used exclusively by Function 0Ah, and the *template pointer* also is part of the function's own internal data, keeping track of which character in the template matches the currently displayed cursor position on-screen.

As the user types input characters, they are temporarily stored in the input area. When the user presses Enter to signal end of input, the bytes in the input area up to the Enter character itself are copied back to your own buffer, becoming the edit template for the next call to this function. A bit later we show how you can create special effects based on knowing just what the edit template really is.

Function/Cursor Key	Function
F1, Right Arrow	Copies to input area one character from edit template and advances template pointer to next character.
F2 `char`	Copies to input area all characters of edit template from current position of template pointer up to, but not including, next occurrence of `char`. Leaves template pointer on first character not copied.
F3	Copies to input area all remaining characters of edit template from current position of template pointer to end. Leaves pointer at end of template so no more characters can be copied from it.
F4 `char`	Advances edit template pointer up to next occurrence of `char` without copying anything to input area, skipping over intervening characters of template.

Function/Cursor Key	Function
F5	Copies all characters from input area to edit template, then outputs @ followed by CR and LF and resets both pointers to start of their areas. The effect is to copy what is already on the display into the edit template, then restart the input process just as if Esc had been pressed. The difference is that the user's input replaces the original edit template and so can be put back in the input area by the other editing keystrokes.
F6	Inserts Control-Z, the old-style text EOF marker character, into the input area.
BkSp, Left Arrow	Deletes character immediately left of the cursor from input area and backs up template pointer. If at first character, has no effect.
Delete	Advances template pointer by one character without copying anything, giving the illusion of having deleted the character from the template.
Insert	Toggles the link between input area (cursor position) and template pointer. Initially both pointers are connected and advance or retreat in unison except when specific editing keys move one without affecting the other. The first use of Insert disconnects the template pointer so that it does not advance as characters are typed into the input area and is moved only by specific editing keys. Use of any editing key returns the link to its connected state.

Function/Cursor Key	Function
Esc	Echoes a `\`, `CR`, and `LF` character sequence to the display to acknowledge the user's actions, then sets both the input area pointer and the template pointer back to the start of their respective buffers. This effectively deletes all the user's input and permits starting afresh.

The buffer that you pass to Function 0Ah must be 2 bytes longer than the longest string of characters you expect to receive, but cannot be longer than 257 bytes (255 plus the added two). The first 2 bytes of the buffer contain control information.

The first byte, filled in by your program, tells the function the maximum number of characters your buffer can hold. If the user attempts to type in this many characters (because the final byte is reserved for the terminating Enter byte), each additional keystroke is stored in the next-to-final byte location, and a `BEEP` character is sent to `STDOUT`.

The second byte, filled in by Function 0Ah, tells your program how many characters were actually returned from the user. If the user presses Enter as the very first keystroke, this byte will be zero, and the third byte of your buffer (the first data byte) will contain the Enter character, a byte of 0Dh.

If you want to supply a built-in edit template on your program's initial call to Function 0Ah, as for example to supply a default filename in an installation routine, you can do so by filling the data area of your buffer with the desired string of bytes, followed by the `0Dh` terminating character, and setting the second control byte to the count of characters in your string.

Function 0Ah examines the byte found by adding the value in that second control byte to the actual offset of the first data byte of your buffer. If that byte does *not* contain the expected 0Dh value, the function assumes that no valid edit template exists. This undocumented fact can cause the edit capability to appear to fail, if you modify the input string in the buffer itself rather than copying it to another area for any changes you want to make.

The calling sequence, in assembly language, for this function is:

```
mov ah,0Ah   ; Function 0Ah
push ds     ; optional, see text
mov dx,seg Buffer
mov ds,dx
mov dx,offset Buffer
int 21h     ; call MS-DOS
pop ds     ; optional, see text
```

In the calling sequence, if `Buffer` is in a data segment that is already referenced by the DS register, the three instructions to modify DS before the call, and the single instruction to restore it after returning, are unnecessary and can be omitted.

Function 0Ah returns no indication of error; the only errors that can occur during execution of this function are dealt with automatically by the DOS Critical Error Handler.

Function 3Fh: Read Device

When the whole idea of *handles* rather than *file control blocks* was introduced into MS-DOS in Version 2.0, one of the major advantages it was supposed to bring was the capability to treat files and devices in exactly the same way within application programs. The capability is what makes redirection possible and also greatly simplifies most application programming.

The MS-DOS function that reads devices or files by the handle technique is *Function 3Fh.* This is the function that Microsoft recommends be used rather than Function 0Ah for all new programming, effective with DOS 5.0.

Function 3Fh requires a bit more setup to use than does Function 0Ah. In addition to setting the address of the data buffer to be used into the DS:DX registers and the function number into AH, you must also set BX to the predefined `STDIN` handle value of zero, and put the maximum size of your input buffer into CX, before making the call. This takes the place of the special buffer format that is used by Function 0Ah.

Function 3Fh returns the number of characters in the input string in the AX register rather than in a dedicated part of the input buffer, and unlike Function 0Ah, this count includes both the 0Dh byte that signaled `end of input` and any 0Ah byte that was added to it automatically by the DOS ASCII-mode translation. Thus where the older function would return a count of zero when the user pressed Enter with no other keystrokes, Function 3Fh normally returns a count of two under the same condition.

Like Function 0Ah, Function 3Fh permits editing of the input data with the same set of function and cursor keys. The edit template used by Function 3Fh, however, is not your own buffer space, so you cannot preload it with any default value. On your initial call to this function, the edit template remains empty; it's only available on the second and subsequent calls.

In addition, DOS maintains only one edit template for all calls to this function, so if your program requires string input at two different locations, the call at the second location will use the edit template that was filled in by the first call, even if the two calls provide individual buffers to keep the returned strings separated. Function 0Ah keeps the edit templates separate so long as you provide separate buffers for the various calls.

Also unlike Function 0Ah, which discards excess input characters, beeping at the user all the while, Function 3Fh silently accepts them and stores them as the initial series of keystrokes for the next call to the function.

Because the terminating `Enter` character is stored, that next call will not wait for the user to do anything. Because of this, your application must be prepared to deal with such a situation. You can do so by always testing the final two characters of the string (based on the count returned in AX) to verify that they are actually 0Dh and 0Ah; if not, the user overran the buffer and a second call will be necessary to clear it of the leftover excess input.

Even so, once the buffer overruns its space, the edit template frequently loses track of just which input is valid, making its use confusing at best.

Finally, Function 3Fh requires that you be prepared to deal with error conditions although these can occur only if input is redirected from a file that has somehow become unreadable.

The calling sequence, in assembly language, for this function is:

```
mov ah,3Fh  ; Function 3Fh
mov bx,00h  ; STDIN handle
mov cx,BufSize   ; maximum length
push ds    ; optional, see text
mov dx,seg Buffer
```

```
mov ds,dx
mov dx,offset Buffer
int 21h     ; call MS-DOS
pop ds     ; optional, see text
jc  errorhandler
mov NbrRead,ax    ; actual length
```

In the calling sequence, if `Buffer` is in a data segment that is already referenced by the DS register, the three instructions to modify DS before the call, and the single instruction to restore it after returning, are unnecessary and can be omitted.

Is Function 0Ah Obsolete?

As of DOS Version 5.0, Microsoft has labeled Function 0Ah as being "superseded," and recommends Function 3Fh instead. As noted in the discussion of Function 3Fh, however, significant differences exist between its operation and that of Function 0Ah. Therefore programs that follow the Microsoft recommendation are exposed to a number of potential disasters.

These include loss of the capability to automatically ignore user overruns of the allocated buffer space, the possibility that the program may fail to wait for user input, and the need to set additional registers which adds, no matter how slightly, to the complexity of your programs.

You can illustrate the `failure to wait` situation with a rather simple program that calls Function 3Fh with the buffer size set to a very small value, such as one byte. On the first call, no matter how many characters you type, the function will not return until you press Enter. It then copies the first character you typed into your buffer.

On the next call, you will get the second character with no opportunity to change your input. This continues until your input buffer gets the Enter byte itself. The next call after that will return to the initial condition, enabling you to type a new string.

You don't need assembly language to demonstrate this quirk, because most C and C++ compilers implement their `getchar()` library function as just such a call to Function 3Fh. The following small C program, when compiled with either Microsoft or Borland compilers (from MSC 4 on, or any Borland compiler), shows the problem:

```
#include <stdio.h>
void main( void)
{  int c;
   while( (c = getchar()) != 27 )
     putchar;
}
```

When you run this program, nothing will happen as you type input characters, until you press Enter. It will then echo back all your typed characters. Press Esc followed by Enter to break the loop and end program operation.

Besides the repeated-input quirk, a more serious problem with using Function 3Fh rather than 0Ah as Microsoft recommends is that DOS uses only a single internal buffer for all calls to read `STDIN`. Because of this, you are no longer able to keep edit templates uniquely associated with specific calls for input.

Instead, your input during one call becomes the edit template for the next, even if that next call comes from a totally different part of your program. The accompanying screen displays compare what happens when you use Function 0Ah, and when you use Function 3Fh, for the same sequences of input.

```
D:\WINWORD\D6DG>rd0a
Demo program for INT 21/0A testing:
1>test 1
test 1
2>test 2
test 2

1>test 1 again
test 1 again
2>test 2 again
test 2 again

1>this is an attempt to overflow the input buffer c
this is an attempt to overflow the input buffer c
2>

1>^C
D:\WINWORD\D6DG>
```

Figure 7.1. When Function 0Ah is used to obtain keyboard input, the results look like this. The edit templates for each separate input call remain distinct, and the user is unable to cause overflow of the input buffer.

```
D:\WINWORD\D6DG>rd3f
Demo program for INT 21/3F testing:
1>test1
test1
2>test2
test2

1>test2 again
test2 again
2>test2 again again
test2 again again

1>this is an attempt to overflow the input buffer completely.
this is an attempt to overflow the input buffer co
2>

mpletely.

1>^C
D:\WINWORD\D6DG>
```

Figure 7.2. When Microsoft's recommendation to use Function 3Fh is followed, keyboard input looks more like this. Your response to one prompt becomes the edit template for the next one, and the user is allowed to run past the end of the buffer. What's worse, the overrun becomes the input used by your next call.

To generate these displays, I wrote simple programs that request one input string, display it, and then request a second string using a separate buffer, display that string, and finally loop back to the first request. The only significant differences between the two programs were the functions used to obtain input.

In both examples, the first string input was `Test1` and the second was `Test2`. On the second pass around the loop, the F3 function key was used at each prompt to recover the content of the edit template, and the word `again` added to the recovered string. Finally, on the third pass, I attempted to type in a string of characters that would exceed the 50-character limit I had placed on the input buffers, using the same string in both tests.

The results speak for themselves.

Because using Function 3Fh makes programs both less friendly and more error-prone, most experienced developers have chosen to disregard Microsoft's official recommendation in this matter. They continue to use Function 0Ah for user input. You will be well advised to follow their example, at least for now.

Function 0Bh: Check Keyboard Status

One of the reasons we presented Function 06FFh was that it permitted you to determine whether any keystrokes were available from the `STDIN` data stream, rather than simply waiting for one to appear if none happened to be waiting when the function was called.

The same capability is provided by *Function 0Bh*, which does nothing but test the `STDIN` input status. If at least one character is waiting to be taken, this function returns the value `0FFh` in the AL register. If no character is present, AL contains zero on return.

Unlike Function 06FFh, Function 0Bh does not itself set any flags. You must test the value returned in AL to determine the condition.

This, like most of the other low-numbered functions of MS-DOS, is a heritage from the CP/M operating system, which always indicated success or failure of a BDOS function by the content of the A register (the 8-bit 8080 did not divide the registers into high and low sections) upon returning.

Function 0Bh has no effect on the character waiting to be read, if one exists; you must still call one of the other functions in order to actually read the character. By using this function first, however, you can be sure that no wait will result even when you call a function that waits for a character. After all, you only call that function when you know that a character is waiting.

The calling sequence, in assembly language, for this function is:

```
mov ah,0Bh  ; Function 0Bh
int 21h     ; call MS-DOS
cmp al,0    ; flag returns in AL
je  NoCharYet ; no char available
```

Function 0Ch: Flush Buffer, Read Keyboard

When users become familiar with your program, many of them will capitalize on this familiarity by "typing ahead" even before your application requests its input data. Because they know what item will be asked for next, they type their responses blindly, and the system then picks the keystrokes up from the keyboard buffer when your program asks for them.

In normal situations this is usually a tendency that you should encourage, because it makes your application seem more "willing" to let the user decide how to use it. If the program runs into some exceptional condition that requires an unexpected response from the user, however, having these pending keystrokes in the buffer can be inconvenient at best, and might even prove disastrous.

If, for example, the program encounters an error for which the most reliable solution would be to erase your data files, it obviously should ask the user's consent before taking such a drastic step. Your routine for getting that consent might easily accept a single "Y" or "N" keystroke as its acceptable responses.

But if the "normal" next input that the user expected the program to ask for is `Customer's last name` and the user has already anticipated that need and typed `Youngblood` into the keyboard buffer, your routine will get the `Y`, interpret it as consent, and destroy the data files without giving the user any chance to intervene. Disastrous results such as this must be avoided if you want to build a reputation for creating reliable software.

Fortunately the designers of DOS anticipated such a need, and gave us Function 0Ch for just such occasions. This function actually has five different versions, which enable you to use it to both clear the keyboard buffer of all pending input and then automatically continue with any of four other functions for single-key input. The fifth version simply clears the buffer and returns immediately, when you want to use one of the string input techniques to get the actual response.

The four functions that can be called automatically via Function 0Ch are Functions 01h, 06FFh, 07h, and 08h. You specify which of these is to be called by placing its number in AL (rather than AH). If you load 6 into AL, you must also place 0FFh into DL so that Function 06h will have the correct subfunction indicator. If AL contains any value other than 1, 6, 7, or 8, then Function 0Ch will not call anything else, but will return to your program immediately after clearing the keyboard buffer.

If one of the four keyboard input functions is called automatically, then the keystroke obtained by the input function is returned in AL. If the clear-only action is specified, AL will contain zero when Function 0Ch returns.

The calling sequence, in assembly language, for this function is:

```
mov ah,0Ch   ; Function 0Ch
mov al,01h   ; or 6 or 7 or 8
int 21h      ; call MS-DOS
mov chr,al   ; keystroke returns in AL
```

BIOS Int 16h for Keyboard Functions

The ROM BIOS contains eight functions dealing with keyboard services. Of these, three are available on all IBM-BIOS-compatible systems, three are available only on systems equipped with the 101-key enhanced keyboards that provide 12 function keys and additional cursor-keys separate from the numeric keypad, one is available only on the PCjr, and one is unavailable on original 8086/8088 systems such as the XT but can be used on the PCjr and 286+ systems. Because the PCjr is, for all practical purposes, extinct, I omit the details of its functions here.

The three functions that are available on all systems permit you to determine whether a keystroke is available in the keyboard buffer, to obtain a keystroke from that buffer (waiting until one becomes available if none is already present), and to access the eight flag bits maintained by the BIOS to indicate status of the keyboard Shift, Control, Alt, and assorted Lock keys.

Like the DOS functions, the BIOS keyboard services are called by placing a service code in the AH register and then invoking a software interrupt. For the keyboard BIOS services, Interrupt 16h is used.

To wait for a key to become available, and then extract it from the buffer and return its value, service code 00h is used. Following, in assembly language, is the calling sequence for this function:

```
mov ah,00h   ; get keystroke
int 16h      ; call BIOS keyboard svc
mov chr,ax   ; keystroke returns in AX
```

Unlike the DOS functions, the BIOS function returns both the ASCII value (in AL) and the key's scancode (in AH). Thus by using this function to get single key values, you eliminate the confusion that DOS incurs between the ASCII value of a key and its scancode value, that can cause false tripping of the Control-P toggle.

You pay a price for this, however, and only you can decide whether the advantage is worth the cost: none of the trapping for Control-C is done at the

BIOS level (although Control-Break will still be detected), nor can you redirect input from a file when you use the BIOS to read the keyboard.

The BIOS keyboard service code to use when you need only know that a key is available is 01h. Following is the calling sequence, in assembly language, for this function:

```
mov ah,01h  ; get key status
int 16h     ; call BIOS keyboard svc
jz  NoChr   ; no key available
mov chr,ax  ; keystroke returns in AX
```

Even though this function, like Function 00h, returns the full keystroke value in the AX register, it does not remove it from the keyboard buffer. A subsequent call to Function 00h will get this same character a second time. The most usual use of this BIOS function is to simply determine whether to call Function 00h or not, in situations such as modem routines where your program must avoid waiting indefinitely for a key to be hit.

The final BIOS function available on all systems is Function 02h, which gets the shift-status byte from the BIOS scratchpad area in low RAM. Following is the calling sequence, in assembly language, for this function:

```
mov ah,02h  ; get shift flags
int 16h     ; call BIOS keyboard svc
mov Flags,al ; status byte in AL
```

The bits returned in the AL register correspond to the following Shift-key conditions, if nonzero:

Bit	Meaning
80h	Insert is active.
40h	CapsLock is active.
20h	NumLock is active.
10h	ScrollLock is active.
08h	(Either) Alt key is pressed.
04h	(Either) Ctrl key is pressed.
02h	Left Shift key is pressed.
01h	Right Shift key is pressed.

Systems that support the full 101- and 103-key enhanced keyboards that were introduced with the advent of the AT systems use three similar functions. The codes for these enhanced BIOS services are exactly 10h greater than the codes for the corresponding universal services. The code to wait for a key, for example, is 10h. The calling sequence, in assembly language, for this function is:

```
mov ah,10h  ; get extended keystroke
int 16h    ; call BIOS keyboard svc
mov chr,ax  ; keystroke returns in AX
```

To determine whether a keystroke is available, the enhanced function code is 11h. The calling sequence, in assembly language, for this function is:

```
mov ah,11h  ; get extended key status
int 16h    ; call BIOS keyboard svc
mov chr,ax  ; keystroke returns in AX
```

Finally, to check the extended shift flags, Function 12h is used. The calling sequence, in assembly language, for this function is:

```
mov ah,12h  ; get extended flags
int 16h    ; call BIOS keyboard svc
mov Flags,ax ; status word in AX
```

The bits returned in the AX register correspond to the following Shift-key conditions, if nonzero:

Bit	Meaning
8000h	SysReq key is pressed.
4000h	CapsLock key is pressed.
2000h	NumLock key is pressed.
1000h	ScrollLock key is pressed.
0800h	Right Alt key is pressed.
0400h	Right Ctrl key is pressed.
0200h	Left Alt key is pressed.
0100h	Left Ctrl key is pressed.
0080h	Insert is active.

Bit	Meaning
0040h	CapsLock is active.
0020h	NumLock is active.
0010h	ScrollLock is active.
0008h	Either Alt key is pressed.
0004h	Either Ctrl key is pressed.
0002h	Left Shift key is pressed.
0001h	Right Shift key is pressed.

Function 03h is the one that can be used on both the PCjr and on AT-and-up systems. Only one of its subfunctions, however, applies to the AT-and-up usage. The calling sequence, in assembly language, for this subfunction is:

```
mov ah,03h  ; set repeat values
mov al,05h  ; Set rate and delay
mov bh,Delay
mov bl,Rate
int 16h    ; call BIOS keyboard svc
```

The value set into BH for delay must be in the range 0 to 3, and is one less than the number of quarter-second intervals that must elapse before keymatic repeat action goes into effect. That is, 0 gives 1/4 second delay and 3 gives a full second.

The value set into BL for rate is, similarly, a code, with 0 producing a 30 character per second repetition rate, the default value of 12 (0Ch) producing 10 characters per second, and the maximum value of 31 (1Fh) producing 2 per second.

Function 03h returns no error indications.

The final BIOS keyboard service function we will examine here is one that can be used to determine whether your program is running on a system capable of supporting the enhanced 101-key operations, because it is available only in those versions of the BIOS that also support the enhanced functions.

This is Function 05h, which stuffs a keystroke into the keyboard buffer just as if it had been pressed by the operator. The calling sequence, in assembly language, for this function is:

```
mov ah,05h     ; set keystroke
mov ch,Scancode
mov cl,ASCIIval
int 16h       ; call BIOS keyboard svc
mov Result,al   ; return code in AL
```

You must supply both the scancode and the ASCII value in order for them to be placed in the keyboard buffer, but many programs ignore values of the scancode for ASCII characters. In any event, whatever is in CX when this function is called will go into the buffer. The value in AL upon return will be 00 if the function succeeds, or 01 if the keyboard buffer was already full.

To determine whether an extended keyboard BIOS is present in the system, first clear the keyboard buffer of any waiting input, then use this function to stuff 0FFFFh into the keyboard buffer. Next, use Function 01h to determine whether a keystroke is available. If not, Function 05h failed which means the enhanced BIOS is not present.

If a keystroke is present, use Function 00h to retrieve it, and compare the full value returned in AX with the 0FFFFh that you tried to put there. If they match, the enhanced BIOS exists. Otherwise try Function 00h again, and repeat this loop until you get a definite indication one way or the other. This usually happens on the first pass, unless a user just happens to be sitting on the keyboard when your program makes the test.

Console Output Functions

Output may be displayed on the CRT by any of three different methods. The most desirable, from a theoretical point of view and for ease of program maintenance, is to use DOS functions. Faster, but less desirable, is to use BIOS functions, but then not all MS-DOS machines are guaranteed to be able to run your program. Fastest of all, but also the most restricted in portability, is to write directly into video RAM, bypassing both the BIOS and DOS functions.

The DOS functions described in this section all deal with display of information to the console CRT screen, or more accurately, to the standard output device (in the case of the DOS functions). If redirection is in effect for output, the actual destination may be a file, or some other device.

The BIOS functions described here display information to the CRT and are not capable of redirection to a file or any other device. They will, however, distinguish between the various types of video systems available in MS-DOS machines, and deal with all systems in a reasonable manner.

This section does not address direct writes to video RAM.

Function 02h: Display Character

The usual DOS function for display of a single character is Function 02h, which in addition to sending the character to the `STDOUT` stream also checks for Control-C signals from the keyboard.

Microsoft has labeled this function as "superseded" as of DOS Version 5.0 and suggests using Function 40h instead, with a string length of 1, which seems somewhat less than reasonable because each call to Function 40h requires much more setup code. However Function 02h is still supported in DOS 6.0 and most developers continue to use it.

The calling sequence, in assembly language, for this function is:

```
mov ah,02h  ; Function 02h
mov dl,chr  ; character to display
int 21h    ; call MS-DOS
```

No error indication or other value is returned.

If an ASCII backspace character is sent to the screen by this function (`mov dl,8`) the cursor moves one position to the left, but the character that was on-screen is not erased. To achieve the conventional destructive backspace, the following sequence is required:

```
mov ah,02h  ; Function 02h
mov dl,8   ; output backspace
int 21h    ; call MS-DOS
mov ah,02h  ; Function 02h
mov dl,' '  ; erase previous char
int 21h    ; call MS-DOS
mov ah,02h  ; Function 02h
mov dl,8   ; backspace again
int 21h    ; call MS-DOS
```

Function 06h: Direct Console Output

When you want to send individual characters to the STDOUT stream without performing any checks for Control-C interruptions, you can use Function 06h. This function is capable of displaying 255 of the 256 possible characters in the extended-ASCII character set. Only the byte value 255 (0FFh) cannot be displayed; this value tells the function to get input rather than sending output.

This function is actually a mere wrapper provided by DOS to go around the often-used BIOS interface, to escape some of the problems involved in going directly to BIOS for output. The bell, backspace, tab, linefeed, and carriage-return ASCII codes are interpreted as controls, but all other patterns (except for 0FFh) are displayed or sent to STDOUT.

Following is the calling sequence, in assembly language, for this function:

```
mov ah,06h  ; Function 06h
mov dl,chr  ; character to display
int 21h    ; call MS-DOS
```

Function 09h: Display String

The most frequent string output requirement isn't for individual characters at all, but rather for a function that will output a whole string at one call. That's what Function 09h does. Pass it the address of the first characters of the string, and it will then send the entire string to STDOUT.

Along the way, continual checking is done for Control-C keystrokes. Just as in Function 06h, the bell, backspace, tab, linefeed, and carriage-return ASCII codes are interpreted as controls.

The end of the string is marked by the dollar sign, $; so that's one character that cannot be displayed by Function 09h. The calling sequence, in assembly language, for this function is:

```
mov ah,09h  ; Function 09h
mov dx,offset string
int 21h    ; call MS-DOS
```

Microsoft has labeled this function as "superseded" as of DOS Version 5.0 and suggests using Function 40h instead. While Function 40h does require a bit of additional setup, it does have one advantage: all printable characters, including the dollar sign, can be displayed.

Function 40h: Write Device

Function 40h, the generic one-size-fits-all output routine for files and devices that was introduced in Version 2.0 of MS-DOS as part of the handle technique, is now the recommended primary method for providing output from all applications.

For normal output (that is, replacing Functions 02h or 09h) the handle to use is the predefined stream STDOUT. This handle normally addresses the CON device, that is, the CRT. If redirection of output is in effect, however, it may address any other device, or a file.

The length of the string to be output must be loaded into the CX register prior to the call, and the DS:DX register pair must point to the first character of the string. No special end-of-string marker is needed; the length value in CX tells DOS how many characters to send to STDOUT.

Following is the calling sequence, in assembly language, for this function:

```
mov ah,40h   ; Function 40h
mov bx,01h   ; STDOUT handle
mov cx,strlen ; length of string
push ds    ; optional, see text
mov dx,seg Strg
mov ds,dx
mov dx,offset Strg
int 21h    ; call MS-DOS
pop ds    ; optional, see text
jc  errorhandler
mov NbrSent,ax   ; actual length
```

For normal output situations, no error is likely to be detected. If output is redirected to a disk file, however, and the disk becomes full during the execution of this function, that error will be reported, so it's never completely safe to ignore the error return possibilities even though they have very low probability of ever being needed.

BIOS Int 10h for CRT Output

While DOS itself has only basic functions for providing CRT output, the BIOS functions provide much additional control. The four DOS functions, for example, make no provision for controlling either the colors used for output, or the location on-screen where the output characters appear. The BIOS functions, however, deal with these needs, and also provide the capability to scroll data up or down.

In fact, the BIOS video functions provide far more control capability than we have space to discuss here, so this description is deliberately limited to those functions directly involved with the display of output including color and cursor control. For additional video BIOS functions see Chapter 15, "BIOS Services."

One major disadvantage of the BIOS functions is that they do not support the output-redirection features which their DOS-function counterparts include automatically.

The starting point for any video output is to establish the operating mode for the video system, unless your application can be certain that the mode already set is appropriate for its operation. To establish the mode, use video BIOS Function 00h. Following is the calling sequence, in assembly language, for this function:

```
mov ah,00h  ; Function 00h
mov al,Mode  ; see table
push bp
int 10h     ; call video BIOS
pop bp
```

The `push bp` and `pop bp` instructions are necessary around all calls to Interrupt 10h because the original IBM-PC's BIOS code failed to preserve the BP register when scrolling the screen. Because most modern computer languages make extensive use of this register to preserve stack information, failure to preserve it can cause strange and intermittent problems. Although most BIOS chips in use today treat BP properly, there's always the chance that your programs might be run on an original PC system, so you must practice safe calling techniques in this instance.

While "super VGA" cards, now widely-used, provide many additional nonstandard mode values, the most commonly employed mode settings are those listed in the following table:

Mode	Description
0	40x25x2-color text mode, CGA, EGA, MCGA, VGA
1	40x25x16-color text mode, CGA, EGA, MCGA, VGA
2	80x25x2-color text mode, CGA, EGA, MCGA, VGA
3	80x25x16-color text mode, CGA, EGA, MCGA, VGA
4	320x200x4-color graphics, CGA, EGA, MCGA, VGA
5	320x200x4-color graphics, CGA, EGA, MCGA, VGA
6	640x200x2-color graphics, CGA, EGA, MCGA, VGA
7	80x25 Monochrome text mode, MDA and Hercules
0Dh	320x200x16-color graphics, EGA and VGA
0Eh	640x200x16-color graphics, EGA and VGA
0Fh	640x350x2-color graphics, EGA and VGA
10h	640x350x16-color graphics, EGA and VGA
11h	640x480x2-color graphics, MCGA and VGA
12h	640x480x16-color graphics, MCGA and VGA
13h	320x200x256-color graphics, MCGA and VGA

When you set the video mode using Function 00h, the display clears automatically. You can take advantage of this to achieve a quick clearing of the CRT if you don't mind the resulting black screen. The BIOS code does not permit you to select a color for the automatic clear-screen action (which actually comes about as a side effect of setting all video RAM locations to 0 as a part of establishing the mode).

Newer versions of the video BIOS provide the capability to prevent this automatic clearing from taking place. If you set the high bit of the AL register to 1, by `OR`ing 80h into the register after selecting your desired mode, the screen content will be left unchanged. Note, however, that if you are switching from a text to a graphics mode, or from one graphics mode to another, the result may be totally unreadable garbage when you do this.

Because the primary thrust of this chapter involves text output to the display, the rest of the functions described in this section all apply only to text modes of operation. See Chapter 15 for BIOS functions used in graphics modes.

Function 01h controls the cursor's shape and, with some video systems, its visibility and blink rate. Be warned, however, that some video BIOS code is extremely buggy in its handling of this function. Unless you absolutely must use it, your best practice is to avoid it.

The cursor shape and size is determined by telling the video controller chip at which scanline of the character box to start the cursor, and at which to end it. These values are loaded into the CH and CL registers, respectively.

Because no standard character box exceeds 32 scanlines in height, only five bits are required to specify the starting line number in CH, so the high three bits of the register are used to specify the cursor blink rate on MDA cards, or its visibility on EGA/VGA systems. The high bit should always be zero. Bits 6 and 5 should be set to 00 for normal cursor action. On the MDA, setting these bits to 01 makes the cursor invisible, 10 produces erratic results, and 11 gives a slow blink rate. On EGA and VGA systems, any nonzero value for these two bits hides the cursor.

In other words, you can usually hide the cursor by `OR`ing 32 into CH on this call, and make it visible by `AND`ing 31. A bit later I show sample code to do this. The calling sequence, in assembly language, for Function 01h is:

```
mov ah,01h   ; Function 01h
mov ch,CurTop ; see text
mov cl,CurBot ; see text
push bp
int 10h     ; call video BIOS
pop bp
```

To set the cursor location to a specific column of a specific row on the display, use Function 02h. Both the row and column values start at zero; the "home position" at the top left corner of the screen is Row 0, Column 0. Most displays extend to Column 79 and to Row 24, although some are much larger.

In addition to the row and column values, Function 02h requires that you specify which video page you are dealing with. Actually, many other functions of the video BIOS services also need to know the video page involved, so let's take time out at this point to see what it's all about.

Displaying detailed multi-color graphics on the CRT requires much greater amounts of video RAM that does the display of text. Because of this, most video systems provide at least 32K of storage in order to deal with graphics (super-VGA systems may go as high as a megabyte).

Text storage, however, takes only two bytes per character, one for the attribute and one for the character code itself, so a 40x25 text display such as that produced by video modes 0 and 1 needs only 2000 bytes of video RAM. The standard 80x25 display uses twice as much, or 4000 bytes. This means that the video cards have enough video RAM available to store several screens of data rather than just one.

These individual screens of data are known as *video pages* and every card, no matter what mode is in use, always has at least one video page available: Page 0. This is the only screen available when operating in any graphics mode, but in the various text modes additional screens can be used.

If the video mode is 0 or 1, you can use video pages 0 through 7. In the more usual mode 2 or 3, you can use only pages 0 through 3. And in mode 7, you have only two pages available, 0 and 1.

Use of pages other than Page 0 (the usual default because it is the only page that is guaranteed to always be available no matter what kind of system is in use) carries a few dangers. The one most likely to bite you is the fact that all pages, not just the currently active page, are cleared automatically by a mode change, and also are cleared when a scrolling function is used to erase the screen.

The reason that Function 02h must be told the video page to use is that each of the up to 8 pages available has its own cursor, and the location of each is tracked separately. All, however, have the same shape, so Function 01h did not need to know which page to deal with. Following is the calling sequence, in assembly language, for Function 02h:

```
mov ah,02h  ; Function 02h
mov bh,VidPag ; see text
mov dh,Row
mov dl,Col
push bp
int 10h    ; call video BIOS
pop bp
```

Function 03h gets cursor data for you, both the current location and the start and stop scanlines. All you need to pass to this function is the number of the video page involved.

Following is the calling sequence, in assembly language, for this function:

```
mov ah,03h   ; Function 03h
mov bh,VidPag ; same as Function 02h
push bp
int 10h     ; call video BIOS
pop bp
mov CurTop,ch       ; info from Function 01h
mov CurBot,cl
mov Row,dh   ; info from Function 02h
mov     Col,dl
```

All the information you might need in order to restore a cursor state later can be obtained by this single call, though two calls are needed to do the restoring.

You can produce a pair of useful subroutines for hiding and showing the cursor by combining BIOS functions 01h and 03h. The routines look like this in assembly language:

```
HideCur  proc       ; Hides cursor
     push bp
     mov ah,03h  ; Get current data
     mov bh,VidPag ; same as Function 02h
     int 10h
     or  ch,32      ; mark as invisible
     mov ah,01h  ; Put it back, modified
     int 10h
     pop bp
     ret
HideCur  endp
ShowCur  proc       ; Shows cursor
     push bp
     mov ah,03h  ; Get current data
     mov bh,VidPag ; same as Function 02h
     int 10h
     and ch,31      ; mark as visible
     mov ah,01h  ; Put it back, modified
     int 10h
```

```
    pop bp
    ret
ShowCur  endp
```

Simply call `HideCur` (after setting a global variable `VidPag` appropriately; many programs use only Page 0 by default) to make the cursor invisible. Even if it's already invisible no harm will be done. Similarly, you can call `ShowCur` when the cursor is already visible without creating any problems. I find these routines invaluable, and have wondered for years why DOS never provided such functions for applications programmers to use.

To scroll up or scroll down you can call BIOS Function 06h or 07h, respectively. The only difference in these two functions is the direction in which the scroll moves. Both require you to define a window on-screen in terms of its top row, left column, bottom row, and right column, and to provide an attribute to establish the color of the blank line that will move into this window (from the bottom in Function 06h, or from the top in Function 07h).

You must also specify how many lines to scroll. If you specify 0, or any value larger than the actual height of the window that will be scrolled, the window will be cleared. To clear the entire screen, set CX to 0, DH to the number of rows minus one, DL to the number of columns minus 1, and AL to 0. Note that this will also clear any inactive video pages as well as the visible area.

The attribute byte moved into BH for these functions specifies both the foreground and background colors for the blank characters that move into the vacated space on the bottom or top line. The high bit of this byte determines whether the character is to be steady or blinking, the next three bits determine the background color, Bit 3 specifies the intensity of the foreground color, and the low three bits specify the color to be used for the character itself (the foreground color). It looks like this:

```
 7  6   5   4   3   2   1   0

Blink   Background Color   Inten.   Foreground Color
```

The codes for the eight possible colors are:

Code	Color
0	Black
1	Blue
2	Green

Code	Color
3	Cyan
4	Red
5	Magenta
6	Brown/Yellow
7	Gray/White

If the intensity bit is 1, the foreground colors become much brighter. In particular, the gray tone produced by attribute 7 becomes bright white with attribute 0Fh, and the dirty brown color of attribute 6 becomes an attractive yellow with attribute 0Eh.

Every character displayed on-screen has an accompanying attribute byte, and the attribute for each character is independent of all other characters. You can change the appearance of the screen significantly just by changing the attribute bytes with no need to modify the actual characters, but doing so requires direct access to video RAM; neither the BIOS nor DOS provides any function to change attributes only.

Following is the calling sequence, in assembly language, for Function 06h:

```
mov ah,06h  ; Function 06h
mov al,Lines ; number to scroll
mov bh,Attrib ; see text
mov ch,TopRow
mov cl,LeftCol
mov dh,BotRow
mov dl,RtCol
push bp
int 10h    ; call video BIOS
pop bp
```

Following is the calling sequence, in assembly language, for Function 07h:

```
mov ah,07h  ; Function 07h
mov al,Lines ; number to scroll
mov bh,Attrib ; same as Function 06h
mov ch,TopRow
mov cl,LeftCol
mov dh,BotRow
```

```
mov dl,RtCol
push bp
int 10h     ; call video BIOS
pop bp
```

Function 08h enables you to read a single character together with its attribute. The character that is read will be the one at which the cursor is currently located. This function can be used to get input that has been displayed on-screen, but its most common use is to pick up the attribute for use in a subsequent scrolling operation.

Following is the calling sequence, in assembly language, for this function:

```
mov ah,08h   ; Function 08h
mov bh,VidPag ; same as Function 02h
push bp
int 10h     ; call video BIOS
pop bp
mov Attrib,ah ; same as Function 06h
mov chr,al
```

To write a single character and its attribute byte, you use Function 09h. Just as Function 08h reads from the location addressed by the cursor for the specified page, Function 09h writes at the cursor position. Neither function changes the cursor's position. This means that when you want to write a string of characters using Function 09h, you must advance the cursor to the next column after each character is written. And when you do this, you must also check to determine that you did not move the cursor off the right side of the screen.

If advancing to the next column did move the cursor off the edge of the screen, you have the option of either ignoring the rest of the string to give the effect of clipping the output at the screen edge, or of wrapping to the next line even though this may cause a single word to be broken into two chunks. But if you wrap to the next line, then you must make the same kind of test on the row, to be certain that you didn't run off the lower edge.

While Function 09h accepts a repeat count in the CX register, this actually only writes repeated copies of the single character. It bears little relation to the way that the CX register is used by DOS Function 40h to specify the length of a string to be written. In most cases, you will set CX to 1 when using Function 09h.

Following is the calling sequence, in assembly language, for this function:

```
mov ah,09h   ; Function 09h
mov al,chr   ; to display
mov bh,VidPag ; same as Function 02h
mov bl,Attrib ; same as Function 06h
mov cx,Repeat ; number of copies
push bp
int 10h     ; call video BIOS
pop bp
```

When you want to only write a character to the screen, without making any change to the attribute byte already in place for the location addressed by the cursor, you can use Function 0Ah. This function behaves exactly the same as Function 09h, except that it doesn't require you to load BL with an attribute byte, and it doesn't change the color. All precautions concerning cursor movement and the repeat count still apply, however.

Following is the calling sequence, in assembly language, for this function:

```
mov ah,0Ah   ; Function 0Ah
mov al,chr   ; to display
mov bh,VidPag ; same as Function 02h
mov cx,Repeat ; number of copies
push bp
int 10h     ; call video BIOS
pop bp
```

Possibly the most frequently used BIOS video output function is the one called `TTY output` in the original IBM-PC BIOS listings, Function 0Eh. This is the function used by DOS itself to report significant errors during the boot process, and by many device drivers for the same purpose. It's used, in preference to DOS functions, because it's implemented completely within the ROM-BIOS and thus can always be counted on to be available when needed.

Function 0Eh uses a default attribute byte of 07h (gray on black) for all output, and interprets control characters BEL (07h), backspace (08h), LF (0Ah), and CR (0Dh), but displays all others. After each character displays, this function automatically advances the cursor to the next visible position, wrapping at the end of each line and scrolling upward at the end of the screen, much as the older paper teleprinters did.

This similarity in action to a classic TTY machine is what gave Function 0Eh its name. Following is the calling sequence, in assembly language, for this function:

```
mov ah,0Eh   ; Function 0Eh
mov al,chr   ; to display
mov bh,VidPag ; same as Function 02h
push bp
int 10h     ; call video BIOS
pop bp
```

Before your program makes any changes to the video mode, it should use Function 0Fh to get the existing mode so that it can restore things when it's through. Well-mannered programs, like well-mannered people, should always leave things in the condition that they found them (unless the purpose of the program is to make permanent changes).

In addition to reporting the current video mode, this function will also tell you the screen width in columns, and the current video page. Because it cannot encounter an error and makes no changes to the state of the system, you can use it at any time to obtain any or all the three values that it returns. Following is the calling sequence, in assembly language, for Function 0Fh:

```
mov ah,0Fh   ; Function 0Fh
push bp
int 10h     ; call video BIOS
pop bp
mov NumCols,ah
mov VidMode,al
mov VidPag,bh ; same as Function 02h
```

Possibly the most versatile of all the video BIOS output functions is one that isn't often encountered: write string, Function 13h. Because this function was not available on original PC and XT systems using the 8086/8088 processor unless the system had an EGA or more advanced video system installed, most developers simply did not consider it for use.

Now that the 80286 is considered a minimum system by many users, it's possible that you could find this powerful function attractive should you need to output strings, rather than individual characters, via the BIOS. Function 13h combines the "individual attribute" capability of Function 09h with a "mass attribute" capability, and gives you the choice of updating the cursor position to the first unused location after the string is displayed, or leaving the cursor pointing to the first character that was output.

These choices are specified by the bit pattern you load into the AL register. Only the two least significant bits of this byte are meaningful. Bit 0 should be set to 1 to specify that the cursor position should be updated after the last character is written, or to 0 to indicate that the cursor should be left on the first character of the string. Bit 1 should be 0 if the attribute byte loaded into BL is to be used for all characters in the string, or 1 if the string consists of alternate data characters and attribute bytes.

If Bit 1 is set to 0, the common attribute byte should be loaded into BL and the string itself should contain only data characters. If Bit 1 is set to 1, the content of the BL register will be ignored by Function 13h, and the string should have an attribute byte following each data character.

In either case, the four control characters (bell, backspace, LF, and CR) are recognized and acted upon while all other characters are displayed. Attribute bytes for these control characters may have any value, but must be supplied if Bit 1 of AL is set to 1.

Following is the calling sequence, in assembly language, for this function:

```
mov ah,13h  ; Function 13h
mov al,WrtMode ; see text
mov bh,VidPag ; same as Function 02h
mov bl,Attrib ; same as Function 06h
push bp
mov cx,seg Buf ; far pointer to string
mov es,cx
mov bp,offset Buf
mov cx,StrLen ; length of string
mov dh,Row  ; location to put string
mov dl,Col
int 10h    ; call video BIOS
pop bp
```

Cursor and Color Control via ANSI.SYS

While you can use BIOS calls to make your own programs display text output at any location on-screen that you desire, and in any color scheme that the actual video system can support, these decisions are made when you create the program. The people who use your program don't get any chance to modify your decisions about these things.

In addition, only your applications are affected when you set color schemes using the BIOS calls. However, many users find that they need to establish color schemes that are tailored to their own visual preferences, or, in some cases, needs.

You may, for example, choose to call attention to a warning message by making it bright red against a black background. On many laptop systems equipped with the orange-and-black plasma displays, however, this gets translated to black on black, making your warning invisible!

That's not a hypothetical example. It happened to me during the week this chapter was being written and brought home to me the importance of avoiding, to the greatest extent possible, having any unchangeable color information embedded in an application.

As we shall see in the sample program at the end of this chapter, it's possible to achieve this goal and still use color as a means of highlighting information displays that you consider important. And you can do this while still avoiding virtually all use of BIOS functions, if your application needs to do so for any reason. The secret is the ANSI.SYS installable device driver that is furnished as a part of MS-DOS itself and so can be assumed to be available to all users of your application, although because it is not automatically installed when MS-DOS is installed or upgraded, they will have to take some actions to make it usable.

ANSI.SYS is a driver that enables you to use certain escape sequences standardized by ANSI (the American National Standards Institute) for control of screen and keyboard actions. Among other things, you can move the cursor up, down, sideways, or to a specified row and column location. You can save the current location of the cursor, and restore its location after you display a message elsewhere on-screen.

You can clear the screen. And finally, you can control the video display mode and the colors in which information is displayed. For full details of the installation and use of ANSI.SYS, refer to your MS-DOS User's Guide or to the on-line help supplied with Version 6.0.

All ANSI.SYS escape sequences begin with the ESC character (1Bh) followed by the left bracket ('[', 5Bh). This may be followed by optional numeric values, separated by semicolons. The final character in the sequence is a command code that tells the driver what to do.

The sequence to save the present location of the cursor, for example, is `ESC [ s` (with no embedded spaces). The s must be lowercase; ANSI.SYS uses case to distinguish between commands at times, although not frequently. When you want to save the present cursor position, simply output those three characters to the CON device (using any of the standard DOS output functions if redirection is not in effect). They will not appear on-screen, but the driver will save the row and column values internally.

When you're ready to put the cursor back where it was, send the sequence `ESC [ u` to CON, and the cursor will return to the last saved position.

You cannot save several locations and return to them in sequence; the driver has only one internal storage cell for the information, so each time you issue the save-cursor-position sequence, the previously saved information is overwritten.

To set the cursor to a specific location, you can use either of two sequences. The original and still most widely used is `ESC [ r;c H` but you also can substitute `f` for the `H` and achieve the same effect. Replace the `r` with the actual number of the row, and the `c` with the actual column number. Both the row and column numbering, like that of the BIOS functions, start at zero rather than at 1.

To set the location to row 9, column 15, the sequence would be `ESC [ 9 ; 15 H` (and as always, the spaces shown here to make things more legible should be omitted from the sequence you actually send). If either number is omitted, it defaults to zero, so you can use just `ESC [ H` to return the cursor to the top left corner of the display, or `ESC [ 5 H` to put it at the first column of the sixth line down.

You also can move the cursor relative to its current position with no need to know just where it really is. The sequence `ESC [ n A` will move it up by `n` lines. If `n` is omitted or is zero, the cursor moves one line higher on-screen. If already at the top line, the sequence is ignored.

Similarly, replacing the `A` with `B` reverses direction and the cursor moves down. If already on the bottom line, the request is ignored. Changing the letter to `C` causes movement to the right by `n` columns (except from the last column of a line) and a `D` moves the position to the left.

Both color values and text display attributes are set by the sequence `ESC [ n ; n ; n m` where you can have any number of `n` values you need. Valid codes, and their effects, are as follows:

Value	Attributes	Value	FG Color	Value	BG Color
0	All OFF	30	Black	40	Black
1	Bold ON	31	Red	41	Red
4	Underline ON	32	Green	42	Green
	(MDA only)	33	Yellow	43	Yellow
5	Blink ON	34	Blue	44	Blue
7	Inverse video ON	35	Magenta	45	Magenta
8	Hide text ON	36	Cyan	46	Cyan
		37	White	47	White

To display text in bright red on black, for example, you would output the sequence `ESC [ 1 ; 30 ; 41 m` to device CON, using any of the DOS output functions. Turning the `bold` display attribute `ON` causes the foreground color to become bright, and the other two codes specify black background and red foreground respectively.

The sequence `ESC [ 2 J` clears the screen and positions the cursor to the upper left corner. In this case, the `2` is a modifier that tells ANSI.SYS to clear the entire screen area. While ANSI.SYS itself has no other option available, some alternative drivers will clear only from the present position to the end of the screen when the `2` is omitted, and in this case leave the cursor position unaffected.

To clear from the present cursor location to the end of the current line, use the sequence `ESC [ K` with no modifier digits. All the `clear` sequences use whatever color and display attributes have been set by the `m` command sequence; these default to all attributes `OFF`, black background, and white foreground if no `m` sequence has been sent.

To change video modes, use one of the sequences `ESC [ = n h` or `ESC [ = n l` (the final character of the second sequence is a lowercase `L`).

These sequences differ only when the value of `n` is 7; in this case, the `h` sequence enables wrapping of lines at the right side of the screen, rather than simply truncating output at that point, and the `l` sequence disables the wrapping action.

Other values for n and the mode set by each are as follows:

Value	Resulting Video Mode
0	40x25 monochrome text mode (all systems)
1	40x25 16-color text mode (all systems)
2	80x25 monochrome text mode (all systems)
3	80x25 16-color text mode (all systems)
4	320x200 4-color graphics mode (CGA, EGA, VGA systems)
5	320x200 2-color graphics mode (all systems)
6	640x200 2-color graphics mode (all systems)
13	320x200 16-color graphics mode (EGA, VGA systems)
14	640x200 16-color graphics mode (EGA, VGA systems)
15	640x350 2-color graphics mode (EGA, VGA systems)
16	640x350 16-color graphics mode (EGA, VGA systems)
17	640x480 2-color graphics mode (MCGA, VGA systems)
18	640 x 480 16-color graphics mode (VGA systems)
19	320x200 256-color graphics mode (MCGA, VGA systems)

Control-C and Control-Break

The standard tool that MS-DOS provides to its users for interrupting a running program consists of two separate but related keystrokes. Actually, like the input and output services, one of these is a BIOS service while the other is part of MS-DOS itself.

The BIOS service is the detection of the Control-Break combination. When the keyboard service routines inside of BIOS detect the Break key while either of the Control keys is pressed, they call Interrupt 1Bh rather than performing normal keystroke processing. What happens next depends on the service routine for Interrupt 1Bh, but the default routine that is set up during the system bootstrap loading forces a Control-C character into the keyboard input buffer as the very first keystroke.

The DOS service deals with Control-C characters when one is detected, whether it arrived because the user pressed Control and C at the same time or whether it resulted from the normal action of Interrupt 1Bh.

Because the only significant effect of the BIOS action is to make sure that the DOS action is invoked at the earliest possible opportunity, there's no need to examine it in any detail. All that it really does, at least in my own BIOS, is to force the Control-C character into the input stream.

The DOS service, however, is somewhat more complicated. Part of it is built into DOS itself in such a way that it's impractical to modify, and part of it is handled by a default handler for Interrupt 23h that is actually an integral part of the user's command interpreter (usually COMMAND.COM). Before issuing the call to Interrupt 23h, however, MS-DOS stops action on any system function that was in process when the Control-C was detected, changes the stack pointer back to the user program's area rather than DOS' internal stack, and clears all internal variables so that all DOS services will be available to the Interrupt 23h handler routine.

In addition to all these actions, which are not visible to your users and can have no permanent effect on your program's operation because DOS will not look for the Control-C at any time when a delay could damage data, the system also echoes the familiar `^C` followed by a carriage return and linefeed to the screen. Only after this has been done is Interrupt 23h called.

The default handler provided in the command interpreter for Interrupt 23h terminates the application immediately unless a batch file is being executed. If a batch file is being processed, the user gets a message asking whether to cancel the execution or ignore the keystroke, and the handler acts accordingly once the user has responded.

Sometimes, such as during the entry of a password in order to gain entry to the system or to a sensitive data file, you want to make it impossible for any user to interrupt the program's actions. You have several means available to prevent Control-C and Control-Break from being used.

By far the simplest technique is to modify the interrupt vectors for Interrupt 23h (Control-C) and Interrupt 1Bh (Control-Break) right inside your program. Here's the little test program I wrote to verify that this would work for Interrupt 23h; I used essentially the same code to test Interrupt 1Bh also, but if you prevent Control-C from having any effect, that will automatically take care of Control-Break too:

```
.model small

.data

OLDPTR DD   0  ; save original vector

.stack

.code

START:

   MOV AX,3523h    ; get old vector
   INT 21h
   MOV WORD PTR OLDPTR,BX
   MOV WORD PTR OLDPTR+2,ES

   PUSH DS        ; preserve DS
   MOV AX,CS       ; set new one
   MOV DS,AX       ; to do nothing
   MOV DX,OFFSET DUMMY
   MOV AX,2523h
   Interrupt 21h

go: MOV AH,01h     ; read and echo...
   INT 21h        ; test loop, put
   CMP AL,1Bh      ; your code here
   JNZ GO

   POP DS        ; get DS back now
   LDS DX,OLDPTR    ; restore original
   MOV AX,2523h
   INT 21h

   MOV AX,4C00h    ; exit to DOS
   INT 21h

dummy:
   iret

   end   start
```

This code assembles with any version of MASM from 5.1 on, or with any version of TASM, and links using the corresponding linker programs. When you run it, and type in characters during the go read-and-echo loop, you can see that pressing Control-C causes the ^C to be put on-screen but has no other effect. The program continues to read characters until you press the Esc key (1Bh) to signal that you're ready to quit.

```
D>tst23
This is TST23.EXE and I am about to press Control-C^C
which did echo to the screen but did not have any effect on the program.
I now do the same with Control-Break and as you can see it had no effect at
all on the program's action. I end the program by pressing ESC
D>
```

Figure 7.3. Here's what happens when TST23.EXE is run, and you press Control-C.

If you replace all three occurrences of 23h with 1Bh and reassemble, you will find that pressing Control-Break has absolutely no effect, but that Control-C causes the program to halt immediately.

To keep the ^C from being displayed may not be possible in all cases, because even totally disabling Control-C checking itself will not also disable the Control-Break action. You can minimize the chances of it appearing, however, by setting both Interrupt 23h and Interrupt 1Bh to point to a dummy IRET instruction (the same dummy can be used for both of them), and also disabling actual checking for Control-C.

To disable the Control-C checks, you can either write your programs to use the input and output functions that do not perform any checking (such as DOS Function 06h for both input and output), or you can set the CON device into RAW mode using the IOCTL functions that are discussed in the next section of this chapter.

Contrary to popular belief, placing the command BREAK=OFF in the CONFIG.SYS file does not disable checking for Control-C. All it does is to set the initial condition of DOS' internal break flag to show that such checking should be performed only for DOS Functions 01h through 0Ch. This is the same thing your program can do via DOS Function 33h subfunction 1, with DL set to zero. Similarly, placing the line BREAK=ON in CONFIG.SYS is equivalent to using Function 3301h with DL set to 1.

You can get the current setting of the flag with Function 3300h by including code such as this within your program:

```
mov ax,3300h ; Function 33h, sub 0        int 21h    ; call DOS

mov Flg,dl   ; 0=OFF, 1=ON
```

You can use Function 3301h within your program to set the flag by including code such as the following:

```
mov ax,3301h ; Function 33h, sub 1
mov dl,Flg   ; 0=OFF, 1=ON
int 21h      ; call DOS
```

When the break flag is set to 1, DOS performs the Control-C tests on every disk action in addition to doing so whenever console I/O is called for. When the break flag is 0, the tests are done only for console I/O actions. But the only way to totally suppress the tests is to set RAW mode using the `IOCTL` functions.

Device Control and IOCTL

It's often necessary to determine or control specific characteristics of a device that's attached to a data stream by means of a handle. The predefined standard handles `STDIN`, `STDOUT`, and `STDERR`, for example, refer to a single device, identified by the name CON, that combines the keyboard and CRT interfaces.

Similarly `STDAUX` refers to device `AUX` and `STDPRN` refers to device `PRN`. Note that none of these device names includes a colon (:) as its final character, although many versions of the BASIC language have required it and many writers seem to be unaware of the difference. While many areas within DOS will accept device names both with and without the colon, many others refuse to recognize devices if the colon is added to the name.

To provide the ability to communicate with the device itself, rather than merely reading data from or passing data to it, DOS includes Function 44h, known as `IOCTL` for Input/Output Control. This is possibly the most complicated single function of all those available in the DOS group accessed through Interrupt 21h. Like many other functions, it has subfunctions (although it has more than most). But even its subfunctions, in many cases, are subdivided into still finer distinctions.

The IOCTL function applies to both character devices, such as CON, AUX, and PRN, and to block devices (usually known as *disk drives* but other kinds of block devices also exist). Because the function does so many different things, I discuss only those parts of it that apply to character devices in this chapter. We will return to IOCTL and examine its block-device features when we look at the details of disk I/O techniques.

You can use Function 44h to determine whether a handle refers to a character device or to a block device, but this is not always adequate to detect whether a stream has been redirected from its usual device. You can do a better job of detecting redirection when you know how this function works. You also can tell when a device is in RAW or COOKED mode, and set it into whichever mode your application needs.

The subfunctions of IOCTL Function 44h are identified by the value set into the AL register at the time the function is called. The nine that are meaningful for character devices are:

Al Value	Subfuntion Action
0	Gets device attribute data for this handle
1	Sets device attribute data for this handle
2	Receives control data from device
3	Sends control data to device
6	Checks input status of device
7	Checks output status of device
0Ah	Determines whether file or device is remote
0Ch	Generic character device interface
10h	Queries whether function is supported

To determine whether a handle refers to a character device or to a block device, or to determine the RAW/COOKED status or detect redirection, subfunction 00h is what you use. The calling sequence, in assembly language, for this subfunction is:

```
mov ax,4400h ; Function 4400h
mov bx,Handle ; for device to access
```

```
int 21h      ; call MS-DOS
jc  ErrHdlr  ; must deal with errors
mov Atribs,dx ; attribute data
```

If bit 7 in the DX register upon return is `0`, the handle refers to a file and none of the information presented in the following paragraphs is applicable. If bit 7 is `1`, then the handle refers to a character device. In this case, the remaining bits have the following meanings if set to 1 (all bits not listed are immaterial but will usually be 0):

Bit	Meaning
0 (01h)	Device is STDIN default device
1 (02h)	Device is STDOUT/STDERR default device
2 (04h)	Device is NUL device
3 (08h)	Device is CLOCK$ device
4 (10h)	Device supports Interrupt 29h fast output service
5 (20h)	Device is in binary (RAW) mode
6 (40h)	Device has not reached end of input stream

To determine whether STDIN has been redirected, use the subfunction like this:

```
mov ax,4400h
mov bx,STDIN
int 21h
jc  ErrHdlr   ; must deal with errors
and dl,81h  ; char dvc and STDIN bits
cmp dl,81h  ; are both set to 1?
jne IsReDir   ; no, is redirected
```

To determine whether STDOUT has been redirected, use the subfunction like this:

```
mov ax,4400h
mov bx,STDOUT
int 21h
jc  ErrHdlr   ; must deal with errors
and dl,82h  ; char dvc, STDOUT bits
cmp dl,82h  ; are both set to 1?
jne IsReDir   ; no, is redirected
```

To determine whether STDOUT is in RAW or COOKED mode, use the subfunction like this:

```
mov ax,4400h
mov bx,STDOUT
int 21h
jc  ErrHdlr   ; must deal with errors
test dl,80h   ; char dvc bit
jnz NotChar   ; is a block device
test dl,20h   ; RAW/COOKED bit
jnz IsRaw    ; device is in RAW mode
```

In case of error, AX contains an error code upon returning. This call can return only three error conditions: `invalid function` (1), `access denied` (5), or `invalid handle` (6). Only the last of these is likely to occur, and that only when accessing a handle other than one of the predefined five.

The distinction between RAW and COOKED modes (which Microsoft officially calls Binary and ASCII mode, but everyone else refers to by the names that originated for their UNIX counterparts) is that in COOKED mode, which is the normal default for all character devices, any CR character is translated to a CR/LF character pair, any horizontal tab character (09h) is expanded into an appropriate number of blanks on output, the Control-Z end-of-file marker is recognized and terminates the data transfer, and, possibly the most significant, the system checks for a Control-C keystroke every time a character is taken from the keyboard or written to the screen.

You can achieve significantly greater output speed from the normal DOS functions by setting STDOUT into RAW mode and thus eliminating the usual Control-C checking. You also can prevent the user from interrupting your program by going to RAW mode. However, you will have to handle the character translations in your code, if you do.

Another area in which the RAW/COOKED distinction becomes critical is the output of raster graphics data to a printer, as when your program is printing a received FAX image for example. Graphics data is quite likely to contain pixel patterns that match the sequences which are translated in COOKED mode, so you should always set the printer device to RAW operation before sending it graphics data streams.

To set the mode, you use subfunction 4401h, which is the exact counterpart of the `get mode` operation of subfunction 4400h but requires that you load DX with the desired attributes before calling the function. Following is the calling sequence, in assembly language, for this subfunction:

```
mov ax,4401h ; Function 4401h
mov bx,Handle ; for device to access
mov dx,Atribs ; attribute data
int 21h      ; call MS-DOS
jc  ErrHdlr  ; must deal with errors
```

Possible error codes for this subfunction are `invalid function` (`1`), `access denied` (`5`), `invalid handle` (`6`), or `invalid data` (`0Dh`). The most likely of these is `invalid data` and this usually results from calling the function with DH not having all bits set to zero.

The normal procedure for using subfunction 4401h to set `RAW` or `COOKED` mode is to first call `4400h` to load the DX register with the correct bits for the device (and to verify that the handle does not refer to a block device because of redirection). You then zero the DH register, which refers to bits that DOS will not let you modify, set bit 5 to the desired state (`1` for `RAW` or `0` for `COOKED`) and use subfunction `4401h` to change the attributes. The following is typical code for setting `STDOUT` to `RAW` mode:

```
mov ax,4400h ; get attributes
mov bx,STDOUT
int 21h
jc  ErrHdlr  ; must deal with errors
test dl,80h  ; char dvc bit
jnz NotChar  ; is a block device
xor dh,dh    ; blank high bits
or  dl,20h  ; set RAW mode bit
mov ax,4401h ; set attributes
mov bx,STDOUT
int 21h
jc  ErrHdlr  ; must deal with errors
```

Some, but not all, character devices provide a capability for your application to pass control information to and from the driver by means of the `IOCTL receive control data` and `send control data` functions. Many image scanners, for example, use this technique to pass all control and status information.

While the format of the two IOCTL subfunctions that are used (4402h to read and 4403h to write) is clearly specified, all that these functions really do is move data from a buffer in your application into the driver, or from the driver into your buffer. Nothing in DOS itself controls the format or use of the information that is moved. That, unfortunately, depends entirely upon the author of the device driver involved.

What this means is that to use these functions, you must not only know how to call them at the DOS level, but you must also have full documentation from the driver's creators telling you the format and meaning of the information that is passed.

Following is the calling sequence, in assembly language, for subfunction 4402h:

```
mov ax,4402h ; Function 4402h
mov bx,Handle ; for device to access
mov cx,BufSiz ; size of transfer bfr
push ds    ; save segment reg
mov dx,seg Buf; set buffer address
mov ds,dx
mov dx,offset Buf
int 21h    ; call MS-DOS
pop ds    ; restore seg reg
jc  ErrHdlr  ; must deal with errors
mov ResCnt,ax ; bytes actually read
```

Possible error codes for this subfunction are `invalid function` (1), `access denied` (5), `invalid handle` (6), or `invalid data` (0Dh).

Following is the calling sequence, in assembly language, for subfunction 4403h:

```
mov ax,4403h ; Function 4403h
mov bx,Handle ; for device to access
mov cx,BufSiz ; size of transfer bfr
push ds    ; save segment reg
mov dx,seg Buf   ; set buffer address
mov ds,dx
mov dx,offset Buf
int 21h    ; call MS-DOS
pop ds    ; restore seg reg
jc  ErrHdlr  ; must deal with errors
mov ResCnt,ax ; bytes actually sent
```

Possible error codes for this subfunction are `invalid function` (1), `access denied` (5), `invalid handle` (6), or `invalid data` (0Dh).

You can see that the formats for the two functions are essentially identical, differing only in the subfunction number and the direction of transfer.

To determine the ready/not ready condition of an input device you can use subfunction 4406h. Following is the calling sequence, in assembly language, for this subfunction:

```
mov ax,4406h ; Function 4406h
mov bx,Handle ; for device to access
int 21h     ; call MS-DOS
jc  ErrHdlr  ; must deal with errors
mov Result,al ; 0FFh if ready, else 0
```

Possible error codes for this subfunction are `invalid function` (1), `access denied` (5), or `invalid handle` (6).

To check the output status of a character device, use subfunction 4407h. Following is the calling sequence, in assembly language, for this subfunction:

```
mov ax,4407h ; Function 4407h
mov bx,Handle ; for device to access
mov dx,Result ; attribute data
int 21h     ; call MS-DOS
mov Result,al ; 0FFh if ready, else 0
```

Possible error codes for this subfunction are `invalid function` (1), `access denied` (5), or `invalid handle` (6).

When your application runs on a network, it may become necessary to determine whether a specific device is local (at the station running the program) or remote (at some other network location). That's the purpose of subfunction 440Ah, which applies to both files and devices. Following is the calling sequence, in assembly language, for this subfunction:

```
mov ax,440Ah ; Function 440Ah
mov bx,Handle ; for device to access
int 21h     ; call MS-DOS
jc  ErrHdlr  ; must deal with errors
test dx,8000h ; local/remote bit
jnz IsRemote ; remote if nonzero
```

Possible error codes for this subfunction are `invalid function` (1) or `invalid handle` (6).

The most complicated of the `IOCTL` subfunctions discussed in this chapter is 440Ch, the `generic I/O` for character devices. This subfunction has, within itself, nine `minor codes` that control various aspects of character device operation. Four of them get existing values of parameters, and five of them change these values.

The values that can be modified via this function are the iteration count (the number of times the driver should try to send output before concluding that the device is busy), the code page (for localization features), and the display mode.

The iteration count is read via subfunction 440Ch, minor code 65h, and is set by minor code 45h. Following is the calling sequence, in assembly language, for minor code 65h:

```
mov ax,440Ch ; Function 440Ch
mov bx,Handle ; for device to access
mov ch,Category
mov cl,65h  ; minor code
push ds    ; save segment reg
mov dx,seg Buf   ; set buffer address
mov ds,dx     ; to receive count
mov dx,offset Buf
int 21h    ; call MS-DOS
pop ds    ; restore seg reg
jc  ErrHdlr  ; must deal with errors
```

The calling sequence for minor code 45h is identical except that CL gets the value 45h rather than 65h.

The `Category` loaded into CH must be 01h if referring to a serial device, 03h if referring to the console, and 05h if referring to a parallel printer. `Buf` refers to a two-byte location that can receive a 16-bit count value (for 65h) or already contains the value to be set (for 45h). Possible error codes for this subfunction are `invalid function` (1) or `invalid handle` (6). The function also may return other error codes as defined by the specific driver being addressed.

The display mode is read via subfunction 440Ch, minor code 7Fh, and is set by minor code 5Fh. Following is the calling sequence, in assembly language, for minor code 7Fh:

```
mov ax,440Ch ; Function 440Ch
mov bx,Handle ; for device to access
mov ch,037Fh ; screen, minor code
push ds     ; save segment reg
mov dx,seg Buf    ; set buffer address
mov ds,dx      ; to receive count
mov dx,offset Buf
int 21h     ; call MS-DOS
pop ds     ; restore seg reg
jc  ErrHdlr  ; must deal with errors
```

The calling sequence for minor code 5Fh is identical except that CL gets the value 5Fh rather than 7Fh.

`Buf` refers to a `DISPLAYMODE` structure that contains full mode information. Following is the format of this structure:

```
DISPLAYMODE  STRUC
   InfoLevel db  0  ; must be zero
   Reserved1 db  ?
   DataLengthdw  14  ; number of bytes
   Flags    dw  ?  ; 1 for bright
   Mode    db  ?  ; 1=text, 2=graphic
   Reserved2 db  ?
   Colors   dw  ?  ; number of colors
   Width    dw  ?  ; in pixels, graphic only
   Length   dw  ?  ; in pixels, graphic only
   Columns   dw  ?  ; text mode
   Rows    dw  ?  ; text mode
DISPLAYMODE  ENDS
```

Only those combinations that are listed in the ANSI.SYS discussion are valid for inclusion in the `DISPLAYMODE` structure. Minor code 7Fh will fill the addressed structure with the current values, while minor code 5Fh sets the video system to match the values in the structure.

Possible error codes for this subfunction are `invalid function` (1), `access denied` (5), or `invalid handle` (6). The function also may return other error codes as defined by the specific driver being addressed. If ANSI.SYS is not present, the `invalid function` error will be returned.

The remaining five minor codes of subfunction 440Ch deal with code page manipulation. Minor code 6Ah reads information about the selected code page for a specified device into a buffer, 6Bh reads the list of prepared code pages into a buffer, 4Ah selects a code page from information in its buffer, 4Ch starts code page preparation, and 4Dh ends the preparation process.

All five of these functions are used only in connection with National Language Support features and require extensive additional information about the structures and drivers involved. This information takes a full chapter of the MS-DOS Programmer's Reference Manual for DOS 5.0, and has not undergone any detectable changes in Version 6.0.

Because use of these minor codes is so closely interwoven with the other considerations involved in international support, they are discussed in Chapter 12 rather than in this chapter.

The final `IOCTL` subfunction for now is 4410h, `Query IOCTL Handle`, which is used to determine whether a specific device handle is capable of supporting the iteration-count functions. Following is the calling sequence, in assembly language, for this subfunction:

```
mov ax,4410h ; Function 4410h
mov bx,Handle ; for device to access
mov ch,Category  ; as for 45/65
mov cl,FCode ; 45h or 65h
int 21h    ; call MS-DOS
jc  NotSupported
```

Possible error codes for this subfunction are `invalid function` (1) or `access denied` (5). Invalid function is returned if the driver does not support `IOCTL` functions at all; `access denied` is returned if the specified subfunction is not supported. The distinction is not usually important.

Other Device I/O

The three functions described in this section correspond in most ways to Functions 01h and 02h, but rather than taking input from `STDIN` or sending output to `STDOUT`, address other devices: `STDAUX` is the default serial port, usually `COM1`, and STDPRN is the default printer, normally LPT1. In addition to these functions, Functions 3Fh and 40h can be used for input and output, respectively, by placing the predefined standard handle value for the desired device in the BX register, rather than using the STDIN or STDOUT handles shown in the preceding discussions. All other details for these functions remain unchanged.

Function 03h: Auxiliary Input

Function 03h, which receives input from the STDAUX device, is hardly ever used in practice, because it waits for a character to arrive.

Most terminal programs cannot afford such a delay, and instead use neither DOS nor BIOS functions to access the serial ports. I include the function here only to be complete.

Following is the calling sequence, in assembly language, for this function:

```
mov ah,03h  ; Function 03h
int 21h     ; call MS-DOS
mov chr,al  ; character returns in AL
```

Function 04h: Auxiliary Output

Function 04h, which sends output to STDAUX in much the same way that Function 02h sends it to STDOUT, is more usable than its input counterpart, but again because most programs that deal with the serial port provide their own hardware-level interfacing, this function sees little actual use and is included here only to be complete. Following is the calling sequence, in assembly language, for this function:

```
mov ah,04h  ; Function 04h
mov dl,chr  ; char to print
int 21h     ; call MS-DOS
```

Function 05h: Print Character

The final character-device function we present is *Function 05h*, which sends a single character to STDPRN. Following is the calling sequence, in assembly language, for this function:

```
mov ah,05h  ; Function 05h
mov dl,chr  ; char to print
int 21h     ; call MS-DOS
```

An Example Program

To illustrate the use of the functions discussed in this chapter, and also to make it easier for you to apply them in your own applications, let's build a color management system. It consists of a configuration program that will let your users pick any three color combinations they like and save the ANSI.SYS control sequences for them, and a set of support routines you can include in your programs to retrieve this stored information and use it to establish standard colors for displaying "normal" output, highlighted messages, or status information.

Let's look first at the configuration program, CHAP07.C. When run, it clears the screen and displays all 128 possible color combinations on-screen, in an 8x16 matrix where each of the 8 rows provides a different background color, and each of the 16 columns provides a different foreground color. One color pair in each row is, of course, invisible: the one where both foreground and background colors are the same. It is, however, still a perfectly valid pair of colors, and can even be useful when you want to prevent any echoed information from becoming visible on-screen!

Once the color matrix is showing, the program prompts you to select a `NORMAL` color set. You do so by using the arrow keys to move up, down, left, or right. As you move the selection point, the displayed prompt changes color to match. This shows you what a message in that color scheme will look like in actuality, because some color combinations make only certain letters difficult to read.

When you press Enter to choose the selected color pair as your `NORMAL` color set, the program then prompts you to choose colors for `HILITE` use, and after you have chosen a pair, finally asks you to choose a `STATUS` set. After you press Enter to specify your `STATUS` colors, the program asks if you want to save your selections.

If you press **Y** or **y** (case does not matter here) the program writes the ANSI.SYS control sequences for the three color pairs to a file named COLORCFG.DAT in the current working directory, clears the screen using your `NORMAL` color set, and returns to the DOS prompt. If you press any other key, control returns to the `NORMAL` prompt so that you can select three different color sets. Figure 7.3 shows the program in action while it waits for the first color set to be chosen.

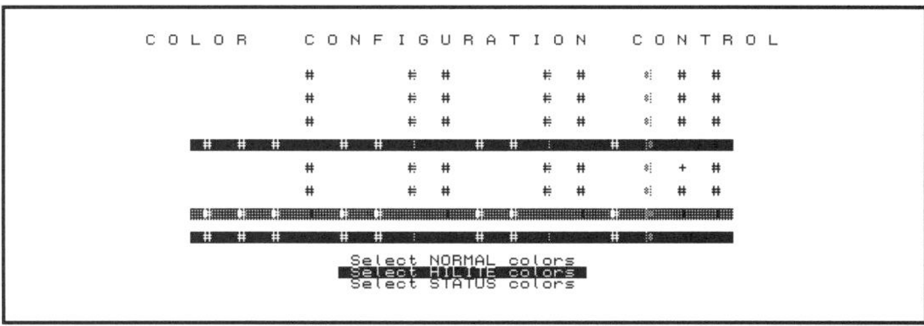

Figure 7.4. This view shows CHAP07.EXE in action, while awaiting user input at the "NORMAL" color set prompt.

Now that you have seen the configuration program in action, let's look at the way it does its job. It's actually far simpler than you might expect.

CHAP07.C uses the BIOS interfaces, rather than DOS functions, to achieve much of its simplicity. Each BIOS function used is "wrapped" inside a C function, so that it can be easily called by C functions.

This keeps the logic much simpler than it would be were the whole example written in assembly language, while retaining the straightforward ability to achieve cursor positioning and color control that exists only at the BIOS level. The BIOS function wrappers themselves use inline assembly language, available in both Microsoft and Borland's C and C++ compilers, to access the BIOS.

Listing 7.1. Chap07.C.

```
/***********************************************************
 *                           *

 *   CHAP07.C - Sample Program for Chapter 7        *

 *                           *

 ***********************************************************/
#include <stdio.h>
#include <stdlib.h>
#include <string.h>

/***********************************************************
```

continues

Listing 7.1. continued

```
 *
 *   compiler compatibility kludge for inline assembly
 */
#ifdef _MSC_VER
#define ASM _asm
#else
#ifdef __TURBOC__
#define ASM asm
#endif
#endif

/**********************************************************
 *
 *   global values for simplicity
 */
unsigned char CurAtr = 0x0F;
unsigned char MaxRow = 24;
unsigned char MaxCol = 79;
unsigned char CurRow, CurCol;
unsigned char NormalAtr, HiLiteAtr, StatusAtr;

/**********************************************************
 *
 *   character constants to build ANSI.SYS data
 */
char *fg[] =
{ "30", "34", "32", "36", "31", "35", "33", "37",
 "1;30", "1;34", "1;32", "1;36", "1;31", "1;35", "1;33", "1;37"
}, *bg[] =
{ ";40", ";44", ";42", ";46", ";41", ";45", ";43", ";47"
};

/**********************************************************
 *
 *   Clear the screen using BIOS scroll function
 */
void ClearScr( void )
{ ASM { mov ah,6
    mov al,0
    mov bh,CurAtr
    xor cx,cx
```

```
    mov dh,MaxRow
    mov dl,MaxCol
    push bp
    int 0x10
    pop bp
   }
}

/**********************************************************
 *
 *   Position the cursor at row and column via BIOS
 */
void GoRC( unsigned char row, unsigned char col )
{ ASM { mov ah,2
    mov bh,0
    mov dh,row
    mov dl,col
    push bp
    int 0x10
    pop bp
   }
}

/**********************************************************
 *
 *   Put character and attribute via BIOS
 */
void PutCA( unsigned char c, unsigned char a )
{ ASM { mov ah,9
    mov al,c
    mov bh,0
    mov bl,a
    mov cx,1
    push bp
    int 0x10
    pop bp
   }
}

/**********************************************************
 *
 *   Output entire string via PutCA() call in loop
 */
```

continues

Listing 7.1. continued

```
void BiosStrg( unsigned char r, unsigned char c, char * s )
{ while( *s )
  { GoRC( r, c++ );
   PutCA( *s++, CurAtr );
  }
}

/************************************************************
 *
 *   Center a string on specified row of screen
 */
void Center( unsigned char r, char * s )
{ BiosStrg( r, (80 - strlen(s)) >> 1, s );
}

/************************************************************
 *
 *   Get a keystroke via BIOS, waiting for it
 */
int GetKey( void )
{ int Key;
 ASM { mov ah,0
     int 0x16
     mov Key,ax
    }
 return Key;
}

/************************************************************
 *
 *   Move chosen combination in display matrix
 */
int MoveChoice( void )
{ int Key;

 CurAtr = ( CurRow << 4 ) + CurCol + 128;
 BiosStrg( 3 + (CurRow << 1), (16 + 3*CurCol), " + " );
 Key = GetKey();
 CurAtr = ( CurRow << 4 ) + CurCol;
 BiosStrg( 3 + (CurRow << 1), (16 + 3*CurCol), " # " );
 GoRC( 3 + (CurRow << 1), 17 + 3*CurCol );
```

```
 switch( Key )
  {
  case 0x4800:  /* up  */
   CurRow—;
   CurRow &= 7;
   break;
  case 0x4B00:  /* left */
   CurCol—;
   CurCol &= 15;
   break;
  case 0x4D00:  /* right*/
   CurCol++;
   CurCol &= 15;
   break;
  case 0x5000:  /* down */
   CurRow++;
   CurRow &= 7;
   break;
  case 0x1C0D:  /* CR  */
   return 0;
  }

 return 1;
}

/***********************************************************
 *
 *   main routine builds matrix, gets choices, then
 *   saves three ANSI.SYS strings to COLORCFG.DAT file
 */
void main( void )
{ FILE *fp;

 ClearScr();
 Center( 0, " C O L O R   C O N F I G U R A T I O N  C O N T R O L " );

 for( CurRow = 0; CurRow < 8; CurRow ++ )
  for( CurCol = 0; CurCol < 16; CurCol ++ )
   { CurAtr = ( CurRow << 4 ) + CurCol;
    BiosStrg( 3 + (CurRow << 1), (16 + 3*CurCol), " # " );
   }
 CurRow = 1;
```

continues

Listing 7.1. continued

```
CurCol = 15;

do {
  do { CurAtr = ( CurRow << 4 ) + CurCol;
     Center( 19, " Select NORMAL colors " );
   } while( MoveChoice() );
  NormalAtr = CurAtr;

  do { CurAtr = ( CurRow << 4 ) + CurCol;
     Center( 20, " Select HILITE colors " );
   } while( MoveChoice() );
  HiLiteAtr = CurAtr;

  do { CurAtr = ( CurRow << 4 ) + CurCol;
     Center( 21, " Select STATUS colors " );
   } while( MoveChoice() );
  StatusAtr = CurAtr;

  CurAtr = NormalAtr;
  Center( 22, " Save This Color Set? " );
  } while( ( GetKey() ¦ 0x20 ) != 0x1579 );

 fp = fopen( "COLORCFG.DAT", "w" );
 fprintf( fp, "%c[%s%sm%c", 27, fg[NormalAtr & 15],
bg[NormalAtr>>4], 0 );
 fprintf( fp, "%c[%s%sm%c", 27, fg[HiLiteAtr & 15],
bg[HiLiteAtr>>4], 0 );
 fprintf( fp, "%c[%s%sm%c", 27, fg[StatusAtr & 15],
bg[StatusAtr>>4], 0 );
 fclose( fp );
 ClearScr();

}
```

The first thing you will notice about the source code is the `#define ASM` macro; while both Microsoft and Borland compilers provide keywords to access their in-line-assembly-language feature, the actual keywords are different. The macro uses special predefined macro names to determine which compiler is processing it, and defines `ASM` as the correct keyword for that compiler. You will encounter this one over and over in the next several chapters, but I will not explain all the details every time.

You also will see, when `ASM` is actually used, that the accompanying opening brace (`{`) character appears on the same line. This is critical, at least so far as the Borland compilers are concerned, because you can use either a semicolon or a carriage-return to terminate a single assembler operation and if a return is encountered by the compiler before it finds the `{` that starts the assembly language block, it considers the `{` and what follows to be just more C code.

Following the ASM macro definition you will see a number of global variables defined. While most authorities on program design frown on the use of globals, and with good reason, in a small utility such as this they can greatly simplify program structure and, if used with care, will do no harm.

As always, rules should be bent to fit the job at hand, not vice versa. When you must sacrifice any program requirements just to follow an arbitrary rule, the rule should be discarded; one of the requirements for this program is to keep things clear enough for you to see exactly what is being done and the globals prevent clutter that would be created by any attempt to avoid them.

The four functions `ClearScr()`, `GoRC()`, `PutCA()`, and `GetKey()` all provide wrappers for BIOS functions that were described in detail earlier in this chapter. Only `GetKey()` returns a value; its return value is the full scancode-ASCII combination of the keystroke that it obtains.

In contrast to these, the functions `BiosStrg()` and `Center()` are strictly C code, although BiosStrg uses the wrapper functions `GoRC()` and `PutCA()` to display a full string on the CRT. When you call `BiosStrg()` you must pass it the row and column position for the first character, together with a pointer to the string to be displayed. The routine then uses `GoRC()` to position the cursor and automatically advance the column position for the next character, followed by `PutCA()` to display one character. Again, the pointer is automatically advanced, and the routine loops until reaching the all-zeroes end-of-string marker byte.

Note that, for simplicity, `BiosStrg()` makes no checks at all to determine whether the column position has moved off the screen. Adding such checks would have obscured the major points being illustrated.

To use this technique in your own code, however, you should add a test to see if the `c` parameter ever becomes greater than the maximum valid column number and, if so, increment `r` and reset `c` to zero.

This, in turn, adds a requirement that `r` be tested after it is incremented, and if it goes beyond the highest valid row number for the screen mode, the screen must scroll up by one line.

The `Center()` routine simply calculates a value for `c` that will cause the supplied string to be centered horizontally, by subtracting the string's length from the screen width and then dividing by two. It then passes `r`, `c`, and the string to `BiosStrg()` for display.

The real heart of this program is the `MoveChoice()` function. This first changes the currently selected color indicator to a blinking + rather than the steady # which normally appears, then uses `GetKey()` to wait for a keystroke. When one is obtained, the indicator is changed back to a steady # so that it will need no additional action if the selection point moves. The involved arithmetic used to set `CurAtr` and the row and column positions for the two `BiosStrg` calls simply maps the row and column positions into color attributes and screen locations. Then a 5-way `switch()` statement determines if the keystroke is one of those the program recognizes.

If it is, and is not the Enter key, then either the `CurRow` or `CurCol` global variable is adjusted depending on the direction (up or down, left or right). If the adjustment moved the value outside the range of 0 through 7 for `CurRow` or 0 through 15 for `CurCol`, it is reset to the other range limit. In any of these cases, `MoveChoice()` returns the value of 1 to tell its caller that nothing final has yet happened. This value also is returned if none of the five valid keys were pressed.

If the keystroke was the Enter key, however, `MoveChoice()` simply returns `0` to indicate that a choice has been made.

The whole thing is pulled together by the `main()` routine. This first clears the screen, then centers a banner line on its top row. Next it builds the matrix display using two nested `for()` loops, one to advance the rows and the other to establish the columns within each row. With the matrix displayed, `main()` sets a default value for the starting `NORMAL` set at `bright white (15)` on `blue (1)` by selecting Row 1 and Column 15.

The loop that follows simply does three inner loops, one for each color set. Each of these sets the color of the prompt, displays the prompt, and calls `MoveChoice()` to get your response. So long as `MoveChoice()` returns a nonzero value, the loop continues to set color and redisplay the prompt. When `MoveChoice` does return `0`, indicating that you have pressed Enter, the current `CurAtr` value is saved in one of three dedicated globals, one for each set, and control advances to the next inner loop which repeats the process with a different prompt and dedicated global.

After the third inner loop, `CurAtr` is reset to the value you picked as `normal`, and you are asked if you want to save your selections. If you press any key other than Y or y (the two are made to give the same result by the `(GetKey() | 0x20 ) != 0x1579` expression in the `while()` loop) then the outer loop returns to its start and reissue the `NORMAL` prompt. The Y keystroke, in either lower or upper case, breaks the loop, enabling the program to open COLORCFG.DAT, write out three control-sequence strings based on the values saved in the three dedicated global variables, and finally close the file, clear the display, and return to the DOS prompt.

You cannot exit from CHAP07.EXE without writing a new file. Neither Control-C nor Control-Break has any effect on its operation, because this program uses only BIOS functions for console I/O and the interrupt signal works only at the DOS level. Remember that Control-Break just forces a Control-C into the input buffer; the BIOS functions used by CHAP07.EXE merely ignore it.

You can compile this program with either Borland or Microsoft compilers. Figures 7.5 and 7.6 show the command lines used in each case, and the messages reported by the compilers.

```
 9:39:06, Tue  Feb 9, 1993
F:\BC>bcc chap07.c
Borland C++  Version 3.00 Copyright (c) 1991 Borland International
chap07.c:
Turbo Link  Version 5.0 Copyright (c) 1991 Borland International

        Available memory 3988208

 9:39:27, Tue  Feb 9, 1993
F:\BC>
```

Figure 7.5. This view shows CHAP07.C being compiled by Borland's BC++ Version 3.0.

To use the information written into COLORCFG.DAT by the CHAP07.EXE program, your applications need the second half of this chapter's sample package: CH07U.OBJ and CH07U.H. The OBJ file provides four functions together with some internal support routines for them. One of these initializes the system, loading the information from COLORCFG.DAT into your application. The other three select one of the three color sets and output its ANSI.SYS control sequence to the CRT. Should your application's `stdout` be redirected to a file or to some non-CRT device such as a printer, or if the COLORCFG.DAT file cannot be read, no control sequence is sent. This prevents the system from generating garbage in your reports or capture files.

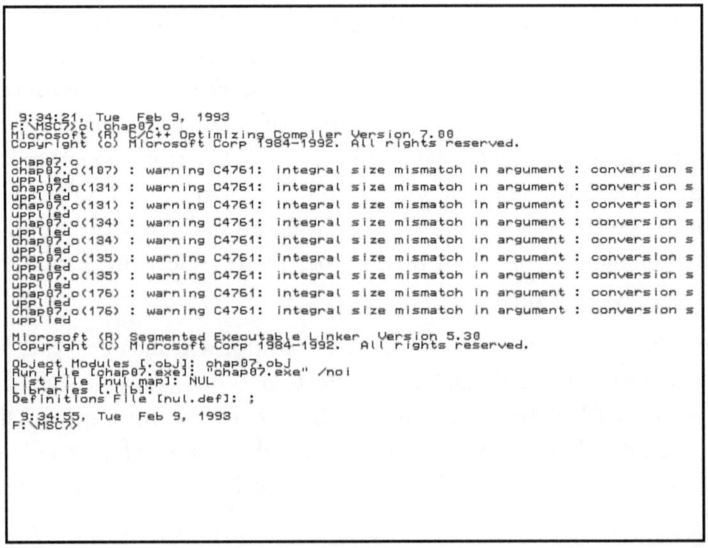

```
 9:34:21, Tue  Feb 9, 1993
F:\MSC7>cl chap07.c
Microsoft (R) C/C++ Optimizing Compiler Version 7.00
Copyright (c) Microsoft Corp 1984-1992. All rights reserved.

chap07.c
chap07.c(107) : warning C4761: integral size mismatch in argument : conversion s
upplied
chap07.c(131) : warning C4761: integral size mismatch in argument : conversion s
upplied
chap07.c(131) : warning C4761: integral size mismatch in argument : conversion s
upplied
chap07.c(134) : warning C4761: integral size mismatch in argument : conversion s
upplied
chap07.c(134) : warning C4761: integral size mismatch in argument : conversion s
upplied
chap07.c(135) : warning C4761: integral size mismatch in argument : conversion s
upplied
chap07.c(135) : warning C4761: integral size mismatch in argument : conversion s
upplied
chap07.c(176) : warning C4761: integral size mismatch in argument : conversion s
upplied
chap07.c(176) : warning C4761: integral size mismatch in argument : conversion s
upplied

Microsoft (R) Segmented Executable Linker  Version 5.30
Copyright (C) Microsoft Corp 1984-1992.  All rights reserved.

Object Modules [.obj]: chap07.obj
Run File [chap07.exe]: "chap07.exe" /noi
List File [nul.map]: NUL
Libraries [.lib]:
Definitions File [nul.def]: ;

 9:34:55, Tue  Feb 9, 1993
F:\MSC7>
```

Figure 7.6. This view shows CHAP07.C being compiled by Microsoft's C/C++ Version 7.0 compiler. While many warning messages are displayed, none of them is critical and the program operates exactly the same as when compiled using BC++3.0.

The source file for CH07U.OBJ is CH07U.C, which follows:

Listing 7.2. CH07U.C.

```
/**********************************************************
 *                            *
 *   CH07U.C - Sample Program for Chapter 7, part 2  *
 *                            *
 *********************************************************/
#include <stdio.h>

/**********************************************************
 *
 *   compiler compatibility kludge for inline assembly
 */
#ifdef _MSC_VER
#define ASM _asm
#else
```

```
#ifdef __TURBOC__
#define ASM asm
#endif
#endif

static int CFlag = 0;      /* TRUE if control okay */
static char NCtl[32];
static char HCtl[32];
static char SCtl[32];

/***********************************************************
 *
 *   Put character to STDOUT via DOS, with tests
 */
static void Put( char c )
{ ASM { mov ah,6
    mov dl,c
    int 0x21
   }
}

/***********************************************************
 *
 *   Test for STDOUT being redirected from CON device
 */
static int Chk( void )
{ int retval = 0;
 ASM { mov ax,0x4400  /* use IOCTL function  */
    mov bx,1    /* STDOUT handle value */
    int 0x21
    and dx,0x82   /* mask to the critical bits  */
    mov retval,dx  /* to test with C operations  */
   }
 return retval == 0x82 ? 1 : 0;
}

/***********************************************************
 *
 *   Output entire string via Put() call in loop
 */
static void PutStrg( char * s )
{ while( *s )
  Put( *s++ );
}
```

continues

Listing 7.2. continued

```
/***********************************************************
 *
 *   ColorInit() sets up routines for action and loads
 *   the ANSI.SYS strings from COLORCFG.DAT file
 */
void ColorInit( void )
{ FILE *fp;
 long start;

 fp = fopen( "COLORCFG.DAT", "rb" );
 if( fp )
  { if( fread( NCtl, 1, 32, fp ))
   { start = (long)strlen( NCtl ) + 1;
    fseek( fp, start, 0 );
    if( fread( HCtl, 1, 32, fp ))
    { start += ((long)strlen( HCtl ) + 1);
     fseek( fp, start, 0 );
     if( fread( SCtl, 1, 32, fp ))
      CFlag = Chk(); /* true if not redirected  */
    }
   }
   fclose( fp );
  }
}

/***********************************************************
 *
 *   Output NORMAL color scheme (only if Cflag OK )
 */
void SetNorm( void )
{ if( CFlag )
  PutStrg( NCtl );
}

/***********************************************************
 *
 *   Output HILITE color scheme (only if Cflag OK )
 */
void SetHigh( void )
{ if( CFlag )
  PutStrg( HCtl );
}
```

```
/*************************************************************
 *
 *   Output STATUS color scheme (only if Cflag OK )
 */
void SetStat( void )
{ if( CFlag )
  PutStrg( SCtl );
}
```

Like CHAP07.C, this program uses the ASM macro, but unlike the previous example, this time we use DOS functions to send our string to `STDOUT`. The global variable `CFlag` determines whether any sequences are actually sent. The `Put()` function writes one character, using DOS Function 06h. The `PutStrg()` function calls `Put()` for each character of its string. Because nothing will actually be displayed (ANSI.SYS intercepts the control sequences and acts on them rather than displaying them) no cursor control is needed. Finally `Chk()` determines whether `STDOUT` still refers to the CRT, as described earlier, by testing two bits returned by DOS Function 4400h.

All these variables and functions are declared as `static` so that their names will not be visible outside of the single CH07U.OBJ module and thus cannot conflict with any names you choose to use within your application. Only the `ColorInit()` function and the three control-sequence functions `SetNorm()`, `SetHigh()`, and `SetStat()` can be called from outside the module.

To compile CH07U.C into an OBJ file with the Borland C++ compiler, use the `bcc -c cho7u.c` command. To compile CH07U.C into an OBJ file with the Microsoft compiler, use the `cl /c cho7u.c` command.

The file CH07U.H contains prototype declarations for these four functions, and should be included in any application that will use them.

Listing 7.3. CH07U.H.

```
/*************************************************************
 *
 *   Prototypes for color control package
 */
void ColorInit( void );
void SetNorm( void );
void SetHigh( void );
void SetStat( void );
```

To see how your applications might use this module, look at the `C7TEST.C` listing which follows. This 15-line demonstration program simply calls `ColorInit()` to load your defined color sets, and then selects each set in turn and sends one line of output to the screen using the standard C library function `puts()`. Finally, it restores the color setting to your `normal` set and returns to the DOS prompt.

Listing 7.4. C7TEST.C.

```
/************************************************************
/*
 * testbed for CH07U.OBJ package
 */
#include <stdio.h>
#include "ch07u.h"

void main( void )
{ ColorInit();
 SetNorm();
 puts( "This string should be displayed in NORMAL color\n" );
 SetHigh();
 puts( "This string should be displayed in HILITE color\n" );
 SetStat();
 puts( "This string should be displayed in STATUS color\n" );
 SetNorm();
}
```

To compile and link C7TEST with the Borland C++ compiler, use the `bcc c7test.c cho7u.obj` command. To compile and link C7TEST with the Microsoft compiler, use the `cl c7test.c cho7u.obj` command.

In either case the result should be a file C7TEST.EXE, which you can run to obtain a display that resembled Figure 7.7.

If you are writing your applications with Pascal or BASIC, you may still be able to use the CH07U.OBJ module, but you will have to create declarations for its four subroutines that are compatible with your language. For BASIC, this means that you will need the following four statements at the beginning of your program:

```
DECLARE SUB ColorInit;

DECLARE SUB SetNorm;

DECLARE SUB SetHigh;

DECLARE SUB SetStat;
```

```
10:42:37, Tue  Feb 9, 1993
F:\BC>bcc -c ch07u.c
Borland C++  Version 3.00 Copyright (c) 1991 Borland International
ch07u.c:

        Available memory 3950944

10:42:46, Tue  Feb 9, 1993
F:\BC>bcc c7test.c ch07u.obj
Borland C++  Version 3.00 Copyright (c) 1991 Borland International
c7test.c:
Turbo Link  Version 5.0 Copyright (c) 1991 Borland International

        Available memory 3956836

10:43:01, Tue  Feb 9, 1993
F:\BC>c7test
This string should be displayed in NORMAL color



10:43:03, Tue  Feb 9, 1993
F:\BC>
```

Figure 7.7. C7TEST.EXE illustrates what can be done with this chapter's sample programs.

Within your program, simply call these subroutines just as you would any other library routine. When linking your compiled application's OBJ files, be sure to include CH07U.OBJ in the file list.

You might find it necessary to recompile the file in a medium or large memory model if your compiler cannot use files created in the small model, however.

For use with Turbo Pascal, refer to your Borland manuals for details of using mixed-language object files.

When linking your compiled application's OBJ files, be sure to include CH07U.OBJ in the file list.

You might find it necessary to recompile the file in a medium or large memory model if your compiler cannot use files created in the small model, however.

For use with Turbo Pascal, refer to your Borland manuals for details of using mixed-language object files.

Summing Up

In this chapter, you have seen a selection of techniques for performing input from, and output to, the standard console devices, such as the screen and the keyboard.

In Chapter 8, our attention moves to the management of time and space. More specifically, we examine techniques for dealing with the clocks and calenders within MS-DOS, and those for managing memory allocation.

Managing Time and Space

8

When MS-DOS appeared upon the scene in 1981, a PC memory as large as 256K bytes was considered huge, and nobody considered it at all out of place for the computer to forget both the time and the date any time it lost operating power (whether by being turned off intentionally, becoming accidentally unplugged, or because of a utility failure).

Not so today. Memory sizes are commonly measured in *megabytes*, with tens of megabytes not uncommon, and the always-running clock and calendar (which didn't appear until 1983) are now taken for granted. But, as always, the increase in both capacity and capability over the years has led to corresponding increases in complexity, so as a developer you must know how to manage both the time and space aspects of the systems in which your applications will run.

Fortunately, the two are nowhere near as closely related in the universe of personal computing as they are in Einstein's physics, so the main reason for grouping them together in a single chapter is convenience. They do, however, share one physical component, which we'll examine in some detail (since most reference sources seem to ignore it altogether).

In this chapter, we look first at the techniques you can use to control the system clocks and calendars (yes, there are at least two of each in most modern systems, and you must be aware of both sets). Then we dive into the often mystifying area of memory management, and see how to deal not only with conventional RAM space, but also Expanded Memory, Extended Memory, UMB's, the HMA, and a host of other acronyms.

Controlling the Clock and Calendar

The original PC architecture in IBM's first unit kept track of both the time and the date by the simple expedient of asking the operator to supply them each time the system was turned on, and then counting cycles of an internal constant-frequency signal to keep them up to date as long as the system continued to run.

While this approach was the accepted standard for the times, it did have a number of serious shortcomings. The worst was that an impatient or careless operator could simply press Enter in response to both the `Time?` and `Date?` prompts, establishing the time as midnight and the date as January 1, 1980 (the defaults when the internal counters were both set to zero).

Impartial (and quite possibly equally inaccurate) observers have estimated that at least two-thirds of all files ever written through the MS-DOS operating system carry, as a direct result, date-time stamps for the pre-dawn hours of

New Year's Day 1980, since many folk turn off their systems each time they walk away, and then turn them back on to resume work.

Serious as it was, this problem could be overcome easily by anyone who seriously cared about keeping file dates and times accurate. All that was required was to enter the date and time accurately each time the system was turned on. A more serious problem, and one over which the user had little or no control, stems from inaccuracy of the internal clock signal source.

According to the 1981 IBM-PC Technical Reference manual, the internal time register's count was derived from a video reference frequency, which was in turn generated by a quartz crystal oscillator. In this age of electronic marvels, it's easy to lose sight of the fact that the quartz crystal frequency standard is a mechanical device, and like all mechanical devices involves manufacturing tolerances and is also affected by temperature changes.

The basis for the internal time register is, of course, the 18.2-times-per-second "tick" created by servicing Interrupt 08h. Each time this interrupt occurs, the BIOS code increments the internal counter by one "tick", and then resets a counter chip which will, in turn, generate another INT 08h when it counts back down to zero. The counter chip is driven by the video reference signal.

This action divides the high-frequency video reference signal by 65,536, and the internal counter uses 24-bit arithmetic to maintain the count of ticks. When the count reaches 1800B0h, that marks exactly 24 hours (assuming perfect accuracy of the reference signal's frequency) and the internal tick counter is cleared back to zero to indicate the arrival of midnight. At the same time, a flag is set to notify the calendar procedures that a new day needs to be tallied.

The crystal from which the clock's count is derived is one of the most accurately machined mechanical devices in existence, but its accuracy is still only about one part in 20,000 (0.005%). That might not sound like much, but in one day, 86,400 seconds go by. If the clock signal is just one part in 20,000 slower than it should be, the clock will lose four seconds every 24 hours.

The effects of heat within the case are even more dramatic, and in practice can cause the time as indicated by the original clock circuit to be wrong by as much as 10 to 15 seconds in only a few hours of operation.

For most purposes this error can be ignored, but in some applications it can't be tolerated. If your application really requires accurate time information, you ought not depend on the standard counter-based clock built into the PC.

To overcome both sets of problems, third-party vendors developed special *clock-calendar* units that could be plugged into any empty system adapter slot. These units, based on the electronic circuits developed for digital watches, were powered by on-board batteries and made it possible to maintain more accurate time values.

By adding commands to their AUTOEXEC.BAT files, users could establish their system's internal date and time values from the add-on board each time they powered up, and the prevalence of files dated January 1, 1980 began to decrease.

The popularity of these third-party circuits did not escape the notice of IBM's system architects, and when the PC-AT appeared in 1983, it featured a built-in clock-calendar circuit, combined with a 128-byte CMOS memory that holds setup information about the specific system configuration. Later in this chapter, when we look at memory management, we'll discuss the CMOS features in some detail. For now, think of it as a built-in digital watch that allows your system to read time and date directly.

However, for compatibility with the older 8088-based systems that were still in wide use, MS-DOS and the system boot routines still prompt for the date and time each time power is turned on, unless an AUTOEXEC.BAT file is in place. The difference, now, is that rather than setting the internal counters to zero, today's BIOS routines set them from the CMOS chip's registers, so that just pressing Enter at each prompt still provides correct information.

When the Big Hand Is On...

Now that we have the general picture of how an MS-DOS system keeps track of the time and date, let's get down to the business of actually dealing with the clocks. The reasons for doing so are limited only by your imagination.

Many programs display current time and date somewhere on the screen, and go out of their way to update the time at least once every minute if not every second. Doing so can add a professional touch to almost any program that requires large amounts of data entry, and it's a simple operation.

Other programs provide a running count of the amount of time the program has been operating. This feature is especially useful for communications programs that may be used to connect to commercial networks or to make toll calls to bulletin boards, since in both these cases the cost of each call depends on how long one remains connected. It's nice to have a running tally of that time, visible on the screen.

Reading the Clocks

Several techniques exist for obtaining current time information. Possibly the best, however, is also the oldest and the simplest. That's to use MS-DOS Function 2Ch, get system time, which returns the current value from the counter-based clock, in hours, minutes, seconds, and hundredths of seconds

Following is the calling sequence, in assembly language, for this function:

```
mov  ah,2Ch     ; Function 2Ch
int  21h        ; call MS-DOS
mov  hour,ch    ; current hour (0-23)
mov  minit,cl   ; current minute (0-59)
mov  sec,dh     ; current second (0-59)
mov  frac,dl    ; current sec/100 (0-99)
```

You must, however, keep in mind that Function 2Ch does not retrieve time from a clock/calendar chip. It gets the DOS internal time, which is only as accurate as its setting. On most modern systems that are set from CMOS or some other clock/calendar circuit each time they are turned on, this internal counter time will be within a few seconds of the right value, which usually is close enough for all practical purposes.

The count returned in the DL register is not necessarily trustworthy, either. Many systems don't subdivide the 18.2 times per second tick rate. In such a situation, the value returned in DL may jump by several hundredths of a second rather than progressing smoothly.

Function 2Ch is recommended over all the alternatives for several reasons: for one, it returns the time values to you in pure binary format, ready to use in whatever way you may want, while other techniques require you to do some conversion before you have user-friendly hour, minute, and second values.

More importantly, though, this function takes special pains to be sure that the system does not lose track of midnight's passage, which as we shall see later in this chapter has been one of MS-DOS' most persistent problems for a number of years. Not all of the alternatives give you this protection.

Since Version 2.0, MS-DOS has provided an alternate method you can use to obtain the system time and date. This method completely bypasses the *realtime clock* counters if any hardware is present, whether it's a built-in CMOS circuit or a third-party add-on. If no hardware is available, the counters are used by default, so it's guaranteed to always provide the most accurate time or date information that can be had. For some unknown reason, however, almost no applications use this alternate method.

This alternate method is to use the `CLOCK$` device driver, which is built into the IO.SYS hidden file but easily can be replaced by an installable device driver with the same name. To use it, you simply open the device, and then either read from it to get the time and date, or write to it to set new information in. In both cases, a 6-byte buffer must be passed between the application and the driver. Following is sample code, in assembly language, for reading the current time:

```
.data
ClkDev    db      'CLOCK$',0        ; device name
ClkBuf    dw      ?                 ; buffer for data, day count
          db      ?                 ; minutes in BCD
          db      ?                 ; hour in BCD
          db      ?                 ; sec/100 in BCD
          db      ?                 ; seconds in BCD
.code
GetClk    proc
          mov     dx,offset ClkDev
          mov     ax,3D02h          ; open for read/write
          int     21h
          jc      error             ; device not present
          mov     bx,ax             ; put handle in BX
          mov     cx,6              ; buffer size
          mov     dx,offset ClkBuf  ; buffer to use
          mov     ah,3Fh            ; read data; use 40h to write
          int     21h
          jc      error             ; should never happen
          mov     ah,3Eh            ; close device
          int     21h
          ret
GetClk    endp
```

Note that while the initial word, the count of days since January 1, 1980, is in standard integer low-byte high-byte format, the remaining four bytes of information that CLOCK$ deals with are always in BCD format.

BCD, which stands for Binary-Coded Decimal, is a way of representing numbers in the range 00 through 99 by encoding each decimal digit, 0 through 9, as its binary equivalent, 0000 through 1001, and then packing the two 4-bit values into a single byte. Thus, the hex representation of 99 in BCD format looks exactly like its decimal equivalent: 99.

BCD format is popular in business and commercial use because it avoids all of the *round-off error* problems associated with conversion between pure binary and pure decimal formats. It's less popular in other areas because it allows only 100 distinct values to be stored in one byte, in contrast to the 256 values possible when you use pure binary format.

Because CD is used by not only the CLOCK$ device, but also the CMOS memory we'll look at a bit later, following is a small library of C routines to convert back and forth between BCD, binary, and ASCII representations of numbers:

```
/*
 * BCDUTL.C - utilities for dealing with BCD representations
 */
#include <dos.h>

int BCD_ASC( char bcd )
{ asm xor ah,ah;
  asm mov al,bcd;
  asm mov cl,4;                                   /* unpack the BCD */
  asm shl ax,cl;
  asm shr al,cl;
  asm xchg ah,al;                                /* convert to ASCII */
  asm add ax,0x3030;
}

int BCD_Bin( char bcd )
{ asm xor ah,ah;
  asm mov al,bcd;
  asm mov cl,4;                                   /* unpack the BCD */
```

```
  asm shl ax,cl;
  asm shr al,cl;
  asm xor bx,bx;                              /* convert to binary */
  asm xchg bl,al;
  asm xchg ah,al;
  asm mov ch,10;
  asm mul ch;
  asm add ax,bx;
}

char ASC_BCD( char hi, char lo )
{ asm mov ah,hi;                          /* convert to unpacked BCD */
  asm mov al,lo;
  asm and ax,0x0F0F;
  asm mov cl,4;                               /* pack up the BCD */
  asm shl al,cl;
  asm shr ax,cl;
}

char Bin_BCD( char bin )
{ asm mov al,bin;                         /* convert to unpacked BCD */
  asm aam;
  asm mov cl,4;                               /* pack up the BCD */
  asm shl al,cl;
  asm shr ax,cl;
}
```

Here's how the four functions work: `BCD_ASC` takes a single-byte packed BCD input value as its parameter, and returns a packed pair of ASCII characters in `int` format, but with the high character positioned to be stored first. Look at the `BCDTEST.C` sample program which follows to see how this can be useful in your own code; both characters can be stored by a single assignment. The reason for the `XCHG AH,AL` line is to assure correct positioning of the characters so that this can be done.

`BCD_Bin` takes the BCD representation as its input, and then unpacks the two digits into AH and AL, multiplies AH by ten, and adds AL, to convert back to a pure binary representation. The gyrations involving BX simply keep everything straight while doing the arithmetic.

`ASC_BCD` converts two separate ASCII characters into a packed BCD form; it makes no tests to verify that the characters are actually decimal digits, so you must take care not to pass it non-digits. This lack of lowest-level testing is usually not a problem for tools of this sort because they are called only after higher-level routines have verified that all is well.

Finally, the `Bin_BCD` routine takes a pure binary value in the range 0 through 99 (decimal), and converts it to packed BCD format. Again, no tests are made for out-of-range input data.

Because the `BCDUTL` routines all use the `asm` keyword of Borland's compilers, you should have no trouble converting them to other compilers or even to assembly language if you desire. Following is the `BCDUTL.H` file that declares the four routines of the package:

```
/*
 * BCDUTL.H - header file for BCD utilities
 */
#ifndef BCD_UTL_
#define BCD_UTL_

int BCD_ASC( char bcd );
int BCD_Bin( char bcd );
char ASC_BCD( char hi, char lo );
char Bin_BCD( char bin );

#endif
```

Finally, here's a little demonstration program that shows some of the things that `BCDUTL` does. Note particularly how the return value from `BCD_ASC()` is written into a character array, by using type-casting to force a 16-bit assignment. We'll use this same trick later, when we employ these utilities to help deal with some clock and calendar data.

```
/*
 *  BCDTEST.C - demo BCD decoding action
 */
#include <stdio.h>
#include "bcdutl.h"

void main( void )
{ int i, j;
  char c[3];
```

```
  c[2] = 0;
  for(j=0; j<10; j++ )
    for( i=0; i<10; i++ )
      { *(int *)c = BCD_ASC((char)(( j << 4 ) + i ));
        printf( "%5s%3d", c, BCD_Bin((char)(( j << 4 ) + i )));
      }
}
```

Figure 8.1 shows how I compiled BCDTEST, and also illustrates how you can include the utilities in your application. Note that the four warning messages about return values being needed are normal; they result from the fact that the return action is actually established by the assembly language register usage and so the C compiler is unaware of its existence.

```
C:\>bcc bcdtest.c bcdutl.c
Borland C++  Version 3.00 Copyright (c) 1991 Borland International
bcdtest.c:
bcdutl.c:
Warning bcdutl.c 14: Function should return a value in function BCD_ASC
Warning bcdutl.c 28: Function should return a value in function BCD_Bin
Warning bcdutl.c 37: Function should return a value in function ASC_BCD
Warning bcdutl.c 45: Function should return a value in function Bin_BCD
Turbo Link  Version 5.0 Copyright (c) 1991 Borland International

        Available memory 876337

C:\>
```

Figure 8.1. To compile BCDTEST.EXE, I used Borland's BC++ 3.0. By changing the "asm" keyword, you could use Microsoft C instead.

While these messages could be eliminated by using an intermediate variable to hold the data, that would more than double the size of each function. A better way to get rid of the messages if they pose a problem would be to translate the package to pure assembly language, or declare each function to return `void` while leaving the original return values in the header-file declarations.

When you run BCDTEST, as Figure 8.2 shows, you simply get a display of all 99 possible single-byte BCD values. These are the left-hand column of each pair of figures; the right-hand column shows the same values but this time the BCD was converted to binary rather than to ASCII, and printed by the `%3d` format control statement.

```
C:\>bcdtest
   00  0   01  1   02  2   03  3   04  4   05  5   06  6   07  7   08  8   09  9
   10 10   11 11   12 12   13 13   14 14   15 15   16 16   17 17   18 18   19 19
   20 20   21 21   22 22   23 23   24 24   25 25   26 26   27 27   28 28   29 29
   30 30   31 31   32 32   33 33   34 34   35 35   36 36   37 37   38 38   39 39
   40 40   41 41   42 42   43 43   44 44   45 45   46 46   47 47   48 48   49 49
   50 50   51 51   52 52   53 53   54 54   55 55   56 56   57 57   58 58   59 59
   60 60   61 61   62 62   63 63   64 64   65 65   66 66   67 67   68 68   69 69
   70 70   71 71   72 72   73 73   74 74   75 75   76 76   77 77   78 78   79 79
   80 80   81 81   82 82   83 83   84 84   85 85   86 86   87 87   88 88   89 89
   90 90   91 91   92 92   93 93   94 94   95 95   96 96   97 97   98 98   99 99

C:\>
```

Figure 8.2. Following is the output of the BCDTEST sample program.

Now let's get back to the business of reading the clock. The `CLOCK$` driver, like Function 2Ch, keeps track of the calendar and midnight flag properly. This makes it just as useful as Function 2Ch, except for the need to convert from BCD format to binary if you want to perform any calculations with the hour, minute, or second values, and also just as safe.

Another method you can use for getting the system time is to go directly to BIOS, using Function 00h of Interrupt 1Ah, the BIOS Time-Date Service interrupt. Doing so will obtain the unprocessed raw value of the system clock counter in the CX:DX register pair.

Following is the calling sequence, in assembly language:

```
mov   ah,00h          ; Function 00h
int   1Ah             ; call BIOS time service
mov   CountHi,cx      ; approximate hour
mov   CountLo,dx      ; current tick count
mov   MidNite,al      ; save midnight flag
```

Using this function can, however, create serious calendar problems as we shall see later. It's unfortunate that so many commercial products (including Borland's C compilers) use it, because unless they take special care to restore the midnight flag in the BIOS-RAM scratchpad area, the internal calendar can lose a whole day from its count. Fortunately, the Borland compilers do replace the flag properly; not all other products are so considerate of the users.

If you want to read the time maintained by the CMOS clock rather than using the internal counter system, then you will want Function 02h of Interrupt 1Ah. Following is how you can call it, in assembly language:

```
mov   ah,02h          ; Function 02h
int   1Ah             ; call BIOS time service
jc    error
```

```
mov  BCDHour,ch      ; hour in BCD, 00-23
mov  BCDMinute,cl    ; minute in BCD, 00-59
mov  BCDSec,dh       ; seconds in BCD, 00-59
mov  DSTFlag,dl      ; DST in effect if nonzero
```

Not all BIOS versions support the daylight savings time flag return in DL, but most produced after 1985 do so.

If the carry flag is set upon return from this call, the CMOS clock is not functioning and any return values should be ignored.

You also can read these same values directly from the CMOS chip itself, as we shall see in the latter part of this chapter.

How and When to Set the Clocks...

While you seldom need to set new time values into the system clocks, especially with modern systems that automatically synchronize the counter version to the CMOS standard each time power is applied, in most areas it's necessary to do so at least twice a year: when daylight savings time goes into effect each spring, and when standard time comes back each fall.

That, of course, can be done from the command prompt using MS-DOS' `TIME` command, but you also need to be aware of the various techniques for establishing the time of day within a program.

The oldest, and still the simplest, method available is MS-DOS Function 2Dh, the exact inverse of Function 2Ch. Both functions pass the time values in the same formats, allowing you to make minor adjustments by first reading the time using Function 2Ch, and then modifying one or more registers while leaving the rest alone, and finally writing all values back via Function 2Dh.

Following is the calling sequence, in assembly language, for Function 2Dh:

```
mov  ah,2Dh          ; Function 2Dh
mov  ch,hour         ; current hour (0-23)
mov  cl,minit        ; current minute (0-59)
mov  dh,sec          ; current second (0-59)
mov  dl,frac         ; current sec/100 (0-99)
int  21h             ; call MS-DOS
cmp  al,0
jne  error           ; function failed (unlikely)
```

In actual applications, it's often best to just zero out the DL register rather than attempt to achieve fractional-second accuracy. Trying to set hundredths of a second goes beyond what most typical users want.

However, if your program takes its input from CMOS, from a clock/calendar chip, or from a national time service, then it easily can set the time to hundredth-of-a-second accuracy.

Some computers, nevertheless, are unable to return this accuracy on a consistent basis because the real-time clock is not accurate enough. My own systems consistently show a drift of one to two seconds in four hours between the CMOS time value and that maintained by the internal counter.

If the system has a CMOS clock, use of Function 2Dh will cause its time to be set, along with the tick counter, eliminating the need for a second call to any alternate functions.

Just as when reading the time, BIOS provides a function to set the tick counter. And just as for reading, the input value that BIOS Function 01h of Interrupt 1Ah requires is a 32-bit tick-count value. This immediately sets the value of the system clock counter to whatever you specify, with no effect at all on either the CMOS circuits if present, or the calendar data.

Because of the added calculation required, this technique isn't very useful for dealing with clock time, but as we shall see shortly it can be useful to create an elapsed-time counting circuit.

Following is the calling sequence, in assembly language, for Function 01h:

```
mov  cx,CountHi      ; high word (0-24)
mov  dx,CountLo      ; low word
mov  ah,01h          ; Function 01h, set count
int  1Ah             ; call BIOS time service
```

If you want to set the clock to a specific time using BIOS function 01h, you must compute the number of ticks (since midnight) that correspond to that time. This value becomes the new clock setting.

To calculate the number of ticks, you compute the number of seconds since midnight for the desired time setting (3600 seconds for each hour, plus 60 more for each minute past the hour) and then multiply that number by 18.2065 (the approximate number of ticks per second). A much simpler approximation is to multiply by 91 and then divide by 5, but your time may be off by a few seconds because this produces a count of only 1,572,480 (86,400 * 91 / 5) ticks for a full day rather than the "correct" value of 1,573,040 ticks. Your result will be off by 23.33 ticks per hour; this is still closer than the accuracy shown by most counter circuits.

When you use this function, be careful. BIOS makes no effort to protect you from illegal input values. If you specify a value outside a normal day's range (24 hours, or 1800B0h ticks; CX = 0018h, DX=00B0h), the BIOS will accept it with no indication of error.

Occasionally you may want to set the time maintained by the real-time clock without affecting the counter circuits. When that's your requirement, the function to use is Function 03h of BIOS time service Interrupt 1Ah. Following is the calling sequence, in assembly language, for this function:

```
mov  ch,Hour        ; BCD hours (0-23)
mov  cl,Minutes     ; BCD minutes (0-59)
mov  dh,Seconds     ; BCD seconds (0-59)
mov  dl,DSTFlag     ; DST if nonzero
mov  ah,03h         ; Function 03h
int  1Ah            ; call BIOS time service
```

What Day Is This?

The calendar is a bit trickier than the clock itself, because the job of keeping the clock accurate, and that of making sure the calendar is up to date, were split, in the original design, between BIOS and MS-DOS. The result is that it's quite possible for a whole day to fall though a gaping crack that exists in the interfaces.

We've already noted that the BIOS time counters tally time as the number of ticks since midnight, and that "midnight" is defined as the total tick count in a complete day of 86,400 seconds (1,573,040 ticks of the clock, for a total elapsed time of 86,399.9121 seconds).

When the timer interrupt service routine for Interrupt 08h detects the critical count value and decides that midnight has arrived, it sets a flag byte in RAM (at location 0040:0070) to 1. The next call to BIOS Interrupt 1Ah's Function 00h to retrieve the tick count returns the content of that flag byte in the AL register, and at the same time clears the flag byte so that it will not be set again for another 24 hours.

Note that if midnight passes twice, the second time is simply ignored. This is, in my opinion, a true bug in the design; it should count up rather than simply serving as a flag. But that is a separate, though closely related, problem, from the one that causes the first midnight to fall through a crack.

If any program calls Interrupt 1A Function 00h between the time that the flag byte is set and the time that MS-DOS uses that information to tally another day into the day counter, then the calendar loses a day. This happens frequently when a system is left turned on overnight; the next morning the time is correct, but the calendar says it's still yesterday.

Reading the Date

While we don't look at the calendar quite as frequently as we do at the clock, most of the same considerations apply and many data entry screens display both the current date and current time as a convenience to the operator.

If your applications require that a date field be filled out, too, then it's a simple task to read the current system date and plug it in as the default value. The user can then accept it, or in the rare case when some other date is desired, can edit the application's suggestion with little added effort. Touches of this sort help make your applications stand out from the crowd.

Just as in the case of the clocks, you can take your pick of several techniques. And again, the oldest is quite possibly the simplest and best one to use. That's MS-DOS Function 2Ah, which gets the year, month, day, and day of the week from the system's days-since-1980 counter.

Following is the calling sequence, in assembly language, for this function:

```
mov  ah,2Ah          ; Function 2Ah
int  1Ah             ; call BIOS date service
mov  year,cx         ; current year-1980 (0-1019)
mov  month,dh        ; current second (1-12)
mov  day,dl          ; current sec/100 (1-31)
mov  wkdy,al         ; day of week (0=Sunday)
```

Function 2Ah simply returns information about the current system date maintained internally by MS-DOS. Even when a real-time clock/calendar is present, no reference to it occurs. As we've noted, it's not at all uncommon for the internal count of days to miss one or even more passages of midnight, so it's never totally safe to trust the date value unless it has been verified by some means. Once verified, however, it's not likely to change until another midnight comes by, unless some application or program explicitly does so.

If you need to verify the date, and have a CMOS clock/calendar in the system, you can use Function 04h of BIOS Date Service Interrupt 1Ah to read the date maintained by that device. Following is the calling sequence, in assembly language:

```
mov  ah,04h          ; Function 04h
int  1Ah             ; call BIOS date service
jc   error
mov  Century,ch      ; in BCD, 19 or 20
mov  year,cl         ; in BCD, 00-99
mov  month,dh        ; in BCD, 01-12
mov  day,dl          ; in BCD, 01-31
```

If the carry flag is set upon return from a call to this function, the CMOS clock is not functioning and any return values should be ignored.

Sometimes you may want to retrieve the day count, without having it translated into human-oriented calendar form. This can be especially useful when determining whether it's time to generate a regular once-a-month report, for example. Function 0Ah of BIOS Date Service Interrupt 1Ah allows you to do this. Following is the calling sequence, in assembly language, for this function:

```
mov  ah,0Ah          ; Function 0Ah
int  1Ah             ; call BIOS date service
mov  DayCount,cx     ; since 01/01/1980
```

To store the current date so that you can use it later as a basis for calculation, just write it to a file. Then, a week or two later, your program can retrieve that saved value, subtract it from the value returned by Function 0Ah at the later time, and tell exactly how many days have gone by since the first value was saved without any need to correct for wrapping past the end of a month or even a year. Judicious use of this function can save hours of development time trying to deal correctly with all the ins and outs of the many calendars in use.

Resetting the Calendar

Were it not for the tendency of the MS-DOS/BIOS interface to lose a midnight from time to time, there hardly would be any need to reset the calendar, especially in systems that have CMOS or other automatic circuits. However, it does become necessary on occasion, so you should know how it's done.

The simplest method to set the system date to a specified value, and one which does not change the system time, is to use MS-DOS Function 2Bh. Following is the calling sequence, in assembly language:

```
mov  cx,Year         ; binary, 1980-2099
mov  dh,month        ; binary, 1-12
mov  dl,day          ; binary, 1-31
mov  ah,2Bh          ; Function 2Bh
int  21h             ; call MS-DOS
cmp  al,0
jne  error           ; invalid date values
```

If the system has a CMOS chip or clock/calendar device, you can access it to get the current date, then update the system date. Without a clock/calendar, you could prompt the user for input. This is essentially the same thing that MS-DOS does at power-up time to initialize the date correctly.

Using this function in a system equipped with a CMOS clock causes its date, in addition to the internal day counter, to be set accordingly.

Because the date set with this function is used to mark files during file operations, it's essential to you as a developer to be certain that your own system keeps its calendar accurate. That's the only way that such useful utilities as MAKE are able to operate.

When you want to set only the date maintained by the real-time clock, leaving the day counter unchanged, the function to use is 05h (still in the BIOS Date Service Interrupt 1Ah). Following is the calling sequence, in assembly language:

```
mov  ch,Century      ; in BCD, 19 or 20
mov  cl,year         ; in BCD, 00-99
mov  dh,month        ; in BCD, 01-12
mov  dl,day          ; in BCD, 01-31
mov  ah,05h          ; Function 05h
int  1Ah             ; call BIOS date service
```

As always, you must take care when using this function to assure that the values provided to the BIOS are correct, because no checking is done on them. Incorrect values cause unpredictable clock settings.

When you want to set only the date maintained by the internal counter, without any change of the real-time clock, the function to use is BIOS Date

Service Interrupt 1Ah, Function 0Bh. Following is the calling sequence, in assembly language:

```
mov  cx,DayCount      ; since 01/01/1980
mov  ah,0Bh           ; Function 0Bh
int  1Ah              ; call BIOS date service
```

Elapsed Time Measurement

Quite frequently an application can need some method of measuring elapsed time between two events. Less frequently, you will run into a requirement to introduce explicit delay into a program's operation. Both of these needs involve measurement of elapsed time, and as always in the MS-DOS world, you can take your pick from several techniques.

The simplest, and often the most straightforward method by far, is to create your own Interrupt Service Routine and hook into the System Timer Interface that's built into the BIOS as Interrupt 1Ch. This interrupt is called during every performance of the Interrupt 08h routine, which means that except for very special instances, it's called regularly 18.2 times every second on average.

Because Interrupt 1Ch is actually called from inside the Interrupt 08h routine, though, it has a number of stringent constraints placed upon it. You have no way of knowing what the system may be doing in the foreground when this interrupt is active, nor do you know what the contents of any registers other than CS and IP may be. You do, however, know that they should all be preserved for use by the routine that was interrupted (actually most BIOS code saves them, but you can never depend fully upon this being the case). And finally, you cannot count on having any but the barest minimum of stack space available to use.

These constraints make it difficult, though not impossible, to write reliable Interrupt 1Ch handlers in any high level language. Using the `interrupt` keyword available with many modern HLL's causes all registers to be pushed onto the stack; there's no way to check in advance and determine whether there's enough room. Therefore you can't use that feature.

Similarly, because you cannot determine just where the DS register may be steering data retrieval, you can't even access any global variables from within the service routine itself.

The safest way to use this capability is to write a small assembly-language module to link with your main application code that has two (actually three, when you count housekeeping code to install and remove the hook) separate parts that communicate via a single data area in the code segment. Following is what such a module might look like, written for C and using MASM's simplified segment conventions:

```
.model      large, C
.code

Counter     dw        ?     ; notice it's in CODE
OldVec      dd        ?

ISR         proc      far   ; tally a count, no more
            inc       word ptr Counter
            jmp       dword ptr OldVec
ISR         endp

ClrCtr      proc            ; clear the counter
            mov       cs:Counter, 0
            ret
ClrCtr      endp

GetCtr      proc             ; read the counter
            mov       ax,cs:Counter
            ret
GetCtr      endp

InstTmr     proc             ; install timer
            mov       ax,351Ch
            int 21h
            mov       word ptr OldVec,bx
            mov       word ptr OldVec+2,ES
            push      ds
            mov       dx,cs
            mov       ds,dx
            mov       dx,offset cs:ISR
            mov       ax,251Ch
            int 21h
            pop       ds
            ret
InstTmr     endp
```

```
RmvTmr     proc                ; remove timer
           push      ds
           lds       dx,OldVec
           mov       ax,251Ch
           int 21h
           pop       ds
           ret
RmvTmr     endp

           end
```

While it might appear that this is a horribly complicated little kludge just to measure elapsed time, the majority of the code here deals with installing and removing the interrupt hook itself. The ISR itself merely adds one to its count, and then transfers control to the previous service routine so that it can do its thing. The `ClrTmr` procedure zeroes out the counter to start your timing period, and the `GetTmr` function returns the most recent count.

This technique has two major restrictions, one serious and one less so. The less serious of the two is that your time interval must be less than one hour, since the counter will overflow after approximately 60 seconds. So long as you read out the interval more frequently than that, though, and accumulate it in your own data area using a 32-bit variable or floating point (with suitable conversion), and then zero the counter and start it over, you can measure periods of whatever length you may desire.

The more serious restriction is that since the tick occurs only 18.2 times each second, you cannot measure any interval smaller than about 55 milliseconds, and even for periods of several seconds' duration the lack of accuracy is alarmingly large.

Unfortunately, improving the resolution of the event timer is not a trivial task; it requires re-programming the system timer chip to count more rapidly, and then modifying the Interrupt 08h routine by means of a pre-filtering hook to keep it from being misled by the faster timer. Any mistakes in this area can cause the system to lock up tightly, though there's little danger of damage to either the data or the hardware. My recommendation, should you require more precise timing intervals, is to use a commercial or shareware library developed expressly for such tasks.

In my own work, I find the simple tick-based timer perfectly adequate to determine whether I've helped or hurt the performance of a program, and that's about all I ever need an elapsed-time measurement for. However, I do use the alternative command processor 4DOS.COM, from J.P. Software Inc. in Boston, MA, in preference to COMMAND.COM, and 4DOS includes timing capability among the many features it adds to the command processing shell.

With introduction of the PC-AT line in 1983, a totally separate timer driven from the CMOS clock's capabilities became available. You can use it in either of two ways. Function 83h of BIOS System Services Interrupt 15h allows you to start a timer going, and if desired to cancel the timer before it runs down. If the timer does run out, the system will set the high byte of a byte that you provide the address for as notification. Function 86h of Interrupt 15h provides a wait-here delay. In both cases, you specify the timer interval in microseconds as a 32-bit value in the CX and DX registers, but the actual time increment is usually 1/1024 second using the CMOS `fast period` interrupt, or about 977 microseconds.

Function 83h can be used to determine whether a remote device has responded within the specified time. This usage often is called a *watchdog timer* because it watches out for the possibility that your program might try to wait forever for a response from a device that's not even connected. To use it in this manner, establish your time interval and flag byte, and then clear the flag to zero and start the timer. While the timer is running, call your connection routine. If it succeeds in establishing the connection, cancel the wait. If it fails, test the flag byte and if still clear, loop back to call the connection routine again.

By doing this, your routine will keep trying as long as the timer is running (and the timer can be set for periods approaching 4,000 seconds) but when the timer runs down, the loop is broken so it doesn't make futile attempts forever.

The two subfunctions for Function 83h are distinguished by the value set into the AL register when you call it. Following is the calling sequence, in assembly language, for Subfunction 0, set wait interval:

```
mov  al,0             ; set wait interval
mov  cx,WaitHi        ; upper 16 bits of delay
mov  dx,WaitLo        ; count in microseconds
mov  bx,seg Flag
mov  es,bx
mov  bx,offset Flag
mov  ah,83h           ; Function 83h
int  15h              ; call BIOS system services
jc   error
```

The byte pointed to by ES:BX when you call Subfunction 0 is the one that will serve as the rundown flag. Possible error returns from this call, both returned in the AX register if the carry flag is set on return, are 80h and 86h. A return code of 80h indicates that the function is not valid on the current system, and is unlikely to be encountered on an 80286 or later processor. A code of 86h indicates that the service is not supported, and again is unlikely for any system that has CMOS memory.

To cancel the timer's action before the rundown occurs, Subfunction 1 is used. Following is its calling sequence, in assembly language:

```
mov  al,1        ; cancel wait
mov  ah,83h      ; Function 83h
int  15h         ; call BIOS system services
jc   error
```

The wait-now service, Function 86h, is similar to the watchdog timer action, but rather than starting the timer and returning immediately so that your program can do other actions while the timer runs, it remains in its own loop and does not return until the specified time has elapsed. It can be used, for instance, if you want to deliberately slow down some action to give a human time to respond.

Function 86h should be avoided on programs that may be used on multitasking systems, since its tight-loop action tends to hog system resources away from other programs. Following is the calling sequence, in assembly language, for this function:

```
mov  al,0        ; set wait interval
mov  cx,WaitHi   ; upper 16 bits of delay
mov  dx,WaitLo   ; count in microseconds
mov  ah,86h      ; Function 86h
int  15h         ; call BIOS system services
jc   error
```

Along with the Interrupt 15h `wait` and `delay` functions, introduction of the PC-AT line brought an alarm feature that's accessed by way of the Time and Date Services interrupt, 1Ah. These features, though not widely used, allow you to set a system alarm timer to generate an interrupt at some future time, specified in the same hour-minute-second sequence as the CMOS clock functions we've already discussed.

Each time that the specified time arrives, if the alarm is active, a call to Interrupt 4Ah is made. It's up to you to provide a handler and hook the vector for this interrupt to respond to the alarm.

The alarm must be turned off before it can be set. That is, if it's already set, any attempt to set it again will result in an error code and no change will take place. To set the alarm, you use Function 06h of BIOS Time Services Interrupt 1Ah, and to turn it off, you use Function 07h.

Following is the calling sequence, in assembly language, for Function 06h:

```
mov  ch,AlarmHr      ; BCD alarm hour (0-23)
mov  cl,AlarmMin     ; BCD alarm minute (0-59)
mov  dh,AlarmSec     ; BCD alarm second (0-59)
mov  ah,06h          ; Function 06h
int  1Ah             ; call BIOS time services
jc   error
```

If the carry flag is set upon return from this function, either the alarm is already set, or the clock is not functioning correctly.

Before you set the alarm, you must disable it with function 07h, and set up an interrupt handler to deal with the alarm when it occurs.

To turn off the system alarm timer, use Function 07h of the same BIOS Time Services Interrupt. Following is the calling sequence, in assembly language, for this function, which requires no parameters and returns no error codes:

```
mov  ah,07h          ; Function 07h
int  1Ah             ; call BIOS time services
```

Memory Management

One of the most confusing aspects of resource management under MS-DOS is the question of memory management. In the early days, this was a subject that nobody needed to worry about, because there was only one question that could arise: "Is the application too big to run on this system?"

But as time passes and applications became ever more feature-laden, that question brought a "NO!" answer far too frequently, and system makers devised methods for adding additional memory so that larger programs could run properly.

At first, this was simply a matter of adding additional memory chips, since the original PC design left 640 kilobytes of address space free for programs to use. This was 10 times as large as the industry standard in 1981, and at that point it was incomprehensible how anyone could ever need more.

But as more, and larger, RAM chips became available and were plugged into both the motherboard and add-on memory expansion boards, eventually the 640K limit was reached. And programs needed still more memory.

The next step was the invention of *expanded memory* which used additional hardware and software to make the memory on special expansion boards map to a location in the upper memory area. So long as only a few pages of this additional RAM were used at any one moment, the boards and their drivers could switch addresses around so that many pages shared the same address.

This worked fairly well, but then along came the 80286 processor and its capability to run in protected mode and address more than a single megabyte of RAM all at one time. System architects didn't take long to find ways of providing *extended memory* above the one-megabyte mark.

Today's systems can theoretically address more RAM than anyone has yet tried to install in a box: with 32-bit address lines the byte count goes up to a staggering 4 gigabytes. MS-DOS itself, however, still has a few problems addressing anything above the 16-megabyte point, because of some hardware limitations designed into the most common types of motherboards.

Along with all this added capability, of course, we've gotten things more complicated, so that rather than simply wondering "Will my program fit into RAM?", we now must be concerned with such things as the EMS interface, the XMS specification, HMA, UMB's, and a host of other acronyms that serve more to confuse us than to clarify matters.

As a developer you will need to know the techniques of dealing with all of these things. The first step in learning them is to find out exactly what the various words and acronyms mean. Bear with me if I seem to be describing things you already know well; the intent is to create a common vocabulary we can use to discuss the techniques a bit later in this chapter.

Figure 8.3 shows a not-to-scale map of the first 20 megabytes of the MS-DOS system address space, with all its various parts labeled. Not all systems include all of these parts. A user can, for example, configure a system to have no EMS page frame at all, and thereby gain an additional 64K of UMB area.

Similarly, not many systems have both color and mono video attached, so one or the other of these regions also can be turned over for UMB use (although as we shall see a bit later, that can be dangerous).

Over the years developers have experienced much confusion about the exact meanings of various terms that appear on Figure 8.3. The following definitions are taken directly from the official Extended Memory Specification standard jointly developed by Microsoft Corporation, Lotus Development Corporation, Intel Corporation, and AST Research, Inc. at its latest revision (XMS 3.0):

Extended Memory. Memory in 80286 and 80386 based machines which is located above the 1Mb address boundary. (Note: Also in 80486 and Pentium systems.)

Extended Memory Blocks (EMBs). Blocks of extended memory located above the HMA which can only be used for data storage.

High Memory Area (HMA). The first 64K of extended memory. The High Memory Area is unique because code can be executed in it while in real mode. The HMA officially starts at FFFF:10h and ends at FFFF:FFFFh making it 64K-16 bytes in length.

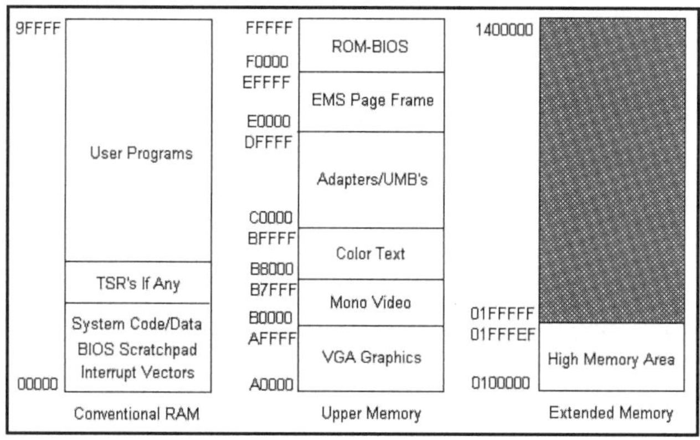

Figure 8.3. This map shows the entire range of memory address spaces possible for today's MS-DOS systems, and is not to scale.

In Figure 8.3, the two columns to the left total only 1 megabyte between them while the one on the right covers a full 19 megabytes. As you can see, *conventional* RAM (the leftmost column) is where many of the system functions, and most application programs, operate. The upper memory area (middle column) is used for video display, memory-mapped peripheral adapters, and whatever space happens to be left over is available for system use. All the rest is extended memory (rightmost column), with the first 64K bytes (minus 16) being used as the HMA so that the DOS kernel code does not take space away from your applications. Addresses are shown in 20-bit form for the first megabyte, and 24-bit form for extended memory.

Upper Memory Blocks (UMB's). Blocks of memory available on some 80x86 based machines which are located between DOS's 640K limit and the 1Mb address boundary. The number, size, and location of these blocks vary widely depending upon the types of hardware adapter cards installed in the machine.

A20 Line. The 21st address line of 80x86 CPUs. Enabling the A20 line allows access to the HMA.

XMM. An Extended Memory Manager. A DOS device driver which implements XMS. XMM's are machine specific but allow programs to use extended memory in a machine-independent manner.

HIMEM.SYS. The Extended Memory Manager currently being distributed by Microsoft.

As you can see, the rules for using the various parts of the address space are much more complicated than they were back in the days when a 512K system had more memory than anyone knew how to use. In the rest of this chapter we'll look at the techniques used to manage all these various kinds of RAM.

First, however, we'll take a short side trip and look at a totally different part of current system memory, which usually gets short shrift in reference books. That's the CMOS memory space associated with the built-in clock/calendar circuitry since the advent of the PC-AT systems in 1983.

Keeping the System Sane

The CMOS circuits generally referred to as the clock/calendar, or sometimes as CMOS RAM, do two barely-related things for the system. First, they maintain the date and time information even when system power is off (at least, they do in most systems, if the battery is alive). Second, and more important although less visible to the user so long as everything is working, they retain a record of just how this specific system is configured: how much memory, how many and what kinds of disk drives are present, and so on.

The actual hardware involved is a highly specialized IC chip that evolved from the technology used to create digital watches. Its timekeeping abilities are essentially identical to those of any electronic watch, but rather than displaying the information it maintains on a display as a watch does, it stores this information in a special on-board RAM that draws so little current that it can be powered indefinitely with a small battery. That RAM can store at least 128 bytes of data.

Because only eight bytes of information are used by the clock and calendar, there's quite a bit of space left over, and the system architects of the PC-AT decided to use it, rather than DIP switches or jumpers on the motherboard, to hold specific system configuration information. Not only did this reduce manufacturing costs by using something already there, it made installation by the end user much simpler because the CMOS locations could be set up by software rather than anyone having to open the case and move jumper connectors.

The data layout used for CMOS information is only partially documented, and much of the documentation contains contradictions. What follows is my own compilation of the data, based on all the input I've been able to find, but it may be less than totally accurate; any errors are my own.

Figure 8.4 shows a hex dump of the content of CMOS for my home system, an 80386DX using an AMI BIOS chip. Only the first 64 bytes are known at all, and not all of them are identifiable.

```
C:\>cmos1

CMOS memory dump - Jim Kyle - March 1993

  00:  30 00 34 01 15 00 00 20 03 93 26 02 50 80 00 00
  10:  24 0C F0 9B 4F 80 02 00 10 23 00 00 00 00 00 00
  20:  00 00 00 00 00 00 00 00 00 00 00 00 00 3D 02 FC
  30:  00 10 19 D3 00 01 80 80 1B 7B 21 00 00 00 04 08
  40:  00 60 00 00 00 00 00 00 00 00 00 00 00 00 00 00
  50:  00 50 20 00 00 00 00 00 00 00 FF 80 00 00 00 01
  60:  B5 8F B2 31 79 40 A2 02 D1 A2 68 CE 59 45 F4 C4
  70:  08 78 DD 1C 66 EB E1 31 02 1A 4B 5A 03 09 5C 0F

C:\>
```

Figure 8.4. This shows a dump of the content of CMOS for my 80386DX home system with AMI BIOS; all values on the bottom four lines of this display are specific to my BIOS chip and nothing like them shows up on a similar dump of my office system, an 80486DX also equipped with AMI BIOS.

The first six bytes are time data, alternating current time and alarm time values. At 00h we have the current value of seconds past the minute, and at 01h we have the current alarm time setting for seconds. Then at 02h we have the current minute, and at 03h the alarm minute. At 04h is the current hour, in 24-hour format, and at 05h the alarm hour.

While the byte at 06h is listed as "day of week" in one reference I have, in my own searching I have not found this byte to be anything other than zero and can only conclude that few, if any, systems support it.

At offset 07h is the current day of the month, at 08h the current month, and at 09h the low two digits of the year. The high two digits are at location 32h.

The bytes at locations 0Ah and 0Bh are internal status flags. Those at 0Ch and 0Dh are connected with the alarm features and other internal status. The next byte that I have been positively able to identify is at location 10h, which indicates the types of floppy drives installed. The two halves of this byte apply to the two possible drives that CMOS recognizes: the high half is Drive A: and the low half is Drive B: A value of 0 indicates that the drive is not present; 1 means a 360K 5.25-inch unit, 2 is a 1.2-meg 5.25-incher, 3 is 720K 3.5 inch, and 4 is 1.44-meg 3.5 inch. The value of `24` shown indicates that I have a 1.2-meg 5.25-inch drive in the A: position, and a 1.44-meg 3.5-inch as drive B:

The following byte is, again, a mystery. One source indicates that it contains the drive type for Fixed Disk 0, but that is patently false in my case. The byte at location 12h maps the Fixed Disk types, using the same hi-lo strategy as for floppies, but if either drive shows as type `F` (hex), then it's necessary to look at byte 19h for Fixed Disk 0 or 1Ah for Fixed Disk 1. In my case that shows that I have a Type 35 drive as C:, and no physical D: drive.

Only three fields of known meaning remain: the byte pair at location 15h and 16h form a 16-bit count of the number of kilobytes of conventional RAM present; in Figure 8.4 you see 0280h for this, or 640K. The following pair, at location 17h and 18h, specify how many K of extended memory are present; my value of 1000K indicates 4096K of extended RAM. The final field is the byte pair at 30h and 31h, which shows the *actual expansion memory* size in kilobytes. In my home system, as you can see, this is also 1000h, but on other systems I have seen different values in this pair.

Knowing the arrangement of CMOS, and the significance of each byte, makes it possible for you to create routines that can display or edit its content. However, when editing, take great care to change only those values that you are absolutely certain will be safe to modify.

Much of this data is BIOS-specific and varies from one system to the next. When in doubt, leave things alone. If the content of CMOS becomes corrupted, it's possible that the system might not be able to boot again. In such a case you might find it necessary to disassemble the unit, remove the CMOS battery, and wait a day or two for all content to vanish. Many systems do run a checksum of CMOS content each time they power up, and give the user an opportunity to correct any errors discovered, but this isn't always totally reliable. Be careful.

While it's always safe to modify the time data, you probably won't want to do so often. Using the BIOS or MS-DOS functions that set the CMOS clock will be much safer, because those functions will preserve the CMOS checksum correctly without any effort on your part. Figure 8.5 shows the three bytes of the CMOS dump that hold the time information.

```
C:\>cmos1

CMOS memory dump - Jim Kyle - March 1993

  00:  30 00 34 01 15 00 00 20 03 93 26 02 50 80 00 00
  10:  24 0C F0 9B 4F 80 02 00 10 23 00 00 00 00 00 00
  20:  00 00 00 00 00 00 00 00 00 00 00 00 00 3D 02 FC
  30:  00 10 19 D3 00 01 80 80 1B 7B 21 00 00 00 04 08
  40:  00 60 00 00 00 00 00 00 00 00 00 00 00 00 00 00
  50:  00 50 20 00 00 00 00 00 00 00 FF 80 00 00 00 01
  60:  B5 8F B2 31 79 40 A2 02 D1 A2 68 CE 59 45 F4 C4
  70:  08 78 DD 1C 66 EB E1 31 02 1A 4B 5A 03 09 5C 0F

C:\>
```

Figure 8.5. The three bytes that are highlighted here are the seconds, minutes, and hours values respectively for the CMOS clock. This snapshot of the content was made at 15:34:30, or shortly after 3:30 p.m.

While it can be dangerous to write to CMOS, you can, however, read from it at any time with no possibility of harming anything. This capability can be most useful, especially when you need to get information about system configuration details that's not stored elsewhere, or if you want to display time or date information from within a TSR that cannot use any DOS functions.

Communicating with the CMOS chip is a simple, but not totally conventional procedure. You must first send a location byte to the address register of the chip, and then read from or write to the data register. The address register is at Port 70h, and the data register at Port 71h.

To simplify the communication task, here's a simple little utility containing just two routines, `GetCMOS` and `PutCMOS`. You can include this as part of your C language program, or link its OBJ file in, and then call them directly.

```
/*
 * CMOSUTL.C - Utilities for reading or writing CMOS
 */
unsigned char GetCMOS( char i )          /* reads value from cell i */
{ unsigned char retval;
  outportb( 0x70, i );
  retval = inportb( 0x71 );
  return retval;
}

void PutCMOS( char i, char v )           /* writes value v to cell i */
{ outportb( 0x70, i );
  outportb( 0x71, v );
}
```

The following header file provides prototypes for both functions:

```
/*
 * CMOSUTL.H - header for CMOS utilities
 */
#ifndef CMOS_UTL
#define CMOS_UTL

unsigned char GetCMOS( char i );         /* reads value from cell i */
void PutCMOS( char i, char v );          /* writes value v to cell i */

#endif
```

To demonstrate how `CMOSUTL` can be used, here's a simple test file that reads various information out, and displays it on the screen. Various techniques for handling the data are shown, including the two-at-once storage trick we first met back in `BCDTEST`:

```
/*
 *  CMOSTEST.C - demo CMOS data recovery
 */
```

```
#include <stdio.h>
#include "bcdutl.h"
#include "cmosutl.h"

static char time[] = "hh:mm:ss";
static char date[] = "mm/dd/ccyy";
static char *Floppy[] = {
 "(none)",
 "5.25-inch 360k",
 "5.25-inch 1.2M",
 "3.5-inch 720k",
 "3.5-inch 1.44M"
};

void main( void )
{ puts( "\nCMOS contains this information:" );

  *(int *)&time[0] = BCD_ASC( GetCMOS( 0x04 ) );
  *(int *)&time[3] = BCD_ASC( GetCMOS( 0x02 ) );
  *(int *)&time[6] = BCD_ASC( GetCMOS( 0x00 ) );
  printf( "\nTime is %s\n", time );

  *(int *)&date[0] = BCD_ASC( GetCMOS( 0x08 ) );
  *(int *)&date[3] = BCD_ASC( GetCMOS( 0x07 ) );
  *(int *)&date[6] = BCD_ASC( GetCMOS( 0x32 ) );
  *(int *)&date[8] = BCD_ASC( GetCMOS( 0x09 ) );
  printf( "Date is %s\n", date );

  printf( "System RAM installed is %dK\n",
          (GetCMOS( 0x16 ) << 8) + (unsigned)GetCMOS( 0x15 ) );

  printf( "Expansion RAM installed is %dK\n",
          (GetCMOS( 0x18 ) << 8) + (unsigned)GetCMOS( 0x17 ) );

  printf( "Floppy drive A: is %s unit, drive B: is %s\n",
          Floppy[ GetCMOS( 0x10 ) >> 4 ],
          Floppy[ GetCMOS( 0x10 ) & 15 ] );

  printf( "First HD is Type %d, second is Type %d\n",
          GetCMOS( 0x19 ),
          GetCMOS( 0x1A ) );
}
```

One of the techniques used in `CMOSTEST.C` that you might want to extract to a separate utility is its reading of time information from CMOS, and then converting this into a string representation for display. The same thing is done for date information, and it would not be a major modification to add an indexed table of month names so that you could show the month in text rather than numeric form. To do this, use the same technique shown for converting the floppy-disk drive types into text, except that rather than shifting the CMOS value over to extract a 4-bit slice, use `BCD_Bin` instead to convert the BCD to binary form.

To compile `CMOSTEST.C`, I used a command line similar to that shown in Figure 8.2 for `BCDTEST.C`, except that I also added a third filename, CMOSUTL.C, to the list of files to be compiled.

When I run `CMOSTEST` on my home system, Figure 8.6 shows what it reveals. I captured this display at 8 seconds past 11 a.m. on March 25, as shown by the time and date displays. Conventional RAM in the system is maxed out at 640K, and 4096K (4 megabytes) of expansion RAM are reported. The system actually contains four 1-megabyte SIMM chips plus one megabyte of RAM in an Intel Above Board that was left over from the previous 80286 system; the missing 384K provide the upper memory blocks that are not recorded in CMOS setup information.

In addition, the display shows one 5.25-inch and one 3.5-inch floppy drive, plus a single physical hard drive of Type 35 (an ancient Seagate model 4096 80-meg unit). All in all, quite a bit of information about the system from just over two dozen lines of code.

```
C:\>cmostest

CMOS contains this information:

Time is 11:00:08
Date is 03/25/1993
System RAM installed is 640K
Expansion RAM installed is 4096K
Floppy drive A: is 5.25-inch 1.2M unit, drive B: is 3.5-inch 1.44M
First HD is Type 35, second is Type 0

C:\>
```

Figure 8.6. This is what the CMOSTEST program shows about my own system. You easily can extract any part of this program to create your own routines for getting information out of the CMOS RAM, which often is both faster and safer than using MS-DOS functions to do the same job.

Now that we know about CMOS interfacing, let's get back to the main subject of managing program and data memory.

Managing Conventional Memory

To control its use of RAM, MS-DOS establishes a chain of *memory control blocks* that is referred to in Microsoft's literature as *the memory arena.* Each control block (MCB) consists of one 16-byte paragraph. The first byte identifies it as a valid MCB by containing the ASCII code for either *M* or *Z* (the initials of Mark Zibrowski, one of the architects of MS-DOS version 2).

The next two bytes, interpreted as a conventional 16-bit word, identify the process which owns the block. That is, these bytes contain the Process ID (PSP segment address) of the process which first allocated the block. The following two bytes contain the size of the block in paragraphs.

Originally, the remaining 11 bytes of the MCB were unused, but at Version 3.0 MS-DOS began adding the bare filename from which the program was loaded as the final 8 bytes of each MCB that was allocated for program loading.

Certain exceptions to the rules just set forth exist, but you will rarely if ever encounter them in practice. In fact, since the MCB was not documented at all prior to MS-DOS Version 5, and still has no functions that will show you its content explicitly, you will never see one of them unless you go beyond the documented limits. One of the exceptions is that an owner code of 0008 is used for the low-RAM region reserved for use by the MS-DOS kernel code. Others include special identification of UMB control blocks in some, but not all, third-party memory managers.

Figure 8.7 shows how the MCB chain works. MS-DOS maintains a 16-bit pointer to the segment address of the very first MCB in the chain, within its SYSVARS area in low RAM. By adding the length word from that chain to the segment address of the block *following* the MCB, the segment address for the next MCB is obtained.

So long as each MCB accessed in this manner carries the `M` identifier byte, it's assumed that the chain is intact and has not reached its end. When the `Z` identifier is found, that's the end of the chain. Any other value in the identifier byte indicates a "corrupted memory arena" error which brings the system to an immediate halt.

If you need to know how much RAM is in a system, one way to determine this value is to trace the MCB chain until reaching the `Z` identifier, and accumulate the size of each block. But simpler techniques exist.

We've already seen one: if the system has CMOS memory, the amounts of both conventional and expansion memory are recorded in it. So you need only look there to obtain the same figure.

Even if the system does not have CMOS, BIOS in newer systems checks memory size during the `Power-On Self Test` procedures it goes through each time you turn the system on, and stores the information in its RAM scratchpad area. (In the original PC and XT models, this information was read from a DIP switch on the motherboard, however, and was not always reliable.) You can use Interrupt 12h to retrieve the BIOS value. Following is the calling sequence, in assembly language:

```
int  12h            ; call BIOS
mov  MemSize,ax     ; in kilobytes
```

Notice that the value returned by Interrupt 12h, and that obtained by reading CMOS location 15h, will usually be identical.

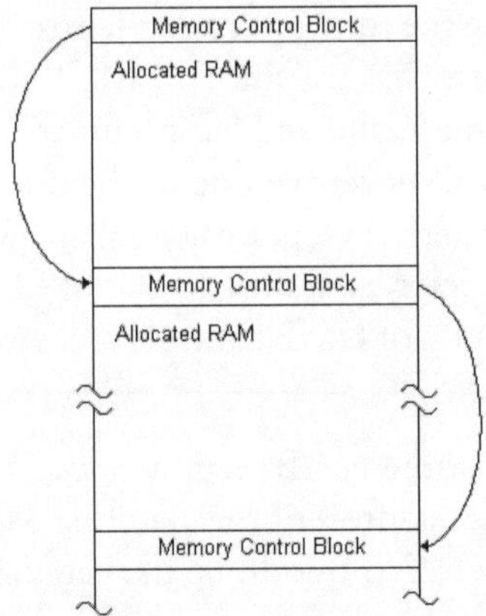

Figure 8.7. This is how the MCB chain works. Each MCB contains a word showing how many paragraphs it controls; these paragraphs always follow it immediately. By adding that length to the segment address of the first controlled paragraph, MS-DOS determines the segment address for the next MCB in the chain.

For many applications, you will never need to be concerned with memory management. Modern high-level languages, and the MS-DOS loader, cooperate to make it essentially invisible most of the time. Only when your task is especially demanding with its memory requirements will you find any need to do your own management of memory.

The tools that MS-DOS provides for this purpose are few in number, but adequately powerful for almost all needs. Three MS-DOS functions allow you to allocate, release, and re-size RAM blocks, and a fourth allows you to establish the strategy that will be used when searching for a block to fill an allocation request.

When you know exactly how much memory you need to allocate, your task is simple and Function 48h can deal with it. This function allocates a block of memory for use and returns the segment address of the beginning of the block. Following is its calling sequence, in assembly language:

```
mov  bx,Size         ; in paragraphs
mov  ah,48h          ; Function 48h
int  21h             ; call MS-DOS
jc   error
mov  BlkSeg,ax       ; seg address of block
```

If the carry flag is set upon return from this function, an error of some type occurred. The size of the largest block found during the search is returned in BX, in this case, and AX contains a code indicating the error type. By far the most frequent error encountered is code 08, not enough memory available to fill the request.

In fact, the way that most command interpreters force *all available RAM* to be allocated to a process is to first request a block of size 0FFFFh; since this is larger than MS-DOS is able to address directly, this request always fails, but it establishes the size of the largest available block in BX, and a subsequent call to Function 48h with no change of the BX value will succeed.

Because most programs are allocated all of memory, by default, this function frequently fails unless memory has first been released after entering the program. To release only a part of the memory assigned to the program, Function 4Ah must be used. Many high-level languages automatically provide this re-sizing action during their start-up code; if, however, you have difficulty using Function 48h, availability of RAM is the first place to look when trying to solve the problem.

To release an entire allocated block of RAM back to MS-DOS so that it can be used by other programs, Function 49h is used. Following is the calling sequence, in assembly language, for this function:

```
mov  ax,BlkSeg       ; block to be released
mov  es,ax
mov  ah,49h          ; Function 49h
int  21h             ; call MS-DOS
jc   error
```

If the carry flag is set upon return from this function, AX will contain a code indicating the type of error that occurred. This code will be either 7, indicating a corrupted memory arena, or 9, indicating that the value passed in ES was not a valid memory block address.

Just as the command interpreter (normally COMMAND.COM) takes care of allocating space for a program when it is first loaded for execution, so does it release all space owned by the program back to MS-DOS when the program terminates, unless it terminates but remains resident as a TSR. In such a case, no automatic release of memory occurs and you must handle it within your program before going resident.

A much more frequent need in many applications is to be able to change the size of an allocated block of RAM, either to expand it to more bytes, or to shrink it back to less. We've already seen that this may be necessary before you can allocate any space at all within a program, if it already owns all available space.

Resizing a memory block previously allocated by Function 48h is the purpose of Function 4Ah. Following is the calling sequence, in assembly language:

```
mov  ax,BlkSeg       ; block to be released
mov  es,ax
mov  bx,NewSize      ; in paragraphs
mov  ah,4Ah          ; Function 4Ah
int  21h             ; call MS-DOS
jc   error
```

If the carry flag is set upon return from this function, AX will contain a code indicating the type of error that occurred. This code will be either `7`, indicating a corrupted memory arena, `8`, indicating that not enough RAM is available to fill the request, or `9`, indicating that the value passed in ES was not a valid memory block address.

If an insufficient-memory error occurs, then BX will contain the largest number of paragraphs that can be allocated, just as when allocating a block initially.

MS-DOS can follow any of several strategies for determining which specific block of RAM to supply in response to an allocation request. These are known as *best fit*, *first fit*, and *last fit* techniques. Regardless of the strategy used, the search routines will go all the way to the end of the MCB chain before doing returning, and while making the search, packs any adjacent free blocks into single larger blocks.

The first-fit method searches from low memory to high looking for the *first* block of memory that is as large as, or larger than, the requested memory size. This is the default condition if no other strategy is specified.

The best-fit strategy finds the *smallest* block that will meet the allocation requested.

The last-fit strategy is the same as the first fit strategy except that the search returns the *last* block found that will meet the requirement.

Naturally, if only one free block of RAM exists, which often is the case, all three strategies give the same result, except that last-fit will allocate the upper end of the block while the other two will allocate the lower end.

Two subfunctions of Function 58h allow you to determine the current allocation strategy, and to set a new strategy. To determine which strategy is currently in use, you call Subfunction 00h. Following is the calling sequence:

```
mov  al,00h          ; get strategy
mov  ah,58h          ; Function 58h
int  21h             ; call MS-DOS
jc   error
mov  Strat,ax        ; coded result
```

If the carry flag is set upon return from Interrupt 21h, the function call was not valid. In general, this can only happen if file sharing is in effect (SHARE.EXE loaded), or if one of the subfunctions added to Function 58h at MS-DOS version 5.0 (and described separately when we look at management of UMB's) is called when a version of MS-DOS prior to 5.0 is running. In these cases, the error code returned in AX will be 1. In addition, if the 386MAX third-party memory manager is running, this function may return an error code of 2.

The strategy code returned in AX will be 0 for first fit, 1 for best fit, and 2 for last fit. Prior to Version 5.0, any other value was interpreted as last fit, but when the upper memory capability was added at that time, six more strategy codes were defined.

Three of the new codes are 80h, 81h, and 82h, indicating first, best, and last fit respectively, with upper memory being searched first. Only if the request cannot be satisfied from upper memory will conventional RAM be searched.

The other three new codes are 40h, 41h, and 42h, which again indicate first, best, and last fit respectively. With these strategies, however, only upper memory is searched. The request will never be filled from conventional RAM.

Each of the various strategies has its place; the default first-fit-low is usually best for most needs, but when loading TSR code it's often advantageous to place it in upper memory so that more space will be available in the conventional RAM area for programs. We'll look at this in more detail when we examine UMB management.

To change the strategy code in effect, Subfunction 01h is used. Following is the calling sequence:

```
mov  bx,Strat        ; strategy code
mov  al,01h          ; set strategy
mov  ah,58h          ; Function 58h
int  21h             ; call MS-DOS
jc   error
```

Error indications and strategy codes are identical to those for Subfunction 00h.

As a general rule, should you need to modify the strategy in any application, you should first retrieve the existing strategy code via Subfunction 00h, and save it, so that you can put things back as you found them when you no longer need your special strategy.

Managing Expanded Memory

As noted earlier, one of the first steps toward alleviating the RAM-cram condition that has plagued MS-DOS applications for a number of years now was development of the Expanded Memory (EMS) technology. Originally known as LIM (for Lotus-Intel-Microsoft, the original creators of the specification) it subsequently merged with a rival solution to the problem and is now most often called just EMS.

True EMS, which can be used with even an original 8088 PC system, uses special hardware coupled with a custom driver package to allow many different blocks of RAM to share a single small address space known as the *EMS page frame.* In our earlier memory map we showed the page frame at address E0000, but it can actually be located any place in the upper memory area where there's a 64K byte block of unused address space.

An EMS adapter board, such as Intel's Above Board, contains its own address and mapping circuits, so that any four 16K blocks of the up to 8 megabytes of storage on the board can be mapped into the page frame at any one time. This memory is accessible to the system only when it is mapped into the page frame by means of special driver calls that go through Interrupt 67h, the "standard" EMS interface hook.

With the advent of the 80286 and later processors able to address extended memory directly, the need for EMS was reduced. However, many popular programs such as Lotus still required it for full performance, so systems still had to have the capability. The resulting compromise was introduction of alternate drivers that required no special hardware; these were able to map areas from the extended memory space down to the page frame on demand, as shown in Figure 8.8.

Use of Interrupt 67h by EMS drivers may conflict with certain SCSI device drivers that also chose that interrupt, and these conflicts may appear unexpectedly under MS-DOS version 6 if you use the MEMMAKER utility to optimize your upper memory use. We look at this in more detail when we examine generic memory managers later in this chapter.

Even though direct access to extended memory space has replaced the use of EMS in many areas, the EMS technology still offers several significant advantages. Not the least is that it's possible to execute program code within the page frame, since that address space is still within the 1-megabyte limit that real-mode (and therefore MS-DOS) can access.

When attempting to execute code in the page frame, you must observe several critical precautions, all of which are intended to assure that your address references are correct, and that what's at those addresses is actually the code that you want to execute.

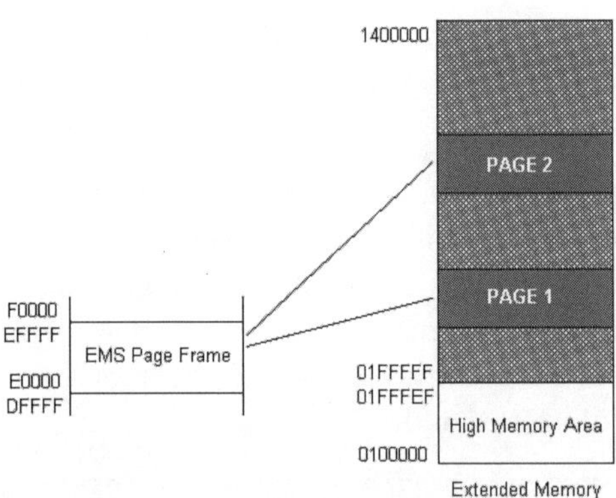

Figure 8.8. This view shows how the 64K page frame for EMS actually refers to unrelated 16K blocks in the extended memory space or, in older systems, on a special EMS expansion board. All programs refer to the page-frame addresses, but the actual memory that's affected is elsewhere. The smoke and mirrors available with on-the-fly remapping make this magic possible.

It's never safe, for example, to install TSR routines or any interrupt service routines into the page frame, because at any given instant the frame may contain data or other procedures rather than the routine you expect to be there.

By the same token, since any other application can remap the page frame to a different set of logical pages, you must always verify that it contains your desired code before calling it, or jumping to it.

While this might not seem to be a serious problem in MS-DOS since it's not a multi-tasking system, it can be fatal if your application ever executes from a Windows DOS box, because then pre-emptive multitasking comes into play and other applications or even Windows itself may change the page frame mapping without your knowledge.

But what are those words about *set of logical pages* and *mapping*? Let's look more closely at the technology that EMS involves.

As already mentioned, the page frame itself consists of four contiguous 16-kilobyte blocks of RAM, each of which is known as a *physical page* and identified by a page number in the range zero through three. Each physical page, moreover, must start at a 16K boundary in the address space (this requirement originally simplified the mapping hardware for the expansion boards and has been retained for compatibility).

The expanded memory can be any multiple of 16K in size, and is similarly divided into *logical pages.* An application that needs to use expanded memory must ask the EMS manager software to allocate memory; the application passes in the number of logical pages desired, and if that much can be allocated, the EMS manager returns a *handle* that uniquely identifies the allocated region. Note that any number of pages can be requested; the application is not restricted to just the four that can fit into the page frame at one time.

To request allocation of EMS, Function 43h of EMS Interrupt 67h is used. Following is its calling sequence, in assembly language:

```
mov  bx,Pages        ; number of pages desired
mov  ah,43h          ; Function 43h
int  67h             ; call EMS manager
cmp  ah,0            ; test for success
jne  error
mov  Handle,dx       ; save handle for use
```

If any nonzero value is returned in AH, some error occurred. The most likely is that the manager is out of either handles (error code 85h) or space (88h).

Once a handle has been obtained by the application, it must be saved for all future communication with the EMS manager. To use the EMS space it represents, the application must ask the EMS manager to map the desired logical page or pages to physical pages in the frame, and here no more than four logical pages can be accessed at once. However, the mapping operation is not time-intensive, so almost no performance penalty is imposed by a need to change mappings frequently when more than four logical pages require access.

To request the necessary mapping, Function 44h of EMS Interrupt 67h is used. Following is its calling sequence, in assembly language:

```
mov  ah,44h          ; Function 44h
mov  al,PhysPage     ; 0 through 3
mov  bx,LogPage      ; logical page number
mov  dx,Handle
```

```
int  67h            ; call EMS manager
cmp  ah,0           ; test for success
jne  error
```

Again, a nonzero value in AH upon return indicates some error. Most likely, for this function, are codes 83h, invalid handle, 8Ah, indicating an invalid logical page number, or 8Bh, indicating an illegal physical page number.

In order to provide program access to the page frame, your application has to know the segment address at which the frame begins. Since this varies from one system to another (it's set by option switches when the EMS driver is installed), the application must obtain the correct value dynamically. This need be done only once, however, since the address does not change during program operation.

To get the page frame's segment address, Function 41h of EMS Interrupt 67h is used. Following is its calling sequence, in assembly language:

```
mov  ah,41h         ; Function 41h
int  67h            ; call EMS manager
cmp  ah,0           ; test for success
jne  error
mov  SegAdr,bx      ; save value for use
```

Only a few error conditions are possible for this call and all of them are unlikely: 80h indicates an internal error in the EMS manager, 81h a hardware malfunction, and 84h indicates an invalid function (which could happen only with a malfunction that altered the value of AH between your call and arrival of control at the EMS manager).

With the segment address for the page frame known, far pointers to each of the four possible physical pages can be created by using an offset value of 0 for Page 0, 4000h for Page 1, 8000h for Page 2, and 0C000h for Page 3. Alternatively, you can adjust the segment values for the four pages by adding 400h (16K bytes = 1024 paragraphs) to the segment address of the previous page, and thus have each offset start at 0.

Since your program can never be certain that some other application has not changed mappings since the last time it referenced the EMS, you should always verify that your own data is in the page frame before any critical actions. One way of doing this is to have your application write a short *signature* pattern into the first few bytes of each logical page, immediately after they are allocated, and then subsequently verify the presence of the signature.

When you're finished using EMS, it's necessary to release the handle back to the EMS manager. Failure to do this makes all the space that you reserved unavailable to any other application, until the system is rebooted; MS-DOS cannot do any automatic release of EMS allocations, since it's a technology that is completely outside of the operating system's reference frame.

To release an allocation back to the EMS manager, Function 45h of EMS Interrupt 67h is used. Following is its calling sequence, in assembly language:

```
mov  dx,Handle       ; handle to release
mov  ah,45h          ; Function 45h
int  67h             ; call EMS manager
cmp  ah,0            ; test for success
jne  error
```

The most likely error return from this function is 83h, invalid handle.

The functions described in this section are only a small part of the complete list defined in the LIM 4.0 specification, but they are the ones you will use most frequently in normal applications. Others that you may need allow you to verify the EMS version, determine how much EMS RAM is available, and find out the condition of the EMS hardware.

To read the version of the EMS manager, Function 46h of EMS Interrupt 67h is used. Following is its calling sequence, in assembly language:

```
mov  ah,46h          ; Function 46h
int  67h             ; call EMS manager
cmp  ah,0            ; test for success
jne  error
mov  Versn,al
```

The version information in AL indicates the major version number in the upper four bytes of the register, and the minor version number in the lower four bytes.

To determine the number of EMS pages available, both total and free, Function 42h of EMS Interrupt 67h is used. Following is its calling sequence, in assembly language:

```
mov  ah,42h          ; Function 42h
int  67h             ; call EMS manager
cmp  ah,0            ; test for success
jne  error
mov  NumFree,bx      ; available page count
mov  TotEMS,dx       ; total page count
```

To determine whether the EMS hardware is functioning properly, Function 40h of EMS Interrupt 67h is used. Following is its calling sequence, in assembly language:

```
mov  ah,40h          ; Function 40h
int  67h             ; call EMS manager
cmp  ah,0            ; test for success
jne  error
```

Any non-zero value in AH upon return indicates an error; the most likely such code is 81h, hardware malfunction.

As you can see, using EMS involves many repetitive operations that really have no connection with the *normal* calculations of your application. And we didn't even discuss the need to verify the existence of an EMS manager before attempting to use any of these functions, but it's something that must always be done. Because of these tedious complications, it's usually better to employ an existing EMS utility library (and hide the details so they don't get in your way) than to attempt to control all the EMS interfacing from your applications.

For several years, Intel has made available at no charge a 4-diskette library of EMS interface functions for both C and assembly language programmers. It's available from their CompuServe forum (GO PCEO) for only the cost of your download time.

The `EMMLIB` package from Intel deals with almost all of the EMS functions, most of which you may never use. You might find the accompanying package, `EMSUTL.C`, adequate for your application's needs. It provides 11 functions which deal with the basics of verifying EMS presence, allocating RAM, mapping it, obtaining physical page pointers, and freeing the RAM after use.

This program requires a Borland compiler to create its OBJ file, because it uses Borland's pseudoregister variables which are not available from other compilers, but the OBJ file should be compatible with all standard C tools. You can compile `EMSUTL.C` using any memory model that you desire; the only critical return values that are model-dependent are the four page-pointer functions, which always return far pointers regardless of model.

As a general rule, however, most programs that use EMS extensively should be designed for the "large" memory model since it readily supports far pointers for both code and data. Models that expect near pointers for data can demonstrate mysterious symptoms when their library functions (such as `strcpy()`) are called with far-pointer argument values.

```
/*
 * EMSUTL.C - compile using Borland or TC
 *
 *      Provide interface to EMS drivers, callable from C programs
 *
 */
#include <dos.h>

static int Have_EMS = 0;            /* flags that EMS driver present */
static int Total_pages = 0;
static int Avail_pages = 0;

int EMS_here( void )                  /* test for presence of driver */
{ static char *device_name = "EMMXXXX0";
  char far * drvrp;
  int i;

  if( ! Have_EMS )
    { asm mov ah,0x35;                           /* get vector contents */
      asm mov al,0x67;                             /* EMS vector number */
      asm int 0x21;                                         /* call DOS */
      drvrp = MK_FP( _ES, 10 );      /* pointer to device name field */
      for( i=0; i < 7; i++ )                     /* compare to standard */
        if( drvrp[i] != device_name[i] )
          break;                                         /* on mismatch */
      Have_EMS = ( drvrp[i] == device_name[i] );    /* true if match */
    }
  return Have_EMS;                          /* EMS manager loaded status */
}

int EMS_hardware_OK( void )               /* test hardware, true if OK */
{ if( Have_EMS )
    { asm mov ah,0x40;
      asm int 0x67;
      if (_AH == 0)
        return 1;
    }
  return 0;
}

int EMS_avail( void )             /* return number of pages available */
{ if( Have_EMS )
```

```
    { asm mov ah,0x42;                      /* GET_FREE_COUNT opcode */
      asm int 0x67;
      asm jc a;                                        /* call failed */
      Avail_pages = _BX;
      if( ! Total_pages )              /* set size also if not done */
        Total_pages = _DX;
    }
  a:
  return ( Avail_pages );
}

int EMS_total( void )
{ if( Have_EMS && ! Total_pages )
    { asm mov ah,0x42;                      /* GET_FREE_COUNT opcode */
      asm int 0x67;
      asm jc a;                                        /* call failed */
      Total_pages = _DX;
    }
  a:
  return ( Total_pages );
}

char far * EMS_pg0_ptr( void )
{ char far * cptr = (char far *)MK_FP( 0, 0 );
  if( Have_EMS )
    { asm mov ah,0x41;               /* GET_PAGE_FRAME_BASE opcode */
      asm int 0x67;
      if ( ! _AH )
        cptr = (char far *)MK_FP( _BX, 0 );            /* phys page 0 */
    }
  return (cptr);                             /* NULL indicates failure */
}

char far * EMS_pg1_ptr( void )
{ char far * cptr = (char far *)MK_FP( 0, 0 );
  if( Have_EMS )
    { asm mov ah,0x41;               /* GET_PAGE_FRAME_BASE opcode */
      asm int 0x67;
      if ( ! _AH )
        cptr = (char far *)MK_FP( _BX+1024, 0 );       /* phys page 1 */
    }
  return (cptr);                             /* NULL indicates failure */
}
```

```
char far * EMS_pg2_ptr( void )
{ char far * cptr = (char far *)MK_FP( 0, 0 );
  if( Have_EMS )
    { asm mov ah,0x41;                /* GET_PAGE_FRAME_BASE opcode */
      asm int 0x67;
      if ( ! _AH )
        cptr = (char far *)MK_FP( _BX+2048, 0 );     /* phys page 2 */
    }
  return (cptr);                          /* NULL indicates failure */
}

char far * EMS_pg3_ptr( void )
{ char far * cptr = (char far *)MK_FP( 0, 0 );
  if( Have_EMS )
    { asm mov ah,0x41;                /* GET_PAGE_FRAME_BASE opcode */
      asm int 0x67;
      if ( ! _AH )
        cptr = (char far *)MK_FP( _BX+3072, 0 );     /* phys page 3 */
    }
  return (cptr);                          /* NULL indicates failure */
}

unsigned EMS_alloc( int numpages )        /* allocate logical pages */
{ if( Have_EMS )
    { if( numpages <= EMS_avail() )
        { asm mov ah,0x43;                 /* ALLOCATE_PAGES opcode */
          asm mov bx,numpages;
          asm int 0x67;
          if ( ! _AH )
            return _DX;                                   /* handle */
        }
    }
  return 0;                                               /* failed */
}

int EMS_free_handle( unsigned handle )     /* release logical pages */
{ if( Have_EMS && handle )
    { int i;
      for ( i=0; i < 5; i++)          /* try 5 times if unsuccessful */
        { asm mov ah,0x45;               /* DEALLOCATE_PAGES opcode */
          asm mov dx,handle;
```

```
          asm int 0x67;
          if( ! _AH )
            return 1;                                         /* success */
        }
    }
  return 0;                                                   /* failure */
}

int EMS_map_page( unsigned handle,                         /* EMS handle */
                  char phy_page,                  /* physical page (0-3) */
                  int log_page )                   /* logical page (0-N) */
{ if( Have_EMS && phy_page >= 0 && phy_page <= 3 )
    { asm mov ah,0x44;                              /* MAP_PAGES opcode */
      asm mov al,phy_page;
      asm mov bx,log_page;
      asm mov dx,handle;
      asm int 0x67;
      if ( ! _AH )
        return 1;                                             /* success */
    }
  return 0;                                                   /* failure */
}
```

Most of the 11 functions in `EMSUTL.C` are direct implementations of the assembly language versions described earlier. The only significant variation is the `EMS_here()` function that's used to determine the presence or absence of an EMS manager.

`EMS_here()` works by verifying that Interrupt 67h points into a segment that contains a standard EMS device driver; all such standard drivers are identified by the name `EMMXXXX0`, and all device drivers' names are located at offset 0010h within the segment. If offset 10h of the segment pointed to by the Interrupt 67h vector contains anything other than the standard name, `EMS_here()` returns a value of zero, and leaves the static internal variable `Have_EMS` also zero (or false). Each of the other functions, then, calls the EMS manager only if `Have_EMS` is nonzero (true), thereby satisfying the requirement that the manager be called only if present.

Prototypes for the 11 functions are provided by the file `EMSUTL.H`:

```
/*
 * EMSUTL.H - header file for EMS utilities
 */
```

```
#ifndef EMS_UTL_
#define EMS_UTL_

int EMS_here( void );                /* test for presence of driver */
int EMS_hardware_OK( void );            /* test hardware, true if OK */
int EMS_avail( void );          /* return number of pages available */
int EMS_total( void );
char far * EMS_pg0_ptr( void );
char far * EMS_pg1_ptr( void );
char far * EMS_pg2_ptr( void );
char far * EMS_pg3_ptr( void );
unsigned EMS_alloc( int numpages );        /* allocate logical pages */
int EMS_free_handle( unsigned handle );     /* release logical pages */
int EMS_map_page( unsigned handle, int phy_page, int log_page );

#endif
```

To give you some ideas of how EMSUTL can be used, here's a brief program called EMSTEST.C which uses EMSUTL functions to determine the amount of EMS memory available, displays that value, and then allocates several pages and checks again, and finally releases the memory back to the EMS manager. While this program is not in itself useful, it did show me a few interesting things about the way Windows works (which we'll examine shortly):

```
/*
 * EMSTEST.C - Demonstrate use of XMSUTL package
 * Jim Kyle - March 1993
 */
#include <stdio.h>
#include "emsutl.h"

void main( void )
{ int total_EMS;
  int total_free;
  char far * p1;
  unsigned handle;

  puts( "\nEMSTEST - demonstrates EMSUTL routines\n" );
  if( EMS_here() )
    { total_EMS  = EMS_total();                  /* gather size data */
      total_free = EMS_avail();
```

```
   printf( "Total EMS present: %8lu bytes (%5d pages)\n",
           total_EMS * 16384L,
           total_EMS );
   printf( "          EMS free: %8lu bytes (%5d pages)\n",
           total_free * 16384L,
           total_free );
   printf( "\nAllocating 5 pages now ... " );
   handle = EMS_alloc( 5 );
   if( handle )
     printf( "returned handle: %u\n", handle );
   else
     puts( "Allocation failed" );
   printf( "\nFree page count now is %d\n", EMS_avail() );
   printf( "\nReleasing those pages..." );
   if( EMS_free_handle( handle ))
     puts( "okay" );
   else
     puts( "failed" );
   printf( "\nFree page count now is %d\n", EMS_avail() );
  }
 else
  puts( "No EMS Driver could be found." );
}
```

To compile `EMSTEST.C`, follow the same pattern already used for `BCDTEST` and `BCDUTL` as shown in Figure 8.9.

```
C:\>bcc emstest.c emsutl.c
Borland C++  Version 3.00 Copyright (c) 1991 Borland International
emstest.c:
emsutl.c:
Turbo Link  Version 5.0 Copyright (c) 1991 Borland International

        Available memory 2263772

C:\>
```

Figure 8.9. Compilation of EMSTEST, with EMSUTL.C, follows the same pattern used for BCDTEST and BCDUTL described earlier. This time, however, no warnings result.

Running EMSTEST.EXE from a DOS box under Windows 3.1, and from the command prompt outside of Windows completely, shows drastic differences in the amount of EMS available to programs under these conditions. As you can see in Figure 8.10, captured from the Windows DOS box, only one megabyte, 64 logical pages, of EMS is available under Windows. Remember that this must be shared among all DOS programs that use EMS; it's a serious limitation.

```
C:\>emstest
EMSTEST - demonstrates EMSUTL routines
Total EMS present:  1048576 bytes (   64 pages)
         EMS free:  1048576 bytes (   64 pages)
Allocating 5 pages now ... returned handle: 1
Free page count now is 59
Releasing those pages...okay
Free page count now is 64
C:\>
```

Figure 8.10. When called from the MS-DOS box under Windows 3.1, EMSTEST shows that Windows permits only 64 pages of EMS to be used and restricts the available RAM to a bit more than a megabyte. Contrast this with Figure 8.11, showing the result when run outside of Windows on the same system.

When run outside of the Windows environment, from the MS-DOS command prompt itself, the result (on the same system) is drastically different as Figure 8.11 shows. Now there are a total of 276 pages in the system, rather than 64, and 161 of them are available for use.

```
C:\>emstest
EMSTEST - demonstrates EMSUTL routines
Total EMS present:  4521984 bytes (  276 pages)
         EMS free:  2637824 bytes (  161 pages)
Allocating 5 pages now ... returned handle: 1
Free page count now is 156
Releasing those pages...okay
Free page count now is 161
C:\>
```

Figure 8.11. With Windows out of the act, EMSTEST reports much more available EMS memory and more than four times as many pages available.

The exact amount of EMS that's available under Windows, it turns out, can be adjusted by proper tuning of individual system parameters. The thing you must remember, as a developer, is simply that such restrictions exist, and your applications must be prepared to deal with them at run time on an individual-system basis.

Managing Extended Memory

Since MS-DOS is inherently limited to operating only in real mode, which limits its address space to the first megabyte of memory, Extended Memory is inherently less useful to it than is Expanded or Conventional Memory. Only data can be placed in extended memory; no code can execute there.

However this limitation on the utility of extended memory has not stopped its acceptance or use, and when you need relatively large amounts of rapid-access temporary storage in an application, this is the area to look into.

Over the years, a number of competing (and conflicting) methods for obtaining access to the extended memory region have been developed. We've already seen how it can be used to emulate EMS, and thus made more amenable to the real-mode limitations of MS-DOS.

When Version 3.0 of MS-DOS made its appearance, source code for a virtual disk device driver named VDISK.SYS was part of the package. VDISK.SYS showed a primitive method for gaining access to extended memory that gained fairly widespread popularity before its faults became obvious. The major fault of the VDISK technique was that no standard for its use existed, and so attempts to run more than one program based on VDISK in a single system often led to total crashes.

The VDISK approach since been superseded by the Extended Memory Specification known as XMS. Nevertheless, when MS-DOS versions 5 or 6 install themselves high, they still include a small prefix that masquerades as the VDISK.SYS driver header, to prevent any program that attempts to use the VDISK technique from causing problems to the MS-DOS kernel code.

Interfaces for dealing with extended memory appeared in BIOS at about the same time as VDISK. We'll look at them briefly before turning our attention to the methods based on XMS, but only to familiarize you with them should you encounter them. For new applications, the XMS specification provides the only safe way to deal with extended memory.

The BIOS functions dealing with extended memory made their appearance in the PC-AT line in 1983, and are functions of Interrupt 15h, the BIOS system service interface. One allows you to determine how much extended memory is present while the other allows a block of data to be moved to or from extended memory,

To determine how much extended RAM the system contains, use Function 88h. Following is the calling sequence, in assembly language:

```
mov   ah,88h          ; get extended mem size
int   15h             ; call BIOS system services
jc    error
mov   ExMemSz,ax      ; contiguous kilobytes
```

Note that this function assumes that all the extended memory is contiguous, and is located in the address space immediately following the 1-megabyte mark. The VDISK technique was based on this function: the device driver first used this function to determine how much memory was available, and then installed itself at the upper end of the space, and hooked the BIOS interrupt to force subsequent calls to return a smaller-than-actual value.

To copy data into or out of the extended memory region, things were a bit more complicated. Because the only way that the extended memory can be directly addressed in the 80286 processors is by switching into protected mode, the BIOS function had to take the CPU into protected mode, do the transfer using 24-bit full linear addresses, and then restore operations to real mode. During this time, all interrupts had to be disabled, because the interrupt vector table assumes real-mode addressing rather than protected mode.

The BIOS function that does all these things is 87h, and here's its calling sequence, in assembly language:

```
mov   ah,87h             ; copy extended memory
mov   cx,NbrWords        ; maximum is 8000h
mov   si,seg DescTbl     ; point to table for move
mov   es,si
mov   si,offset DescTbl
int   15h                ; call BIOS system services
jc    error
```

Note that almost no information is passed to this function in the registers. Instead, a far pointer to a *descriptor table* is provided in ES:SI. The `DescTbl` structure that must be supplied has this format:

```
DescTbl   db   16 dup(0)      ; must be zeroes
          dw   ?              ; source length in bytes
          db   3 dup(?)       ; 24-bit source address
          db   93h            ; source access rights
          dw   0
```

```
dw   ?                  ; destination length, bytes
db   3 dup(?)           ; 24-bit dest address
db   93h                ; destination access rights
db   18 dup(0)          ; must be zeroes
```

The two 24-bit addresses are stored in the table low byte first. The *access rights* bytes allow reading and writing at both ends of the transfer.

Because interrupts must remain disabled during the entire time of each data transfer, this function turned out to be incompatible with many high-speed modem applications.

When the XMS standards appeared, they acknowledged the prevalence of programs already using the BIOS functions by imposing two requirements. All XMS drivers are required to hook Interrupt 15h and watch for calls to functions 87h (Block Move) and 88h (Extended Memory Available).

The Interrupt 15h Block Move, Function 87h, must be hooked so that the state of the A20 line is preserved across the call. The Extended Memory Available function must be hooked to return 0h and thus prevent the HMA from being overwritten by accident.

For the vast majority of your applications, you will use XMS exclusively to access extended memory. Doing so will tend to assure compatibility with anything that may be developed later, since XMS is now the accepted industry standard.

You'll probably want to use a tried and true library to get your XMS support, rather than rolling your own, for the reasons already cited in respect to EMS interfacing. However you still need at least passing familiarity with XMS, especially because it differs in several important details from anything we've yet examined.

To find out whether an XMS driver is present in the system, we use Function 43h of Multiplex Interrupt 2Fh. Subfunction 00 checks for presence of the XMS driver. Following is the calling sequence, in assembly language:

```
mov  ax,4300h        ; verify XMS presence
int  2Fh             ; call multiplex interrupt
cmp  al,80h          ; test for driver located
jne  error           ; no driver found
```

If the value returned in AL is anything other than 80h, no valid XMS driver is available in the system and the rest of the XMS functions cannot be used. If a valid driver is present, the next step is to obtain a far pointer to its entry point.

For this, subfunction 10h of the same function is what we need. Following is the calling sequence:

```
mov  ax,4310h              ; get XMS entry address
int  2Fh                   ; call multiplex interrupt
mov  word ptr HMM,bx       ; save far pointer
mov  word ptr HMM+2,es
```

The far pointer referenced in our example as HMM is then used to actually invoke the XMS driver's functions, which are not limited only to management of extended memory blocks. The XMS driver also controls access to the HMA, the state of the A20 line, and can provide access to upper memory blocks.

In all these cases, the XMS function is specified by loading its code into the AH register, and then (after putting any required parameters into other registers) doing an indirect call through the pointer at HMM. The XMS specification at version 3.0 specifies 19 functions, but only the first 16 are required.

To get the version number of the driver, for instance, Function 00h is used. Following is the calling sequence:

```
mov  ah,00h         ; get XMS version
call far ptr HMM    ; call XMS manager
mov  Version,ax     ; in BCD
mov  Revision,bx    ; internal number
mov  HasHMA,dx      ; 1 if HMA exists, else 0
```

The internal revision number returned in the BX register may not be meaningful. The HMA flag returned in DX will be 1 if a high memory area exists, or 0 if there is none. Lack of an HMA indicates that the system has no contiguous extended memory immediately above the 1-megabyte address.

Functions 01h through 07h deal with the HMA and access to it via the A20 address line. Because most applications should always leave the HMA free for use by MS-DOS itself, we don't explore these functions here.

Function 08h tells you how many kilobytes of extended memory you have free, and the size of the largest free block. Following is its calling sequence:

```
mov  ah,08h         ; query amount free
call far ptr HMM    ; call XMS manager
cmp  bl,0           ; test for success
jne  error
mov  Largest,ax     ; in kilobytes
mov  Total,dx       ; in kilobytes
```

The XMS manager returns its error codes in the BL register, unlike most of the other functions with which we deal. A value of 0 in BL indicates that no error occurred, but we don't usually test for that because most of the XMS functions also return an error flag in AX, which is set to 1 for success, or 0 if an error occurred. The error codes you may encounter in the BL register upon return from one of the EMB functions are all in the range A0h through ADh:

Code	Meaning
A0	All extended memory has already been allocated.
A1	All extended memory handles have already been used.
A2	Invalid handle supplied to function.
A3	Source handle (for move) is not valid.
A4	Source offset is not valid.
A5	Destination handle is not valid.
A6	Destination offset is not valid.
A7	Length value is not valid.
A8	Move has an invalid overlap condition.
A9	Parity error detected.
AA	Block is not locked.
AB	Block is locked.
AC	Block lock count overflowed.
AD	Lock failed.

To allocate a block of extended memory Function 09h is the right tool. Its calling sequence follows:

```
mov  ah,09h          ; allocate an EMB
mov  dx,Kilobytes    ; size desired
call far ptr HMM     ; call XMS manager
cmp  ax,1            ; test for success
jne  error
mov  Handle,dx       ; save for use
```

The handle returned by Function 09h must be saved so long as the allocated block is in use. When we're through with the block, we use the handle to release it via Function 0Ah:

```
mov  ah,0Ah          ; free an EMB
mov  dx,Handle       ; block to free
call far ptr HMM     ; call XMS manager
cmp  ax,1            ; test for success
jne  error
```

Since in the general case, we can only store data in the EMB and cannot actually access it directly, we must move that data into the EMB to store it, and back into conventional RAM to use it. Function 0Bh does both tasks:

```
mov  ah,0Bh          ; move data
mov  si,offset MovStruc
call far ptr HMM     ; call XMS manager
cmp  ax,1            ; test for success
jne  error
```

This is the `MovStruc` organization expected by Function 0Bh:

```
MovStruc  dd   ?    ; number of bytes to move, even
          dw   ?    ; source block's handle
          dd   ?    ; offset into source block
          dw   ?    ; destination block's handle
          dd   ?    ; offset into destination block
```

If either handle's value is zero, the associated offset is interpreted as an absolute segment:offset address in real-mode memory space. Thus this function can move data in either direction between conventional RAM and an EMB, or between different EMBs.

Functions 0Ch and 0Dh permit us to lock an EMB into place so that its mapping does not change while we work with it. This is not one of the main facets of XMS operation so I've skipped over them. Function 0Eh, given an EMB handle, returns all significant information connected with that handle:

```
mov  ah,0Eh          ; get handle information
mov  dx,Handle
call far ptr HMM     ; call XMS manager
cmp  ax,1            ; test for success
jne  error
mov  LockCount,bh    ; number of locks on block
mov  FreeHdls,bl     ; number handles left free
mov  BlkSize,dx      ; size in kilobytes
```

Function 0Fh, given an EMB handle, enables you to change the size of the EMB to which that handle refers:

```
mov  ah,0Fh          ; reallocate EMB
mov  dx,Handle
mov  bx,NewSize      ; in kilobytes
call far ptr HMM     ; call XMS manager
cmp  ax,1            ; test for success
jne  error
```

The remaining three XMS functions deal with upper memory blocks and are discussed under that heading later in this chapter.

Like the EMS we previously examined, making effective use of XMS requires that many repetitive details be handled, so a library is the simplest way to deal with it. Following is a simplified library package, XMSUTL.C, which although stripped to the absolute essentials, may still suffice for most of your XMS needs:

```
/*
 * XMSUTL.C - translated from a Microsoft example
 *            compile using Borland or TC
 *            small memory model only
 *
 *      Provide interface to XMS drivers, callable from C programs
 *      All calls except XMS_Vers() return >= 0 if successful
 *              or < 0 for error, error code in low word.
 *
 */
#include <dos.h>                    /* for pseudoregister features */

static int Init = 0;                  /* flags whether init required */

static void NotInit( void )          /* default safety valve routine */
{ asm mov bl,0x80;                  /* "Not Implemented" return code */
  asm xor ax,ax;                                   /* signal failure */
}

static void (far * Entry)() = NotInit;       /* link to driver code */

int XMS_Present( void )           /* TRUE if driver ready to operate */
{ if( !Init )                                  /* if not initialized */
    { _AX = 0x4300;                              /* check for driver */
```

```
      geninterrupt( 0x2F );
      if( _AL == 0x80 )                        /* if XMS driver here */
        { _AX = 0x4310;                           /* get entry point */
          geninterrupt( 0x2F );
          Entry = MK_FP( _ES, _BX );
          Init = 1;                       /* set to TRUE if all okay */
        }
    }
  return Init;
}

long XMS_Vers( void )      /* returns version number or 0 if no XMS */
{ _AH = 0;                                     /* opcode VERSION */
  (*Entry)();                                 /* call the driver */
  return (long) _AX;                            /* version level */
}

long XMS_Avail( void )                 /* returns count or status */
{ long retval;
  _AH = 8;                                  /* XMS opcode QUERY */
  (*Entry)();                                 /* call the driver */
  if( _BL == 0 )                             /* if no error found */
    retval = (long) _AX;                      /* number of K free */
  else
    retval = 0xFFFF0000L + _BL;              /* return error value */
  return retval;
}

long XMS_Biggest( void )               /* returns count or status */
{ long retval;
  _AH = 8;                                  /* XMS opcode QUERY */
  (*Entry)();                                 /* call the driver */
  if( _BL == 0 )                             /* if no error found */
    retval = (long) _DX;                    /* biggest free block */
  else
    retval = 0xFFFF0000L + _BL;              /* return error value */
  return retval;
}

long XMS_Alloc( int n )               /* returns handle or status */
{ long retval;
```

```
  _AH = 9;                                          /* opcode ALLOCATE */
  _DX = n;                                         /* how many blocks? */
  (*Entry)();                                       /* call the driver */
  if( _AX )                                       /* if no error found */
    retval = (long) _DX;                   /* plug handle into return */
  else
    retval = 0xFFFF0000L + _BL;                  /* return error value */
  return retval;
}

long XMS_Free( unsigned handle )                     /* returns status */
{ long retval = 0L;
  _AH = 10;                                             /* opcode FREE */
  _DX = handle;                                 /* handle to be freed */
  (*Entry)();                                       /* call the driver */
  if( ! _AX )                                              /* if error */
    retval = 0xFFFF0000L + _BL;                   /* return its value */
  return retval;
}

long XMS_Move( void *MvBlok )                        /* returns status */
{ long retval = 0L;
  _SI = (unsigned) MvBlok;                 /* pass in parameter block */
  _AX = 11;                                             /* opcode MOVE */
  (*Entry)();
  if( ! _AX )                                              /* if error */
    retval = 0xFFFF0000L + _BL;
  return retval;
}

long XMS_Size( unsigned handle )            /* returns count or status */
{ long retval = 0L;
  _AH = 14;                                             /* opcode INFO */
  _DX = handle;                                 /* handle to get size */
  (*Entry)();                                       /* call the driver */
  if( _AX )                                       /* if no error found */
    retval = (long) _DX;                     /* plug size into return */
  else
    retval = 0xFFFF0000L + _BL;                  /* return error value */
  return retval;
}
```

```
long XMS_Left( unsigned handle )          /* returns count or status */
{ long retval = 0L;
  _AH = 14;                                          /* opcode INFO */
  _DX = handle;                                  /* handle to check */
  (*Entry)();                                    /* call the driver */
  if( _AX )                                     /* if no error found */
    retval = (long) _BL;                /* plug count into return */
  else
    retval = 0xFFFF0000L + _BL;               /* return error value */
  return retval;
}
```

Although XMSUTL was based on an assembly-language package originally published by Microsoft several years ago, I've translated it to C and trimmed it back somewhat. You must use a Borland compiler to create the OBJ file, because of the pseudoregister variables, but once you have the OBJ file (which is on the companion diskette) the actual library is compatible with all standard C compilers and linkers.

The nine functions within XMSUTL allow you to determine whether an XMS manager is present, to read its version data, and to determine both the total amount of XMS space free and the size of the largest free block. You can allocate a block, move data in either direction (using the MOVSTRUC parameter block defined in XMSUTL.H), and determine the size of any allocated EMB given its handle.

Prototypes for these functions are in XMSUTL.H, together with a type definition for the MOVSTRUC parameter block that must be used to move data into or out of an EMB.

```
/*
 * XMSUTL.H - header file for XMS utilities
 */
#ifndef XMS_UTL_
#define XMS_UTL_

int  XMS_Present( void );        /* TRUE if driver ready to operate */
long XMS_Vers( void );     /* returns version number or 0 if no XMS */
long XMS_Avail( void );                  /* returns count or status */
long XMS_Biggest( void );                /* returns count or status */
long XMS_Alloc( int n );                /* returns handle or status */
long XMS_Free( unsigned handle );                 /* returns status */
```

```
long XMS_Move( void *MvBlok );                        /* returns status */
long XMS_Size( unsigned handle );           /* returns count or status */
long XMS_Left( unsigned handle );           /* returns count or status */

typedef struct {
     long count;    /* number of bytes to move, must be even */
     int  SrcHdl;                /* source block's handle */
     unsigned long SrcOff;          /* offset into source block */
     int  DstHdl;           /* destination block's handle */
     unsigned long DstOff;     /* offset into destination block */
} MOVSTRUC;

#endif
```

Several features of this library are demonstrated by the `XMSTEST.C` program which follows:

```
/*
 * XMSTEST.C - Demonstrate use of XMSUTL package
 * Jim Kyle - March 1993
 */
#include <stdio.h>
#include "xmsutl.h"

void main( void )
{ int vers;
  unsigned hdl;
  long total_free, total_used = 0L;

  puts( "\nXMSTEST - demonstrates XMSUTL routines\n" );
  if( XMS_Present() )
    { vers = (int)XMS_Vers();                     /* report the version */
      printf( "XMS Version is %d.%d%d\n",
              vers >> 8,
              (vers & 0xF0) >> 4,
              vers & 0xF );

      total_free = XMS_Avail();                     /* gather size data */
      printf( "   XMS still free: %8lu bytes (%5dK)\n",
              total_free << 10,
              total_free );
```

```
        printf( "    Largest block: %8lu bytes (%5dK)\n",
                XMS_Biggest() << 10,
                XMS_Biggest() );

        for( hdl = 1;                 /* count and report blocks in use */
             hdl < 65535;
             hdl++ )
          { long size = XMS_Size( hdl );
            if( size > 0 )
              { printf( "\tHandle %4X uses %8lu bytes (%5dK)\n",
                        hdl,
                        size << 10,
                        size );
                total_used += size;
              }
          }
        printf( "Total XMS present: %8lu bytes (%5dK)\n",
                ( total_free + total_used ) << 10,
                ( total_free + total_used ) );
      }
    else
      puts( "No XMS Driver could be found." );
}
```

The only unusual feature that shows up here is the brute-force approach taken to determining how much XMS memory is in use, and thereby calculating the total amount present in the system. Because the XMS specification provides no function that reports this information directly, it's necessary to cycle through all possible EMB handles, calling the handle-info function `XMS_Size()` for each. If the handle is not valid, an error results. Otherwise, the returned size is added to the total being accumulated.

This loop makes the program take an appreciable amount of time to run, even on a fast system, but at present no more direct method to obtain the information seems to exist. Possibly some future version of the XMS specification will give us such a function.

To compile `XMSTEST`, it's necessary to use a Borland compiler if you compile `XMSUTL` at the same time as shown in Figure 8.12. However, there's nothing in `XMSTEST.C` itself that is vendor-specific, so you also can use it under Microsoft compilers without change if you link in XMSUTL.OBJ after the compilation.

```
C:\>bcc xmstest.c xmsutl.c
Borland C++  Version 3.00 Copyright (c) 1991 Borland International
xmstest.c:
xmsutl.c:
Warning xmsutl.c 20: Suspicious pointer conversion
Turbo Link  Version 5.0 Copyright (c) 1991 Borland International

        Available memory 2116568

C:\>
```

Figure 8.12. XMSTEST with XMSUTL.C compiles just as cleanly as did EMSTEST; as you can tell from the source code, both follow essentially the same pattern except that one deals with expanded memory while the other manages extended memory.

When XMSTEST.EXE is run from within a Windows 3.1 DOS box, it shows results that are little short of amazing. For instance, Figure 8.13 shows the report obtained in a system that has only 5120 kilobytes of RAM total, and of that amount, the low 640K are occupied by MS-DOS even when Windows is running so the total XMS size cannot physically exceed some 4480 kilobytes.

Nevertheless, the illustration shows that XMS finds 4069 kilobytes of EMB's in use but still shows 996 kilobytes free, for a total of 5054K XMS in the system: this is just 66K less that the total of physical RAM, so obviously there's some kind of discrepancy present.

There is, of course, and it's the result the Windows "virtual memory" features that were in use when Figure 8.13 was captured from the screen. Some of the XMS handles listed here no longer referred to physical locations in extended memory, but instead to areas that had been swapped out to a swapfile on disk. This can happen because Windows provides its own built-in drivers for both EMS and XMS, which take the place of the DOS versions and permit virtual memory to operate.

When the program is run in the same system, but from outside the Windows environment, the report obtained is significantly different. Figure 8.14 shows only some 4 megabytes of XMS memory present. This is all physical memory.

You can see that the first two handles remain unchanged between the two captures, but from that point on there's little similarity. The megabyte at handle A912 is the cache provided by SMARTDRV, which reduces itself automatically to half size when Windows is invoked.

```
C:\>xmstest

XMSTEST - demonstrates XMSUTL routines

XMS Version is 2.00
   XMS still free:  1019904 bytes (  996K)
    Largest block:  1019904 bytes (  996K)
      Handle A8FE uses     557056 bytes (  544K)
      Handle A908 uses     103424 bytes (  101K)
      Handle A912 uses     524288 bytes (  512K)
      Handle A91C uses     545792 bytes (  533K)
      Handle A926 uses    2398208 bytes ( 2342K)
      Handle A930 uses      26624 bytes (   26K)
Total XMS present:  5175296 bytes ( 5054K)

C:\>
```

Figure 8.13. This capture from within a Windows 3.1 MS-DOS box underscores Windows' profligate use of extended memory. Contrast it with Figure 8.14, which shows the same system without Windows running.

```
C:\>xmstest

XMSTEST - demonstrates XMSUTL routines

XMS Version is 3.00
   XMS still free:  2393088 bytes ( 2337K)
    Largest block:  2393088 bytes ( 2337K)
      Handle A8FE uses     557056 bytes (  544K)
      Handle A908 uses     103424 bytes (  101K)
      Handle A912 uses    1048576 bytes ( 1024K)
      Handle A91C uses      26624 bytes (   26K)
Total XMS present:  4128768 bytes ( 4032K)

C:\>
```

Figure 8.14. This is how MS-DOS Version 6 uses XMS in my home system when Windows is not running. The megabyte being used by handle A912 is the SMARTDRV cache area.

Managing Upper Memory Blocks

One of the major changes introduced to MS-DOS in Version 5.0, and not significantly changed in version 6.0, was the ability to use upper memory blocks (UMB's) interchangeably with conventional memory.

While the most usual use of UMB's is to load TSR programs, via the `LOADHIGH` facility of COMMAND.COM or compatible alternate command interpreters, you also can use them from within your applications in exactly the same way that conventional RAM is allocated and released.

The key to using the UMB area is to control the link between upper memory and conventional RAM that is maintained by the XMS driver or memory manager that actually controls them. You do this by using subfunctions of MS-DOS Function 58h that were added to the system in Version 5.0.

Subfunction 02h gets the current state of the link, while subfunction 03h establishes a new state. Both functions return an error code of 1 if they are not supported by the version of MS-DOS that is being used. Following is the calling sequence, in assembly language:

```
mov  ah,58h          ; memory strategy
mov  al,2            ; get link state
int  21h             ; call MS-DOS
jc   error
mov  LinkFlag,al     ; 1=linked, 0=unlinked
```

If the upper memory chain is linked to the chain in conventional RAM, `LinkFlag` will contain 1 upon executing this code fragment. If the link is broken, the result will be 0.

The official MS-DOS Programmer's Reference for Version 5.0 indicates that the carry flag will be clear upon return if the upper memory chain is linked but is unclear about its condition otherwise. To make it easier to determine just what you can expect in such cases, I and a CompuServe friend, Jim Harrington, did a bit of experimenting. Jim reports that he found only two error codes to be returned no matter what kind of problem he created prior to making a call:

If no XMS driver is loaded under MS-DOS Version 5.0 or 6.0, or if the call is attempted under earlier versions of the operating system, the carry flag is set and the code returned in AX is 1.

If upper memory is being controlled by the third-party program 386MAX (which we'll meet in another few pages), no UMB linkage can be done. The carry flag is set, and the error code in AX is 2.

Although some references indicate that Subfunction 2 will return an error code of 7 if it encounters a corrupt memory arena condition, Jim wrote, "I have been unable to get Subfunction 2 to return an error under any condition (except under 386MAX)."

Even after going to such extremes as deliberately destruction of a link in the MCB chain, every call to the function returned the correct `LinkFlag` value and no indication of error. Of course, the system was unusable after each such attempt until it was rebooted, because it would lock up on the next attempt to allocate RAM, but Subfunction 2 failed to report the problem.

Setting a new link state condition is the job of Subfunction 3 of MS-DOS Function 58h. Following is the calling sequence:

```
mov  bl,LinkFlag     ; 1=linked, 0=unlinked
mov  al,03h          ; set link
mov  ah,58h          ; Function 58h
int  21h             ; call MS-DOS
jc   error
```

The error codes returned by this subfunction also appear to differ from those that its documentation suggests. While it is supposed to return 1 if loaded without `DOS=UMB` being in effect, or 7 if the arena is corrupted, like Subfunction 2 it appears to ignore the corrupt memory arena condition completely, and to return 1 as its only error code regardless of the reason for the error. Possible causes of an error would be the absence of an XMS driver, the lack of an enabling `DOS=UMB` line in CONFIG.SYS, or a corrupted memory arena.

To enable use of UMB's with the normal MS-DOS allocation functions, first call Subfunction 2 to determine the current link state, and save the value that it returns. Next, call Subfunction 0 to obtain the current allocation strategy, and save that value also. Then call Subfunction 3 with BL set to 1, to link the UMB chain, and Subfunction 1 with an appropriate value in BX to establish your allocation strategy. Before leaving your program, restore the saved conditions for both link state and allocation strategy, to avoid surprising your users with strange results from the program that they run *after* yours is done.

Once the upper memory chain has been linked into the allocation strategy, and the strategy set appropriately as discussed under conventional RAM earlier (usually using code 80h, which searches upper memory first and moves on to use conventional RAM only if a request cannot be satisfied with a UMB), then UMB space is allocated and released via the conventional functions 48h, 49h, and 4Ah. Any space allocated by this technique will be automatically freed when the program terminates along with the conventional-RAM area that the program uses.

If an XMS driver is present, it's possible to allocate and release UMB's without using the MS-DOS functions. This permits a program to make use of them without relying on `DOS=UMB` activating the linkage feature, or even under versions of MS-DOS prior to 5.0.

Direct allocation and release of UMB's is handled through the XMS driver in much the same manner as XMS allocation, but using different subfunctions. Subfunction 10h of the XMS interface allocates a UMB of specified size. Following is the calling sequence, in assembly language:

```
mov  ah,10h          ; get UMB
mov  dx,Size         ; desired, in paragraphs
call far ptr HMM     ; call XMS manager
cmp  ax,1            ; test for success
jne  error
mov  UMBSeg,bx       ; segment address of block
mov  BlkSize,dx      ; actual size in paragraphs
```

It's always best to test the returned block size in DX against the size you asked for, to be certain that you actually obtained the amount requested. In some cases an XMS driver may fail to provide the full block size requested, yet also fail to detect the error.

It's also always necessary to verify that UMB's are actually present before making any attempt to obtain them directly. If `DOS=UMB` is in effect, making it possible to allocate the space conventionally, then no more blocks will be available for direct allocation. During the boot process, MS-DOS itself uses this interface to snatch up all available UMB's so that it will retain full control over their allocation.

To release an allocated UMB back to the XMS manager, Subfunction 11h of the XMS interface is needed. Following is the calling sequence:

```
mov  ah,11h          ; release UMB
mov  dx,UMBSeg       ; block to release
call far ptr HMM     ; call XMS manager
cmp  ax,1            ; test for success
jne  error
```

You can change the allocated size of a UMB with Subfunction 12h of the XMS interface. It's called as follows:

```
mov  ah,12h          ; reallocate UMB
mov  bx,NewSize      ; in paragraphs
mov  dx,UMBSeg       ; block to reallocate
call far ptr HMM     ; call XMS manager
cmp  ax,1            ; test for success
jne  error
```

Three possible errors can result from this call. An error code of 80h indicates that the function is not implemented in the XMS manager, a code of B0h means that no UMB large enough to satisfy the request is available, and a code of B2h indicates that the supplied UMB segment number is not valid.

If a code of B0h, indicating no block large enough to fill the request is available, is returned, then DX contains the size in paragraphs of the largest block that *is* available.

Managing the High Memory Area

The final area of memory above conventional RAM that may require management is the High Memory Area (HMA), the 65,520 bytes immediately above the 1-megabyte mark that can be accessed from real mode although technically a part of the extended memory.

Users of MS-DOS versions 5.0 and 6.0 usually turn the HMA over to MS-DOS for its own use, by including the line `DOS=HIGH` in the CONFIG.SYS file. This frees a significant amount of conventional RAM for use by applications. However, the XMS specification provides methods for direct allocation of the HMA, and you should be aware that such techniques exist although we don't explore them here in any detail.

General-Purpose Memory Managers

In MS-DOS Version 6.0, you can use two drivers furnished with the system, HIMEM.SYS and EMM386.EXE, to provide complete memory management. They deal with the HMA, UMB's, XMS, and even emulate EMS. But with older versions of MS-DOS, especially those prior to Version 5.0, it was necessary to turn to a third-party memory management program for full capabilities.

Two such programs, QEMM.SYS from Quarterdeck Office Systems and 386MAX from Qualitas, are still widely used and both still offer some performance bonuses over those available from the system-supplied drivers.

Because your applications should not be sensitive to the specific memory management software installed in any user's system, as long as that software meets the accepted standards, it's important to you as a developer to know how the systems vary from each other, and all areas in which any of them departs from standards.

Both QEMM and the Microsoft-supplied drivers provide full support for the UMB linkage subfunctions 2 and 3 of MS-DOS Function 58h, but 386MAX does not and instead returns an undocumented error code of `2`.

This departure of 386MAX from accepted standards means that in order to create truly bulletproof code that deals with upper memory block allocation, you must first check to determine whether 386MAX is installed in the system. If it is, UMB allocation cannot be done.

While no explicit function to test for the presence of 386MAX is known, an indirect test can be performed easily, by attempting to open the character device named `386MAX$$` and if a device or file by that name is located, checking via `IOCTL` to verify that it is actually a character device rather than a file. Following is typical code to perform such a test:

```
.model tiny                         ; so that DS=CS
.data
     name db    '386MAX$$',0
.code
          mov  ax,3D00h            ; open file/device
          mov  dx,offset name
          int  21h
          jc   No386MAX
          mov  bx,ax
          mov  ax,4400h            ; IOCTL get attributes
          int  21h
          push dx             ; save the results
          mov  ah,3Eh              ; close it in any case
          int  21h
          pop  dx
          test dx,128              ; char/device bit
          jz   No386MAX            ; block, not 386MAX
```

This fragment of code first attempts to open the device by means of MS-DOS Function 3Dh. If it cannot do so, then obviously 386MAX cannot be present in the system. If the open attempt succeeds, though, there's an outside chance that the system might actually contain a file of that name, rather than having such a device in place, so the additional test using MS-DOS Function 44h is necessary.

After calling Function 4400h to obtain the attributes associated with the handle, the next step is to close the handle since no more reference to it will be made no matter which way the test turns out. Then the bit in the attribute word that distinguishes between character and block device drivers can be tested; if it's not a file, the only safe assumption is that 386MAX is, in fact, present in the system.

All of this may sound as if 386MAX is a product to be avoided; that's definitely not a valid conclusion. I've used all three of the top memory managers, 386MAX, QEMM, and EMM386. Prior to MS-DOS Version 6, there was no question in my mind that 386MAX was the best for my way of working. With the advent of added capability for EMM386 in Version 6, the decision becomes a bit more difficult, but to me 386MAX still has the edge for a developer's use.

QEMM, however, has many devoted followers, and the differences between the products are actually much like the differences between one make of automobile and another. All of them give good results. But to avoid unexpected error returns, don't try using UMB allocation via MS-DOS Function 48h if 386MAX is present, because it doesn't support all the functions required.

Jim Harrington advises me that everything said regarding 386MAX also holds true for Qualitas' BlueMax memory manager, a special version of 386MAX for use in MicroChannel Architecture systems.

UMB memory can still be allocated directly from the XMS driver, when 386MAX is present, using direct calls to XMS. Both the other managers (QEMM or EMM386.EXE plus HIMEM.SYS) give the results one expects when an XMS driver is present.

Another disquieting situation can arise when general purpose memory managers are present in a system. All three memory management packages include optimization programs which attempt to determine the best arrangement of material in conventional RAM and the UMB space, and rewrite CONFIG.SYS and AUTOEXEC.BAT files based on their findings.

The analysis program included with QEMM is called OPTIMIZE, and is called by Quarterdeck "one of the most important features" of the package. With 386MAX, you get MAXIMIZE, and with MS-DOS Version 6.0 itself you get MEMMAKER.

All these programs follow the same general approach. They first create temporary CONFIG.SYS and AUTOEXEC.BAT files to be sure that all TSR and driver programs are loaded in conventional RAM, and hook a driver into the MS-DOS loader function that can determine the amount of space required to load each program, and the amount occupied when loading is finished. Neither value bears any necessary relation to the size of the program's actual executable file.

The programs then reboot the system, with all instrumentation in place, and obtain the needed size data. They then try many different combinations of program sequence, attempting to find the single combination that maximizes the amount of space left in conventional RAM.

When this stage of their action is done, they again modify CONFIG.SYS and AUTOEXEC.BAT to reflect their findings, remove all the instrumentation hooks, and reboot the system once more. The expected result at this time is that you will have more conventional RAM available than you did before running the analyzer, and that system operation will not be affected in any other way.

Unfortunately, all three analyzer programs fail to take into full account possible interactions between different drivers, which may require one of the drivers to be loaded first before the other can work. One such case appears when a SCSI disk controller driver uses Interrupt 67h for its own purposes, while the EMS manager requires this same interrupt vector.

That conflict is normally handled by a special small driver that must be installed in CONFIG.SYS ahead of the line that installs the EMS manager, but most of the analyzers fail to recognize this situation and put the EMS manager in front of nearly everything else.

If your system happens to boot from the SCSI disk that lost its critical setup information because of this, you will be unable to boot from the disk until the conflict is repaired by moving the special SCSI back above the EMS manager.

Fortunately, MS-DOS Version 6.0 provides escapes via function keys F5 and F8 to bypass part or all of CONFIG.SYS, making it much easier to get out of such traps than it was with prior versions, but it's still a problem and you must be aware of its potential to confuse your users, who may run an analyzer yet have no knowledge of all the things that can go wrong.

Especially if your application installs as a TSR or driver and has any such dependencies upon other things being present, you will find this blind rearrangement of sequence to be one of the largest creators of technical support calls from end users. You can save many headaches by eliminating every such dependence that you possibly can.

The final aspect of general purpose memory managers that we examine here involves the use of protected mode on 80386 and later systems. Many current programs require more memory than real mode can provide, and so make use of DOS extenders. A number of different such extenders exist, and several volumes have been written exclusively on the subject of their use.

A standard for interfacing DOS and protected mode, however, has evolved and many of the most recent programs use it. It's known as the DOS Protected-Mode Interface, or DPMI. Any program that requires protected mode but makes all reference to it via the documented DPMI interface can operate under any memory manager that provides full DPMI support, making such programs independent of any specific DOS extender utility.

Currently, both 386MAX and QEMM provide DPMI managers, so using either of them allows use of compilers such as Borland C++ and Microsoft's Visual C++, both of which require DPMI, from the MS-DOS command line.

On the other hand, the memory managers supplied with MS-DOS version 6.0 do not support DPMI, making it necessary to either change to one of the other managers for development operations, or to do all development from within the Windows 3.1 environment, since Windows 3.1 is itself a DPMI provider.

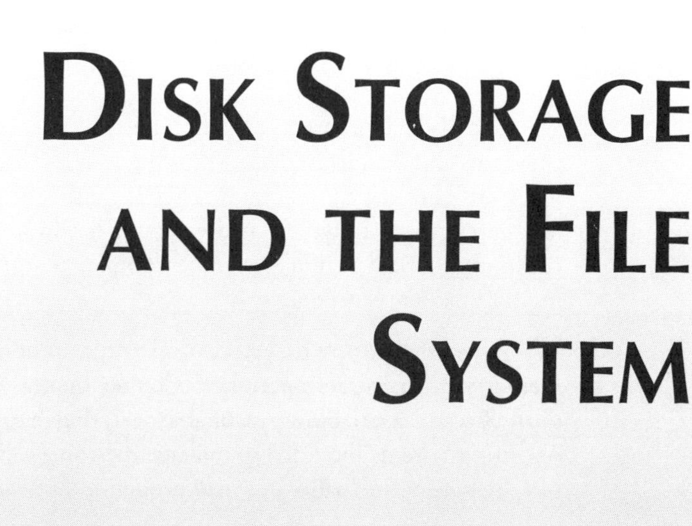

Disk Storage and the File System

In the very earliest days of personal computing, when the "console" was a clattering Teletype machine and four kilobytes was an unbelievably large amount of RAM, the only type of storage available was punched paper tape. Slow and bulky as it was, this was still far better than the only alternative: setting each byte of a program into front-panel switches!

One of the first targets of the pioneers was to devise a method for keeping programs and data from one computing session to another; their first solution was to use ordinary audio tape cassettes, and this worked quite well. Within only a few years, however, as the cost of hardware dropped steadily and the computing tasks became ever more complex, computer hobbyists were looking for a better technique.

When the floppy diskette, originally intended as a form of read-only memory for mainframe peripherals rather than as a serious data storage medium, became available at reasonable cost, they had what they needed. Several operating systems intended to manage the complexities of disk input and output, including the loading of new programs, appeared soon thereafter.

One of these, Gary Kildall's *CP/M* (Control Program for Microcomputers), became an industry standard despite its requirement for special custom adaptation to every different system in which it was installed. Its architecture, which divided the system into a *Basic Input Output System* (BIOS), a *Basic Disk Operating System* (BDOS), and a *transient program area* (TPA) survives to this day in MS-DOS. For that matter, CP/M itself remains alive and well, though it's no longer the industry standard system.

At a time when the systems were built primarily by people who used them as a hobby, the requirement for individual customization was no drawback. Creating your own version of BIOS was half the fun of building a new system, and patching it to work with a new video terminal or disk controller board just added to the enjoyment.

But the advent of CP/M also gave rise to the desktop computer industry. The emphasis began to shift away from the hobbyists, and toward small and midscale business users who had no interest in dealing with the system software or the hardware. These users did not want a toy; they wanted only a machine that would perform useful work.

This trend was already firmly established when MS-DOS made its appearance with the original IBM Personal Computer in 1981. The availability of a huge variety of business-oriented CP/M software that could easily be translated to work with the new system propelled MS-DOS to a position of leadership over the other two systems that IBM offered for its new line.

Through all this history, the subject of data storage and retrieval on magnetic disks is the common factor. This capability is the main reason that MS-DOS exists, and your applications will use it extensively.

As a developer, you must be familiar with the conventional techniques for dealing with disk storage, as well as many that you may need only rarely. This chapter is intended to introduce you to all these techniques. It does not, however, delve deeply into the darker mysteries of disk interfacing that should never affect your applications. Neither does it explore the murky world of network disk interfacing, which varies from one brand of network to another and would require a volume in itself for accurate coverage.

This chapter begins with the physical fundamentals of information storage on magnetic media, with particular emphasis on the disks most commonly used. Next, we examine the logical structures involved, including the new Microsoft Realtime Compression Interface introduced with MS-DOS version 6.0.

With this background, we can approach the file system itself and see how it organizes data so that storage and retrieval can be done easily. Here we discuss the multi-level directory system and how to deal with it.

Finally, we discuss the various techniques for actual storage and retrieval, including the original methods based on File Control Blocks, the more versatile functions that make use of "handle" identifiers, and how to deal with errors that may occur at runtime.

Physical Fundamentals

While the audio tape cassette was still in wide enough use at the time IBM introduced its first PC, and the BIOS includes routines for dealing with it, use of tapes for primary data storage never gained significant acceptance under MS-DOS. From the beginning, the magnetic disk has been the standard medium for information storage.

Today, magnetic tapes are used for backing up fixed disk drives, but for primary storage the disk still has no serious competitor. In the sections that follow, we look at how disk capacity grew, from the 160,000 bytes available on the first floppy diskettes to the multi-megabyte fixed disk drives commonly used now, and develop a vocabulary for defining disk interface requirements. We also begin discussion of actual techniques by dispelling some myths that surround write verification, and see how to control this seldom-useful feature.

The Historical Record

While the floppy diskette sprang full-grown into the world of desktop computing, it had significant history in its native universe, that of the mainframes. In this universe, the mammoth *Direct Access Storage Device* (IBM's term for any fixed disk drive) ruled supreme. The floppy originated at IBM in 1971 as a "cheap-and-dirty" variant of the DASD idea intended to provide read-only memory as a program loading device.

The earliest DASDs were unbelievably huge. They were mounted in cabinets the size of a large refrigerator. Because they required actuating mechanisms that were capable of creating as much as 100 G's of acceleration, if something happened to go wrong with one, it could walk itself right across the floor of the computer room and crash through walls like an insane robot. (If you have ever watched a washing machine with an unbalanced load attempt to shake itself to death, you've seen a small sample of what happened on more than one occasion.)

For that matter, the first floppy diskettes used by CP/M systems weren't so small themselves. Eight inches in diameter and recorded on only one surface, they deserved the diminuitive "ette" suffix to their name only by comparison to their monster brothers. This variety of floppy disk appeared in 1973 and established Shugart Associates as the leading manufacturer of small floppy disk drives. When the microprocessor appeared two years later, the firm was ready.

In 1976, Shugart launched its model SA400, a 5.25-inch mini floppy drive that had been designed at the express request of a personal-computer firm. The SA400 had a capacity of 110K bytes, only 1/8 that of the 8-inch double-density units, but its small size rapidly made it the standard unit for personal-computer applications, five full years before the advent of IBM's PC.

The SA400 had only one recording/playback head and so could use only one surface of the diskette. The rotation speed (300 RPM) and the limitations of the medium and existing head technology allowed no more than about 5000 bytes of information to be recorded on a single track.

The rated capacity of 110K resulted from the standards accepted at that time for speed tolerance and hardware response times together with the use of IBM's standard 128-byte sector size. Experimenters soon discovered, though, that increasing the sector size while reducing the number of sectors per track would reduce the amount of space lost to inter-record gaps, and when they reached eight 512-byte sectors on each track, the result was a capacity of 160K bytes.

The 160K size was still accepted as standard when the IBM PC appeared in 1981, but not long afterward, speed tolerances were tightened. This permitted sectors to be placed closer to each other on the track, which made room for 9 sectors rather than 8 and raised the capacity to 180K. The next improvement was to add a second head to the drive so that both sides of the diskette could be used, creating the 360K format still in wide use.

At about the same time, Sony introduced a 3.5-inch floppy disk drive with a capacity of 438K, a 600-RPM rotation speed, and an innovative diskette package that totally protected the fragile recording surface. Nothing much happened immediately.

Several years passed without additional major changes to diskette format. The 80-track drives for ordinary diskettes that had been commonly used with some other operating systems failed to gain acceptance with MS-DOS.

With the introduction of the PC-AT line, an entirely new diskette and format appeared. Called *high density* to distinguish it from the older device, this drive spun its diskettes at higher speed and packed much more information on each of its 80 tracks, providing 1.2 megabytes of storage.

It took until 1987 for Sony's 3.5-inch design to catch on in the MS-DOS world. Along the way its capacity was increased to 720K and the spindle speed reduced to 300 RPM, but it still fits easily into a shirt pocket. Almost immediately, a doubled version offering 1.44 megabytes showed up and now is standard for the distribution of compilers and other development tools. By 1989, shipments of 3.5-inch drives had passed those of 5.25-inch units.

As the time of this writing, another major extension of diskette capabilities appears to be taking place. A 2.88-megabyte diskette is available, and also a 20-megabyte "Floptical" using the 3.5-inch format. Both require special drives, and neither is yet supported by any version of MS-DOS, but can be added by using special device drivers furnished with the drives. One drawback to them is that even Version 6.0 of MS-DOS treats these devices as fixed disks and refuses to acknowledge that they have removable media.

Even before the appearance of today's file structure, in MS-DOS version 2.0, fixed disks were available as third-party add-on devices. The most widely-used unit was Shugart's 5.25-inch unit which appeared in 1980. The first IBM unit to include a fixed disk was the XT, with its 10-megabyte unit. At the time, it seemed like more than anyone could reasonably hope to fill.

But Parkinson's Law about work expanding to consume available time has a corollary applicable to disk storage devices: needs expand to surpass available space. Soon, 20-megabyte drives were the standard. Not long after that, program sizes took another quantum leap, and disk sizes followed suit. Today a 100-megabyte drive is hardly large enough for serious software development.

All magnetic storage devices commonly used with MS-DOS, whether floppy diskette, fixed disk, or magnetic tape, transfer their information between the magnetic medium itself and the computer system as a serial stream of signals which take the form of voltage fluctuations. A disk controller circuit converts these signals to and from the familiar byte-oriented format that our programs deal with.

Through the years, several different recording formats have been used, and in addition, a number of interface standards exist. These formats and interface standards have created a veritable jungle of alphabet soup. The most common recording formats are *MFM* and *RLL*. The interface standards include ST-506, IDE, EDSI, and SCSI. And all these may, or may not, make use of DMA. Let's delve into these acronyms and see what they mean, before we deal with the disk storage formats themselves.

The recording format abbreviations stand for *modified frequency modulation* and *run length limited*. Without going into excessive technical detail, it's necessary to maintain extremely accurate timing information on the disk in order to separate the continuous stream of signals into individual bytes. These two formats represent two different ways of doing that.

Because the rotation speed of the disk itself may vary, the only reliable method of providing sufficiently accurate timing is to combine a clock signal right into the data stream. Both MFM and RLL formats do this. With MFM, a regular stream of clock pulses is fed in, and the data bits are represented by pulses at the midpoint of each clock interval. This means that a byte of all zero bits would be represented as 8 clock pulses with no intermixed data pulses, while a byte of all ones would total 16 pulses, alternating between clock and data.

This format works, and works well. It's still the standard for all four of the official floppy-diskette types. But it's not really necessary to provide all 8 clock pulses. Information theorists discovered back in the 1960s that at least half of them could be eliminated by proper intermediate coding, and that's what the RLL technique does. Rather than using up to 16 pulses to represent each byte, it uses a maximum of 12 together with lookup-table encoding and decoding in the disk controller circuits. An RLL controller can store approximately half again more data on the same platter as can the MFM approach, but for successful use of RLL, much higher quality in the recording medium itself is necessary.

Several years ago the distinction between MFM and RLL was controversial, but today's high-capacity drives universally use some variant of the RLL technique together with very high mechanical precision to pack as many bytes into as small a physical space as they do.

Now, what about the interface standards? The ST-506 standard originally was a proprietary interface developed by Seagate, but became so widely-used that it was the de facto industry standard for many years. If you have a disk controller that doesn't claim to be of some other type, it's probably an ST-506.

One of the distinguishing characteristics of the ST-506 interface was that most of the electronic circuits were concentrated on the disk controller board. The drive itself contained only enough circuitry to boost the signal to levels that could be sent through the connecting cable, and to permit positioning and writing of data.

As ever-greater storage capacity was sought, designers explored the use of much higher recording densities. Packing many more bits into each time interval, however, involved signals of higher frequency, and the distance travelled by the raw signal between the drive's head and the controller board was recognized as a limiting factor.

The first attempt to improve transfer rates involved redesigning the venerable ST-506 interface, and resulted in something called the *Enhanced Small Device Interface* or ESDI. Appearing on the scene about 1986, this system (like ST-506) directly interfaces the system bus to the disk controller, but both the controller and the disk drives were designed with emphasis on speed. The ESDI approach remains unmatched for speed of data transfer, though its lead is no longer a commanding one.

A disadvantage of ESDI was that it appeared only on high-capacity drives. Nevertheless, it has been widely used, notably on the large disk drives for the PS/2 line's high-end models.

For smaller drives, the ST-506 interface was eventually replaced by moving most of the electronics from the controller into the drive itself. This technique, termed *Integrated Drive Electronics* or IDE, today is possibly the most widely-known of all the formats.

For large drives, ESDI is rapidly being displaced by another standard which began at Seagate, like ST-506, in 1979 to connect 8-inch Winchester drives to minicomputers, and later became ANSI standard X3.131-1986.

This rising standard now is known as the *Small Computer System Interface* or SCSI. Long used in the Macintosh world, it's gaining prominence in MS-DOS also. The major advantage of SCSI over IDE or ESDI is that one SCSI Host Adapter on your system bus can handle up to seven different drives, whereas with IDE each drive must have its own adapter and with ESDI only two drives can be connected to a single controller.

Additionally, the SCSI standard is defined for magnetic tape units, printers, CD-ROM readers, and image scanners, as well as for disk drives. A single SCSI Host Adapter can provide the interface for all these different kinds of units, which is a definite advantage for a development system. Most developers find their first major hardware problem to be a severe shortage of adapter slots to handle all the peripherals required.

From the standpoint of MS-DOS, it makes no difference at all whether a device is MFM or RLL, or whether it uses the ST-506, IDE, ESDI, or SCSI interface standard. The only thing that matters is that it has a block device driver which meets MS-DOS standards. The driver built into the IO.SYS hidden file handles ST-506 and IDE devices without assistance; drives that use other interfaces usually have appropriate drivers included with them.

What about DMA? What is it all about? This acronym stands for *direct memory access* and refers to the method by which blocks of data are transferred between the MS-DOS buffers and the disk drive itself. Your application, when it uses MS-DOS functions, places data into or removes it from these buffers. The job of MS-DOS itself is moving the data between the buffers and the drives.

When DMA is used, the disk controller can initiate a block transfer, and then return control to MS-DOS so that other tasks can be performed while the transfer takes place. In the absence of DMA, the controller must move data into the buffers one byte at a time as it is received from the drive, and no other significant actions can occur.

In practice, unless special drivers are used, it really makes almost no difference whether DMA is used because the only other task performed by the standard MS-DOS code is to ask the controller if the transfer is complete yet. This situation, however, may change with the next generation of high-performance operating systems, so it's still useful to know what DMA means.

Geometry, Yet!

Regardless of the kind or size of disk involved, all data storage and retrieval from magnetic disks uses a standard set of terms to describe how the information is arranged, and to address specific data records for retrieval.

The basic unit of storage is a surface of a rotating disk. Sometimes disk engineers will speak of the number of *platters* in a unit, meaning the number of separate disks in the stack. Many small fixed disks have three platters, providing four surfaces. The top of the upper platter and the bottom of the lower one are not used; the surfaces are the bottom of the upper disk, both sides of the center one, and the top of the lower one.

Each surface has an associated *head* and the surface is addressed by its head number. Heads are numbered conventionally, starting with 0. A double-sided floppy drive has two heads, 0 and 1. A 4-surface fixed disk has 4, numbered 0 through 3.

If the head remains in one position, it traces a circle on the surface as the disk rotates. This circle, shown greatly exaggerated in Figure 9.1, is known as a *track*. Each surface has many tracks; the heads move laterally, toward or away from the center of the disk, to be positioned over each track in turn. Floppy drives have either 40 or 80 tracks, while fixed disks may have up to 1023 (more are possible, but most BIOS code imposes this limit).

The tracks on each surface are separated from each other by *guard bands* of unused space. Each time data is written to the disk, the write head actually records the entire track plus some spillover into both guard bands, and the erase head then trims the track width back to normal. This keeps the guard bands free of noise pulses.

In a fixed disk with multiple heads, all heads are attached to a single actuator assembly often called a *comb* so that they all move together. Thus when any head is positioned over a specific track on its surface, all other heads are over the similarly-numbered tracks on their own surfaces.

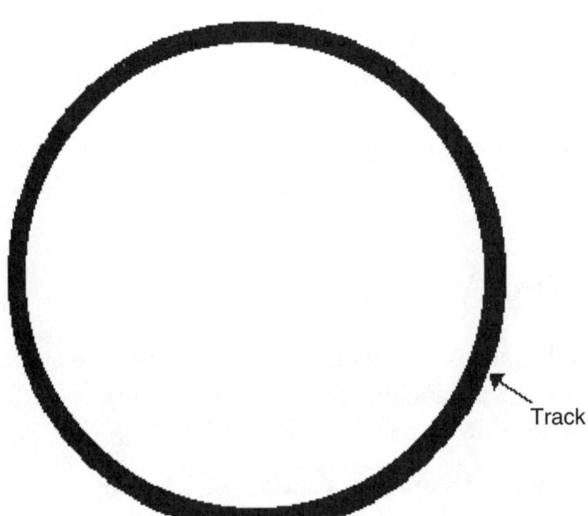

Figure 9.1. This exaggerated view of a single track on one surface of a disk is the starting point toward understanding physical disk addressing conventions. The track is traced by the drive's head, remaining fixed in one position while the disk rotates beneath it. Each surface has many such tracks, with unused space between them.

This combined movement of all heads together creates a virtual cylinder that expands and contracts in radius, and as a result the conventional method of specifying track addresses is by *cylinder* rather than by track number (see Figure 9.2). Both cylinders and tracks are numbered starting at the outer edge with 0 and moving in toward the center. Floppies with 40 tracks are numbered 0 through 39, and so on.

The cylinder convention came from mainframe usage, where multiple-track reads were normally done by remaining on the same cylinder as long as possible and switching to the next head when the current track was exhausted. This was much faster than the alternative of physically moving the actuator to a new track. In the MS-DOS world we don't take full advantage of this at all times, although it's certainly possible to do so.

A full track, on a 360K floppy diskette, holds approximately 5,000 bytes of data; with a fixed disk, the figure is even larger. This is far more than we usually want to read or write at one time, so each track is logically subdivided into sectors as shown in Figure 9.3. While this illustration shows only eight sectors in the track, current practice for 360K diskettes uses nine sectors per track, and high-density 1.2-megabyte diskettes use 17. The principle remains the same in all cases, though.

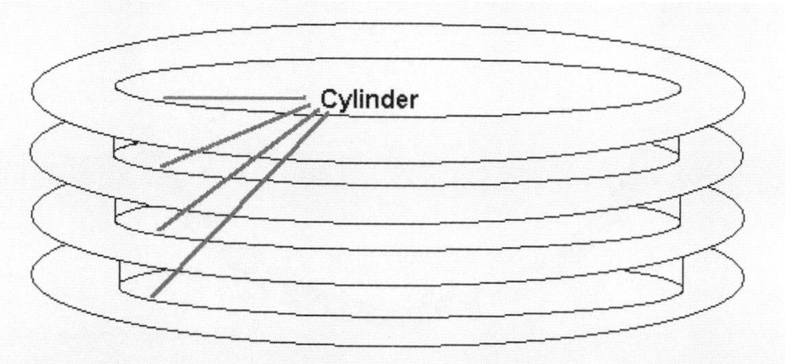

Figure 9.2. The "cylinder" that's used in specifying physical disk addresses consists of all tracks at the same distance from the spindle. This convention arose because switching from one head to another within the same cylinder is much faster than moving the actuator mechanism to a new track would be; multiple-sector reads can be done more efficiently as a result.

Unlike head, track, and cylinder numbering, sector numbering starts at 1. The location of Sector 1 is established by an index pulse (generated by a small hole near the disk hub in the case of most floppies, or by a magnetic sensor in the drive mechanism for fixed disks) that occurs once per revolution.

When a disk is formatted, this pulse determines the location at which the first sector is recorded, and precise timing (plus intersector gaps large enough to allow for all tolerances) takes care of the rest. When the disk is read or written, the pulse tells the controller to watch for *address marks* placed in the gaps by the formatting process. These marks contain the physical sector numbers. When the desired sector is found, the read or write head is switched into action.

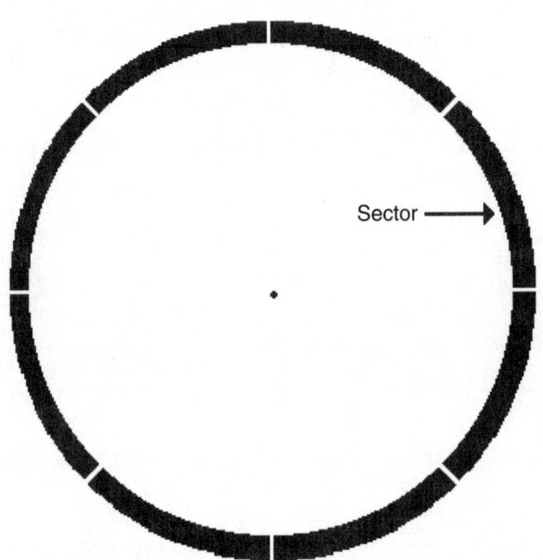

Figure 9.3. Each track is arbitrarily subdivided into sectors as shown here for improved convenience of use. This allows smaller chunks of data to be moved back and forth between the disk and RAM, but the more sectors a track contains, the more space must be "wasted" in intersector gaps to allow time for write heads to be switched off without damaging data on the next sector. The choice of sector size always involves this compromise between convenience and efficiency.

Physical Disk Addressing

Physical disk addresses may be expressed in either of two conventions, and the techniques for direct disk access we'll examine later in this chapter use both. The most explicit convention, used by both BIOS and the `IOCTL` functions of MS-DOS, specifies cylinder, head, and sector numbers separately, together with the number of sectors affected. A less obvious convention uses the *logical sector number* which ranges from 1 up to the maximum count of sectors on the device. This convention is used by Interrupts 25h and 26h.

Either convention can be converted to the other if you know the number of sectors per track, the number of heads, and the sector size (almost always

512 bytes in MS-DOS). You must also know how many reserved and hidden sectors exist in order to calculate the cylinder, head, and sector for Logical Sector Number 1.

The advantage of the separate addressing is that it makes possible access to any part of the disk, including the master boot record. The LSN method can address only non-hidden portions of the disk. For normal access to data, however (as opposed to reading or writing the administrative areas such as the MBR), the methods are essentially equivalent.

Write Verification

Before we go any deeper into the theory of disk organization, let's take time out to dispel a widely believed myth about writing data to the disk surface.

Since mainframe days, disk controllers have featured two forms of the *write* command, known as *write* and *write with verify*. These variants exist in the MS-DOS device drivers also, and the general belief is that using "verify" (by executing the command VERIFY ON, or adding the /V switch to COPY commands) provides total verification that the writing was done correctly.

Nothing could be less true. The *verify* action actually just causes the disk controller to do a dummy read of the data after it has been written, and compare the CRC byte that was generated by the controller at that time with the one that was written onto the record originally. No actual comparison of the data itself is attempted.

The major effect, therefore, is to test not the write action, but the disk controller, to see if it performs the same calculation twice running. And the cost of doing so is to cut disk throughput exactly in half, because every write must be followed by a read, and it will take one revolution of the disk to get the data back into position to read it.

It's far safer to do explicit byte-for-byte comparisons of the data written with that still in RAM, when accuracy is essential, and simply ignore the question at other times. For that reason, you should not have much need for the following two MS-DOS functions, which allow you to determine whether verify mode is in effect or not, and to control it.

To determine the current state of verification, use MS-DOS Function 24h. Following is the calling sequence, in assembly language:

```
mov     ah,24h          ; get verify flag
int     21h             ; call MS-DOS
mov     VfyFlag,al      ; 0=off, 1=on
```

To turn verification on or off, Function 2Eh is the one to use. Following is its calling sequence:

```
mov     al,VfyFlag      ; 0=off, 1=on
mov     ah,2Eh          ; set verify flag
int     21h             ; call MS-DOS
```

In both cases, 0 means that verification is not being done, and 1 means that it will be. When verification mode is on, every write to any disk gets the full verification treatment and accompanying delay in completion.

Logical Drive Structures

Most modern MS-DOS systems contain several physical disk drives. A typical configuration might include one 5.25-inch floppy, one 3.5-inch floppy, and one fixed disk. However, while this list shows only three drives, the system may have many more than just three logical drives, each of which appears to MS-DOS as if it were a physically separate unit. Before we move into the details of the file system, let's spend a few pages exploring the logical drive structures that may be present in any MS-DOS installation.

Identifying Disk Units

The most apparent logical drive units we see when we look at an MS-DOS system are the various letters used to reference the drives. By convention we know that Drive A: is the boot floppy, and if a second floppy is present it will be Drive B: (if not, B: becomes an alternate name for the A: drive, which can cause confusion; we'll get back to this later). The fixed disk is usually C:

It wasn't always so, however. In the early days it wasn't unusual to find four floppies on a system, set up as A: through D:, followed by a fixed disk known as Drive E:. The current conventions date from the introduction of the XT, when C: was hard-coded into the BIOS as the boot drive.

A number of MS-DOS functions deal with drive selection and housekeeping, and we might as well become familiar with them before moving on into more arcane aspects of the logical drive structures.

A common action, in CP/M days, was the *resetting* of the disk system; in that operating system, you were expected to manually perform this reset by pressing Control-C, each time you changed diskettes in any drive. The reset forced all old information out of the operating system's internal tables and replaced it with new data from the new disk.

While it's handled more or less automatically for you by MS-DOS, it's nice to remember that you can still use Control-C at the prompt to force all disk buffers to be flushed, and directory information reloaded. And you also can do this from within a program, by using MS-DOS Disk Reset Function 0Dh.

Following is the calling sequence, in assembly language, for this function:

```
mov     ah,0Dh              ; disk reset
int     21h                 ; call MS-DOS
```

It's really that simple. No return value, no error code, but all disk systems are fully reset.

One of the most fundamental operating assumptions within MS-DOS is the existence of a *current* or *default* drive. That's the drive that is used whenever you don't explicitly specify a drive letter.

When the system first starts up, the current drive is automatically set to the drive from which the system booted, usually C for a fixed-disk system or A if only floppies are available. The default command prompt displays the current drive's letter to let you know where you are. You can then "log into" any other drive by simply typing its letter and the colon identifier.

Programs, too, can ask MS-DOS to tell them the current default drive, or to log into another drive. These capabilities can be used together to make the program's drive switch totally invisible to the user, by first getting the default drive and saving it, then switching to a new drive to do the work, and finally switching back to the original drive before leaving the program.

The functions of Interrupt 21h that deal with the default drive are Function 19h, Get Current Default Drive, and Function 0Eh, Select Default Drive. The calling sequence, in assembly language, for Function 19h is:

```
mov     ah,19h          ; get default drive
int     21h             ; call MS-DOS
mov     CurDrv,al       ; current drive, A=0
```

Note that the drive numbers used here are zero-based, so that A: is represented by zero, B: by one, and so on. Many of the other drive functions we'll meet use 0 as the number for the current default drive, and represent A: by one. You have to continually be aware of which system is used by which function to stay out of trouble.

To select a new default drive, use this assembly language calling sequence:

```
mov     dl,CurDrv       ; zero-based, A=0
mov     ah,0Eh          ; set default drive
int     21h             ; call MS-DOS
mov     LogDrvs,al      ; number of drives
```

When Function 0Eh returns, the value in the AL register indicates the number of potentially valid drive letters, but this usually has little if anything to do with the actual number of drives present in the system. For example, under Novell's NetWare, the value is always 32 because that's the number of drive *letters* available (NetWare uses the punctuation marks having ASCII codes of 5Bh through 5Fh to indicate temporary drive assignments). Under normal MS-DOS from version 3.1 on up, the value is the greater of 5, the number associated with the `LASTDRIVE=` statement in CONFIG.SYS, or the number of actual drives present in the system, but you have no way to tell which of these three values is actually used.

Another aspect of drive "housekeeping" involves the buffer known as the Disk Transfer Area. This is a 128-byte space that MS-DOS will use as a scratchpad during such operations as `FindFirst` and `FindNext`. Each time a process begins execution, the DTA is set by default to offset 80h of its PSP. Interrupt 21h provides two functions to manipulate the DTA: Function 2Fh gets the current DTA address as a far pointer returned in ES:BX, while Function 1Ah sets a new DTA address.

Whenever your program uses one of the functions that employs the DTA, it's best to explicitly save the existing address, change to your own data space, and then restore the original address after calling the function that writes to the DTA.

Following is the calling sequence, in assembly language, to get the Disk Transfer Area address:

```
mov     ah,2Fh          ; get DTA
int     21h             ; call MS-DOS
mov     DTASeg,ES       ; current DTA segment
mov     DTAOff,BX       ; current DTA offset
```

To set the Disk Transfer Area address, use this calling sequence:

```
push     ds            ; save data segment
mov     ds,NewSeg      ; new DTA segment
mov     dx,NewOff      ; new DTA offset
mov     ah,1Ah         ; set DTA
int     21h            ; call MS-DOS
pop     ds             ; restore data segment
```

Neither of these functions returns any error code; the DTA simply is a far pointer that MS-DOS maintains in its own data area, and this far pointer always has some value. The value is always assumed to be valid. Thus you should take care to keep from passing invalid values to Function 1Ah, because any value you pass will be accepted without additional checking.

Partitioning

When fixed disks were first introduced to MS-DOS, the normal size limit for a single drive was fixed at 32 megabytes by the 16-bit maximum size for representing the sector number. This figure was still much larger than the original drives, though, and was very much larger than anyone anticipated could possibly be used by a single operating system.

There was, however, much interest in placing several different operating systems, such as MS-DOS, UNIX, and even CP/M-86, on a single fixed disk, and selecting which of the system to be used at boot time.

Since the file structures used by these different systems were not compatible with each other, it was necessary to partition the single disk into several logically different drives in order to support multi-system use. That was the original reason for establishment of the Master Boot Record (MBR), also known as the partition table (although the partition table itself is only a part of the full MBR).

As drives became larger, and passed the 32-megabyte limit in capacity, another reason for having multiple partitions came into existence: they permitted the use of all the capacity of a larger physical drive, even though all of its partitions were assigned to MS-DOS rather than being spread across several different operating systems.

The full-use reason for partitions rapidly supplanted the original multi-system need. Both needs, however, remain fully supported.

The Master Boot Record, by general convention, is located on the very first sector of the first track of the first surface of the physical disk. This is the same location where a floppy diskette has its *boot sector* and like the boot sector of a floppy, the MBR of a fixed disk begins with executable code that comes into play as soon as the system is powered up and finishes its internal self-tests.

Unlike the boot code, though, that of the MBR simply reads the information from the partition into RAM, where it controls the *visibility* of data on the disk. The partition table can hold a maximum of four partitions; each defines a separate logical drive in terms of a physical starting address and a size. It also specifies the operating system for which that logical drive is formatted, and only those logical drives that are formatted for the operating system in use will be visible to the system when it comes into operation.

One, and only one, of the four partitions is tagged as being the bootable partition; the operating system for which that partition is set up is the one that will be used. Multi-booting systems such as those used to share a system between MS-DOS and OS/2, for example, usually work by changing the tag in the partition table and then re-booting, although it's also possible for them to move in between the MBR and any of the normal logical drives, and from that vantage point select which partition to use each time you boot the system.

In MS-DOS, the tool that manipulates the MBR is FDISK.EXE. This tool identifies all *foreign* partitions (such as those for systems other than MS-DOS itself) simply as *non-DOS partitions* and does not allow you to modify them. This is a safety precaution; to change a UNIX partition, you must use the corresponding tool in your UNIX system.

Standard MS-DOS file routines cannot access the MBR, since they can only read from and write to the logical drives that it defines, and the MBR itself is outside all the logical drives. The record can, however, be dealt with via BIOS Interrupt 13h, and also through the special `IOCTL` functions of MS-DOS Interrupt 21h Function 440Dh.

Because access to everything on a fixed disk is controlled through its MBR, this record is a favorite target of virus writers. By destroying the MBR, they can effectively erase all the data from the disk in the time it takes to write a single sector.

The `MBR` structure is fully defined in Chapter 4. Later in this chapter we present a sample program that can read, save, list, and restore the MBR. While the program is discussed as an example of most disk I/O techniques, it is especially useful for anticipating and repairing damage that may be done by those virus programs which mangle the MBR.

The New MRCI Capability

One of the few truly new features found in MS-DOS Version 6.0 is MRCI, the *Microsoft Real-time Compression Interface.* MRCI (pronounced *Merci*) allows an application (the *client*) to request compression services from an engine that uses the *Microsoft Real-time Compression Format* (the *server*). This establishes a compression standard, which may be implemented either totally by software, or with hardware assistance.

MRCI servers implemented totally in software are provided as part of MS-DOS Version 6.0 (the DoubleSpace compressed file system includes a software MRCI server). Hardware implementations, also, are expected to appear before long. When they do, the MRCI standard will assure that your programs need not change to take full advantage of the increased performance.

MRCI consists of three major components: the Query API, the Compress and Decompress APIs, and the Compression Format.

The Query API consists of a rendezvous API that lets an application check for the presence of MRCI-compliant compression services. These services may be implemented in either software or hardware.

The Compress and Decompress APIs allow an application to use any MRCI server that may be present in the system. Using the address returned from the query, the application can transfer data to be compressed to, and that to be decompressed from, the MRCI server located by the Query API.

The Compression Format assures that, given the same stream of uncompressed bytes as input, all MRCI-compliant servers will output identical streams of compressed bytes, and vice-versa for decompression. The standardized format, a variant of Lempel-Ziv encoding, enables compressed data to be exchanged between systems.

The Query API

The `MRCQuery` API permits either a client or another server to establish communication with an existing MRCI server. This API consists of two software interrupts, one used to query for a RAM-based (software-only) server and the other to query for a ROM-based (hardware-assisted) server.

The MRCI specification permits a new server to install itself in the system, partially or fully replacing a previously installed server. Only the last MRCI server installed will respond to `MRCQuery`. If you create a server, you may find it useful to preserve the location of any previous server so that it can be restored if your server subsequently removes itself from the system.

The following subroutine is adapted from an example in the MRCI specification. When called, it returns zero in AX if an MRCI server of either variety has responded to the query, and a pointer (in ES:DI) to the server's `MRCINFO` structure (described in Chapter 4). If no server responds, the routine returns with AX equal to 1 and the content of ES:DI is meaningless.

The routine can be assembled with MASM Version 5.1 or later, or any other assembler that follows the same simplified-segment conventions.

```
;***    MRCQuery - Detect presence of MRCI server, return MRCINFO
;
;       Detect presence of MRCI server safely, and if present
        return
;       pointer to the server's MRCINFO structure. NOTE that we
        check
;       first for a RAM-based server, and then for a ROM-based
;       server.
;
;       If successful, returns:
;               ax = 0, MRCI server is present.
;               es:di -> MRCINFO structure
;
;       If no server identified, returns:
;               ax = 1, NO MRCI server is present.

MRCQueryproc    near
```

```
        push    ax
        push    bx
        push    cx
        push    dx
        push    si
        push    bp
        push    ds
;*      Check intMRCI vector before we issue the interrupt.
        xor     ax,ax           ; Segment of vector table
        mov     ds,ax
        lds     si,ds:[2Fh*4]   ; ds:si -> MRCI server
        mov     ax,ds
        or      ax,ax           ; Vector hooked?
        jz      mdr             ;   NO, make another check
        mov     ax,04A12h       ; Function
;       A signature technique is used to verify that the response
;       is coming from an MRCI server, and not some other code. The
;       server must change CX/DX, so that the caller can trust that
;       an actual MRCI server was responding, rather than some
;       other interrupt hook.
        mov     cx,'MR'          ; Signatures for validation
        mov     dx,'CI'
        int     2Fh              ; Call server
        cmp     cx,'IC'          ; Signature match?
        jne     mdr              ;   NO, make another check
        cmp     dx,'RM'          ; Signature match?
        je      mdp              ;   YES, have server

;*      Server not present, check for ROM based server
mdr:    xor     ax,ax
        mov     ds,ax
        lds     si,ds:[1Ah*4]    ; ds:si -> ROM MRCI server
        mov     ax,ds
        or      ax,ax            ; Vector hooked?
        jz      mde              ;   NO, fail
        mov     ax,0B001h        ; Function
;       Same signature check as before is made for ROM server too.
        mov     cx,'MR'          ; Signatures for validation
        mov     dx,'CI'
        int     1Ah              ; Call ROM server
        cmp     cx,'IC'          ; Signature match?
        jne     mde              ;   NO, failed
```

```
        cmp     dx,'RM'             ; Signature match?
        jne     mde                 ;   No, failed
mdp:    xor     ax,ax               ; Indicate success
        jmp     short mdx           ; Go exit
mde:    mov     ax,1                ; Indicate failure
mdx:    pop     ds                  ; restore registers and return
        pop     bp
        pop     si
        pop     dx
        pop     cx
        pop     bx
        pop     ax
        ret
MRCQueryendp
```

You may notice that the MRCQuery API makes no use of Interrupt 21h for accessing the interrupt vectors. This allows it to be called from routines that are, themselves, invoked while Interrupt 21h is in use, but also can create problems if you attempt to use this code unchanged within a Windows virtual device driver or other protected-mode application. Should that occur, modify the code while retaining the specific interrupt values, register content, and checks upon return from the two interrupts.

Upon successful return from this routine, your program should store the pointer returned in ES:DI in the MRCINFO structure (Chapter 4) so that it can be used by the Compress and Decompress APIs.

The Compress and Decompress APIs

The compression and decompression APIs (MRCCompress, MRCUpdateCompress, MRCMaxCompress, MRCDecompress, and MRCIncrementalDecompress) allow a client to call a server to compress and decompress data in the MRC Format. These services are invoked by direct calls to the server, using the address obtained by MRCQuery, for maximum performance.

While all five listed services are defined by the MRCI specification, only MRCCompress and MRCDecompress are actually necessary for use of MRCI.

Following is one way to invoke the MRCCompress service, adapted from an example presented in the specification:

```
;***    MRCCompress - Compress an uncompressed data buffer
;
;       Returns:
```

```
;               ax = 0, operation completed
;               ax = non-zero error code

MRCCompress proc
        push    bx                          ; Save registers
        push    cx
        push    dx
        push    bp
        push    si
        push    di
        push    ds
        mov     ds,seg MRCREQUEST           ;(see Chapter 4)
        mov     si,offset MRCREQUEST        ;(see Chapter 4)
        mov     es,seg MRCINFO              ;(see Chapter 4)
        mov     bx,offset MRCINFO           ;(see Chapter 4)
        mov     ax,1                        ; Standard compression
        mov     cx,0                        ; application is calling
        call    dword ptr es:[bx].mi_pfnOperate   ; Call Server
        pop     ds
        pop     di
        pop     si
        pop     bp
        pop     dx
        pop     cx
        pop     bx
        ret
MRCCompress endp
```

Before making this call, the `MRCINFO` structure's `mi_pfnOperate` pointer must have been filled with the entry point returned by `MRCQuery`, and the `MRCREQUEST` structure (fully described in Chapter 4) must be set up to point to the data to be compressed (`mr_pbSrc`, `mr_cbSrc`) and to appropriate buffer space (`mr_pbDst`, `mr_cbDst`). Upon return, the value in AX must be tested for possible error conditions. It will be zero if the call succeeds; meanings for nonzero return codes are listed following the `MRCDecompress` example.

To decompress a buffer of data, the `MRCDecompress` service is called in similar fashion:

```
;***    MRCDecompress - Decompress a compressed data buffer
;
;       Returns:
;               ax = 0, operation completed
```

```
;               ax = non-zero error code

MRCDecompress proc near
        push    bx                          ; Save registers
        push    cx
        push    dx
        push    bp
        push    si
        push    di
        push    ds
        mov     ds,seg MRCREQUEST           ;(see Chapter 4)
        mov     si,offset MRCREQUEST        ;(see Chapter 4)
        mov     es,seg MRCINFO              ;(see Chapter 4)
        mov     bx,offset MRCINFO           ;(see Chapter 4)
        mov     ax,2                        ; Decompress bit
        mov     cx,0                        ; application is calling
        call    dword ptr es:[bx].mi_pfnOperate    ; Call Server
        pop     ds
        pop     di
        pop     si
        pop     bp
        pop     dx
        pop     cx
        pop     bx
        ret
MRCDecompress endp
```

Before making this call, the `MRCINFO` structure's `mi_pfnOperate` pointer must have been filled with the entry point returned by `MRCQuery`, and the `MRCREQUEST` structure (fully described in Chapter 4) must be set up to point to the data to be decompressed (`mr_pbSrc`, `mr_cbSrc`) and to appropriate buffer space (`mr_pbDst`, `mr_cbDst`). Upon return, the value in AX must be tested for possible error conditions. It will be zero if the call succeeds; meanings for nonzero return codes are as follows:

```
MRCI_ERROR_NONE              equ 0  ; No error
MRCI_ERROR_NOT_SUPPORTED     equ 1  ; Unsupported operation requested
;       Server does not support this operation.
MRCI_ERROR_BUSY              equ 2  ; Server is busy
;        Server is busy with another operation. Try again later.
MRCI_ERROR_BUFFER_OVERFLOW   equ 3  ; Destination buffer too small
```

```
;        The destination buffer size (mr_cbDst) was not large enough
;        to hold the compressed data.
MRCI_ERROR_NOT_COMPRESSIBLE  equ 4 ; Data could not be compressed
;        The data was not compressible; the size of the compressed
;        data would have been greater than (mr_cbDst - mr_cbChunk).
MRCI_ERROR_BAD_MRC_FORMAT    equ 5 ; Compressed data format is bad
```

The Compression Format

No information about the compression format itself is available at the time of writing, although Microsoft has promised to license the MRCI software libraries (the same libraries used for MS-DOS 6's DoubleSpace and Backup programs, which provide fast, real-time compression-decompression services in software, and adhere to the MRCI compression format) to independent software vendors at no fee.

File System Organization

Possibly the most important single task that an operating system such as MS-DOS (any system, not just this one in particular) performs is to simplify the storage and retrieval of information. Almost without exception, the first step taken toward that simplification is to establish a system of identifying the information by grouping it into collections called *files* and to identify each file by a unique name.

Only a few systems have tried to bypass the convention of organizing information into named files. One that did was Forth, which divided its disk space into *blocks* and assigned a unique number to each block. Rather than remembering that the text for this chapter is filed as CHAP09.DOC in a subdirectory of my WINWORD directory, if I were working in Forth, I would have to keep in mind that it started at Block 7329 on Diskette 99324.

That totally arbitrary *naming* technique might, all by itself, go a long way toward explaining why Forth never achieved even a tenth the acceptance level of MS-DOS. However, this book is about MS-DOS, not Forth, so let's return to the way files are named and organized into directories.

Lately, many critics have attacked the MS-DOS naming conventions, which allow eight characters for a base name plus three more as a type or extension, as being too limited to permit assignment of meaningful names. In point of fact, the MS-DOS standards (inherited unchanged from CP/M) were less limited than the standards in effect for commercial mainframe use. Many of them restricted filenames to just six characters rather than eight, and some of them did not permit any extensions.

Even today, files placed in the library areas of CompuServe are restricted to six-character names, which often result in extremely strained contractions as uploaders attempt to indicate something about the file in just 6 letters.

However, by the time that MS-DOS reached Version 2.0, its designers had realized that business users would need a more versatile data storage organization than the simple directory of named files provided, and so the capability of organizing an entire disk's content into a hierarchy of directories and subdirectories was added at that time.

In this section, we'll see how space is allocated for storage of data and programs, and how the directory structure is managed. First, though, let's take another of our side trips to see how absolute disk I/O techniques, which totally bypass the directory structure and naming conventions, work.

Absolute Disk I/O

Absolute disk input and output techniques are essential parts of any operating system, since as we have already seen the actual hardware can only accept commands that express storage addresses either in terms of Logical Sector Numbers, or in sector/head/cylinder form. Normally, MS-DOS transforms your name-based references into one of these two equivalent forms and then passes the request on to BIOS for action.

Sometimes, though, you may run into a real requirement to perform absolute disk I/O from your own program. Examples of such a need include programs such as the example which closes this chapter and reads or writes your Master Boot Record data, because the MBR is not part of any logical disk known to MS-DOS. Instead, it's outside of the MS-DOS universe, in a never-never area that only BIOS (and the BIOS-escape functions provided in newer versions of MS-DOS) can address.

Other examples include disk editors such as those included in utilities like PC Tools from Central Point or Symantec's Norton Utilities, which allow direct modification of any data anywhere on the disk. Although such editors are dangerous in the hands of inexperienced users, they can be essential when you need to recover a munged set of files and have the knowledge to make proper use of them.

It's also necessary to use absolute disk I/O if your program will do any disk reformatting actions, whether for copy protection or to repair possible damaged areas. Again, these actions are extremely dangerous unless you know what you are up to, and can easily destroy all information on an entire disk, so we will not cover them in any detail within this section.

The place that you should definitely NOT try to use absolute disk I/O is for normal file access; while it's possible to duplicate everything that MS-DOS does, why bother to do so when it's faster and safer to just let the normal functions do what they are designed to accomplish?

When you do have a true need for absolute disk I/O, you can choose from three groups of techniques to deal with it. Each has its own set of peculiarities, with its own advantages and disadvantages. The three techniques, each of which we examine in its own section, are:

1. Use of BIOS, via Interrupt 13h, which is the most generic method and is completely independent of the MS-DOS version in use, but which may run into problems with some makes of BIOS chips.
2. Use of MS-DOS Interrupts 25h and 26h, which can deal with absolute I/O to any logical disk known to MS-DOS but which cannot access the MBR or other *hidden* sectors of a physical disk.
3. Use of MS-DOS Interrupt 21h Function 440Dh, Generic `IOCTL` for Block Devices, and its subfunctions which provide what is essentially a transparent interface to the BIOS capabilities.

Using BIOS

The BIOS interface provided by Interrupt 13h is the most general, by far, of the three techniques, but has its pitfalls. One of the most bothersome is that this technique is the favorite method of many virus creators, and consequently antivirus programs tend to be accusatory of any program that uses Interrupt 13, especially if it writes to the disk at any time.

Far more serious, though, is the simple fact that using the BIOS interface bypasses all the error-checking that is built into MS-DOS functions, and makes it much easier for your program to accidentally destroy all information on a user's fixed disk. Because of this, you should take extreme caution when using these techniques.

The full Interrupt 13h interface permits you to reformat one track, or an entire disk, with consequent loss of all data. Because of the complexity of performing this operation correctly, and the dire consequences if it's done incorrectly, we don't provide details of these functions. Our examination of the BIOS interface is limited to those functions you're most likely to need: resetting the disk system, reading one or more sectors, writing those sectors back out, and checking the disk status. For more complicated operations, use the IOCTL alternative discussed later in this section, which provides at least slight improvements in safety.

The simplest use of the BIOS interface is to reset the disk system. That's done by Function 00h, which forces each drive associated with the addressed controller to pull its heads to track 0 and to start the next I/O operation from track 0.

When Function 00h is called, the disk system does not react instantly. Instead, a flag is set in the controller to *recalibrate the drive* the next time it is used. The recalibrate command, when issued, takes the heads to Track 0 and causes the grinding sound you frequently hear after a disk error.

Unlike many of the MS-DOS functions, which use drive codes in a sequence `0, 1, 2, 3` or `1, 2, 3, 4` in which Drive C would be either drive 2 or drive 3, the BIOS interface drive code maintains different sequences for floppy and fixed drives. Floppy drive codes are zero based, so drive code 2 would be the third floppy drive in the system without regard to drive lettering. Fixed disk codes are similarly zero based, but the high bit is set so that the first fixed disk (normally Drive C in MS-DOS conventions) would be drive code 0x80 or 128.

If the drive number you specify has the high bit set, indicating that it is a fixed disk, the diskette system may be reset anyway, before the fixed disk controller is reset. Any error return code will refer to the fixed disk action. Diskette status can be found in the BIOS data area, at 0040:0041h.

This function often is used when any critical error has been detected. You may want to do several retries in such situations, resetting the system each time, in case the error is one that the user can correct. If you get consistent failure, however, you should notify the user and quit the program.

Following is the calling sequence, in assembly language, for Function 00h:

```
mov     dl,DriveCode      ; see text for details
mov     ah,00h            ; Reset Disk System
int     13h               ; call BIOS Disk Service
jc      error
```

If the carry flag is set upon return, the error code in AH will be one of those listed for Function 01h, Get Status. Generally, errors can occur in this function only if you provide an invalid drive code in DL when calling it.

Whenever one of the BIOS functions detects an error condition, it returns with the carry flag set and an error code in the AH register. You also can interrogate BIOS to learn the result of the last action, using Function 01h. Following is its calling sequence, in assembly language:

```
mov     ah,01h           ; Get Status
int     13h              ; call BIOS Disk Service
```

Upon return, AH will contain one of the following codes:

0	No error
1	Invalid value passed or unsupported function
2	Cannot locate address mark
3	Floppy write protected
4	Sector not found
5	Hard Disk reset failed
6	Floppy changed line on (1.2Mb drives)
7	Hard Disk activity failed
8	DMA overrun occurred
9	DMA attempted across 64K byte boundary
0Ah	Bad sector detected (hard disk)
0Bh	Bad track (hard disk)
0Ch	Media type not found
0Dh	Invalid number of sectors on format (hard disk)
0Eh	Control data address mark detected (hard disk)
0Fh	DMA level out of range (hard disk)
10h	CRC read error
20h	Controller failure
40h	Seek operation failed
80h	Floppy drive not ready
AAh	Fixed disk drive not ready

To read data from any sector on the disk, whether it is within an MS-DOS partition or not, use Function 02h of the BIOS interface. This function reads one or more sectors from the disk into memory.

Note that, like all functions of the Interrupt 13h BIOS interface, Function 02h does no checking at all on any of its input data. You must carefully check all input parameters before you call it, because an invalid value will lead to unpredictable and confusing results.

Following is the calling sequence, in assembly language, for this function:

```
mov     es,seg Bfr        ; data buffer, must
mov     bx,offset Bfr     ; be at least 512 bytes
mov     ch,Track          ; physical address
mov     cl,Sector         ;   on disk
mov     dh,HeadNbr        ;   of data to read
mov     dl,DriveCode      ; Bit 7 set if fixed
mov     ah,02h            ; Read Sectors
mov     al,NbrSectors     ; number to read
int     13h               ; call BIOS Disk Service
jc      error
```

If the carry flag is set upon return, the error code in AH will be one of those listed in the discussion of Function 01h.

It's possible for this function to return a DMA Boundary Error, when the DMA operation crosses a memory offset address that is, in its 20-bit absolute representation, a multiple of 4096 (1000h). Such a memory address must correspond to a sector boundary in the disk read, because of limitations of the Direct Memory Access hardware in some designs. This DMA boundary problem is especially apparent with the FORMAT.COM program in some versions of DOS, generating an error message to the effect that Track 0 is bad and the disk is unusable, for every diskette tried. If it appears, it can be cured by adding or removing `FILES=` or `BUFFERS=` values from the CONFIG.SYS file, and rebooting, to change the position in memory of the disk buffer used by FORMAT.COM. The same remedy can be applied if the problem appears in programs you create.

To write one or more sectors from memory to the disk, Function 03h of BIOS Interrupt 13h is the one to use. Except for the disk drive number, no value passed to this function is checked for validity, so you must check them in your own program. Passing an invalid value may lead to confusing and unpredictable results, and could cause damage to other data on the disk.

Following is the calling sequence, in assembly language, for Function 03h:

```
mov     es,seg Bfr          ; data buffer, must
mov     bx,offset Bfr       ; be at least 512 bytes
mov     ch,Track            ; physical address
mov     cl,Sector           ;   on disk
mov     dh,HeadNbr          ;   of data to read
mov     dl,DriveCode        ; Bit 7 set if fixed
mov     ah,03h              ; Write Sectors
mov     al,NbrSectors       ; number to write
int     13h                 ; call BIOS Disk Service
jc      error
mov     NumWrote,al         ; Number sectors transferred
```

If the carry flag is set upon return, the error code in AH will be one of those listed in the discussion of Function 01h.

The DMA Boundary Error mentioned previously can occur in this operation also, and the same cure applies.

Two Special Services

In the original version of MS-DOS, two interrupts were assigned for absolute disk I/O actions. Interrupt 25h was reserved for reading the disk, and 26h for writing to it. Both functions access the disk in terms of Logical Sector Numbers, and consequently are able to address only those sectors which are within a logical drive known to MS-DOS. Neither can deal with the Master Boot Record as a result.

When Version 4.0 added support for drives larger than 32 megabytes in capacity to MS-DOS, both functions were enhanced to deal with the larger volume sizes. Then, as of Version 5.0, they were both listed as *superseded* and the IOCTL functions described later in this section were recommended as their replacements.

Both Interrupts leave the CPU flags register on top of the stack when returning; this was apparently an oversight in the coding of Version 1.0 which has subsequently been preserved faithfully to avoid breaking the workaround that was required by the original version. Whenever either of these is used, the flags must be popped from the stack immediately after returning from the INT, but your program should check the carry flag to determine if an error occurred, before restoring the original flag settings. Alternatively, you can simply adjust the stack pointer, as our example sequences do.

Following is the calling sequence, in assembly language, to read MS-DOS volumes of 32 megabytes or less using the original version of Interrupt 25h:

```
mov     al,DriveCode          ; 0=A, 1=B, 2=C, etc.
mov     bx,seg Buffer         ; set far pointer to
mov     es,bx
mov     bx,offset Buffer      ;   disk buffer in ES:BX
mov     cx,NbrSectors         ; how many to read
mov     dx,FirstLSN           ; where to start
int     25h                   ; Absolute Disk Read
add     sp,2                  ; flush flags from stack
jc      error
```

If the carry flag is set upon return, the error code in AH will indicate BIOS errors and that in AL will indicate driver errors, as described at the end of this section.

To read MS-DOS volumes larger than 32 megabytes, a different calling sequence is required. First, in the data area, a `DISKIO` structure must be set up:

```
DISKIO      struc
diStart     dd     ?     ; sector number to start, 32-bit form
diCount     dw     ?     ; number of sectors to read or write
diBufr      dd     ?     ; far pointer to buffer
DISKIO      ends
```

Then, this calling sequence is used, after filling in the three elements of the `DISKIO` structure:

```
mov     al,DriveCode          ; 0=A, 1=B, 2=C, etc.
mov     bx,seg DISKIO         ; set far pointer to
mov     es,bx
mov     bx,offset DISKIO      ;   parameter block
mov     cx,0FFFFh             ; indicates big volume call
mov     dx,FirstLSN           ; where to start
int     25h                   ; Absolute Disk Read
add     sp,2                  ; flush flags from stack
jc      error
```

If the carry flag is set upon return, the error code in AH will indicate BIOS errors and that in AL will indicate driver errors, as described at the end of this section.

To write to volumes of 32 megabytes or less, use Interrupt 26h as follows:

```
mov     al,DriveCode          ; 0=A, 1=B, 2=C, etc.
mov     bx,seg Buffer         ; set far pointer to
mov     es,bx
mov     bx,offset Buffer      ;   disk buffer in ES:BX
mov     cx,NbrSectors         ; how many to write
mov     dx,FirstLSN           ; where to start
int     26h                   ; Absolute Disk Write
add     sp,2                  ; flush flags from stack
jc      error
```

If the carry flag is set upon return, the error code in AH will indicate BIOS errors and that in AL will indicate driver errors, as described at the end of this section.

For volumes larger than 32Mb, the `DISKIO` structure is filled just as for reading, and then this calling sequence is used to write data:

```
mov     al,DriveCode          ; 0=A, 1=B, 2=C, etc.
mov     bx,seg DISKIO         ; set far pointer to
mov     es,bx
mov     bx,offset DISKIO      ;   parameter block
mov     cx,0FFFFh             ; indicates big volume call
mov     dx,FirstLSN           ; where to start
int     26h                   ; Absolute Disk Write
add     sp,2                  ; flush flags from stack
jc      error
```

If the carry flag is set upon return from any of these calls, the error code in AH will indicate BIOS errors and that in AL will indicate driver errors, as follows:

```
AH: ROM-BIOS errors
        01h     Bad command
        02h     Address mark not found
        03h     Write-protection fault (26h only)
        04h     Sector not found
        08h     (not used)
        10h     CRC (data) error detected
        20h     Controller failure
        40h     Seek failure
        80h     Drive did not respond
```

```
AL: Driver errors
        00h     Write-protect violation (26h only)
        01h     Unknown unit
        02h     Drive not ready
        04h     Data (CRC) error
        06h     Seek error
        07h     Unknown media
        08h     Sector not found
        0Ah     Write Fault (26h only)
        0Bh     Read Fault (25h only)
        0Ch     General failure
        0Fh     Invalid media change
```

If a critical error is detected, these services do not invoke Critical Error Handler Interrupt 24h; they simply return the appropriate error code.

The MS-DOS Equivalent to BIOS

At version 3.2, the *generic* IOCTL family of subfunctions was added to MS-DOS Interrupt 21h, Function 44h. Separate subfunctions are provided for dealing with character devices and with block devices. The block-device subfunction, 440Dh, is in essence a transparent window to the BIOS functions but adds some error checking that BIOS lacks, and removes some of the complexity from some actions such as formatting a track. While a number of functions are available, in this section we examine only four: reading, writing, formatting, and verifying.

Interrupt 21h/440Dh (generic block-device IOCTL) uses subfunction 0861h to read from any location on a disk, whether in an MS-DOS logical volume or not, and subfunction 0841h to write. Both subfunctions use the RWBLOCK structure to pass parameters. Layout of the structure, in assembly language, is as follows:

```
RWBLOCK     struc
rwSpecFunc          db    0     ; must be zero
rwHead              dw    ?     ; head to start read/write
rwCyl               dw    ?     ; cylinder to start read/write
rwFirstSec          dw    ?     ; first sector to read/write
rwSecCount          dw    ?     ; number of sectors to read/write
rwBuffer            dd    ?     ; far pointer to data buffer
RWBLOCK     ends
```

The `RWBLOCK` structure must be filled in with physical address information, and a far pointer to the data buffer area, before calling either of the `IOCTL` subfunctions. Having done so, you can read one or more sectors from any disk regardless of size by using the following assembly language calling sequence:

```
mov     ax,440Dh            ; block IOCTL
mov     bx,DriveCode        ; 0=current, 1=A, 2=B, 3=C
mov     cx,0861h            ; read track
mov     dx,seg RWBLOCK      ; point to parameter block
push    ds                  ; save data segment
mov     ds,dx
mov     dx,offset RWBLOCK
int     21h                 ; call MS-DOS
pop     ds                  ; restore data segment
jc      error
```

Following is the calling sequence, in assembly language, to write data using the `IOCTL` interface after filling in the `RWBLOCK` structure with the details of where and what to write:

```
mov     ax,440Dh            ; block IOCTL
mov     bx,DriveCode        ; 0=current, 1=A, 2=B, 3=C
mov     cx,0841h            ; write track
mov     dx,seg RWBLOCK      ; point to parameter block
push    ds                  ; save data segment
mov     ds,dx
mov     dx,offset RWBLOCK
int     21h                 ; call MS-DOS
pop     ds                  ; restore data segment
jc      error
```

To format a track, or verify that a track is properly formatted, you can use subfunctions 0842h (format) and 0862h (verify). Both of these use the `FVBLOCK` structure to specify their parameters:

```
FVBLOCK struc
fvSpecFunc      db      0       ; must be zero
fvHead          dw      ?       ; head to start
fvCyl           dw      ?       ; cylinder to start
FVBLOCK ends
```

Following is the calling sequence, in assembly language, to format a single track. Note that this will destroy all information stored on that track; use this function only with extreme caution.

```
mov     ax,440Dh          ; block IOCTL
mov     bx,DriveCode      ; 0=current, 1=A, 2=B, 3=C
mov     cx,0842h          ; format track
mov     dx,seg FVBLOCK    ; point to parameter block
push    ds                ; save data segment
mov     ds,dx
mov     dx,offset FVBLOCK
int     21h               ; call MS-DOS
pop     ds                ; restore data segment
jc      error
```

To verify accuracy of formatting for a track, use this calling sequence after filling in the FVBLOCK data correctly:

```
mov     ax,440Dh          ; block IOCTL
mov     bx,DriveCode      ; 0=current, 1=A, 2=B, 3=C
mov     cx,0862h          ; verify track
mov     dx,seg FVBLOCK    ; point to parameter block
push    ds                ; save data segment
mov     ds,dx
mov     dx,offset FVBLOCK
int     21h               ; call MS-DOS
pop     ds                ; restore data segment
jc      error
```

If the carry flag is set upon return from any of these subfunctions, the error code in AX will be either `1`, indicating an invalid function, `2`, indicating that the drive code supplied was not valid, or `5`, access denied, which indicates that the addressed area could not be accessed.

Allocation Issues

Now that we've examined the three different ways of performing absolute disk I/O, let's turn our attention to another major function of the operating system: how it allocates space for use by individual files, and reclaims that space when a file is erased or deleted.

Automatic allocation and control of space is an absolute necessity for a modern operating system, but the early mainframe systems didn't provide this feature. They required that the programmer do space allocation manually, when a system was created, and offered no way to expand a file if the original allocation wasn't large enough. It was necessary to rewrite the program just to expand a file!

Space allocation is managed by creating a table of *available space* when a disk is initially formatted for use, and then taking space from this table as required, or putting it back when the space is no longer being used.

Different systems have used different methods for keeping track of the space available; MS-DOS has, from the beginning, maintained a File Allocation Table (FAT) to accomplish this goal. The FAT tracks space in terms of clusters, which simply are groups of adjacent sectors on the disk. Let's look at both of these in more detail.

Clusters

Most users of MS-DOS encounter the term *cluster* only when they run the CHKDSK utility and see a report that some number of *lost clusters* have been detected. As a developer, you need to be able to give the users of your programs accurate answers when they ask you to explain such things, but even more than that, you need to understand what clusters are used for in order to comprehend the way in which MS-DOS manages its disk space. First let's see what clusters are and then we can explore just how they can managed to get lost in the rather limited confines of a disk drive.

A cluster is a group of adjacent disk sectors that is allocated as a single entity. The size of a cluster can range from a single sector, often used in RAM emulations of disk drives, up to as much as 32 sectors (16 kilobytes). Normally, however, the largest cluster size used is 8K or 16 sectors, and most fixed disk drives use 2K (4-sector) clusters while the clusters on floppies are more often 1K or 2 sectors.

Why bother with clusters at all, rather than just allocating space one sector at a time? The major reason is to provide better use of memory. By making allocations in bigger chunks, the allocation table needs fewer entries.

Some actual examples here may help make the point: the 80-megabyte fixed disk on the system I am using right now contains 156,502 sectors in its MS-DOS partition. To represent this number requires a minimum of 18 bits, so an allocation table that could keep track of the status of each sector would have to have at least 18 bits in each entry; calculations would be much less complex if the entry was some power of two, which would result in 32-bit items.

But to store 156,500 entries, each 32 bits long, would take 626,000 bytes just for the table. That's over half a megabyte that would not be usable for data storage.

By grouping the space into clusters, each 2K bytes or four sectors in size, only one-quarter as many entries are required in the allocation table, and, more importantly, each entry can be represented in a 16-bit item rather than requiring 32 bits. These two effects work together to reduce the total size of the allocation table to 39,126 entries of 2 bytes each, or just under 40 kilobytes. That's much more efficient use of the space than the alternative.

The downside of this approach is that a single-byte file, when stored, will occupy one sector in the first system, but will take up four sectors in the second. On average, if the file sizes are completely random, each file can be expected to waste half a cluster in unused space between the end of data and the end of the cluster.

Thus the expected wastage would be 256 bytes per file with single-sector allocations, as opposed to 1024 bytes per file with the usual 2K cluster size. Sounds bad, but when you consider the total number of files on most systems (usually under 2,000 at any one time) and compare to the fixed requirements of larger allocation tables when smaller clusters are used, actually it's quite acceptable. And in addition, many applications create files of distinctly non-random sizes; this can totally invalidate "average" expectations.

To see how clusters can become lost we'll have to wait until we've looked at the File Allocation Table in the next subsection. However, at this point we have all we need to comprehend how the new MRCI disk compression utility can report such high compression ratios as "16:1" when most other compression techniques seldom do better than 2:1.

The 16:1 report is comparing the number of sectors occupied in the compressed volume file to the number that would be used by the same file, uncompressed, in a disk volume with the same cluster size as the CVF. And the cluster size for all DoubleSpace CVF's is fixed at 8K or 16 sectors.

The minimum threshold used by DoubleSpace when compressing files is one sector. If the file cannot shrink by at least this much, it will be stored with no compression at all. But it's precisely the tiny, less-than-one-sector files such as small batch files, that show the 16:1 compression values on a `DIR/C`. That happens because DoubleSpace stores the file, uncompressed, in a single sector of the CVF, but the compression report compares the one sector actually used to the 16 that would be required by a conventional file of the same cluster size.

The CVF is, itself, stored using the normal cluster size for the host drive, usually 2K or 4 sectors. When you issue a `DIR /CH` command, the report you get will compare on the basis of that cluster size and will show 4:1 for the same file. Older third-party compression utilities show their performance using the inflated technique, so Microsoft had to use the same approach in order not to appear less effective.

When compression actually does take place, the report is still based on the number of sectors occupied by the compressed version compared to the number that would be needed for an uncompressed one, but the ratios are much less extreme.

Now that we've seen how the choice of cluster size can affect not only the actual amount of space used by a file, but how it is reported, let's move on and examine the File Allocation Table's organization and use.

File Allocation Tables

We've already noted that MS-DOS has used a File Allocation Table (FAT) to keep track of the space available for allocation and to know what has already been assigned for use. However the FAT does more than this. It also provides the glue that holds the various clusters that a file is using together in the correct sequence. The way in which this is accomplished is one of the features that was unique to MS-DOS when it was introduced.

When MS-DOS formats a disk for use, before anything is stored on it, it creates a FAT (most usually, two identical copies of the FAT) and a *root directory* between the boot sector, and the first space used for file storage.

The FAT used only 12 bits in versions prior to 3.0. At that point the option of using 16-bit FAT entries was introduced. When the 12-bit limit was in place, large cluster sizes were necessary with high-capacity drives, but when 16 bits became available, it was possible to reduce the cluster size to the 2K standard most widely used today.

The reason for creating two copies of the FAT rather than depending on just one was to keep the disk usable even if an error should develop in the FAT area. If an error is detected by MS-DOS when reading the FAT, it attempts to read from the second copy before giving up. Any time that data is being written to the FAT, both copies are modified.

Each entry in the FAT corresponds to a single cluster on the disk, and initially, all entries are zeroed out to indicate that the corresponding cluster is available for use.

Each time a cluster is allocated to a file, its entry in the FAT is made nonzero. The special values 0xFF8 (or 0xFFF8 for 16-bit FATs) through 0xFFF (0xFFFF) indicate that the cluster is the last one in the file. Values 0xFF0 through 0xFF6 are reserved, and 0xFF7 marks bad clusters which cannot be used. The value 0x001 is never used for a file but is written into the FAT temporarily when allocating space. All other values are valid cluster numbers, and indicate that the file continues at the indicated cluster.

Thus a file that has more than one cluster need not consist of adjacent clusters, but may be scattered out all over the disk. It makes no difference, so long as the FAT entries for the file correctly link each cluster in turn to the next in sequence. This scattering is called *fragmentation* and special utilities known as *defraggers* can be used to reorganize each file into contiguous clusters. Doing so makes it easier to undelete a file if it is erased by accident, and may also provide slight increases in access speed by reducing the amount of head motion required to read the entire file.

As we shall see when we examine how files can be accessed by name, the directory entry for each file includes the number of the cluster on which it starts. From there, MS-DOS accesses the FAT, transparently and invisibly behind the scenes, to locate each cluster in turn when it's needed, until reaching the final one.

When a file is being written, the clusters it requires are allocated to it as necessary, but the directory entry is not always written to disk immediately. In fact, in most cases the directory entry is not written out until the file is closed. If, during the time between space allocation and file closing, anything happens to cause a system reboot or an abnormal program termination, the directory entry may not ever get written.

When that happens, the clusters assigned to the file have been allocated to it, and their entries in the FAT are no longer zero, but the link to the first cluster doesn't exist. These clusters, then, are *lost* from visibility to the normal

MS-DOS functions. That's what CHKDSK means when it reports finding a number of lost clusters, in one or more chains. It's telling you it has found space marked as allocated, but not reachable through any directory entry.

If you tell CHKDSK to save the clusters, it will create directory entries for each chain in the root directory of the affected drive, using the default filename FILE*nnnn*.CHK (where *nnnn* is a serial number that varies for each file). With a directory entry assigned, the clusters are no longer lost. You can then examine them, and decide whether to delete the files or to rename them.

Most references that describe the MS-DOS FAT structure tell you how to translate the cluster number contained in the FAT into either a Logical Sector Number, or a head/cylinder/sector physical address. This information really isn't worth wasting time with, as a developer; the MS-DOS functions tell all you need to know about the FAT, and any attempt to bypass them and go directly to the structure simply increases the chances that your application will fail on some user's unusual configuration of hardware.

Three functions of Interrupt 21h provide all essential information from the FAT. Two of them tell you the number of sectors per cluster, bytes per sector, and total number of clusters on a drive; one, Function 1Bh, acts on the default drive only while the other, Function 1Ch, acts on any drive that you specify, including the default drive (1Bh just forces the default specification, then jumps into the code for 1Ch). The other tells you the amount of space that remains free for use.

To get the allocation information for the default (current) drive, use this assembly language calling sequence:

```
mov     ah,1Bh              ; get alloc info
push    ds                  ; save data segment
int     21h                 ; call MS-DOS
cmp     al,0FFh             ; test for error
je      error               ; must pop DS there too
mov     SecClust,al         ; sectors per cluster
mov     BytesSec,cx         ; bytes per sector
mov     NumClust,dx         ; number of clusters
mov     al,byte ptr [bx]    ; get media descriptor
mov     MediaCode,al        ; save for use
pop     ds                  ; restore data segment
```

To get this same data for a specific drive, here's the calling sequence, in assembly language:

```
mov     dl,DriveCode          ; 0=current, 1=A, 2=B, etc.
mov     ah,1Ch                ; get alloc info
push    ds                    ; save data segment
int     21h                   ; call MS-DOS
cmp     al,0FFh               ; test for error
je      error                 ; must pop DS there too
mov     SecClust,al           ; sectors per cluster
mov     BytesSec,cx           ; bytes per sector
mov     NumClust,dx           ; number of clusters
mov     al,byte ptr [bx]      ; get media descriptor
mov     MediaCode,al          ; save for use
pop     ds                    ; restore data segment
```

If AL is equal to 0FFh upon return from either of these functions, an error has occurred and the information is not valid. Note that the error handler must still pop DS back from the stack. If you have no need for the media descriptor value that these functions return, you can move the `pop ds` up to immediately follow the invocation of INT 21h, and eliminate the two lines that retrieve and store the descriptor.

Effective with Version 5.0, both of these functions were labelled *superseded* and Function 36h was recommended instead. Function 36h gets the same information, except for the media descriptor, and in its place returns the number of clusters available for use. Following is its calling sequence, in assembly language:

```
mov     dl,DriveCode     ; 0=current, 1=A, 2=B, etc.
mov     ah,36h           ; get free space
int     21h              ; call MS-DOS
cmp     ax,0FFFFh        ; test for error
je      error            ; must pop DS there too
mov     SecClust,al      ; sectors per cluster
mov     BytesSec,cx      ; bytes per sector
mov     NumClust,dx      ; number of clusters
mov     FreeClust,bx     ; number clusters available
```

If AX is equal to 0FFFFh upon return, the drive code supplied at entry was not valid. This is the only error that can result from this function.

To convert the number of clusters into a number of bytes, first multiply by the number of sectors per cluster, then multiply that result by the number of bytes per sector. This is the calculation that DIR uses to display the amount of free space each time you list a directory's contents.

Note that when extremely large disk capacities (greater than 250 megabytes) are involved, the space calculation may fail because the number of bytes exceeds the largest value that can be represented in 32 bits. The same thing often happens if this function is used to determine the size of a CD-ROM or optical WORM-disk volume. The workaround simply is to report the space in terms of *sectors* rather than *bytes* so that the numbers involved will be smaller by several orders of magnitude.

Directory Management

When you format a disk, MS-DOS automatically creates a root directory for it along with the FATs. However, the size of a root directory is severely limited, and no matter how much space is available on the disk, when the root directory becomes full any attempt to create one more file will result in a rather misleading `disk full` error message. The disk really is full, but it's the directory area, rather than the more usual storage space, that has been used up.

To prevent this from happening, and to allow disks to be organized along lines that reflected each user's individual needs, the subdirectory functions were added in Version 2.0 of MS-DOS. Unlike the root directory, the size of each subdirectory is limited only by the amount of room available on the disk. This comes about because each subdirectory is organized just like a file, except that rather than the usual program or data, it contains directory entries. These entries may, in turn, lead the system to still lower subdirectory levels, or to files.

Figure 9.4 shows just a small portion of my D: drive; each of the displayed names is a subdirectory. The *BC* directory is where I keep my Borland C++ compiler, and the multitude of subdirectories that descend from it show how the tree can help keep highly complex data structures organized.

By keeping the root directory for each disk relatively empty, and restricting its content to just top-level subdirectories, you can permit virtually unlimited growth of your data structures. All applications that you develop should allow this kind of organization, and when you plan more complex applications, it's usually best to organize them along these lines too.

Four functions of MS-DOS Interrupt 21h provide all housekeeping needs for the directory tree of each drive. They permit you to create new directories as desired, to switch between directories, to determine the current directory for any drive, and to destroy unwanted directories when they are no longer needed. All these functions duplicate actions that can be done from the command prompt, but permit your programs to perform them automatically and, if you desire, without the user even knowing what is happening.

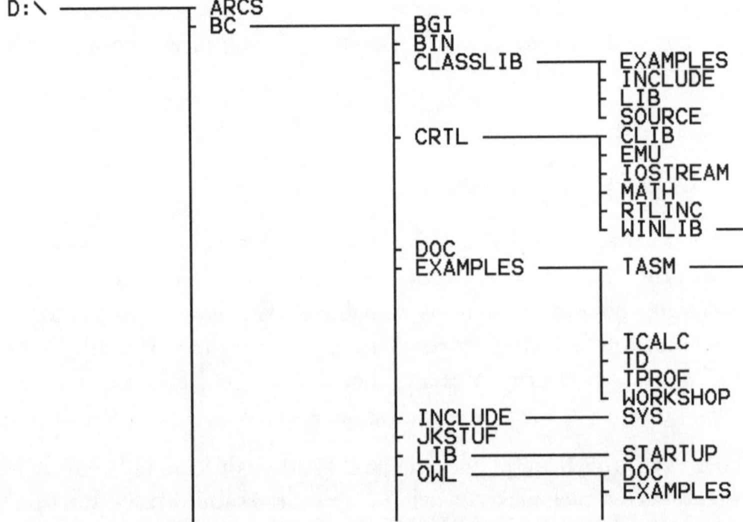

Figure 9.4. This illustration shows only a small portion of the directory tree for my D: drive, where most of my "in process" files and my development tools reside. Every directory name shown here, except for "ARCS", "BC", and "JKSTUF", is part of the standard structure created by Borland C++ when it is installed.

Making New Directories

To create a new directory, you'll use Function 39h of Interrupt 21h. Load a buffer with a full or relative pathname for the directory to be created; this name cannot include any wildcard characters such as *?* or *** and must be a valid name although it must not end with an existing directory or file. Then use the following calling sequence, in assembly language:

```
push    ds                  ; save data segment
mov     dx,seg PathName     ; far pointer to name
mov     ds,dx
```

```
mov     dx,offset PathName
mov     ah,39h                 ; make directory
int     21h                    ; call MS-DOS
pop     ds                     ; restore data segment
jc      error
```

If the carry flag is set upon return, the error code in AX will be either 2, indicating an error in the supplied pathname, 3, indicating that some higher-level directory in the supplied pathname could not be found, or 5, indicating that a file or directory with the requested name already exists.

Changing Directories

To change the current directory for a drive, use Interrupt 21h Function 3Bh, Set Current Directory. Just as when creating a new directory, the pathname supplied must not contain wildcard characters, and must refer to a valid path.

Following is the calling sequence, in assembly language, for this function:

```
push    ds                     ; save data segment
mov     dx,seg PathName        ; far pointer to name
mov     ds,dx
mov     dx,offset PathName
mov     ah,3Bh                 ; set current directory
int     21h                    ; call MS-DOS
pop     ds                     ; restore data segment
jc      error
```

If the carry flag is set upon return, the error code in AX will be 3, indicating that the specified path could not be found.

To determine the current directory established for a drive, use Interrupt 21h Function 47h, Get Current Directory. Set aside a buffer of at least 66 bytes (to allow the maximum 65 characters for the pathname plus a terminating all-zero byte), then use this calling sequence:

```
mov     dl,DriveCode           ; 0=current, 1=A, 2=B, etc.
push    ds                     ; save data segment
mov     si,seg PathName        ; far pointer to name buffer
mov     ds,si                  ;    to receive pathname
mov     si,offset PathName
mov     ah,47h                 ; get current directory
int     21h                    ; call MS-DOS
pop     ds                     ; restore data segment
jc      error
```

If the carry flag is set upon return, the error code in AX will be 15, indicating that the specified drive could not be found.

You can use Function 47h to determine whether the current directory is a subdirectory or the root, by examining the first byte of the PathName buffer upon return. If this byte is zero, then no subdirectory path exists, which implies that the addressed drive must be logged into its root directory. Otherwise, it is in a subdirectory, and the buffer contains the full name of the path but without the drive letter or leading \ character.

Destroying Directories

To remove a subdirectory from the file system, use Interrupt 21h Function 3Ah, passing it the name of the subdirectory to be destroyed. The subdirectory must be completely empty or you will get an `access denied` error. Following is the calling sequence, in assembly language, for this function:

```
push    ds                    ; save data segment
mov     dx,seg PathName       ; far pointer to name
mov     ds,dx
mov     dx,offset PathName
mov     ah,3Ah                ; remove directory
int     21h                   ; call MS-DOS
pop     ds                    ; restore data segment
jc      error
```

If the carry flag is set upon return, the error code in AX will be either 3, indicating that the specified directory could not be found, 5, indicating that access was denied (usually because the directory still contains files or subdirectories), or 16, indicating an attempt to remove the current directory, which is not permitted.

Data Storage and Retrieval

Now that we've seen how the file system is organized in terms of drives and directory trees, we can turn our attention to what is probably one of the most frequently performed tasks of every meaningful application: data storage and retrieval, using the file system.

The original method for dealing with the file system was by using File Control Blocks (FCBs), which were a direct inheritance from the CP/M system. Although this method was supplemented in Version 2.0 of MS-DOS by the *handle* technique which enables us to deal with files and character devices as if they were identical (at least in many respects), it's still in use by some of Microsoft's own programs, notably COMMAND.COM itself.

The reason is simple: for a few, specific, tasks, the FCB version of the task is still much more powerful than is the handle-based equivalent. When that's the case, COMMAND.COM uses the older but more effective technique; when it's not, the recommended newer methods are used. You'd be well advised to ignore Microsoft's recommendations and follow their example instead, in your own material.

In the following sections of this chapter we examine first the older FCB techniques, followed by the newer handle-based functions. In discussing the FCB functions, while all are shown, only those which may still be of value to you for performance reasons are explored to any degree of detail.

The "Bad Old Days" of FCB's

The basis of the FCB approach was the File Control Block itself, which was in essence simply a memory copy of the directory entry for the specified file, with a few fields added for housekeeping purposes. Later, the Extended FCB (XFCB) was defined to permit additional information to be specified. Both `FCB` and `XFCB` structures are fully described in Chapter 4.

As mentioned on the previous page, while most of the `FCB` functions have fallen into almost total disuse because the handle-based functions are far more powerful, some of them are still extremely useful because they either have no exact handle-based equivalent, or have far more effective power. The first group of FCB functions we examine here form that first group: those with no exact equal in the handle-based collection.

Still Without Equal

Because the text-string representation of any filename is markedly different from the format in which it must be converted for use in the FCB, the parsing of a filename into FCB format was an obvious "natural" candidate for being turned into a common subroutine. Interrupt 21h Function 29h, Parse Filename into FCB, was the result.

The original motivation for this function was for the parsing of the command tail, into the default FCB provided in the PSP area (see the PSP structure description in Chapter 4 for details). Function 29h accepts as input far pointers to the text string itself (in DS:SI) and to the FCB to receive the parsed result (in ES:DI), plus a "parse control byte" in the AL register. The exact action and status returns are determined by the low four bits of the parse control byte; the high four bits are reserved and must always be set to zero.

Each of the four bits controls a different part of the action, and the four are independent of each other. Thus you have 16 possible combinations of conditions that can be performed by this single function.

If Bit 0 is set to 1, the parse will skip over exactly one *separator* character within the string, if the character appears before any other non-white-space character. If set to 0, the parse stops when it encounters a separator character even if it has not yet reached the actual filename. The separator characters are : , ; .= and +.

If Bit 1 is set to 0, the parse will set the *drive* byte in the `FCB` structure to 00 (default drive) if the input string does not contain a drive letter; if the bit is set to 1, the *drive* byte in the structure is left unchanged unless a drive letter is specified in the input string.

Bit 2 performs a similar function for the 8-character *filename* field of the FCB. If set to 0, the parse will set this field to all blanks if the input string does not contain a filename or a wildcard character. If set to 1, the field is left unchanged in the absence of a new filename.

Finally, Bit 3 controls replacement of the 3-character *extension* field by the same rules. If set to 0, the field is blanked when no extension is supplied. If set to 1, it is left unchanged.

Upon return from Function 29h, the FCB will have been completely cleared except for the drive, name, and extension fields, and these will have been set as specified by the control byte and the parse of the input string. The DS:SI registers will be pointing to the next byte of the input string (i.e. the first character after the last one parsed) and ES:DI will point to the FCB itself.

Status is returned in AL, which will be FFh if the input string contained a drive letter that did not refer to a valid drive, 01h if either the filename or the extension contains at least one wildcard character, and 00h if all went well and no wildcards are involved.

Following is the calling sequence, in assembly language, for Function 29h:

```
push    ds                  ; save data segment
mov     si,seg P_Bfr        ; far pointer to name
mov     ds,si
mov     si,offset P_Bfr
mov     di,seg FCB          ; far pointer to FCB
mov     es,di
mov     di,offset FCB
mov     ah,29h              ; parse filename
mov     al,Control          ; see text
int     21h                 ; call MS-DOS
pop     ds                  ; restore data segment
```

Note that this sample code saves and restores DS but does not preserve the pointer to the next input character first; if you are performing multiple parses, as for the `RENAME` function we'll examine a few pages hence, you'll want to keep track of just where your parse pointer really is. In a COM file, where CS, DS, SS, and ES all contain the same segment address, the save and restore really are not needed and the problem vanishes. Otherwise you may want to save just the offset part, and reload DS from the unvarying segment address each time around.

It might seem that this function is as obsolete as all the other `FCB` functions, but that overlooks one highly important point. It's one of a very few known methods able to verify that a drive letter is actually valid, without attempting to access the physical drive. That is, to check whether a system has a floppy drive, you can point DS:SI at the simple string `A:`, ES:DI to a 32-byte buffer area (the actual FCB created will not be used, but the buffer will be written to in any event), set AL to zero, and call Function 29h.

Upon return, AL will be zero if the floppy drive letter was valid, and will be FFh if it is not, but since the system never accesses the drive to make the check, no critical error can result if the drive happens to be empty. Most of the more widely known techniques for verifying drive-letter validity require that a disk be installed.

Certain variants of the `IOCTL` handle-based function can return the same information but are considerably more complicated to set up and interpret, which retains the place of Function 29h as a valuable tool in the developer's arsenal. In addition, you can use it to set up the FCB structure properly for those few other FCB functions that are still of more than historical interest.

Two more FCB functions without exact equivalents in the handle-based group are FindFirst and FindNext, which search the current directory of the specified drive for the first entry that matches the supplied FCB, and for any subsequent entries, respectively.

While similar functions that work with handle-based techniques exist, and we'll examine them later, the FCB versions have one feature that's missing in the newer methods. They provide a direct value for the starting cluster of each file that they find, while the newer versions do not. This value is necessary in order to calculate the compression ratio for files stored using disk compression (such as DoubleSpace, Stacker, SuperStor, or DoubleDisk) because the compression information is associated with it.

For this reason, COMMAND.COM still uses the FCB methods to implement the DIR command; performance is much better as a result, than it would be if the handle techniques were used. In that case it's possible to use undocumented bytes of the FILEINFO structure to determine just where in the directory itself the file's entry appears, but to learn the starting cluster so that a compression ratio can be calculated, it's necessary to do a disk read of the directory itself.

The function to find the first matching file using FCB techniques is 11h. Before you call this function, you must establish a current Disk Transfer Area (DTA, discussed earlier in this chapter) which will receive the search results, unless you want to use the default area, and you should initialize either an FCB or an XFCB to specify your search pattern. To list all files within a directory, use the input string *.* and parse it into the FCB via Function 29h. Then call Function 11h. Following is the calling sequence, in assembly language, for it:

```
push    ds              ; save data segment
mov     dx,seg FCB      ; far pointer to FCB
mov     ds,dx
mov     dx,offset FCB
mov     ah,11h          ; find first (FCB)
int     21h             ; call MS-DOS
pop     ds              ; restore data segment
cmp     al,0            ; test for error
jne     error
```

If AL is nonzero upon return, an error has been detected. The only error reported by this function is `file not found` which indicates that the `FCB` contained an invalid name or extension.

If the function is successful, the `DTA` will be filled with the drive number used in the search (which will never be 0; the actual number is used), followed by the following structure (which is the actual directory entry for the first matching file):

```
DIRENTRY          struc
    deName        db     8 dup (?)       ; filename
    deExtension   db     3 dup (?)       ; extension
    deAttributes  db     ?
    deReserved    db     10 dup (?)      ; actually unused
    deTime        dw     ?
    deDate        dw     ?
    deStartClstr  dw     ?               ; starting cluster
    deFileSize    dd     ?
DIRENTRY          ends
```

If an `XFCB`, rather than an `FCB`, was supplied to this function, then the extended FCB header is copied into the `DTA` in front of the `DIRENTRY` structure, rather than the drive number.

Once Function 11h has returned the first matching file's data successfully, you can use Function 12h to obtain the data for the next, and all following, matching files. To do so, you must leave the `FCB` or `XFCB` undisturbed between the calls, because it will contain information that tells the next call where to resume its search.

Following is the calling sequence, in assembly language, for Function 12h:n

```
push    ds                  ; save data segment
mov     dx,seg FCB          ; far pointer to FCB
mov     ds,dx
mov     dx,offset FCB
mov     ah,12h              ; find next (FCB)
int     21h                 ; call MS-DOS
pop     ds                  ; restore data segment
cmp     al,0                ; test for error
jne     error
```

If AL is nonzero upon return, an error has been detected. This usually indicates that no more matching files can be found.

Note that if you call these functions within a loop that is also creating new files, or new copies of old ones, you may appear to get duplicates. This happens because the search proceeds linearly through the directory, from its first entry to its last, and if the directory is fully packed with no unused entries, any newly-created file will be added to the end. If a file already found in the search is deleted and the new entry renamed to use the old name, that old name will be found again when the search reaches the new entry.

And this doesn't always happen, because if old files have been deleted, their entries will be used before new ones are added to the end of a directory. If the search has passed that point in the directory, such entries will not be reported again. It looks inconsistent to a casual observer, but the action is really quite logical.

Creating or Retrieving Files

Since the `FCB` techniques are rarely used to create or open files, and should be avoided in new programs in favor of the handle-based methods, we simply show you the calling sequences that are used without going into much detail.

Both functions described in this section require that you provide a pointer to an unopened `FCB` structure that has the appropriate drive, filename, and extension filled in properly and all other bytes of the structure set to zero. The simplest way to create such a structure is to allocate the space for it and use Interrupt 21h Function 29h to parse an ASCII file specification into it. Note that none of the FCB functions recognize subdirectories; if you use these, you must switch to the correct subdirectory first by explicit calls to the directory functions already described.

To open a file for FCB techniques, use Interrupt 21h Function 0Fh. Following is the calling sequence, in assembly language:

```
push    ds              ; save data segment
mov     dx,seg FCB      ; far pointer to FCB
mov     ds,dx
mov     dx,offset FCB
mov     ah,0Fh          ; open file (FCB)
int     21h             ; call MS-DOS
pop     ds              ; restore data segment
cmp     al,0            ; test for error
jne     error
```

If AL is nonzero upon return, an error has been detected. The only error returned is `file not found` and is indicated by AL containing 0FFh.

To create or truncate a file for `FCB` techniques, use Interrupt 21h Function 16h. Following is its calling sequence, in assembly language:

```
push    ds              ; save data segment
mov     dx,seg FCB      ; far pointer to FCB
mov     ds,dx
mov     dx,offset FCB
mov     ah,16h          ; make file (FCB)
int     21h             ; call MS-DOS
pop     ds              ; restore data segment
cmp     al,0            ; test for error
jne     error
```

If AL is nonzero upon return, an error has been detected. No error analysis is made; AL will contain 0FFh in case of any possible error. The most usual reason for this call to fail is that the current directory is full.

One use for these functions is to create a volume label for a disk or diskette which does not have one. To do so you must use an Extended FCB rather than a plain FCB, and after parsing the desired volume label into it via Function 29h, explicitly set the `extAttribute` field to `ATTR_VOLUMEID`, 08h. Then invoke Function 16h to create the directory entry, and if successful, close the `FCB` as described later in this chapter.

A volume label can exist only in the root directory of a drive; attempting to create one in a subdirectory may not result in an immediate error, but the label will not be detected as such by any of the MS-DOS utilities such as DIR.

In addition, only one volume label can appear. Again, no error may be reported if you attempt to create another, but only the first will have any effect. You can test for existence of a volume label by setting up a wildcard filename and extension in an `XFCB` that has its attribute field set to `ATTR_VOLUMEID`, and performing a FindFirst search. If a label already exists, it can be renamed via the `XFCB` already established; if not, you can create one.

Reading, Writing, and 'Rithmetic

The eight `FCB`-based functions presented in this section allow sequential reads from or writes to a file, random-access read or writes using either records or blocks of records, selection of the point at which to begin a random access, or determination of the file's size. All have been superseded by handle-based techniques so their major importance in MS-DOS Version 6 is historical.

All these functions require a pointer to an opened FCB at entry. They will modify reserved fields within the FCB while they work, so the FCB should remain undisturbed between successive calls to the functions.

To read a file sequentially, use Interrupt 21h Function 14h. Two fields of the FCB structure (`fcbCurBlockNo` and `fcbCurRecNo`) indicate where in the file to read from, and the `fcbRecSize` field will determine the number of bytes that are read. Incoming data will be placed in the current DTA. Following is the calling sequence, in assembly language:

```
push    ds              ; save data segment
mov     dx,seg FCB      ; far pointer to FCB
mov     ds,dx
mov     dx,offset FCB
mov     ah,14h          ; read seq (FCB)
int     21h             ; call MS-DOS
pop     ds              ; restore data segment
cmp     al,0            ; test for error
jne     error
```

If AL is nonzero upon return, an error has been detected. The error code in AL will be 1 if the end of the file has been reached, 2 if a segment-boundary error occurred (the read will be incomplete in this event), or 3 if a premature end of file was reached (an incomplete record; the buffer will be padded with zero bytes).

If successful, the record number and block number fields will be automatically advanced to point to the next record in the file. Note that records are of fixed length and bear no relation to text-string input lines; reading is always in binary mode, with no automatic translation of such control characters as CR or LF, also. When FCB techniques are used, you must provide all translations in your program; none are supplied automatically as they are with handle-based operations in ASCII mode.

To perform sequential writes, which work exactly like sequential reads, from the DTA to the current position in the file, use this assembly language calling sequence:

```
push    ds              ; save data segment
mov     dx,seg FCB      ; far pointer to FCB
mov     ds,dx
mov     dx,offset FCB
```

```
mov     ah,15h          ; write seq (FCB)
int     21h             ; call MS-DOS
pop     ds              ; restore data segment
cmp     al,0            ; test for error
jne     error
```

If AL is nonzero upon return, an error has been detected. If AL is 1, the disk (or directory) is full, while 2 indicates a segment-boundary error.

To read or write at *random* addresses rather than sequentially, it's first necessary to set the random record number to be accessed. The *random read* and *random write* functions work with a different field within the FCB than do the "sequential" operations, and a special function is used to set this field to the same location as the sequential fields specify. Following is the calling sequence, in assembly language, to do so:

```
push    ds              ; save data segment
mov     dx,seg FCB      ; far pointer to FCB
mov     ds,dx
mov     dx,offset FCB
mov     ah,24h          ; set rand rec (FCB)
int     21h             ; call MS-DOS
pop     ds              ; restor e data segment
```

No error can occur during this function, since it merely transfers data from one area of the FCB to another without performing any analysis of what it moves.

Once the random record number is set, you can use the following functions to repeatedly access that record. Unlike the sequential functions, no automatic incrementing occurs. This permits you to read a random record, update the copy in the DTA, and write the updated record back to the file at the same location.

To read a random record into the DTA, use this assembly language calling sequence:

```
push    ds              ; save data segment
mov     dx,seg FCB      ; far pointer to FCB
mov     ds,dx
mov     dx,offset FCB
mov     ah,21h          ; read rand (FCB)
int     21h             ; call MS-DOS
pop     ds              ; restore data segment
cmp     al,0            ; test for error
jne     error
```

To write the record back, use this calling sequence:

```
push    ds              ; save data segment
mov     dx,seg FCB      ; far pointer to FCB
mov     ds,dx
mov     dx,offset FCB
mov     ah,22h          ; write rand (FCB)
int     21h             ; call MS-DOS
pop     ds              ; restore data segment
cmp     al,0            ; test for error
jne     error
```

If AL is nonzero upon return from either function, an error has been detected. The error codes in both cases are identical to those for the sequential functions.

The final pair of read/write functions for the FCB techniques permit you to read a block of multiple records in semi-random fashion by specifying the initial record's location the same way as for "random" reading/writing, and also specifying the number of records in the block. The specified record, and those immediately following, will be transferred to or from the DTA.

Following is the calling sequence, in assembly language, to read a block of records:

```
push    ds              ; save data segment
mov     cx, NumRecs     ; number of records in block
mov     dx,seg FCB      ; far pointer to FCB
mov     ds,dx
mov     dx,offset FCB
mov     ah,27h          ; rand blk read (FCB)
int     21h             ;  call MS-DOS
pop     ds              ; restore data segment
cmp     al,0            ; test for error
jne     error
```

Following is the calling sequence to write the block back to the file:

```
push    ds              ; save data segment
mov     cx, NumRecs     ; number of records in block
mov     dx,seg FCB      ; far pointer to FCB
mov     ds,dx
mov     dx,offset FCB
mov     ah,28h          ; rand blk write (FCB)
```

```
int     21h             ; call MS-DOS
pop     ds              ; restore data segment
cmp     al,0            ; test for error
jne     error
```

If AL is nonzero upon return from either function, an error has been detected. The error codes in both cases are identical to those for the sequential and random functions.

The final `FCB` function we examine in this section allows you to determine the number of records in a file, when you specify the size of each record. It is passed an unopened `FCB`, with the drive, name, and extension fields set up as done by Function 29h, and also having its `fcbRecSize` field set to the record size.

The function then obtains the file size in bytes from the directory entry, divides this by the specified record size, and places the result in the fcbRandomRecNo field of the `FCB`. If you specify a record size of 1, this function will give you the file size in bytes.

Following is the calling sequence, in assembly language:

```
push    ds              ; save data segment
mov     dx,seg FCB      ; far pointer to FCB
mov     ds,dx
mov     dx,offset FCB
mov     ah,23h          ; get file size (FCB)
int     21h             ; call MS-DOS
pop     ds              ; restore data segment
cmp     al,0            ; test for error
jne     error
```

If AL is nonzero upon return, an error has been detected. No analysis of the error is done, but the most likely reason would be that the specified file could not be found.

Updating Directory Information

Since the directory provides the only link between a file's name and its physical characteristics such as disk address and size, it's essential that the information in the directory entry for the file be kept up-to-date whenever it changes. In the `FCB`-based functions, the only tool available to update the directory is the `Close File` function, Interrupt 21h Function 10h. Any time a file is created or modified, it must be closed afterward in order to write the changes into its directory entry. Should the system fail or reboot before this occurs, "lost clusters" are a certain result.

Following is the calling sequence, in assembly language, to close a file that has been created or modified by FCB techniques:

```
push    ds              ; save data segment
mov     dx,seg FCB      ; far pointer to FCB
mov     ds,dx
mov     dx,offset FCB
mov     ah,10h          ; close file (FCB)
int     21h             ; call MS-DOS
pop     ds              ; restore data segment
cmp     al,0            ; test for error
jne     error
```

If AL is nonzero upon return, an error has been detected. The only such error would be `file not found` and that, in turn, indicates serious problems in the file system since such a file could not have been opened in the first place.

Note that in all versions of MS-DOS since introduction of the handle-based techniques, the FCB methods are actually implemented by an emulation process within the MS-DOS kernel itself, and the "system FCB" resources available for this emulation are limited.

The default number of system FCBs available is four, although you can change it by using the FCBS= command in your CONFIG.SYS file. Because of the limited resources available, you should close all files that are opened for FCB access as soon as possible, even if they are not modified, in order to release the resources for subsequent use.

File Renaming and Deletion

To rename or delete files using FCB techniques, special functions are used. Both of them are still useful even under MS-DOS Version 6.

The rename function is used when you need to modify an existing volume label. For other renaming, the handle-based methods are preferred, since they allow you to "move" a file from one directory to another so long as it remains on the same drive.

To rename a file or volume, you must modify the normal FCB structure (or XFCB, for working with a volume label) to match the following pattern. Note that this structure is the same size as the standard FCB, but defines a different set of fields. You can fill in these fields using Function 29h. Following is the layout:

```
RENAMEFCB       STRUC
  renDriveID    db ?            ; Drive (0=default, 1=A)
  renOldName    db 8 dup(?)     ; Existing name
  renOldExt     db 3 dup(?)     ;   and extension
  renReserv1    db 5 dup(?)     ; Set to zero
  renNewName    db 8 dup(?)     ; New name
  renNewExt     db 3 dup(?)     ;   and extension
  renReserv2    db 9 dup(?)     ; Set to zero
RENAMEFCB       ENDS
```

Once you have filled in all the non-reserved fields, use this calling sequence:

```
push    ds              ; save data segment
mov     dx,seg FCB      ; far pointer to FCB
mov     ds,dx
mov     dx,offset FCB
mov     ah,17h          ; rename file (FCB)
int     21h             ; call MS-DOS
pop     ds              ; restore data segment
cmp     al,0            ; test for error
jne     error
```

If AL is nonzero upon return, an error has been detected. No analysis of the error is done.

To delete a file from the current directory, using FCB methods, fill in an unopened FCB or XFCB structure for it, and then use this calling sequence:

```
push    ds              ; save data segment
mov     dx,seg FCB      ; far pointer to FCB
mov     ds,dx
mov     dx,offset FCB
mov     ah,13h          ; delete file (FCB)
int     21h             ; call MS-DOS
pop     ds              ; restore data segment
jc      error
```

If AL is nonzero upon return, an error has been detected. The only error reported is "file not found."

This function, unlike the handle-based equivalent, can handle wildcard characters in the filename and extension fields, making it possible to delete all files in the current directory with a single call.

For this reason, it's still used by COMMAND.COM even in the latest version of MS-DOS to service the DEL and ERASE commands. Despite Microsoft's recommendations to use Function 41h, the handle-based equivalent, you should do the same in any of your own applications that need to do mass deletion, such as erasing temporary files upon exit.

Handle I/O Techniques

The handle-based I/O techniques, which apply both to disk files and to character devices such as the keyboard, the CRT, and the printer, were added to MS-DOS in Version 2.0 along with subdirectories and a host of other extensions. The most apparent difference between these techniques are the older FCB function is that your application no longer provides the control block that handles all the bookkeeping for file I/O. Instead, it moved into the MS-DOS data area, allowing many processes to share a single file/device control block.

The linkage between your own file I/O needs, and the control block assigned by the system to deal with those needs, is provided by a "handle" that is returned by any function that creates a new file or opens an existing one. This handle is a 16-bit value, but official documentation tells us virtually nothing else about it. Before we get into the details of the handle-based techniques, let's step behind the scenes and get a quick overview of just what a handle really is, and how it ties everything together.

In Chapter 4, in the discussion of the Program Segment Prefix (PSP) structure, we noted that this structure includes a "handle table" of 20 single-byte values. The handle that is provided when you successfully open or create a file simply is an index into that table. Handle 0 addresses the first byte of the handle table, handle 1 the second, and so on.

The first five handles are preassigned when the PSP is created. In the primary command shell, they are assigned by opening the CON device three times to create handles 0, 1, and 2 (STDIN, STDOUT, and STDERR respectively), then opening the `AUX` device to create handle 3, and finally the `PRN` device for handle 4. After their initial creation, subsequent `PSPs` create them by using the `force duplicate` function we'll see a bit later, so that only one set of system file tables is used no matter how many processes may exist.

The values contained in the handle table are, in turn, indexes into the undocumented System File Table structure in the MS-DOS data area of low RAM. The number of SFT entries provided in the table is established by the `FILES=` line of CONFIG.SYS and defaults to only eight if no such line exists. To allow a full 20 handles in each of 3 processes, it would be necessary to have a `FILES=48` line in CONFIG.SYS. (Only 48 are required, rather than 60, because the five predefined handles would use the same 3 SFT entries for all 15 handles generated. The remaining 15 handles in each process might need one SFT entry each, though, since the `force dupe` function is seldom used by applications.)

It's possible to add to the number of `SFT` entries at any time, by running a special TSR program that locates the existing table and chains new entry space to its end. No such program is furnished with MS-DOS itself, but the QEMM memory management package provides one, FILES.COM, and similar utilities are available as shareware. It's also quite feasible to put these added `SFT` entries into Upper Memory, thus saving conventional RAM for program use.

Now that we have some idea of just what a handle is and how it connects to the control blocks for the associated file or device, let's return to the subject of how to use them. But on the way, we need to explore one of the major advantages that the handle-based functions offer: something that's called "device independence" in the literature, which can be extremely useful.

Device Independence: What It Means

Device independence simply means that a handle can refer to a file, or to a character device, and most of the functions will produce the same results in either case. Of course, you must apply a bit of common sense at times, such as when you want to issue a "read" command to the printer, or a "write" to the keyboard (both of which, in certain special cases, are sensible commands that serve a purpose, but they're definitely not the sort of things that are commonly encountered). Also, a couple of the subfunctions in the `IOCTL` function we'll meet later in this chapter are not device-independent; they come in one flavor for block devices and another complementary flavor for character devices.

In general, though, the handle-based functions neither know nor care whether the handle they accept or return refers to a file, or to a character device. They simply do their thing, and return appropriate status and/or data to their caller.

This device independence is what makes it possible to redirect command input normally obtained from the keyboard to come from an ASCII file instead, similarly to redirect output to go to the printer or to a file rather than to the CRT, and finally to "pipe" the standard output from one process into the standard input of another, all without any need to notify the processes involved. They simply take input from STDIN via handle-based functions, and send output to STDOUT the same way. Device independence does the rest.

Because of device independence, any character devices in your system will appear to exist simultaneously as files in all of your directories, and on all of your drives. Any attempt to create a file, or open one, with a name that matches that of any character device you have loaded, will instead wind up addressing that device. This can be most confusing if you open CON and attempt to read from it; everything that you type from the keyboard will show up as input. Similarly, writing to CON results in CRT display.

The effect can be useful when you know what's happening, but is more likely to generate panic for any user who doesn't know what is happening. We'll see a bit later how it can be used for some rather unconventional tests.

One of the most powerful of the handle-based housekeeping functions is Interrupt 21h, Function 4Eh, Find First File. This function, given a pointer to a search-pattern or mask, and a set of search attributes in bitmap form, will return into the current DTA a structure that provides the filename and extension of the first file found that matches the pattern, in text-string form, ready to be copied to your own buffer for use in opening a file, together with the file's date and time stamp, and size. This function provides everything that's needed to complete the usual DIR display for a single file.

The search pattern or mask must be an `ASCIIZ` string (that is, a string of ASCII characters terminated by an all-zero end-of-string byte, which is the normal C-language convention) and may contain wildcard characters in the filename, the extension, or both. Unlike its `FCB` equivalent function, the mask for Function 4Eh also can contain subdirectories to specify the path to the directory to be searched; it's not restricted to the current directory on the specified drive.

The search-attributes bitmap can be any combination of the following bits:

ATTR_NORMAL	0000h	Normal files
ATTR_READONLY	0001h	Read/only files
ATTR_HIDDEN	0002h	Hidden files
ATTR_SYSTEM	0004h	System files
ATTR_VOLUMEID	0008h	Volume Label directory entry
ATTR_DIRECTORY	0010h	Subdirectory entry

To find only directories matching the search mask, a bitmap of 0010h would be used. To exclude directories, you could use a bitmap of 000Fh. If the bitmap is set to ATTR_NORMAL, all matching entries regardless of attributes will be returned. If any combination of ATTR_SYSTEM, ATTR_HIDDEN, and ATTR_DIRECTORY is specified, normal files will be returned also and their individual attribute bits in the returned FILEINFO structure must be tested if you want to ignore such files.

Following is the calling sequence, in assembly language, for this function:

```
mov     cx,Attribs      ; search attributes
push    ds              ; save data segment
mov     dx,seg Mask     ; far pointer
mov     ds,dx
mov     dx,offset Mask
mov     ah,4Eh          ; find first (handle)
int     21h             ; call MS-DOS
pop     ds              ; restore data segment
jc      error
```

If the carry flag is set upon return, the error code in AX will be one of two values: 2 indicates that no file matched the mask, and 3 indicates that one or more of the directories specified could not be located.

If the function is successful, a FILEINFO structure is created in the current DTA. The reserved portions of this structure contain information that will be required for any subsequent calls to Function 4F, Find Next File, so the DTA should not be disturbed if successive calls will be made.

Once a Find First File call has returned successfully, repeated searches using the same mask and attributes are simple (providing that you have kept the DTA from being distributed in the meantime). Following is the calling sequence:

```
mov     ah,4Fh          ; find next (handle)
int     21h             ; call MS-DOS
jc      error
```

If the carry flag is set upon return, the error code in AX will most likely be 12h, no more files. It also can be 2, file not found, or 3, path not found, but since those codes were not returned by the required Find First File Call at the start, they cannot happen unless something has made major changes to the file system in the meantime, such as renaming a directory along the path specified by the search pattern.

Handle Management

The first step toward use of the handle-based functions is to obtain a handle, which is done either by creating a new file or opening an existing one. The `create` function also can be used to open an existing file or device, and if it's a file that is opened, all existing content will be discarded.

To create a new file or truncate an existing one, point DS:DX to a path specification (which can include drive and directory information in addition to the filename and extension) in ASCIIZ format, and load CX with the bitmap of attributes (the same as described earlier for Find First File, Function 4Eh). Then use a calling sequence like this:

```
mov     cx,Attrib               ; File attributes
push    ds                      ; save data segment
mov     dx,seg FileSpec         ; far pointer
mov     ds,dx
mov     dx,offset FileSpec
mov     ah,3Ch                  ; create file
int     21h                     ; call MS-DOS
pop     ds                      ; restore data segment
jc      error
mov     Handle,ax               ; The Handle
```

If the carry flag is set upon return, the error code in AX will be one of three values: 3 indicates that a directory in the specified path could not be located, 4 that the maximum number of open files had already been reached leaving no handle or SFT available for this function's use, and 5 means that access has been denied, either because a read-only file of the specified name already exists, or because the file is being created in a root directory that is already full.

If the function succeeds, the file is opened in read-write mode even though you specified that it be read-only; the read-only attribute does not take effect until the file is closed. Sharing mode will be set to "compatibility mode" and if you desire other attributes you must close the handle and reopen it using Function 3Dh, with the specified sharing attributes.

This function can be used to create a volume label for a disk that does not already have one, by specifying `ATTR_VOLUMEID` in the attribute bitmap. The volume label must be located in the disk's root directory.

To open an existing file without losing its contents (the normal way, in other words) use Function 3Dh. In addition to the ASCIIZ pathspec required when creating a file, this function requires that you specify the access mode to be used, in the AL register. The low two bits specify read-write mode, Bits 4 through 6 specify sharing mode, and the most significant bit specifies inheritance mode. The codes used are:

`READONLY`	0	File cannot be written to while open.
`WRITEONLY`	1	File cannot be read, only written.
`READWRITE`	2	Normal read-write actions permitted.
`COMPATIBILITY`	00h	Allow other programs full access while open.
`DENYALL`	10h	Prohibit any other program from opening file.
`DENYWRITE`	20h	Allow only read-only access by other program.
`DENYREAD`	30h	Allow only write-only access by others.
`DENYNONE`	40h	Allow other programs that specify sharing mode full access to file but prohibit use of compatibility mode by them.
`NOINHERIT`	80h	Prohibit child process from inheriting this handle; if not set, handle will be passed on to any child process.

Following is the calling sequence, in assembly language, for Function 3Dh:

```
mov     al,AccessBits        ; access modes
push    ds                   ; save data segment
mov     dx,seg FileSpec      ; far pointer
mov     ds,dx
mov     dx,offset FileSpec
mov     ah,3Dh               ; open handle
int     21h                  ; call MS-DOS
pop     ds                   ; restore data segment
jc      error
mov     Handle,ax            ; The Handle
```

If the carry flag is set upon return, the error code in AX will be one of five values: 2 indicates that the file could not be found, 3 means that one of the directories in the specified path could not be located, 4 indicates that the maximum number of files were already open, 5 indicates that access has been denied, and 0Ch indicates `invalid access`.

Access may be denied (error code 5) for several reasons. You may have attempted to open a directory or a volume label, or you may have requested write access to a read-only file. The `invalid access` code is returned when you specify a sharing mode and the file is already opened by another process in a mode that prohibits your requested access mode.

Function 3D can be used to determine whether a directory actually exists or not, by attempting to open the CON device using the directory whose existence is to be tested. Since CON is actually a character device, and as such appears to exist in all directories of all drives, the attempt to open it will succeed if the directory does exist. If the directory is not there, however, the attempt will fail with error code 3. If the attempt does succeed, be sure to immediately close the handle you obtain, to prevent waste of limited resources.

We've already noted that MS-DOS re-uses the SFT entries for the five predefined handles so that all processes share the same SFT for each of the three devices involved. You can force a new handle to be assigned that shares the SFT of an already-open handle, by using Function 45h, Duplicate File Handle. Following is the calling sequence, in assembly language, for this function:

```
mov     bx,Handle          ; the existing handle
mov     ah,45h             ; duplicate handle
int     21h                ; call MS-DOS
jc      error
mov     NewHandle,ax       ; the duplicate
```

If the carry flag is set upon return, the error code in AX will be either 4, indicating that the limit for the number of open files had already been reached, or 6, indicating that the handle passed into the function in BX was not valid.

The new handle returned duplicates all characteristics of the original including write, access, and inheritance modes. Using either handle to read or write moves the file pointer for both.

The primary use of this function in applications, prior to Version 5 of MS-DOS, was to force immediate writing of data to the disk without waiting for the file to be closed and reopened. A duplicate handle can be created by Function 45h, then closed, and all buffers will be flushed to disk and the directory data updated. The original handle, however, remains open for use. This action is much faster than closing the file and opening it again. A special function to do the same thing now is available, and we'll examine it in a few more pages.

An alternate to the simple `Force Duplicate` function allows you to specify the handle to be assigned to the duplicate, rather than simply taking the next one available from the handle table. If the requested handle is already in use, the file or device to which it refers is closed before the handle is assigned as a duplicate. Following is the calling sequence, in assembly language, for this function:

```
mov     bx,Handle       ; existing handle
mov     cx,NewHandle    ; desired duplicate
mov     ah,46h          ; force dup handle
int     21h             ; call MS-DOS
jc      error
```

If the carry flag is set upon return, the error code in AX will be one of the same two that may be returned for Function 45h. If the function succeeds, all the caveats noted above with regard to duplicates created by Function 45h will apply.

This function is used primarily by command shells to force redirection of `STDIN` and `STDOUT`, and to restore the original `SFT` values when the redirection ends. The `STDERR` predefined handle is used as the "existing handle" when ending redirection; that's why COMMAND.COM does not permit it to be redirected.

All four of these methods of obtaining a handle require you to store the returned handle value someplace for future reference, because it's the only link you have with the SFT that actually controls file operations for the functions described in the rest of this chapter.

More Ways to Open a Handle

As MS-DOS applications grew more advanced, the simple open and create calls turned out to be somewhat less than convenient to use in many cases, so additional ways to open a handle were added in subsequent versions of the operating system.

One of the first special functions added was Function 5Ah, which assigns a unique name for a temporary file and creates the file. Rather than passing to it an ASCIIZ full filespec, you provide it with only the path, ending in a backslash followed by the all-zero terminating byte, but with 13 more bytes available in the buffer. The function creates a unique name for the file, and returns it in this buffer.

That's the only difference between this function and Function 3Ch, but using Function 5Ah makes it impossible to destroy an existing file by accidentally truncating it. Following is the calling sequence:

```
mov     cx,Attributes         ; same as for 3Dh
push    ds                    ; save data segment
mov     dx,seg TempPath       ; far pointer
mov     ds,dx
mov     dx,offset TempPath
mov     ah,5Ah                ; make tempfile
int     21h                   ; call MS-DOS
pop     ds                    ; restore data segment
jc      error
mov     Handle,ax             ; The Handle
```

If the carry flag is set upon return, the error code in AX will be either 3, 4, or 5, just as when using Function 3Ch.

MS-DOS does not automatically delete any temporary file created by this function. Your program must save the returned filename and explicitly delete the file when you are through with it. This permits temporary files to be used as auxiliary "pipes" between cooperating processes that are all spawned as child processes of a parent "dispatching" application.

Sometimes it's handy to be able to create a new file, using a name of your choice, while still preventing accidental truncation of the file if it already exists. That's the purpose of Function 5Bh, which is identical to Function 3Ch except that this function will fail if the file already exists rather than truncating it to zero length.

Following is the calling sequence, in assembly language, for Function 5Bh:

```
mov     cx,Attributes        ; same as for 3Dh
push    ds                   ; save data segment
mov     dx,seg FileSpec      ; far pointer
mov     ds,dx
mov     dx,offset FileSpec
mov     ah,5Bh               ; make new file
int     21h                  ; call MS-DOS
pop     ds                   ; restore data segment
jc      error
mov     Handle,ax            ; The Handle
```

If the carry flag is set upon return, the error code in AX will be one of the three described for Function 3Ch, or 50h meaning that the file already existed.

Both Function 5Ah and 5Bh behave identically to Function 3Ch if successful; the new file is created with read-write access and opened in compatibility mode. If read-only access is specified, it does not take effect until the file is closed.

The multiplicity of various ways to create or open handles was finally pulled together by introducing Function 6Ch, which combined them all into a single call. This is the function to use for all new program development, but you still need to be aware of the older methods because many existing programs have not yet been rewritten to use Function 6Ch.

Function 6Ch uses bitmaps in the BX, CX, and DX registers to specify all the possible combinations of actions desired. The bitmap in BX specifies the access, sharing, inheritance, and control modes to be used (control modes are new, introduced with this function). That in CX defines the attributes to be used in creating the file. The one in DX specifies what to do if the file exists, or if it does not.

The bitmap in BX is identical to that used in AL by Function 3Dh, with the addition of two new codes:

`NO_CRIT_ERR`	2000h	Do not call Critical Error Handler, instead just fail and return error code to caller.
`AUTO_COMMIT`	4000h	Force buffers to be flushed to disk and directory entry to be updated each time the file is written to.

The attribute code loaded into CX is identical to that used by the FCB entries and by Function 3Ch, but the ATTR_VOLUMEID and ATTR_DIRECTORY bits are not valid.

The codes used in the DX register are as follows:

FILE_OPEN	0001h	Open the file if it exists, without truncation. Fail if file does not exist.
FILE_TRUNCATE	0002h	Open the file if it exists and truncate it to zero length. Fail if file does not exist.
FILE_CREATE	0010h	Create a new file if the file does not already exist. Fail if file exists.

When these codes are combined, failure will occur only if none of the specified conditions is met. For example, you can use 0012h to duplicate the actions of Function 3Ch, or 0010h to duplicate those of Function 5Bh.

A status code is returned in CX to let your program determine just what action was taken if the call is successful.

Following is the calling sequence, in assembly language, for this function:

```
mov     bx,OpenMode           ; see text
mov     cx,Attributes         ; see text
mov     dx,Action             ; see text
push    ds                    ; save data segment
mov     si,seg FileSpec       ; far pointer
mov     ds,si
mov     si,offset FileSpec
mov     ah,6Ch                ; generic open handle
int     21h                   ; call MS-DOS
pop     ds                    ; restore data segment
jc      error
mov     ActionStatus,cx       ; status code
```

If the carry flag is set upon return, the error code in AX will be one of five values. A code of 1 indicates that the function's syntax was not followed, 2 means that the file was not found, 3 that the specified path was invalid, 4 that the maximum number of open files had already been reached, and 5 that access was denied (probably due to one of the reasons cited for Function 3Dh).

The action status code returned in CX will be 1 if an existing file was opened with truncation, 2 if a new file was created, and 3 if an existing file was truncated.

Establishing File Position

When your application makes use of indexed access into files, it's often necessary to position the file pointer accurately rather than just reading from or writing to the next available byte. That's the purpose of the LSEEK capability, Function 42h.

For simple sequential reads or writes, you will not need to use this function. When any file is opened its file pointer is automatically set to the first byte of the file, and the read and write functions move the pointer by the number of bytes read or written.

But when you want to append information to the end of an existing file, rather than overwriting what is already there, you'll need to position the pointer to the first position after the last byte of the file. And if you're using an index for faster access, as do many database-oriented programs, you'll need to set the pointer to the first byte of the desired record as shown by your indexing technique.

Function 42h provides three reference points for determining the new position. You can specify the location with regard to the first byte of the file, the last byte of the file, or the current position. This last capability can be useful if you read a record and then want to replace it with new data of exactly the same length; just set the position back by the number of bytes in the record, using the current-position reference.

The location is specified as a 32-bit signed offset from the reference point. Neither specifying a negative offset from the front of the file nor a positive offset from the end of the file is considered an error. However any position before the front of the file will generate an error on the next operation. If the position is past the end of the file then if the next request is for a read action, it will return an end-of-file indication, but a write operation will skip over the specified number of bytes, leaving undefined values in those locations. This is a common way to reserve file space when writing a file so that you can subsequently position back to the skipped space and fill it with valid data.

Following is the calling sequence, in assembly language, for Function 42h:

```
mov     bx,Handle           ; the file handle
mov     cx,Hi16Offset       ; upper half of offset
mov     dx,Lo16Offset       ; lower half
mov     al,RefPoint         ; 0=BOF, 1=here, 2=EOF
mov     ah,42h              ; set position
int     21h                 ; call MS-DOS
jc      error
mov     Hi16Here,dx         ; new current position
mov     Lo16Here,ax         ; for the file
```

If the carry flag is set upon return, the error code in AX will be either 2, 3, or 5. These indicate file not found, invalid path, or access denied, respectively.

Function 42h can be used to determine the length of a file, and may be more convenient for this purpose than using Find First File if you already have the file opened for any other reason. Simply set CX and DX both to zero, and AL to 2, then call the function to position to the last byte. Store the 32-bit value returned in AX and DX, then return the pointer to its original position. Since all action for this function is done in RAM by manipulating the associated SFT data and no disk accesses are required, it permits speedy performance.

Input, Output, and Translation

The whole purpose of any kind of disk I/O techniques is to accomplish input and output. That's done, in the handle-based methods, by Functions 3Fh and 4Fh, respectively. Both functions require that you supply the handle to be used for input or output, a far pointer to your buffer area, and a count of the number of bytes to be transferred, and both return the number of bytes actually moved if the transfer succeeds.

During the transfer, automatic translation of certain control characters will be done if the handle refers to a character device that is set to operate in ASCII mode. No such automatic translation takes place, however, when dealing with files. This is one of the areas in which operation of the handle-based functions falls somewhat short of true device independence.

Sometimes the results of such action are a bit strange, such as when a program designed to write to a file (and which consequently does its own control-character translation) sends output to a device instead (and MS-DOS translates some of the already-translated characters again, turning CR/LF pairs into triplets of CR/CR/LF).

Following is the calling sequence, in assembly language, to read data from a handle into your buffer area:

```
mov     bx,Handle           ; the handle to use
mov     cx,MaxBytes         ; number to transfer
push    ds                  ; save data segment
mov     dx,seg Buffer       ; far pointer
mov     ds,dx
mov     dx,offset Buffer
mov     ah,3Fh              ; read handle
int     21h                 ; call MS-DOS
pop     ds                  ; restore data segment
jc      error
mov     NumRead,ax          ; number actually read
```

If the carry flag is set upon return, the error code in AX will be either 5, indicating that access was denied, or 6, indicating that the handle passed into the function was not valid.

If the value returned in AX was zero, this means that the end of the file had already been reached and consequently no data was moved into your buffer. If the value is less than the number you requested in CX at entry, then the end of the file was reached during the read. In either case no error is returned.

The calling sequence to write data is almost identical:

```
mov     bx,Handle           ; the handle to use
mov     cx,MaxBytes         ; number to transfer
push    ds                  ; save data segment
mov     dx,seg Buffer       ; far pointer
mov     ds,dx
mov     dx,offset Buffer
mov     ah,40h              ; write handle
int     21h                 ; call MS-DOS
pop     ds                  ; restore data segment
jc      error
mov     NumWrote,ax         ; number actually written
```

If the carry flag is set upon return, the error code in AX will be one of the same two as for Function 3Fh, access denied (5) or invalid handle (6). If the number of bytes written, as returned in AX, is less than the number you requested in CX at entry to the function, the disk has run out of room. Note that this is not reported as an error, but nevertheless is a failure so far as your application is concerned.

If you call this function with CX set to zero at entry, the file will be truncated at its current file pointer position and all disk space beyond that point may be returned to the system for reuse. This is a standard method for cutting a file short, but was not formally documented until Version 5.0 of MS-DOS.

Special Control Capabilities

One special aspect of the handle-based functions involves the IOCTL capability, which permits all kinds of detailed manipulations of the SFT data to be performed and also allows you to access disk devices at the BIOS level while remaining at the much higher (and more defined) conceptual level of MS-DOS functions.

We've already encountered four of the special IOCTL capabilities while looking at absolute disk I/O techniques. Now we'll examine many, but not all, of the rest. The ones we leave out are seldom, if ever, used by applications.

The most general capability of the group is represented by the first two subfunctions: 4400h, Get Device Information, and 4401h, Set Device Information. These allow you to read the device attributes that are set in the SFT entry for a specified handle, and to change those that are not read-only in nature.

Following is the calling sequence, in assembly language, for Subfunction 4400h:

```
mov     bx,Handle          ; the file handle
mov     ax,4400h           ; get device information
int     21h                ; call MS-DOS
jc      error
mov     DevData,dx         ; the attributes
```

If the carry flag is set upon return, the error code in AX will be 1, 5, or 6. A value of 1 indicates some error in the syntax of your call, 5 that access is denied, and 6 that you have passed the function an invalid handle.

If successful, the device data is returned in DX. The bits have the following meanings:

Bits	Meaning
0-5	Drive number (0=A, 1=B, 2=C, and so on).
6	If set, file has not been written to; if clear, it has been.

Bits	Meaning
7	Always 0 for a file; 1 indicates a device. This can be used to detect redirection.
8-15	Always 0 for a file.

Note that the drive number specified by bits 0 through 5 may not be valid, if the file is a network file that is not associated with a redirected drive.

While Subfunction 4401h can be used with a file handle, it cannot change how MS-DOS uses that file and is essentially a useless operation in this case. Following is the calling sequence for Subfunction 4401h:

```
mov     bx,Handle          ; the file handle
mov     dx,DevData         ; the new attributes
mov     ax,4401h           ; set device information
int     21h                ; call MS-DOS
jc      error
```

If the carry flag is set upon return, the error code in AX will be one of four values: 1 indicates that the function is not valid in the context in which it was called, 5 that access was denied, 6 that the handle was not valid, and 0Dh that the data supplied was not valid.

Two subfunctions, 4404h and 4405h, permit you to read from or write to the *control channel* of a block device. The actions performed by these two functions depend entirely on the specific device driver involved; there's no standard. The drivers supplied with MS-DOS version 6.0 for the normal disk drives return error code 1 for both cases.

Note that both subfunctions refer to entire drives rather than to specified handles associated with the drive.

Following is the calling sequence, in assembly language, for Subfunction 4404h:

```
mov     bl,DriveCode       ; 0=current, 1=A, 2=B
mov     cx,MaxBytes        ; size of buffer
push    ds                 ; save data segment
mov     dx,seg Buffer      ; far pointer
mov     ds,dx
mov     dx,offset Buffer
mov     ax,4404h           ; read block control
int     21h                ; call MS-DOS
```

```
pop     ds                  ; restore data segment
jc      error
mov     BytesRead,ax        ; number actually read
```

Following is the calling sequence for Subfunction 4405h:

```
mov     bl,DriveCode        ; 0=current, 1=A, 2=B
mov     cx,MaxBytes         ; size of buffer
push    ds                  ; save data segment
mov     dx,seg Buffer       ; far pointer
mov     ds,dx
mov     dx,offset Buffer
mov     ax,4405h            ; write block control
int     21h                 ; call MS-DOS
pop     ds                  ; restore data segment
jc      error
mov     BytesWrote,ax       ; number actually written
```

If the carry flag is set upon return from either of these, the error code in AX will be one of the same four described for Subfunction 4401h.

Two subfunctions, 4406h and 4407h, allow testing of input and output status for a handle, respectively. Subfunction 4406h tests input status, and 4407h is supposed to do the same for output status (it doesn't). Following is the calling sequence, in assembly language, for Subfunction 4406h:

```
mov     bx,Handle           ; the file handle
mov     ax,4406h            ; get input status
int     21h                 ; call MS-DOS
jc      error
mov     InStat,al           ; the status
```

If the carry flag is set upon return, the error code in AX will be either 1, 5, or 6, indicating that the function is not supported, access has been denied, or the handle was not valid, respectively.

If the carry flag is not set, the status returned in AL has the following meanings for a file handle (those for a character device are different):

Value	Meaning
00h	File pointer is at end of file.
FFh	Ready.

Following is the calling sequence, in assembly language, for Subfunction 4407h:

```
mov     bx,Handle          ; the file handle
mov     ax,4407h           ; get output status
int     21h                ; call MS-DOS
jc      error
mov     OutStat,al         ; the status
```

If the carry flag is set upon return, the error code in AX will be either 1, 5, or 6, indicating that the function is not supported, access has been denied, or the handle was not valid, respectively.

This function always returns `ready` for an output file, even if the disk is full or no disk is in the drive, making it worse than useless. Avoid it, if you want to create reliable programs.

The next two subfunctions refer to drives rather than to handles. Subfunction 4408h tells whether a drive's media is removable (i.e. floppy) or not. Following is the calling sequence:

```
mov     bl,DriveCode       ; 0=current, 1=A, 2=B
mov     ax,4408h           ; is media removable?
int     21h                ; call MS-DOS
jc      error
mov     FixedMedia,ax      ; 1=fixed, 0=removable
```

If the carry flag is set upon return, the error code in AX will be either 1, function not supported, or 0Fh, invalid drive.

If the carry flag is not set, the value returned in AX has the following meanings:

Value	**Meaning**
0000h	Device media removable.
0001h	Media not removable.

Subfunction 4409h reports whether a block device is remote, plus many other characteristics that may be of interest. Following is the calling sequence:

```
mov     bl,DriveCode       ; 0=current, 1=A, 2=B
mov     ax,4409h           ; is device remote?
int     21h                ; call MS-DOS
jc      error
mov     Stat,dx            ; drive status bitmap
```

If the carry flag is set upon return, the error code in AX will be either 1, function not supported, or 0Fh, invalid drive.

If the carry flag is not set, the bitmap returned in DX has the following meanings:

Bit	Meaning
1	If set, drive uses 32-bit addressing.
6	If set, drive accepts subfunctions 440Dh, 440Eh, and 440Fh.
7	If set, drive accepts subfunction 4411h.
9	If set, drive is local but shared by other computers in network.
11	If set, drive accepts subfunction 4408h.
12	If set, drive is remote and all other bits are zero. If clear, drive is not remote and other bits have indicated meanings.
13	If set, drive required Media Descriptor in FAT.
14	If set, drive accepts subfunctions 4404h and 4405h.
15	If set, drive is SUBST drive (part of another drive).

All other bits of the word are set to zero.

Subfunction 440Ah can be used to determine if a specific handle is remote, and also returns other information about the handle. Following is the calling sequence:

```
mov     bx,Handle           ; the file handle
mov     ax,440Ah            ; is handle remote?
int     21h                 ; call MS-DOS
jc      error
mov     FileStat,dx         ; bitmap of status
```

If the carry flag is set upon return, the error code in AX will be either 1, function not supported, or 0Fh, invalid drive.

If the carry flag is not set, the bitmap returned in DX has the following meanings:

Bit	Meaning
0-5	Drive number (0=A, 1=B, 2=C, and so on).
6	If set, file has not been written to.
7	Always 1 for file; if 0, handle refers to a character device.
12	If set, handle will not be inherited by child processes. If clear, handle is inherited normally.
14	If set, file's date and time will not be updated when file is closed.
15	If set, file is remote. If clear, file is local.

All other bits of the word are set to zero.

Subfunction 440Bh sets the number of times that MS-DOS will repeat a failing disk operation if the failure is due to a sharing conflict. Unlike the other IOCTL functions, this one applies to the entire file system and does not require that either a handle or a drive be specified. Following is the calling sequence, in assembly language, for this function:

```
mov     cx,Loops            ; number of times to loop
mov     dx,Retries          ; number of retries
mov     ax,440Bh            ; set retry count
int     21h                 ; call MS-DOS
jc      error
```

If the carry flag is set upon return, the error code in AX will be 1, indicating that the function is not supported. This function is meaningful only if SHARE is loaded.

Default values are 3 for Retries and 1 for Loops. If your program changes them with this function, you should restore the default values before terminating your program.

One of the most versatile of the IOCTL subfunctions is 440Dh, "Generic IOCTL for block devices." This subfunction includes the four absolute I/O capabilities we examined earlier, but also provides much more. When CX is set to 0860h, for example, it can read off the parameters for a specified drive. Following is the calling sequence:

```
mov     bx,DriveCode        ; 0=current, 1=A, 2=B
push    ds                  ; save data segment
mov     dx,seg Buffer       ; far pointer
mov     ds,dx
mov     dx,offset Buffer
mov     ax,440Dh            ; generic IOCTL
mov     cx,0860h            ; get device parameters
int     21h                 ; call MS-DOS
pop     ds                  ; restore data segment
jc      error
```

If the carry flag is set upon return, the error code in AX will be either 1, 2, or 5 (`invalid function`, `file not found`, or `access denied`). The `file not found` code is returned rather than `invalid drive` if the drive number passed in is not valid.

Operation of this capability is most easily described by means of a working example. The following C program, which also appears on the companion diskette, demonstrates the kinds of information you can obtain:

```
/*
 *      DPARM.C - Jim Kyle - April 1993
 *
 *      Requires Borland compiler unless "asm" changed to "_asm"
 *      throughout the file.
 */
#include <stdio.h>
#include <dos.h>

void main( void )
{ char far *fcb1;
  int Drive;
  struct {
    unsigned char dpSpecFunc;              /* DEVICEPARMS struct   */
    unsigned char dpDevType;
    unsigned int  dpDevAttr;
    unsigned int  dpCylinders;
    unsigned char dpMediaType;
    unsigned int  dpBytesPerSec;
```

```
  unsigned char dpSecPerClust;
  unsigned int  dpResSectors;
  unsigned char dpFATs;
  unsigned int  dpRootDirEnts;
  unsigned int  dpSectors;
  unsigned char dpMedia;
  unsigned int  dpFATsecs;
  unsigned int  dpSecPerTrack;
  unsigned int  dpHeads;
  unsigned long dpHiddenSecs;
  unsigned long dpHugeSectors;
  unsigned int  dpSkip1[3];          /* unused words to test */
  unsigned int  dpTrkLayout;           /* used only by 0840h */
} dparm;
unsigned int segptr, offptr;

dparm.dpSpecFunc = 1;          /* get current info            */

fcb1 = MK_FP( _psp, 0x5C );    /* use FCB trick to get drive   */
Drive = *fcb1;
segptr = FP_SEG( (void far *)&dparm );
offptr = FP_OFF( (void far *)&dparm );

asm mov bx,Drive;              /* call the DOS function        */
asm mov cx,0x0860;
asm mov dx,offptr;
asm mov ax,segptr;
asm push ds
asm mov ds,ax
asm mov ax,0x440D;
asm int 0x21;
asm pop ds

printf( "Parameters for drive %i:\n", Drive );
printf( "     dpSpecFunc: %6i      dpDevType: %6i\n",
        dparm.dpSpecFunc, dparm.dpDevType );
printf( "      dpDevAttr: %6i    dpCylinders: %6i    ",
        dparm.dpDevAttr, dparm.dpCylinders );
printf( "dpMediaType: %6i\n", dparm.dpMediaType );
printf( "  dpBytesPerSec: %6i  dpSecPerClust: %6i\n",
        dparm.dpBytesPerSec, dparm.dpSecPerClust );
printf( "   dpResSectors: %6i         dpFATs: %6i\n",
```

```
        dparm.dpResSectors, dparm.dpFATs );
  printf( "  dpRootDirEnts: %6i      dpSectors: %6i       ",
        dparm.dpRootDirEnts, dparm.dpSectors );
  printf( "dpMedia: %6X\n", dparm.dpMedia );
  printf( "      dpFATsecs: %6i  dpSecPerTrack: %6i       ",
        dparm.dpFATsecs, dparm.dpSecPerTrack );
  printf( "dpHeads: %6i\n", dparm.dpHeads );
  printf( "   dpHiddenSecs: %6li  dpHugeSectors: %6li    ",
        dparm.dpHiddenSecs, dparm.dpHugeSectors );
  printf( "dpTrkLayout: %5i\n", dparm.dpTrkLayout );
}
```

To compile `DPARM.C`, use any of the Borland compilers (for Microsoft compilers, edit the `asm` keyword to be `_asm` every place it appears). If you invoke the program by its name alone, it will return the parameters for the current default drive. If you supply a drive letter, it will return the parameters for that drive.

Note that the `FCB` trick of retrieving from the default `FCB`'s set up in the `PSP` is used to determine the drive letter. While this is not, in general, a good technique to use, it's still perfectly valid for special cases such as this one. It should not be used, however, when a subdirectory reference might be involved.

This program returns values from DoubleSpaced drives, under MS-DOS version 6.0, as well as from normal drives, but several of the fields show interesting differences. Figure 9.5 shows the display of my Drive C, the normal uncompressed drive, together with that for Drive D, which is a DoubleSpace compressed volume.

Note the differences in the `dpMediaType` and `dpTrkLayout` fields; all other differences shown are reasonable, and result from the actual differences between the two drives in terms of effective capacity, special functions, and so on. These two fields, however, don't show such differences. The value returned for `dpTrkLayout` from a normal drive (though it's not obvious from Figure 9.5) simply is whatever value was in those two bytes of the buffer originally, while the call zeroes out this field when a DoubleSpaced drive is involved.

The `dpMediaType` field appears to be a simple coding error in the return when a DoubleSpaced drive is involved, since the "240" returned is identical with the content of the `dpMedia` field, 0F8h.

```
C:>dparm c:
Parameters for drive 3:
      dpSpecFunc:        1       dpDevType:      5
       dpDevAttr:        1     dpCylinders:   1023    dpMediaType:       0
  dpBytesPerSec:       512  dpSecPerClust:      4
    dpResSectors:        1         dpFATs:      2
  dpRootDirEnts:       512       dpSectors:      0        dpMedia:      F8
       dpFATsecs:      153  dpSecPerTrack:     17        dpHeads:       9
   dpHiddenSecs:        17  dpHugeSectors: 156502    dpTrkLayout:    1220

C:>dparm d:
Parameters for drive 4:
      dpSpecFunc:        4       dpDevType:      5
       dpDevAttr:        0     dpCylinders:   4096    dpMediaType:     248
  dpBytesPerSec:       512  dpSecPerClust:     16
    dpResSectors:       20         dpFATs:      2
  dpRootDirEnts:       512       dpSectors:      0        dpMedia:      F8
       dpFATsecs:      156  dpSecPerTrack:     17        dpHeads:       9
   dpHiddenSecs:         0  dpHugeSectors: 237764    dpTrkLayout:       0
```

Figure 9.5. Following is the information returned by DPARM when run for my normal drive C:, and for DoubleSpaced drive D:. The differences are discussed in the text.

The fields labelled as `dpSpecFunc`, `dpDevType`, `dpDevAttr`, and `dpMediaType` can be interpreted to learn many details about the drive. For example, `dpDevType` tells specifically what kind of block device contains the drive:

Value	Device Type
0	320K or 360K 5.25-inch floppy diskette drive.
1	1.2M 5.25-inch floppy diskette drive.
2	720K 3.5-inch diskette drive.
3	8-inch single-density diskette drive.
4	8-inch double-density diskette drive.
5	Fixed disk drive.
6	Tape drive.
7	1.44M 3.5-inch diskette drive.
8	Read/write optical drive.
9	2.88M 3.5-inch diskette drive.

The `dpDevAttr` field tells some attributes of the device in bitmap form:

Bit	Device Attributes
0	If set, medium is not removable, else it is removable.
1	If set, change-line feature is supported (door-lock for floppy drives).

The `dpSpecFunc` field is used at entry to the function to specify special actions via bitmapped instructions. Some of the requests apply only when setting the information, not when reading:

Bit	Action Requested
0	If set, use device's BPB for all subsequent BuildBPB requests; if clear, use data from supplied fields to establish BPB.
1	If set, use `dpTrkLayout` information at end of structure and ignore all other fields; if clear, read all fields.
2	If set, all sectors in a track are the same size, and are in the range 1 through the number of sectors on a track (i.e. no number omitted or out of range). If clear, nonstandard formatting is permitted. This bit should always be set.

Finally, the `dpMediaType` field tells what types of medium the drive currently accepts, and applies only to those drives having removable media:

Bit	Acceptable Media
0	If set, drive is set up for lower-density media (360K if 5.25-inch, 720K if 3.5-inch). If clear, drive is set for higher density.

The complementary subfunction, when CX is set to 0840h, writes new parameters for the specified drive. Following is the calling sequence:

```
mov     bx,DriveCode       ; 0=current, 1=A, 2=B
push    ds                 ; save data segment
mov     dx,seg Buffer      ; far pointer
```

```
mov     ds,dx
mov     dx,offset Buffer
mov     ax,440Dh          ; generic IOCTL
mov     cx,0840h          ; set device parameters
int     21h               ; call MS-DOS
pop     ds                ; restore data segment
jc      error
```

If the carry flag is set upon return, the error code in AX will be 1, 2, or 5, just as for `Get Device Parameters`.

Note that misuse of this call (along with any of the 084* functions which alter disk characteristics) can destroy all data on the referenced disk. Be sure that you know exactly what you are doing, and test all programs that use such calls with extreme care.

To read the volume label or serial number from a drive into an `MID` structure (see Chapter 4), use Subfunction 440Dh with CX set to 0866h and ES:DX pointing to the buffer in which the structure will be written. Following is the calling sequence:

```
mov     bx,DriveCode      ; 0=current, 1=A, 2=B
push    ds                ; save data segment
mov     dx,seg Buffer     ; far pointer
mov     ds,dx
mov     dx,offset Buffer
mov     ax,440Dh          ; generic IOCTL
mov     cx,0866h          ; get Media ID
int     21h               ; call MS-DOS
pop     ds                ; restore data segment
jc      error
```

If the carry flag is set upon return, the error code in AX will be 1, 2, or 5, just as for `Get Device Parameters`. If successful, the buffer will contain a filled-in `MID` structure containing the serial number, volume label, and file system type name.

The complementary call to create a new serial number, volume label, and file system type name is with CX set to 0846h. Note that while this changes the information contained in the boot record of the addressed drive, it has no effect on the `VolumeLabel` entry in the root directory, which is the one that `DIR` uses to report the label. The label kept in the boot record is actually of little or no use. Following is the calling sequence, in assembly language, to write out a MID structure:

```
mov     bx,DriveCode        ; 0=current, 1=A, 2=B
push    ds                  ; save data segment
mov     dx,seg Buffer       ; far pointer
mov     ds,dx
mov     dx,offset Buffer
mov     ax,440Dh            ; generic IOCTL
mov     cx,0846h            ; set Media ID
int     21h                 ; call MS-DOS
pop     ds                  ; restore data segment
jc      error
```

If the carry flag is set upon return, the error code in AX will be 1, 2, or 5, just as for `Get Device Parameters`.

The final minor code from Subfunction 440Dh that we'll look at is one that tells what type of media is currently in a drive that is capable of dealing with more than one type. Following is the calling sequence; the buffer supplied here is only two bytes long:

```
mov     bx,DriveCode        ; 0=current, 1=A, 2=B
push    ds                  ; save data segment
mov     dx,seg Buffer       ; far pointer
mov     ds,dx
mov     dx,offset Buffer
mov     ax,440Dh            ; generic IOCTL
mov     cx,0868h            ; get media type
int     21h                 ; call MS-DOS
pop     ds                  ; restore data segment
jc      error
```

If the carry flag is set upon return, the error code in AX will be either invalid function (the specified drive does not allow different media types) or access denied. If the function succeeds, the first byte of the buffer will be set to 1 if the drive currently holds its default media type, or 0 if the media is any type other than the default. The second byte indicates the type of media presently in the drive; it will be set to 2 for 720K disks, 7 for 1.44M disks, and 9 for 2.88M disks.

One of the most perplexing problems that DOS developers who work with floppy diskette drives must face is how to handle the single-floppy system that uses two different drive letters, A and B, to refer to its single drive. If their program refers to the drive by the wrong letter, their carefully crafted screen layout will be disrupted by a message from MS-DOS telling the user to place a diskette in the drive, even if one is already there.

The message, of course, refers to the drive by the letter that the program used, rather than the one that MS-DOS knew was currently in use. The problem the developer must solve is how to determine which letter the system is using at any given instant. When this is known, the program can use that reference, or can just as easily switch the system to use the other designation. But how can you tell who's on first?

Subfunction 440Eh, introduced to MS-DOS with version 3.2, can solve the problem. Following is its calling sequence, in assembly language:

```
mov     bl,DriveCode        ; 0=current, 1=A, 2=B
mov     ax,440Eh            ; get drive map
int     21h                 ; call MS-DOS
jc      error
mov     ActiveCode,al       ;
```

If the carry flag is set upon return, the error code in AX will be either 1 (`invalid function`), 2 (`access denied`), or 0Fh (`invalid drive`). If successful, the currently active drive code will be returned in AL. If the physical drive has only one number, no error is reported but the code returned in AL will be 0.

The code supplied in BL at entry can be either of those that might be in use by the drive in question; the one returned in AL is the one that is currently active.

To adjust the active code to refer to the drive letter you want, should it not be a match already, you can use Subfunction 440Fh. Following is the calling sequence:

```
mov     bl,DriveCode        ; 0=current, 1=A, 2=B
mov     ax,440Fh            ; set drive map
int     21h                 ; call MS-DOS
jc      error
```

If the carry flag is set upon return, the error code in AX will be the same as for Get Drive Map. Otherwise the active code for the drive will be set to match the value you provided in the BL register.

Use of these two functions together permits your applications to switch the drive reference, completely transparent so far as the users are concerned. The following assembly language routine shows how:

```
; DRVFIX.ASM - based on routine written by Brian Bayorgeon

; this will eliminate the MS-DOS message "Insert Disk for Drive A/B"
; call with 1-based drive number as parameter (A=1, B=2)
; returns 0 if any error, 1 if all is well

.model small,c                  ; create module for C use

.code

drvfix    proc    drvnbr:word
          public  drvfix
          cmp     drvnbr,2      ; see if we need to worry about remap
          jg      okay          ; not a: or b: so skip whole thing
          mov     ax,440Eh      ; get logical device (drive) map
          mov     bl,drvnbr     ; check out drive for read/write
          int     21h           ; call MS-DOS
          cmp     al,0          ; see if remapping possible
          je      okay          ; if al=0 two floppy drives exist
          cmp     al,drvnbr     ; see if floppy is remapped
          je      okay          ; not remapped, all is well
          mov     ax,440Fh      ; set logical device (drive) map
          mov     bl,drvnbr     ; remap floppy
          int     21h           ; call MS-DOS
          jnc     okay
          xor     ax,ax         ; return 0 if error
          jmp     short   exit
okay:     mov     ax,1          ; return 1 if okay
exit:     ret
drvfix    endp
          end
```

While based, by permission, on a routine written by Brian Bayorgeon and posted on CompuServe, any problems introduced in the version presented here are strictly my own. Note that you may need to edit the `.model` line at the start of this routine, to define the memory model and language conventions you want to use it with. As shown (and as supplied on the companion diskette) it is for use with C in the small memory model.

When the object file that results from assembling this program (using either MASM 5.1+ or TASM in MASM51 mode) is linked into your application and called with a drive code of either 0, 1, or 2, it will remap the corresponding drive if necessary and then return 1 to indicate success. A return value of 0 indicates that the remapping could not be performed.

The final subfunction we examine is 4411h, introduced to MS-DOS at version 5.0. This subfunction tests to determine whether any desired variation of the generic capability in Subfunction 440Dh is supported for a specific drive. The minor code for 440Dh, as described in the preceding pages for each capability, is placed into CX (that is, to query the availability of the Get Media ID capability, you would load CX with 0866h), and then Subfunction 4411h is called. Following is the calling sequence:

```
mov     bl,DriveCode        ; 0=current, 1=A, 2=B
mov     cx,IOCTLCode        ; see text
mov     ax,4411h            ; query generic
int     21h                 ; call MS-DOS
jc      CannotUse
```

If the carry flag is set upon return, the error code in AX will be 1 if the device driver does not support `IOCTL` functions at all, 5 if the driver supports `IOCTL` but does not support the specific function requested, and 6 if the drive specified is not valid. If the carry flag is clear, the function can be called.

Preventing Loss of Handles

We've already noted that by default, each process in the system is limited to a maximum of 20 handles, but that the total number of handles available in the system is also limited by the number of SFTs available, as set by the `FILES=` line in CONFIG.SYS.

Because the number of handles available in the system is a resource with definite limits, it behooves us to take special care to avoid wasting any of them. One of the most common ways in which handles are wasted is by losing them during installation of TSR programs.

Many users redirect the standard output of all TSR programs they install to the NUL device in order to suppress any output to the CRT when the program installs. Because of the way that COMMAND.COM deals with redirection, an additional handle is used to provide access to the target device. And when any process terminates and stays resident, all of its handles remain open. This effectively "loses" them so far as the rest of the system is concerned.

For the five predefined handles, it makes little difference that TSR processes are adding to their usage count; they use only three of the SFTs between them no matter how many users are tallied for each. But each time a TSR redirects output to NUL and goes resident without closing all 20 of its possible handles, one more handle is lost from the system pool.

You cannot do much about other developers' TSR programs, but you can keep your own from adding to the damage by explicitly closing all 20 possible handles just before going resident. This will release any handles being used to keep track of redirection, and will also tally down the usage count of the shared SFTs.

The function you call to do this is 3Eh, Close Handle. Following is the calling sequence:

```
mov     bx,Handle       ; the file handle
mov     ah,3Eh          ; close handle
int     21h             ; call MS-DOS
jc      error
```

If the carry flag is set upon return, the error code in AX may be 6, invalid handle. This indicates that you attempted to close a handle that was not open. Since this error is harmless, you can simply ignore it in the loop that closes all handles before going resident. Any other error reported may indicate serious problems in the file system, though, since MS-DOS flushes to the disk all buffers connected with a file when the file is closed and any error that is detected during these disk writes will be reported as an error closing the file.

If the file was opened using Function 6Ch, with the `AUTO_COMMIT` bit set in its OpenMode bitmap, then no buffers will remain to be flushed at close time and consequently no errors are likely to be reported.

If you choose not to use the `AUTO_COMMIT` feature to force all buffers to be flushed each time the file is written to, you can still force such cleanup at critical points within your application by using Function 68h, introduced to MS-DOS at Version 3.3. Following is the calling sequence, in assembly language, for this function:

```
mov     bx,Handle       ; the file handle
mov     ah,68h          ; commit file now
int     21h             ; call MS-DOS
jc      error
```

If the carry flag is set upon return, the error code in AX will be the same as those returned by Function 40h, Write File.

If your program needs more than 20 handles (an unlikely situation, but possible) you can create a larger handle table by using Function 67h, introduced in Version 3.3. Following is the calling sequence for this function:

```
mov     bx,NumHandles       ; number of handles wanted
mov     ah,67h              ; set handle count
int     21h                 ; call MS-DOS
jc      error
```

If the carry flag is set upon return, the error code in AX will indicate what went wrong. The only value normally to be expected is 1, invalid function.

The expanded handle table is not inherited by any child processes that your application might launch, and the new number of handles requested in BX must be larger than 20. If fewer than 20 are requested, it is changed to 20 automatically.

Renaming and Deleting Files

In addition to all the usual file I/O functions we've seen, the handle-based techniques include a number of housekeeping capabilities. One of them permits you to rename a file, including changing its directory as well, so long as it remains on the same drive. Others allow you to delete files (but only one at a time if you follow documented methods), to get and set the file's attributes, and to get and set its date and time stamp.

To rename a file, use Function 56h. Following is the calling sequence:

```
push    ds                  ; save data segment
mov     dx,seg OldName      ; far pointer
mov     ds,dx
mov     dx,offset OldName
mov     di,seg NewName      ; far pointer
mov     es,di
mov     di,offset NewName
mov     ah,56h              ; rename via handle
pop     ds                  ; restore data segment
int     21h                 ; call MS-DOS
jc      error
```

Both `OldName` and `NewName` must be `ASCIIZ` strings. They may be either full absolute path specifications, or relative specifications. Neither can include any wildcard characters. This is a major difference between this function, and its `FCB`-based equivalent, Function 17h, which can use wildcards.

If the carry flag is set upon return, the error code in AX will be 2, 3, 5, or 11h. A value of 2 indicates that `OldName` could not be found, 3 that one of the directories specified in OldName could not be located, 5 that access to the file has been denied, and 11h that `NewName` and `OldName` did not specify the same drive.

To delete a file, use Function 41h, passing in a far pointer to an `ASCIIZ` string that specifies the file to be deleted. Following is the calling sequence:

```
push    ds                      ; save data segment
mov     dx,seg FileName         ; far pointer
mov     ds,dx
mov     dx,offset FileName
mov     ah,41h                  ; delete file
int     21h                     ; call MS-DOS
pop     ds                      ; restore data segment
jc      error
```

If the carry flag is set upon return, the error code in AX will be either 2 (`file not found`), 3 (`path not found`), or 5 (`access denied`). Access denied will be returned if you attempt to delete a directory, a volume label, or a read-only file.

To read the current attributes held by a file, use Function 4300h, passing in a far pointer to an `ASCIIZ` string that specifies the file of interest. Following is the calling sequence:

```
push    ds                      ; save data segment
mov     dx,seg FileName         ; far pointer
mov     ds,dx
mov     dx,offset FileName
mov     ax,4300h                ; get file attributes
int     21h                     ; call MS-DOS
pop     ds                      ; restore data segment
jc      error
mov     Attributes,cx           ; bitmap of attributes
```

If the carry flag is set upon return, the error code in AX will be either 1 (`invalid function`), 2 (`file not found`), 3 (`path not found`), or 5 (`access denied`).

The attribute bits returned in CX have the following meanings:

Value	Meaning
0000h	ATTR_NORMAL, Normal file.
0001h	ATTR_READONLY, Read-only file.
0002h	ATTR_HIDDEN, Hidden file.
0004h	ATTR_SYSTEM, System file.
0008h	ATTR_VOLUMEID, Volume Label directory entry.
0010h	ATTR_DIRECTORY, Subdirectory entry.
0020h	ATTR_ARCHIVE, File has been modified.

Any combination of the four bits referring to file attributes is acceptable. The system files for MS-DOS itself carry three of the four attribute bits: system, hidden, and archive.

To modify the attributes, use Function 43h, passing in the new attribute bitmap in CX. Following is the calling sequence:

```
mov     cx,Attributes       ; attribute bits
push    ds                  ; save data segment
mov     dx,seg FileName     ; far pointer
mov     ds,dx
mov     dx,offset FileName
mov     ax,4301h            ; set file attributes
int     21h                 ; call MS-DOS
pop     ds                  ; restore data segment
jc      error
```

If the carry flag is set upon return, the error code in AX will be one of the four values described for Function 4300h.

To get a file's date and time as shown in the directory, open the file, then use Function 5700h, passing in the file handle. Following is the calling sequence, in assembly language, for Function 5700h:

```
mov     bx,Handle          ; the file handle
mov     ax,5700h           ; get file date,time
int     21h                ; call MS-DOS
jc      error
mov     FileTime,cx        ; see text
mov     FileDate,dx
```

If the carry flag is set upon return, the error code in AX will most likely be 6, invalid handle. Any other error condition would have prevented the file from being successfully opened.

The time value returned in CX packs the hour, minute, and second into 16 bits, as follows:

Bits	Meaning
0-4	Seconds after minute, divided by 2 (0-29).
5-10	Minutes after hour (0-59).
11-15	Hours after midnight (0-23).

The date value returned in DX packs the day, month, and year into 16 bits, as follows:

Bits	Meaning
0-4	Day of month (1-31).
5-8	Month (1-12).
9-15	Year - 1980 (0 for 1980, 13 for 1993, and so on).

To set a file's date and time, use Function 5701h. Following is the calling sequence:

```
mov     bx,Handle         ; the file handle
mov     cx,FileTime       ; see text
mov     dx,FileDate
mov     ax,5701h          ; set file date,time
int     21h               ; call MS-DOS
jc      error
```

If the carry flag is set upon return, the error code in AX will most likely be 6, invalid handle.

Miscellaneous Disk Functions

We've almost completed our examination of Disk I/O techniques now, but we still have a couple of functions left that didn't seem to fit into any of the earlier subject headings.

The first involves record locking and unlocking. So long as your application will never be used in a network or other multi-user environment you will not need to be concerned about this, but with the rapid rise in popularity of networks that "never used" situation is quite likely to become rarer than hens' teeth in the very near future.

MS-DOS provides a single function to handle both the locking and unlocking of a "record", which may actually be anything from a single byte in length up to the entire file. This function does nothing, and in fact returns error code 1 (invalid function), if used on a system where SHARE.EXE has not been loaded to enable the file-sharing capabilities,

To lock a region of a file, you must first open the file in the appropriate sharing mode in order to get a handle for it. You then load CX:DX with a 32-bit offset to the first byte of the region to be locked, SI:DI with a 32-bit length value (in bytes) for the region, and call Function 5Ch with AL set to zero.

To unlock the region, you must make an identical call except that AL must be set to one. If the offset and length values do not match, the region will not be unlocked.

Following is the calling sequence, in assembly language, for this function:

```
mov     bx,Handle          ; the file handle
mov     cx,HiOffset        ; upper 16 bits of offset
mov     dx,LoOffset        ; lower 16 bits
mov     si,HiLength        ; upper 16 bits of length
mov     di,LoLength        ; lower 16 bits
mov     ah,5Ch             ; lock record
mov     al,LockUnlock      ; 0=lock, 1=unlock
int     21h                ; call MS-DOS
jc      error
```

If the carry flag is set upon return, the error code in AX will be 1 (invalid function, if SHARE not loaded), 6 (invalid handle), 21h (lock violation, file was already locked), or 24h (sharing buffer exceeded).

Error 21h will result from an attempt to unlock a file when the length and offset fail to match those used when the file was locked, or from an attempt to lock a file if any part of the specified region is already locked. It's perfectly valid for different users to lock the same file, so long as their regions do not overlap.

Sometimes a program needs to lock the entire file, for a process that may cause the file's size to increase. To accomodate this situation, Function 5Ch permits you to specify a length greater than that of the file itself. To lock the entire file, you can set CX to 0, DX to 1, SI to 7FFFh, and DI to FFFFh. This will lock 2,147,483,647 bytes, starting with the very first byte in the file, which should be ample for current applications. And if it's not, you can set CX to 8000h and DX to 0, then repeat the call, to lock that many more.

In addition to a need for locking abilities, applications sometimes need to know the actual, full path for a file that has been specified as being on a drive that has been given a "shorthand" name via the DOS SUBST command. Since version 3.0, MS-DOS has had the capability of expanding such names, but it has not yet been officially documented.

To determine the full pathname for a file, point DS:SI to an `ASCIIZ` string containing the name to be expanded, and ES:DI to an empty buffer capable of holding at least 67 bytes (to allow for drive letter and terminating zero byte plus up to 64 bytes of path specification). Then call Interrupt 21h Function 60h. Upon return, the destination buffer will contain the true name of the file. If it is a network file, the drive letter may be replaced by a volume name. On the other hand, if the name was fully expanded to start with, the two versions will be identical.

Following is the calling sequence, in assembly language, for this function:

```
push    ds                  ; save data segment
mov     si,seg FileSpec     ; far pointer
mov     ds,si
mov     si,offset FileSpec
mov     di,seg Buffer       ; far pointer
mov     es,di
mov     di,offset Buffer
mov     ah,60h              ; expand filename
int     21h                 ; call MS-DOS
pop     ds                  ; restore data segment
```

Error Handling

One facet of Disk I/O overshadows all others: it's where the vast majority of all system errors happen. The disk storage medium is inherently the most fragile part of the entire computer system, and most developers are firmly convinced that Murphy's famous law ("If anything can go wrong, it will.") was first discovered while dealing with disk I/O.

Because most errors tend to be associated with the disk interface, this is the most logical place to address the entire subject of error handling. It's a subject big enough for an entire book of its own, so all that we can do here is scratch its surface, but at least you can get an idea of what's required for dealing with errors in a professional application.

Errors can be grouped by several different criteria. For example, you could divide them into "preventable errors" and "unavoidable ones" if you desired, and we'll look at ways of preventing errors where possible as the final part of this section. But even if all preventable errors could be avoided by your program, you'd still be faced with the questions of dealing with those that could not be escaped.

The unavoidable errors can be subdivided into another two groups, *critical* and *non-critical* errors. A critical error, in MS-DOS, is defined as a failure that prevents a requested operation from being completed. A typical example of a critical error is what happens if you issue the command `DIR A:` when drive A: contains no diskette. Without a diskette, the DIR command cannot be executed.

Non-critical errors, then, are all the rest that can happen. They can prevent the system from operating, but are not necessarily "critical" even when they are fatal, such as the accidental corruption of the memory control block chain.

Let's look in a bit more detail at the two categories of unavoidable errors.

Critical Errors: Their Detection and Treatment

MS-DOS provides automatic trapping of the error conditions that it considers to be critical errors, and whenever such a condition is detected, Interrupt 24h is invoked by the system code. The entire purpose of Interrupt 24h is to deal with these critical errors.

By default, a standard handler for such errors is provided as part of the COMMAND.COM shell, and each time an application is launched from the shell, the vector for Interrupt 24h is set to this default handler. That's the code that pops up to tell you that the system is `Not ready reading Drive A` and asks if you want to `Abort, Retry, or Fail?` when you do issue that `DIR` command with no diskette in the drive.

Whenever the MS-DOS system code invokes Interrupt 24h, it sets up the AX, DI, BP, and SI registers to provide information about the error in a standard form to the handler. Full details of this are provided in Chapter 5, "Other DOS Interrupts."

If you don't want your carefully crafted screens to be disrupted by messages from the default Critical Error Handler, you'll need to provide your own to replace it. Depending on your own needs, you can create similar functionality and ask the user what to do about the situation, or you can simply cause any such error to return to your program with an error code.

If you do replace the default handler, you don't have to worry about preserving the original vector and replacing it before leaving your program. Interrupt 24h is one of the three that is automatically replaced by MS-DOS each time a program runs.

Detailed Error Information

If you do create your own critical error handler, or for that matter when you are handling non-critical errors within your application, you'll often find it useful to have a bit more information about any detected error than the bare minimum that you can get from the error code itself. That's the job that Interrupt 21h Function 59h was designed to do.

When called, this function returns a large amount of additional information concerning the most recently detected error. The data you get back includes an extended error code, an indication of the general type of error that it falls into, a recommended procedure for dealing with it, and finally an indication of which part of the system is involved.

Following is the calling sequence, in assembly language, for Function 59h:

```
mov     ah,59h          ; detail error info
int     21h             ; call MS-DOS
cmp     ax,0
je      no_error
mov     ExtErr,ax       ; more detailed error code
mov     Class,bh        ; kind of error
mov     Action,bl       ; suggested recovery action
mov     Locus,ch        ; where it happened
```

If the value returned in AX is zero, no detailed error information is available.

The extended error code returned in AX from this function will have one of the following 71 meanings:

Value	Meaning	Value	Meaning
0001h	Invalid or unsupported function.	0026h	EOF reached during handle function.
0002h	File not found.	0027h	Disk full during handle function.
0003h	Path not found.	0032h	Not supported.
0004h	Too many open files (out of handles or SFT entries).	0033h	Remote not on valid list.
0005h	Access denied.	0034h	Duplicate name.
0006h	Invalid handle.	0035h	Bad network path.
0007h	Memory arena trashed.	0036h	Network busy.
0008h	Not enough memory.	0037h	Device does not exist.
0009h	Invalid block.	0038h	Too many commands.
000Ah	Bad environment.	0039h	Adapter hardware error.
000Bh	Bad format.	003Ah	Bad network response.
000Ch	Invalid access.	003Bh	Unexpected network error.
000Dh	Invalid data.	003Ch	Bad remote adapter.
000Fh	Invalid drive.	003Dh	Print queue is full.
0010h	Attempted to delete current directory.	003Eh	No spooler space is available.
0011h	Attempted to rename to a different drive.	003Fh	Print job cancelled.

Value	Meaning	Value	Meaning
0012h	No more files (end of wildcard Find Next File search).	0040h	Net name deleted.
0013h	Write protection error.	0041h	Network access denied.
0014h	Bad unit.	0042h	Bad device type.
0015h	Not ready.	0043h	Bad net name.
0016h	Bad command.	0044h	Too many names.
0017h	CRC error detected.	0045h	Too many sessions.
0018h	Bad length.	0046h	Sharing paused.
0019h	Seek error.	0047h	Request not accepted.
001Ah	Not a MS-DOS disk.	0048h	Redirector paused.
001Bh	Sector not found.	0050h	File already exists.
001Ch	Out of paper.	0051h	Duplicate FCB.
001Dh	Write fault.	0052h	Cannot make requested item.
001Eh	Read fault.	0053h	Interrupt 24h signalled failure.
001Fh	General Failure.	0054h	Out of structures.
0020h	Sharing violation.	0055h	Already assigned.
0021h	Lock violation.	0056h	Invalid password.
0022h	Wrong disk.	0057h	Invalid parameter.
0023h	FCB is not available.	0058h	Network write fault.
0024h	Sharing buffer exceeded.	005Ah	System component not loaded.
0025h	Code page mismatched.		

The error-type code returned in the BH register will have one of these values, with the corresponding meaning:

Value	Meaning
01h	A resource, such as storage, has been exhausted.
02h	A temporary condition that is expected to end, such as a file being locked against access.
03h	Problem with authorization.
04h	Internal system error.
05h	Hardware failure detected.
06h	System software failure not due to program detecting error, such as missing or wrong configuration files.
07h	Error caused by application.
08h	File or item specified was not found.
09h	File or item had invalid format or type.
0Ah	File or item was interlocked.
0Bh	Storage medium problem such as wrong disk in drive or bad spot on disk.
0Ch	File or item already exists.
0Dh	Type of error cannot be identified.

The recommended action code returned in the BL register can be any of the following values. In most cases, the action recommended will be the one most appropriate for handling the error condition.

Value	Meaning
01h	Retry failed operation immediately.
02h	Wait briefly, then retry operation.
03h	Bad user input, request new values be supplied.
04h	Cannot recover, terminate in orderly fashion.
05h	Cannot recover, terminate as rapidly as possible; continued operation may cause serious damage to data or hardware.

Value	Meaning
06h	Ignore the condition and proceed.
07h	Prompt the user to take appropriate corrective action and then retry the failed operation.

The error location code returned in the CH register may be any of the following values, which indicate the most likely area but cannot always be totally accurate:

Value	Meaning
01h	Location unknown.
02h	Disk drive or other random access storage device.
03h	Network error.
04h	Serial port or modem error.
05h	Memory system.

In general, your handler can branch to one of seven courses of action based on the action recommendation returned in the BL register; the other values will be useful in only some of these actions. If the "panic" course (terminate as rapidly as possible to avoid additional damage) is recommended, for example, you will not really care what the exact area involved might have been.

While it's tempting to write error handlers so that they deal with all errors as invisibly as possible and do not even let the user know that any problem existed unless they have to request additional input, it's often much better to let your users know of all errors that might be detected. If the program is able to deal with them on its own, your notification message can include a line to tell the user `corrected satisfactorily and operation continuing` but this can alert your users to the possibility that they may need to check their hardware, if error frequency increases.

Prevention: the Best Policy

The best kinds of errors, of course, are those that don't happen at all. Every program that you write should be made as bulletproof as possible, against all kinds of errors.

That term *bulletproof* is one that's commonly used among the developers with whom I work to refer to a program or application's resistance to errors, especially user errors. It's also used as a verb: *bulletproofing* a program is the process of adding error checks to it, so that user actions cannot cause the program to fail.

While no program can ever be made totally bulletproof, you can come close; if you provide any explicit bulletproofing at all you'll be doing far better than many would-be developers, who allow unrestricted input and trust that user's will not do any serious damage as a result.

One kind of error that you should watch out for especially is the kind that results from wrong or even malicious user inputs. Every value that is obtained from user input should be tested to verify that it's acceptable, if any known limits exist for you to test it against.

If possible, input choices should be taken from list boxes or menus rather than having the user type in any commands; this not only simplifies your parsing problems, but eliminates bad input due to typing errors.

Before your program starts any operation that cannot readily be reversed, such as copying data out to disk, it should ascertain that there's enough space available to accommodate all the data that will be written. This check, alone, can prevent many of the most frequently encountered kinds of fatal but non-critical errors.

A word of warning here, too: this is a case of "do as I say, not as I do" because most of the example programs contained in this volume were deliberately short-changed in the error-checking department. The reason was because these programs are intended to illustrate the primary techniques discussed in each chapter, and had I included really adequate error-checking, the only techniques you would be able to learn much about would have been those used to do the checking. The primary techniques would have been hidden beneath the multiple layers of error testing.

Many years ago someone told me jokingly that "Every program is too big, too slow, and contains at least one bug; this will remain true no matter how much you cut it back, speed it up, or debug it." I can add one more item to the list: every program has too little bulletproofing, and this will remain true no matter how much you may add to it.

An Example Program

We've covered lots of ground in this chapter, and it's hardly possible to illustrate all the techniques we've explored in a single useful program of reasonable size.

However, MBRTOOLS.C shows some of the most useful and least-documented techniques, while using standard C runtime disk interfaces for more normal file access.

The purpose of this program is to let you read the Master Boot Record from any of your fixed disk drives, to save it to a file (which can be copied to a floppy for safekeeping, to display its partition table contents on the screen, to load it back from a previously saved file copy, and finally to write it back to the fixed disk should anything have damaged the original copy.)

Unlike some of the other samples, this program can be compiled equally easily with either Microsoft or Borland compilers. The embedded #ifdef statements account for the small differences between the two vendors' products, and you can use these as examples to modify all the other samples on the companion diskette for similar flexibility.

```
/**********************************************************************
 *                                                                    *
 *  MBRTOOLS.C - Jim Kyle, April, 1993                                *
 *                                                                    *
 *  Compile with either Microsoft or Borland compilers:               *
 *      cl mbrtools.c                                                 *
 *      bcc mbrtools.c                                                *
 *                                                                    *
 **********************************************************************/
#include <stdio.h>
#include <ctype.h>
#include <string.h>

#ifdef __TURBOC__
#define ASM asm
#pragma warn -rvl
#else
#ifdef _MSC_VER
```

```
#define ASM _asm
#pragma warning( disable:4035 )
#else
#error WORKS ONLY WITH MICROSOFT AND BORLAND COMPILERS
#endif
#endif

#define BYTE unsigned char
#define WORD unsigned short int

typedef struct {
  BYTE t, l, h, w;
} RECT;

RECT main_win = { 0, 0, 25, 80 };
RECT sub_win = { 6, 15, 15, 50 };
BYTE main_color=0x1F, sub_color = 0x3F;
WORD DriveCode;
int  havedata = 0;

BYTE bfr[512];                                   /* buffer for MBR */
BYTE *bfp;
static char *FileSys[] = {             /* File System Name strings */
  "(unknown)",
  "MS-DOS with 12-bit FAT",
  "type 2",
  "type 3",
  "MS-DOS with 16-bit FAT ( < 32M )",
  "Extended MS-DOS partition",
  "MS-DOS with 16-bit FAT ( >= 32M )",
};

void clear( RECT wn, BYTE c )          /* clears window on screen */
{ BYTE t, b, l, r;
  t = wn.t;                                  /* calculate corners */
  l = wn.l;
  b = wn.t+wn.h-1;
  r = wn.l+wn.w-1;
  ASM mov bh,c                                  /* call video BIOS */
  ASM mov bl,0
  ASM mov ch,t
  ASM mov cl,l
  ASM mov dh,b
```

```
  ASM mov dl,r
  ASM mov ax,0x0600
  ASM int 0x10
}

void posn( RECT wn, BYTE x, BYTE y )   /* position cursor in window */
{ x += wn.l;
  y += wn.t;
  ASM mov ax,0x0200                                 /* call video BIOS */
  ASM mov bh,0
  ASM mov dh,y
  ASM mov dl,x
  ASM int 0x10
}

void putchr( char c, BYTE a )    /* output character with attribute */
{ BYTE x, y;

  ASM mov ax,0x0300
  ASM mov bh,0
  ASM int 0x10                                      /* call video BIOS */
  ASM mov x,dl                                       /* save positions */
  ASM mov y,dh

  ASM mov ah,0x09
  ASM mov al,c
  ASM mov bh,0
  ASM mov bl,a
  ASM mov cx,1
  ASM int 0x10                                      /* call video BIOS */

  x++;
  ASM mov ax,0x0200
  ASM mov bh,0
  ASM mov dh,y
  ASM mov dl,x
  ASM int 0x10                                      /* call video BIOS */
}

void putstr( char * s, BYTE a )        /* display string w/attribute */
{ while( *s )
    putchr( *s++, a );
}
```

```
void SayAt( RECT wn, BYTE y, BYTE x, char * s, BYTE a )
{ posn( wn, x, y );
  putstr( s, a );
  posn( wn, (BYTE)(x + strlen(s)), y );
}

int GetKey( void )                          /* get key and return it */
{ ASM mov ax,0
  ASM int 0x16
  ASM or  al,al
  ASM jz  fini                           /* keep scancode if not ASCII */
  ASM xor ah,ah
fini:   ;
}

void Write_MBR( WORD disk )
{ bfp = &bfr[0];                             /* set to top of buffer */
  ASM mov ax,0x301;                               /* write 1 sector */
  ASM mov bx,bfp;
  ASM mov cx,1                                       /* to sector 1 */
  ASM mov dx,disk;
  ASM int 0x13;                                /* use BIOS for this */
}

void Save_MBR( void  )                       /* write MBR to save file */
{ FILE *fp;
  char fn[] = { "MBRFD0.SAV" };
  fn[5] = '0' + (127 & DriveCode);
  fp = fopen( fn, "wb" );
  if( fp )
    { fwrite( bfr, 1, 512, fp );
      fclose( fp );
    }
}

void DoWrite( void )                        /* write record back out */
{ int c;
  if( havedata )
    { clear( sub_win, sub_color );
      SayAt( sub_win, 2, 20, "WRITE MENU", sub_color );
      SayAt( sub_win, 5,  5, "write to Disk", sub_color );
```

```
    SayAt( sub_win, 7,  5, "write to File", sub_color );
    SayAt( sub_win, 9, 20, "Choose (d/f)? ", sub_color );
    c = GetKey();
    c = toupper( c );
    switch( c )
      {
      case 'D':
        Write_MBR( DriveCode );           /* write to disk itself */
        break;
      case 'F':
        Save_MBR();
        break;
      default:
        SayAt( sub_win, 13,  5,
               "Sorry, unrecognized keystroke", sub_color );
        while( GetKey() != 13 )
          ;                   /* wait for ENTER after error report */
      }
  }
else
  { SayAt( main_win, 2, 0, "Nothing to write!", main_color );
    while( GetKey() != 13 )
      ;                                   /* then wait for ENTER */
  }
}

void Report_Part( int i )
{ BYTE fs, begs, ends;
  WORD begc, endc;

  printf( "\nPartition %i is", i+1 );
  bfp = &bfr[ 446 + (i << 4) ];          /* calculate start of entry */
  if( *(long *)(bfp+12) )
    { fs = *(bfp+4);                       /* get filesystem code */
      if( fs > 6 )
        fs = 0;
      begs = *(bfp+2);                       /* get sector range */
      ends = *(bfp+6);
      begc = *(bfp+3) + ((begs & 0xC0) << 2 );        /* cylinders */
      endc = *(bfp+7) + ((ends & 0xC0) << 2 );
      begs &= 63;                                     /* trim heads */
      ends &= 63;
```

```
      printf( " %s.", (*bfp==0x80 ? "bootable" :
                                   ( *bfp ? "bad" : "not bootable" )));
      printf( "\n  File system is %s.", FileSys[fs] );
      printf( "\n  starts at head %i, ", *(bfp+1) );
      printf( "sector %i, ",  begs );
      printf( "cylinder %i.", begc );
      printf( "\n  ends with head %i, ", *(bfp+5) );
      printf( "sector %i, ",  ends );
      printf( "cylinder %i.", endc );
      printf( "\n  starts with sector %lu,", *(long *)(bfp+ 8) );
      printf( " total sectors = %lu\n",      *(long *)(bfp+12) );
    }
  else
    puts( " not used." );
}

void Report_All( void )
{ int i;

  for( i=0; i<4; i++ )
    Report_Part( i );
}

void DoList( void )                     /* display partition content */
{ clear( main_win, main_color );
  SayAt( main_win, 1, 5, "PARTITIONS:", main_color );
  SayAt( main_win, 2, 0, "", main_color );
  if( havedata )
    Report_All();
  else
    SayAt( main_win, 3, 0,
           "Nothing to list, READ first!", main_color );
  while( GetKey() != 13 )
    ;                                   /* either way, wait for ENTER */
}

void Read_MBR( WORD disk )
{ bfp = &bfr[0];                             /* set to top of buffer */
  ASM mov ax,0x201;                                 /* read 1 sector */
  ASM mov bx,bfp;
  ASM mov cx,1                                      /* from sector 1 */
  ASM mov dx,disk;
  ASM int 0x13;                                 /* use BIOS for this */
}
```

```
int Load_MBR( void )                        /* get MBR from saved file */
{ int retval = 0;
  FILE *fp;
  char fn[] = { "MBRFD0.SAV" };
  fn[5] = '0' + (127 & DriveCode);
  fp = fopen( fn, "rb" );
  if( fp )
    { fread( bfr, 1, 512, fp );
      fclose( fp );
      retval = 1;
    }
  return retval;
}

void DoRead( void )                         /* get MBR into RAM buffer */
{ int c;
  clear( sub_win, sub_color );
  SayAt( sub_win, 2, 20, "READ MENU", sub_color );
  SayAt( sub_win, 5,  5, "read from Disk", sub_color );
  SayAt( sub_win, 7,  5, "read from File", sub_color );
  SayAt( sub_win, 9, 20, "Choose (d/f)? ", sub_color );
  c = GetKey();
  c = toupper( c );
  switch( c )                                 /* dispatch on keystroke */
    {
    case 'D':
      Read_MBR( DriveCode );                  /* read from disk itself */
      havedata = 1;
      break;
    case 'F':
      havedata = Load_MBR();                 /* load from a saved file */
      break;
    default:
      SayAt( sub_win, 13,  5,
             "Sorry, unrecognized keystroke", sub_color );
      while( GetKey() != 13 )
        ;                          /* wait for ENTER if error reported */
    }
}

int ShowMain( void )         /* display main menu, return keystroke */
```

```
{ int c;
  clear( main_win, main_color );
  SayAt( main_win,  3, 24,
         "MASTER BOOT RECORD MAINTENANCE", main_color );
  SayAt( main_win,  7, 15, "Read into memory", main_color );
  SayAt( main_win,  9, 15, "List partitions", main_color );
  SayAt( main_win, 11, 15, "Write from memory", main_color );
  SayAt( main_win, 13, 15, "Quit program", main_color );
  SayAt( main_win, 18, 36, "Choose (r/l/w/q): ", main_color );
  c = GetKey();
  return toupper( c );
}

void main( int argc, char ** argv )
{ int c;
  if( argc < 2 )
    DriveCode = 0x80;                    /* default to Fixed Disk 0 */
  else
    DriveCode = 0x80 + (( *argv[1] & 15 ) - 3 );
  do
    { c = ShowMain();              /* display main menu and get key */
      switch( c )                    /* dispatch based on keystroke */
        {
        case 'R':
          DoRead();                             /* read into memory */
          break;
        case 'L':
          DoList();                                /* list contents */
          break;
        case 'W':
          DoWrite();                              /* write back out */
          break;
        case 'Q':
          SayAt( main_win, 24, 0,
                 "Thanks for using the program!", main_color );
          break;
        }
    } while( c != 'Q' );                     /* continue until QUIT */
}
```

This program illustrates many of the principles of modularity discussed back in Section 1, along with exercising the BIOS disk interface. The `main()` routine, for example, simply establishes a value for `DriveCode`, and then drops into an event loop which executes the `ShowMain()` module to obtain an action code in variable `c`, then selects one of the three action modules (`DoRead()`, `DoList()`, or `DoWrite()`) or quits, based on the value of the action code.

Each time `ShowMain()` is executed, it clears the entire screen and displays the screen shown in Figure 9.6, and then waits for the user to press a key. If the key pressed is not one of the four indicated keys, the switch statement in `main()` does nothing, and so `ShowMain()` executes again. The only action visible to the user in this case is a momentary blink as the screen is cleared and redrawn.

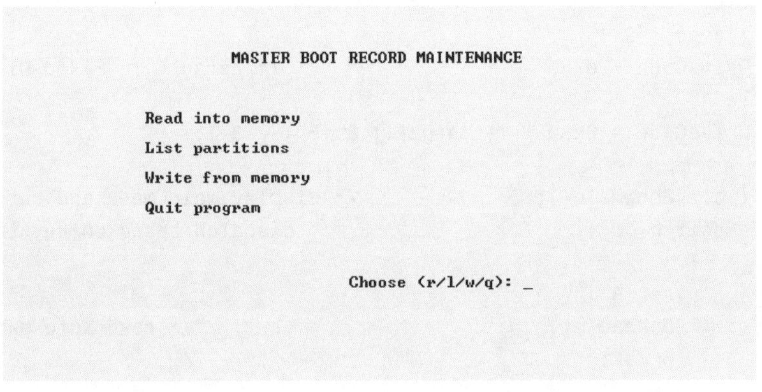

Figure 9.6. This is the display created by the ShowMain() routine in MBRTOOLS.EXE. Only the four keys indicated in parentheses after the "Choose" prompt will cause anything other than display of this screen to happen.

If the user presses *r* in response to the `ShowMain()` screen, the switch statement selects `DoRead()` as the action procedure to execute. This overlays the `ShowMain()` list and prompt with a smaller menu in a contrasting color, which appears as light gray in Figure 9.7.

Like the main menu in `ShowMain()`, this procedure paints its options within its window, then waits for the user to press a key. However, if the user presses any key other than the *d* and *f* indicated by the prompt, an error message will be shown and the system will then wait for Enter to be pressed before returning to `ShowMain()`.

If one of the two valid keys is pressed, either `Read_MBR()` or `Load_MBR()` will be executed. `Read_MBR()` uses the BIOS interface to read the MBR into a one-sector buffer, while `Load_MBR()` reads a file whose name is created automatically from the low four bits of `DriveCode` (which identify the specific fixed disk involved, in the BIOS numbering scheme) to load the same buffer.

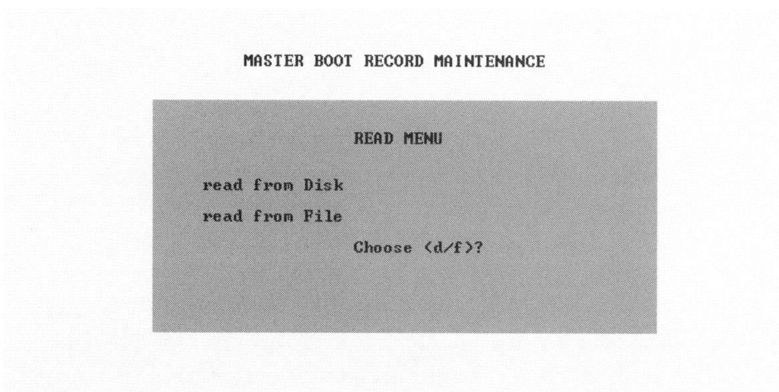

Figure 9.7. This is the submenu displayed by the DoRead() procedure of MBRTOOLS.EXE after the user chooses "read into memory" as the desired action.

Either routine, if successful, sets the variable `havedata` to 1, to signal that a list or write choice now is valid. Until the buffer has been loaded initially, neither list nor write can do anything useful.

Once `havedata` is set, the user can select `list partitions` as the desired action from the `ShowMain()` display of Figure 9.6, and obtain a display such as that shown in Figure 9.8. This display shows the partition table for one of the twin "67-megabyte" Toshiba drives in my office system. The display for the other drive is similar but shows that Partition 1 is not bootable, and that the File system is "Extended MS-DOS partition" rather than "MS-DOS with 16-bit FAT."

The other information shown indicates that the single partition on my drive uses heads 1 through 6 and cylinders 0 through 731, for a total of 4,386 tracks of information. It shows also that each of these tracks is divided into sectors 1 through 26, and that the first 25 sectors are not part of the partition (one of them contains the partition table itself and in most cases, the remainder of the first track is left outside of all partitions). The total number of sectors available to MS-DOS for storage, then, is 133,198, and since each sector is 512 bytes this means that the partition's maximum capacity is 68,197,376 bytes.

```
    PARTITIONS:

Partition 1 is bootable.
  File system is MS-DOS with 16-bit FAT ( >= 32M ).
  starts at head 1, sector 1, cylinder 0.
  ends with head 6, sector 26, cylinder 731.
  starts with sector 26, total sectors = 133198

Partition 2 is not used.

Partition 3 is not used.

Partition 4 is not used.
_
```

Figure 9.8. Partition listing for one of my fixed disks as shown by MBRTOOLS.EXE. This drive is rated at 67 megabytes but actually has space for slightly more than 68 million bytes of data within its bootable MS-DOS partition.

When the user selects **w** as the action choice from the `ShowMain()` screen, the system displays a `WRITE MENU` submenu similar to that shown in Figure 9.8. Choosing *f* causes the buffer containing the `MBR` to be written to the same save file from which the `READ MENU` would load it, while *d* causes the buffer to be written to the fixed disk itself, overwriting the existing record.

> **Note:** Note that this program is NOT bulletproof in this area; nothing will stop you from reading in an invalid file, should it exist, and writing its content back over the MBR of your fixed disk. This can make it impossible to boot your system until a valid MBR has been restored to it. Until you have a valid saved copy that you can use for restoring the MBR, avoid all temptation to experiment with this action! The penalty may be loss of all programs and data on your disk, if you find it necessary to run FDISK and reformat the drive.
>
> Simply reading or listing the data, however, cannot cause any harm to your system. The "disk" action from the WRITE MENU screen is the only one that has any risk at all involved.

Selecting **q** from the `ShowMain()` screen returns to the command line prompt.

The remaining modules in this program all deal with the screen and keyboard input actions. They are deliberately made somewhat different from those shown in Chapter 7, to show you alternative techniques that can be used if you desire.

Serial Communications

With ever-increasing frequency, applications are being required to include serial communications capabilities as standard operating features, just as they are capable of accepting keyboard input. This is due in no small part to the worldwide cultural revolution brought about by the ubiquitous FAX machine. However, useful sources of information which can help you integrate such communications capabilities into your programs are relatively rare. This chapter concentrates on the most common serial communications interface, how it works, and how you can apply it in your programs.

10

In an ideal world, MS-DOS would provide you a standard method for sending data to, and retrieving data from, the communications interface, just as it does for disk storage. However, the real world in which we must develop our applications is far from ideal, and the few primitive functions included in MS-DOS itself for dealing with the serial interface are almost unusable. Those supplied in the industry-standard ROM-BIOS are not much better, though we'll use them as the key elements of a truly useful utility before this chapter ends.

Before we get into the rather dirty details required to successfully integrate serial communications into your applications, we briefly look at just why the MS-DOS functions aren't much help, so that you can explain why you have to bypass them, should you be asked. Then we take a quick refresher tour through the BIOS functions (all of which are described in detail in Chapter 6).

Next we examine the distinctions between "synchronous" and "asynchronous" communications paths, review the basic vocabulary used in connection with serial communications functions, and go through the operation of the serial interface chip supplied in the original IBM PC async adapter (the type 8250 UART). This chip and its faster successors are still the backbone for the vast majority of serial communication tasks in MS-DOS systems.

Finally, we put together a sample program that combines direct hardware access and the BIOS functions to help you keep your system's time and date information current; you'll use this utility at least twice a year, spring and fall, at the start and end of Daylight Savings Time.

Why MS-DOS Can't Be Used

We've noted that the services provided by MS-DOS itself for serial communications are essentially unusable; now let's see why this is so.

Two distinct factors contribute to the problem. One of them is that the only specific communications-oriented functions built into MS-DOS provides only a polling approach to I/O; if no byte is currently available, the input function will wait forever, if necessary, for the number of characters that you requested to arrive.

But serial communications, by their very nature, are always much slower than are parallel data transfers, and users simply won't accept applications that require them to watch a blinking cursor for minutes on end while the system waits for data to arrive from a slow serial link. They demand systems that can be doing something else while waiting for the data to arrive.

The other fatal shortcoming, which applies to the BIOS services also (since the MS-DOS functions simply call the appropriate BIOS functions), is that nothing can be allowed to happen behind the scenes while serial data is being received by the standard methods. Even something so simple as scrolling the screen up by one line will cause three or four characters to be lost, and trying to write anything out to disk is a guarantee of total disaster.

Even though these basic services are totally inadequate for high-performance communications, we'll explore them briefly before moving on closer to the actual hardware. Sometimes, as in our sample program for this chapter, simplicity is more important than raw speed.

STDAUX: No Substitute for a Communications Package

Interrupt 21h Functions 03h and 04h, available since MS-DOS Version 1, can be used to receive a character from, or send a character to, the first serial port (STDAUX beginning with DOS V2). However, they are no substitutes for a full-fledged capability within your application, should you need to deal with remote users or systems via serial communications.

Function 03h is of such little practical use that I won't waste space here by describing it again; it's discussed in Chapter 7 if you're really interested.

You may find Function 04h perfectly adequate for such tasks as sending an automatic-dialing sequence to a desk telephone, from a generic office-organization program. In a situation of this sort, speed is of no importance, but convenience of programming quite well may be.

To send one eight-bit character to `STDAUX`, simply load the character into DL and then invoke the function. Here's the calling sequence:

```
mov     dl,character      ; character to send
mov     ah,4              ; send to STDAUX
int     21h               ; call MS-DOS
```

Since MS-DOS Version 2.0, the output from this call has gone to the standard auxiliary device (`STDAUX`), which is one of the five predefined handles that every process is given automatically when it is launched.

`STDAUX` defaults to the first serial port in most systems. This port is usually initialized to operate at 2400 bps, 8 data bits, no parity, and 1 stop bit. (If these terms are confusing, just read on; we'll explain them all very soon now.) Your version of MS-DOS may differ but in any event you can customize the settings via the MODE command from the command line.

If `STDAUX` is busy when output is attempted, this function waits until it becomes free, then sends the character and returns. If `STDAUX` never becomes available, the system will appear to freeze solid. This shortcoming makes the function have extremely limited value to the serious developer. Serious work with serial ports is done either at the BIOS level, or more often at the hardware level with custom interrupt software to handle everything.

You also can send a character out the AUX port by using Function 40h with the predefined handle 03 (the value of `STDAUX`). Similarly, to bring data in, you can use Function 3F with the predefined handle.

The CTTY Command and Its Limitations

One of the internal commands within COMMAND.COM is `CTTY`, which is defined by the `HELP` command as `Permits you to change the device that controls your system.`

What the `CTTY` command actually does is to switch the `STDIN` and `STDOUT` predefined handles, at the level of the primary shell, so that they read from and write to whatever device is specified in the command line.

If you issue the command `CTTY COM1` the screen and keyboard immediately go dead, and all input and output is obtained through serial port COM1. This results in all of the shortcomings already noted for the `STDAUX`-output function, and also makes it impossible to regain control of your system should anything go wrong on the serial channel.

At one time I used `CTTY NUL` at the top of certain batch files to suppress all output without wasting any handles by individual redirection, followed by a `CTTY CON` to restore control to the keyboard at the end of the batch file. I quit doing so, however, after finding it necessary to reboot from an emergency floppy diskette whenever any error occurred during the batch file's execution.

My recommendation concerning use of the `CTTY` command is quite simple: DON'T.

How to Use BIOS or Custom Coding

With the MS-DOS functions effectively eliminated from consideration for serial communications use, we're left with two choices: we can either try to get by with what the BIOS functions provide (the simpler approach if it can be used) or we can bite the bullet, drag out our assembly-language skills, and go all the way to the metal by programming the UART directly.

The area of serial communications is one of the few remaining parts of PC software development where bypassing all the vendor-supplied systems may still be acceptable. Fortunately, Windows and the competing GUI platforms have all recognized the problems created by lack of a usable standard in MS-DOS, and consequently they all include effective serial communications capabilities.

You also might consider a third option, which is actually a thinly disguised variation of the second: use of a commercial third-party toolkit such as those from Greenleaf or Blaise. These all go direct to the hardware in order to provide good performance, but if you use them you don't need to get your hands quite so dirty at the bit-shift and critical-timing level.

If communications capability forms only a small part of your applications, and you're really not all that interested in the details of how it's done, by all means get and use one of the commercial toolkits. They will save you as much time as does the use of a good compiler compared to doing all programming in assembly language, and you'll get performance every bit as good for your needs. You can skip to Chapter 11 now if you like.

But if you're one of the people who can't rest until you know just how things work, even if you never want to actually build your own widgets, stick with us for the rest of the chapter. We're about to open the hood and crawl right inside the engine to see how serial communications happen.

BIOS Functions Revisited

As noted in Chapters 6 and 15, the BIOS polled interface is more than just a bit primitive, but BIOS functions are still useful in a number of situations. For instance, it's far easier to initialize a port properly via Interrupt 14h Function 00h than it is to create your own initialization procedures.

For more detail on the use of these functions refer to Chapter 15; here we simply summarize the six common functions and what they do. Our sample program near the end of this chapter also shows details of using some of these BIOS functions.

Function 00h initializes the serial port, establishing its bit rate, parity, number of stop bits, and data word length. Parameters for the port are passed as a bitmap and port status is returned as a bitmap, as it is from the first four BIOS functions.

Function 01h places a character into the transmitter holding register of the addressed port, to be transferred automatically to the transmitter shift register and sent, as soon as the character presently going out is finished.

Function 02h waits for a character to become available in the receive data register of the addressed port, then returns that character. In many BIOS's, this function times out if the Data Set Ready (Modem Status Register bit 5) condition is false, even when Function 03h shows data in the receive register.

Function 03h returns both the Port status and the Modem status of the addressed serial port.

Function 04h, first made available on the short-lived IBM Convertible line and subsequently on all later models, extends the initialization capability provided by Function 00h to allow control of response to BREAK signals, and to permit a higher maximum bit rate.

Function 05h, like Function 04h first made available on the IBM Convertible and then on all later models, allows control of the Modem Control Register within the addressed serial port.

Custom Coding

For full performance at speeds greater than 300 BPS (painfully slow by modern standards although considered blazingly fast back in 1981), or if you want to transfer more data than your RAM can hold, at any speed, you'll need to use custom interrupt-driven coding for at least the receiving portions of your application, though the BIOS functions may serve satisfactorily for everything else.

In order to add custom code, you need to know the vocabulary involved, and to gain at least a little familiarity with the UART device that's the heart of a serial port, with adapter conventions, and with modem actions. That's what the next section addresses.

UART Requirements

The heart of most serial communications techniques used in the MS-DOS world (and all of those that we'll examine here) is a special IC chip known as the *UART* (Universal Asynchronous Receiver Transmitter). But before we can look at the details of how the most commonly used UART works, we have to take a little time to find out what that polysyllabic mouthful means.

Any serial interface technique's primary function is to convert the parallel internal format of data (normally an eight-bit byte) that the computer uses into a serial format (one bit at a time, one after another) that can be transmitted over a single wire.

While this conversion can be accomplished by software, and was, in some of the earliest experimental microcomputers, it's far more effective to use special hardware to perform the parallel-to-serial conversion when transmitting data, and the reverse serial-to-parallel conversion when receiving. Today virtually all computer systems use such special hardware; because it's mass-produced, the cost is amazingly low considering what it does. We call it a "serial port."

Since all data that is transmitted in serial fashion moves over the wire just one bit at a time, with the only distinction between one bit's value and that of the following bit being the amount of time that goes by, accurate timing is absolutely essential to accuracy. Losing track of just one bit on a byte will tend to scramble not only that byte, but all subsequent bytes as well, until the transmitter and receiver are brought back into synchronization with each other again.

This need to assure constant synchronization between both ends of the data path has given rise to two entirely different techniques for serial data transfers, known as *synchronous* and *asynchronous* communication.

Both names refer to the timing method used; the synchronous technique maintains tight control of the timing throughout the entire transfer, by sending clocking information right along with the data so that reception can be synchronized. This type of communication, though often used in mini- or mainframe computer applications, is almost unknown in the MS-DOS world so we'll ignore it here.

The asynchronous communication technique breaks the transfer up into individual small information packets, which are then placed on the line with no precise timing between them. The usual packet size is just one eight-bit byte. Each packet is framed by a *start bit* and one or more *stop bits* that are not part of the data but instead signal the hardware at the other end of the line where the packet starts and stops, as shown in Figure 10.1. In the few bits that make up each packet, there's little chance for the timing to lose synchronization.

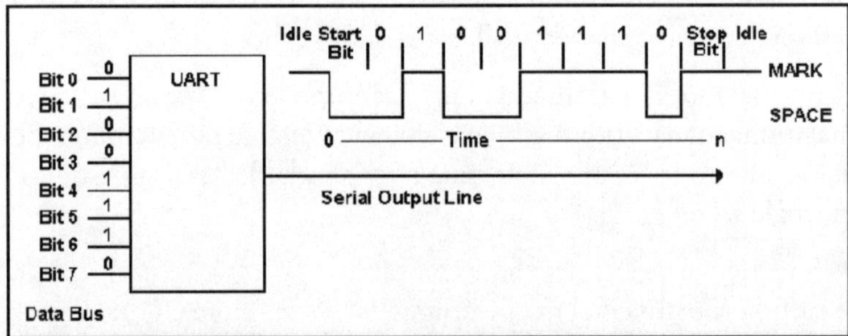

Figure 10.1. This shows how a parallel bit pattern from the system's data bus can be applied to a UART chip to be converted into an asynchronous serial bit stream with the addition of a start bit (at left of waveform) and a stop bit (at right). Bits are always sent out least-significant-bit first, and any parity bit that is appended goes between the last data bit and the stop bit.

The asynchronous method is the one used in most microcomputers, including those which run MS-DOS software. It's called "asynchronous" ("asynch" is the usual shorthand term) because the transmitting and receiving ends are *not* kept in continual synchronization.

Now that we've seen the difference between the two communications methods, let's continue with a short glossary of terms that have special meanings in this highly specialized area. These terms make it much easier to discuss all the unusual things that take place during async communication sessions. These terms include special names for the parts of each async packet, plus descriptions of some operating characteristics:

Start bit: A bit automatically sent by the serial device before the actual character data to notify the receiver that data will follow immediately. The start bit is always represented by a SPACE condition (the opposite of the line's condition when idle) and starts the bit clock of the receiver to clock in the data bits that follow.

Data bits: The bits of the character being transmitted. The usual serial communications chip on a MS-DOS system can handle from five to eight data bits. The only thing that distinguishes one data bit from its neighbors is the passage of time as noted by the receiver's bit clock.

Parity: Parity provides a rudimentary error check of the data within the packet; it can be specified to be EVEN, ODD, MARK, SPACE, or NONE. If EVEN or ODD parity is in use, the system counts the number of data bits set to 1, then appends a parity bit that, when included in the count, will result in the count being the specified EVEN or ODD type. That is, if EVEN parity is in use and five data bits were 1's with 3 being 0's, the appended parity bit would be 1, raising the total count of 1-bits to 6, an even number. Conversely, for ODD parity, the result must be an odd number, so the appended parity bit would be 0. The MARK specification causes the parity bit to always be set to 1, SPACE always sets it to 0, and NONE causes the parity bit to be completely ignored.

Stop bits: At least one Stop Bit is sent at the end of the information packet to guarantee that the line returns to the MARK or idle condition so that the receiver will be able to detect the start bit of the next information packet. At the bit rates that are now common for data communications, a single stop bit is normal.

Baud rate: This technical term actually refers to the signaling (or transfer) rate of a communications line, but is often incorrectly used to refer to the bit rate. Most "2400-baud" communications actually use 600-baud signaling to move 2400 bits per second.

Bit rate: The transmission speed of the communications path, expressed in bits per second (BPS).

Full duplex: A communication convention in which all data that is displayed on your screen is actually transmitted back to you from the remote computer. Most modern systems use full-duplex (usually abbreviated FDX), because it verifies exactly what data reached the other end of the path.

Half duplex: A communication convention (usually abbreviated HDX) in which the information displayed on your screen is actually echoed within your computer. Thus it will continue to display even if the circuit to the remote computer is broken.

DTE: Data Terminal Equipment (DTE) is the term used by telecommunications technicians to refer to any equipment that provides a human interface to the line, such as a dumb terminal or the computer system. It's also used sometimes to distinguish the serial port adapter itself from the associated modem.

DCE: Data Communications Equipment (DCE) is the term used by telecommunications technicians to refer to what we know as a modem.

To allow one computer to communicate with another, both must operate by the same predefined parameters. Each must provide the bit rate, duplex convention, number of data bits per packet, and parity information that the other expects to receive, or their communications will not be reliable.

Fortunately, over the years a few fairly standard configurations have become accepted. In most cases, either eight data bits, no parity, and one stop bit (8N1) or seven data bits, EVEN parity, and one stop bit (7E1) will work. The bit rate will probably be 1,200 or 2,400 BPS, although 4,800 and 9,600 BPS modems also are coming into wide use. Most systems support a variety of bit rates, and many automatically configure themselves based on the first character that they receive (usually a carriage-return).

Within each packet of information transmitted, the timing is critical. Initially, the communication line is idle (in what telecommunications technicians call the MARK state) until a start bit is received. Once the start bit arrives, the line must be sampled at precise intervals to accumulate the individual data bits into a character. The parity bit, if one is used, follows the data. Finally, the stop bit or bits return the line to its idle MARK state, and the receiver waits for another start bit to appear.

In addition to the serial conversion that takes place for data communications, most serial ports also recognize and respond to certain status signals that are generated by most modems. These signals correspond to changes of conditions on the transmission path. Not all systems use these signals, but many do. The four that are handled by all serial ports are:

Signal	Meaning
`CTS`	**Clear to send**: The modem is ready to receive data from the computer.
`DSR`	**Data set ready**: The modem is powered on and ready to operate but is not necessarily in contact with another system.
`RI`	**Ring indicator**: The telephone line is ringing. As the line rings, RI pulses on and off so that your computer can "hear the bell."
`DCD`	**Data carrier detect**: The modem has confirmed two-way communication with another modem and is ready for full operation.

Now that we know the vocabulary and the basic operating principles for async communications, we can turn our attention to the "standard" UART device which forms the basis for virtually all MS-DOS data communications software: the type 8250 chip.

Basics of the 8250 Series

The 8250 began its existence as the Intel 8250 Asynchronous Communications Controller, part of the support hardware for the model 8080 microprocessor which was the ancestor of the 80x86 family used in MS-DOS systems. This single IC chip handles all details of data conversion both to and from the communications line, which is why the generic term for it is a "universal async receiver transmitter" device.

Operation of the 8250 is controlled by 10 programmable single-byte registers. Only a few of these registers are used regularly; most deal only with initialization. All 10 registers are accessed through seven I/O port addresses, which are offset from a base address that is always a multiple of 8. The base address determines which communications port is used. Base addresses for the original "industry standard architecture" based on the IBM PC are different from those used in IBM's MicroChannel Adapters; the ISA addresses for COM1 through COM4 are:

Communications Port	Base Address
COM1:	03F8h
COM2:	02F8h
COM3:	03E8h
COM4:	02E8h

Note that only the first two of these ports were specified originally; the other two were added later and may vary from one system to another. When possible, your applications should try to use either COM1 or COM2 to avoid possible problems.

In the MCA designs, these Base Addresses are used:

Communications Port	Base Address
COM1:	03F8h
COM2:	02F8h
COM3:	3220h
COM4:	3228h
COM5:	4220h
COM6:	4228h
COM7:	5220h
COM8:	5228h

Control Registers and Status

While the 8250 has 10 registers, it needs only seven port addresses for all 10. Two of the seven addresses apply to more than one register, depending on other conditions, and one of these serves three registers rather than two.

When bit 7 of the Line Status Register is set to 0, register offset 0 addresses the *transmitter holding register* (THR) whenever you write to the port, and the receiver data register (RDR) whenever you read from it. Because neither register requires both read and write access, this combination makes sense.

When bit 7 of the Line Status Register is set to 1, register offsets 0 and 1 access the Baud Rate registers. The Baud Rate registers are accessed only during initialization of the chip, and are not needed during normal operations.

The specific offsets for each register, with respect to the base address of the port itself, are:

Offset	LSR Bit 7	Register
0	0	Transmitter holding register (THR) and receiver data register (RDR)
0	1	Baud rate divisor, low byte (BRL)
1	0	Interrupt enable register (IER)
1	1	Baud rate divisor, high byte (BRH)
2	1 or 0	Interrupt identification register (IIR)
3	1 or 0	Line control register (LCR)
4	1 or 0	Modem control register (MCR)
5	1 or 0	Line status register (LSR)
6	1 or 0	Modem status register (MSR)

Let's see now just what each register in the 8250 does.

The Transmitter Holding Register holds the byte of data to be sent. You can write data to this register whenever bit 5 of the *line status register* (LSR) indicates that the register is empty, or when an interrupt results from the THRE (THR Empty) condition.

The Receiver Data Register holds the byte of data most recently received from the communications line. You need to read this register whenever LSR bit 0 indicates that a byte is ready, or when an interrupt results from this condition.

The Baud Rate Divisor Registers hold a 16-bit number, which specifies the bit rate (not the baud rate, despite the official name given by the designers of the UART) used, and is divided between two 8-bit ports (BRL and BRH). The values loaded into each register for typical bit rates are:

Bit Rate (BPS)	BRH	BRL
50	09h	00h
110	04h	17h
300	01h	80h
1200	00h	60h
2400	00h	30h
4800	00h	18h
9600	00h	0Ch
19200	00h	06h

To set these registers, you must first set bit 7 of the LCR to 1. After you have set both BRH and BRL, you should immediately clear bit 7.

The Interrupt Enable Register (IER) controls the interrupts that the UART can generate. You can enable one, all, or none of the four possible interrupts, depending on how you design your interrupt handler.

Whenever this register enables an interrupt, your program must take some specific action to clear it. The four conditions which can create interrupts, the corresponding bits in the register to enable them, and the appropriate action needed to clear each are as follows:

Bit	Activated When	Action to Clear
0	Data is received.	Read RDR
1	THR is empty.	Output to THR
2	Data error or break detected.	Read LSR
3	MSR changes.	Read MSR
4-7	Never	Always set to zero

Whenever one of the activating conditions shown in this list takes place, and the corresponding IER bit is set to 1, an interrupt request is generated on the IRQ line assigned to the port involved.

The *Interrupt Identification Register* (IIR) contains a bitmap which can be used to determine which condition caused the IRQ. More than one bit may be set at the same time. Here's what each bit in the IIR means:

Bit	Meaning
0	More than one interrupt has occurred
1-2	Interrupt ID 00 = Change in modem status register (MSR) 01 = Transmitter holding register (THR) empty 10 = Data received 11 = Data reception error or break

The Line Control Register (LCR) is the primary control register for the conversion process. It specifies the number of data bits in each information packet, the minimum number of stop bits to be sent at the end of each, what parity convention to use, and toggles the meanings of register offsets 0 and 1. Here's how the bits of the LCR are used:

Bit(s)	Values	Meaning
0-1		Number of bits in each information packet:
	00	5 bits
	01	6 bits
	10	7 bits
	11	8 bits

Bit(s)	Values	Meaning
2		Number of stop bits to follow last data bit
	0	1 bit
	1	1.5 bits (If using 5-bit characters)
	1	2 bits (If using 6-, 7-, or 8-bit characters)
3-5		Parity convention
	000	NONE
	100	ODD
	110	EVEN
	101	MARK
	111	SPACE
6		Break Condition (Carrier dropped momentarily)
	0	Disabled
	1	Enabled
7		Port Toggle
	0	Normal (Use THR/RDR and IER registers)
	1	Alternate (Use BRDL and BRDH registers)

The *Modem Control Register* (MCR) controls signals sent to the modem to indicate that the computer is ready to operate. Only the low five bits of the MCR are used:

Bit	Meaning
0	Set Data Terminal Ready (DTR) line active
1	Set Request To Send (RTS) line active
2	User output #1 (Hayes Reset)
3	User output #2 (Enable Ints)
4	UART loopback
5-7	Unused, set to zero

The DTR line indicates that the computer is ready to receive information. The RTS line originally indicated that the computer is ready to send something to the line, but newer modems use this line as part of a data-control technique that we'll look at a bit later.

Bit 2 (user output #1) is used by the Hayes Smartmodem internal board to reset the modem and should be initialized to 0.

Bit 3 (user output #2) is tied (in the original IBM async communications adapter, and all designs which followed its lead slavishly) to the 8250 interrupt servicing and prevents any interrupt handling unless it is set to 1.

Bit 4 allows you to test things without any actual communications being done. When this bit is set to 1, all data that you tell the port to send out reappears as input, as if it had been received from the external line.

The *Line Status Register* (LSR) indicates the condition of the individual characters being sent or received:

Bit	Meaning
0	Data has been received, byte in RDR is ready to take out.
1	Overrun error occurred; the previous byte had not been read from the RDR before another byte arrived.
2	Parity error has been detected.
3	Framing error occurred; the transmission was not in sync (no stop bit was found after the character had been read).
4	Break detected.
5	THR is empty, a new character may be loaded for output to the line.
6	Transmitter shift register (TSR) is empty. (The TSR takes the character from the THR and places it on the line, one bit at a time.) This indicates that the UART has no data to send.
7	Timeout was detected while receiving.

The *Modem Status Register* (MSR) indicates the condition of the four modem lines described earlier in this chapter. The high four bits indicate present status of each line (high or low) and the low four bits indicate whether the status on a line has changed since the last time this register was read:

Bit	Meaning if 1
0	Change in clear to send (CTS)
1	Change in data set ready (DSR)
2	Change in ring indicator (RI)
3	Change in data carrier detect (DCD)
4	Clear to send (CTS) set high
5	Data set ready (DSR) set high
6	Ring indicator (RI) set high
7	Data carrier detect (DCD) set high

Newer variations of the 8250 design add more registers to this list as we shall see in the next section, but this subset is enough to allow useful work with any serial hardware commonly available for today's MS-DOS systems. Before we look at the changes that have been brought about in the never-ending quest for performance, though, let's examine the two techniques that can be used for basic data transfer operations.

Data Transfer by Polling

The polling technique is what the BIOS uses for both sending and receiving data to/from a serial port. All that *polling* means is that the program repeatedly reads the port status and waits for the desired event to be noted, then does what's requested.

A polling routine for receiving data, for example, would repeatedly check the Line Status Register, testing the Data Ready bit, until this bit is set to 1 indicating that the Received Data Register now contains a fully assembled byte or character. That condition would break the loop, and the routine would then read the character from the UART (automatically clearing the Data Ready status bit) and return to its caller.

In any polling loop, it's good practice to establish time limits so that the system does not hang and wait indefinitely should the communications link be broken and thus prevent the expected condition from ever taking place.

In the following sample routine, which shows a polling loop for sending characters to the communications line, this timeout is provided by counting down the CX register. If the Transmit Holding Register fails to empty after 65,536 passes around the loop, the routine returns with the carry flag set to indicate a timeout error.

The routine can be assembled using MASM 5.1 or later, TASM, or any other assembler supporting simplified segment directives, and then linked into your application in order to provide polling service for outgoing data. You can follow it as a model to add receive service also, but it's usually far better to deal with incoming data using the interrupt techniques we discuss in the next subsection.

```
;;
=================================================================
;;
;;    XPOLL.ASM - Jim Kyle - April 1993
;;
;;    masm /mx xpoll;
;;
;;
=================================================================
.model small,C

.data
com_base  dw   ?              ; base port address

.code
CP_inst   proc cport:word     ; sets up com_base from BIOS RAM
     public CP_inst

     mov  bx,cport            ; get port number...
     dec  bx                  ; ...convert to zero-based
     add  bx,bx               ; ...word index
     mov  ax,40h              ; ...for use in BIOS RAM area
     mov  es,ax
     mov  ax,es:[bx]          ; get port address
     mov  com_base,ax
```

```
        or   ax,ax                  ; test for valid port
        jnz  inst1
        stc                         ; no such port, flag as error and
                                      quit
        ret
inst1:  clc                         ; flag no error, all okay
        ret

CP_inst   endp

CP_putc   proc chr:byte             ; sends character to line
        public CP_putc

        xor  cx,cx                  ; set timeout at 65,536 passes
        mov  dx,com_base            ; LSR is at base+5
        add  dx,5
putc1:  in   al,dx                  ; read character
        test al,020h                ; THR empty bit
        jnz  putc2                  ; wait for it to be set
        loop putc1
        stc                         ; indicate timeout error
        ret

putc2:  mov  al,chr                 ; get the character
        mov  dx,com_base            ; THR is at base+0
        out  dx,al                  ; send it out
        clc                         ; flag success
        ret

CP_putc   endp

        end
```

The two routines contained in XPOLL consist of one that initializes internal storage and checks to be certain that the addressed serial port exists, and another that sends a single character to the port each time it is called. The initialization routine, CP_inst, must be called before the first use of the transmit routine, CP_putc.

The CP_inst routine simply gets the base address of the requested port from the table maintained by BIOS, and stuffs it into the local variable com_base for use by the `CP_putc` function when it's called. If the address is zero, indicating that no hardware for the requested port is present in the system, this routine returns with the carry flag set; the flag is cleared to indicate success. If you call these procedures from assembly language you can test the flag upon return; if the routine is called from C or another high level language, no error check is possible. You could, however, declare `CP_inst` to return an integer, and test its return value. It will be the actual base address, or zero.

The `CP_putc` routine requires a single parameter to be supplied: the character to be sent to the port. This routine polls the Line Status Register, testing the bit that indicates that the Transmitter Holding Register is empty. The polling loop is monitored by a countdown in the CX register which permits 65,636 passes around the loop before declaring a timeout error. This is ample time for the THR to empty, even at 300 BPS data rates.

When the THR becomes empty, `CP_putc` moves the character to be sent into it, and returns.

Again, the carry flag is set to indicate error, or cleared for success, but this flag can be tested only from assembly language callers. You might want to modify the two return points to return zero for success and nonzero for error.

Successful Interrupt Service Techniques

If your software is interrupt driven, your program must first specify the type of interrupts it will be prepared to accept, adjust the hardware interrupt vector involved to point to its own interrupt service routine (first saving the original content of the vector so that it can be restored before your program ends), and set up the Interrupt Enable Register accordingly (first saving it also, for later restoration). Then, whenever an interrupt request is received, your program must examine the Interrupt Identification Register to determine the type of interrupt that triggered the request. Finally, when your program terminates, it should restore the hardware interrupt vector and the IER content to their original values.

Any time that you change either the hardware interrupt vectors or the IER, you should first disable interrupts by the assembly language CLI instruction, and leave them disabled until you have the new values in place.

The hardware interrupts used by the various serial ports, like the base addresses for the ports themselves, are different for the original *industry standard architecture* based on the IBM PC than for IBM's MicroChannel Adapters; the ISA interrupts for COM1 through COM4 are:

Communications Port	Interrupt Number
COM1:	0Ch
COM2:	0Bh
COM3:	0Ch
COM4:	0Bh

In the MCA designs, these interrupts are used:

Communications Port	Interrupt Number
COM1:	0Ch
COM2:	0Bh
COM3:	0Bh
COM4:	0Bh
COM5:	0Bh
COM6:	0Bh
COM7:	0Bh
COM8:	0Bh

The following routines can be assembled using MASM 5.1 or later, or any other assembler supporting the simplified segment directives, and then linked into your application in order to provide interrupt-driven service for incoming data. You can follow it as a model to add transmit service also, but there's usually no performance penalty for dealing with outgoing data on a polling basis.

Note that the port number to be used is passed into the `CI_inst` procedure as a parameter. The `CR_inst` routine then sets up the port address, interrupt number, and PIC mask bit, based on the BIOS RAM table and standard conventions for ISA systems. For use with MCA equipment, both the INTVALS and MSKVALS tables must be changed and the BIOS port-address table cannot be used for COM5 through COM8.

```
;;
================================================================
;;
;;   RINTS.ASM - Jim Kyle - April 1993
;;
;;   masm /mx xpoll;
;;
;;
================================================================
.model    small,C

bufsiz    =    256

.data
com_base  dw   ?                    ; base port address
oldvec    dd   ?                    ; storage for original vector
intvals   db   0Ch,0Bh,0Bh,0Ch
mskvals   db   10h,08h,08h,10h
com_int   db   ?                    ; interrupt to use
int_mask1 db   ?                    ; mask bit for PIC off
int_mask2 db   ?                    ; mask bit for PIC on
asc_in    dw   ?                    ; buffer input pointer
asc_out   dw   ?                    ; buffer output pointer
asc_buf   db   bufsiz dup(?)        ; the buffer itself

.code
CI_inst   proc cport:word           ; installs private ISR (receive
                                      only)
     public CI_inst
     mov  bx,cport                  ; get port number
     dec  bx                        ; convert to zero-based index
     mov  al,intvals[bx]            ; get interrupt number
     mov  com_int,al
     mov  al,mskvals[bx]            ; get mask bits for PIC
     mov  int_mask1,al
     not  al
     mov  int_mask2,al
     add  bx,bx                     ; make into word index now
     mov  ax,40h                    ; for use in BIOS RAM area
     mov  es,ax
```

```
    mov  ax,es:[bx]              ; get port address
    mov  com_base,ax
    or   ax,ax                   ; test for validity
    jnz  inst1
    stc                          ; no such port, flag as error and
                                   quit
    ret
inst1:   cli                     ; disable interrupts for now
    mov  ah,35h                  ; Get Vector function
    mov  al,com_int              ; interrupt number, see text
    int  21h                     ; get existing vector
    mov  word ptr oldvec+2,es
    mov  word ptr oldvec,bx
    mov  ah,25h                  ; Set Vector function
    push ds                      ; save data segment
    push cs                      ; DS not valid now!
    pop  ds
    mov  dx,offset CI_isr
    int  21h                     ; install new handler
    pop  ds                      ; restore data segment
    mov  cs:our_ds,ds            ; save it for use by ISR
    mov  dx,com_base
    add  dx,4                    ; set MCR...
    mov  al,0Bh                  ; ...DTR and OUT2 bits
    out  dx,al
    sub  dx,3                    ; set IER...
    mov  al,1                    ; ...for RDR interrupt only
    out  dx,al
    in   al,21h                  ; set 8259 mask...
    and  al,int_mask2            ; ...for COM port
    out  21h,al                  ; and write back to PIC
    xor  ax,ax                   ; clear both pointers
    mov  asc_in,ax
    mov  asc_out,ax
    sti                          ; then re-enable interrupts
    clc                          ; flag no error, all okay
    ret                          ; back to caller
CI_inst   endp

CI_isr    proc far               ; interrupt service routine, RDR
only
```

```
        push ax                     ; save registers
        push bx
        push dx
        push ds
        mov  ax,cs:our_ds           ; use our own data segment
        mov  ds,ax
        mov  dx,com_base            ; RDR is at base+0
        in   al,dx                  ; read character
        mov  bx,asc_in              ; get buffer pointer
        mov  [asc_buf+bx],al        ; store character
        inc  bx                     ; advance pointer
        cmp  bx,bufsiz              ; at end of buffer?
        jne  ascint1                ; no, jump
        xor  bx,bx                  ; yes, reset to front
ascint1:   mov  asc_in,bx           ; store pointer
        sti                         ; now turn interrupts back on
        mov  al,20h                 ; ...and send EOI to PIC
        out  20h,al
        pop  ds                     ; restore all registers
        pop  dx
        pop  bx
        pop  ax
        iret                        ; return from interrupt
our_ds     dw   ?                   ; for interrupt service, must be
                                      in CS
CI_isr     endp

CI_getc    proc                     ; gets character from buffer
        public CI_getc
        mov  bx,asc_out             ; look for a character
        xor  cx,cx                  ; timer for loop check
getc1:     cmp  bx,asc_in           ; any in buffer?
        jne  getc2                  ; yes, take it
        loop getc1                  ; no, wait for one (CI_isr will
        mov  ax,8000h               ; advance asc_in when it's here)
        ret                         ; return with 8000h if timeout

getc2:     mov  al,[bx+asc_buf]     ; get the character
        inc  bx                     ; and advance the buffer pointer
        cmp  bx,bufsiz              ; at end of buffer?
        jne  getc3                  ; no, all okay
```

```
     xor   bx,bx                    ; yes, set back to front
getc3:     mov  asc_out,bx          ; store pointer for next call
     xor   ah,ah                    ; zero out AH for safety
     ret
CI_getc    endp

CI_rmv     proc                     ; removes private service
     public  CI_rmv
     mov   dx,com_base              ; MCR is at base+4
     add   dx,4
     in    al,dx
     and   al,0FEh                  ; clear DTR to hang up
     out   dx,al
     in    al,21h                   ; read PIC mask
     or    al,int_mask1             ; disable COM port bit
     out   21h,al                   ; write new mask
     mov   ah,25h                   ; Set Vector function
     mov   al,com_int
     push  ds                       ; save data segment
     lds   dx,oldvec                ; get saved address
     int   21h                      ; put original back
     pop   ds                       ; restore data segment
     ret                            ; back to caller
CI_rmv     endp

     end
```

Only three of the four routines in RINTS are accessible to other programs. These are `CI_inst`, which installs the interrupt service routine after setting up internal storage and verifying that the requested serial port exists, `CI_getc`, called to get a single character from the internal buffer that is maintained by the interrupt service routine, and `CI_rmv`, which uninstalls the interrupt service routine and disables its hooks into the operating system. `CI_inst` must be called before the first use of `CI_getc`, and `CI_rmv` must be called before your program terminates. The interrupt service routine itself, `CI_isr`, is totally encapsulated within the `RINTS` module.

The `CI_inst` routine sets up certain internal variables used when installing and removing the interrupt service routine, and while doing so, verifies that the requested serial port exists in the system. If not, it sets the carry flag and returns without installing any hooks. Like the `XPOLL` module, though, this error indication cannot be tested by a high level language, and unlike `XPOLL`, this routine as printed returns a zero value whether an error occurred or not. You might want to add a line `MOV AX,1` immediately after the `CLC` at the end of the routine, so that it will return nonzero if successful just as does the corresponding `CP_inst` function in `XPOLL`.

If the serial port exists, then `CI_inst` obtains the current values from the vector for the interrupt associated with that port and saves them for restoration by `CI_rmv` before exit, then sets the address of `CI_isr` into the vector instead. With the vector address changed, the routine then enables the Data Ready interrupt from the serial port, and the associated IRQ via the system's PIC port (at 21h). Finally, it sets both the `asc_in` and `asc_out` pointers into the 256-byte data buffer to zero, indicating that the buffer is empty.

The buffer size can be changed by editing the second line of the program, but 256 bytes is usually ample for most applications.

The `CI_isr` routine is called each time that the UART sends a Data Ready interrupt request, and when called, saves all the registers it will be using, since there is no way to predict exactly what the system may be doing when the interrupt occurs. It then sets DS to the segment address of its own data area, which was saved within the code segment by `CI_inst`, takes the ready character from the UART's RDR, stores the character in the buffer at the offset indicated by asc_in, then increments `asc_in` to point to the next character of the buffer. If this takes the offset past the end of the buffer, it's reset to zero, turning the buffer into an endless carousel with 256 slots available.

The routine then sends an End Of Interrupt code to the PIC at port 20h, re-enables interrupts (which were automatically disabled by the interrupt request itself, and allowed to remain that way while all the critical changes were made), restores the saved registers, and returns to the point of interruption via an IRET opcode.

An important error check has been omitted from the procedure in the interest of keeping the code simple: no test is made to see if the new value for `asc_in` has caught up with the `asc_out` offset, which points to the first character still not removed from the buffer via `CI_getc`. This means that if more than 256 characters arrive between calls to `CI_getc`, the oldest ones will be lost and only the most recent 256 characters will be retained.

If the pointers ever do catch up with each other, which means that the buffer is full, there's no simple universal way to prevent data from being lost. Your only choice in such a situation is whether to lose the oldest data, or the newest, since you cannot be certain that you can control the other end of the line and make it stop sending until your program catches up.

If you'd prefer to lose the newest data instead of the oldest in such a situation, you need to add code at the label `ascint1` to compare BX with the `asc_out` pointer, and if the values are equal, simply don't store BX back in asc_in. This will cause the next incoming character to replace the one just stored, in the buffer, and if the value of `asc_out` has not changed in the meantime, the one after that will replace it. Every incoming character will overwrite the previous one until some of the older data is read out of the buffer.

The ideal situation, of course, would be to detect that such an overlap is imminent and signal the sender to hold up until further notice. That's the area known as *flow control* or *handshaking* and doing it right requires far more detailed knowledge of communications techniques than can be supplied in this volume. Done wrong, flow control can create more problems than it solves. That's why this sample routine begs the question, and simply lets the oldest data get lost if the buffer fills.

You can delay the onset of the problem by increasing bufsiz to create a bigger buffer, but that's not really a cure in all cases. In any event, don't try to make the buffer any bigger than 64K; even that would leave no room for most programs to store any other data. The best rule is to keep the buffer as small as possible while preventing it from filling up in normal use.

Note, also, that the `CI_isr` routine is written specifically to deal with the 8250 UART and has no provision for accepting multiple bytes on a single interrupt. It cannot, as a result, be used with the FIFO buffers we'll meet a bit later, although the modification to allow this would be relatively simple: test the LSR's `Data Ready` bit after each pointer update (just past label "ascint1") and if the bit is nonzero, loop back to the previous `MOV DX,COM_BASE` line to get another character. With this change, all available characters would be read into the buffer from the UART, each time an interrupt occurred.

The `CI_getc` routine is called by your program to get one character from the buffer. If no character is available when this function is called, it will wait for 65,536 passes around its internal loop for one to arrive, and if none shows up by that time, will return the value 8000h as the received character to indicate that it timed out while waiting. Since any valid character will be in the range from 00h through 00FFh, the timeout code is easy to distinguish.

When a character is available, it is returned, and the asc_out pointer is stepped past it just as is the asc_in pointer for incoming data. In this routine, the two pointers being equal indicates that the buffer is empty, since asc_out always points to the next byte available to take, while asc_in points to the first vacant space. When the available byte is vacant then the buffer is empty.

The CI_rmv routine must be called before your program terminates, to disconnect the interrupt service routine from the system and to restore the previous ISR's vector. This routine first drops the Data Terminal Ready line, to force the UART to disconnect the external communication, then disables all the hooks that were enabled by CI_inst, and finally restores the saved address in the interrupt vector. Failure to call this routine before exit can cause strange system crashes at some later time, if the serial port should generate an interrupt when the address pointed to by its vector no longer contains valid code.

Testing These Samples

To test the polling and interrupt routines, I created a small C program I call COMMDEMO. It also illustrates still another routine to initialize the serial port via the BIOS function, with a 1200-BPS bit rate and 8N1 operating mode hard-coded in:

```
#include <stdio.h>
#include <string.h>

void CP_inst( int portnum );                          /* in XPOLL.OBJ
*/
void CP_putc( char c );                               /* in XPOLL.OBJ
*/

void CI_inst( int portnum );                          /* in RINTS.OBJ
*/
int  CI_getc( void );                                 /* in RINTS.OBJ
*/
void CI_rmv( void );                                  /* in RINTS.OBJ
*/

void BI_inst( int portnum )              /* initialize via BIOS call
*/
{ asm mov dx,portnum
  asm dec dx
```

```
  asm mov ax,0x83                                     /* 1200 8N1
*/
  asm int 0x14
  printf( "BIOS init done..." );
  CP_inst( portnum );
  printf( "polling set up..." );
  CI_inst( portnum );
  printf( "ISR installed..." );
}

void main( void )
{ char ToModem[80];                   /* buffer for keyboard input
*/
  char *S_Ptr;
  int workword;

  printf( "\n installing..." );
  BI_inst( 1 );                                 /* test using COM1
*/
  puts( "success!" );
  ToModem[0] = 1;

  for( ; ; )                            /* loop until input empty
*/
    { printf( "\nInput: " );           /* prompt for input string
*/
      gets( ToModem );
      workword = strlen( ToModem );
      if( workword < 1 )            /* detect empty input to get out
*/
        break;
      strcat( ToModem, "\r" );                        /* append CR
*/

      S_Ptr = ToModem;                /* send whole string to port
*/
      while( *S_Ptr )
        CP_putc( *S_Ptr++ );

      printf( "\nResponse:\n" );       /* report response received
*/
```

```
      for( workword=CI_getc(); workword > 0; workword=CI_getc() )
        putchar( workword & 127 );

    }

  printf( "\n removing ISR now..." );
  CI_rmv();
  puts( "successful." );
}
```

To compile this program you can use the MAKEFILE for Chapter 10 that is included on the companion diskette as shown in Figure 10.2, or you can simply invoke your compiler and supply the two OBJ filenames (XPOLL.OBL and RINTS.OBJ) on the command line in addition to the program name. Note that as presented, COMMDEMO is written specifically for Borland compilers; to use it with Microsoft compilers you will need to replace all occurrences of the asm keyword with _asm instead. No other change should be necessary.

```
C:>make commdemo
MAKE Version 3.6  Copyright (c) 1992 Borland International

Available memory 7696384 bytes

        D:\BC\BIN\BCC -ms -c -ID:\BC\INCLUDE -LD:\BC\LIB commdemo.c
Borland C++  Version 3.1 Copyright (c) 1992 Borland International
commdemo.c:

        Available memory 718870
        D:\BC\BIN\TASM xpoll;
Turbo Assembler  Version 3.1  Copyright (c) 1988, 1992 Borland International

Assembling file:   xpoll.ASM
Error messages:    None
Warning messages:  None
Passes:            1
Remaining memory:  368k

        D:\BC\BIN\TASM rints;
Turbo Assembler  Version 3.1  Copyright (c) 1988, 1992 Borland International

Assembling file:   rints.ASM
Error messages:    None
Warning messages:  None
Passes:            1
Remaining memory:  366k

        D:\BC\BIN\TLINK -TDE -LD:\BC\LIB c0s+commdemo+xpoll+rints,commdemo,nul,c
s
Turbo Link  Version 5.1 Copyright (c) 1992 Borland International

C:>
```

Figure 10.2. Here's what happens when you run MAKEFILE and specify that you want to build only COMMDEMO. If none of the necessary object files exists in the current directory, MAKE will invoke the compiler and assembler as necessary to create them all, then run the linker to create COMMDEMO.EXE.

When you run COMMDEMO you'll quickly notice that it's far less convenient than most terminal programs. It is not intended as a real utility, so I made no effort to imitate one. All input is line-oriented rather than character-oriented. Figure 10.3 shows what happens when the program runs, and you type the modem reset command ATZ at the Input prompt.

Typing an empty line in response to the prompt ends the program's operation.

```
C:>commdemo

 installing...BIOS init done...polling set up...ISR installed...success!

Input: ATZ

Response:
ATZ
OK

Input:

 removing ISR now...successful.

C:>
```

Figure 10.3. A sample run of COMMDEMO.EXE, with only the modem reset command "ATZ" entered at the "Input:" prompt. The reports at entry and exit let you know what the program is doing.

Differences for Higher Speed

With the advent of high-speed modems, ever-faster modem technologies, and easily-installed multitasking systems such as Desqview and Windows, serial ports themselves have been hard-pressed to keep up. Standard serial ports were designed when speeds of up to 4800 BPS were considered extremely fast. With current speeds more than twice that figure, they frequently develop problems.

The problems with serial ports result from two primary causes:

1. The 8250 (or equivalent) UART is simply too slow to run at the high speeds required by fast modems. While the chips are rated for high speed use, that assumes a simple and fully dedicated enviroment such as might be found in a chip-maker's test lab, not the busy architecture of a MS-DOS-based PC that is running disk drives, a keyboard, and a screen in addition to the UART itself.

2. The PC architecture requires that many interrupts receive service and some of them cannot themselves be interrupted. If a serial port is running at high speed, the system may lose incoming data because it is servicing some other interrupt when a byte arrives. Since the UART has nowhere to put the incoming byte, it stays in the UART and gets overwritten by the next byte received. This is known as an overrun error.

The faster you drive the port, the more such errors you get. This becomes a serious problem if your application should be multitasked using Windows or Desqview, because the rapid task switching required keeps the system almost totally occupied simply juggling all the different tasks and leaves too little time available for necessary housekeeping.

The 16550 UART

To deal with both of these problems, the designers at National Semiconductor Corporation came up with a better, 8250-compatible UART dubbed the *16550.* This chip is designed for high speed and incorporates an internal buffer that reduces the service demands made on the system by up to 16 times. If your serial port contains an 8250 that is plugged into a socket rather than soldered into place, you can probably replace it just by plugging in a 16550 to replace the original UART.

Since the new chip was originally introduced, many manufacturers have entered the market, and some have buffers that don't work. The "genuine" 16550 is made by National Semiconductor, and its full part number is NS16550AFN. There is an older NS model, but make sure to order the `AFN` type. If your supplier stocks some different version, make certain that it is totally compatible with the NS16550AFN, and if possible, get a guarantee that you can return the chip for a full refund if you find that it isn't.

The FIFO Buffer

The internal buffer of the NS16550AFN provides space that can hold up to 16 bytes. If the system isn't able to take the current byte as soon as it's ready, the UART can hold it in the buffer until the system can deal with it. While the 16-byte space allows some margin to ensure that no received data is lost, it's still good practice to empty the *FIFO* buffer whenever possible, rather than taking only one byte per interrupt.

The buffer on the UART is called a `FIFO` buffer, which means that the first byte put into it will be the first byte taken out (literally, First In First Out). Such buffers are sometimes called *push-through* buffers also, but FIFO is the standard name for them. The alternate action, *LIFO* (Last In First Out) is more often referred to as "the stack" but this would be useless for handling data that arrives in sequence.

Programming the FIFO

The 16550 chip adds additional registers to the 10 contained in the 8250 design. These are the FIFO Control Register (FCR), which shares the offset address of the IIR just as the RDR and THR share the same offset since one is read-only and the other is write-only, and the Scratch Register (SCR) at offset 7 from the port's base address, which was not used by the 8250 design. The SCR actually made its appearance in the 16450 design, which shares the speed limitations of the 8250 and so we won't look any closer at it.

The offsets for each added register, with respect to the base address of the port itself, are:

Offset	Register
2	FIFO Control Register (FCR) when written to.
7	Scratch Register (SCR) not used by 8250 or 16550.

The FIFO Control Register (FCR) programs the manner in which the FIFO buffer operates:

Bit	Meaning
0	FIFO enabled if 1, disabled if 0; default is disabled.
1	Clear receiving FIFO if 1.
2	Clear transmitting FIFO if 1.
3	Mode selection, always set to 1 for MS-DOS systems.
4-5	Always set to zero.
6-7	Sets threshold at which interrupt will be generated: 00 = 1 byte in FIFO 01 = 4 bytes in FIFO 10 = 8 bytes in FIFO 11 = 14 bytes in FIFO

The FIFO buffer on a 16550 chip can be enabled and disabled via software. Initially, at power-up, it will be disabled. To enable it, Bit 0 of the FCR must be set to 1.

To program the FIFO's operation, the usual procedure is to output 0CFh to the FCR. This clears both FIFO buffers, enables the operation, and tells the UART to generate a Data Ready interrupt (if enabled) when 14 characters have been received into the FIFO. This still provides time for two more characters to be received before an overrun error will occur.

If the communications link is running at such a high speed that a two-character safety margin is not enough, you can use 08Fh as the control pattern to select a threshold of eight bytes, leaving an eight-byte margin. In most cases, however, the two-character margin is adequate.

When you use a 16550 UART with Windows 3.1, even if it is properly configured, you may run into problems. If you enable the FIFO buffers by using an external command before entering Windows, then Windows won't recognize the COM port. If your Windows software is 16550 aware, then it will deal with the situation so you won't need to enable the buffers ahead of time, but otherwise you may have to use a replacement COM driver, or different software. As a developer, this is an additional reason to make sure that any communications capabilities you put into your programs are able to identify the presence of a 16550 UART and if one is encountered, to properly deal with its FIFO buffering.

Modem Conventions

As the speed capabilities of the UART designs and the serial adapters advanced, so too did those of modems. A number of techniques are now available to permit speeds that were once deemed impossible to be supported reliably over normal dial-up telephone circuits. Two of the most widely used families of these techniques are the MNP conventions, and the CCITT "speed modulation" standards.

MNP Protocols

The Microcom Networking Protocol, MNP, is a communications protocol designed to support interactive and file-transfer applications. Despite being considered proprietary by Microcom when it was first introduced, parts of this protocol have gained wide acceptance.

MNP is designed to conform to the Open System Interconnection (OSI) Network Reference Model created by the International Organization for Standardization (IOS). This model is a network protocol divided into seven standardized layers, which assist in the interconnection of different vendors' equipment. The OSI Model allows users to choose how their networking systems are partitioned and implemented.

In the OSI Model the Link Layer must provide reliable data transfer, using the Physical Layer to transmit information through the data path. In dial-up communications, the Physical Layer is provided by "traditional" modems. But these modems cannot provide guaranteed error-free communications. The Link Layer must, as a result, provide for error detection and control. In some situations, such as binary file transfers, error detection is provided for file transfers by an error-correcting protocol (such as Xmodem, for example) but there is no such protocol present when dealing with plain ASCII text.

Microcom's MNP fills this gap, when communicating with other equipment that also uses MNP. (It's still possible for errors to occur in a MNP-to-MNP connection, if they occur at either end in the cable or in the computer itself, but the probability for error is far lower here than while the data is moving between modems.) The protocol can be implemented in either hardware (the original and still preferred method) or in software.

A primary rule within the protocol is that each implementation communicates with all other implementations. When an MNP communications link is first established, the implementations at each end negotiate with each other to determine the highest mutually supported class of MNP service, then maintain this level for the remainder of the connection. While nine classes have been defined, few systems today support anything above Class 6.

The following summaries of the first six levels of MNP are based on a paper prepared by Mike Focke in August 1988, from Microcom product description brochures. Each level offers better performance than its predecessor:

Class 1. This is the lowest level of MNP performance. MNP Class 1 uses an asynchronous byte-oriented half-duplex method of exchanging data. The protocol efficiency of a Class 1 implementation is only about 70 percent. That is, a device using MNP Class 1 with a 2400 BPS modem will realize 1690 BPS throughput. Modern microprocessors have become so powerful that MNP Class 1 is seldom implemented alone.

Class 2. MNP Class 2 also uses asynchronous byte-oriented data exchange, but in a full-duplex mode. Almost all microprocessor- based hardware is capable of supporting MNP Class 2 performance. The efficiency of a Class 2 implementation is about 84 percent. A device using MNP Class 2 with a 2400 BPS modem will realize 2000 BPS throughput.

Class 3. MNP Class 3 uses synchronous bit-oriented full-duplex exchange, which is inherently more efficient than the asynchronous byte-oriented data format because 10 bits are required to represent 8 data bits in the asynchronous format. The synchronous data format eliminates the need for start and stop bits. The user still sends data asynchronously to the Class 3 modem, but the modems communicate with each other synchronously.

The efficiency of a Class 3 implementation is about 108 percent. A device using Class 3 with a 2400 bps modem will realize 2600 bps throughput. At Class 3 performance, the MNP protocol "rewards" the user for using an error-correcting modem by producing 8 percent extra throughput over an ordinary modem without MNP.

Class 4. MNP Class 4 introduced two new concepts to further improve performance. During data transfer, MNP-4 monitors the reliability of the transmission medium. If the data channel is relatively error-free, this class will assemble larger data packets to increase throughput. If the data is introducing many errors, then smaller data packets will be transmitted. While smaller data packets increase the protocol overhead, at the same time they decrease the time required by retransmissions and reduce the probability of any one packet being hit by an error. The net result is that more data is transmitted on the first try.

The efficiency of a Class 4 implementation is about 120 percent. A device using MNP Class 4 with a 2400 bps modem will realize approximately 2900 bps throughput. With Class 4 performance, the MNP protocol produces 20 percent more throughput than an ordinary modem without MNP.

Many of today's modems feature MNP-4 operation, under license from Microcom. No modification of your software is needed to achieve these benefits.

Class 5. MNP Class 5 adds Data Compression to MNP Class 4 service. This class uses a real-time adaptive algorithm to compress data. The real-time aspects of the algorithm allow the data compression to operate on interactive terminal data as well as file-transfer data. Data compression delivers faster screen updates to the user. The adaptive nature of the compression algorithm continuously analyzes the user data and adjusts parameters to maximize data throughput.

Data compression algorithms, like sort algorithms, are sensitive to the data pattern being processed. Most information transmitted will benefit from data compression. The user will see compression vary between 1.3 to 1 and 2 to 1 (some files may be compressed at even higher ratios). Some kinds of files, though, notably those that have been compressed with such programs as LHA, PKZIP, ARC, ZOO, or the like, may actually expand when sent by MNP-5, so most modems that incorporate this feature also permit it to be turned off under software control.

A realistic estimate of the overall compression factor a user can expect is 1.6 to 1 or 63 percent. This is equivalent to a net efficiency of 200 percent for an MNP Class 5 implementation. A device using MNP Class 5 with a 2400 bps modem may realize 4800 bps throughput.

Class 6. MNP Class 6 adds Universal Link Negotiation and Statistical Duplexing to MNP Class 5 service. Universal Link Negotiation allows MNP modems to begin operations at a common slower speed and negotiate the use of an alternate high speed modulation technique. An MNP Class 6 modem based on V.29 technology can deliver maximum performance in file transfer applications; up to 19.2 kbps throughput is possible on dial-up circuits.

CCITT Conventions

One of the major differences between various kinds of modems is the *modulation technique* that they use. Through the years, these techniques have tended to be somewhat provincial in nature, and at one time modems that could be used in the U.S. were unable to communicate over international circuits because their modulation technique differed from those in other countries.

That happened because the U.S. standards were set by a private firm, AT&T (the Bell System), without regard to international practice (which was, at the time the standards were first developed, almost non-existent). Not one, but several, standards were developed, each identified by the model number of the first AT&T Data Set (modem) to use it. The most common Bell modulation standards still used are:

Standard	Bit Rate	Description
103	300 bps	Incompatible with CCITT V.21
212A	1200 bps	Partially compatible with CCITT V.22
208	4800 bps	Used mostly on leased lines Likely to disappear

The CCITT (Comite Consultatif International Telephonie e Telegraphique, the international body that standardizes telecommunications practices) is the focus of all work now. The speed modulations established by the CCITT are known as the V series, and you see them listed in the characteristics of all newer modems. Here's a list, compiled by Earle Robinson, forum administrator of CompuServe's IBMEUR forum, of those most commonly used:

CCITT Code	Bit Rate	Description
V.21	300 bps	Incompatible with the Bell 103 modulation.
V.22	1200 bps	Partially compatible with the Bell equivalent, 212a.
V.22bis	2400 bps	Universally used in the U.S. and elsewhere.
V.23	1200/75 bps	Asymmetric protocol used only overseas.
V.26ter	2400 bps	Full duplex plus echo cancellation. Seldom used today.
V.29	9600 bps	Half duplex protocol, used for group 3 faxes, and in some modems, but with proprietary additions.
V.32	9600 bps	Full duplex. Lower manufacturing costs will soon make this speed the standard. Planned enhancements will increase speed, using some asymmetricity for file transfers.
V.34	>14400 bps	Proposed asymmetric high speed modulation.

Further CCITT recommendations which may be of interest include:

V.42	Error correction, in two parts, the main one plus an annex which provides compatibility with MNP classes 2, 3, and 4.
V.42bis	Compression enhancement to V.42. Recently approved by CCITT.

V.25	For parallel automatic dialers, the 2100 hz answer tone.
V.25bis	Serial automatic dialing.
V.24	More or less the CCITT equivalent to RS232.

Use of V.32, V.22bis or any other speed modulation doesn't preclude the use of an error correction method, be it MNP or V.42. Error correction can be done at any speed, though you find it most often in high-speed equipment.

FAX-Modem Considerations

A variation of the classic modem that has taken the market by storm in the past year is the combination FAX-modem, which combines a modem with 2400-BPS or higher speed capability with circuitry that meets CCITT FAX standards, enabling the single adapter to serve as both a FAX card and as a modem.

Most of the popular varieties of FAX-modem cards are based on a Rockwell chip set, although Intel also produces a highly reliable unit using their own chip designs. Before the Rockwell chipset catapulted the combination card into the forefront of the market, a number of FAX-only cards were available. Much of the following information applies to both dedicated FAX cards, and to the FAX-modem combination.

While providing support for direct FAX transmission and reception can be a definite plus feature for many applications, right now the information necessary in order to develop reliable FAX interfacing is not widely available. Here, we simply give you a taste of what's involved.

CAS, FAXBIOS, and Other Standards

One of the first attempts to establish a standard for use with facsimile software was mounted by the Intel Corporation and Digital Communications Associates as a joint effort. This Communicating Applications Specifications, abbreviated to CAS, was widely adopted in the early stages of FAX-card development, but its use seems to be diminishing with the passage of time.

CAS defined six data-communication events, and specified how each should be dealt with. The six were SEND, when the local computer transmitted information to a remote fax machine or other computer; RECEIVE, when the local computer received information from a remote site; POLLED SEND, in which the local system waits for a remote device to call, then automatically sends information to it; POLLED RECEIVE, where the local system initiates the call; GROUP SEND, in which a group of remote systems are sent the same data one after the other; and finally GROUP POLLED RECEIVE, like polled receive except that a group of remotes is called in sequence rather than just a single system.

To handle these events, CAS defined a Resident Manager program and an API to it via Multiplex Interrupt 2Fh using the Program ID Code of CBh. Applications themselves must communicate with the Resident Manager through this API in order to submit documents for transmission or to obtain received documents.

The complete specification, obtainable from either Intel or DCA, fills 58 pages. It also can be downloaded from the Intel Electronic Bulletin Board by calling (503) 645-6275, or from Intel's forum area on CompuServe (GO PCEO).

Another attempt at standardizing the fax interface, this one by a larger group of companies, was FAXBIOS. At this writing, status of the FAXBIOS project is unclear; preliminary versions of the specification have been circulated for comment, but no details are publicly available at the present time and progress seems to have slowed from the initial enthusiastic efforts. The FAXBIOS group conducts at least some of its business in the Telecommunications forum of CompuServe and can be reached by the command GO FAXBIOS.

The most popular standards at this time appear to be two created by the Electronics Industry Association (EIA) and popularly identified as Class 1 and Class 2. Let's look at these in a bit more detail.

Class 1 Systems

Most FAX-modem cards, and almost all external combination FAX-modem units, depend on the Class 1 standard defined by document EIA/TIA-578.

This standard was accepted by the CCITT TR29.2 committee in 1988 for communication between FAX software and FAX modems. Class 1 FAX software handles all of the T.4 FAX image and T.30 session protocol information and timing, leaving little for the modem to do. Thus, the ability to communicate properly with various FAX machines is more a function of the software than the FAX modem. This makes it easy for an external modem to work with Class 1 software, if it is capable of recognizing the special "AT" commands that form the FAX interface.

The Class 1 standard I/O interface supports asynchronous serial and parallel interfaces. The interface rate is 19,200 bps. Start and stop elements are removed from the transmit data and added to the receive data. Both transmit and receive data are buffered. Flow control using XON/XOFF (DC1/DC3) or RTS/CTS is provided.

Unique control character strings are identified, filtered, or reinserted into the I/O data stream. The way these strings are used can be illustrated by the following chart, which summarizes the five phases and many steps required for a Class 1 package to receive a FAX from a remote machine:

DTE Commands	DCE Responses	Remote Fax	Notes
AT+FCLASS=1	OK		Sets system up to accept incoming FAXes
PHASE A			
		Fax machine dial	
	RING		
ATA	modem answers		
	send HDLC flags	receive flags	+FTH=3 implied by answering
	CONNECT		
PHASE B			
<NSF>	send NSF frame	receive NSF	last frame bit=0
	CONNECT		
<CSI>	send CSI frame	receive CSI	last frame bit=0
	CONNECT		

DTE Commands	DCE Responses	Remote Fax	Notes
<DSI>	send DSI frame	receive DSI	last frame bit=1
	OK, drop carrier		
AT+FRH=3	CONNECT		
		send TSI frame	last frame bit=0
	<TSI>,OK		
AT+FRH=3	CONNECT		
		send DCS frame	last frame bit=1
	<DCS>,OK	drop carrier	
AT+FRM=96			
		send v.29	
	CONNECT	send TCF frame	
	<TCF>	drop carrier	
	NO CARRIER		
AT+FTH=3	CONNECT		
<CFR>	send CFR frame	receive CFR	last frame bit=1
	OK,drop carrier		
PHASE C			
AT+FRM=96			
		send page data	
	<page data>	drop carrier	
	NO CARRIER		

DTE Commands	DCE Responses	Remote Fax	Notes
PHASE D			
AT+FRH=3	CONNECT		
		send EOP frame	last frame bit=1
	<EOP>,OK		
AT+FTH=3	CONNECT		
<MCF>	send MCF frame	receive MCF	last frame bit=1
	OK,drop carrier		
AT+FRH=3	CONNECT		
		send DCN frame	last frame bit=1
	<DCN>,OK		
PHASE E			
ATH0	OK,hang up	hang up	

Here's a brief description of just what each of the DTE commands and DCE responses listed in the chart accomplishes:

The AT+FCLASS=1 DTE command that begins the whole sequence is sent from the computer system to the modem, to tell it to enter the FAX interface mode of operation rather than the usual modem conditions. Nothing more happens until after the remote machine has dialed in and the modem has detected an incoming ring signal, in response to which it sends RING status to the computer. This incoming call's origination establishes PHASE A of the sequence.

The computer's `ATA` command directs the modem to answer the call, which it does. Since it is in FAX mode, it automatically sends tone sequences to the caller to indicate its capabilities. The remote system responds to those sequences with tones of its own, and if the two systems are capable of communicating with each other as indicated by these sequences, PHASE A ends with the modem sending `CONNECT` status to the computer.

PHASE B begins with additional handshaking, and more CONNECT status messages, as the modem and the remote machine negotiate for mutually acceptable transmission speeds (bit rates) to be used. The CCITT standard recommends that the highest bit rate that both can handle be used unless its error rate becomes excessive, but permits the bit rate to be as low as 300 BPS if nothing faster can be used. When both ends of the circuit have exchanged the necessary housekeeping information and identifiers (the DSI, TSI, DCS, TCF, and CFR frames) PHASE B gives way to PHASE C.

In PHASE C, the page image data (at a pixel resolution of 203 dots per inch horizontally and 96 lines per inch vertically) is sent. PHASE D follows immediately, beginning with transmission of an EOP frame followed by MCF and DCN frames which signal that the transaction has been completed. In PHASE E, the computer sends "ATH0" to terminate the connection, and both the modem and the remote machine hang up as a result.

You can see from this that the complete set of exchanges required to receive just one page of data is a complicated process. And this description is only an overview; the actual EIA specification requires much more detail to be sent in each of the frames mentioned, and in addition the image must be compressed and decompressed using the CCITT Group 3 algorithm, which gives excellent compression performance but is more difficult to comprehend than are the algorithms used for the LHA and PKZIP programs!

Class 2 Support

EIA/TIA-592, not yet released although it has been in process since 1988, defines the "Class 2" standard FAX-modem interface. Class 2 FAX software is intended to generate a T.4 FAX page image and send it to the FAX modem a page at a time. The FAX modem then handles the T.30 session protocol information and timing. This relieves the computer of some work. Unlike the situation with the Class 1 standard, in Class 2 the ability to communicate properly with various FAX machines is more a function of the FAX modem than the software. However, to complicate matters, Class 2 FAX software can issue Class 1 commands and take over some of the duties of the Class 2 FAX modem.

When the CCITT committee accepted Class 1 back in 1988, it also voted on, but for various technical reasons did not accept, the Class 2 standard. A year later, they had slightly revised the standard but again did not accept it. Nevertheless, some software and hardware manufacturers decided to unofficially adopt this standard until the TR29.2 committee could develop an acceptable standard. Since so many companies have used the unofficial standard, the TR29.2 committee has designated that when the standard is officially adopted it will be known as Class 2.0.

Since 1989, the TR29.2 committee has voted on several revisions to the Class 2 standard. Every time, it has been rejected for technical reasons. The TR29.2 committee is still reviewing the technical issues that were raised.

The Class 2 documentation will not be available to developers until approximately one month after the TR29.2 committee accepts it, if that ever happens. Most of those companies which have already released "Class 2" FAX software either sit on the TR29.2 committee or know someone who does. However, it's a bit difficult to adhere to a "standard" that is still in the process of being written.

An Example Program

One of the best ways to become familiar with effective techniques for incorporating data communications into your programs is to work through a complete communications-based program and see how the various bits and pieces fit together.

While our sample program for this chapter, NEWTIME.ASM, stops short of getting into the more esoteric areas such as dealing with interrupt handlers, it will give you an introduction to some of the factors that all communications packages must deal with, and also will provide a useful tool to help you keep your system's time and date information accurate despite unavoidable variations in your hardware's accuracy from one week to the next.

NEWTIME: Its Plan and Purpose

NEWTIME is a program that automatically dials into a national time service and extracts the time and date information that such a service transmits automatically. As published, it calls the National Institute of Standards and Technology (formerly NBS) number in Boulder, Colorado; however, the program is written to allow you to easily modify it for use with any other service, even those outside the USA.

When you call into the NIST number, using a standard communications program, you get something like this:

```
                              D  L D
MJD    YR MO DA HH MM SS ST S UT1 msADV        <OTM>
49109 93-05-02 02:21:18 50 0 -.2 045.0 UTC(NIST) *
49109 93-05-02 02:21:19 50 0 -.2 045.0 UTC(NIST) *
49109 93-05-02 02:21:20 50 0 -.2 045.0 UTC(NIST) *
49109 93-05-02 02:21:21 50 0 -.2 045.0 UTC(NIST) *
49109 93-05-02 02:21:22 50 0 -.2 045.0 UTC(NIST) *
49109 93-05-02 02:21:23 50 0 -.2 045.0 UTC(NIST) *
```

The data keeps coming until you disconnect, or until 56 seconds have elapsed. Each line takes exactly one second to transmit at 1200 BPS, and the precise boundary of the indicated second is defined by the stop bit of the "OTM" character at the end of each line. Here's some of the information you get when you press "?" for help:

```
DST = Daylight savings time characters, valid for the continental
U.S., are set as follows:
  00 = We are on standard time (ST).
  50 = We are on DST.
  99 to 51 = Now on ST, go to DST when your local time is 2:00 am
and the count is 51.  The count is decremented daily at 00 (UTC).
  49 to 01 = Now on DST, go to ST when your local time is 2:00 am
and the count is 01.  The count is decremented daily at 00 (UTC).
The two DST characters provide up to 48 days advance notice of a
change in time.  The count remains at 00 or 50 at other times.
```

```
LS = Leap second flag is set to "1" to indicate that a leap second
is to be added as 23:59:60 (UTC) on the last day of the current UTC
month.  The LS flag will be reset to "0" starting with 23:59:60
(UTC).  The flag will remain on for the entire month before the
second is added.  Leap seconds are added as needed at the end of
any month.  Usually June and/or December are chosen.
```

```
DUT1 = Approximate difference between earth rotation time (UT1) and
UTC, in steps of 0.1 second.        DUT1 = UT1 - UTC
```

MJD = Modified Julian Date, often used to tag certain scientific data.

The full time format is sent at 1200 Baud, 8 bit, 1 stop, no parity. The format at 300 Baud is also 8 bit, 1 stop, no parity. At 300 Baud the MJD and DUT1 values are deleted and the time is transmitted only on even seconds.

Maximum on line time will be 56 seconds. If all lines are busy at any time, the oldest call will be terminated if it has been on line more than 28 seconds, else, the call that first reaches 28 seconds will be terminated.

Current time is valid at the "on-time" marker (OTM), either "*" or "#". The nominal on-time marker (*) will be transmitted 45 ms early to account for the 8 ms required to send 1 character at 1200 Baud, plus an additional 7 ms for delay from NIST to the user, and approximately 30 ms "scrambler" delay inherent in 1200 Baud modems. If the caller echoes all characters, NIST will measure the round trip delay and advance the on-time marker so that the midpoint of the stop bit arrives at the user on time. The amount of msADV will reflect the actual required advance in milliseconds and the OTM will be a "#". The NIST system requires 4 or 5 consecutive delay measurements which are consistent before switching from "*" to "#". If the user has a 1200 Baud modem with the same internal delay as that used by NIST, then the "#" OTM should arrive at the user within +-2 ms of the correct time. However, NIST has studied different brands of 1200 Baud modems and found internal delays from 24 ms to 40 ms and offsets of the "#" OTM of +-10 ms. For many computer users, +-10 ms accuracy should be more than adequate since many computer internal clocks can only be set with granularity of 20 to 50 ms. In any case, the repeatability of the offset for the "#" OTM should be within +-2 ms, if the dial-up path is reciprocal and the user doesn't change the brand or model of modem used. This should be true even if the dial-up path on one day is a land-line of less than 40 ms (one way) and on the next day is a satellite link of 260 to 300 ms. In the rare event that the path is one way by satellite and the other way by land line with a round trip

```
measurement in the range of 90 to 260 ms, the OTM will remain a "*"
indicating 45 ms advance.
```

```
For user comments write:
NIST-ACTS
Time and Frequency Division
Mail Stop 524
325 Broadway
Boulder, CO  80303
```

While it's quite possible to use the service by calling with a conventional terminal program, it's much more convenient to have a program that extracts the time and date information, adjusts for your local time zone, and even makes the allowance for Daylight Savings Time when needed. That's what NEWTIME does.

Note that since NEWTIME uses the BIOS function (implemented by the polling technique) for receiving characters from the time service, the program cannot be used in a MS-DOS session under Windows in Enhanced mode. The preemptive multitasking treatment that Windows applies will cause characters to be lost and the program will become completely confused. Used from the command prompt only, with pure MS-DOS and no multitasker involved, it works perfectly.

The Program and How to Assemble It

NEWTIME is written in assembly language rather than C for no compelling reason except that when I first wrote it, the use of assembly language seemed more fitting to the kinds of actions the program performs. When I chose it for inclusion in this volume, I left it in its original language rather than translating into C primarily to offer you some variety in the examples.

I have compiled it with both MASM 5.1, and with TASM; the results are indistinguishable from each other. Most other assemblers also should work with it, since it does not make any use of simplified segment directives or other unique language features:

```
;           NEWTIME
;           Created:   23-Sep-92
```

```
;          Version:   2

seg_a      segment    byte public
           assume     cs:seg_a, ds:seg_a

           org        100h

newtime    proc       far

start:     mov        ax,10Dh                ; send CR to modem
           mov        dx,portnbr
           int        14h
           and        ax,8000h               ; sent okay?
           jz         go_ok
           mov        ax,4CFFh               ; quit with error code 255
           int        21h
go_ok:     jmp        Do_It

initval    db         83h                    ; 1200 8N1
max_sec    db         25
GMTzone    dw         6                      ; Central timezone
portnbr    dw         0                      ; COM1

dialcmd    db         'ATDT 1 303-494-4774
diallen    dw         13h
rst_cmd    db         '~+++~~ATZ             '
rst_len    dw         9
send_cr    db         0Dh

rcv_bfr    db         '48889 '               ; modified julian date
date_in    db         '92-09-24 '
time_in    db         '02:14:26 '
dst_flg    db         '32 0 +.3 045.0 UTC(NIST) *', 0Dh, 0Ah
mon_day    db         4
day_adj    dw         0
yearval    dw         1900

timeout    dw         0

banner1    db         'NIST Time Setter$'
banner2    db         ' - Free Program from Jim Kyle', 0Dh
           db         0Ah, '$'
redials    db         're$'
```

```
dialing   db      'dialing...', 0Dh, 0Ah, '$'
alldone   db      7, ' <<<== Carrier Still Present ==>>>', 0Dh, 0Ah
          db      '[NIST will disconnect within 60 sec]', 0Dh, 0Ah
warn      db      'Operation complete.', 0Dh, 0Ah, '$'

monthtbl  db      31, 28, 31, 30, 31, 30
          db      31, 31, 30, 31, 30, 31
newtime   endp

;==================================================================
;                      SUBROUTINE
;==================================================================
setport   proc    near
          push    es
          push    si
          mov     dx,40h                 ; use BIOS-RAM area
          mov     es,dx
          mov     si,portnbr             ; index into table
          add     si,si                  ; convert to word
          mov     dx,es:si               ; get port base address
          pop     si
          pop     es
          ret
setport   endp

;==================================================================
;                      SUBROUTINE
;==================================================================
mcr_s     proc    near                   ; set Data Terminal Ready
          push    ax
          push    dx
          call    setport
          add     dx,4                   ; modem control port offset
          in      al,dx
          or      al,1
          jmp     short $+2              ; delay for I/O
          out     dx,al
          pop     dx
          pop     ax
          retn
mcr_s     endp
```

```
;==================================================================
;                       SUBROUTINE
;==================================================================
timer    proc     near
         cmp      al,0
         je       tmr2                ; test for timeout
         push     ax                  ; else set time interval
         mov      ah,2Ch              ; get time
         int      21h
         pop      ax
         mov      dl,dh
         mov      dh,cl
         add      al,dl               ; add specified seconds
         cmp      al,59
         jle      tmr1                ; still same minute
         sub      al,60               ; next minute, adjust
         inc      dh
tmr1:    mov      dl,al
         mov      timeout,dx          ; save for use later
         retn
tmr2:    mov      ah,2Ch              ; get time
         int      21h
         mov      dl,dh               ; set up to compare
         mov      dh,cl
         mov      ax,timeout
         cmp      ax,dx               ; caller will check flags
         retn
timer    endp

;==================================================================
;                       SUBROUTINE
;==================================================================
waits    proc     near                ; countdown delay
         push     cx
         mov      cx,0Fh
wait1:   push     cx                  ; Outer loop
         mov      cx,0FFFFh
wait2:   loop     wait2               ; Inner loop
         pop      cx
         loop     wait1               ; Outer loop
         pop      cx
         retn
waits    endp
```

```
;==================================================================
;                       SUBROUTINE
;==================================================================
get_c   proc        near
        mov         ah,2
        int         14h
        retn
get_c   endp

;==================================================================
;                       SUBROUTINE
;==================================================================
get_s   proc        near
        push        ax
        push        dx
        mov         dx,portnbr          ; select COM port
        push        di
        mov         di,offset rcv_bfr
gets1:  call        get_c               ; wait for close paren
        cmp         al,29h
        jne         gets1
gets2:  call        get_c               ; wait for linefeed
        cmp         al,0Ah
        jne         gets2
        mov         cx,51               ; set to take 51 bytes
gets3:  call        get_c               ; get a character
        stosb                           ; save it in buffer
        loop        gets3               ; back for next one
        call        setport             ; now clear DTR bit
        add         dx,4                ; modem control port offset
        in          al,dx
        and         al,0FEh             ; clear the bit
        jmp         short $+2           ; delay for I/O
        out         dx,al               ; send back to modem
        pop         di
        pop         dx
        pop         ax
        retn
get_s   endp
```

```
;===================================================================
;                          SUBROUTINE
;===================================================================
snd_s   proc         near                 ; send string of chars
        push         ax
        push         dx
        mov          dx,portnbr           ; select COM port
nextchar:
        lodsb                             ; get a char
        cmp          al,'~'               ; special delay?
        jne          ischar               ; no, send it out
        call         waits                ; yes, wait a while
        jmp          short cwait          ; then go close loop
ischar:mov           ah,1                 ; send char to port
        int          14h
        test         ah,80h               ; sent okay?
        jz           cwait                ; yes, keep going
        stc                               ; no, flag an error
        jmp          short sent           ; and get out now
cwait: push          cx
        mov          cx,4000h
        loop         $
        pop          cx
        loopz        nextchar             ; character countdown

sent:   pop          dx
        pop          ax
        retn
snd_s   endp

;===================================================================
;                          SUBROUTINE
;===================================================================
get_n   proc         near
        lodsw        ; String [si] to ax
        sub          ax,3030h
        xchg         ah,al
        aad          ; Ascii adjust
        retn
get_n   endp
```

```
;=================================================================
;                       MAIN PROGRAM
;=================================================================
Do_It:
        call        mcr_s                   ; set DTR bit
        mov         ah,9
        mov         dx,offset banner1
        int         21h
        mov         dx,offset banner2
        int         21h

        mov         ah,0
        mov         al,initval              ; 1200 8N1
        mov         dx,portnbr
        int         14h                     ; reset port

tryagn:mov          dx,offset dialing       ; show status message
        mov         ah,9
        int         21h
        mov         si,offset dialcmd       ; dial Boulder, CO
        mov         cx,diallen
        call        snd_s
        mov         si,offset send_cr
        mov         cx,1
        call        snd_s
        mov         al,max_sec
        call        timer                   ; set timer-up count
listen:mov          dx,portnbr              ; wait for answer
        mov         ah,3
        int         14h                     ; get status al=modem, ah=line
        and         al,80h
        jnz         answer                  ; carrier detected
        xor         al,al
        call        timer                   ; check for timer-up
        jnc         listen                  ; no, keep listening
        mov         si,offset send_cr       ; yes, clear modem
        mov         cx,1
        call        snd_s
        mov         ah,6
        mov         dl,0FFh                 ; get key if pressed
        int         21h
        jz          no_esc
```

```
        cmp        al,1Bh              ; ESC keystroke
        jne        no_esc
        jmp        getout
no_esc:mov         al,3
        call       timer               ; set wait time
holdup:xor         al,al
        call       timer               ; check for time up
        jnc        holdup
        mov        dx,offset redials
        mov        ah,9
        int        21h                 ; display string
        jmp        short tryagn

answer:call        get_s               ; read data from NIST
        mov        si,offset dst_flg   ; check for DST
        call       get_n
        cmp        al,1
        jle        notDST
        cmp        al,51
        jg         notDST
        dec        GMTzone             ; apply DST adjustment
notDST:mov         si,offset time_in   ; get time value
        call       get_n
        sub        ax,GMTzone          ; convert GMT to local time
        cmp        ax,0                ; check for midnight wrap
        jge        noback              ; none occurred
        add        ax,24               ; reset to next day
        mov        day_adj,1           ; and back up date
noback:mov         ch,al               ; hours
        inc        si
        call       get_n
        mov        cl,al               ; minutes
        inc        si
        call       get_n
        mov        dh,al               ; seconds
        xor        dl,dl
        mov        ah,2Dh              ; set time, cx=hrs/min,
dh=sec
        int        21h
        mov        dx,portnbr
        mov        ah,3                ; check to see if hangup yet
        int        14h
        and        al,80h              ; still have carrier?
```

```
        jz          offlin              ; no, no action needed
        mov         si,offset rst_cmd   ; yes, hang up
        mov         cx,rst_len
        call        snd_s
        mov         si,offset send_cr
        mov         cl,1
        call        snd_s
offlin:mov          si,offset date_in   ; convert the date informa-
                                          tion
        call        get_n               ; year
        add         ax,1900
        mov         yearval,ax
        inc         si
        call        get_n               ; month
        mov         mon_day,al
        inc         si
        call        get_n               ; day
        sub         ax,day_adj          ; apply midnite correction
        cmp         ax,0                ; did day back out of month?
        ja          settime             ; no
        dec         mon_day             ; yes, correct the month
        jnz         prvmon              ; did that affect the year?
        dec         yearval             ; yes, so go to previous one
        mov         mon_day,12          ; Dec 31
prvmon:mov          bl,mon_day
        xor         bh,bh
        mov         al,byte ptr monthtbl[bx]
settime:
        mov         dl,al
        mov         dh,mon_day
        mov         cx,yearval
        mov         ah,2Bh              ; set date
        int         21h
        mov         dx,portnbr
        mov         ah,3                ; check if hangup yet
        int         14h
        mov         dx,offset warn
        and         al,80h
        jz          no_car              ; yes
        mov         dx,offset alldone   ; no, change message
no_car:mov          ah,9
        int         21h
```

```
getout:mov          ax,4C00h
       int          21h

seg_a  ends

       end          start
```

To assemble and link NEWTIME.COM, you can use the MAKEFILE by typing MAKE NEWTIME at the command prompt (provided that MAKE.EXE is on your execution path). All that's necessary to use it with an 80286 or later system is to run the program; the CMOS clock-calendar will be set automatically by the system time and date setting calls. If you are using an 8088 system, you'll need to transfer the settings that NEWTIME has made for your current system values into your clock and calendar hardware; the method for achieving this varies from one make of add-on clock card to another.

What the Subroutines Do

Here's what the subroutines contained in NEWTIME.ASM accomplish. The descriptions appear in the sequence that they are invoked when the program runs, rather than that in which they appear in the source code.

The MCR_S Routine

The MCR_S routine calls SETPORT, adds 4 to the base address returned in DX in order to access the MCR, reads the content of the MCR, then sets Bit 0 to 1 in order to make the DTR line to the modem active. The routine performs an apparently unnecessary jump, which actually serves to delay things long enough for the slowest UART to recover from the previous access, then sends the modified content of the MCR back out to the UART.

This routine is called only once, as soon as the program has determined that a modem is indeed present on the specified COM port, to signal the modem that the program is ready for action.

The SETPORT Routine

The SETPORT routine uses the value stored in the PORTNBR variable to index into the table of port addresses maintained by BIOS in its RAM workspace, and loads the specified port's base address into the DX register. This allows the calling routines to add an appropriate offset to DX in order to access any of the UART registers for either input or output.

This routine is called from several locations within NEWTIME. Its use by MCR_S is the first.

The SND_S Routine

The SND_S routine is called with DS:SI pointing to a string of characters to be transmitted to the modem, and CX containing the count of characters to be sent. This routine first loads DX with the port number to be used, then uses the LODSB opcode to get the current character of the string into the AL register and simultaneously increment SI for the next access. If the character is ~ (tilde), which calls for a short delay, the WAITS routine is called; otherwise, the character is sent to BIOS Function 01h, which will wait for the UART to become ready for the character and will then return with status flags in AH.

On return from the BIOS function, this routine tests AH for an error indication. If none is found, the routine uses the LOOP opcode to decrement CX and if it's still nonzero, jump back to get the next character. When LOOP brings CX to zero, the routine has done its work and will return normally.

If any error occurs on one of the BIOS calls, the carry flag is set (LOOP automatically clears it on the normal exit condition) and control passes to the return code. The routine that called SND_S can then test the carry flag to determine if a detectable modem error occurred.

Using the BIOS function here, instead of programming the UART directly, avoided all the problems of testing to see whether the THR was ready for a new character, and greatly simplified the procedure. Polling is used rather than the more complex interrupt-driven procedures because high performance in this part of the program isn't needed.

The WAITS Routine

The WAITS routine is called from within SND_S, whenever a ~ (tilde) character is encountered in the string being sent to the modem. The purpose of this is to allow a time delay to be introduced to the modem commands. It simply sets up two nested loops and counts down at both levels. The delay will vary with system CPU speed but will approximate one-half second per delay character.

Routines such as this are frequently needed when dealing with data communications, to allow for slow response from the far end of a telephone circuit, and for variations in hardware from one system to another.

The TIMER Routine

The `TIMER` routine performs two different functions. If AL is nonzero when the routine is called, it sets up the `TIMEOUT` variable by getting the current system time and adding whatever value AL contains to the seconds indicated. If the addition creates a total of 60 or more, it's adjusted by subtracting 60 from the seconds and incrementing the minutes by one.

If AL is zero when the routine is called, `TIMER` gets the current time value and compares its seconds reading to the value stored in `TIMEOUT`. If the current reading is still less than the value that `TIMEOUT` contains, the carry flag will be clear when TIMER returns from this call. If the carry flag is set, the specified time has elapsed.

`TIMER` is called from several locations in the main procedure, to prevent waiting indefinitely for a response from the called modem, and to time the delays between repeated dialing attempts.

The GET_C Routine

The `GET_C` routine simply encapsulates a call to BIOS Function 02h, used in preference to interrupt-driven techniques in the interest of simplicity and because performance is not an issue with this program. As already noted, this did make it impossible to use the program in a MS-DOS session from the Windows desktop, however. If you're adventurous, you might want to graft in the RINTS module to overcome this problem.

The GET_S Routine

The `GET_S` routine is tailored specifically to the characteristics of the NIST time service, and may require slight modifications if the program is to be used with some other national time reporting facility. After initializing DX with the port number and pointing DI to the RCV_BUF data reception buffer, this routine calls GET_C repeatedly until it receives a close parenthesis character, which is one of the last characters sent by NIST on each line. It then waits again until a line-feed character is received, which informs it that the next character received will be the start of a new line.

At this time CX is set to 51, the number of characters contained in each NIST text line, and the real reception loop begins. Each character received by GET_C is stored in the RCV_BUF area, and the loop continues until all 51 characters have been received and stored.

Then GET_S calls SETPORT and adds 4 to the port address returned, in order to access the MCR and turn off the DTR line. Normally, this will cause the modem to hang up instantly and thus break the connection to the time service. The code here is identical to that in the MCR_S routine except that it forces Bit 0 to zero rather than to 1.

The GET_N Routine

The final routine, GET_N, is called with DS:SI pointing to a two-digit numeric value in the RCV_BUF area. The routine uses LODSW to load both digits into the AX register, substracts the constant 00 from them to convert them from ASCII format to unpacked BCD representations, exchanges AH and AL to undo the sequence reversal done automatically when they were loaded, and finally uses the AAD opcode to convert the unpacked BCD representation to a pure binary value.

This routine is called from a number of locations in the main procedure, to convert the received time and date information from ASCII to binary form suitable for passing to the system date and time functions. It's about as simple an ASCII-to-binary conversion routine as can be written; it works only for two-digit numbers, but fortunately that's the only kind with which NEWTIME must deal.

The Main Program

When you run NEWTIME.COM, it will first verify that modem is there by attempting to send a carriage-return character to it. If this attempt times out, the program concludes that no modem is connected to the specified port and quits operation, returning an ERRORLEVEL code of 255 to the shell.

If the attempt is successful, operation jumps to the DO_IT label (which follows all the subroutines). There, the program calls the MCR_S routine to activate the Data Terminal Ready line to the modem, displays a two-line sign-on message, and calls BIOS Interrupt 14h Function 0 to initialize the port using the assembled-in value stored in INITVAL.

Next, the program displays the status message `dialing...` and sends the modem the `dial` command stored in `DIALCMD`, followed by a carriage return. Both are sent via routine `SND_S`. The timer is then set for a delay that is specified by `MAX_SEC` (25 seconds as presented here), and the `LISTEN` loop is entered. This loop uses BIOS Function 03h to check port status, testing Bit 7 of the AH register (line status) for a nonzero value that will indicate receipt of a carrier from the time service (which means that a connection has been established). When the carrier is detected, control jumps to `ANSWER`.

If no carrier is found, the `LISTEN` loop next checks the timer to see if its 25-second period has elapsed. If not, control returns to `LISTEN` and the port status check is repeated. If the time is up, one CR is sent to the modem, the keyboard is sampled by means of Interrupt 21h Function 06FFh (to allow the user to interrupt the re-dial loop by pressing ESC), and an additional 3-second wait takes place. When this time is up, the prefix "re" is displayed on the screen and control returns to the TRYAGN label, where "dialing..." is once again displayed and the dial loop continues.

Once the system has connected with the time service and control reaches the `ANSWER` label, the `GET_S` routine is called to wait for a carriage return from the time service and then accept one full 51-character line of data. After `GET_S` has received 51 bytes, it drops the DTR signal to the modem to initiate a disconnect action and returns to the main routine.

The first action taken upon return from `GET_S` is to check the DST field of the received line. The `GET_N` routine is used to convert this two-character field to a numeric value, which will always be in the range 00 through 99. If the value is anything from 1 to 50 inclusive, Daylight Savings Time is in effect; any other value indicates standard time.

If DST is in effect, the `GMTZONE` variable is decremented by one hour to automatically apply the adjustment when the actual time is converted. The `GMTZONE` variable indicates your local time zone's offset from GMT, when standard time is in effect. The value shown, 6, applies to the Central time zone of the USA; for the Eastern zone, it would be 5, for Mountain time, 7, and for the Pacific zone, 8. Elsewhere you'll need to calculate your own value and change the program accordingly.

With the DST adjustment applied to the in-memory copy of `GMTZONE` (which won't affect the value stored in the executable program file) the main routine then extracts the time value from the received line, taking the hours first by setting SI to point to the time field in the buffer area, calling `GET_N` to convert to a number, and subtracting `GMTZONE` to correct to local time.

If the value is negative after subtracting the GMT offset, that means that midnight is somewhere between your zone and Greenwich, so 24 hours are added to the time and 1 is stored in `DAY_ADJ` (which was initialized at assembly time to be zero) for use later.

The values for the minutes and seconds are obtained similarly; the incrementing of SI before each call to `GET_N` skips over the : separator character. With the hour, minute, and seconds all converted, the main routine then calls MS-DOS Interrupt 21h Function 2Dh to set the system time to match. On 80286 and later systems, this automatically updates the CMOS clock-calendar's setting at the same time.

After setting the time, the main routine checks the port status to determine whether the time service has disconnected yet. This check was included just in case the modem failed to drop the connection when DTR was turned off by the `GET_S` routine; some modems ignore the DTR condition. If carrier is still present, a reset command is sent to the modem to force it to hang up.

Then the date is processed in much the same manner as was done for the time. The value in `DAY_ADJ` is subtracted from the day value, just in case a midnight correction is necessary, and then if the day has become less than 1, the month also must be backed up. The `MONTHTBL` array is used in this case to set the day to the last day of the previous month. (No leap-year test is made here; avoid using this program during the evenings of February 29th because it will set your calendar to February 28 instead if a midnight correction occurs.) If the month backs off to zero, then the day and month are set to 31 and December, respectively, and the year is decremented.

When all date corrections have been applied, Function 2Bh of MS-DOS Interrupt 21h is called to set the system date. Like Function 2Dh, this action automatically adjusts the CMOS calendar also for 80286 and later systems. If you are using an 8088 system, you'll have to transfer the new system date and time information into your clock-calendar manually.

Finally, one more check of port status is made, to determine which of two exit messages to display. The selected message is then sent to the screen, and the program terminates with an exit code of zero to indicate success.

Customizing to Fit Your Needs

The best way to make changes to `NEWTIME` in order to fit your needs is to change the source file, NEWTIME.ASM, and then reassemble and link it to generate a modified copy of the program.

However, all of these data constants are stored in an 80-byte area near the front of the program, and you can patch them easily by using DEBUG, should you need to make only minor changes. Figure 10.4 shows the entire area involved, and the rest of this section provides detailed instruction for making such patches. This technique, too, is one that you can use in your own applications, especially if they are intended for users who won't be frightened by the hexadecimal conventions that DEBUG uses; it was common practice in the days of CP/M communications programs.

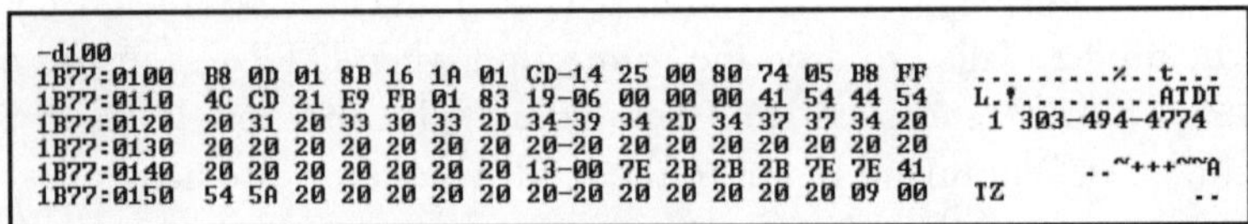

```
-d100
1B77:0100  B8 0D 01 8B 16 1A 01 CD-14 25 00 80 74 05 B8 FF   .........%..t...
1B77:0110  4C CD 21 E9 FB 01 83 19-06 00 00 00 41 54 44 54   L.!.........ATDT
1B77:0120  20 31 20 33 30 33 2D 34-39 34 2D 34 37 37 34 20    1 303-494-4774
1B77:0130  20 20 20 20 20 20 20 20-20 20 20 20 20 20 20 20
1B77:0140  20 20 20 20 20 20 20 13-00 7E 2B 2B 2B 7E 7E 41          ..~+++~~A
1B77:0150  54 5A 20 20 20 20 20 20-20 20 20 20 20 20 09 00   TZ            ..
```

Figure 10.4. If you type **DEBUG NEWTIME.COM**, then at the "-" prompt issued by DEBUG, type **d100** as shown here, these are the first six lines displayed. Refer to this illustration to identify the specific fields or bytes involved for each of the custom modifications to the program described in this section.

The general approach for all five changes is the same: load the executable file into DEBUG with the command `DEBUG NEWTIME.COM`, identify the address at which the field starts, decide exactly what byte patterns will be needed, and then use the E (edit) command of DEBUG to make the change. You can use `D 100 15F` to verify that your changes went in properly, and can repeat the `E` command as often as necessary until you are satisfied with the result. Then issue the `W` command to write the patched version of the file back to disk, replacing the original copy (it's always a good idea to save the original under a different name just in case you want to restore it).

Now let's see just what's involved for each change.

Changing Your Port Number

The port number is stored in a two-byte field that's at offsets 011A and 011B (all offsets and other values used by DEBUG are expressed in hexadecimal so I don't include the `h` or `0x` indicators in this section) in the standard Intel reversed-byte representation. Since the port number will always be less than 255, you'll change only the byte at 011A to change the number.

The value stored here should be one less than the port number. The `00` value shown in Figure 10.4 indicates COM1. To change to COM2 instead, type `E 11A 01` at the `-` prompt and press Enter. Then verify that the change took place by using `D 100 15F` and comparing the resulting display with Figure 10.4.

If this is the only change you are making, type **W** to write the patched file back to disk, and **Q** to exit from DEBUG. If you have other changes to make at the same time, make them before writing the file back and quitting.

Changing Your Time Zone

The `GMTZONE` variable is a two-byte field that's at offset 0118 and 0119. If you're in the western hemisphere, the values will range from 0 through 12 and you'll change only the byte at 0118. If you're to the east of Greenwich, though, this value will be negative, in the range -1 to -12, so the byte at 0119 must be changed from 00 to FF, and the one at 0118 must be FF for -1, through F4 for -12.

To patch the time zone, first determine the number of hours' difference between the standard (not daylight) time for your zone, and Greenwich. Then use the command `E 118 05 00` to change to a +5 hour difference (Eastern zone of U.S.A.) or `E 118 FE FF` for a -2 hour adjustment. In every case the values that follow the `118` should be those for the difference expressed in hex, low byte first.

If this is the only change you are making, type **W** to write the patched file back to disk, and **Q** to exit from DEBUG. If you have other changes to make at the same time, make them before writing the file back and quitting.

Changing Your Timeout Delay Value

The timeout delay value is stored at offset 0107 as a one-byte entry. To change from the default value of 25 seconds (19 hex), use `E 107` *nn* where *nn* is your new value expressed in hex. Do not set this value to zero, because that may cause the program to keep your phone line tied up for an extended period of time (if the system time should roll from one minute to the next in the interval between the setting of the program timer, and the first time it is checked; if that happens, the program will keep trying until the same minute and second of the NEXT hour are reached).

If this is the only change you are making, type W to write the patched file back to disk, and Q to exit from DEBUG. If you have other changes to make at the same time, make them before writing the file back and quitting.

Changing the Number to Call

The full dialing command and number to call are stored in a 43-character field that starts at offset 011C, and the number of characters used is stored in a 2-byte field at offsets 0147 and 0148. To change the command or the number, write out your new command and number and convert the ASCII characters to their hex equivalents, then use the E 11C command to enter the editor dialog.

When you do not specify a new value on the line with the E command, DEBUG goes into an interactive mode in which it displays the existing value at each location and waits for you to type in a new value. To retain the existing value unchanged, press the space bar. After each new value, or space, DEBUG will step to the next byte and repeat the dialog. This continues until you press Enter to end the editing action.

Alternatively, you can use the A (assemble) command to enter ASCII data and not have to manually convert from ASCII to hex. For instance, to change the existing command and number to "ATDT 1-800-555-1212," you could type the following:

```
-a11C
xxxx:011C     db 'ATDT 1-800-555-1212'
xxxx:012F
-
```

Note that single quote characters, rather than double quotes, are required around the string to be entered, and that you signal completion by an empty line (Enter only, at the next address prompt).

If you change the length of the dialing command string, you also must patch the byte at offset 0147 to show the new string length in hex. If you use the `A` command to patch the string itself, you can have DEBUG calculate the new length's hex value for you also by using the `H` command as follows:

```
-h 12F 11C
024B 0013
```

This command displays both the sum and the difference of the two hex values you supply to it. Use the second of them, the difference, as the new string length. In this case, since the new length is identical to the original one, there's no need to change the byte at 0147.

If this is the only change you are making, type **W** to write the patched file back to disk, and **Q** to exit from DEBUG. If you have other changes to make at the same time, make them before writing the file back and quitting.

Changing the Modem-Reset Command

The modem-reset command is stored in a 21-byte field that begins at offset 0149, and its length is at offset 015E and 015F. To change this field, use either the interactive version of the E command, or the A command, just as described for modifying the dialing command, and don't forget to update the length if it changes. The `~` characters contained in the original reset command introduce the delay that's necessary for most modems to respond to the `+++` request to switch from `online` to `command` operating mode, which is necessary before the `ATZ` reset command can be recognized.

If this is the only change you are making, type **W** to write the patched file back to disk, and **Q** to exit from DEBUG. If you have other changes to make at the same time, make them before writing the file back and quitting.

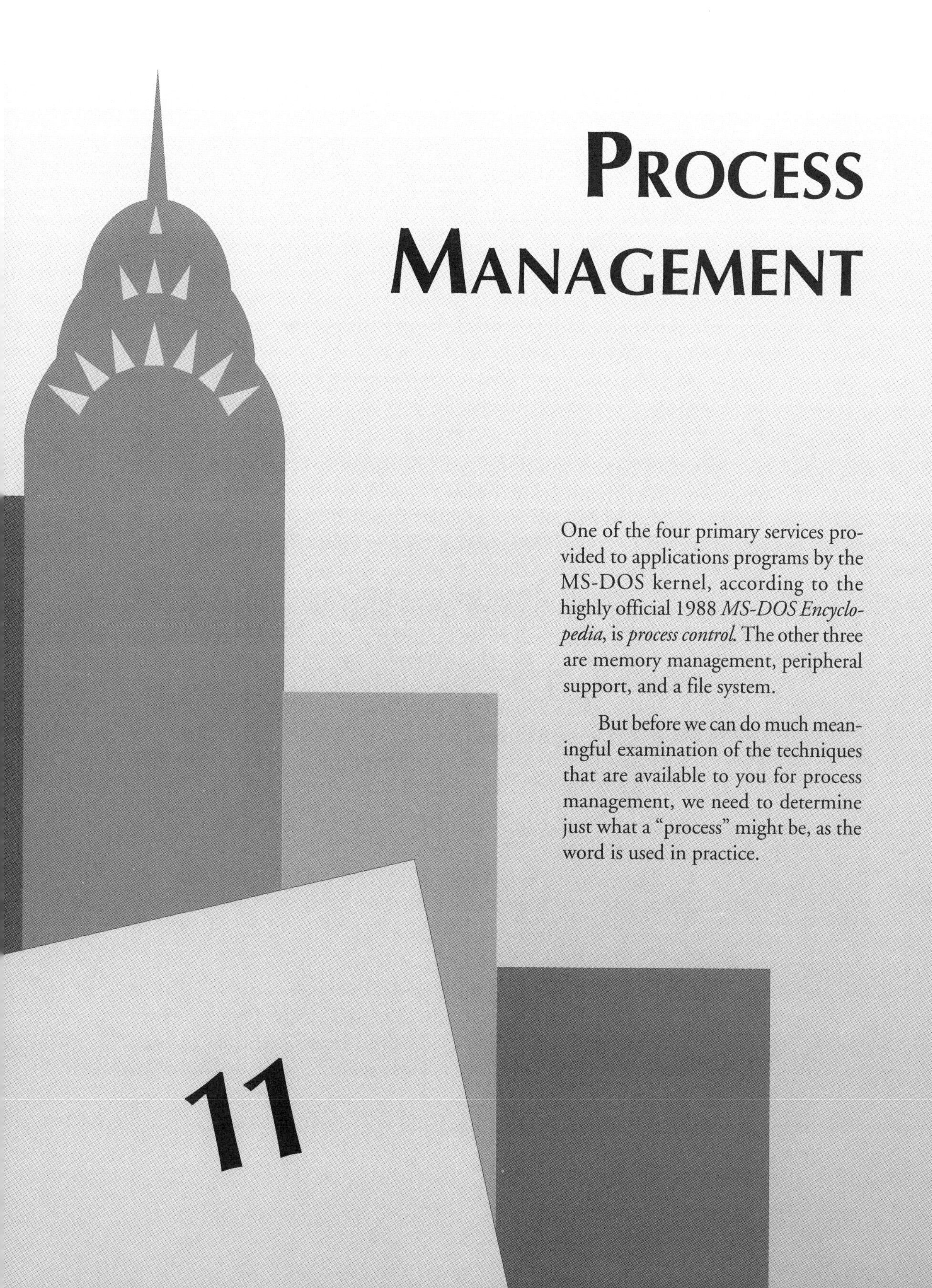

Process Management

One of the four primary services provided to applications programs by the MS-DOS kernel, according to the highly official 1988 *MS-DOS Encyclopedia*, is *process control.* The other three are memory management, peripheral support, and a file system.

But before we can do much meaningful examination of the techniques that are available to you for process management, we need to determine just what a "process" might be, as the word is used in practice.

The Encyclopedia isn't a lot of help in this regard. It says simply "Process, or task, control includes..." and goes on to list the five major areas of control that are provided. But nowhere does it spell out what a "process, or task," might consist of, or how to recognize one should it dart out from under a disk drive and attack your program.

The equally-thick *Encyclopedia of Computer Science and Engineering* does little better. Under the heading "Process" is a simple cross-reference to the article for "Task," and that article, in turn, begins by stating that "A task (or process) is an atomic unit of activity in a computer system." From that start, the definition gets murkier as it proceeds.

So for the purposes of this chapter, we've got to establish a workable, understandable definition of just what this "process" that we'll be managing really is. The final sentence of the rather murky definition in our second reference gives us a start: "The word 'process' is most often to describe programs in execution...."

But that's only a start, because in any MS-DOS system no more than one program can be "in execution" at any specific instant, while the only limit on the number of processes which can simultaneously exist is that set by the amount of storage space available to the system. So rather than beat around the bush any longer, let's use this as our definition of *process*: "A program that has been loaded and is capable of execution." And let's add to that a requirement that each process have a means of identifying it that suffices to distinguish it from all other processes that may be in the system at the same time.

The difference between *in execution* and *capable of execution* is minute, but it's critical to our discussions. A "program" can exist in any of several forms: even when it's only a file of source code that has not yet been compiled, it's a program. After it has been compiled but before linking, it's turned into an object file, but remains a program. After linking, it becomes an executable file, but that's still not a process.

Not until the loader has actually allocated memory space to it, brought the executable code into memory, and assigned a process identification symbol to it, does the program become a process. Once that happens, it remains a process until its memory space is relinquished and its identification symbol cancelled.

This definition implies that each process has a distinctly limited lifespan that extends from the time it is launched until it terminates. It's not quite so obvious that more than one process may be using the same program, but it's common practice in such environments as Windows (where different terms are often used to separate the single code process from the various data instances when multiple invocations of an application occur).

Close examination of the way the power-on *bootstrap* system operates will reveal that MS-DOS, itself, can be considered to be a process. It's loaded automatically when you power up the system, initially assigned all the RAM it can deal with and manage, and then proceeds to launch subsidiary or "child" processes to perform specific tasks.

One of the first such processes to be launched is the primary command interpreter, or *shell*, that issues the familiar prompt, accepts your commands, and in turn launches any other processes necessary to carry out those commands.

But we don't have to explore all the undocumented internal workings of the system initialization code to make use of the process management techniques that MS-DOS provides for us. Almost everything we will need to handle all application needs is documented, though some parts of the information are more readily accessible than others.

In this chapter, we examine each of the major facets of process management separately. First we look at how each process is identified by MS-DOS and how new processes are launched. Next we deal with the techniques that permit the "current process" that MS-DOS deals with to be switched, so that we can select which of several processes that may exist will be the one of which the MS-DOS kernel is aware. Then we see how you can terminate a process when it reaches the end of its useful life.

From that point it's a natural step to explore TSR technology, since that's the technique used to create multiple simultaneous processes. And since TSR technology can involve you in a mystifying mess of support problems, we then look at some very workable alternatives to it that can often sidestep many of the troubles associated with the TSR techniques.

Finally, we conclude with an example program that uses one of the alternative techniques and which reveals some interesting by-products of process management.

Process Launching

Some sort of process identifier is required by the definition we chose earlier; in any MS-DOS system, the identifier that is used is the segment address of the 256-byte area associated with each process that's called the *Program Segment Prefix* (PSP). This segment address is often referred to as the Process ID, or abbreviated simply as PID.

The PSP structure is fully described in Chapter 4. Much of the information contained in the PSP is there to assist MS-DOS in managing the specific process with which the PSP is associated. For instance, each process has its own individual handle table for file and device I/O, and this table is located by default in the PSP. Each has its own copy of the environment block, and the address of that copy is stored in the PSP. And the list goes on.

In Version 1 of MS-DOS, no *program loader* service had yet been defined, so a special function (Function 26h) was provided to create a new PSP upon demand. Any process that needed to spawn another process (for example, the primary shell routine's dispatching code) had to allocate memory for that new process and then call Function 26h, which in effect copied the existing process' own PSP data into the first 256 bytes at the specified address.

The spawning program then had to make any changes necessary, and finally take care of reading the executable program into memory following the PSP, setting up the segment registers and stack pointer properly, and transferring control to it.

By the time Version 2 of MS-DOS appeared, it had become obvious to all developers that the use of Function 26h wasn't the most effective way to work; a new, undocumented, function, number 55h, appeared. Its purpose was to create a child PSP, and it was somewhat simpler to use. However, since a much better and documented function called `Load and Execute` also came out at the same time, Function 55h was never widely used.

Today, neither Function 26h nor Function 55h is worth wasting time with. Anything that either of them could do can be done much more easily and automatically by using one of the four variations available with Function 4Bh.

The two most often-used variations are Function 4B00h, Load and Execute, which launches the process, then automatically starts it and does not return until the process terminates, and Function 4B01h, Load, which allocates memory and loads the process but does not launch it. Instead, control returns to the calling process, with two fields of the supplied control block filled in to provide far pointers for setting the stack segment and pointer, and the code segment and instruction pointer, when the new process is to be launched.

Both variations require that you provide a 22-byte `LOAD_CB` control block which contains such essential information as the address of the environment block, and any parameters to be passed to the process. The structure of this control block is fully described in Chapter 4. The `Load-and-Execute` function uses only the first four fields of this structure. Two additional fields, used only by the `Load` function, are filled in by the loader after it has set the program up for execution.

The `LOAD_CB` structure's layout, for quick reference, looks like this:

```
LOAD_CB             struc
    ldEnvironment   dw   ?     ; segment address, or 0
    ldCommandTail   dd   ?     ; pointer to count byte of string
    ldFCB_1         dd   ?     ; pointer to FCB, or 0
    ldFCB_2         dd   ?     ; pointer to FCB, or 0
    ldCSIP          dd   ?     ; used only by LOAD
    ldSSSP          dd   ?     ; used only by LOAD
LOAD_CB             ends
```

If the `ldEnvironment` word is set to 0, then the loader will automatically copy the environment block of the calling process into a new area of RAM that will be allocated for it. If either or both of the FCB pointers is set to 0, the associated FCB in the new process' PSP area will be cleared to 0. The only field that must be supplied is the `ldCommandTail` far pointer, which may point to a two-byte buffer containing 00 0D as a minimum to represent an empty command line, if no arguments are to be provided.

The two functions use the same calling sequence, except for the content of the AL register. Here's the sequence for Function 4B00h, `Load and Execute`:

```
push    ds                ; save data segment
mov     dx,seg pgm        ; program to run
mov     ds,dx
mov     dx,offset pgm
mov     bx,seg LoadCB     ; control block structure
mov     es,bx
mov     bx,offset LoadCB
mov     ax,4B00h          ; Load and Execute
```

```
int     21h             ; call MS-DOS
pop     ds              ; restore data segment
jc      error
```

Here's the sequence for Function 4B01h, `Load`:

```
push    ds              ; save data segment
mov     dx,seg pgm      ; program to run
mov     ds,dx
mov     dx,offset pgm
mov     bx,seg LoadCB   ; control block structure
mov     es,bx
mov     bx,offset LoadCB
mov     ax,4B01h        ; Load, Don't Execute
int     21h             ; call MS-DOS
pop     ds              ; restore data segment
jc      error
```

If the carry flag is set upon return from either function, the AX register will contain one of eight error codes. Possible return values are 1 to indicate invalid use of the function, 2 to show that the specified file could not be found for loading, 3 to indicate an error in the specified path to the file, 4 if the limit on the number of open files had already been reached, 5 if access to the file is denied for any other reason such as a sharing error, 8 if the loader was unable to allocate the required amount of memory for the new process, 0Ah for an error in allocating or copying the environment, and 0Bh to indicate that the specified file was not in either of the recognized executable formats (COM or EXE).

By far the most frequent error encountered when using either of these functions is error `8`, `ERROR_NOT_ENOUGH_MEMORY`. By default, MS-DOS usually allocates all available RAM to a process when it is launched. If your application has not explicitly freed some of its allocated space, before attempting to load or launch another process, an error 8 is sure to result. Techniques of memory management are described in Chapter 8. In addition, modern linkers offer control parameters that let you specify the maximum amount of RAM to be allocated to your application, thus preventing the default use of "all available" as the allocated amount.

Most applications, including the primary shell itself (and even the MS-DOS initialization code that launches that primary shell), use Function 4B00h. It makes the entire loading and activation sequence essentially automatic; you simply set up the control block, specify the file to be used, invoke the function, and the new process takes over from there.

The `Load` function, 4B01h, is used primarily by debugging and diagnostic tools such as DEBUG.EXE itself. This permits a program being tested to be set up for running, but then allows the debugger to retain control and execute the child process on a single-step basis if desired. Prior to MS-DOS Version 5, this function was not documented, but it has been present since the introduction of the Load family of functions at Version 2.0.

Some systems, notably Novell's NetWare, replace the normal MS-DOS shell with totally different code that handles loading and execution differently. However, even in these systems, parts of MS-DOS remain active and they need to be informed of the "execution state" of each process.

To support the SETVER capability, for example, the version number reported by MS-DOS must be set as specified for each program. Other information, also, must be initialized before a program can execute.

To make that information available, Function 4B05h was added to MS-DOS at Version 5.0. Here's the calling sequence, in assembly language, for this function:

```
push    ds                  ; save data segment
mov     dx,seg ExecState
mov     ds,dx
mov     dx,offset ExecState
mov     ax,4B05h            ; Set Execution State
int     21h                 ; call MS-DOS
pop     ds                  ; restore data segment
```

The `ExecState` structure pointed to by DS:DX when this function is called specifies the esecution state and conditions, and is laid out as follows:

```
EXECSTATE       STRUC
    esReserved  dw    ?    ; reserved, must be zero
    esFlags     dw    ?    ; type flags
    esProgName  dd    ?    ; points to ASCIIZ program name
    esPSP       dw    ?    ; PSP segment of the new program
    esStartAddr dd    ?    ; starting cs:ip of the new program
    esProgSize  dd    ?    ;program size, including PSP
EXECSTATE       ENDS
```

The six fields of this structure have the following meanings:

Fields	Meaning
`esReserved`	Reserved; must be zero.
`esFlags`	This bitmap can be any combination of the following values: **Bit** — **Meaning** Bit 0 — 0 = Program is in .COM format. 1 = Program is in .EXE format. Bit 1 — 1 = Program is an overlay. Bits 2-7 — Reserved, must be zero.
`esProgName`	Points to an ASCIIZ string that specifies the name of the program file. The string must be a valid MS-DOS filename.
`esPSP`	Specifies the segment address of the program segment prefix (PSP) that will be used for the program.
`esStartAddr`	Specifies initial values of CS and IP for the program (starting address).
`esProgSize`	Specifies program size in bytes, including the 256-byte PSP.

Once Function 4B05h has been called, your program must transfer control to the new program as quickly as possible. In particular, before the new program begins, your program cannot call MS-DOS system functions, ROM BIOS functions, or system interrupts. When Function 4B05h returns, MS-DOS has been told that the new program, rather than yours, is the "current" process.

If MS-DOS is loaded into the high-memory area (HMA), this function turns off the A20 line, thus making the HMA inaccessible. If the new program needs access to the HMA before its first call to an MS-DOS function, the program must explicitly activate the A20 line by using Interrupt 2Fh Function 4310h. MS-DOS automatically turns this line on, however (and usually leaves it on), when carrying out other system functions. It's extremely unlikely that your applications will need to do anything, or, for that matter, that you will ever use Function 4B05h since it's meant primarily for system implementation tools.

Process Switching

We've already noted that MS-DOS uses the segment address of the PSP associated with a process as the Process Identifier or PID. In conventional MS-DOS applications, the PID uniquely identifies one process, although it's valid only for the life of that process. In particular, just about every process that's launched directly from the primary shell will have the same PID, because when one process terminates, its memory space is released, and then the `Load-and-execute` function will get that same segment address for the next PSP that is created.

But while these sequential PID's may have the same value since they refer to the same segment address, they still uniquely identify their associated processes, because no two of them are valid at the same time.

This is not necessarily the case when you start dealing with such multitasking environments as Windows in its Enhanced mode of operation, or DesqView. Since these have the capability of swapping a process out to "virtual memory" that's really somewhere on a disk, they may assign the same PID to several processes, and all of these may be valid simultaneously. When this happens, the PID is no longer a unique identifier; you have to associate it with some other information, such as the process' position in the task queue, to distinguish one of the processes from another.

For now there's no need to worry about this, because when you deal with such environments, they take care of keeping process identification untangled; the only reason to mention it is to keep from giving you false information to the effect that the PID is always unique. Most of the time it is, but there are exceptions to the rule.

It takes only a moment's thought to realize that whenever your application is running, at least two processes (and possibly more) must exist in the system. Your application itself forms one of them, and when it's actually running, it's the "current" process. But the primary shell is another, which is active but in a sort of limbo while Function 4B00h has turned the system over to your process.

If a print spooler or some other background TSR is active, it forms still another process, and when it takes over the system momentarily, MS-DOS must switch its attention away from your application and to that other process. To make this possible, we have three functions devoted to process switching.

Closely related to process switching is the use of the overlay technique, which makes it possible to run programs that are far too large to fit into memory all at once by splitting them up into different modules, each of which can run without the others, and letting these modules share memory between themselves.

Swapping Out Processes

The three functions that deal with process switching are Functions 50h, 51h, and 62h of Interrupt 21h. While three function numbers exist, code exists for only two of them. Function 62h uses the same code as does Function 51h.

While Functions 50h and 51h have been available since MS-DOS Version 2.0, they were not documented until the official MS-DOS Programmer's Reference for Version 5.0 was published. Meanwhile, Function 62h was introduced and documented in Version 3.0.

Prior to Version 3.0, these functions could not be called safely from inside a TSR because the MS-DOS dispatcher had already switched to its internal stack. Now, however, they can be called at any time because they bypass the register-saving area of the dispatcher.

Function 50h establishes the "current" PID by placing a PSP segment address into the internal variable from which the MS-DOS kernel code determines what process is current. Whenever any action is to be taken dealing with the current process, the kernel code obtains the PID from this variable and performs the action for that process.

This means that just by setting your own process' PID into that variable, by means of a call to Function 50h, you can take over the system. This is done automatically by Function 4B00h when it makes the new process current. If you use this function to change the current process, though, you should always first determine what process is already using MS-DOS, by calling Function 51h or 62h, and save that PID so you can restore things when you finish.

Here's the calling sequence, in assembly language, to establish a new value for the current PID:

```
mov      bx,NewPID
mov         ah,50h       ;        Set Process ID
int            21h       ;        call MS-DOS
```

Since this function simply stores BX in a dedicated location, no error can result from calling it. MS-DOS performs no check at all to verify that the PID you store is valid, and in fact at least one Microsoft application package sets a deliberately invalid PID of 0000h as "current" momentarily while attempting to determine what operating system is in use, which creates nasty system crashes when that application is used on a Novell network.

To determine the current PID value, you can use either undocumented Function 51h or documented Function 62h; they produce identical results since they use the same code to do so. Here's the calling sequence for 51h:

```
mov      ah,51h          ;        Get Process ID
int      21h             ;        call MS-DOS
mov      CurrentPID,bx   ;        current Process
```

The calling sequence for 62h is almost identical.

```
mov      ah,62h          ;        Get Process ID
int      21h             ;        call MS-DOS
mov      CurrentPID,bx   ;        current Process
```

Again, no error can occur from calling either function, and you have no real guarantee that the value returned is a valid PID (although in most uses you can assume this to be true, because it will be the value that MS-DOS has been using unless you have just stored an invalid PID for test purposes).

The primary use for all three of these functions is in TSR programming. We'll examine that subject a little farther down this chapter.

Using Overlays

When your application becomes so large that it won't all fit into memory at once, it may be time to consider organizing it into a series of overlays. The idea behind overlays is that you can break an application up into a number of modules, each of which is essentially independent of the others, and then use the same memory area for all of those modules by having only one of them in memory at one time. When another is needed, it's read in from disk, replacing the one that had been there.

Any program that uses overlays must have a "root" module that is always in memory, that controls which overlay is to be used at any time. It's best, also, to keep your data in memory rather than in the overlaid area, because by doing so you never need to save anything from the overlay area when you need to read another overlay in for execution. This greatly speeds the overlay action.

Designing an application to use overlays effectively takes some extra thought up front, to partition it properly so that all the code needed for each action is in memory as part of the same overlay. However, if you've followed the principles set forth in Section 1 concerning modularity, cohesion, and coupling, you'll find that your application requires little additional effort to convert to overlay usage.

A number of linker programs provide overlay support that's essentially automatic; Borland's compilers, also, include a `VROOM` capability that handles overlay partitioning for you, invisibly. However, you may find it instructive, and sometimes even more effective than the alternatives, to use the original overlay technique: partition your application into several different executable files, and provide a function in your root module that will load each of them into the overlay area of your memory space, as needed, by calling Function 4B03h of Interrupt 21, which is designed specifically for loading overlays into RAM.

If you try this, you should design each overlay module to have either the entry point, or a pointer to the entry point, at the very first byte of the module after it is loaded. Doing this lets you execute the module's code by just calling that first byte of the overlay area, and also permits you to maintain your root and overlay modules easily, because the root module will never contain any detailed knowledge of addresses within any overlay segment.

If an overlay module may contain several different routines rather than just one, you can store a count of the number of routines as the first byte or bytes of the overlay module, and follow that immediately with a table of pointers to the various entry points. You also can add special overlay signature codes, so that your application can verify that the expected module was loaded.

Each overlay module can be stored in either the COM or EXE file format, but the EXE format is more convenient for large projects. It's also helpful to make all overlay modules use the large or huge memory model, so that they are called using full `segment:offset` addressing rather than just by offset.

When you store overlay modules in executable format, though, you need to take precautions against your users accidentally running one of them directly from the command line without the root module being present. The simplest way to accomplish this is to assign each overlay module a filename extension other than COM or EXE, so that the shell will not load it.

One of the most convenient naming conventions is to use the same filename as the root segment, but a different extension, such as .OV1, .OV2, and so on. The numbers help you distinguish which overlay module is which.

To use the overlay technique, you need to reserve a paragraph-aligned overlay space within your program, where each overlay module will be loaded. This space must be at least as large as the largest overlay, and it would not hurt to have a few bytes of safety margin. You might consider allocating this space dynamically, but it may prove more reliable to build the space reservation right into your program itself so that the application simply won't start if there's not enough memory for the root module plus the overlay area. In either event, the memory that will be used for the overlay area must be allocated to your process, whether that's done at load time by Function 4B00h when your root module loads, or at run time by Function 48h when you allocate memory dynamically.

Once this is done, here are the steps that your root module must perform each time it needs to load in a different overlay file:

1. Set up the parameter block for Function 4B03h to use. This block must contain the segment address of the block that will receive the overlay (usually not the same as the PID of the process; instead, it's normalized so that the first byte is at offset 0 relative to this segment address), and also a segment relocation value that will be applied to the contents of the overlay file if it is in EXE format. These values are normally the same.

2. Call Function 4B03h to load the overlay into memory.

3. Upon return from Function 4B03h, check the carry flag to determine whether any error occurred; if it did, deal with the error as required by your program. The flag will be clear if the overlay was found and loaded.

4. If the flag is clear, execute the overlay code by transferring to it with a far call.

This sequence must be performed each time a new overlay is to be loaded. The parameter block used has this layout:

```
LOADOVERLAY         STRUCT
    loStartSegment  dw    ?    ; segment address
    loRelocFactor   dw    ?    ; amount to add to segments
LOADOVERLAY         ENDS
```

To set up the block prior to calling Function 4B03h, you can use code that looks like this:

```
mov    ax,seg OvlArea               ; get segment address
mov    parms.loStartSegment,ax      ; into both words of block
mov    parms.loRelocFactor,ax
```

Here's the calling sequence, in assembly language, for Function 4B03h:

```
push    ds                ; save data segment
mov     dx,seg ovrlay     ; name of overlay to load
mov     ds,dx
mov     dx,offset ovrlay
mov     bx,seg parms      ; parameter block
mov     es,bx
mov     bx,offset parms
mov     ax,4B03h          ; Load Overlay
int     21h               ; call MS-DOS
pop     ds                ; restore data segment
jc     error              ; failed to load
```

If the carry flag is set upon return from the call, the error code in AX can be any of those listed for Functions 4B00h and 4B01h, except for 0Bh (bad format). If any error occurs, you should assume that the overlay was not loaded and must not attempt to execute the code that the module contains. Only if the carry flag is clear upon return should you call the overlay's entry point.

To transfer control to the overlay's entry point, modify the value stored at `parms.loRelocFactor` to reflect the offset of the entry point, then do an indirect call using the block as a far pointer, with code similar to this:

```
mov    ax,0         ; establish offset of zero
mov    parms.loRelocFactor,ax
push   ds
call   dword ptr parms.loStartSegment
pop    ds
```

Ending a Process

All things eventually end, and that's true of processes in the MS-DOS system too. Every process that's launched should terminate when it has finished its work, and return control back to the process that launched it.

The primary shell might seem to be an exception to that rule, but in Version 6 even the shell has a capability of returning to the process that launched it (the initialization code within hidden file IO.SYS). Of course, that return happens only if the primary shell cannot load from the file you specify; the initialization code then asks you where to find COMMAND.COM and uses the path you specify to try again. It will keep this up indefinitely until it either finds a loadable copy of the command interpreter, or you power the system down and start troubleshooting. This is a great improvement over older versions, which simply complained about not finding the shell, then locked solid without giving you a chance to specify an alternate path.

All other processes, however, need to keep track of what process launched them, and have a method to return control to that process when the current process ends.

This bookkeeping is done by the *parent* field in the PSP, which holds the PID of the process that launched this one. The exception is the shell itself, which has its own PID in this field. The reason for a shell being its own parent is so that the default critical error handler can deal properly with the `Abort` choice at run time; this handler always resets the current process to the PID in the parent field, and then transfers to the termination address stored at offset 0Ah of the PSP. By having the shell serve as its own parent, it remains current even if `Abort` is selected when an internal command is being processed.

The termination address is stored at offset 0Ah when the PSP is created, by copying the content of the vector for Interrupt 22h. The contents of the vectors for Interrupts 23h and 24h are also stored in the PSP immediately following that for Interrupt 22h.

When Function 4B00h executes, it places its own return address (taken from the stack) into the vector for Interrupt 22h, before the new PSP is created. When the process terminates, it restores all three interrupt vectors from its PSP, then transfers control to the termination address by using the Interrupt 22h vector as a far pointer.

Your applications can take advantage of this to guarantee that any necessary clean-up actions, such as restoring other interrupt vectors, get done, by moving the four bytes from PSP offset 0Ah into another far pointer, and then replacing them with a far pointer to your own clean-up code. This code should end by doing a far jump to the original termination address, and it should not call any DOS functions that deal with I/O because the "current process" may have already been switched away from your process at the time it is executed.

When MS-DOS terminates a process by any of the standard methods, all files opened by that process are closed and all memory allocated to the process is released back to the pool of free RAM for reallocation. The file closing deals with inherited handles in such a manner that they actually remain open; that's because they were not re-opened when the process was launched, but instead had their "user count" incremented. The MS-DOS `Close File` function first decrements that count in the system file table entry reached from the specified handle, and only when the count reaches zero is the file actually closed. Note that the automatic closing and release of RAM are performed only for normal termination; the TSR functions discussed later in this chapter bypass both of these actions.

Processes can terminate or end by any of several techniques. All of them end up at the same code within MS-DOS itself, but some get there more cleanly than others.

The oldest technique for terminating a process, dating from MS-DOS Version 1.0, is to invoke Interrupt 20h. Here's the call, in assembly language:

```
int          20h        ;        Terminate process
```

This has the same effect as the End Program function we'll see a bit later, called with a return code of zero. The hex bytes for `INT 20h` are `CD 20` and they are the two bytes at offset 0 of the PSP. They're there to emulate the older CP/M technique of jumping to location 0 to end a program; when a COM-format program, in which all four segment registers contain the same address, executes a jump to location 0, it finds the INT 20h that terminates the process.

About the same age as INT 20h is Function 00h of Interrupt 21h, and it does exactly the same thing. Both calls end up at the same byte of code in the MS-DOS kernel. Here's the calling sequence, in assembly language, for this function:

```
mov          ah,0       ;     Terminate program
int          21h        ;     call MS-DOS
```

Since its introduction in Version 2.0, the recommended technique for terminating a process is to use Function 4Ch of Interrupt 21h, known as `End Program`. This function allows your application to return a value to its parent that can indicate the reason for process termination. The usual convention is to return a value of 0 to indicate successful program execution, and any of the 255 possible non-zero values to encode various error conditions.

Here's the calling sequence, in assembly language, for this function:

```
mov        ah,4Ch         ;     Terminate w/Exit Code
mov        al,ExitCode
int        21h            ;     call MS-DOS
```

To determine what exit code was returned by a child process, the parent can call Function 4Dh. This function returns in the AL register the process' exit code, and in AH an indication of the type of termination that occurred. Since Function 4Dh automatically zeroes the return-code storage space, it can be called only once for each process; the value returned should be stored for future reference if it may be needed again. Here's the calling sequence, in assembly language, for this function:

```
mov        ah,4Dh         ;     Get Return Code
int        21h            ;     call MS-DOS
mov        SaveCode,ax    ;     save for future use
```

The value that's returned in AH will be zero for "normal termination" because of any of the explicit termination methods we've discussed here, 1 if the process was terminated by a Control-C keystroke, 2 if it was terminated by the default Critical Error handler, or 3 if the process "ended" with a call to the Keep Program (TSR) function, 31h, that we'll examine in the next section.

TSR Technology

Long before the advent of the desktop computer for personal use, mainframe architects had discovered it made sense to perform certain relatively slow operations such as printing as background tasks while other things were done with the majority of a processor's time; the result of this discovery was something called *multitasking,* meaning that a single processor was dealing with multiple tasks concurrently although not simultaneously. Another result was creation of the verb *to spool* and the noun *spooler* both based on IBM's acronym for its implementation of the idea: *Simultaneous Peripheral Operation On Line.*

After the desktop system made its debut, but before MS-DOS entered the picture, the pioneering wordprocessing program WordStar had demonstrated (in its CP/M versions) that the level of multitasking necessary to do printer spooling was quite achievable on the desktop, too. This early implementation, however, had one major shortcoming: you had to remain in the WordStar program until your print was finished, although you could edit some other document if you desired. The reason was that all the multitasking support was built into WordStar itself, rather than being furnished by the operating system.

So when MS-DOS was created, one of the features added to it that had not existed before was operating-system support for print spooling, via a program named PRINT.COM and several system functions, not all of them even documented at all, and the others described only sketchily.

The major undocumented feature was Interrupt 28h, which finally came to light in the official MS-DOS Programmer's Reference for Version 5.0 and which we'll discuss a bit later. The primary documented function involved was Interrupt 27h, described as `Terminate and Stay Resident` but not otherwise discussed to any degree. We examine it, also, together with additional functions added in later revisions, later in this chapter.

MS-DOS had been around for quite some time before experimenters discovered just how PRINT.COM worked, and came up with other ways of using the functions to add custom capabilities to the system. But by the time that Borland introduced SideKick, the first widely accepted pop-up TSR, to a waiting world, a number of other resident programs had been made available through the press and via bulletin board postings.

Function 27h gave its name to the entire technology that evolved, and today both the technology and the programs that are based on it are known as TSRs. However not all TSRs are alike. In the *MS-DOS Encyclopedia*, Microsoft's first concession of legitimacy to the technology, Richard Wilton grouped the category in two divisions he called "active" and "passive" but his "active" group can be subdivided again, resulting in the three general classes of TSRs that we'll examine: Pop-Ups, Displays, and Adapters.

The TSR technology is not the only way to provide these three classes of support; alternates include the use of *wrappers* which we'll go into later in this chapter, and Installable Device Drivers, discussed in Chapter 12.

One of the complaints heard frequently from MS-DOS users who migrate to Windows is that Windows doesn't get along with TSR's. This is true, because the Windows kernel itself serves as a "wrapper" for all the applications being run, and conventional TSR functions can be done just as well by another application running concurrently. It's still possible, however, to supply adapter functions to Windows applications via TSR technology; it's only the Pop-Up and Display classes that become less useful there.

TSR Pop-Ups

One of the first TSRs to gain wide acceptance, SideKick, typifies the pop-up class of TSR functions. Once installed, the program simply lies dormant, out of sight and mind, until you press its *hotkey* to wake it up and bring it into action.

Once awakened, though, the pop-up TSR takes over both the keyboard and the display. Whatever process was executing at the time gets pushed to the background, and you do what you want with the pop-up.

One of the features that made SideKick such an instant success was the number of things it allowed you to do: you could take notes, refer to previous notes, consult reference tables, or even use it to dial a telephone number.

Then when you were ready to return to the original task, another keystroke would put the pop-up back to sleep, and restore the original job at the exact point where it had been interrupted.

SideKick was by no means the only pop-up TSR or even the first. A similar program was published in one of the early issues of *PC Magazine.* Later shareware authors added calculator popups and other reference-table-lookup routines to the list of those available. Borland provided a pop-up help capability for its compilers when Turbo Pascal 4.0 arrived, and it has been a feature of all their language tools ever since. This provides instant context-sensitive help no matter what editor you use with their tools.

Another quite useful pop-up utility is *CTRLALT,* created by two professors of physics at the University of Southern California and originally distributed as *potware* (the registration fee was simply a postcard telling them you were using their program). The program became so popular that it was eventually rewritten to include most of the enhancements requested by its users, and was then released as shareware. The professors, Barry Simon and Rick Wilson, are still at USC but have created an organization called CtrlAlt Associates to provide support. This program does essentially everything done by SideKick, plus more: cut-and-paste, multiple monitor support, calculation in most any number system, system control, display color variations, keyboard redefinition, and the list goes on.

TSR Displays

While pop-ups are what most folk think of when the phrase *TSR* is mentioned, another class actually came before them. This class of TSR is not at all invisible. Instead, it provides an ongoing display of some information on the screen.

One of the first examples was an on-screen clock described by John Socha in a now-defunct magazine called *SofTalk* and since reinvented countless times by other programmers. This routine simply installs itself, hooks into the system clock routines, and once every second, displays the current time in one corner of the screen.

Variations of this class may display information other than the time. One developed by the author as part of a larger commercial application serves as a notification system in a network-based office information system. Every five seconds, the TSR (if installed) checks a central message file located on the network file server.

This file contains one record for each username authorized on the network, with three fields (besides the name) in each record. One field is used to notify the user that a message is waiting in that user's InBasket area, another does the same for incoming FAX messages, and the third is for phone messages.

Each time the TSR checks and finds a message flag set for the current user, it displays a white-on-red `M`, `P`, or `F` in the upper right corner of the screen. Once set, the flag can be cleared only when the user reads the message, so even if someone is not logged onto the network when the message is posted, he or she will be notified as soon as they log in and their login script installs the TSR.

Similar notification systems form part of a number of *E-mail* systems for office use. All of them are based on the display class of TSR.

TSR Adapters

The final class of TSRs neither pop up in response to a hotkey nor display any information on the screen. Instead, they simply provide special functionality that's not normally a part of MS-DOS itself. The special software used with networks, such as Novell's IPX and NETX interface programs, is one example of this sort of TSR.

Members of this adapter class of TSRs are functionally similar to device drivers and to wrappers (discussed later in this chapter) in many ways, and can sometimes be interchanged with them. The design choice between implementing an adapter's functions in TSR form, as a device driver, or as a wrapper depends to a large degree on just when the functions need to take effect.

An adapter intended to prevent a user from ever gaining full control of the system by means of the Control-C or Control-Break keystrokes, for example, even during the power-up bootstrapping sequences, would have to be implemented as a device driver so that it would be active before the first point in the bootstrap sequence at which a keystroke could be detected.

The network software, however, mentioned a few paragraphs back is better done as a TSR, giving the user the opportunity to leave it inactive until it's really wanted.

The critical factors involved in deciding which of the three implementations (TSR, driver, wrapper) to use for a specific function revolve around the installation and removal of the function from the system. A TSR's installation can be delayed indefinitely after the system is powered up, and many TSRs can be removed when no longer needed. A device driver takes over automatically at power up, and removing one requires that the user modify CONFIG.SYS and reboot (or use the multi-configuration option of MS-DOS Version 6.0, but in any event requires the reboot action). A wrapper is more transient, and removes its functionality automatically when the program finishes.

TSR Coding Techniques

The original method of installing a TSR was to use Interrupt 27h, which returns control to wherever the process was launched but does not close any open handles nor does it automatically release the memory allocated to the process. A newer method is to use Interrupt 21h Function 31h, which accomplishes exactly the same function but can deal with larger programs.

Interrupt 27h was designed at a time when no program was expected to exceed 64K in size; it therefore assumes the COM-format condition of having all four segment registers pointing to the same 64K block. To use it, you load the DX register with the offset in that block to the first byte to be released, then invoke the interrupt. Here's the calling sequence, in assembly language:

```
mov         dx,offset Scrap    ;     RAM to release
int         27h                ;     TSR Interrupt
```

Normal practice when using this function is to place all data areas that must remain resident immediately after the start of the program, but locate those that are required only during the installation process at the end of the program. The installation code, together with any routines that are used only at that time, are placed just in front of that second data area. Then, when going resident, the offset loaded into DX can be that of the first byte of installation-only code.

As programs continued to grow in size, the 64K assumption on which Interrupt 27h's design had been based lost its validity, so Function 31h was added to Interrupt 21h at MS-DOS Version 2.0 to both allow for larger resident processes, and to permit return of an exit code to the launching process.

The significant differences between the two are that the content of DX became a count of paragraphs to be retained, rather than an offset of the first location to release, and an exit code (identical to that used by Function 4Ch, described previously) was added.

Here's the calling sequence, in assembly language, for Function 31h:

```
mov       dx,Paragraphs     ;      RAM to retain
mov       al,ExitCode
mov       ah,31             ;      Terminate, Stay Resident
int       21h               ;      call MS-DOS
```

Keep in mind that neither of these techniques for going resident will close open files, nor will they release any RAM that was not originally allocated to the process when it was launched. In particular, they will not release the private copy made of the environment block when the process was launched, nor will they close the predefined handles.

Leaving the private environment copy allocated simply wastes memory; if your TSR does make any use of the environment data, that should be done at the time it installs, and the result stored as data within the TSR's own data area so that the block itself can be released before going resident.

Since failure to close open files can result in lost handles as described back in Chapter 9, every TSR should close all 20 possibly-open handles before going resident. This can be done by means of a loop that ignores any error code returned by the `Close File` call; that's exactly the way the `normal termination` code inside the system kernel deals with the situation and no harm will result. Of course, if you specifically require that a file remain open, it should not be closed by such a loop, but this is an exception rather than the rule.

A pair of utility functions, both originally undocumented, provide special support for TSR programs. One was officially recognized by the MS-DOS Programmer's Reference for Version 5.0 but the other still remains in limbo. Both apply primarily to TSRs of the pop-up variety, but may be useful in others also.

The still-undocumented Function 34h obtains the address of an internal flag that the system kernel uses to determine whether it's already doing something. This flag has become known as the INDOS flag; if it's non-zero, then MS-DOS is already executing an Interrupt 21h and no other call to it can be allowed. If the flag is zero, however, it's perfectly safe to invoke any MS-DOS function.

Since the very first implementation of this function could not, itself, be called safely if Interrupt 21h was already executing, your TSR should only call Function 34h from its installation code when there's no chance that another Interrupt 21h call might be in progress. It can then save the address as a far pointer, and at pop-up time use the pointer to check the flag. Here's the calling sequence, in assembly language, for this function:

```
mov     ah,34h                  ;   Get INDOS Flag Pointer
int     21h                     ;   call MS-DOS
mov     word ptr FlagPtr,BX
mov     word ptr FlagPtr+2,ES
```

Within the MS-DOS kernel code, a number of functions provide `wait until ready` operation. One example is the keyboard-input function, which can wait indefinitely until a keystroke becomes available in the input buffer.

This wait is implemented as a call to the BIOS function that checks for data availability, followed by a jump back to that call if no data is yet ready. Such a loop is known, generically, as an *idle loop* and every one of the MS-DOS functions that can "wait until ready" has an idle loop somewhere deep within it.

If the idle loop were implemented in the simple form just described, though, it would be impossible for any TSR to gain control of the system and pop up or do anything else it needed to do, while the loop was running.

To avoid this impasse, Interrupt 28h was added to the system in Version 2.0. Every idle loop within the system kernel code includes an invocation of this interrupt inside the loop itself, so that immediately after discovering no data is ready, Interrupt 28h is invoked before closing the loop.

The default handler supplied for Interrupt 28h is the single machine instruction `IRET` which simply returns from the interrupt without changing the system state in any way. The only effect, then, is a slight delay, and this isn't significant because the whole purpose of the loop in the first place is to waste time until the program has something to do.

Every TSR that may need to pop up or display data while MS-DOS is in an idle loop, though, can provide and install a replacement handler for Interrupt 28h, so that it gets control at this point. This technique, originally implemented by Microsoft's own PRINT.COM background print spooler, was the original secret of making pop-up TSRs such as Sidekick work.

When Interrupt 28h is called, MS-DOS may be in use, but if it is, you can still safely use all functions numbered 0Dh and above (except that you should avoid using the handle I/O functions with handles that refer to character devices such as CON). In particular, it's safe to do disk access. Be sure to switch the Process ID to your own TSR's PSP, though, so that you use your own handle table rather than that of the process in control when your TSR popped up.

When you install a handler for Interrupt 28h, you should always preserve the original address, and jump to it when your own handler's processing is done. This preserves the integrity of the interrupt chain. It also permits you to restore the vector to its original value should your TSR later remove itself from the system.

Removing a TSR

It's often possible to remove a TSR from the system after it has been in use for a while, but this isn't always the case. The capability to remove a TSR depends upon many factors, and not all of them are under your control as a developer.

Many TSRs, for example, `hook` existing interrupt vectors and replace or supplement them with new code. If two such TSRs are installed in a system, one after the other, then even if both TSRs try to be well behaved and preserve the vector contents that were present at installation time, the second routine to be installed will find the vector pointing to the first TSR's hook rather than to the original code.

This is no problem should the second TSR need to be removed, but it makes the first one installed impossible to remove successfully. It's providing the only link between the second TSR's handler for the interrupt in question, and the original code. If this link should be removed, then the remaining TSR would be chaining its hook to an address that would no longer be valid, and as a result the system would crash.

The only way that the first TSR could be removed safely would be to remove the second one first, so that nothing remained in the system to refer to the hook in the first TSR. The first TSR can then restore the vector from its own saved copy, putting the system back to its initial condition.

In generic terms, then, this situation means that a TSR can be removed from the system safely only if none of the interrupt vectors that it has hooked has been hooked again by some other routine, whether TSR, program, or wrapper code. It's quite safe, however, to have a TSR disable itself instantly when it's told to remove itself, and you can even provide code in an Interrupt 28h handler that will check to see if it's safe yet to do the actual removal. Some of the commercial libraries provide just such capability.

If you're not using a library, the way to verify that removal can be safely done is to compare the content of each and every interrupt vector that your TSR has hooked with the full address (segment and offset both) of the TSR itself. Only if every such vector matches in all bits will it be safe to remove the TSR and release its memory.

To do the actual removal, first restore all vectors that were hooked at install time, so that they have their original values once more. Then just call one of the regular `terminate` functions such as Interrupt 21h, Function 4Ch. They will take care of releasing memory and closing any open files, all automatically.

You can initiate such removal action either by means of a pop-up hotkey, or by another process that uses your TSR's executable file but searches memory to locate the resident copy (the copy of the program that is doing the removal can serve as a *signature template* since all offsets will be the same in the portion that goes resident; only the segment addresses will differ between the resident and transient copies). There's no clear cut technical advantage of one of these methods compared to the other.

TSR Pitfalls

While TSR programs have achieved deserved popularity and their use is widespread, they also can run into pitfalls which are sometimes of major proportions.

A poorly designed TSR, for example, can destroy all data on the user's system. While this is admittedly an extreme case and seldom happens in practice, it's not at all unusual to find inexperienced users completely baffled by problems that arise frequently when installing one more TSR in an already crowded system.

One of the most frequent such problems is that some program that has been running satisfactorily for months or even years will suddenly, and inexplicably, start producing garbage or even refuse to run with no error message to indicate why. Either of these symptoms usually indicates that the system had little or no RAM space to spare, and adding a new TSR took the space below the minimum required for the other program to run properly.

Many end users don't recognize the difference between RAM space and disk space, much less the fine points that distinguish XMS, EMS, and conventional RAM areas; when you try to explain to them that they just don't have enough memory available, they will insist that "I have over 100 megabytes free when I take a directory, so I can't be out of memory."

Even experienced developers can run into mysterious dead-end conditions when dealing with a mix of TSR code from many different sources, since no single standard for TSR programming exists. Most of the time, it's necessary to take the failing system back to a "plain vanilla" configuration (with all drivers and TSRs other than those absolutely necessary to run the system temporarily removed), and add things back one at a time until the specific combination that causes the problem can be isolated. On a complicated system this may take weeks rather than hours of troubleshooting.

Because of the potential for problems, it's best to avoid the use of TSR functions if any alternate way of doing the job exists. Sometimes, of course, there's no acceptable alternate. But when that happens, be prepared to deal with puzzling problems, and remember the full meaning of the ancient Chinese curse: "May you live in interesting times!"

TSR Libraries

Creation of successful TSR routines, free from most problems that can result from inadequate documentation of the many internal functions of MS-DOS which can affect TSR programs more than most others, is greatly simplified by adopting one of the several commercial libraries that have become available in recent years. In this section I summarize the features of several such libraries; most of the descriptions come from literature supplied by the publishers involved, but in some cases they reflect personal involvement also.

I participated in some early development and testing of the TTSR package (and have written other software for its publisher although I had no part in developing the current version). I have also done beta testing for TurboPower, and my company uses many of MicroHelp's products. Because of these many connections, I have attempted to eliminate all implications of relative quality from this section and simply list those products which you may find useful. All of them have good reputations; the choice is yours.

CodeRunneR

The *CodeRunneR* libraries from Omega Point, Inc., 25 Birch Road, Framingham, MA 01701, offer the widest range of capabilities, but you'll find that it costs nearly a thousand dollars to buy that entire range even though the main package costs less than $200.

This library (the unusual capitalization is part of the product identity, which seems to be a rule for TSR-library publishers) is for use with the C language only, but works with all major C compilers.

The $195 main package contains "quick start" templates and sample TSR programs with sources to help you get started, with a 300-page reference manual and a 60-page starting manual. Its main feature, of course, is the library itself, which has drawn rave reviews from the leading programming journals.

For additional capabilities, three "Professional Developer's Kits" priced at $99 each are available, or you can buy the library plus all three kits for a combination price of $429.

PDK-1 provides a serial communications library that permits communications to run in the background while other applications are running, plus support for EMS memory, print spooling, and registration and copy protection of your applications.

PDK-2 provides an EXE-file "merge" feature that lets you combine EXE files into a single application that swaps memory among the different executables, plus "spawn over" capability that swaps a process out so that its RAM can be used by another spawned process, XMS support, keyboard and time slicing functions, and a number of other smaller features.

PDK-3 supports in-depth support for spawning processes, including graphics save and restore so that your TSR can pop up over a graphics-based screen and restore it properly at exit, and also furnishes a mouse API for event-based programming.

The top-of-the-line option, though, is the "Advanced Developer's Kit" ADK-1 priced at $995. This kit creates multi-application swappers and provides all the capabilities already listed for the PDK series.

For more information about these products, you can write to Omega Point at the address above, or call them at (508) 877-1819. Their FAX number is (508) 877-0915, and they maintain a technical support BBS at (508) 875-8009.

TesSeRact TTSR Library

One of the pioneering efforts to establish industry-wide standards for TSR interfacing was a group dubbed the *Ringmaster Development Team* that met on CompuServe for several months back in 1986 and 1987 under the leadership of Chip Rabinowitz. The team included many of the pioneers of TSR programming.

The goals set by the group, however, turned out to be too ambitious to be practical, and after a time the plan appeared to have died.

It hadn't. Rabinowitz single-handedly resurrected the idea and later in 1987 established Innovative Data Concepts, Inc., to market a library that embodied much of the team's original intent. This library, renamed *TesSeRact* and originally distributed as shareware, formed the foundation for IDC's line of products, which has expanded to include a host of development tools which are now commercial products.

The TTSR Library, as the original product was renamed to give it an identity within the product line, is now at revision 2.02 and is priced at $149. Like the competing CodeRunneR package, it provides automatic loading into Upper Memory; the capability to swap RAM to EMS, XMS, or disk, so that the TSR takes only 6K of memory when not active; the ability to pop up over graphics screens; and background processing capabilities.

The library uses a standard interface via Multiplex Interrupt 2Fh for determining whether the TSR is already installed, and for communicating with the TSR from an external program. This interface has been made widely available and its use is encouraged for TSRs that make no other use of the TTSR package, so that the original goal of standardization can be achieved.

Your author was a member of the original Ringmaster Development Team, and shares byline credit with Rabinowitz for the description of how to use the standard interface that still appears in the TTSR manual, but his only participation in the design of the most recent version of the library was to create a Turbo Pascal example of its use.

For additional information about the TTSR library, contact IDC at 122 North York Road, Suite 5, Hatboro, PA, 19040. You can telephone them at (215) 443-9705 or reach them via FAX at (215) 443-9753. And finally, their products are supported on CompuServe in the PCVENC forum, section 6.

TSRs and More

The least costly TSR library of which I'm aware is *TSRs Made Easy* from TurboPower Software, P.O. Box 49009, Colorado Springs, CO 80949. This $49 package, for use only with Turbo (and Borland) Pascal, bundles the TSR-related features of TurboPower's more general library (Object Professional) into a single economical package.

The TSRs Made Easy library provides routines for TSR swapping to EMS, XMS, or disk, as available; selectable hotkeys; keystroke playback; swapping Exec function; ISR handling, and more. It also includes several useful demo programs, including a memory resident programmer's assistant (reference chart, calculator, file browser, text editor, phone book) that fits into only 6K of RAM, and in addition to both 3.5 and 5.25-inch diskettes, is accompanied by 200 pages of printed documentation, complete source code, a disk of bonus units, responsive technical support, and a royalty-free license for use in commercial applications.

The library supports Turbo Pascal Versions 5.0, 5.5, 6.0, and 7.0, as well as Borland Pascal 7.0 for real mode DOS applications only. You can obtain additional information about it by calling 1-800-333-4160 from 9 a.m. to 5 p.m. Mountain time, by writing to TurboPower Software at the address given earlier, or by visiting their CompuServe area in the PCVENB forum, section 6.

If your location does not support "800" telephone numbers, TurboPower can be reached at 719-260-9136. Their FAX number is 719-260-7151, and CompuServe mail can be addressed to 76004,2611.

TurboPower was founded and is operated by Kim Kokkonnen, author of the widely circulated TSR utilities "MARK" and "RESTORE" which permit unloading of TSRs that don't in themselves provide a removal capability. These utilities, complete with source code, are supported in TurboPower's CompuServe support section where they may be downloaded at no charge other than usual connect time.

Stay-Res

Stay-Res is a TSR library from MicroHelp Inc., one of the leading makers of support libraries for the entire line of Basic languages, that makes it possible to write full-fledged pop-up TSR's in Basic rather than having to deal with C, Pascal, or assembly language.

While the resulting programs, like most Basic programs, will certainly take no prizes for small size, it's often useful to be able to create a TSR in the same language you use for all other development. If that language happens to be Basic, then Stay-Res will make it easy for you to create TSR routines.

You can contact MicroHelp at 4636 Huntridge Drive, Roswell, GA, 30075, or telephone them at (404) 552-0565.

The Wrapper Technology

While the TSR approach seems to be the first thing anyone suggests when a need to extend normal MS-DOS capabilities arises, it's not always the best solution to every problem. Any TSR introduces many opportunities for trouble to creep into a system. The pitfalls can include such relatively simple things as running out of memory for normal programs, and interrupt conflicts, but also can extend to downright malicious activity on the part of older TSRs that may be installed in the system.

At least one commercial TSR, for example, periodically checked to see if any other program had taken over the interrupt it had hooked, and if so, unceremoniously grabbed it back (thus creating an infinite loop that brought the system to an immediate halt).

For these reasons, and also because doing commercial-quality bulletproofing of any TSR requires extended testing on hundreds of different types of systems which is usually beyond the capability of any individual developer or even a small software company, you're better off to consider a TSR as the last-ditch solution, rather than as the preferred way to proceed. If at all possible, use a wrapper instead.

A wrapper is simply a small program that includes the TSR functionality within itself, but rather than going resident so that you can launch another process, it spawns the other process itself. Once that spawned process completes its actions and returns to its parent, the wrapper program, the parent itself unhooks its TSR functionality from any interrupt vectors and then terminates itself, passing the child's Exit Code back as its own.

If the spawned process launched by the wrapper is actually another copy of the command interpreter, the action is indistinguishable from normal TSR usage, but the wrapper package is much easier to bulletproof since it never needs to play tricks on the internal code of MS-DOS itself.

To spawn the child process, the wrapper can use library routines such as Turbo Pascal's `EXEC` function, or the *spawn/exec/system* family of functions in C. One sample implementation of such a library routine is presented in the next section as part of the example program for this chapter. Before attempting to launch the process, the wrapper should take care to reduce its RAM usage to the absolute minimum in order to leave room for the child process to load.

An interesting variation of the wrapper approach has resulted in the creation of "swapping dispatchers" such as XSPAWN, DRSWITCH, DOSSWAP, and a number of others. These products all, in one way or another, swap most of the process that calls them out to EMS, XMS, or disk, to leave adequate room for almost any other program to run. When that program terminates, the swapped-out material is restored to memory.

XSPAWN, written by Jack Whitney, was originally sold commercially and later distributed as shareware before being released into the public domain by Whitney in Version 1.33. This package, available on many BBSs, essentially replaces the *spawn/exec/system* family of functions for most C compilers. This permits you to create a dispatching application that can serve as its own wrapper, and select which of several large programs to run. I have used the commercial version for just this purpose since mid-1990, without problems.

DOSSWAP, originally written by Nico Mak, is distributed by IDC as a shareware package. It is a separate program that installs as a TSR and can then be invoked at any later time to free up all RAM that has been allocated since DOSSWAP itself was loaded, bringing in another program to execute, and then restoring everything afterward. I have used it to make more than 500K free when shelled out from within Microsoft's WORD word processor, a program not noted for parsimonious use of memory.

An Example Program: TIMEFOR

For this chapter's example here's a wrapper program that times the execution of its child process. Since it uses the 18-tick-per-second counter of the system time-of-day clock as its standard, the minimum resolution is approximately 55 milliseconds. This is far too long to provide any meaningful measurements as you attempt to fine-tune an application for maximum performance, but works nicely to compare two significantly different approaches to a problem.

The program, `TIMEFOR`, is written in C. While it has been tested only with the Borland compiler, it contains no vendor-specific code and should work equally well with any other ANSI-compliant package.

The Program Source

As you can see, a wrapper program is a simple thing to put together. That's because most of the complexity involved is wrapped up in the library routine `system()` that does the actual launch of a child process. Here's the source code:

```
/*******************************************************************/
/*                                                                 */
/*      TIMEFOR.C - Jim Kyle - April 1993                          */
/*                                                                 */
/*      BCC TIMEFOR.C                                              */
/*              or                                                 */
/*      BCC TIMEFOR.C SYSTEM.OBJ                                   */
/*                                                                 */
/*******************************************************************/
#include <stdio.h>
#include <stdlib.h>
#include <string.h>

long get_ticks( void )     /* read current tick count from BIOS RAM
*/
{ long far *t = (long far *)(unsigned long)0x0040006c;
  return *t;
}

void report( long diff )                /* print DIFF as hh:mm:ss.ff
*/
{ long sec = (diff * 5L)/91L;
  int fract = (int)(diff - ((sec * 91L)/5L));
  unsigned int mins = (unsigned int)(sec/60L);
  unsigned int hrs = mins/60;

  sec %= 60;
  mins %= 60;
  if( fract < 0 )
    fract = 0;
  printf( "%2i:%02i:%02u.%02i", hrs, mins, (int)sec, (fract*500)/91
);
}
```

```
void usage( void )                           /* print usage and get out
*/
{ puts( "Provide the command to be timed on the command line:" );
  puts( "\texample:\tDIR D: /W" );
  exit( 1 );
}

void main( int argc, char ** argv )
{ long starttime,
       exectime,
       finaltime;
  int i;
  char cmdbfr[128];

  if( argc < 2 )
    usage();                                      /* tell how to use it
*/

  strcpy( cmdbfr, argv[1] );                    /* rebuild command line
*/
  for( i = 2; i < argc; i++ )
    { strcat( cmdbfr, " " );
      strcat( cmdbfr, argv[i] );
    }
  strcat( cmdbfr, "\r" );                  /* be sure to end it with CR
*/

  starttime = get_ticks();
  system( "CALIB" );                      /* empty task to time loading
*/
  exectime  = get_ticks();
  system( cmdbfr );                             /* the real job to time
*/
  finaltime = get_ticks();

  printf( "\n\nTiming of %s", cmdbfr );      /* now report results
*/
  printf( "\n\nStarted at " );
  report( starttime );
  printf( ",\nCalibration ended at " );
  report( exectime );
```

```
    printf( ",\nExecution ended at " );
    report( finaltime );
    printf( ".\n\nExecute time was " );
    report( finaltime - exectime - ( exectime - starttime ) );
    puts( "." );
}
```

You can compile this program with either the Borland or Microsoft compilers, in either of two ways. One way uses the compiler's own library code for the `system()` function, while the other uses an independent SYSTEM.OBJ module to provide the same action. As discussed later in this section, both are functionally identical. Figure 11.1 shows how to compile using the compiler library. To use the independent version discussed later in this section, add the filename "system.obj" to the command line as a fourth argument.

```
C:>bcc /ms timefor.c
Borland C++  Version 3.1 Copyright (c) 1992 Borland International
timefor.c:
Turbo Link  Version 5.1 Copyright (c) 1992 Borland International

        Available memory 1545384
```

Figure 11.1. This shows compilation of TIMEFOR.C using Borland's C++ Version 3.1, to use the library version of `system()`.

What Each Module Does

Let's see how the `TIMEFOR` program is put together. While the program itself is written in C for simplicity, even though this causes it to be significantly larger than a similar program could be if written in assembly language, we'll include in this examination of each module an equivalent assembly language routine to replace the `system()` function of the usual C libraries, since that's the call that actually invokes Function 4B00h to spawn a child process for us.

The Usage Function

The `usage()` function is called by the main routine if you simply invoke `TIMEFOR` without supplying anything for it to do. This routine displays a two-line message explaining how to use the system, then returns directly to the MS-DOS prompt without returning to `main()`.

Whenever possible, it's good practice to provide such a handy reminder so that your users can refresh their memories about just what your application expects in the way of input. Of course, it's not always practical to do so; some applications, such as menu programs, won't be expecting any inputs in their normal operation, and then no `usage()` function would be needed.

The Get_Ticks Function

The `get_ticks()` function simply encapsulates the hardware interface to the dedicated BIOS tick counter at address 0040:006C. It contains a far pointer to this address, and when called, returns the current value of the tick counter as a long integer. Since the high word of the counter will never have a value greater than 24, there's no need to declare the value as unsigned.

The CALIB Program

The two-byte `CALIB.COM` function that's included on the companion diskette, and launched by `TIMEFOR`, is intended to be used as a measurement of the time it takes your system to load a child process, and to terminate it once it has run. By measuring the total time taken to do this for `CALIB.COM`, and then subtracting that tick count from the one recorded for the real program that you are timing, your final report will reflect only the actual execution time used.

The two bytes of CALIB.COM are `CD 20`, the hex version of `INT 20`, which invokes the MS-DOS termination routines by the shortest and fastest route. You can create this program via DEBUG, by typing the following lines:

```
C:> debug CALIB.COM
File not found
-a
xxxx:0100 int 20
xxxx:0102
-rcx
CX 0000
:2
-w
```

This example shows the prompts and messages that `DEBUG` will provide, in addition to the data that you should type. The `file not found` message is normal and simply means that the file does not yet exist; when you type the `w` as the last line of this dialog, the file will be created in the current directory, and both bytes will be written to it. DEBUG will then tell you it has done so, and you can type q and press Enter to end the session. The *xxxx* will actually be four hex digits that will depend on just what your system has loaded into RAM.

The SYSTEM Module

The actual work of spawning the child processes, one for CALIB.COM and the other for the program that you are timing, is handled by the system() function. This routine is normally supplied as a part of the standard runtime library, with your compiler. However, in order to show you just how the module works, here's a functionally equivalent version that you can assemble using either MASM or TASM, and link into TIMEFOR in place of the standard library procedure.

If you try building TIMEFOR both ways, you'll see that the total elapsed times from start to finish are significantly longer using this version of the system() module than they are when you use the one that comes with your compiler, but the measured elapsed times should be almost identical in both cases so long as the program that you are timing has similar operating conditions for both runs.

The reason why this version is slower is that the library package takes advantage of things that are done automatically via the C library start-up code, so it does not need to search the environment for COMSPEC every time it is called. This routine, however, includes everything in itself so that you can see what happens:

```
;;
;;      SYSTEM.ASM - Implements C's "system()" function via 4B00h
;;
;;              MASM /mx SYSTEM;
;;              TASM /mx SYSTEM
;;
.model small,c

        extrn   _psp:word               ; created by C startup code

.data

com_var db      'COMSPEC=',0            ; environment variable name

com_spec db     80 dup (0)              ; copied from environment
```

```
cmd_tail db     0,' /C '               ; command tail for using
cmd_copy db     128 dup (0)            ; shell as a transient

par_blk dw      0                      ; environment segment address
par_cmd dd      cmd_tail               ; command line pointer
        dd      0                      ; FCB1 pointer
        dd      0                      ; FCB2 pointer

.code

system  proc    cmd:ptr byte           ; size adjusted by ".model"
        public  system

        mov     si,offset com_var      ; locate COMSPEC variable

        mov     ax,_psp                ; set pointer for environment
        mov     es,ax
        mov     ax,es:[002Ch]
        mov     es,ax
        xor     di,di

sys1:   mov     bx,si                  ; initialize pointer to name
        cmp     byte ptr es:[di],0     ; at end of environment yet?
        jne     sys2                   ; no, try this one
        ret                            ; yes, no COMSPEC, return

sys2:   mov     al,[bx]                ; get character from name
        or      al,al                  ; at end of name yet?
        jz      sys4                   ; yes, name matched
        cmp     al,es:[di]             ; no, compare to environment
        jne     sys3                   ; jump if match failed
        inc     bx                     ; advance environment
        inc     di                     ; and name pointers
        jmp     sys2

sys3:   xor     al,al                  ; skip rest of this variable
        mov     cx,-1
        cld
        repnz scasb
        jmp     sys1                   ; go compare next string

sys4:   push    ds                     ; save data segment
        push    ds                     ; swap segment pointers
        push    es
        pop     ds
        pop     es
```

```
        mov     si,di               ; DS:SI points past "="
        mov     di,offset com_spec  ; ES:DI = local buffer

sys5:   lodsb                       ; copy COMSPEC variable
        stosb                       ; into command buffer
        or      al,al               ; is the copy complete?
        jnz     sys5                ; no, get next character

        if      @DATASIZE           ; model-dependent code
        lds     si,cmd              ; pointer is FAR for large
        else
        push    es                  ; set DS back to DGROUP
        pop     ds
        mov     si,cmd              ; pointer is NEAR if here
        endif                       ; end of model-dependent area

        mov     di,offset cmd_copy  ; copy command from input
        mov     cx,128
        cld
        rep movsb                   ; into command tail area

        pop     ds                  ; restore saved data segment
        mov     al,0Dh              ; count tail characters
        mov     cx,130              ; by scanning for CR
        mov     di,offset cmd_tail+1
        repnz scasb

        mov     ax,di               ; calculate command-tail
        sub     ax,offset cmd_tail+2 ; length without CR

        mov     cmd_tail,al         ; set up parm block
        mov     word ptr par_cmd,offset cmd_tail

        mov     dx,offset com_spec  ; spawn system call
        mov     bx,offset par_blk
        mov     ax,4B00h            ; load and execute
        int     21h

        ret                         ; back to caller

system  endp

        end
```

When control reaches this function, the routine first searches the environment for the COMSPEC variable. If the variable cannot be found, the routine returns immediately without doing anything more. If it is located, though, it's copied into the local buffer area com_spec for use by Function 4B00h.

The search begins at the first byte of the environment space, after ES is set to the environment by way of the pointer at offset 002Ch in the PSP. Use of the _psp variable is the only external information that this version of system() relies upon. The first character of the first variable is compared to the C of COMSPEC, and if they differ, the loop at sys3 skips all of the current variable and brings DI to the first character of the next one. The jump back to label sys1 repeats the initial-character test. The first thing done there is to check for an all-zero byte, that flags the end of the environment. If found, it means that the entire environment has been searched without finding a variable named COMSPEC.

If the byte is non-zero, though, it's compared to the C of COMSPEC again, at label sys2. So long as the byte pointed to by BX (the COMSPEC reference string in the program) is non-zero, and the characters match, both BX and DI are incremented and the loop checks the next character pair. When the byte addressed by BX is zero, then the first eight letters of the variable name have matched the string COMSPEC= and the routine transfers control to label sys4. If any mismatch takes place, control goes to label sys3 which skips the rest of the current variable.

At sys4, the function swaps the DS and ES segment registers after first saving DS for later restoration, so that it can easily copy the content of the COMSPEC variable into a local buffer. When it reaches the zero byte that marks the end of the variable, the loop breaks and control falls into the only model-dependent code of the routine.

If you compile in large or huge model, your pointer to the input command will be a far pointer that must be retrieved via an LDS operation, while if you use medium, small, or compact models, the pointer will be near. The @DATASEG value that is tested is set up by the assembler (either MASM or TASM) automatically to indicate which model is in use, and so selects the appropriate code for getting the source address into DS:SI. The ES register already points to the local buffer area, so it's correct regardless of model. The input command string is then copied into the command tail buffer, which has a permanent " /C " string as its first four characters. When this is finished, the DS register is restored to point to the local area along with ES.

The function next searches the copied command for its terminating CR character, calculates and adjusts the string length, and sets up the first byte of the command buffer as required by Function 4B00h. The job is almost complete at this point.

The final actions are simply to load BX and DX with the path to the program to be executed (as obtained from `COMSPEC`) and the parameter block to use, then invoke Function 4B00h.

Function 4B00h loads the specified program, which will be a child copy of the command interpreter, and that program in turn will execute whatever command you passed in as the input string, whether it's an internal command or the name of a program to run. When the execution terminates, the command interpreter also terminates, returning to this function. And when that happens, the function returns to its caller.

The Report Function

The `report()` function, given as input a long integer containing a tick count, converts that tick count to hours, minutes, seconds, and hundredths of seconds, and displays the result on the CRT. It consists of relatively straightforward arithmetic operations, using four internal variables to split the time up into the appropriate units. The 91/5 conversion factor is only an approximation, but it's more than close enough for all practical purposes.

Don't be misled, by the two-decimal-place display of the result, into thinking that the reported times are accurate to 1/100 second. The ticks on which this entire program are based are some 55 milliseconds apart, so the maximum accuracy is something less than 0.05 second. The two-digit display is intended only to reflect the tick count more closely than could be done by a single-digit result.

Notice the test for `fract` being less than zero just before actually displaying the report. This prevents a confusing result from being displayed as the final elapsed time when internal commands are being analyzed. Because MS-DOS normally buffers the most recently accessed disk sectors, it's quite possible that the second launch of the command shell may take significantly less time than did the first one, and the command execution itself to use less than a tick. When this happens, the "difference" passed into this function for the final elapsed-time report is actually negative, and violates the assumptions on which the arithmetic is designed. By forcing `fract` to zero when this happens, you get a reported zero-duration instead.

Because of the relatively large interval between ticks, it's quite possible to run a program twice in succession and get reports that appear to be significantly different from each other. Close examination usually reveals that one of them has measured one tick less in both the calibration and the timing phases, and the round-off introduced in the `report()` routine has then magnified that difference to look like three or four ticks rather than one.

Some Revelations

Running `TIMEFOR` brings to light some interesting situations. A couple of them are shown in Figure 11.2.

```
C:>timefor path
PATH=H:\MSC7\BIN;Q:\CTOR\BIN;D:\CALERA\BIN;K:\WINDOWS;X:\NPO;D:\BC\BIN;D:\UTIL;C
:\MAX6;D:\UU;D:\STACKER;C:\DOS;E:\BUILDER\BLD2;Z:\PUBLIC;


Timing of path

Started at 14:19:49.60,
Calibration ended at 14:19:49.93,
Execution ended at 14:19:50.10.

Execute time was  0:00:00.00.

C:>timefor donothing
Unknown command "DONOTHING"


Timing of donothing

Started at 14:20:00.93,
Calibration ended at 14:20:01.27,
Execution ended at 14:20:02.98.

Execute time was  0:00:01.38.
```

Figure 11.2. This shows two consecutive experiments using the `TIMEFOR` program. The first timed the internal command `PATH`, and measured out to zero elapsed time because the shell program was buffered by MS-DOS after the calibration pass. The second shows the effect of the maximum-size `PATH` list as all named directories had to be searched to determine that the "command" given was not, in fact, valid.

The first run executed the internal command `PATH`, to display the currently active `PATH` environment variable of the author's office system when it's logged into a Novell network with drives mapped to every letter in the alphabet. As you can see, this path is about as long as it's possible to have without some fancy behind-the-scenes manipulation, and it addresses eight different drives, five of which are network drives.

One of the interesting things, however, is that the *execution time* for this internal command was reported as 00.00 seconds, or no time at all. That's normal for any internal command that does not require disk access, because

`TIMEFOR` calibrates out the time required to access the primary shell; any internal command that does not require disk access usually will complete within a single tick of the system clock, so the reported elapsed time will be either 00.00 or 00.05 seconds. If you compare the actual times reported, you will see that the calibration took 0.33 seconds while the execution itself used only 0.17 seconds (6 ticks for calibration versus 3 for execution, because the shell was buffered by MS-DOS after the calibration pass).

The second capture shown in Figure 11.2 illustrates the effect of the long path when a non-existent command or program name is given. Before the system could determine that `donothing` was not a known command, it had to search every subdirectory listed in the path, and despite having a disk cache active and an adequate supply of MS-DOS buffers defined, that search took 1.38 seconds to perform. If you duplicate this experiment, don't expect to see the `Unknown command` report unless you use 4DOS; COMMAND.COM will tell you `Bad command or file name` in this situation.

The moral of this little experiment is that if you consider your time worth anything, avoid the use of long paths where possible. While 1.38 seconds may not sound like much, if you're like most developers you'll mistype commands rather often, and losing more than a second each time you do can quickly add up to several minutes of lost time each day.

The long path shown in Figure 11.2 exists on the author's system only when logged into the network, and provides access to a number of interoffice communication utilities. Most of each day, however, the system is logged out of the network, and the path in use is much shorter.

12

Miscellaneous Functions and Structures

The techniques addressed in the previous chapters by no means cover everything that's possible in MS-DOS applications, but they do provide solid foundations on which you can build. This final chapter of the *Techniques* section deals with three more essential techniques: how to get information about the current system's configuration, how to localize applications for international use, and how to create and apply device drivers for tasks other than their obvious I/O functions.

System Configuration Details

If an application includes a special installation procedure, that procedure probably will need to obtain certain critical information about what hardware is present in the current system, not to mention other configuration details. Several functions are provided in the BIOS and by MS-DOS to make much of this information available.

What Hardware Is Present?

The BIOS functions include two that can be used to determine most of the necessary information about the hardware configuration of the system. They are Interrupt 11h, which has been present since the first IBM PC sold, and Interrupt 15h Function C0h, introduced at the advent of the PC-AT line in 1983.

Following is the calling sequence, in assembly language, for Interrupt 11h:

```
int  11h        ; Get Equipment List
mov  Equip,ax   ; save equipment bitmap
```

The equipment list bitmap returned in AX contains a host of relevant data, but it's all packed into 16 bits and must be unpacked with care to extract the desired information.

The bits of AX have the following significance (note that certain bits are used differently by the PC BIOS and by the BIOS of the PS/2 line):

Bit(s)	Significance
0	1 if floppy disk drive(s) is installed
1	1 if math coprocessor is installed
2-3	System board RAM size (used only by the BIOS for the original IBM PC with the 64K system board, and for the PCjr)

Bit(s)	Significance
	00 = 16 KB
	01 = 32 KB
	10 = 48 KB
	11 = 64 KB
2	1 if pointing device is installed (PS/2)
3	Unused by PS/2 BIOS
4-5	Initial video mode
	00 = Unused
	01 = 40-by-25 color text
	10 = 80-by-25 color text
	11 = 80-by-25 monochrome
6-7	Number of floppy disk drives present (if bit 0 = 1)
	00 = 1
	01 = 2
	10 = 3
	11 = 4
8	Unused
9-11	Number of RS-232 ports installed
12	1 if game adapter is installed
13	1 if internal modem is installed (PC and XT only)
	1 if serial printer is attached (PCjr)
14-15	Number of printers installed

For information about the exact model of system (in genuine IBM hardware only) and the availability of certain BIOS enhancements, the function to use is Interrupt 15h, Function C0h, which returns a far pointer to the actual system configuration table stored in the ROM BIOS area. Following is the calling sequence, in assembly language:

```
mov  ah,0C0h        ; Get Configuration
int  15h            ; System Interface
mov  TblPtr,bx      ; save table pointer
mov  TblPtr+2,es
```

The format of the system configuration table is as follows:

Byte(s)	Contents	
00h01h	Length of table in bytes.	
02h	System model:	
	Value	**Model**
	F8h	PS/2 Model 70
	F8h	PS/2 Model 80
	F9h	PC Convertible
	FAh	PS/2 Model 30
	FBh	PC/XT
	FCh	PC-AT
	FCh	PC/XT-286
	FCh	PS/2 Model 50
	FCh	PS/2 Model 60
	FDh	PCjr
	FEh	PC/XT
	FFh	PC
03h	System submodel:	
	Submodel	**Value**
	PS/2 Model 30	00h
	PC/XT	00h or 01h
	PC-AT	00h or 01h
	PS/2 Model 80	00h or 01h
	PS/2 Model 50	04h
	PS/2 Model 70	04h or 09h
	PS/2 Model 60	05h

Offset	Bit	Significance (if set)
04h	BIOS revision level	
05h	Configuration flags:	
	0	Not used
	1	Micro Channel is implemented
	2	Extended BIOS data area is allocated.
	3	Wait for External Event is available.
	4	Keyboard intercept (Interrupt 15h Function 4Fh) is available.
	5	Real-time clock is available.
	6	Slave 8259 is present (cascaded IRQ2).
	7	DMA channel 3 is used.
06h09h		Not used

This function may not be available in all systems, and the model and submodel information certainly will not apply to systems other than those built by IBM.

Establishing the MS-DOS Version

Any application that uses functions which were not available in all versions of MS-DOS needs to verify that it is running under a version that actually contains all the functions it uses. Since Version 2.0, Interrupt 21h Function 30h has been available to verify the system version actually in use.

At Version 5.0, however, the SETVER capability was added to MS-DOS, with the result that the information returned by Function 30h is no longer trustworthy. To put it bluntly, the purpose of SETVER is to cause Function 30h to lie about the version that is present. As a result, the value returned can differ from the true MS-DOS version number for the system. To obtain the true value, use Get MS-DOS Version (Function 3306h).

There's good reason to do so; many applications that used Function 30h under older versions tested for an exact match of both the major and minor version numbers, rather than simply verifying that the values returned were at least as high as those required by the program. The result was that such a program, if designed for use with Version 3.2, would refuse to run after the system was upgraded to Version 3.3.

The reasoning behind SETVER was to allow the user to specify, for each such program in the system, the version number that it expected. Function 30h would then, for that specific program, return the expected version number rather than the actual one for the system. (Making this happen is rather complicated; it involves the SETVER TSR and special actions by the MS-DOS loader, Interrupt 21h Function 4B00h.)

For more information about SETVER, see the MS-DOS User's Guide and Reference.

In addition to returning the MS-DOS version number set by SETVER for the program, Function 30h also returns the MS-DOS version flag or the original-equipment-manufacturer (OEM) number. The choice of which of these to return is made by the value in AL when the function is invoked. Following is the calling sequence, in assembly language:

```
mov  al, ValueSwitch            ; 01h = version flag, 00h = OEM
                                  number
mov  ah, 30h                    ; Get Version Number
int  21h
mov  MajorV, al                 ; major version (06h for version 6.0)
mov  MinorV, ah                 ; minor version (00h for version 6.0)
mov  VerOrOEM, bh               ; version flag or OEM number
mov  byte ptr [UserNum+2], bl ; 24-bit user serial number
mov  word ptr [UserNum], cx
```

The values returned in the AX, BX, and CX registers have the following significance:

Register	Contents
AL	Major version, such as 03h for Version 3.31, 05h for Version 5.0.

Register	Contents
AH	Minor version, such as 1Eh for Version 3.3, 00h for Version 5.0. Note that this is always expressed as the binary value of a 2-digit decimal number.
BH	Either the OEM number or the version flag, depending on which was requested by the value of AL at the call. A version flag value of 08h indicates that MS-DOS is running in ROM; otherwise, MS-DOS is in RAM. All other bits are set to zero.
BL:CX	A 24-bit user serial number. The user serial number is OEM-dependent, and few systems use this capability. If not used, the number is set to zero.

Because the value returned by Function 30h cannot be trusted, it became necessary to provide another function that would always return the actual version number. Otherwise, applications that really are totally version-specific (such as COMMAND.COM) would have no way of verifying that they could run safely. Subfunction 6 was added to the existing Function 33h of Interrupt 21h to serve this purpose. Following is the calling sequence:

```
mov  ax, 3306h            ;Get MS-DOS Version
int  21h
mov  MajorV, bl           ;major version (05h for version 5.0)
mov  MinorV, bh           ;minor version (00h for version 5.0)
mov  RevisionNum, dl      ;revision number in bits 0 through 2
mov  VersionFlags, dh     ;version flags
```

The BX and DX registers contain the following information upon return from this function:

Register	Contents
BL	Major version, such as 05h for Version 5.0.
BH	Minor version, such as 00h for Version 5.0.
DL	In the low three bits, the revision number. All other bits are set to zero.
DH	Version flags, which may be any combination of the following values:

Value	Meaning
08h	MS-DOS runs in ROM; otherwise, MS-DOS runs in RAM.
10h	MS-DOS is in the high memory area; otherwise, MS-DOS is in conventional memory.
All other bits are set to zero.	

Other Configuration Information

Some applications may need to determine specifically which drive from which the system was booted. One reason for needing such information might be to locate the CONFIG.SYS and AUTOEXEC.BAT files in case an installation routine needs to modify them (although such modification should never be done without the user's permission, obtained via a "Mother May I" message).

Before Version 4.0 of MS-DOS, it was almost impossible to determine the boot drive. However, with that release, Subfunction 5 was added to Interrupt 21h Function 33h for the specific purpose of retrieving this information. Following is the assembly language calling sequence:

```
mov  ax, 3305h          ;Get Startup Drive
int  21h
mov  StartupDrive, dl   ;drive (1=A, 2=B, and so on)
```

Becoming International

The market for software knows few, if any, national boundaries, and the trend for worldwide use of applications without regard to their birthplace seems to be increasing steadily.

One complaint concerning programs that bear the "Made in the USA" label, however, seems to be nearly universal: Developers in the USA seem to be convinced that the entire world speaks, reads, and types using North American English. As a result, these developers create programs that often are difficult, and sometimes impossible, to translate into the local idiom wanted by non-technical computer system users.

The problem has been recognized for some time, and since Version 3.3, MS-DOS has included features to provide National Language Support. However, so little detail concerning the techniques of using these features has been available that the majority of developers still ignore the availability. This section explores those techniques. Much of the information presented here is based on material provided by Microsoft in their Far East Software Developer's Kit but not available elsewhere.

The Language of Languages

In order to discuss the techniques used to enable programs or applications for localization to a specific part of the worldwide marketplace, it's necessary to define several terms that have special meanings in this area. This section provides such definitions. Many of them were adapted from the notes issued by Microsoft.

Code Page. A term specific to MS-DOS, which refers to a table that defines the character set to be used when displaying to the screen or a printer. Each code page contains 256 characters and is identified by means of a 3-digit number. Code Page 437, for example, applies to the USA. In many respects the terms *Code Page* and *character set* are synonymous.

Country Code. A 3-digit code that defines the country for which a specific system's NLS features are currently tailored. Each country code is the same as that used for the country's international telephone prefix. MS-DOS uses this code when preparing and assigning default code pages for the system. The actual NLS setup is described in the user manuals and on-line help for MS-DOS Version 6.0 and requires several specific entries in both CONFIG.SYS and AUTOEXEC.BAT to establish the correct country code and code page to be used. The country codes currently defined are as follows:

Code	Country	Code	Country
001	United States	042	Czechoslovakia
002	Canadian-French	044	United Kingdom

Code	Country	Code	Country
003	Latin America	045	Denmark
031	Netherlands	046	Sweden
032	Belgium	047	Norway
033	France	048	Poland
034	Spain	049	Germany
036	Hungary	055	Brazil
038	Yugoslavia	061	International English
039	Italy	351	Portugal
041	Switzerland	358	Finland

CPI File. One of several files supplied as part of the MS-DOS NLS system. Each of the files contains the following standard code pages (older versions of MS-DOS do not include Code Page 852):

Code Page	Country
437	United States
850	Multilingual (Latin I)
852	Slavic (Latin II)
860	Portuguese
863	Canadian-French
865	Nordic

Enabling. The process of designing and coding a product so that it can inexpensively and easily be made to function for international use. A product is enabled if a national language version can be created at minimal expense, and if it does not interfere with current or planned national language support of other products.

Internationalization. Synonymous with *enabling.*

Locale. The local conventions, culture, and language for any specific geographic region. This may or may not be synonymous with *country* because any country may contain multiple locales, and a locale may span several countries. A locale is specified by the language used (English, French, Spanish, and so on), by the country or geographic region involved, and by the encoding system used to represent the language symbols within the system (such as DBCS, Kanji, and Hongeul for Far Eastern locales). MS-DOS is country-oriented rather than locale-oriented, but international standards are based on locale rather than on national boundaries.

Localization. The process of translating and adding functions to an enabled product to accommodate a specific national language, conventions, and culture.

National Language. A language or dialect spoken by any group of people. This definition is not restricted to those languages that are officially recognized by governments, nor does it apply to groups of languages such as "English." The English spoken in the United States and that used in the United Kingdom are distinct national languages under this definition, as are Parisian French and the French spoken in Quebec.

National Language Support. Those features of a product that accommodate a specific country, national language, local convention, or culture. More specifically, a system of features introduced into MS-DOS in Version 3.3 in order to facilitate such accommodation.

National Language Version. Any variant of an original product that implements national language support and is targeted to a particular national market.

Retrofitting. Redesign and modification of a product that is not already enabled, in order to enable the product.

Enabling International Support

Even though your application is intended strictly for domestic use, it never hurts to spend the time necessary to enable it. And should an unforeseen export market for the product appear later, the fact that the program already is enabled will greatly simplify the process of localizing it as required for export.

Many of the rules to be followed when enabling a program are simply good design practices that were discussed in Chapter 2, "Analysis and Design." For example, you should never mix functional code with strings, messages, or any other information that would have to be modified to localize the package. Instead, the material that must change for localization should be in its own, separate module.

Tight coupling between such enabling modules and the associated code modules which use them is acceptable. The idea is to prevent any need for recompiling the code itself during localization. Instead, only the localization module or modules need be compiled, and then the package can be relinked. Because the code did not change, no bugs can be introduced by this process (although it's possible to introduce cosmetic errors, such as misspellings in the messages, so careful attention to quality is still required).

Windows applications can use the stringtable resource to handle this need for isolation. While no equivalent function is a part of MS-DOS itself, it's quite simple to collect all text information into a separate *message file* that can be assembled or compiled into an object module. Each specific string can be identified by name. The code modules then use these string names to refer to the text, and the linker takes care of resolving the linkages. To localize such an application, a copy of the message file is translated to meet the new language needs and then assembled or compiled. Linking the new object file rather than the original one does the trick.

Whether the module is created as a stringtable resource or as a message file, anything that might turn out to be a localization item should be included. It's far better to have excess information in the localization module than it is to have even one needed item hard-coded into the program itself. The format strings used with the C language, for example, might be considered part of the code rather than part of localization, but some languages require that the sequence in which parts of speech appear to be changed. This makes the format strings just as sensitive to locale as are the text messages themselves.

Another rule to follow when enabling an application is to leave plenty of space for strings to expand. Many, if not most, languages are more verbose than English and consequently require more characters to express the same idea. The longer the English text, the less extra space will be required, however. Microsoft provides the following table as a guide for the amount of extra space to leave, as a function of the string length in English:

Length in characters	Additional space required
1-10	200%
11-20	100%
21-30	80%
31-50	60%
51-70	40%
70+	30%

Here are a few more rules to help prepare applications for enabling. When dealing with foreign languages, make no assumptions about usage. The word sequence often differs, and non-English languages frequently require more words to express the same meaning.

Because some words have different translations (different gender and number) depending on the context, avoid all temptations to save space by using the same word in more than one message, or creating plurals by adding "s". Make each text string contain a single message, and create a distinct string for every message rather than trying to re-use parts.

The Localization Functions of MS-DOS

MS-DOS provides a number of special functions to assist in localization of programs and complete applications. Following is a list of the MS-DOS NLS-related functions:

Function	Description	Version
38h	Get/Set Country Information	2.0
440Ch	Generic Device IOCTL	3.3
6501h	Get Extended Country Information	3.3
6502h	Get Uppercase Table	3.3
6504h	Get Filename Uppercase Table	3.3

Function	Description	Version
6505h	Get Filename-Character Table	3.3
6506h	Get Collate-Sequence Table	3.3
6507h	Get Double-Byte Character Set	3.3
6520h	Convert Character	3.3
6521h	Convert String	3.3
6522h	Convert ASCIIZ String	3.3
6601h	Get Global Code Page	3.3
6602h	Set Global Code Page	3.3

The Localization Structures

Two structures find frequent use with the MS-DOS localization functions. They provide much the same information, but in slightly different formats.

The `COUNTRYINFO` structure contains country-specific information that programs use to format dates, times, currency, and other information.

The `COUNTRYINFO` structure has the following form:

```
COUNTRYINFO     STRUC
     ciDateFormat   dw  ?           ;date format
     ciCurrency     db  5 dup (?)   ;currency symbol (ASCIIZ)
     ciThousands    db  2 dup (?)   ;thousands separator (ASCIIZ)
     ciDecimal      db  2 dup (?)   ;decimal separator (ASCIIZ)
     ciDateSep      db  2 dup (?)   ;date separator (ASCIIZ)
     ciTimeSep      db  2 dup (?)   ;time separator (ASCIIZ)
     ciBitField     db  ?           ;currency format
     ciCurrencyPlaces   db  ?       ;places after decimal point
     ciTimeFormat   db  ?           ;12-hour or 24-hour format
     ciCaseMap      dd  ?           ;address of case-mapping routine
     ciDataSep      db  2 dup (?)   ;data-list separator (ASCIIZ)
     ciReserved     db  10 dup (?) ;reserved
COUNTRYINFO     ENDS
```

The fields of this structure are used as follows:

The 2-byte `ciDateFormat` field contains a value that specifies the format to be used for the date. This field value is 0, indicating USA format (month/day/year); 1, indicating European format (day/month/year); or 2, indicating Japanese format (year/month/day).

The 5-byte `ciCurrency` field contains a zero-terminated ASCII (ASCIIZ) string containing the currency symbol.

The 2-byte `ciThousands` field contains an ASCIIZ string containing the thousands separator.

The 2-byte `ciDecimal` field contains an ASCIIZ string containing the decimal separator.

The 2-byte `ciDateSep` field contains an ASCIIZ string containing the date separator.

The 2-byte `ciTimeSep` field contains an ASCIIZ string containing the time separator.

The 1-byte `ciBitField` field contains a value that specifies the format for currency. This field can be either 0, meaning that the currency symbol precedes the amount and no space appears between currency symbol and amount, 1, meaning that the currency symbol follows the amount and no space appears between currency symbol and amount; 2, meaning that the currency symbol precedes the amount and one space appears between currency symbol and amount; or 3, meaning that the currency symbol follows the amount and one space appears between currency symbol and amount.

The 1-byte `ciCurrencyPlaces` field contains a value that specifies the number of digits that appear after the decimal place in currency figures.

The 1-byte `ciTimeFormat` field contains a value that specifies the format for time. This field can be either 0, indicating 12-hour time format; or 1, for 24-hour time format.

The 4-byte `ciCaseMap` field contains a far pointer to the case-conversion routine, which performs country-specific lowercase-to-uppercase mapping for character values in the range 80h through 0FFh and does not convert characters with values less than 80h. To convert a character, a program copies the character value to the AL register, and then calls the routine using the address in the ciCaseMap field. If there is a matching uppercase character, the routine returns it in the AL register. Otherwise, the routine returns the initial value unchanged. AL and FLAGS are the only registers altered.

The 2-byte ciDataSep field contains an ASCIIZ string containing the data-list separator.

The10-byte ciReserved field is not to be used.

The EXTCOUNTRYINFO structure contains country-specific information that programs use to format dates, times, currency, and other information.

The EXTCOUNTRYINFO structure has the following form:

```
EXTCOUNTRYINFO      STRUC
    eciLength           dw  ?              ; size of structure, in
                                             bytes
    eciCountryCode      dw  ?              ; country code
    eciCodePageID       dw  ?              ; code-page identifier
    eciDateFormat       dw  ?              ; date format
    eciCurrency         db  5 dup (?)      ; currency symbol (ASCIIZ)
    eciThousands        db  2 dup (?)      ; thousands separator
                                             (ASCIIZ)
    eciDecimal          db  2 dup (?)      ; decimal separator
                                             (ASCIIZ)
    eciDateSep          db  2 dup (?)      ; date separator (ASCIIZ)
    eciTimeSep          db  2 dup (?)      ; time separator (ASCIIZ)
    eciBitField         db  ?              ; currency format
    eciCurrencyPlaces   db  ?              ; places after decimal
                                             point
    eciTimeFormat       db  ?              ; 12- or 24-hour format
    eciCaseMap          dd  ?              ; ptr to case-mapping
                                             routine
    eciDataSep          db  2 dup (?)      ; data-list separator
                                             (ASCIIZ)
    eciReserved         db  10 dup (?)     ; reserved
EXTCOUNTRYINFO      ENDS
```

The fields of this structure are used as follows:

The 2-byte eciLength field contains the length in bytes of the structure, not including this field.

The 2-byte `eciCountryCode` specifies the country code for the given information. This can be any of the values listed earlier in this chapter.

The 2-byte `eciCodePageID` identifies the code page for the given information. This field can be any of the values listed earlier in this chapter.

The 2-byte `eciDateFormat` field contains a value that specifies the format to be used for the date. This field value is either 0, indicating USA format (month/day/year); 1, indicating European format (day/month/year); or 2, indicating Japanese format (year/month/day).

The 5-byte `eciCurrency` field contains a zero-terminated ASCII (ASCIIZ) string containing the currency symbol.

The 2-byte `eciThousands` field contains an ASCIIZ string containing the thousands separator.

The 2-byte `eciDecimal` field contains an ASCIIZ string containing the decimal separator.

The 2-byte `eciDateSep` field contains an ASCIIZ string containing the date separator.

The 2-byte `eciTimeSep` field contains an ASCIIZ string containing the time separator.

The 1-byte `eciBitField` field contains a value that specifies the format for currency. This field can be 0, meaning that the currency symbol precedes the amount and no space appears between currency symbol and amount; 1, meaning that the currency symbol follows the amount and no space appears between currency symbol and amount; 2, meaning that the currency symbol precedes the amount and one space appears between currency symbol and amount; or 3, meaning that the currency symbol follows the amount and one space appears between currency symbol and amount.

The 1-byte `eciCurrencyPlaces` field contains a value that specifies the number of digits that appear after the decimal place in currency figures.

The 1-byte `eciTimeFormat` field contains a value that specifies the format for time. This field can be 0, indicating 12-hour time format; or 1, for 24-hour time format.

The 4-byte `eciCaseMap` field contains a far pointer to the case-conversion routine, which performs country-specific lowercase-to-uppercase mapping for character values in the range 80h through 0FFh and does not convert characters with values less than 80h. To convert a character, a program must load the character value into the AL register, and then call the conversion routine using the address in the `ciCaseMap` field. If a matching uppercase character exists, the routine returns it in the AL register. Otherwise, the routine returns the initial value unchanged. AL and FLAGS are the only registers altered.

The 2-byte `eciDataSep` field contains an ASCIIZ string containing the data-list separator.

The 10-byte `eciReserved` field is not to be used.

These structures allow programs and applications to use the MS-DOS NLS functions to retrieve and set country information, such as the time format, the currency symbol, and the screen and printer code pages.

Function 38h Get/Set Country Information

While PC-DOS Version 2.0 made it possible for programs to get country-specific information, not until Version 3.0 did the capability to set the country code become universally available. Function 38h of Interrupt 21h does the trick, and in all versions of both PC-DOS and MS-DOS from 3.0 on, either returns country information or sets the country code, depending on the contents of the DX register. Following is the calling sequence in assembly language:

```
        cmp   CountryCode, 0FEh          ; test for 16-bit code
        ja    code2
        mov   al, byte ptr CountryCode   ; country code if less than 254
        jmp   doit
code2:  mov   bx, CountryCode            ; code if greater than 254
        mov   al, 0FFh                   ; flag that code is in BX
doit:   mov   ah, 38h                    ; Get/Set Country Information
        push  ds                         ; save data segment
        lds   dx, InfoAddress            ; far pointer to structure
        int   21h
        pop   ds                         ; restore data segment
        jc    error                      ; carry set means error
```

When the `DX` register contains any value other than `0FFFFh`, this function fills in a supplied `COUNTRYINFO` structure with the country information that MS-DOS uses to control the keyboard and screen. When the `DX` register contains `0FFFFh`, this function sets the country code that MS-DOS uses to determine country information for the keyboard and screen.

The CountryCode parameter can be any of the country code values listed earlier in this chapter. To get country information for the current country, set CountryCode to zero. When the country code is less than 254, the AL register contains the code. Otherwise, the BX register contains the country code and the AL register contains the value 0FFh.

The InfoAddress parameter specifies whether this function gets country information or sets the country code. When the parameter points to a COUNTRYINFO structure, the function copies country information to the structure. If the low 16 bits of the parameter is 0FFFFh, the function sets the country code. If the DX register contains any value other than 0FFFFh, the function returns the country code in both the AL and BX registers. In this case, the AL register contains the low 8 bits of the country code.

If the carry flag is set on return from this function, the AX register contains an error value, which may be 1 (Invalid Function) or 2 (File Not Found).

Code Page Actions of Function 440Ch

Function 440Ch of Interrupt 21h, Generic Character Device IOCTL, includes five subfunctions known as *minor codes* that deal with preparing, selecting, and refreshing code pages for a character device, which must be open when the functions are called. These subfunctions all require that the BX register be set to the handle returned by Function 3Dh (or 6Ch) when the device was opened, and that the CH register contain a Category value which specifies the type of device. The Category value must be either 1, indicating a Serial device; 3, indicating the Console (screen); or 5, indicating a Parallel printer. The Minor Code indicating which of the five subfunctions is desired must be loaded into the CL register, while DS and DX point to a structure or buffer the details of which vary from one subfunction to another.

To select the code page to be used by a device, use Minor Code 4Ah. The code page must be in the list of prepared code pages for the device. Following is the calling sequence, in assembly language:

```
mov  bx, Handle            ; device handle
mov  ch, Category          ; device category
mov  cl, 4Ah               ; Select Code Page
mov  dx, seg CodePageID
push ds                    ; save data segment
mov  ds, dx
```

```
mov  dx, offset CodePageID ; points to CODEPAGE structure
mov  ax, 440Ch             ; Generic Character Device IOCTL
int  21h                   ; call MS-DOS
pop  ds                    ; restore data segment
jc   error
```

For this minor code, `DS:DX` points to a `CODEPAGE` structure containing the identifier of the code page to be selected. The `CODEPAGE` structure has the following form:

```
CODEPAGE  STRUC
cpLength  dw 2 ;structure size, (always 2)
cpId      dw ? ;code-page identifier
CODEPAGE  ENDS
```

The value in `cpId` may be any of those listed as Code Pages earlier in this chapter.

To instruct a device driver to begin to prepare a new code-page list, use `Minor Code 4Ch`.

After calling `Minor Code 4Ch`, a program must write device-specific data defining the code-page fonts to the device driver by using `Function 4403h`. The program must then end the code-page preparation by using `Minor Code 4Dh`.

Following is the calling sequence, in assembly language, for `Minor Code 4Ch`:

```
mov  bx, Handle          ; device handle
mov  ch, Category        ; device category
mov  cl, 4Ch             ; Start Code-Page Prepare
mov  dx, seg PrepIDs
push ds                  ; save data segment
mov  ds, dx
mov  dx, offset PrepIDs  ; address of CPPREPARE structure
mov  ax, 440Ch           ; Generic Character Device IOCTL
int  21h                 ; call MS-DOS
pop  ds                  ; restore data segment
jc   error
```

For this minor code, `DS:DX` points to a `CPPREPARE` structure that contains information for the new code-page list. The `CPPREPARE` structure has the following form:

```
CPPREPARE   STRUC
cppFlags       dw 0                  ; flags (device-specific)
cppLength      dw (PAGE_IDS+1)*2     ; structure length, in bytes,
                                     ; excluding first two fields
cppIds         dw PAGE_IDS           ; number of code pages in list
cppId          dw PAGE_IDS dup(?)    ; array of code pages
CPPREPARE   ENDS
```

The symbolic constant `PAGE_IDS` should be replaced by the actual number of code pages to be used. The maximum number is 12.

When code-page preparation is complete, `Minor Code 4Dh` is called to end the action. Following is the calling sequence, in assembly language:

```
mov  bx, Handle                  ; device handle
mov  ch, Category                ; device category
mov  cl, 4Dh                     ; End Code-Page Prepare
mov  ax, 440Ch                   ; Generic Character Device IOCTL
int  21h                         ; call MS-DOS
jc   error
```

The remaining two minor codes return information rather than making actual changes. `Minor Code 6Ah` returns the currently selected code page for the device. Following is the calling sequence:

```
mov  bx, Handle                  ; device handle
mov  ch, Category                ; device category
mov  cl, 6Ah                     ; Query Code Page
mov  dx, seg CodePageID
push ds                          ; save data segment
mov  ds, dx
mov  dx, offset CodePageID       ; point to CODEPAGE structure
mov  ax, 440Ch                   ; Generic Character Device IOCTL
int  21h                         ; call MS-DOS
pop  ds                          ; restore data segment
jc   error
```

For this minor code, `DS:DX` points to a `CODEPAGE` structure that receives the identifier for the selected code page. The `CODEPAGE` structure has the following form:

```
CODEPAGE    STRUC
cpLength    dw  2                ; structure size, excluding this
                                 ; field (always 2)
cpId        dw  ?                ; code-page identifier
CODEPAGE    ENDS
```

Minor Code 6Bh returns a list of currently prepared code pages for the device. The call may return up to 12 hardware code-page identifiers and 12 prepared code-page identifiers. Following is the calling sequence:

```
mov  bx, Handle         ; device handle
mov  ch, Category       ; device category
mov  cl, 6Bh            ; Query Code-Page Prepare List
mov  dx, seg ListIDs
push ds                 ; save data segment
mov  ds, dx
mov  dx, offset ListIDs ; address of structure
mov  ax, 440Ch          ; Generic Character Device IOCTL
int  21h                ; call MS-DOS
pop  ds                 ; restore data segment
jc   error
```

For this minor code, DS:DX points to a CPLIST structure that receives the list of prepared code pages. The CPLIST structure has the following form:

```
CPLIST  STRUC
cplLength dw ((HARDWARE_IDS+1)+(PREPARED_IDS+1))*2
                                       ; structure length, in bytes,
                                       ;   excluding this field
cplHIds    dw HARDWARE_IDS             ; number of hardware code pages
cplHid     dw HARDWARE_IDS dup(?)      ; array of hardware pages
cplPIds    dw PREPARED_IDS             ; number of prepared code pages
cplPid     dw PREPARED_IDS dup(?)      ; array of prepared pages
CPLIST  ENDS
```

The symbolic constants HARDWARE_IDS and PREPARED_IDS in this definition reflect the actual number of each type of code page that have been prepared in the system, but will not exceed 12 in each case. To use this function it's necessary to know the actual numbers for each type.

Get Extended Country Information: Function 6501h

To read the country information that MS-DOS employs to control the keyboard and screen, use *Function 6501h* (Get Extended Country Information) of Interrupt 21h. Following is the calling sequence for this function:

```
mov  bx, CodePageID     ; code page
mov  cx, InfoSize       ; size of buffer for country info
mov  dx, CountryCode    ; country code
mov  di, seg Info
```

```
mov  es, dx
mov  di, offset Info      ; address of structure
mov  ax, 6501h            ; Get Extended Country Information
int  21h
jc   error_handler        ; carry set means error
```

The variables used in this example have the following meanings:

CodePageID specifies the code page for which country information is to be returned. This parameter can be any of the code page values listed earlier in this chapter. If this parameter is 0FFFFh, MS-DOS returns information about the current console/screen code page.

InfoSize contains the size in bytes, which must be at least 5, of the buffer for the country information.

CountryCode identifies the country code for which country information is to be returned. This parameter can be any of the country code values listed earlier in this chapter. If this parameter is 0FFFFh, MS-DOS returns the table for the current country.

Info is the far-pointer address of a buffer into which MS-DOS copies the requested country information. The buffer consists of a single byte followed by an `EXTCOUNTRYINFO` structure.

If the carry flag is clear upon return, the country information has been copied to the EXTCOUNTRYINFO structure. If the InfoSize value is greater than 5 but less than the size of the country information, the information is truncated and no error is returned.

If the carry flag is set upon return, the AX register contains an error code, either 1 if the value specified in InfoSize is less than 5, or 2 if MS-DOS cannot retrieve country information for the specified code page and country code.

Get Uppercase Table: Function 6502h

To obtain the address of the uppercase table for a specified code page and country code, use *Function 6502h* (Get Uppercase Table) of Interrupt 21h. The table maps extended ASCII characters (ASCII values greater than 128) to the uppercase equivalents. Following is the calling sequence, in assembly language, for this function:

```
mov  bx, CodePageID       ; code page
mov  cx, 5                ; size of buffer (at least 5)
```

```
mov  dx, CountryCode      ; country code
mov  di, seg Table
mov  es, dx
mov  di, offset Table     ; address of table
mov  ax, 6502h            ; Get Uppercase Table
int  21h                  ; call MS-DOS
jc   error
```

The variables used in this example have the following meanings:

CodePageID specifies the code page for which the uppercase table is to be returned. This parameter can be any of the code page values listed earlier in this chapter. If this parameter is 0FFFFh, MS-DOS returns information about the current console/screen code page.

CountryCode identifies the country code for which the uppercase table is to be returned. This parameter can be any of the country code values listed earlier in this chapter. If this parameter is 0FFFFh, MS-DOS returns the table for the current country.

Table is the far-pointer address of a buffer, which must be at least 5 bytes long, into which MS-DOS will copy the value 02h (the 8-bit identifier for the uppercase table) and the address (in segment:offset far pointer format) of the table.

If the carry flag is clear upon return, the address of the uppercase table has been copied into the buffer pointed to by the `Table` parameter. The uppercase table itself, in an MS-DOS data area, begins with a 16-bit value that specifies the length of the table (normally 128), followed immediately by that many bytes which specify the uppercase equivalents of the ASCII characters from 80h to 0FFh.

If the carry flag is set upon return, the `AX` register contains an error code, which will be either 1 if the buffer size specified by the `CX` register is less than 5, or 2 if MS-DOS cannot retrieve country information for the specified code page and country code.

Get Filename Uppercase Table: Function 6504h

To obtain the address of the filename uppercase table for a specified country code and code page, use *Function 6504h* (Get Filename Uppercase Table) of Interrupt 21h. The table maps extended ASCII characters in filenames (ASCII values greater than 128) to their uppercase equivalents. Following is the calling sequence:

```
mov  bx, CodePageID      ; code page
mov  cx, 5               ; size of buffer (at least 5)
mov  dx, CountryCode     ; country code
mov  di, seg Table
mov  es, dx
mov  di, offset Table    ; address of table
mov  ax, 6504h           ; Get Filename Uppercase Table
int  21h                 ; call MS-DOS
jc   error
```

The variables used in this example have the following meanings:

CodePageID specifies the code page for which the filename uppercase table is to be returned. This parameter can be any of the code page values listed earlier in this chapter. If this parameter is 0FFFFh, MS-DOS returns information about the current console/screen code page.

CountryCode identifies the country code for which the filename uppercase table is to be returned. This parameter can be any of the country code values listed earlier in this chapter. If this parameter is 0FFFFh, MS-DOS returns the table for the current country.

Table is the far-pointer address of a buffer, which must be at least 5 bytes long, into which MS-DOS will copy 04h (the 8-bit identifier of the filename uppercase table) and the address (in segment:offset format) of the table.

If the carry flag is clear upon return, the 32-bit address of the filename uppercase table has been copied into the buffer pointed to by the *Table* parameter. The filename uppercase table itself, in a MS-DOS data area, begins with a 16-bit value that specifies the length of the table (normally 128). The remainder of the table specifies uppercase equivalents of the ASCII characters from 80h to 0FFh for use in filenames, which may not be identical to the equivalents used elsewhere.

If the carry flag is set upon return, the `AX` register contains an error code, which will be either 1 if the buffer size specified by the `CX` register is less than 5, or 2 if MS-DOS cannot retrieve country information for the specified code page and country code.

Get Filename-Character Table: Function 6505h

To obtain the address of the filename-character table for a specified code page and country code, use *Function 6506h* (Get Filename-Character Table) of

Interrupt 21h. This table specifies which characters must not be used in filenames. Following is the calling sequence:

```
mov  bx,CodePageID      ; code page
mov  cx,5               ; size of buffer (at least 5)
mov  dx,CountryCode     ; country code
mov  di,seg Table
mov  es,di
mov  di,offset Table     ; address of table
mov  ax,6505h            ; Get Filename-Character Table
int  21h
jc   error_handler       ; carry set means error
```

The variables used in this example have the following meanings:

CodePageID specifies the code page for which the filename-character table is to be returned. This parameter can be any of the code page values listed earlier in this chapter. If this parameter is 0FFFFh, MS-DOS returns information about the current console/screen code page.

CountryCode identifies the country code for which the filename-character table is to be returned. This parameter can be any of the country code values listed earlier in this chapter. If this parameter is 0FFFFh, MS-DOS returns the table for the current country.

Table is the far-pointer address of a buffer, which must be at least 5 bytes long, into which MS-DOS will copy the value 05h (the 8-bit identifier for the filename-character table) and the address (in segment:offset far pointer format) of the table.

If the carry flag is clear upon return, the address of the filename-character table has been copied into the buffer pointed to by the *Table* parameter. The table starts with a 16-bit value that specifies the length of the table, followed by the characters that are not valid for use in filenames.

If the carry flag is set upon return, the AX register contains an error code, either 1 if the buffer size specified in the CX register is less than 5, or 2 if MS-DOS cannot retrieve country information for the specified code page and country code.

Get Collate-Sequence Table: Function 6506h

To obtain the address of the collate-sequence table for the specified code page and country code, use *Function 6506h* (Get Collate-Sequence Table) of

Interrupt 21h. This table is a character array of 256 elements, each of which specifies the sorting weight of the corresponding character.

Sorting weight determines where a character appears with respect to other characters in a sorted list, and bears no necessary relation to character values. In a hypothetical code page, sorting weights for the characters A, a, B, and b might be 1, 1, 2, and 2, even though their character values are 65, 97, 66, and 98. This would cause a sort to ignore the case of each letter, and if the sorting weights for punctuation and numeric characters were all greater than 26, would cause such characters to follow the letters rather than preceding them as happens when the ASCII value is used as the sorting weight.

Following is the calling sequence, in assembly language, for `Function 6506h`:

```
mov  bx, CodePageID       ; code page
mov  cx, 5                ; size of buffer (at least 5)
mov  dx, CountryCode      ; country code
mov  di, seg Table
mov  es, di
mov  di, offset Table     ; address of table
mov  ax, 6506h            ; Get Collate Table
int  21h                  ; call MS-DOS
jc   error
```

The variables used in this example have the following meanings:

CodePageID specifies the code page for which the table is to be returned. This parameter can be any of the code page values listed earlier in this chapter. If this parameter is 0FFFFh, MS-DOS returns information about the current console/screen code page.

CountryCode identifies the country code for which the table is to be returned. This parameter can be any of the country code values listed earlier in this chapter. If this parameter is 0FFFFh, MS-DOS returns the table for the current country.

Table is the far-pointer address of a buffer, which must be at least 5 bytes long, into which MS-DOS will copy 06h (the 8-bit identifier of the collate-sequence table) and the address (in segment:offset format) of the table.

If the carry flag is clear upon return, the 32-bit address of the collate-sequence table has been copied into the buffer pointed to by the *Table* parameter. The collate-sequence table begins with a 16-bit value that specifies the length of the table; the remainder of the table specifies the sorting weight for each character.

If the carry flag is set upon return, the AX register contains an error code, which will be either 1 if the buffer size specified in the CX register is less than 5, or 2 if MS-DOS cannot retrieve country information for the specified code page and country code.

Get Double-Byte Character Set: Function 6507h

Function 6507h (Get Double-Byte Character Set) returns the address of a buffer containing values that specify the valid ranges for lead bytes in the given double-byte character set (DBCS). Except in the Far East, DBCS functions aren't likely to be encountered; they require special versions of MS-DOS. Following is the calling sequence, in assembly language, for this function:

```
mov  bx, CodePageID      ; code page
mov  cx, 5               ; size of buffer (at least 5)
mov  dx, CountryCode     ; country code
mov  di, seg DBCS
mov  es, di
mov  di, offset DBCS     ; address of table
mov  ax, 6507h           ; Get Double-Byte Character Set
int  21h                 ; call MS-DOS
jc   error
```

The variables used in this example have the following meanings:

CodePageID specifies the code page for which the table is to be returned. This parameter can be any of the code page values listed earlier in this chapter. If this parameter is 0FFFFh, MS-DOS returns information about the current console/screen code page.

CountryCode identifies the country code for which the table is to be returned. This parameter can be any of the country code values listed earlier in this chapter. If this parameter is 0FFFFh, MS-DOS returns the table for the current country.

DBCS is the far-pointer address of a buffer, which must be at least 5 bytes long, into which MS-DOS will copy 07h (the 8-bit identifier of the DBCS table) and the address (in segment:offset format) of the table.

If the carry flag is clear upon return, the 32-bit address of the DBCS values has been copied into the buffer pointed to by the DBCS parameter. The DBCS values, located in a MS-DOS data area, begin with a 16-bit value that specifies the length of the table. The remainder of the table consists of pairs of bytes with each pair specifying the low and high character values for a valid range of lead byte values.

If the carry flag is set upon return, the AX register contains an error value, which may be either 1 if the buffer size specified in the CX register is less than 5, or 2 if MS-DOS cannot retrieve information for the specified code page and country code.

Convert Character: Function 6520h

To convert a specified character to uppercase via the current uppercase table, use *Function 6520h* (Convert Character) of Interrupt 21h. Following is the calling sequence:

```
mov  dl, Character  ; character to convert
mov  ax, 6520h      ; Convert Character
int  21h            ; call MS-DOS
jc   error
```

In this example, Character specifies the character to convert. If a corresponding uppercase character exists, the function copies it to the DL register. If no corresponding character exists, the register is not changed.

Convert String: Function 6521h

To convert each character in a specified string to uppercase via the current uppercase table, use *Function 6521h* (Convert String) of Interrupt 21h. Following is the calling sequence:

```
mov  cx, StringLength    ; length of string in bytes
mov  dx, seg String
push ds                  ; save data segment
mov  ds, dx
mov  dx, offset String   ; address of string to convert
mov  ax, 6521h           ; Convert String
int  21h                 ; call MS-DOS
pop  ds                  ; restore data segment
jc   error
```

In this example, `String` points to the string to convert and `StringLength` specifies the length, in bytes, of the string. The function replaces the original characters with corresponding uppercase characters. If no corresponding uppercase character exists, the original remains unchanged.

Convert ASCIIZ String: Function 6522h

To translate each character of a specified string to uppercase via the current uppercase table, *use Function 6522h* (Convert ASCIIZ String) of Interrupt 21h. Following is the calling sequence, in assembly language:

```
mov  dx, seg String
push ds                    ; save data segment
mov  ds, dx
mov  dx, offset String     ; address of string to convert
mov  ax, 6522h             ; Convert ASCIIZ String
int  21h                   ; call MS-DOS
pop  ds                    ; restore data segment
jc   error
```

In this example, `String` points to a zero-terminated string. The function replaces the original characters of the string with corresponding uppercase characters. If no corresponding uppercase character exists, the original character is unchanged.

Get Global Code Page: Function 6601h

To identify the code page currently used by all programs, use *Function 6601h*, (Get Global Code Page), of Interrupt 21h. Following is the calling sequence, in assembly language:

```
mov  ax, 6601h             ; Get Global Code Page
int  21h                   ; call MS-DOS
jc   error
mov  UserCodePageID, bx    ; user code page
mov  SysCodePageID, dx     ; system code page
```

If the carry flag is clear upon return, the `BX` register contains the active code page (the code page set by the user), and the `DX` register contains the number of the system code page (the code page specified at startup). The code page values returned can be any of those listed earlier in this chapter.

If the carry flag is set upon return, the AX register contains an error code, which will be 2 if MS-DOS cannot read the COUNTRY.SYS file (or another specified country-information file).

Set Global Code Page: Function 6602h

To set the code page for all programs, use *Function 6602h* (Set Global Code Page) of Interrupt 21h. Before a code page can be selected for a device, the device must be prepared for code-page switching. The selected code page must also be compatible with the country code specified in CONFIG.SYS.

Following is the calling sequence, in assembly language, for Function 6602h:

```
mov  bx, CodePageID ; code page to set
mov  ax, 6602h      ; Set Global Code Page
int  21h            ; call MS-DOS
jc   error
```

CodePageID specifies the code page to be set. This parameter can be any of the code page values listed earlier in this chapter.

If the carry flag is set upon return, the AX register contains an error code, which will be 2 if MS-DOS cannot read the COUNTRY.SYS file (or another specified country-information file).

Device Drivers

The *installable device driver*, introduced to MS-DOS in Version 2.0, may be the single most significant factor that propelled MS-DOS to its present position of dominance. The capability to easily install a driver for newly-designed hardware that had not even been dreamed of when the system itself was released provided a flexibility that few other operating systems have even approached.

Installable device drivers can be contained in binary image (COM-format) files, containing absolute load images, or in .EXE-format files. Binary image files for device drivers often are given the extension .SYS to distinguish them from other binary images, such as .COM program files. While most device-driver files contain only one device driver, some contain more, and in such a case the file must contain one header for each driver and the link field of each header should contain the offset of the next within the file, as a 32-bit value.

The Two Kinds of Drivers

MS-DOS classifies all I/O devices into one of two types: *character* and *block*. A character device deals with input and output one character at a time, and can process streams of characters with no defined structure other than length. Examples are the keyboard, screen, serial port, and parallel port. A block device performs input and output in tightly structured pieces called blocks; each block is always the same size and has the same characteristics as all other blocks for that device (the division of a disk's tracks into sectors is an example of a block structure). Block devices include all disk drives and most other high-capacity storage devices on the computer.

A device driver can be designed to support either a character device or a block device, but can never deal with both since MS-DOS handles the two kinds of devices very differently.

The type of device a driver supports determines many important characteristics of the driver. Both the functions the driver implements, and the information the driver returns to MS-DOS when initialized, differ significantly between the two driver categories.

Character Device Drivers

A *character-device driver* handles input and output for a device that can generate or accept an unstructured stream of individual bytes, such as a keyboard, screen, or serial port.

Every character-device driver includes a device name that identifies the driver and is used by programs to open the device. These names are not required to be unique, but MS-DOS will access only the most recently initialized driver if two or more drivers have the identical name. When opening a named device, MS-DOS searches the driver chain until it finds a driver with a matching name. Because the last driver initialized is always the first to be found, MS-DOS stops its search there.

This is not necessarily a design flaw; resident device drivers can be replaced, just by giving an new installable driver the same name as the original resident driver. The popular ANSI.SYS driver, for example, does just this to take the place of the resident version of the keyboard and video driver, CON.

While many programmers (and even some writers who should know better) believe that driver names always end with a colon, because that's the way they must be specified in the Basic language, the names actually do not include the colon at all and when a driver is accessed by name via MS-DOS functions. Including the colon will prevent the search from succeeding.

Block Device Drivers

A *block-device driver* handles input and output for a device that can generate or accept only a structured organization of bytes, such as a disk drive which can transfer data only in sectors rather than as single bytes.

Each block-device driver controls one or more units. A unit can be a physical drive, such as a floppy disk drive, or a logical drive, such as a partition on a hard disk. In either case, MS-DOS assigns each unit a unique drive number that programs use to access it. The driver must report to MS-DOS the number of units it supports when it returns from initializing itself.

MS-DOS allows only 26 drives for the entire system. To allow the driver to verify that it will not exceed this limit, MS-DOS passes the next assignable drive number to the driver at initialization. If this number plus the number of units set up by the driver is less than 26, the initialization will succeed. If the limit is exceeded, MS-DOS will reject the driver even though initialization may appear to be successful.

No block-device driver can be replaced by an installable device driver as character-device drivers are, because they are referenced by drive numbers rather than by name. MS-DOS always initializes resident block-device drivers before installable drivers, and always assigns drive numbers in the same order as it initialized the drivers.

Required Driver Functions

While many different command functions have been defined for MS-DOS device drivers, only nine of them are required for both character and block device drivers. The remaining functions all apply to only one of the two kinds of drivers. Even if a function is not required, a driver of either type should respond to all valid function codes, although this response may do no more than set the `done` flag in the request header's status word.

Some of the functions are required only when specific bits of the attribute word for the driver are set. If a driver leaves those bits clear, it need not respond to the corresponding function codes.

The nine functions that apply to both kinds of drivers are as follows:

Code	Function	When Required
00h	Initialize	Always
03h	IOCTL Read	Only when bit 14 is set in attribute word
04h	Read	Always
08h	Write	Always
0Ch	IOCTL Write	Only when bit 14 is set in attribute word
0Dh	Open Device	Only when bit 11 is set in attribute word
0Eh	Close Device	Only when bit 11 is set in attribute word
13h	Generic IOCTL	Only when bit 6 is set in attribute word
19h	IOCTL Query	Only when bit 7 is set in attribute word

The following seven functions apply only to drivers for character devices:

Code	Function	When Required
05h	Non-destructive Read	Always
06h	Input Status	Always
07h	Input Flush	Always
09h	Write with Verify	Always
0Ah	Output Status	Always
0Bh	Output Flush	Always
10h	Output Until Busy	Only when bit 13 is set in attribute word

Finally, the following six functions are applicable only to block device drivers:

Function	Name	Comments
01h	Media Check	Always
02h	Build BPB	Always
09h	Write with Verify	Always
0Fh	Removable Media	Only when bit 11 is set in attribute word
17h	Get Logical Device	Only when bit 6 is set in attribute word
18h	Set Logical Device	Only when bit 6 is set in attribute word

Device Driver Format Requirements

Every device driver, whether it supports a character device or a block device, follows a consistent format. Each consists of a device-driver header, a strategy routine, and an interrupt routine. These elements provide the information and code needed to carry out requests from MS-DOS for device input and output.

The header, described in Chapter 4, "DOS Itself: Interrupt 21h," contains a far pointer to the next driver in the chain maintained by MS-DOS, followed by an attribute word, 16-bit near offsets to the two routines, and an 8-byte name field. For block devices, which are not named, the first byte of the name field specifies the maximum number of units that the driver can support.

Device Driver Attributes

The *attribute word* in the device driver header is a bitmap which specifies whether the driver is for a character device or a block device, and provides additional information to MS-DOS.

Bit 15 of the attribute word indicates the device type; it is set to 1 for a character device, or 0 for a block device. The remaining 15 bits in this field have the following meanings (note that the meanings of certain bits vary between the two types of drivers, while other bits have identical meanings for both types):

Bit	Meaning
0	For a character-device driver, this bit is set to 1 if the driver replaces the resident device driver for the standard input device (`stdin`). For a block-device driver, this bit is unused and is set to 0.
1	For a character-device driver, this bit is set to 1 if the driver replaces the resident device driver for the standard output device (`stdout`). For a block-device driver, this bit is set to 1 to indicate that the driver supports 32-bit sector addressing, and must be set to 0 if the device supports only 16-bit sector addresses.
2	For a character-device driver, this bit specifies that the device is the NUL device (which cannot be replaced). This bit must be zero for all other device drivers.
3	For a character-device driver, this bit is set to 1 if the driver replaces the resident driver for the clock device. For a block-device driver, this bit is unused and is set to 0.
4	For a character-device driver, this bit specifies that the driver supports fast character output. If this bit is set to 1, the driver has installed a handler for Interrupt 29h which replaces the resident facility for fast output. Normally, Interrupt 29h is used only for output to the screen, but this bit can be used (with a corresponding handler in the driver) to route fast output to any destination. For a block-device driver, this bit is unused and is set to 0.
6	For all drivers, this bit specifies whether logical-drive mapping or generic `IOCTL` functions, or both, are supported. This bit is set to 1 if the driver implements functions 17h and 18h (Get Logical Drive and Set Logical Drive) or function 13h (Generic `IOCTL`).

Bit	Meaning
7	For all drivers, this bit specifies whether `IOCTL` queries are supported. This bit is set to 1 if the device driver implements `IOCTL Query` (Function 19h).
11	For all drivers, this bit is set to 1 if the driver implements functions 0Dh, 0Eh, and 0Fh (Open Device, Close Device, and Removable Media). Only block-device drivers can support Removable Media.
13	For a character-device driver, this bit is set to 1 if the driver implements Function 10h (Output Until Busy). For a block-device driver, this bit is set to 1 if the driver requires MS-DOS to supply the first sector of the first file allocation table (FAT) when it calls `Build BPB` (Function 02h). Drivers with no other method to detect the current medium type use the first byte of the FAT.
14	For all drivers, this bit is set to 1 if the driver implements Function 03h and 0Ch (`IOCTL Read` and `IOCTL Write`).

Communicating with the Driver

Communication between MS-DOS and a device driver follows a complicated process that was originally intended, apparently, to provide for simple expansion into a multitasking environment, but that never happened and the only heritage it left was in the names "strategy routine" and "interrupt routine."

MS-DOS first builds a request packet that will tell the driver what action is desired and will provide all information necessary to perform it, and then makes a far call to the driver's strategy routine, passing (in the `ES:BX` registers) a far pointer to the first byte of the packet. The strategy routine saves this pointer and returns immediately by using a far return.

MS-DOS next calls the interrupt routine. At this point, the driver interprets the packet and performs the function requested. When done, the interrupt routine sets the status value in the packet and returns to MS-DOS.

Despite its name, the interrupt routine has no connection with any interrupt. The routine is always explicitly called by MS-DOS. The name apparently derives from a never-implemented plan to defer actual execution until some later interrupt was being serviced, which could have allowed multiple requests to be posted in a queue.

Both the strategy and interrupt routines must preserve any registers they use, including flags. The direction flag and interrupt-enable bits are especially critical and must be preserved in all cases; saving the flags register as the first step at entry and restoring it as the last step before return will do this automatically.

Both routines can use the stack to save registers, but space on the stack is limited when these routines are called. Usually no more than 40 to 50 bytes are free to use. If a driver requires more space than this, it should set up its own stack.

The usual implementation of the strategy routine simply stores ES and BX in a dedicated location within the driver's own memory space, which has no effect on the flags or any other register, so no register save is required for it. The interrupt routine, however, is a different matter; it should preserve all registers just to be on the safe side.

The Device Driver Interface

The details of creating a hardware-specific installable device driver are far too complex to cover in detail here. They could fill an entire book, and have done so. However, the complications are virtually all in the area of hardware-specific actions, and the fundamental device driver interface is even simpler to work with than is the TSR concept.

It's highly unlikely that you will write many device drivers for the original purpose of providing a uniform hardware interface between MS-DOS and specific peripheral equipment, but you may find the device driver mechanism an excellent replacement for the adapter class of TSR routines.

To take the place of a TSR, just follow the device driver format requirements discussed in the previous section, and put all resident code between the header and the initialization routine. Then have the initialization routine do all the work of hooking interrupt vectors as required and so on, before returning. That's all there is to it. Later in this chapter, the example program shows just how simple such a device driver can be.

The Initialization Function

Initialization Function 00h, which directs the driver to initialize itself, is required for all device drivers but is called only once, immediately after the driver is loaded during the processing of CONFIG.SYS. The request packet sent to the driver with this call has the following structure:

```
INITREQUEST         STRUC
     irLength       db   ?          ; length of record, in bytes
     irUnit         db   ?          ; not used
     irFunction     db   00h        ; function number: Initialize
     irStatus       dw   ?          ; status
     irReserved     db   8 dup(?)   ; reserved, never used
     irUnits        db   ?          ; see text for rest of these
     irEndAddress   dd   ?
     irParamAddress dd   ?
     irDriveNumber  db   ?
     irMessageFlag  dw   ?
INITREQUEST         ENDS
```

The fields of this structure have the following significance:

Field	Significance
`irLength`	Specifies the length, in bytes, of the `INITREQUEST` structure.
`irUnit`	Not used.
`irFunction`	Specifies the Initialization Function; value must be 00h on this call.
`irStatus`	Returns the status of the completed function. If the function is successful, the driver will set the done bit (bit 8). Otherwise, the driver is expected to set both the error and done bits (bits 15 and 8) and copy an error value to the low-order byte.
`irReserved`	Reserved; do not use.

Field	Significance
`irUnits`	Specifies the number of units (block devices only) supported by the driver. MS-DOS uses this number to assign sequential drive numbers to the units. The driver must set this field. Character-device drivers should set this field to zero.
`irEndAddress`	Tells the driver the address, in far pointer format, of the end of memory available to the device driver, and returns the address of the first byte past the initialized driver that can be released, also in far pointer form. Following is more detail about the input and output conditions for this field: Input: During initialization, the driver may use any memory between its own starting address and this address. The driver may also retain any or all of this memory for use after initialization. This field was not used for input in MS-DOS versions earlier than 5.0. Output: The driver must set this field to an address that is not greater than the end of available memory (as passed in via this field). If the initialization fails, the driver should set this field to its starting address, which will tell MS-DOS to remove the driver and free all associated memory.
`irParamAddress`	Tells the driver the address, in far pointer format, of its initialization parameters, and returns the address, also in far pointer form, of an array of pointers to BPB structures (for block drivers only). Following is more detail about the input and output conditions for this field:

Field	Significance	
	Input	Points to the initialization parameters for the driver as copied from the CONFIG.SYS file. That is, to all text on the corresponding `device` or `devicehigh` command line up to the terminating carriage-return (ASCII 0Dh) or linefeed (ASCII 0Ah) character, but not including the `device` or `devicehigh` command and equal sign.
	Output	For block device drivers, points to an array of pointers to BPB structures. These structures specify the BIOS parameters for each unit supported by the drive. Character device drivers must set this field to zero.
`irDriveNumber`	For block device drivers, this field will contain (upon entry) the zero-based drive number for the driver's first unit as assigned by MS-DOS. MS-DOS supplies this number so that the driver can decide if MS-DOS, which allows no more than 26 units in the system, will accept all its units.	
`irMessageFlag`	Directs MS-DOS to display an error message on initialization failure. To display the message (which happens only if the driver also sets the `irStatus` field to indicate failure), the driver must set this field to 1. If the field is left set to 0, its value at entry, no message will be displayed.	

A Device Driver Template

To simplify creation of device drivers, a template that forces all the necessary elements to be included in the correct sequence becomes useful. DDSKEL.ASM, which follows and is also provided on the companion diskette, serves the purpose.

This template can be used with any assembler that supports simplified segment directives; it has been tested with both MASM 5.1 and TASM 3.0.

```
;=====================================================================
;
;       DDSKEL.ASM - Device Driver template
;
;       Jim Kyle - April, 1993
;
;=====================================================================
.model large

.code

ddskel          proc    far

;=====================================================================
;
;                       The header (character device version)
;
;=====================================================================
link_field      dd      0FFFFFFFFh      ; link to next driver
attributes      dw      08000h          ; char device
pointers        dw      offset strategy
                dw      offset commands
device_name     db      '<DDSKEL>'      ; device name

;=====================================================================
;
;                       Additional driver data
;
;=====================================================================
pkt_ptr         dd      0               ; packet pointer storage
                                        ; function dispatch table
disp_tbl        dw      offset Init     ;  0 - Initialize driver
                dw      offset ErrExit  ;  1 - Build DPB
                dw      offset ErrExit  ;  2 - Media ID
                dw      offset ErrExit  ;  3 - IOCTL Read
                dw      offset ErrExit  ;  4 - Read
                dw      offset ErrExit  ;  5 - Non-Destr Read
                dw      offset ErrExit  ;  6 - Input Status
                dw      offset ErrExit  ;  7 - Input Flush
```

```
                dw      offset ErrExit  ;  8 - Write
                dw      offset ErrExit  ;  9 - Write and Verify
                dw      offset ErrExit  ;  A - Output Status
                dw      offset ErrExit  ;  B - Output Flush
                dw      offset ErrExit  ;  C - IOCTL Write
                dw      offset ErrExit  ;  D - Open Device
                dw      offset ErrExit  ;  E - Close Device
                dw      offset ErrExit  ;  F - (not used)
                dw      offset ErrExit  ; 10 - Output Until Busy
                dw      offset ErrExit  ; 11 - (not used)
                dw      offset ErrExit  ; 12 - (not used)
                dw      offset ErrExit  ; 13 - Geieric IOCTL
                dw      offset ErrExit  ; 14 - (not used)
                dw      offset ErrExit  ; 15 - (not used)
                dw      offset ErrExit  ; 16 - (not used)
                dw      offset ErrExit  ; 17 - (not used)
                dw      offset ErrExit  ; 18 - (not used)
                dw      offset ErrExit  ; 19 - IOCTL Query
Nbr_Codes       equ     ($ - disp_tbl) / 2

;==================================================================
;
;                       The strategy routine
;
;==================================================================
strategy        proc    far
                mov     word ptr cs:pkt_ptr,bx
                mov     word ptr cs:pkt_ptr+2,es
                retf
strategy        endp


;==================================================================
;
;                       The interrupt routine
;
;==================================================================
commands        proc    far
                pushf                   ; save all registers
                push    ax
                push    bx
                push    cx
```

```
                push    dx
                push    ds
                push    es
                push    si
                push    di
                push    bp
                mov     ax,cs           ; set DS to this segment
                mov     ds,ax
                les     bx,pkt_ptr      ; point ES:BX to packet
                mov     al,es:[bx+2]    ; get FUNCTION code
                cmp     al,Nbr_Codes    ; is it supported?
                jae     ErrExit         ; no, get out with error
                cbw                     ; yes, jump to its code
                add     ax,ax
                mov     si,ax
                jmp     word ptr disp_tbl[si]

ErrExit:        mov     ax,8103h        ; error exit
Exit:           mov     es:[bx+3],ax    ; normal exit, set status
                pop     bp              ; restore all registers
                pop     di
                pop     si
                pop     es
                pop     ds
                pop     dx
                pop     cx
                pop     bx
                pop     ax
                popf
                retf                    ; return to MS-DOS

;=====================================================================
;
;                       The resident routines
;
;=====================================================================
                ;       any code to stay resident goes here.
                ;
                ;       this can include interrupt handlers, etc.
```

```
;===================================================================
;
;                       The initialization procedure
;
;===================================================================
Init:           ;       do whatever needs doing
                ;       in case of error jump to failed

                mov     ax,offset cs:ErrExit
                mov     cs:disp_tbl,ax  ; make Init illegal next
time
                mov     ax,100h         ; set DONE bit for status
                jmp     short okay

failed:         mov     ax,8100h        ; set ERROR and DONE status

okay:           les     bx,cs:pkt_ptr   ; release Init space for
use
                assume  es:nothing
                mov     word ptr es:[bx+0Eh],offset cs:Init
                mov     es:[bx+10h],cs
                jmp     Exit

commands        endp

ddskel          endp

                end
```

To use the template, make a copy of it under any name you like. Then use a text editor to change the name `<DDSKEL>` (at the label `device_name` near the front of the file) to a new name for your driver. The name must always be exactly eight characters long. The "<" and ">" characters in the template are there to prevent any possibility of conflict with anything typed in at a command prompt; because these are the redirection characters, no name containing them can be supplied in response to the prompt.

Next, add any resident routines needed. These will, of course, vary from one driver to the next and are the heart of the driver. Be sure to edit the appropriate label references in the dispatch table if your driver will communicate with programs by means of the standard driver command packets. You can delete all the entries between the last one that you customize and the label Nbr_Codes at the end of the list, because the dispatch code will return an error for any command code greater than that established by Nbr_Codes. This means that if you don't use any of the command packet codes, the only entry in the dispatch table will be that for Init; an example of this appears later in this section.

The final step is to modify the Init routine to add anything that needs to be done when the driver is installed. Then the driver is ready to be assembled and linked into a SYS-format file (identical to COM format except that the origin offset is 0000h rather than 0100h).

The object file produced by the assembler can be linked by any of the linker tools described in Chapter 3, "Languages, Compilers, Assemblers, and the Like." With TLINK or OPTLINK it's possible to create the desired SYS-file format directly; other linkers may generate an EXE file that must then be processed through EXE2BIN or EXECOM to create the loadable driver file. EXE2BIN.EXE was furnished with older versions of MS-DOS but was dropped several revisions back; EXECOM is an exact equivalent created by Chris Dunford (author of PCED and many other utilities) to take its place and can be downloaded from CompuServe or many bulletin boards at no cost other than connect time.

A Simple Tracing Driver

To show just how easy it is to create a driver using the template, and also to provide a handy tool to help debug other device drivers by forcing the system to pause when processing CONFIG.SYS, here's an example of template use.

The HOLDUP.ASM driver which follows (and also appears on the companion diskette) is a do-nothing driver. It contains no resident code, and even removes itself completely when it returns to MS-DOS after its initialization code executes (this is done by setting the break address to the very first byte of the driver, its link address).

To use HOLDUP for debugging, place a line in CONFIG.SYS, just in front of that for the driver that is causing problems, which specifies DEVICE=HOLDUP.SYS ABOUT TO LOAD and then place another similar line, DEVICE=HOLDUP.SYS LOADING COMPLETE, following the problem driver's DEVICE= line.

Upon rebooting, the system will display HOLDUP.SYS ABOUT TO LOAD and pause when the first line is processed, and if the problem driver does not crash the system, the second HOLDUP.SYS line will cause another display, `HOLDUP.SYS LOADING COMPLETE`, and pause, when it is reached.

After CONFIG.SYS completes its action, however, no trace of HOLDUP.SYS can be found in memory. This makes this example a truly useful tool for driver development.

```
;===================================================================
;
;       HOLDUP.ASM - Device Driver to echo its parameters and wait
;
;       Jim Kyle - April, 1993
;
;===================================================================
.model large

.code

holdup          proc    far

;===================================================================
;
;                       The header (character device version)
;
;===================================================================
link_field      dd      0FFFFFFFFh      ; link to next driver
attributes      dw      08000h          ; char device
pointers        dw      offset strategy
                dw      offset commands
device_name     db      '<HOLDUP>'      ; device name

;===================================================================
;
;                       Additional driver data
;
;===================================================================
pkt_ptr         dd      0               ; packet pointer storage
                                        ; function dispatch table
disp_tbl        dw      offset Init     ;  0 - Initialize driver
Nbr_Codes       equ     ($ - disp_tbl) / 2
```

```
;=================================================================
;
;                       The strategy routine
;
;=================================================================
strategy        proc    far
                mov     word ptr cs:pkt_ptr,bx
                mov     word ptr cs:pkt_ptr+2,es
                retf
strategy        endp


;=================================================================
;
;                       The interrupt routine
;
;=================================================================
commands        proc    far
                pushf                           ; save all registers
                push    ax
                push    bx
                push    cx
                push    dx
                push    ds
                push    es
                push    si
                push    di
                push    bp
                mov     ax,cs                   ; set DS to this segment
                mov     ds,ax
                les     bx,pkt_ptr              ; point ES:BX to packet
                mov     al,es:[bx+2]            ; get FUNCTION code
                cmp     al,Nbr_Codes            ; is it supported?
                jae     ErrExit                 ; no, get out with error
                cbw                             ; yes, jump to its code
                add     ax,ax
                mov     si,ax
                jmp     word ptr disp_tbl[si]

ErrExit:        mov     ax,8103h                ; error exit
Exit:           mov     es:[bx+3],ax            ; normal exit, set status
```

```
                pop     bp              ; restore all registers
                pop     di
                pop     si
                pop     es
                pop     ds
                pop     dx
                pop     cx
                pop     bx
                pop     ax
                popf
                retf                    ; return to MS-DOS

;=====================================================================
;
;                       The initialization procedure
;
;=====================================================================
Init:           lds     si,es:[bx+12h]

again:          lodsb
                cmp     al,' '
                jb      done
                mov     ah,0Eh
                int     10h
                jmp     again

done:           xor     ax,ax
                int     16h
                cmp     al,0Dh
                jne     done

                mov     ax,100h         ; set DONE bit for status
                les     bx,cs:pkt_ptr   ; release all space for use
                mov     word ptr es:[bx+0Eh],offset cs:link_field
                mov     es:[bx+10h],cs
                jmp     Exit

commands        endp

holdup          endp

                end
```

Making HOLDUP.ASM from DDSKEL.ASM was largely a matter of deleting material. The only unusual points are the loading of DS:SI from the command packet, at the very first instruction of the `Init` routine, which provides access to the content of the DEVICE= line, and the setting of the break address to the first byte of the `link_field`, just before the jump to `Exit` at the end of the routine.

Note that BIOS functions 10h and 16h are used for all input and output in order to avoid any possibility of problems caused by interaction with MS-DOS itself. This permits HOLDUP to function even around drivers which may modify MS-DOS' own actions with respect to console I/O.

An Example Program

Just as HOLDUP shows the use of a device driver as a tracing tool for debugging other driver problems, so can the device driver technique be applied to solve other problems. For example, a driver can be used to extend the size of the BIOS keyboard buffer beyond the miserly 15-byte limit imposed by the original PC design.

XKB.ASM follows the same pattern as DDSKEL and HOLDUP, and, like them, appears on the companion diskette and can be assembled using either MASM 5.1 or later, or any version of TASM (set to MASM51 mode).

The resulting driver must be installed within 64K bytes of the BIOS RAM area at segment address 0040h, because the BIOS code assumes the use of near pointers within that segment. This is not normally a limitation, however. Because the driver uses less than 500 bytes of RAM and has no interaction with any part of the system other than BIOS keyboard processing, it can (and should) be installed by the first `DEVICE=` line that appears in CONFIG.SYS; this normally assures that it is located within the required area.

```
;======================================================================
;
;       XKB.ASM - Device Driver for larger keyboard buffer
;
;======================================================================
.model large

.data
```

```
BIOS_DATA       SEGMENT PARA AT 0040h

        db      0001Ah dup (?)
kbgp    dw      ?       ; kb get pointer
kbpp    dw      ?       ; kb put pointer
        db      00062h dup (?)
kbfb    dw      ?       ; bfr beg
kbfe    dw      ?       ; bfr end

BIOS_DATA       ENDS

.code

xkb             proc    far

link_field      dd      0FFFFFFFFh
attributes      dw      08800h          ; char device, no open/
close
pointers        dw      offset strategy
                dw      offset commands
device_name     db      '<KBXTND>'
pkt_ptr         dd      0

;====================================================================
;
;                       The big keyboard buffer itself
;
;====================================================================

Kbufbeg         dw      128 dup (0)
Kbufend         equ     this byte

;====================================================================
;
;                       External Entry Point
;
;====================================================================

strategy        proc    far
                mov     word ptr cs:pkt_ptr,bx
                mov     word ptr cs:pkt_ptr+2,es
                retf
strategy        endp
```

```
;======================================================================
;
;                             External Entry Point
;
;======================================================================

commands          proc     far
                  pushf
                  push     ax
                  push     bx
                  push     cx
                  push     dx
                  push     ds
                  push     es
                  push     si
                  push     di
                  push     bp
                  mov      ax,cs
                  mov      ds,ax
                  les      bx,cs:pkt_ptr
                  mov      di,es:[bx+2]
                  les      bx,cs:pkt_ptr
                  and      di,0FFh
                  jz       Init
                  mov      ax,8103h
 Exit:            mov      es:[bx+3],ax
                  pop      bp
                  pop      di
                  pop      si
                  pop      es
                  pop      ds
                  pop      dx
                  pop      cx
                  pop      bx
                  pop      ax
                  popf
                  retf

 ;
 ;        install the keyboard pointers
 ;
```

```
Init:           mov     ax,seg BIOS_DATA
                mov     es,ax
                assume  es:BIOS_DATA

                mov     dx,cs
                sub     dx,ax             ; calc difference
                cmp     dx,0FB0h          ; check for within range
                jnb     OutOfRange

                mov     cl,4
                shl     dx,cl             ; convert to byte offset
                mov     ax,offset cs:Kbufbeg
                add     ax,dx             ; convert to BIOS-based
                cli
                mov     es:kbgp,ax        ; set into BIOS area
                mov     es:kbpp,ax
                mov     es:kbfb,ax
                mov     ax,offset cs:Kbufend
                add     ax,dx             ; convert to BIOS-based
                mov     es:kbfe,ax
                sti
                mov     ax,100h
                jmp     short okay

OutOfRange:     mov     ax,8100h

okay:           les     bx,cs:pkt_ptr
                assume  es:nothing
                mov     word ptr es:[bx+0Eh],offset cs:Init
                mov     es:[bx+10h],cs
                jmp     Exit

commands        endp

xkb             endp

                end
```

New points illustrated in XKB include the use of a separate data segment to define a based RAM area in the BIOS memory space (segment 0040h), although the actual buffer itself is still defined along with other driver data inside the code segment.

Also, rather than using the dispatch table approach when no command packets will be received once installation is complete, this program shows the alternate approach of jumping to `Init` for command code 0, and returning an error for any other command. This is preferable in many cases.

The initialization code is relatively straightforward. It calculates the byte offset necessary for the buffer start and finish addresses to allow for the difference between its own code-segment address and the BIOS data segment address of 0040h, and then stuffs the adjusted values into the BIOS pointers. This abandons the original 32-byte, 15-character keyboard buffer area and uses instead the 256-byte, 127-character buffer located in the driver.

Notice that `CLI` and `STI` operations are used to bracket all the actions that actually modify the pointers used by BIOS. By disabling interrupts entirely for the time in which the pointers are being changed, the program prevents loss of keystrokes that might happen if an Interrupt 09h were to take place in the middle of this modification sequence.

It is still possible, however, that a keystroke might occur just before these actions (thus being stored in the original buffer); such a keystroke would not be visible to BIOS after the pointer change. While not exactly "lost" (it would still be in the old buffer area) it might as well be because it would not be available to any program. Fortunately, such an event is not likely during the CONFIG.SYS processing.

Summing Up

This concludes Section 3 of this book, the discussion of detailed techniques. In Section 4, "Reference Material," which begins with Chapter 13 and continues through chapters 14 and 15, summarized references organized in numeric sequence rather than functionally are provided for your convenience.

Section 4: Reference Material

The three chapters that form this final section contain reference listings for all documented functions present in DOS 5 and 6. They do not attempt to provide comprehensive coverage of functions that were present prior to DOS 5 but were not retained at that level, nor of undocumented functions, although these are accounted for in the numbering system.

This section consists of three chapters: Chapter 13, "Interrupt 21h: The DOS Interface," Chapter 14, "Other DOS Interrupts," and Chapter 15, "BIOS Services." Within each chapter, functions appear in numeric sequence, and significant conditions (including register contents) at entry to the function and at exit are shown where applicable. When a function requires more detailed discussion than the format of this section allows, its entry here contains one or more references back to such discussions in Section 3, "The Techniques."

13

Interrupt 21h: The DOS Interface

Version 6.0 of MS-DOS, like Version 5.0, accepts a total of 109 function codes through the INT 21h interface, from 00h to 6Ch inclusive. Not all these codes are meaningful, however, because some of them have never done anything, and some, while useful in older versions of MS-DOS, have been disabled.

A number of these function codes are undocumented; the official MS-DOS documentation ignores them, or shows the code but calls it *reserved* with no hint as to what it might do.

Existence of the undocumented codes always has intrigued developers, and has led to speculation that use of such functions may be something used to give Microsoft an unfair edge in the applications-program marketplace. The truth, however, is much more prosaic.

A fair percentage of the once-undocumented functions did receive official blessing in the MS-DOS Programmer's Reference for Version 5.0. Those that remain *outside the fold* duplicate the functions of existing, documented codes do nothing, or have such strange quirks that their general use is considered highly unsafe.

This chapter lists all 109 functions; however, no detail is given for those that are placeholders. For some of the other codes, only a summary list is provided.

Function 00h: Terminate Process

Entry Conditions: AH equals 00h.

Exit Conditions: Never returns from function.

Results: Current process terminates and control returns to next higher process in DOS hierarchy. Errorlevel code is set to 0.

Related to: INT 20h; INT 27h; Functions 31h and 4Ch

Function 01h: Read Character From STDIN, With Echo

Entry Conditions: AH equals 01h.

Exit Conditions: AL equals character read.

Results: If CONTROL-C or CONTROL-BREAK are detected, INT 23h is executed. Redirection is honored. Character read is echoed to STDOUT stream.

Related to: Functions 06h, 07h, 08h, and 3Fh

Function 02h: Write Character To STDOUT

Entry Conditions: AH equals 02h, DL equals character to write.

Exit Conditions: Not significant.

Results: If CONTROL-C or CONTROL-BREAK are detected, INT 23h is executed. Redirection is honored.

Related to: Functions 06h, 09h and 40h

Function 03h: Read Character From STDAUX

Entry Conditions: AH equals 03h.

Exit Conditions: AL equals character read.

Results: If CONTROL-C or CONTROL-BREAK are detected in the STDIN stream, INT 23h is executed. This function waits for an input character to appear from STDAUX, without limit on the wait time.

Related to: Function 3Fh

Function 04h: Write Character To STDAUX

Entry Conditions: AH equals 04h, DL equals character to write.

Exit Conditions: Not significant.

Results: If CONTROL-C or CONTROL-BREAK are detected in the STDIN stream, INT 23h is executed. If STDAUX is busy, this function will wait indefinitely for it to become available.

Related to: Function 40h

Function 05h: Write Character To STDPRN

Entry Conditions: AH equals 05h, DL equals character to write.

Exit Conditions: Not significant.

Results: If CONTROL-C or CONTROL-BREAK are detected in the STDIN stream, INT 23h is executed. If STDPRN is busy, this function will wait indefinitely for it to become available.

Related to: Function 40h

Function 06h: General Console I/O

This function normally provides for output without testing; this is similar to the use of BIOS, but differs in that redirection of the STDOUT stream will be honored.

Entry Conditions: AH equals 06h, DL equals any value other than 0FFh

Exit Conditions: Not significant

Results: Character in DL is output to STDOUT stream

Related to: Functions 02h, 06h, 09h and 40h

If the value in DL is 0FFh, however, this function provides for input rather than output. This duplicates the use of BIOS in that no tests are made of the received character, but differs in that redirection of the STDIN stream will be honored.

Entry Conditions: AH equals 06h, DL equals 0FFh

Exit Conditions: ZR flag set if no keystroke available. NZ if keystroke available, AL equals ASCII value.

Results: Combines test for available keystroke from STDIN stream with access of that keystroke. Returns immediately without waiting in either event. If flag indicates keystroke but AL is zero, the function should immediately be called again to retrieve scancode for a special key. Character read is not echoed to STDOUT stream.

Related to: Functions 01h, 07h, 08h, and 3Fh

Function 07h: Untested Character Input Without Echo

Entry Conditions: AH equals 07h

Exit Conditions: AL equals character read

Results: Function waits for a keystroke from the STDIN stream, and then returns it without testing for CONTROL-C or CONTROL-BREAK. Character read is not echoed to STDOUT stream.

Related to: Functions 01h, 06h, 08h, and 3Fh

Function 08h: Character Input Without Echo

Entry Conditions: AH equals 08h

Exit Conditions: AL equals character read

Results: Function waits for a keystroke from the STDIN stream. If CONTROL-C or CONTROL-BREAK are detected in the STDIN stream, INT 23h is executed. Character read is not echoed to STDOUT stream.

Related to: Functions 01h, 06h, 07h, and 3Fh

Function 09h: Print String

Entry Conditions: AH equals 09h, DS:DX points to $-terminated character string

Exit Conditions: Not significant

Results: String is written to STDOUT stream, up to but not including the terminating $ character. If CONTROL-C or CONTROL-BREAK are detected in the STDIN stream, INT 23h is executed.

Related to: Functions 02h, 06h, and 40h

Function 0Ah: Input With Editing

Entry Conditions: AH equals 0Ah, DS:DX points to input buffer in which first byte indicates maximum number of characters allowable and second byte indicates number of bytes of existing input that can be recalled by standard DOS edit keys (F1, F2, F3, and F4). Rest of buffer may contain recallable input string.

Exit Conditions: Buffer filled and second byte indicates number of valid characters, excluding CR that terminates input. First character of input is located in third byte of buffer.

Results: Input comes from STDIN and redirection is honored. If first byte of buffer is 0, then function returns immediately with no input action. If second byte is 0, then DOS edit keys cannot be used during input. If CONTROL-C or CONTROL-BREAK are detected in the STDIN stream, INT 23h is executed.

Related to: Functions 01h, 06h, 08h, and 3Fh

Function 0Bh: Check for Input Available From STDIN

Entry Conditions: AH equals 0Bh

Exit Conditions: AL equals 00h if no input available from STDIN, or FFh if input available.

Results: If CONTROL-C or CONTROL-BREAK are detected in the STDIN stream, INT 23h is executed.

Related to: Function 06h

Function 0Ch: Flush Buffer, Then Read STDIN

Entry Conditions: AH equals 0Ch; AL equals 01h, 06h, 07h, 08h, or 0Ah

Exit Conditions: As appropriate for specified read function

Results: STDIN input buffer (keyboard buffer in usual case) is emptied of typeahead material, and then the function specified by the AL register is called. Results depend on the specified read function.

Related to: Functions 01h, 06h, 07h, 08h, and 0Ah

Function 0Dh: Disk Reset

Entry Conditions: AH equals 0Dh

Exit Conditions: Not significant

Results: All modified disk buffers are physically written to disk before function returns. Directory entries are not updated.

Related to: None

Function 0Eh: Select Default Drive

Entry Conditions: AH equals 0Eh, AL equals new default drive (0 equals A:, 1 equals B:, 2 equals C:, and so on)

Exit Conditions: AL equals LASTDRIVE value stored by DOS

Results: Specified drive becomes current drive for all disk I/O operations. Return value bears no direct relationship to number of drives actually present in system.

Related to: None

Function 0Fh: Open File via FCB

Entry Conditions: AH equals 0Fh, DS:DX point to unopened File Control Block

Exit Conditions: AL equals status, 00h if successful, FFh if an error occurs

Results: File opens in compatibility mode. This call is not supported by the Windows DOSX.EXE DOS extender.

Related to: Functions 3Ch, 3Dh, 5Ah, 5Bh, and 6Ch

Function 10h: Close File via FCB

Entry Conditions: AH equals 10h, DS:DX point to unopened File Control Block

Exit Conditions: AL equals status, 00h if successful, FFh if an error occurs

Results: Disk buffers are flushed and directory entry for file is updated. This call is not supported by the Windows DOSX.EXE DOS extender.

Related to: Function 3Eh

Function 11h: Find First via FCB

Entry Conditions: AH equals 11h, DS:DX point to unopened File Control Block that may contain ? or * wildcard characters.

Exit Conditions: AL equals status, 00h if successful, FFh if no file found or an error occurs

Results: If successful, then current Disk Transfer Area contains unopened FCB for first file that matches mask passed into this function's FCB.

Related to: Function 4Eh

Function 12h: Find Next via FCB

Entry Conditions: AH equals 12h, DS:DX point to same File Control Block used by prior call to Function 11h or 12h

Exit Conditions: AL equals status, 00h if successful, FFh if no more files match.

Results: If successful, then current Disk Transfer Area contains unopened FCB for next file that matches mask passed into this function's FCB.

Related to: Function 4Fh

Function 13h: Delete File via FCB

Entry Conditions: AH equals 13h, DS:DX point to unopened File Control Block which may contain ? or * wildcard characters.

Exit Conditions: AL equals status, 00h if successful, FFh if no deletions occur.

Results: All files in current directory of specified drive that match filename and extension mask of FCB are deleted. This function can delete directories without deleting files contained in that particular directory. This function should be used with extreme caution, if at all.

Related to: Function 41h

Function 14h: Sequential Read via FCB

Entry Conditions: AH equals 14h, DS:DX point to opened File Control Block.

Exit Conditions: AL equals status: 00h if successful, 01h if end of file and no data, 02h if segment wrap occurrs in DTA, or 03h if EOF with partial record.

Results: One record of size specified in FCB (128 bytes by default) is read into the Disk Transfer Area if function successful. This call is not supported by the Windows DOSX.EXE DOS extender.

Related to: Functions 21h, 27h, and 3Fh

Function 15h: Sequential Write via FCB

Entry Conditions: AH equals 15h, DS:DX point to opened File Control Block

Exit Conditions: AL equals status: 00h if successful, 01h if disk is full, or 02h if segment wrap occurrs in DTA.

Results: One record of size specified in FCB (128 bytes by default) is written from the Disk Transfer Area if function successful. Record is written to current file position, and FCB is updated. Data is moved to DOS buffer but not necessarily written to disk immediately. This call is not supported by the Windows DOSX.EXE DOS extender.

Related to: Functions 22h, 28h, and 40h

Function 16h: Create or Empty File via FCB

Entry Conditions: AH equals 16h, DS:DX point to unopened File Control Block which may not contain ? or * wildcard characters.

Exit Conditions: AL equals status, 00h if successful, FFh if directory is full or specified file exists and is read-only.

Results: Specified file is truncated to zero length if it exists, or is created if it does not. If an extended FCB is used and specified attributes are assigned. This call is not supported by the Windows DOSX.EXE DOS extender.

Related to: Functions 3Ch, 5Ah, 5Bh, and 6Ch

Function 17h: Rename File via FCB

Entry Conditions: AH equals 17h, DS:DX point to modified File Control Block that contains old name in normal location and new name and extension in the 11 bytes starting at offset 11h. Both old and new names may contain ? or * wildcard characters.

Exit Conditions: AL equals status, 00h if successful, FFh if no file matches FCB, matching file is read-only, or specified name already exists.

Results: Old name in directory entry is replaced with a new name. This function may be used to rename subdirectories by using an extended FCB with the appropriate attribute set.

Related to: Function 56h

Function 18h: Reserved for CP/M Compatibility

Entry Conditions: AH equals 18h

Exit Conditions: AL equals 00h

Results: This function performs no task in any version of MS-DOS.

Related to: None

Function 19h: Get Current Drive Number

Entry Conditions: AH equals 19h

Exit Conditions: AL equals number of current drive (0 equals A:, 1 equals B:, 2 equals C:, and so on)

Results: No change to system condition results from this call.

Related to: None

Function 1Ah: Set Disk Transfer Address

Entry Conditions: AH equals 1Ah; DS:DX point to buffer to be used as new Disk Transfer Area.

Exit Conditions: Not significant

Results: Default DTA at program startup is offset 80h in Program Segment Prefix. This function assigns user's buffer instead and should be called before using Functions 4E or 4F.

Related to: Function 2Fh

Function 1Bh: Get Allocation Information for Current Drive

Entry Conditions: AH equals 1Bh

Exit Conditions: AL equals number of sectors per cluster, CX equals number of bytes per sector, DX equals total number of clusters on drive, and DS:BX point to Media ID byte indicating characteristics for removeable media.

Results: No change to system condition results from this call.

Related to: Function 1Ch

Function 1Ch: Get Allocation Information for Specified Drive

Entry Conditions: AH equals 1Ch, DL equals 1-based drive number (0 equals current drive, 1 equals A:, 2 equals B:, 3 equals C:, and so on)

Exit Conditions: AL equals number of sectors per cluster, CX equals number of bytes per sector, DX equals total number of clusters on drive, and DS:BX point to Media ID byte indicating characteristics for removeable media.

Results: No change to system condition results from this call.

Related to: Function 1Bh

Function 1Dh: Reserved for CP/M Compatibility

Entry Conditions: AH equals 1Dh

Exit Conditions: AL equals 00h

Results: This function performs no particular task in any version of MS-DOS.

Related to: None

Function 1Eh: Reserved for CP/M Compatibility

Entry Conditions: AH equals 1Eh

Exit Conditions: AL equals 00h

Results: This function performs no particular task in any version of MS-DOS.

Related to: None

Function 1Fh: Get Drive Parameters for Current Drive

Entry Conditions: AH equals 1Fh

Exit Conditions: AL equals status: 00h if successful, FFh if drive not valid; DS:BX point to Drive Parameter Block for current drive if function succeeds, otherwise are not significant.

Results: The Drive Parameter Block contains the same information returned by Function 1Bh, plus additional details.

Related to: Function 32h

Function 20h: Reserved for CP/M Compatibility

Entry Conditions: AH equals 20h

Exit Conditions: AL equals 00h

Results: This function performs no particular task in any version of MS-DOS.

Related to: None

Function 21h: Read Random Record via FCB

Entry Conditions: AH equals 21h, DS:DX point to opened File Control Block.

Exit Conditions: AL equals status: 00h if successful, 01h if end of file and no data, 02h if segment wrap occurred in DTA (no data is read), or 03h if EOF with partial record.

Results: Record is read from current file position as specified by random record and record size fields of the FCB, into current DTA. File position is not changed by this function. If partial record is read, DTA is padded to full record size with zero bytes. This call is not supported by the Windows DOSX.EXE DOS extender.

Related to: Functions 14h, 27h, and 3Fh

Function 22h: Write Random Record via FCB

Entry Conditions: AH equals 22h, DS:DX point to opened File Control Block.

Exit Conditions: AL equals status: 00h if successful, 01h if disk is full, or 02h if segment wrap occurs in DTA.

Results: Record is written from current DTA to current file position as specified by random record and record size fields of the FCB. File position is not changed by this function. If record is located beyond end of file, the file's size is extended, however, the added space is not initialized. This call is not supported by the Windows DOSX.EXE DOS extender.

Related to: Functions 15h, 28h, and 40h

Function 23h: Get File Size via FCB

Entry Conditions: AH equals 23h, DS:DX point to unopened File Control Block which may not contain wildcard characters in the name or extension fields.

Exit Conditions: AL equals status, 00h if successful (matching file found), FFh if no match found.

Results: Record size field of the FCB is filled with the file size in records, and rounded up to next full record, if function succeeds. This call is not supported by the Windows DOSX.EXE DOS extender.

Related to: Functions 4Eh and 4Fh

Function 24h: Set Record Number Into FCB

Entry Conditions: AH equals 24h, DS:DX point to opened File Control Block.

Exit Conditions: Not significant

Results: Random record number corresponding to current record number and record size is computed and stored in random record number field of FCB. This function is used when changing from sequential to random access. This call is not supported by the Windows DOSX.EXE DOS extender.

Related to: Functions 27h and 28h

Function 25h: Set Interrupt Vector

Entry Conditions: AH equals 25h, AL equals interrupt number, DS:DX equal address to be plugged into interrupt vector.

Exit Conditions: Not significant

Results: Address to which specified interrupt transfers control is changed.

Related to: Function 35h

Function 26h: Create New PSP

Entry Conditions: AH equals 26h, DX equals segment address at which to create new PSP.

Exit Conditions: Not significant

Results: This undocumented function is obsolete and should not be used. Use Function 4Bh instead to create PSP and load or execute program.

Related to: Functions 4Bh and 55h

Function 27h: Random Block Read via FCB

Entry Conditions: AH equals 27h, DS:DX point to opened File Control Block, CX equals number of records to read.

Exit Conditions: AL equals status: 00h if successful, 01h if EOF (no data), 02h if segment wrap occurred in DTA (no data), or 03h if EOF reached with partial data record.

Results: Reads multiple records to DTA, starting with record specified in FCB. File position is updated after each record is read. This call is not supported by the Windows DOSX.EXE DOS extender.

Related to: Functions 14h, 21h, and 3Fh

Function 28h: Random Block Write via FCB

Entry Conditions: AH equals 28h, DS:DX point to opened File Control Block, CX equals number of records to write.

Exit Conditions: AL equals status: 00h if successful, 01h if disk was full or file was read-only, or 02h if segment wrap occurred in DTA; CX equals number of records written.

Results: Writes multiple records from DTA, starting with record specified in FCB. File position is updated after each record is written. This call is not supported by the Windows DOSX.EXE DOS extender.

Related to: Functions 15h, 22h, and 40h

Function 29h: Parse File Name Into FCB

Entry Conditions: AH equals 29h, AL equals parsing options, DS:SI point to filename string which may contain drive specifier and ? or * wildcard characters but not directory names, and ES:DI point to FCB to receive results.

Exit Conditions: AL equals status, 00h if successful and no wildcards detected, 01h if successful and wildcards found, FFh if drive specifier invalid; DS:SI point to first unparsed character of input string.

Results: Buffer at ES:DI is filled with unopened FCB with all essential fields set to match input string's specifications. Any * character in filename or extension area of input string expands to series of ? characters in FCB. Note that this function can determine whether a drive letter is valid, without generating a DOS critical error by attempting to read a non-existent drive.

Related to: None

Function 2Ah: Get System Date

Entry Conditions: AH equals 2Ah

Exit Conditions: AL equals day of week (0 equals Sunday), DL equals day, DH equals month, CX equals year (in range 1980-2099).

Results: No change to system condition results from this call.

Related to: Function 2Bh

Function 2Bh: Set System Date

Entry Conditions: AH equals 2Bh, DL equals day, DH equals month, CX equals year (in range 1980-2099).

Exit Conditions: AL equals status: 00h if successful, FFh if registers contain invalid date.

Results: System calendar is set to date specified in registers; if date was not valid (Feb. 30, 1994, for example) calendar remains unchanged. Versions 3.3 and up also set CMOS calendar.

Related to: Function 2Ah

Function 2Ch: Get System Time

Entry Conditions: AH equals 2Ch

Exit Conditions: CH equals hours, CL equals minutes, DH equals seconds, and DL equals 1/100 seconds.

Results: If BIOS midnight flag is set, calling this function will cause the calendar to advance to the next day.

Related to: Function 2Dh

Function 2Dh: Set System Time

Entry Conditions: AH equals 2Dh, CH equals hours, CL equals minutes, DH equals seconds, and DL equals 1/100 seconds.

Exit Conditions: AL equals status, 00h if successful, FFh if registers contain invalid time.

Results: System clock is set to time specified in registers; if time was not valid (25:63:90.25, for example) time remains unchanged. Versions 3.3 and up also set CMOS clock.

Related to: Function 2Ch

Function 2Eh: Set Verify Flag

Entry Conditions: AH equals 2Eh, AL equals flag (0 equals off, 1 equals on).

Exit Conditions: Not significant

Results: If flag is set `ON`, block device drivers are requested to verify all write operations. Most drivers only perform CRC check and do not do actual read-after-write comparisons. Default condition is `OFF`.

Related to: Function 54h

Function 2Fh: Get Disk Transfer Address

Entry Conditions: AH equals 2Fh

Exit Conditions: ES:BX point to first byte of current Disk Transfer Area.

Related to: Function 1Ah

Function 30h: Get DOS Version

Entry Conditions: AH equals 30h, AL equals switch for BH (0 equals return OEM number, 1 equals return DOS location).

Exit Conditions: AL equals major version number (0 if V1.x), AH equals minor version number, BL:CX equals 24-bit user serial number (usually 0), BH equals OEM number (00=IBM, FFh=MS-DOS) if AL was 0 at entry, or RAM location (08=DOS in ROM, 10h=DOS in HMA) if AL was 1.

Results: Results cannot be trusted in Version 5.0 or higher because SETVER will modify them; use Function 33h with AL=6 to obtain true version number.

Related to: Function 33h; Subfunction 06

Function 31h: Terminate and Stay Resident

Entry Conditions: AH equals 31h, AL equals exit code, and DX equals number of paragraphs to keep resident.

Exit Conditions: Never returns to caller.

Results: Unlike normal process termination, no files are closed nor any handles released. Good practice requires that all files be closed before going resident unless they are required to remain open specifically. Value in DX applies only to block identified by PSP; any additional RAM obtained by the program will remain allocated to it (such as the environment block remains allocated).

Related to: INT 27h; Function 4Dh

Function 32h: Get Drive Parameters for Specified Drive

Entry Conditions: AH equals 32h, DL equals 1-based drive number (0 equals current drive, 1 equals A:, 2 equals B:, 3 equals C:, and so on)

Exit Conditions: AL equals status: 00h if successful, FFh if specified drive not valid; DS:BX point to Drive Parameter Block for specified drive if function succeeds, otherwise are not significant

Results: The Drive Parameter Block contains the same information returned by Function 1Ch, plus additional details.

Related to: Function 1Fh

Function 33h: Control Break Checks, Get Boot Drive, True Version

This function includes five subfunctions, which check the state of extended BREAK testing, determine from which drive the system booted most recently, and enable a program to determine the true version of DOS if the SETVER capability introduced in Version 5.0 is returning a false version level via Function 30h. All subfunctions of Function 33h avoid use of any DOS internal stack area and so are fully re-entrant.

Subfunction 00 gets the current state of extended BREAK testing:

Entry Conditions: AH equals 33h, AL equals 00h (get extended break state)

Exit Conditions: DL equals extended break state (0 equals off, 1 equals on)

Results: If extended break state is on (the default condition), every DOS I/O function will check for a CTRL-BREAK keystroke. If one is detected, it will interrupt the process immediately. If the state is off, CTRL-BREAK checks will be performed only during character I/O functions.

Subfunction 01 sets the current state of extended BREAK testing:

Entry Conditions: AH equals 33h, AL equals 01h (set break state), DL equals new break state (0 equals off, 1 equals on)

Exit Conditions: Not significant

Results: If extended break state is on (the default condition), every DOS I/O function will check for a CTRL-BREAK keystroke and if one is detected, will interrupt the process immediately. If the state is off, CTRL-BREAK checks will be performed only during character I/O functions.

Subfunction 02 gets the current state of extended BREAK testing and sets a new state, both in a single call to DOS:

Entry Conditions: AH equals 33h, AL equals 02h (get and set at same time), DL equals new break state (0 equals off, 1 equals on)

Exit Conditions: DL equals old break state (0 equals off, 1 equals on)

Results: If extended break state is on (the default condition), every DOS I/O function will check for a CTRL-BREAK keystroke and if one is detected, will interrupt the process immediately. If the state is off, CTRL-BREAK checks will be performed only during character I/O functions.

Subfunction 05 gets the one-based number of the boot drive:

Entry Conditions: AH equals 33h, AL equals 05h (get boot drive)

Exit Conditions: DL equals 1-based number of drive from which current session was booted (1 equals A: and so on).

Subfunction 06 gets the true version number for MS-DOS Version 5.0 and later:

Entry Conditions: AH equals 33h, AL equals 06h (get true version number).

Exit Conditions: BL equals major version, BH equals minor version, DL equals revision, DH equals location (08 equals DOS in ROM, 10h equals DOS in HMA).

Results: This function is not affected by `SETVER`.

Function 34h: Get INDOS Flag Address (Undocumented)

Entry Conditions: AH equals 34h

Exit Conditions: ES:BX point to single-byte `INDOS` flag.

Results: The `INDOS` flag is incremented each time the DOS kernel is entered, and is decremented at exit from the kernel. If it is zero, no process is executing in the DOS kernel. This flag is used by TSR routines to help determine whether use of DOS functions may be safe when the TSR pops up.

Related to: None

Function 35h: Get Interrupt Vector

Entry Conditions: AH equals 35h, AL equals interrupt number

Exit Conditions: ES:BX point to interrupt service routine for the specified interrupt

Related to: Function 25h

Function 36h: Get Free Disk Space

Entry Conditions:	AH equals 36h, 1-based drive number (0 equals current drive, 1 equals A:, and so on)
Exit Conditions:	AX equals 0FFFFh if invalid drive specified, otherwise AX equals sectors per cluster, BX equals number of clusters free, CX equals bytes per sector, and DX equals total number of clusters on drive.
Results:	Free space on drive, in bytes, is AX times BX times CX, while total drive capacity is AX times CX times DX. Some large drives may cause these calculations to overflow, creating invalid space reports.
Related to:	None

Function 37h: SwitChar and DEV Control

Entry Conditions:	AH equals 37h, AL equals 00h
Exit Conditions:	AL equals status; 00h if successful, FFh if not supported. If successful, DL equals switch character (always / in Version 5 and later).
Entry Conditions:	AH equals 37h, AL equals 01h, and DL equals new switch character.
Exit Conditions:	AL equals status; 00h if successful, FFh if not supported. Version 5 and up returns 00h but does not change the character.
Entry Conditions:	AH equals 37h, AL equals 02h

Exit Conditions: AL equals status; 00h if successful, FFh if not supported. If successful, DL indicates whether \DEV\ prefix required on device names (0 equals required, nonzero equals optional). Version 5 and up always return FFh.

Entry Conditions: AH equals 37h, AL equals equals3h, and DL equals DEV flag (0 equals mandatory, nonzero equals optional)

Exit Conditions: AL equals status; 00h if successful, FFh if not supported

Related to: None

Function 38h: Country-Specific Information

To retrieve the current country-specific information from DOS, use the following format:

Entry Conditions: AH equals 38h, AL equals country code (00 equals current country, FFh equals 16-bit code in BX, other values are all valid 8-bit country codes), BX equals code if AL equals FFh, and DS:DX point to buffer for information.

Exit Conditions: CY set if error and AX equals 02h; CY clear if successful and BX equals country code.

Results: If successful, buffer pointed to by DS:DX is filled with all applicable information for specified country.

To set a new country code in DOS, use the following format:

Entry Conditions: AH equals 38h, AL equals country code (00 equals current country, FFh equals 16-bit code in BX, other values are all valid 8-bit country codes), BX equals code if AL equals FFh, and DX equals FFFFh to set new country code.

Exit Conditions: CY set if error and AX equals error code; CY clear if successful.

Results: Country specified by AL and BX possibly becomes current country.

Related to: Functions 63h, 65h, and 66h

Function 39h: Make Subdirectory

Entry Conditions: AH equals 39h, and DS:DX point to ASCIIZ pathname for directory to be created. Name may be relative to current directory, or absolute.

Exit Conditions: CY clear if directory created, else CY set and AX equals error code.

Results: All directories in specified path, except the final one, must already exist. The final name must not exist previously.

Related to: Functions 3Ah, 3Bh, and 47h

Function 3Ah: Remove Subdirectory

Entry Conditions: AH equals 3Ah. DS:DX point to ASCIIZ pathname for directory to be removed from file system. Name may be relative to current directory, or absolute.

Exit Conditions: CY clear if directory removed, else CY set and AX equals error code.

Results: Directory must be empty of all files and subdirectories before it can be removed from the file system. All directories in specified path must already exist.

Related to: Functions 39h, 3Bh, and 47h

Function 3Bh: Set Current Directory

Entry Conditions: AH equals 3Bh. DS:DX point to ASCIIZ pathname for directory to be made current. Name may be relative to current directory, or absolute.

Exit Conditions: CY clear if successful, else CY set and AX equals error code.

Results: If successful, current directory for specified drive is changed. This, however, does not change the current drive value if the directory was not on the current drive.

Related to: Functions 39h, 3Ah, and 47h

Function 3Ch: Create via Handle

Entry Conditions: AH equals 3Ch, CX equals file attribute bitmap, DS:DX point to ASCIIZ filename or path specification for file to be created.

Exit Conditions: CY clear if file created successfully, and AX contains handle assigned to the file for reference. CY set if file cannot be created, and AX contains error code.

Results: If file already existed, is truncated to zero length by this function.

Related to: Functions 16h, 5Ah, 5Bh, and 6Ch

Function 3Dh: Open via Handle

Entry Conditions: AH equals 3Dh, AL equals access mode bits (see Chapter 9), CL equals attribute mask, and DS:DX point to ASCIIZ filename or path specification for file to be opened.

Exit Conditions: CY clear if file opened successfully, and AX contains handle assigned to the file for reference. CY set if file could not be created, and AX contains error code.

Results: File pointer positioned to start of file. Writing to file overwrites existing information. Pointer may be moved to end of file in order to append new information after existing data.

Related to: Functions 0Fh and 6Ch

Function 3Eh: Close Handle

Entry Conditions: AH equals 3Eh and BX equals file handle.

Exit Conditions: CY set if error, and AX equals error code, else CY clear.

Results: File handle is returned to system for reuse. If file was modified, buffers are flushed to disk and directory entry is updated.

Related to: Function 10h

Function 3Fh: Read via Handle

Entry Conditions: AH equals 3Fh, BX equals handle, CX equals number of bytes to read, and DS:DX point to buffer to receive data.

Exit Conditions: CY set if error, and AX equals error code, else CY clear and AX contains actual number of bytes read.

Results: Specified number of bytes are read into buffer, starting at current file position, and file position is updated to point to first unread byte. If only a partial read was accomplished, value returned in AX may be less than number of bytes requested. If reading from device in RAW mode, read stops at first CR character encountered.

Related to: Functions 14h, 21h, 27h, and 3Fh

Function 40h: Write via Handle

Entry Conditions: AH equals 40h, BX equals handle, CX equals number of bytes to read, and DS:DX point to buffer containing data to be written.

Exit Conditions: CY is set if error, and AX equals error code, else CY clears and AX contains actual number of bytes written.

Results: Specified number of bytes are written from buffer, starting at current file position, and file position is updated to point to first unused byte. If only a partial write was accomplished, value returned in AX may be less than number of bytes requested.

Related to: Functions 15h, 22h, and 28h

Function 41h: Delete File

Entry Conditions: AH equals 41h, DS:DX point to buffer containing full name of file to be deleted.

Exit Conditions: CY set if error, and AX equals error code, else CY clear.

Results: File's data is not erased; directory entry is marked as being erased and FAT chain is released for possible reuse. Unless SHARE is loaded, however, handles that refer to the deleted file are not closed automatically, making it possible to attempt to write to a file that no longer exists and thus corrupt a directory unless any file that is to be deleted is explicitly closed by all users before the delete takes place.

Related to: Function 13h

Function 42h: Set Current File Position

Entry Conditions: AH equals 42h, AL equals reference point (0=start of file, 1=current position, 2=end of file), BX equals handle, CX:DX equals signed 32-bit offset from reference position, with most significant 16 bits in CX.

Exit Conditions: CY set if error, and AX equals error code, else CY clear and new file position in DX:AX as signed 32-bit offset from reference position, with most significant 16 bits in DX.

Results: New position may be negative offset from start of file; no error will be reported by this function in such a situation, but any subsequent attempt to do I/O will result in an error. If new position is beyond end of file, attempts to read will return the EOF condition but attempts to write will extend the file's size and bytes between the current EOF and the new location will be of undefined value.

Related to: Function 24h

Function 43h: Get or Set File Attributes

Entry Conditions: AH equals 43h, AL equals mode (0=get, 1=set), DS:DX point to buffer containing full name of file. If setting attributes, CX contains new attribute values (see Chapter 9) to be assigned.

Exit Conditions: CY set if error, and AX equals error code, else CY clear. If getting attributes and no error, CX contains attribute values (see Chapter 9).

Related to: None

Function 44h: IOCTL Interface

The IOCTL interface function is, in itself, almost as complicated as all the rest of the INT 21h interface put together. It now documents 18 distinct subfunctions, some of which have additional subdivisions in themselves. Refer to Chapters 7 and 8 for discussion and tabulation of this function. Chapter 7 discusses those parts of it which deal with character devices, while Chapter 8 deals with its actions on block devices (usually, disk drives or files).

Function 45h: Create Duplicate Handle

Entry Conditions: AH equals 45h, BX equals handle to be duplicated.

Exit Conditions: CY set if error, and AX equals error code, else CY clear and AX equals new handle referring to same file or device.

Results: Subsequent actions affecting one handle will affect the other identically because both will be using the same internal DOS storage information. In particular, moving current position of one will also move it for the other.

Related to: Function 46h

Function 46h: Force Duplicate Handle

Entry Conditions: AH equals 46h, BX equals handle to be duplicated, CX equals handle to be forced to refer to same file or device.

Exit Conditions: CY set if error, and AX equals error code, else CY clear.

Results: Closes file or device specified by CX at entry if it is open. Subsequent actions affecting one handle will affect the other identically because both will be using the same internal DOS storage information.

Related to: Function 45h

Function 47h: Get Current Directory

Entry Conditions: AH equals 47h, DL equals 1-based drive number (0=current drive, 1=A:, and so on), DS:SI point to buffer at least 65 bytes long to receive the pathname in ASCIIZ format.

Exit Conditions: CY set if error, and AX equals error code, else CY clear.

Results: Returned path does not include a drive letter or the initial '\' character.

Related to: Functions 39h, 3Ah, and 3Bh

Function 48h: Allocate Memory

Entry Conditions: AH equals 48h, BX equals number of paragraphs to be allocated.

Exit Conditions: CY set if error with AX equals error code and BX equals size of largest available RAM block, else CY clear and AX equals segment address of allocated block.

Results: If successful, value in AX should be used as segment portion of a far pointer, and offset set to 0, to identify the allocated RAM. This function merges any adjacent free blocks of RAM while searching for an area to allocate, and goes through entire memory chain before returning a value. See Function 58h to determine search strategy that will be followed.

Related to: Functions 49h, 4Ah, and 58h

Function 49h: Free Memory

Entry Conditions: AH equals 49h, ES equals segment address of block to be freed.

Exit Conditions: CY set if error with AX equals error code, else CY clear.

Results: Freed block is not merged with adjacent blocks when it is released.

Related to: Functions 48h, 4Ah, and 58h

Function 4Ah: Adjust Size of Memory Block

Entry Conditions: AH equals 4Ah, BX equals new block size in paragraphs, ES equals segment address of block to be resized.

Exit Conditions: CY set if error with AX equals error code and BX equals size of largest size block can be given, else CY clear.

Results: If less space is available than was requested, block will be made as large as possible. Asking for block to grow to 0FFFFh paragraphs will make it take all available RAM.

Related to: Functions 48h, 49h, and 58h

Function 4Bh: Load or Exec Process

The five variations of this function are too complex to cover in a reference format; Chapter 11 is devoted entirely to discussion of Function 4Bh.

Function 4Ch: Terminate Process With Exit Code

Entry Conditions: AH equals 4Ch, AL equals exit code.

Exit Conditions: Function does not return to caller.

Results: Exit code is stored in DOS kernel where it can be recovered by a subsequent call to Function 4Dh, and control returns to the process that invoked the one just terminated (at the address stored in offset 0Ah of this process' PSP). In effect, this function forces return from the EXEC variation of Function 4Bh. Unless this process is its own parent, all open handles are closed and all memory allocated to the process is freed.

Related to: INT 20h; Functions 00h, 31h, 4Bh, and 4Dh

Function 4Dh: Get Exit Code

Entry Conditions: AH equals 4Dh.

Exit Conditions: AH equals termination type (0=normal, 1=CTRL-C, 2=critical error, 3=process terminated and stayed resident), AL equals exit code.

Results: Value returned is for last previous process. Internal storage location is cleared when value is obtained so cannot be read again; values returned by this function must be stored immediately if future reference is required.

Related to: INT 20h; INT 27h; Functions 00h, 31h, 4Bh, and 4Ch.

Function 4Eh: Find First Matching Pathspec

Entry Conditions: AH equals 4Eh, CX equals attribute mask, DS:DX point to pathspec mask which may include wildcard characters.

Exit Conditions: CY set if error with AX equals error code, else CY clear.

Results: If successful, FindFirst data block is created in the current DTA. First 21 bytes contain undocumented information: drive number, search template, search attribute bits, and directory and file location. First documented field (at offset 15h from start of DTA) contains file's attribute bits, followed by 16-bit file time and 16-bit file date entries, 32-bit file size, and 13-byte (maximum) filename and extension in ASCIIZ format.

Related to: Function 11h

Function 4Fh: Find Next Matching Pathspec

Entry Conditions: AH equals 4Fh, DTA must not have been altered since previous call to Function 4Eh which set it up.

Exit Conditions: CY set if error with AX equals error code, else CY clear.

Results: If another match found, DTA is set up as for Function 4Eh but with next match to search template. If no more files match the search template, error 12h is returned.

Related to: Function 12h

Function 50h: Set PID

Entry Conditions: AH equals 50h, BX equals PSP address of process to be made current.

Exit Conditions: Not significant

Results: By changing the PSP that is used by DOS operations, this undocumented function changes the significance of all file/device handles.

Related to: Functions 51h and 62h

Function 51h: Get PID

Entry Conditions: AH equals 51h.

Exit Conditions: BX equals PSP segment address of current process.

Results: This undocumented function is identical to, and uses the same code as, documented Function 62h.

Related to: Functions 50h and 62h

Function 52h: Get List of Lists

Entry Conditions: AH equals 52h

Exit Conditions: ES:BX point to DOS internal list of data tables.

Results: Full description of information that may be retrieved by use of this undocumented function is far beyond the scope of this book.

Related to: None

Function 53h: Translate BPB to DPB

Entry Conditions: AH equals 53h, DS:SI point to BIOS Parameter Block in device driver, ES:BP point to buffer big enough to accept Drive Parameter Block.

Exit Conditions: Buffer at ES:BP filled.

Results: Undocumented function used by DOS when loading block device drivers. Seldom, if ever, used in application programs.

Related to: None

Function 54h: Get Verify Flag

Entry Conditions: AH equals 54h

Exit Conditions: AL equals verify flag (0=off, 1=on).

Results: If verify flag is on, then all DOS write requests will direct the driver involved to perform post-write verification. Unfortunately in many cases this action is meaningless, and simply creates a false sense of security. Standard DOS block-device drivers, for example, "verify" write operations by repeating the CRC calculations for the sector, and verifying that this value matches that calculated in the actual write; the data written is never actually read back for verification.

Related to: Function 2Eh

Function 55h: Create Child PSP

Entry Conditions: AH equals 55h, DX equals segment at which to create PSP, SI equals value to place in memory size field.

Exit Conditions: Not significant

Results: This undocumented function is obsolete and its actions are now included within Function 4Bh.

Related to: Functions 26h and 4Bh

Function 56h: Rename File or Directory

Entry Conditions: AH equals 56h, CL equals attribute mask, DS:DX point to name of existing file in ASCIIZ format, ES:BX point to new name for file also in ASCIIZ format.

Exit Conditions: CY set if error with AX equals error code, else CY clear.

Results: Directory entry for named file is modified to reflect new name. This function may be used to move files from one subdirectory to another so long as both directories involved are on same volume (drive).

Related to: Function 17h

Function 57h: Get or Set File Date and Time

Entry Conditions: AH equals 57h, AL equals action (0=get, 1=set), BX equals handle. If setting, CX equals file time and DX equals file date.

Exit Conditions: CY set if error with AX equals error code, else CY clear. If getting and successful, CX equals file time and DX equals file date.

Results: Most significant 5 bits of CX indicate time in hours, next 6 bits indicate minutes, and lowest 5 bits indicate seconds/2. Most significant 7 bits of DX indicate year—1980, next 4 bits indicate month, and lowest 5 bits indicate day. This is same format used in directory entries themselves and by many "packed timestamp" utilities.

Related to: Functions 4Eh and 4Fh

Function 58h: Get or Set Memory Allocation Strategies

Entry Conditions: AH equals 58h, AL equals action (0=get strategy code, 1=set strategy, 2=get UMB link state, 3=set UMB link state), BX equals new value if setting.

Exit Conditions: CY set if error with AX equals error code, else CY clear. If getting, AL equals strategy code (see Chapter 7) or link state (0=UMBs not in chain, 1=UMBs in memory chain).

Results:	UMB actions apply to Version 5 and up only. To allocate memory in UMB if possible, first use function with AX=5803h and BX=1 to add UMB area to chain, then use function again with AX=5880h to specify first fit strategy trying high first, then low. Actual allocation is done by Function 48h.
Related to:	Functions 48h, 49h, and 4Ah

Function 59h: Extended Error Codes

Entry Conditions:	AH equals 59h
Exit Conditions:	AX equals extended error code, BH equals error class, BL equals recommended action, CH equals error locus, other register contents destroyed.
Results:	AX, BH, BL, and CH provide more detail about errors detected by DOS. See Chapter 12 for full explanation.
Related to:	None

Function 5Ah: Create Temporary File

Entry Conditions:	AH equals 5Ah, CX equals file attribute as for Function 43h, DS:DX point to ASCIIZ pathspec that ends with at least 13 zeroed bytes to receive generated filename.
Exit Conditions:	CY set if error with AX equals error code, else CY clear and AX equals file handle, DS:DX buffer is extended to contain name assigned to file.

Results: New file is created using specified path and is opened for read/write access in compatibility mode. File is assigned arbitrary name.

Related to: Functions 3Ch, 5Bh, and 6Ch

Function 5Bh: Create New File

Entry Conditions: AH equals 5Bh, CX equals file attribute as for Function 43h, DS:DX point to ASCIIZ pathspec that ends with name of file to be created.

Exit Conditions: CY set if error with AX equals error code, else CY clear and AX equals file handle.

Results: If named file already exists, returns error condition 50h. Otherwise, new file is created using specified path and is opened for read/write access in compatibility mode.

Related to: Functions 3Ch, 5Ah, and 6Ch

Function 5Ch: Lock or Unlock File Records

Entry Conditions: AH equals 5Ch, AL equals operation (0=lock, 1=unlock), BX equals file handle, CX:DX equals offset in bytes from start of file to beginning of area to be locked (high 16 bits in CX), and SI:DI equals length in bytes of area to be locked (high 16 bits in SI). This function requires that SHARE or a functional equivalent be active.

Exit Conditions: CY set if error with AX equals error code, else CY clear.

Results: An unlock operation must specify the same region as some previous lock operation. Locked areas become totally inaccessible to other processes.

Related to: None

Function 5Dh: Network Support

Function 5Dh provides a wide range of operations, mostly for network support, but only one of them is officially documented:

Entry Conditions: AH equals 5Dh, AL equals 0Ah, DS:SI point to structure containing information to be returned by next call to Function 59h, Get Extended Error.

Exit Conditions: Not significant

Results: Next call to Function 59h will return data from structure set by this call, rather than using the standard DOS error tables. This allows you to create your own extensions to the error reporting system.

Related to: Function 59h

Function 5Eh: Network Printer Control

Although Function 5Eh has at least six subfunctions, only three of them (`get machine name`, `get printer setup string`, and `set printer setup string`) are documented. All require that appropriate network driver software be active, else results are undefined:

Subfunction 0 gets the machine name and NetBIOS number:

Entry Conditions: AH equals 5Eh, AL equals 00h, and DS:DX point to 16-byte buffer to receive name.

Exit Conditions: CY set if error with AX equals error code, else CY clear.

Results: CH equals 0 if name valid, CL equals NetBIOS number for machine name, DS:DX buffer filled with name, blank-padded.

Related to: None

Subfunction 2 establishes a setup string for a printer specified by means of a redirection list index:

Entry Conditions: AH equals 5Eh, AL equals 02h, BX equals redirection list index, CX equals length of string, and DS:SI point to new setup string.

Exit Conditions: CY set if error with AX equals error code, else CY clear.

Results: New string is established for network printer.

Related to: None

Subfunction 3 gets a setup string for a printer specified by means of a redirection list index:

Entry Conditions: AH equals 5Eh, AL equals 03h, BX equals redirection list index, and ES:DI point to buffer to receive setup string.

Exit Conditions: CY set if error with AX equals error code, else CY clear.

Results: CX equals length of setup string, ES:DI buffer contains the string.

Related to: None

Function 5Fh: Network Redirection Support

Although at least nine subfunctions of Function 5Fh exist, only three of them (`get assign-list entry`, `make network connection`, and `delete network connection`) are documented. All require that appropriate network software be in operation to produce meaningful results.

Subfunction 2 gets a list entry:

Entry Conditions: AH equals 5Fh, AL equals 02h, BX equals list index, DS:SI point to 16-byte device name buffer, and ES:DI point to 128-byte network name buffer (subfunctions 2 and 3 only).

Exit Conditions: CY set if error with AX equals error code, else CY clear.

Results: BH equals device status (0=valid, 1=invalid), BL equals device type (3=printer, 4=disk), both buffers filled, content of DX and BP destroyed.

Related to: None

Subfunction 3 makes a connection:

Entry Conditions: AH equals 5Fh, AL equals 03h, BL equals device type (3=printer, 4=disk), CX equals user value, DS:SI point to 16-byte device name buffer, and ES:DI point to 128-byte network name buffer.

Exit Conditions: CY set if error with AX equals error code, else CY clear.

Results: Specified device is redirected to specified network name.

Related to: None

Subfunction 4 deletes a connection:

Entry Conditions: AH equals 5Fh, AL equals 04h, and DS:SI point to 16-byte device name buffer.

Exit Conditions: CY set if error with AX equals error code, else CY clear.

Results: Redirection of specified device is cancelled.

Related to: None

Function 60h: TrueName (Undocumented)

Entry Conditions: AH equals 60h, DS:SI point to ASCIIZ filename or pathspec, and ES:DI point to 128-byte buffer to receive expanded pathspec.

Exit Conditions: CY set if error with AX equals error code, else CY clear.

Results: If successful, buffer at ES:DI is filled with full pathspec in normal form (uppercase letters, effects of JOIN and SUBST included, and so on) and AH=0. Otherwise the buffer's content is unchanged.

Related to: None

Function 61h: (Obsolete)

Entry Conditions: AH equals 61h.

Exit Conditions: Not significant

Results: Not significant

Related to: None

Function 62h: Get Current PID

Entry Conditions: AH equals 62h.

Exit Conditions: BX equals segment address of "current" process' PSP, also known as the Process Identifier.

Results: This function is identical to Function 51h, and was dropped from official documentation when 51h was finally documented at Version 5.0.

Related to: Functions 50h and 51h

Function 63h: International Support (Undocumented for current versions)

This function is meaningful only in the Asian versions of MS-DOS, although the U.S. version has accepted it since Version 4.0 (and returns no error, but no meaningful data either).

Entry Conditions: AH equals 63h, AL equals subfunction (0=get lead table pointer, 1=set Hongeul input mode, 2=get Hongeul input mode), DL equals new mode for subfunction 1 (0=return only full characters, 1=return partial characters).

Exit Conditions: For subfunction 0, CY set if error with AX equals error code, else CY clear and DS:SI point to DBCS table. For subfunctions 1 and 3, AL equals status, 00h if successful, FFh if function not supported or if any error occurred.

Related to: Functions 38h, 65h, and 66h

Function 64h: Control Lookahead Flag (undocumented)

Entry Conditions: AH equals 64h, AL equals flag (0=test input before Functions 01h, 08h, and 0Ah, nonzero=do not perform input tests).

Exit Conditions: Not significant

Results: This function, called by the DOS PRINT.COM TSR code, appears to determine whether DOS should ignore certain console input request functions if input is not already waiting.

Related to: None

Function 65h: Extended Country Information

This function provides a large number of subfunctions to deal with the differences among national alphabets and usage. They may require that `NLSFUNC` be installed to provide information about countries and code pages other than that for which MS-DOS was installed on any specific system.

The first group deals with the most frequent needs encountered in localization of programs. Subfunction 01 gets general localization information in the form of a table:

Entry Conditions: AH equals 65h, AL equals 01h, BX equals CodePageID (437 for U.S.A.), CX equals size of buffer (minimum is 40 bytes), DX equals country code to get information for (001 equals U.S.A., 0FFFFh equals current country), ES:DI point to buffer to receive the information.

Exit Conditions: CY set if error with AX equals error code, else CY clear.

Results: If successful, buffer is filled with EXTCOUNTRYINFO structure described in Chapter 12.

Related to: Functions 38h, 63h, and 66h

Subfunction 02 gets a pointer to the uppercase translation table:

Entry Conditions: AH equals 65h, AL equals 02h, BX equals CodePageID (437 for U.S.A.), CX equals size of table address buffer (5 bytes), DX equals country code to get information for (001 equals U.S.A., 0FFFFh equals current country), ES:DI point to 5-byte buffer to receive the identifier (02h) and address of the actual table.

Exit Conditions: CY set if error with AX equals error code, else CY clear.

Results: If successful, address buffer is filled with address of actual translation table. The table starts with a 16-bit value that specifies the table length. The following bytes are the uppercase equivalents of the extended ASCII characters from 80h to FFh.

Related to: Functions 38h, 63h, and 66h

Subfunction 04 gets a pointer to the filename translation table:

Entry Conditions: AH equals 65h, AL equals 04h, BX equals CodePageID (437 for U.S.A.), CX equals size of table address buffer (5 bytes), DX equals country code to get information for (001 equals U.S.A., 0FFFFh equals current country), ES:DI point to 5-byte buffer to receive the identifier (04h) and address of the actual table.

Exit Conditions: CY set if error with AX equals error code, else CY clear.

Results: If successful, address buffer is filled with address of actual translation table. The table starts with a 16-bit value that specifies the table length. The following bytes are the uppercase equivalents of the extended ASCII characters from 80h to FFh to be used when translating file names, which are not the same values used when converting to normal upper case.

Related to: Functions 38h, 63h, and 66h

Subfunction 05 gets a pointer to the filename terminator table:

Entry Conditions: AH equals 65h, AL equals 05h, BX equals CodePageID (437 for U.S.A.), CX equals size of table address buffer (5 bytes), DX equals country code to get information for (001 equals U.S.A., 0FFFFh equals current country), ES:DI point to 5-byte buffer to receive the identifier (05h) and address of the actual table.

Exit Conditions: CY set if error with AX equals error code, else CY clear.

Results: If successful, address buffer is filled with address of actual translation table. The table starts with a 16-bit value that specifies the table length. The following bytes are the characters that are not valid for use in file names.

Related to: Functions 38h, 63h, and 66h

Subfunction 06 gets a pointer to the collation sequence table:

Entry Conditions: AH equals 65h, AL equals 06h, BX equals CodePageID (437 for U.S.A.), CX equals size of table address buffer (5 bytes), DX equals country code to get information for (001 equals U.S.A., 0FFFFh equals current country), ES:DI point to 5-byte buffer to receive the identifier (06h) and address of the actual table.

Exit Conditions: CY set if error with AX equals error code, else CY clear.

Results: If successful, address buffer is filled with address of actual translation table. The table is a character array of 256 elements, each of which specifies the sorting weight of the character to which it corresponds. Characters with lower sorting weights appear earlier in the collating sequence. This table is used when sorting, to allow for differences in national alphabets.

Related to: Functions 38h, 63h, and 66h

Subfunction 07 gets a pointer to the Double-Byte Character Set (DBCS) table:

Entry Conditions: AH equals 65h, AL equals 07h, BX equals CodePageID (437 for U.S.A.), CX equals size of table address buffer (5 bytes), DX equals country code to get information for (001 equals U.S.A., 0FFFFh equals current country), ES:DI point to 5-byte buffer to receive the identifier (07h) and address of the actual table.

Exit Conditions: CY set if error with AX equals error code, else CY clear.

Results: If successful, address buffer is filled with address of actual translation table. The table starts with a 16-bit value that specifies the table length. The following bytes are paired, with each pair specifying the low and high character values for a valid range of lead byte values.

Related to: Functions 38h, 63h, and 66h

The second group deals with country-dependent capitalization rules. Subfunction 20 converts a character from lowercase to uppercase:

Entry Conditions: AH equals 65h, AL equals 20h, DL equals character to be converted.

Exit Conditions: CY set if error with AX equals error code, else CY clear and DL equals converted character.

Results: If successful, character is converted to uppercase using current country information.

Related to: Functions 38h, 63h, and 66h

Subfunction 21 converts a counted string of characters to all-caps:

Entry Conditions: AH equals 65h, AL equals 21h, DS:DX point to string of characters, CX equals length of string in bytes.

Exit Conditions: CY set if error with AX equals error code, else CY clear.

Results: If successful, characters are converted to uppercase using current country information.

Related to: Functions 38h, 63h, and 66h

Subfunction 22 converts an ASCIIZ string of characters to all-caps:

Entry Conditions: AH equals 65h, AL equals 22h, DS:DX point to string of characters terminated with 00h end-of-string marker.

Exit Conditions: CY set if error with AX equals error code, else CY clear.

Results: If successful, characters are converted to uppercase using current country information.

Related to: Functions 38h, 63h, and 66h

Subfunction 23 (undocumented) determines whether a character stands for "yes" or "no" in the current language and alphabet:

Entry Conditions: AH equals 65h, AL equals 23h, DL equals character to test, DH equals second byte if applicable.

Exit Conditions: CY set if error with AX equals error code, else CY clear.

Results: If successful, AX indicates type of response: 0=no, 1=yes, 2=neither yes nor no.

Related to: Functions 38h, 63h, and 66h

Function 66h: Code Page Table

This function gets or sets the global code page. Code page values are:

437 U.S.A.

850 Multilingual (Latin I)

852 Slavic (Latin II)

860 Portugese

863 Canadian-French

865 Nordic

Before a code page can be selected for use on a device such as a printer, the device must be prepared for code-page switching. The selected code page must also be compatible with the country code specified in CONFIG.SYS.

Entry Conditions: AH equals 66h, AL equals subfunction (1=get, 2=set), if setting page, BX equals Code Page ID (per preceding table).

Exit Conditions: CY set if error with AX equals error code, else CY clear. If getting page, BX equals current user Code Page ID and DX equals current system Code Page ID.

Results: User code page is the one currently active while system code page is the one specified at system startup.

Related to: Functions 38h, 63h, and 65h

Function 67h: Set Handle Count

Entry Conditions: AH equals 67h, BX equals desired number of handles.

Exit Conditions: CY set if error with AX equals error code, else CY clear.

Results: Adjusts maximum number of handles available to current process; default value is 20. Number must be less than total number of System File Table entries created by `FILES=` line in CONFIG.SYS, and greater than 20. If less than 20 handles are requested, the default value of 20 remains in effect.

Related to: Function 46h

Function 68h: Commit File

Entry Conditions: AH equals 68h, BX equals file handle.

Exit Conditions: CY set if error with AX equals error code, else CY clear.

Results: All DOS buffers containing data for the specified file are flushed to disk in the same manner as they are when the file is closed. This action can be made automatic if the file is opened using Function 6C.

Related to: Functions 0Dh, 3Eh, 45h, 6Ah, and 6Ch

Function 69h: Get or Set Volume Serial Number

Entry Conditions: AH equals 69h, AL equals subfunction (0=get, 1=set), BL equals drive (0=current, 1=A, 2=B, 3=C, etc.), DS:DX point to Volume Serial Number buffer.

Exit Conditions: CY set if error with AX equals error code, else CY clear.

Results: If getting serial number, buffer is filled with information read from disk volume. If setting serial number, information in buffer is written to disk volume replacing original data. First two bytes of buffer are both zero, followed by 32-bit volume serial number, 11-byte volume label (`NO NAME` followed by four spaces if volume is not labelled), and 8-byte volume type string (`FAT12` or `FAT16` followed by three spaces).

Related to: Function 440Dh, minor codes 46h and 66h. Function 69h is not documented, but the identical action in Function 440Dh is. Function 69h actually sets up the register content to mimic Function 440Dh, then jumps back to the internal dispatch routine. The only advantage to using this function is that it requires less register setup in advance.

Function 6Ah: Commit File (Undocumented)

Entry Conditions: AH equals 6Ah, BX equals file handle.

Exit Conditions: CY set if error with AX equals error code, else CY clear.

Results: All DOS buffers containing data for the specified file are flushed to disk in the same manner as they are when the file is closed. This action can be made automatic if the file is opened using Function 6CH. Function 6Ah is identical to the documented Function 68h, executing exactly the same internal procedure within DOS. The reason for this function's existence is unknown.

Related to: Functions 0Dh, 3Eh, 45h, 68h, and 6Ch

Function 6Bh: Do Nothing (Undocumented)

Entry Conditions: AH equals 6Bh.

Exit Conditions: AL equals 0, CY is clear.

Results: This undocumented function was introduced at Version 4.0 for unknown reasons. With the release of Version 5.0 its original need had apparently vanished; this do-nothing dummy function appeared instead, presumably to allow any programs that had used the older function to operate without reporting errors. In both 5.0 and 6.0, this function simply executes an `XOR AL,AL` and returns.

Related to: None

Function 6Ch: Extended Open/Create

This function combines the many capabilities of the older `file create/open` routines into a single unified interface. For details refer to Chapter 9, "Disk I/O Techniques."

Entry Conditions:	AH equals 6Ch, BX equals access mode (xxx0=read-only, xxx1=write-only, xxx2=read-write, xx0x=compatibility mode, xx1x=exclusive, xx2x=deny write, xx3x=deny read, xx4x=deny none, xx8x=no inherit, 2xxx=no critical error handler, 4xxx=commit after each write), CX equals attributes (0=normal, 1=read-only, 2=hidden, 4=system, 20h=tag for archiving), DX equals action (1=fail if file does not exist, 2=if file exists replace it else fail, 10h=create new file if file does not exist), DS:SI point to ASCIIZ filespec which may include drive and path information. Access mode groups, and attribute values, may be combined via `OR` functions.
Exit Conditions:	CY set if error with AX equals error code, else CY clear and AX equals file handle, CX equals action taken (1=opened, 2=created, 3=replaced).
Results:	If successful, file is opened with requested access mode and operating conditions. Attribute values apply only if a file is created by this call and have no effect on an existing file.
Related to:	Functions 3Ch, 3Dh, 5Bh, and 68h

Other DOS Interrupts

14

MS-DOS reserves the 32 interrupt vectors in the range 20h through 3Fh for its own use, and actually employs 15 of them (including the two at 30h and 31h that are made unusable by the obsolete CP/M Dispatcher interface). One of them, Interrupt 21h, was described fully in the preceding chapter. This chapter deals with the dozen that remain, and is organized in the same fashion as in Chapter 13.

The purpose of this chapter is not to provide a detailed reference manual, but rather to serve as a rapid reminder you can use when you don't remember which register should contain a specific parameter.

Terminate Process: Interrupt 20h

Interrupt 20h, Terminate Process, was the original interface for terminating operation of a program. It remains a historical remnant, but has been superseded for most purposes by Interrupt 21h Function 4Ch, which permits the process to return an exit code to indicate success or failure.

Entry Conditions:	Undefined
Exit Conditions:	Function never returns
Results:	Current process is terminated, all open handles closed, memory released, Termination Return Address is restored from PSP pointer (see Chapter 4), and control returns to address specified by Termination Return Address (Interrupt 22h vector).
Related to:	Interrupt 21h Functions 00h and 4Ch

Termination Return Address: Interrupt 22h

The Termination Return Address provides the route back to the program that initiated the current program (in developer jargon, its parent). As the last step in completing service for Interrupt 20h, Interrupt 21h Functions 00h, 31h, or 4Ch, or Interrupt 27h, MS-DOS jumps to the termination address.

These routines always restore the vector-table entry from offset 0Ah in the current PSP before transferring control, so changes to the vector-table entry are ignored. This interrupt should never be invoked directly; its only purpose is to standardize the technique by which MS-DOS controls the flow of control between spawned processes.

Control-C Handler: Interrupt 23h

Interrupt 23h is issued automatically by MS-DOS when the Control-C character (ASCII 03h) is detected. This interrupt is invoked from only a few locations within the MS-DOS kernel code, and should never be called by a user program.

Entry Conditions:	All registers contain the values which they had upon entry to the system function in which the Control-C character was detected.
Exit Conditions:	If CY flag is set, MS-DOS terminates the program by calling Interrupt 21h Function 4Ch. If CY is clear, the system function's action starts over from the beginning.
Related to:	Interrupt 1Bh

Critical Error Handler: Interrupt 24h

Interrupt 24h (Critical Error Handler) is called from within MS-DOS system functions that read from or write to files or devices, upon detection of any error that prevents completion of an I/O action. Its default handler is the source of the infamous `Abort, Retry, Ignore?` message.

Entry Conditions:	AH = error locus, AL = drive number, DI = error value, BP:SI point to device driver header for driver that detected the error condition. Stack contains return address to system, all program registers at time system function was called, and return address to retry the failing function.
Exit Conditions:	AL = 0 to ignore error, 1 to retry failing function, 2 to exit from the program with termination type 2, and 3 to force failing function to return error code to calling program.

Results: Depend on action code returned in AL register.

If an exit code of 0 is returned in AL, MS-DOS will ignore the detected error and the system function will return with no indication that any error occurred. An exit code of 1 instructs MS-DOS to repeat the call to the failed function, from its beginning.

To terminate the program entirely, the handler can return an exit code of 2, while the final code, 3, tells the system function to report the error back to the calling program and let the program deal with it.

Absolute Disk Read: Interrupt 25h

Interrupt 25h (Absolute Disk Read), now superseded by Interrupt 21h Function 440Dh Minor Code 61h, bypasses the MS-DOS file system to read directly from one or more Logical Sector Numbers on a drive into a data buffer in RAM. It has two calling conventions, depending on whether the drive being accessed is smaller than 32 megabytes, or larger.

Following are the conventions for drives smaller than 32 megabytes:

Entry Conditions: AL = drive (and so on), DS:BX point to data buffer to receive input, CX = number of sectors to read, DX = first logical sector number to be read.

Exit Conditions: CY set if error with AX = error code, else CY clear. Note that since error indicator is returned in carry flag, the flags register pushed onto the stack by the Interrupt call is still there after returning and the calling program must adjust the stack pointer accordingly.

Results: If successful, number of sectors specified by CX is read into buffer at DS:BX, starting at LSN specified in DX. If error is indicated, AH and AL encode its type as described in the following tables.

Related to: Interrupt 26h

Following are the conventions for drives equal to or larger than 32 megabytes in size:

Entry Conditions:	AL = drive (0 = A, 1 = B, 2 = C, and so on), DS:BX point to DISKIO data structure, and CX = 0FFFFh.
Exit Conditions:	CY set if error with AX = error code, else CY clear. Note that since error indicator is returned in carry flag, the flags register pushed onto the stack by the Interrupt call is still there after returning and the calling program must adjust the stack pointer accordingly.
Results:	If successful, number of sectors specified by DISKIO structure's `diStartSector` field is read into buffer specified in structure's diBuffer field, starting at LSN specified in structure's `diStartSector` field. If error is indicated, AH and AL encode its type as described in the following tables.
Related to:	Interrupt 26

If the carry flag is set when the function returns, then the AX register is interpreted as shown in the following tables. AH and AL are interpreted as separate error codes.

AH Register Codes

Code	Meaning
80h	Attachment failed to respond
40h	Seek operation failed
20h	Controller failed
10h	Data error (bad CRC)
08h	DMA failure
04h	Requested sector not found
03h	Write-protect fault
02h	Bad address mark
01h	Bad command

AL Register Codes

Code	Meaning
00h	Write-protect error
01h	Unknown unit
02h	Drive not ready
03h	Unknown command
04h	Data error (bad CRC)
05h	Bad request structure length
06h	Seek error
07h	Unknown media type
08h	Sector not found
09h	Printer out of paper
0Ah	Write fault
0Bh	Read fault
0Ch	General failure

Absolute Disk Write: Interrupt 26h

The *Interrupt 26h* (Absolute Disk Write), now superseded by Interrupt 21h Function 440Dh Minor Code 41h, bypasses the MS-DOS file system to write directly from a data buffer in RAM to a group of consecutive Logical Sector Numbers on a drive. It has two calling conventions, depending on whether the drive being accessed is smaller than 32 megabytes, or larger.

Following are the conventions for drives smaller than 32 megabytes:

Entry Conditions: AL = drive (0 = A, 1 = B, 2 = C, and so on), DS:BX point to data buffer which contains the information to be written, CX = number of consecutive sectors to write, DX = first logical sector number to be written to.

Exit Conditions: CY set if error with AX = error code, else CY clear. Note that since error indicator is returned in carry flag, the flags register pushed onto the stack by the Interrupt call is still there after returning and the calling program must adjust the stack pointer accordingly.

Results: If successful, number of sectors specified by CX is written to disk from the buffer at DS:BX, starting at LSN specified in DX. If error is indicated, AH and AL encode its type as described in the following tables.

Related to: Interrupt 25h

Following are the conventions for drives equal to or larger than 32 megabytes in size:

Entry Conditions: AL = drive (and so on), DS:BX point to DISKIO data structure, CX = 0FFFFh.

Exit Conditions: CY set if error with AX = error code, else CY clear. Note that since error indicator is returned in carry flag, the flags register pushed onto the stack by the Interrupt call is still there after returning and the calling program must adjust the stack pointer accordingly.

Results: If successful, number of sectors specified by DISKIO structure's `diStartSector` field is written from buffer specified in structure's `diBuffer` field, starting at LSN specified in structure's `diStartSector` field. If error is indicated, AH and AL encode its type as described in the tables for Interrupt 25h.

Related to: Interrupt 25h

Terminate and Stay Resident: Interrupt 27h

This interrupt ends operation of the program that calls it, but preserves the memory area and all resources assigned to the program so that operation can be resumed later.

Entry Conditions:	CS = Segment of PSP; DX = Offset of last byte to remain resident (relative to first byte of PSP), plus 1.
Exit Conditions:	None (does not return).
Results:	Program remains in RAM with all its assigned resources but control returns to process which launched the calling program.

Idle Time: Interrupt 28h

This hook is called regularly during MS-DOS console I/O polling loops to let any programs that need to do so know that it is safe to use file operations and most other system functions above 0Ch.

Entry Conditions:	Undefined
Exit Conditions:	Undefined
Results:	Default action is to do nothing, but may be hooked by user applications and TSRs to perform any type of operation in background.
Related to:	Interrupt 2Fh Function 1680h

Fast CRT Output: Interrupt 29h

Interrupt 29h (Fast CRT Output) is called by DOS output routines when the output is directed to a device, and the device driver's attribute word has bit 3 set to 1. Although introduced to support the ANSI.SYS driver, it also is supported by the standard CON device driver built into IO.SYS.

Entry Conditions: AL = ASCII character to be displayed (CR, LF, and BEL are treated as control characters, all others are displayed).

Exit Conditions: Not significant

Results: Character is displayed on-screen and cursor is advanced to next character position. Redirection does not apply. The default service for this undocumented interrupt simply calls BIOS Interrupt 10h, Function 0Eh, TTY Output.

Related to: Interrupt 10h Function 0Eh

Network Redirector: Interrupt 2Ah

Interrupt 2Ah (Critical-Section Hook) was introduced in Version 3.1 of MS-DOS to provide protection against interference between multiple users on a networked system. Calls to this interrupt appear frequently within the internal code of MS-DOS itself. It should never be called by an application program; doing so may disrupt normal system operation.

Command.Com Hook: Interrupt 2Eh (Not Documented)

Interrupt 2Eh (Command.Com Hook) is not meant for general use. This undocumented service, used in the processing of batch files under COMMAND.COM, provides a direct entry point to reach the command interpreter's main input and parsing procedures.

Entry Conditions: DS:SI point to counted, CR-terminated command string identical to that supplied by Interrupt 21h Function 0Ah.

Exit Conditions: Returns to address pointed to by Interrupt 22h vector.

Results:	Content of buffer pointed to by DS:SI is treated as an input command and processed accordingly by the primary copy of COMMAND.COM. If any other command shell is in use, results are undefined.
Related to:	None

Multiplexing: Interrupt 2Fh

The *Multiplex Interrupt* service is an open-ended method by which any program can tie itself into the structure of MS-DOS, and has found wide acceptance by many third-party toolmakers.

The different services that connect themselves into the Multiplex Interrupt hook are distinguished by Program ID codes, passed into the service in the AH register. Codes 01 through BFh are reserved for use by MS-DOS and those from C0h through FFh are intended for third-party applications. Since the original dividing line, however, was located at 80h rather than at C0h, many third-party applications adopted codes that are now in the MS-DOS-only region, and continue to use them.

It's not possible to compile a comprehensive listing of all Program ID codes and their associated programs, because new applications continue to appear on a near-daily basis.

The most complete source of information available in this area is Ralf Brown's *The Interrupts List* which can be downloaded from the Internet and from many BBS systems. It is updated approximately four times each year, and the only cost for its use is the call or connect time involved in downloading (which may itself be significant, since the file now exceeds a megabyte in size and listed some 4,500 interrupt services in the most recent version).

This chapter attempts only to list those Program ID codes used by MS-DOS itself or by closely associated services such as network software and Windows. In addition, because many of these tend to differ significantly from one version of MS-DOS to another and not all the undocumented material from Version 6.0 has been uncovered at the time of writing, not all the undocumented codes and subfunctions appear.

PRINT.EXE (Program ID 01h)

Program ID 01h for the Multiplex Interrupt provides an interface to the resident portion of the MS-DOS print spooler (PRINT.COM). Subfunction 00h is the usual test for presence of the spooler.

Entry Conditions:	AX = 0100h
Exit Conditions:	AL = status, FFh if program is loaded, 00h if not loaded and safe to install, 01h if not present but unsafe to install.

Subfunction 01h submits a single file to the print spooler for subsequent printing.

Entry Conditions:	AX = 0101h, DS:DX point to packet address (packet contains name of file to submit, in ASCIIZ format).
Exit Conditions:	CY set if error with AX = error code as shown in following list, else CY clear.
Results:	If no error is reported, file has been added to the queue for printing. Queue operates in first-in-first-out fashion.

If the carry flag is set on return from this call, the AX register will contain one of the following error codes:

Code	Meaning
01h	Function invalid
02h	File not found
03h	Path not found
04h	Too many open files
05h	Access denied
08h	Queue full
09h	Spooler busy
0Ch	Name too long
0Fh	Drive invalid

Subfunction 02h removes one or more files from the print queue.

Entry Conditions:	AX = 0102h, DS:DX point to ASCIIZ file specification, which may contain wild card characters "?" or "*".
Exit Conditions:	CY set if error with AX = error code, else CY clear.
Results:	If no error is reported, all files matching the file specification submitted to this subfunction have been removed from the print queue.
Related to:	Subfunction 03h

If the carry flag is set on return from this call, the AX register will contain one of the following error codes:

Code	Meaning
01h	Function invalid
02h	File not found
03h	Path not found
04h	Too many open files
05h	Access denied
08h	Queue full
09h	Spooler busy
0Ch	Name too long
0Fh	Drive invalid

Subfunction 03h stops the current print job, then cancels it and all other files in the print queue.

Entry Conditions:	AX = 0103h
Exit Conditions:	Not significant
Results:	Print spooler action stops as soon as any printer buffers have emptied.
Related to:	Subfunction 02h

Subfunction 04h holds print jobs by stopping print-queue processing and returns status information to the caller.

Entry Conditions:	AX = 0104h.
Exit Conditions:	DX = error count, and DS:SI point to print queue. No error indication is defined for this subfunction for MS-DOS version 5 and later. With earlier versions, CY set if error with AX = error code, else CY clear.
Results:	Print queue processing halts until restarted by explicit command so that error count remains valid.
Related to:	Subfunction 05h

If the carry flag is set on return from this call, the AX register will contain one of the following error codes (prior to Version 5 only):

Code	Meaning
01h	Function invalid
09h	Spooler busy

Subfunction 05h ends the print hold established by subfunction 04h.

Entry Conditions:	AX = 0105h
Exit Conditions:	Not significant for MS-DOS version 5 and later. With earlier versions, CY set if error with AX = error code, else CY clear.
Results:	Print queue processing halted by Subfunction 04h resumes.
Related to:	Subfunction 04h

If the carry flag is set on return from this call (prior to Version 5 only), the AX register will contain one of the following error codes:

Code	Meaning
01h	Function invalid
09h	Spooler busy

Subfunction 06h returns a far pointer to the device driver header for the currently active printing device, and also indicates whether the print queue is empty.

Entry Conditions:	AX = 0106h
Exit Conditions:	CY is clear if queue is and with AX = 0, else CY is set and AX = 8; DS:SI point to address of device driver header in either event.
Results:	This call has no effect on print queue operation.

Critical Error Handler (Program ID 05h, Undocumented)

Program ID 05h for the Multiplex Interrupt provides an (undocumented) interface to the default MS-DOS Critical Error Handler. The subfunctions available through this capability allow a user program to override any or all the messages displayed by the handler in COMMAND.COM. Subfunction 00h is the usual test for presence of the handler.

Entry Conditions:	AX = 0500h
Exit Conditions:	AL = status, FFh if program is loaded, 00h if not loaded and safe to install, 01h if not present but unsafe to install.
Related to:	Subfunction 05h

Subfunction 05h expands an error code into a descriptive message.

Entry Conditions:	AH = 05h, AL = extended error code for versions prior to 4.0 or error type (1=extended error or 2=parameter error) and BX = error code for version 4.0 and later.
Exit Conditions:	CY set if error code cannot be converted, else CY clear and ES:DI point to descriptive message in ASCIIZ format.
Related to:	Subfunction 00h

ASSIGN.COM (Program ID 06h)

Program ID 06h for the Multiplex Interrupt provides an interface to the resident portion of the MS-DOS drive substitution TSR (ASSIGN.COM). Subfunction 00h is the usual test for presence of the TSR.

Entry Conditions:	AX = 0600h
Exit Conditions:	AL = status, FFh if program is loaded, 00h if not loaded and safe to install, 01h if not present but unsafe to install.

Undocumented subfunction 01h obtains the address of the work area used by the ASSIGN TSR when it is present.

Entry Conditions:	AX = 0601h
Exit Conditions:	AX = segment address of ASSIGN work area and drive assignment table.
Results:	The 26 bytes starting at offset 0103h within the segment addressed by AX specify which drive number will be used by references to drive letters A through Z. Initially they are set to 1, 2, 3, and so on through 26, but the values are changed by the ASSIGN command.

ASSIGN is no longer supplied with MS-DOS version 6.0, but is available on a supplemental disk.

DRIVER.SYS (Program ID 08h, Undocumented)

Program ID 08h for the Multiplex Interrupt provides an interface to the undocumented MS-DOS custom disk driver (DRIVER.SYS). Subfunction 00h is the usual test for presence of the driver.

Entry Conditions:	AX = 0800h
Exit Conditions:	AL = status, FFh if program is loaded, 00h if not loaded and safe to install, 01h if not present but unsafe to install.
Related to:	Function h

Subfunction 01h adds a new block device to the internal drive data table maintained by MS-DOS. It should not be called by applications programs.

Entry Conditions:	AX = 0801h, DS:DI point to MS-DOS drive data table located by using subfunction 03h.

Exit Conditions: Not significant
Results: Subfunction moves down internal list of drive data tables, copying and modifying "drive description flags" word for each table that references the physical drive data table just added.
Related to: Subfunction 03h

Subfunction 02h executes a device driver request.

Entry Conditions: AX = 0802h, ES:BX point to device driver request header.
Exit Conditions: Request header is updated by the requested operation. Operation code was part of request header structure.
Results: If no error is reported, requested operation has been performed.

Values for the operation code are described in Chapter 12, "Miscellaneous Functions and Structures," in the discussion of Device Driver techniques. Structure of the header is described in Chapter 4, "DOS Itself: Interrupt 21h."

Subfunction 03h gets the MS-DOS internal drive data table list.

Entry Conditions: AX = 0803h
Exit Conditions: DS:DI point to first drive data table in list.
Results: Not significant
Related to: Subfunction 01h

SHARE.EXE (Program ID 10h)

Program ID 10h for the Multiplex Interrupt provides an interface to the MS-DOS file-sharing facility (SHARE.EXE). Subfunction 00h is the usual test for presence of the facility.

Entry Conditions: AX = 1000h
Exit Conditions: AL = status, FFh if program is loaded, 00h if not loaded and safe to install, 01h if not present but unsafe to install.

Undocumented subfunction 80h, available only under MS-DOS Version 4, turns on file sharing checks.

Entry Conditions:	AX = 1080h
Exit Conditions:	AL = status, FFh if checking was already on, F0h if successful.
Results:	File sharing action is enabled.
Related to:	Subfunction 81h

In MS-DOS Version 4, SHARE performs dual functions: it supplies FCB support for large (greater than 32 megabyte) volumes, and it handles file sharing checks. The undocumented command line switch /NC can be used to disable the sharing code. This subfunction then enables it.

Undocumented subfunction 81h, available only under MS-DOS Version 4, turns off file sharing checks.

Entry Conditions:	AX = 1081h
Exit Conditions:	AL = status, FFh if checking was already off, F0h if successful.
Results:	File sharing action is disabled.
Related to:	Subfunction 80

In MS-DOS Version 4, SHARE performs dual functions: it supplies FCB support for large (greater than 32 megabyte) volumes, and it handles file sharing checks. The undocumented command line flag /NC also can be used to disable the sharing code.

Network Redirector (Program ID 11h)

Program ID 11h for the Multiplex Interrupt provides an interface to the MS-DOS Network Redirector facility. In MS-DOS Version 4, only, these calls are all in IFSFUNC.EXE, not in the Redirector. Version 5.0 moved the calls back into the Redirector. However, the same program ID code is used in all versions.

This Program ID code also was assigned to the MS CD-ROM Extensions, MSCDEX. It's possible to distinguish between the two by checking the word at the top of the stack, which will be 0DADAh if the call is intended for MSCDEX. Any other value indicates that the call is for the Redirector.

Subfunction 00h is the usual test for presence of such a facility, normally supplied as a part of network software.

Entry Conditions: AX = 1100h
Exit Conditions: AL = status, FFh if program is loaded, 00h if not loaded and safe to install, 01h if not present but unsafe to install.

The Network Redirector provides subfunctions that essentially duplicate all the normal MS-DOS file system capabilities used with local drives. The exact results of these subfunctions, however, tend to vary from one brand of network software to another. For more information about the subfunctions of the Redirector, check the latest version of The Interrupts List or refer to your network software reference manuals.

MS CD-ROM Extensions, MSCDEX (Program ID 11h)

Program ID 11h for the Multiplex Interrupt was also assigned to provide an interface to the MS CD-ROM Extensions, MSCDEX. It is distinguished from the identical call for the Network Redirector by presence of a word containing the value 0DADAh on top of the stack when dealing with MSCDEX.

Subfunction 00h is the usual test for presence of MSCDEX.

Entry Conditions: AX = 1100h, stack word = 0DADAh.
Exit Conditions: AL = status, FFh if program is loaded, 00h if not loaded and safe to install, 01h if not present but unsafe to install.
Results: Stack word is changed to 0ADADh if MSCDEX is present rather than Network Redirector.

MS-DOS Internals (Program ID 12h, Undocumented)

Program ID 12h for the Multiplex Interrupt provides an undocumented interface to the internal functions of MS-DOS. It's highly tempting to try to make use of these functions within applications, but it's also very dangerous to do so because they tend to change from one version of MS-DOS to the next and, being undocumented, you will never know the change took place.

In Version 6.0, a total of 48 subfunctions exist, numbered 00h through 2Fh. The only one safe to call, however, is the usual presence test, subfunction 00h. This always returns with the indication that MS-DOS is, in fact, present.

Entry Conditions: AX = 1200h
Exit Conditions: AL = FFh because MS-DOS is always present.

Disk Driver Hooks (Program ID 13h, Undocumented)

Program ID 13h for the Multiplex Interrupt provides an undocumented interface to the hook that MS-DOS installs on the BIOS generic disk I/O service. The internal code for MS-DOS uses this interface to determine the original vector for that service, in order to restore the vector when a system reboot is requested.

When MS-DOS first loads, IO.SYS hooks Interrupt 13h and inserts one or more filters ahead of the original handler for Interrupt 13h that was installed by ROM BIOS code.

The first such filter provides disk change detection on floppy drives, the second tracks formatting calls and corrects DMA boundary errors, and the third corrects certain problems in specific versions of certain models of ROM BIOS. These filters are installed only if needed and if the hardware supports the capabilities, but if installed, must be removed before a successful reboot can take place.

This Multiplex Interrupt function is the means by which MS-DOS installs, and later removes, the filters. Before the first call, ES:BX points at the original BIOS Interrupt 13h; DS:DX also points there unless IO.SYS has installed the third special filter for hard disk reads, in which case it points at the special filter.

Existence of this service provides a dangerous security loophole for any virus-monitoring software that fails to trap this call and verify the code it invokes, since a number of viruses are known to use it to obtain the original ROM entry point just as MS-DOS does, and then call the ROM directly to create mischief without detection by MS-DOS-based monitoring routines.

Entry Conditions: AH = 13h, DS:DX point to interrupt handler for disk driver calls on read/write, and ES:BX = address for restoration of Interrupt 13h on system halt or warm boot (Interrupt 19h).

Exit Conditions: DS:DX contains corresponding values from previous call to this function, and ES:BX contains similar values from previous invocation.

NLSFUNC.SYS (Program ID 14h)

Program ID 14h for the Multiplex Interrupt provides an interface to the NLSFUNC.SYS device driver, which is part of the National Language Support system that also includes DISPLAY.SYS and KEYB.SYS.

This Program ID code was also used in the European Version 4.0 of MS-DOS, never sold in the U.S.A., for its POPUP interface.

The only documented subfunction for this service is 00h, the usual test for presence of the driver.

Entry Conditions: AX = 1400h

Exit Conditions: AL = status, FFh if program is loaded, 00h if not loaded and safe to install, 01h if not present but unsafe to install.

Subfunction 01h is used to change code page information. It should not be called by applications.

Entry Conditions: AX = 1401h, BX = new code page, DX = country code, and DS:SI point to internal code page structure.

Exit Conditions: AL = 00h if successful, else AX = MS-DOS error code.

Results: If successful, internal structure is modified to reflect new codes passed to this call.

Related to: Interrupt 21h Function 65h

Subfunction 02h is used to get country information from the internal code page structure of MS-DOS.

Entry Conditions:	AX = 1402h, BX = code page, CX = size of user buffer, DX = country code, BP = subfunction (same as AL for Interrupt 21h Function 65h), DS:SI point to internal code page structure, and ES:DI point to user buffer.
Exit Conditions:	AL = 00h if successful, else AX = MS-DOS error code.
Results:	If successful, information is copied into user buffer.
Related to:	Subfunction 04h

Subfunction 03h is used to set country information and appears to be essentially identical to Subfunction 01h.

Entry Conditions:	AX = 1403h, BX = code page, DX = country code, and DS:SI point to internal code page structure.
Exit Conditions:	AL = 00h if successful, else AX = MS-DOS error code.
Results:	If successful, internal structure is modified to reflect new codes passed to this call.
Related to:	Subfunction 01h

Subfunction 04h is used to get country information from the internal code page structure of MS-DOS. It appears to be essentially identical to Subfunction 02h.

Entry Conditions:	AX = 1404h, BX = code page, CX = size of user buffer, DX = country code, BP = subfunction (same as AL for Interrupt 21h Function 65h), DS:SI point to internal code page structure, and ES:DI point to user buffer.
Exit Conditions:	AL = 00h if successful, else AX = MS-DOS error code.
Results:	If successful, information is copied into user buffer.
Related to:	Subfunction 02h

European MS-DOS 4 POPUP Service (Program ID 14h)

Program ID 14h for the Multiplex Interrupt is used, in the European version 4.0 of MS-DOS which was never sold in the U.S.A., for its POPUP interface.

This Program ID code also is used as the interface to the NLSFUNC.SYS device driver, which is part of the National Language Support system that also includes DISPLAY.SYS and KEYB.SYS.

The four subfunctions used by the Europe-only version are all undocumented. Subfunction 00h both tests for presence of the capability, and returns the amount of memory that its use will require.

Entry Conditions:	AX = 1400h
Exit Conditions:	AX = FFFFh if installed, BX = maximum memory required by POPUP to save screen and keyboard info.
Related to:	Functions 01h, 02h, and 03h

Subfunction 01h both opens and closes the POPUP screen, depending on the function code passed to it.

Entry Conditions:	AX = 1401h, DH = wait flag (0=block until screen opens, 1=return error if screen not available, 2=urgent, open screen right now), and DL = function (0=open, 1=close).
Exit Conditions:	CY set if error, else CY clear, and BX = amount of memory needed to save screen and keyboard information (0 if default save location can be used).
Results:	Application which was using the screen is frozen until the POPUP screen is subsequently closed.
Related to:	Subfunctions 00h, 02h, and 03h

Subfunction 02h saves the POPUP screen.

Entry Conditions:	AX = 1402h, ES:DI point to save buffer (0000:0000 to use the default buffer in POPUP).
Exit Conditions:	CY set if error with AX = error code (1=process does not own screen, 4=unknown error, or 5=invalid pointer), else CY clear.

Results: Content of screen is preserved in save buffer until restored by subsequent call to subfunction 03h.
Related to: Subfunctions 00h, 01h, and 03

Subfunction 03h restores the POPUP screen from the save buffer.

Entry Conditions: AX = 1403h, ES:DI point to buffer containing saved screen (0000:0000 to use the default buffer in POPUP).
Exit Conditions: CY set if error with AX = error code (1=process does not own screen, 4=unknown error, or 5=invalid pointer), else CY clear.
Results: Content of screen is restored from save buffer.
Related to: Subfunctions 00h, 01h, and 02h

GRAPHICS.COM (Program ID 15h)

Program ID 15h for the Multiplex Interrupt, under MS-DOS Version 4, provides an interface to GRAPHICS.COM, a TSR for using PrintScreen when the screen is in graphics rather than text mode.

This Program ID code was also assigned to the CD-ROM Extensions service and so GRAPHICS.COM was moved to Program ID code ACh at Version 5.0 of MS-DOS.

Subfunction 00h is the installation check but does not return the standard status codes.

Entry Conditions: AX = 1500h
Exit Conditions: AX = FFFFh if program is loaded, and ES:DI point to data used by the TSR.

CD-ROM Extensions, MSCDEX (Program ID 15h)

Program ID 15h for the Multiplex Interrupt, under MS-DOS Version 4, provides an interface to MSCDEX, the CD-ROM Extensions service.

In MS-DOS Version 4, this Program ID code was also assigned to GRAPHICS.COM, a TSR for using PrintScreen when the screen is in graphics rather than text mode. GRAPHICS.COM was moved to Program ID code ACh at Version 5.0 of MS-DOS.

Subfunction 00h is the installation check but does not return the standard status codes.

Entry Conditions:	AX = 1500h, BX=0000h
Exit Conditions:	BX = number of CD-ROM drive letters used, if MSCDEX is loaded, and CX = starting drive number (0=A and so on).

Subfunction 01h creates a drive device list for all devices associated with the CD-ROM driver.

Entry Conditions:	AX = 1501h, ES:BX point to buffer to hold drive letter list (5 bytes per drive letter).
Exit Conditions:	Buffer is filled, for each drive letter first byte is subunit number in driver and next four are far pointer to address of device driver header.

Subfunction 02h copies the copyright filename for a disk into a user supplied buffer.

Entry Conditions:	AX = 1502h, ES:BX point to 38-byte buffer for name of copyright file, and CX = drive number (0=A:).
Exit Conditions:	CY set if drive is not a CD-ROM and AX = error code 15 (invalid drive), else CY clear.
Results:	Buffer is filled with name of copyright file.
Related to:	Subfunction 03h

Subfunction 03h copies the abstract filename for a disk into a user supplied buffer.

Entry Conditions:	AX = 1503h, ES:BX point to 38-byte buffer for name of abstract file, and CX = drive number (0=A:).
Exit Conditions:	CY set if drive is not a CD-ROM and AX = error code 15 (invalid drive), else CY clear.
Results:	Buffer is filled with name of abstract file.
Related to:	Subfunction 02h

Subfunction 04h copies the bibliographic document filename for a disk into a user supplied buffer.

Entry Conditions:	AX = 1504h, ES:BX point to 38-byte buffer for name of bibliographic document file, and CX = drive number (0=A:).
Exit Conditions:	CY set if drive is not a CD-ROM and AX = error code 15 (invalid drive), else CY clear.
Results:	Buffer is filled with name of bibliographic document file.
Related to:	Subfunctions 02h and 03h

Subfunction 05h reads the Volume Table of Contents (VTOC) from a CD-ROM disk into a user supplied 2048-byte buffer.

Entry Conditions:	AX = 1505h, ES:BX point to 2048-byte buffer, CX = drive number (0=A:), and DX = sector index (0=first volume descriptor, 1=second, and so on).
Exit Conditions:	CY set if error with AX = error code (15=invalid drive or 21=drive not ready), else CY clear and AX = volume descriptor type (1=standard, FFh=terminator, 0=other).

Subfunction 06h turns debugging ON. This subfunction is used only when developing a CD-ROM driver.

Entry Conditions:	AX = 1506h, BX = function to enable
Exit Conditions:	Not significant

Subfunction 07h turns debugging OFF. This subfunction is used only when developing a CD-ROM driver.

Entry Conditions:	AX = 1507h, BX = function to disable
Exit Conditions:	Not significant

Subfunction 08h is used to perform an absolute disk read operation.

Entry Conditions:	AX = 1508h, ES:BX point to buffer, CX = drive number (0=A:), DX = number of sectors to read, and SI:DI = starting sector number.
Exit Conditions:	CY set if error with AX = error code (15=invalid drive, 21=not ready), else CY clear.
Related to:	Subfunction 09h

Subfunction 09h is used to perform an absolute disk write operation; however, because CD-ROM means read-only this subfunction presently does nothing.

Entry Conditions:	X = 1509h, ES:BX point to buffer, CX = drive number (0=A:), DX = number of sectors to write, and SI:DI = starting sector number.
Exit Conditions:	Not significant
Results:	None
Related to:	Subfunction 08h

Subfunction 0Ah is reserved and does nothing.

Subfunction 0Bh verifies that MSCDEX.EXE is installed and that a specified drive number is supported by it.

Entry Conditions:	AX = 150Bh, CX = drive number (0=A:).
Exit Conditions:	BX = ADADh if MSCDEX.EXE installed, and AX nonzero if specified drive supported and 0000h if not.
Related to:	Subfunction 0Dh

Subfunction 0Ch gets the version numbers for MSCDEX.EXE. Versions prior to 2.00 do not recognize this function and return zero in BX.

Entry Conditions:	AX = 150Ch
Exit Conditions:	BH = major version number and BL = minor version number.

Subfunction 0Dh copies the list of valid drive numbers into a user supplied buffer.

Entry Conditions:	AX = 150Dh, ES:BX point to buffer for drive letter list (1 byte per drive).
Exit Conditions:	Buffer is filled with drive numbers (0=A and so on). Each byte corresponds to the drive in the same position for subfunction 01h.
Related to:	Subfunctions 01h and 0Bh

Subfunction 0Eh gets or sets volume descriptor preference information into the driver. To get the existing settings, set BX to 0.

Entry Conditions: AX = 150Eh, BX = 0 to get preference, CX = drive number (0=A), and DX = 0.
Exit Conditions: CY set if error with AX = error code (1=invalid function, 15=invalid drive), else CY clear and DX = preference settings.

To modify the settings, place the new settings in DX and set BX to 1.

Entry Conditions: AX = 150Eh, BX = 1 to set preference, CX = drive number (0=A), DH = volume descriptor preference (1=primary volume descriptor, 2=supplementary volume descriptor), and DL = supplementary volume descriptor preference (1=shift-Kanji).
Exit Conditions: CY set if error with AX = error code (1=invalid function, 15=invalid drive), else CY clear and DX = preference settings.

Subfunction 0Fh gets the directory entry on the CD-ROM for a specified file.

Entry Conditions: AX = 150Fh, ES:BX point to ASCIZ path name, CH bit 0 = copy flag (0=direct copy, 1=copy to structure which removed ISO/High Sierra differences), CL = drive number (0=A:), and SI:DI point to buffer for directory entry (minimum size for direct copy is 255 bytes).
Exit Conditions: CY set if error with AX = error code, else CY clear and AX indicates disk format (0=High Sierra, 1=ISO 9660).

Subfunction 10h sends a device driver command packet to the MSCDEX driver. The packet must conform to the commands and structures described in Chapter 12, "Miscellaneous Functions and Structures."

Entry Conditions: AX = 1510h, ES:BX point to command packet header structure, and CX = CD-ROM drive letter (0 = A, 1 = B, and so on).
Exit Conditions: Command packet may be modified by the driver operation requested.
Results: Vary with driver operation requested.

Windows Hooks (Program ID 16h)

Program ID 16h for the Multiplex Interrupt provides an API for non-Windows programs (DOS device drivers, TSRs, and applications) to cooperate with multitasking Windows/386 version 2.*x* and with Windows 3.*x* enhanced mode.

While only subfunction 80h, the MS-DOS idle call, is documented in the MS-DOS Programmer's Reference for Version 5.0, many of the others are fully described in the Windows Software Development Kit. Only a few of the subfunctions for this API are described in this chapter because many apply only when developing specifically for Windows compatibility.

Subfunction 00h is the installation check that will tell whether Windows is active, and if so, which version and mode are current.

Entry Conditions: AX = 1600h

Exit Conditions: AL = 00h or 80h if neither Windows 3.*x* enhanced mode nor Windows/386 2.*x* is running; 01h if Windows/386 2.*x* is running, FFh if Windows/386 2.*x* running, and for all other values greater than or equal to 3, AL = Windows major version number and AH = Windows minor version number.

Related to: Subfunction 0Ah

Subfunction 05h notifies all routines that hook into the Multiplex Interrupt chain that Windows is initializing. Both the Windows enhanced mode loader and Microsoft's 286 DOS extender broadcast this call when initializing. Any MS-DOS device driver or TSR can monitor Interrupt 2Fh for this broadcast and return the appropriate values. If the driver or TSR returns CX not equal to 0, it also is its responsibility to display an error message.

Before processing the call, each handler must first pass it along to the previous handler for Interrupt 2Fh, with registers unchanged, so that all services have an opportunity to be informed.

Entry Conditions: AX = 1605h, ES:BX = 0000:0000, CX = 0000h, DX = flags (bit 0=0 if Windows enhanced-mode initialization, or 1 if Microsoft 286 DOS extender initialization, all other bits reserved), DS:SI = 0000:0000, and DI = version number (major in upper byte, minor in lower).

Exit Conditions: CX = 0000h if okay for Windows to load, or non-zero to prevent Windows from loading (any routine that finds CX non-zero upon returning from the chain should simply exit rather than possibly setting CX to zero while processing), ES:BX point to a startup info structure, and DS:SI point to a virtual86 mode enable/disable callback procedure or both contain zero.

Related to: Subfunctions 06h, 08h, and Multiplex Interrupt Function 4B05

Subfunction 06h is a broadcast notification, similar to Subfunction 05h, that is issued when Windows ends operation. If the initialization broadcast fails, then this notification is issued immediately.

Entry Conditions: AX = 1606h, DX = flags (bit 0=0 if Windows enhanced-mode initialization, or 1 if Microsoft 286 DOS extender initialization, all other bits reserved).

Related to: Subfunction 05h

Subfunction 07h provides a special interface to virtual device drivers and is not discussed here.

Subfunction 08h is broadcast by Windows when all installable devices have completed initialization.

Entry Conditions: AX = 1608h
Exit Conditions: Not significant
Related to: Subfunction 05h

Subfunction 09h is broadcast by Windows at the beginning of a normal exit sequence. This call does not occur in the event of a fatal system crash.

Entry Conditions: AX = 1609h
Exit Conditions: Not significant
Related to: Subfunctions 06h and 08h

Subfunction 0Ah was introduced with Windows 3.1 to identify the Windows version and type more simply that is done by subfunction 00h.

Entry Conditions:	AX = 160Ah
Exit Conditions:	AX = 0 if call is supported. In this case, BH = major version number, BL = minor version number, and CX = current mode (2=standard, 3=enhanced).
Related to:	Subfunction 00h and Function 4680h

Subfunction 0Bh, introduced with Windows 3.1, allows Windows-aware TSR programs to make themselves known to Windows. Windows will issue the call, which the TSR should intercept. If ES:DI are nonzero and do not match the TSR's own allocated communication structure, the call should be passed along the Multiplex chain. If they are zero, the TSR should allocate space for the structure, initialize it, and return the address to Windows. If nonzero and ES:DI point to the TSR's own structure, it should perform any actions defined in that structure.

Entry Conditions:	AX = 160Bh, ES:DI point to a communication structure defined in the Windows SDK or both contain 0.
Exit Conditions:	ES:DI point to communication structure to be used, supplied by the TSR.

Subfunction 80h, the only one of the subfunctions for Program ID code 16h to be described in the official MS-DOS Programmer's Reference for Version 5.0, is used by DPMI version 1.0 and later extenders and by OS/2 in addition to its use by Windows 3.0 and above. It is for use in programs which include idle loops where some routine waits for operator input, and is intended to improve the operation of multitasking systems by releasing the time slice allocated to its process each time it is called. This allows other tasks that are not waiting for input to have a larger share of the available processor time.

Entry Conditions:	AX = 1680h
Exit Conditions:	AL = 00h if the call is supported, otherwise AL is not changed.
Results:	If supported, process making the call surrenders its current time slice but does not lose its position in the multitasking queue. If not supported, has no effect.
Related to:	Interrupt 15h, Functions 1000h and 5305h

Subfunction 86h determines whether Interrupt 31h is available in order to make use of DPMI.

Entry Conditions: AX = 1686h
Exit Conditions: AX = 0000h if operating in protected mode under DPMI (Interrupt 31h is available). AX nonzero if operating in real or Virtual-86 mode or if no DPMI present (Interrupt 31h is not available).
Related to: Subfunction 87

Subfunction 87h obtains DPMI provider version information.

Entry Conditions: AX = 1687h
Exit Conditions: AX nonzero if no DPMI provider installed. Otherwise BX = flags (bit 0: 32-bit programs supported), CL = processor type (02h=80286, 03h=80386, 04h=80486), DH = DPMI major version, DL = two-digit DPMI minor version, SI = number of paragraphs of DOS extender private data, and ES:DI point to DPMI mode-switch entry point.

ANSI.SYS (Program ID 1Ah)

Program ID 1Ah for the Multiplex Interrupt provides an interface to the ANSI.SYS replacement device driver for CON, in MS-DOS version 4 and later. A number of third-party ANSI.SYS equivalent drivers also respond to this service in the same way.

The only documented subfunction for ANSI.SYS is 00h, the standard test for presence.

Entry Conditions: AX = 1A00h
Exit Conditions: AL = status, FFh if program is loaded, 00h if not loaded and safe to install, 01h if not present but unsafe to install.
Related to: Function h

Undocumented subfunction 01h gets or sets display information in the driver using its `IOCTL` interface.

Entry Conditions: AX = 1A01h, CL = 5Fh to set or 7Fh to get, DS:DX parameter block as described for IOCTL service of a character device driver in Chapter 12.
Exit Conditions: CY set if error with AX = error code, else CY clear.
Results: Parameter block may be modified by this call.
Related to: Interrupt 21h Function 440Ch minor codes 035Fh and 037Fh

Extended Memory Manager (Program ID 43h)

Program ID 43h for the Multiplex Interrupt provides an interface to any extended memory manager that conforms to XMS Version 3. HIMEM.SYS is one such manager and is furnished with MS-DOS Version 6.

This Program ID supports two documented subfunctions and two undocumented ones that were added to HIMEM.SYS in Version 2.77 (the version supplied with MS-DOS Version 6 is 3.09). Subfunction 00h tests for presence of the XMS driver but has non-standard return information.

Entry Conditions: AX = 4300h
Exit Conditions: AL = status, 80h if XMS 2.0 driver is loaded, 00h if not.

Undocumented subfunction 08h obtains information from the driver about the A20 handler currently installed.

Entry Conditions: AX = 4308h
Exit Conditions: AL = 43h if this call is supported, BH = A20 handler number, and BH = A20 switching time (0=medium, 1=fast, 2=slow).
Related to: Subfunction 30h

Documented subfunction 10h obtains a far pointer to the address at which the XMS driver should be called.

Entry Conditions: AX = 4310h

Exit Conditions: ES:BX point to driver's entry address. See Chapter 8, "Managing Time and Space," for descriptions of the functions available via this entry point. AL = 80h if external A20 handler installed, and ES:BX point to external A20 handler.

Undocumented subfunction 30h obtains the address of any external A20 handler present in the system.

Entry Conditions: AX = 4330h
Exit Conditions: AL = 80h if external A20 handler installed, and ES:BX point to external A20 handler.

DOSKEY.COM (Program ID 48h)

Program ID 48h for the Multiplex Interrupt provides an interface to the DOSKEY TSR which provides command-line history and macro capabilities to COMMAND.COM.

Subfunction 00h is the installation check but returns a non-standard indication.

Entry Conditions: AX = 4800h
Exit Conditions: AL = status, non-zero if program is loaded, unchanged if not loaded.

Subfunction 10h obtains one line of console input from either the history queue or the keyboard and places it in a user-supplied buffer.

Entry Conditions: AX = 4810h, DS:DX point to input buffer set up exactly as for Interrupt 21h Function 0Ah (see Chapter 7, "Console I/O"). First byte must be 80h or DOSKEY handler will not respond.
Exit Conditions: AX = 0000h if successful and buffer contains input from user. If macro name was put into buffer, or a special parameter, the program must immediately issue this call again to translate the input.

More MS-DOS Internals (Program ID 4Ah, Undocumented)

Program ID 4Ah for the Multiplex Interrupt provides an interface to several internal functions of MS-DOS, all undocumented. One of the most useful is subfunction 00h, which enables you to prevent the annoying `Insert disk` message when a single-floppy system is given the wrong drive letter in reference to the floppy.

Entry Conditions: AX = 4A00h, CX = 0000h, DH = old drive number, DL = new drive number.

Exit Conditions: CX = 0FFFFh if no `Insert Disk` message if desired, otherwise unchanged.

Task Switcher (Program ID 4Bh)

Program ID 4Bh for the Multiplex Interrupt provides an interface to the MS-DOS Shell's task switcher. Though documented in the official MS-DOS Programmer's Reference for Version 5.0, all its functions, except for the presence test, are omitted here because of the complexity of its requirements and the small likelihood that you will be attempting to develop a similar application.

Entry Conditions: AX = 4B00h

Exit Conditions: AL = status, FFh if program is loaded, 00h if not loaded and safe to install, 01h if not present but unsafe to install.

KEYB.COM (Program ID 0ADh)

Program ID ADh for the Multiplex Interrupt provides an undocumented interface to the DISPLAY.SYS driver and a documented interface to the KEYB.COM TSR, both parts of the National Language Support system.

Undocumented subfunction 00h is the installation check for DISPLAY.SYS.

Entry Conditions:	AX = 0AD80h
Exit Conditions:	AL = FFh if DISPLAY.SYS is installed.

Undocumented subfunction 01h sets the active code page for DISPLAY.SYS.

Entry Conditions:	AX = AD01h, BX = new code page.
Exit Conditions:	CY set if error with AX = , else CY clear and AX = 0.
Related to:	Subfunction 02h

Undocumented subfunction 02h gets the active code page for DISPLAY.SYS.

Entry Conditions:	AX = 0AD02h
Exit Conditions:	CY set if code page never set with AX = 1 and BX = FFFFh, else CY clear and BX = current code page.
Related to:	Functions 01h and 03h

Undocumented subfunction 03h gets code page information into a user supplied buffer.

Entry Conditions:	AX = 0AD03h, CX = size of buffer in bytes, and ES:DI point to buffer for code page information.
Exit Conditions:	CY set if error, else CY clear.
Results:	Buffer at ES:DI filled with code page information.
Related to:	Functions 01h and 02h

Documented subfunction 80h is the installation check for KEYB.COM.

Entry Conditions:	AX = 0AD80h
Exit Conditions:	AL = FFh if KEYB.COM installed, BH = major version number, BL = minor version number, and ES:DI point to internal data.

Documented subfunction 81h sets the keyboard code page.

Entry Conditions:	AX = 0AD81h, BX = code page
Exit Conditions:	CY set if error with AX = error code, else CY clear.
Related to:	Subfunction 82h

Documented subfunction 82h sets the keyboard mapping.

Entry Conditions: AX = 0AD82h, BL = new state (00h=US keyboard (Control-Alt-F1), FFh=foreign keyboard (Control-Alt-F2)).
Exit Conditions: CY set if error with AX = error code, else CY clear.
Related to: Subfunctions 81h and 83h

Documented subfunction 83h gets the keyboard mapping.

Entry Conditions: AX = 0AD83h
Exit Conditions: BL = new state (00h=US keyboard, FFh=foreign keyboard)
Related to: Function 82h

GRAFTABL.COM (Program ID 0B0h)

Program ID B0h for the Multiplex Interrupt provides an interface to a TSR that enables display of extended ASCII characters in graphics mode.

Entry Conditions: AX = 0B000h
Exit Conditions: AL = status, FFh if program is loaded, 00h if not loaded and safe to install, 01h if not present but unsafe to install.

APPEND.EXE (Program ID 0B7h)

Program ID B7h for the Multiplex Interrupt provides an interface to the APPEND TSR. Because there has been little standardization in networking over the years, not all networks respond correctly to this service call.

Subfunction 00h is the installation check.

Entry Conditions: AX = 0B700h
Exit Conditions: AL = status, FFh if program is loaded, 00h if not loaded and safe to install, 01h if not present but unsafe to install.

Subfunction 02h checks the version of APPEND that is installed.

Entry Conditions: AX = 0B702h
Exit Conditions: CY set if error with AX = error code, else CY clear and AX = FFFFh if Version 4 or later of APPEND installed.

Subfunction 04h gets the address of APPEND's directory path list.

Entry Conditions: AX = 0B704h
Exit Conditions: CY set if error with AX = error code, else CY clear and ES:DI = Point to active APPEND path.

Subfunction 06h gets the current value of the modes flag bits.

Entry Conditions: AX = 0B706h
Exit Conditions: CY set if error with AX = error code, else CY clear and BX contains a bitmap indicating state of the modes flag bits.
Related to: Subfunction 07h

The bitmap returned in BX has the following meaning:

Bit	Meaning if 0	Meaning if 1
15	/X switch inactive	/X switch active
14	/E switch inactive	/E switch active
13	/PATH inactive	/PATH active
0	APPEND disabled	APPEND enabled

Subfunction 07h sets the current value of the modes flag bits.

Entry Conditions: AX = 0B707h, BX = modes flag bitmap as for subfunction 06h.
Exit Conditions: CY set if error with AX = error code, else CY clear.
Results: Modes flag bits are changed.
Related to: Subfunction 06h

Subfunction 11h sets a flag that affects operation of certain MS-DOS system functions.

Entry Conditions:	AX = 0B711h
Exit Conditions:	CY set if error with AX = error code, else CY clear.
Results:	Subfunction 11h causes APPEND to modify the action of Functions 3Dh, 43h, and 6Ch of Interrupt 21h. When this function is executed, the next call to any of those functions returns the fully qualified filename, in the same buffer in which the filename was passed to the function. You must be sure that the buffer is large enough (67 bytes minimum size) to accept any possible return value.
Related to:	Interrupt 21h, Functions 3Dh, 43h, and 6Ch

The New MRCI Compression Hooks

Use of the MRCI compression interface hooks added to MS-DOS in Version 6 is described in detail in Chapter 5, "Other DOS Interrupts," and Chapter 9, "Disk Storage and the File System." The technique of using this interface is too detailed to summarize in a reference table.

BIOS Services

15

Interrupt vectors usually considered as belonging to BIOS services include the following 25, but not all of them are described in this chapter, nor are all the possible variations listed for those which are included. Only the functions and subfunctions of each that are generally available on current systems (that is, those having 80286 or later processors, and equipped with EGA or later video cards) are tabulated in the detail discussions.

INT	Name/Description
05h	Print Screen Service
08h	System Timer
09h	Keyboard Data Ready
0Ah	Vertical Retrace Notification
0Bh	COM2/COM4 Service Request
0Ch	COM1/COM3 Service Request
0Dh	Fixed Disk Notification
0Eh	Diskette Controller Notification
0Fh	Parallel Printer Notification
10h	Video Services
11h	Hardware Information
12h	Memory Size
13h	Disk Services
14h	Serial Communications
15h	System Interfaces
16h	Keyboard Services
17h	Printer Services
18h	ROM-BASIC Interface
19h	System Reboot
1Ah	Time Services
1Bh	Control-Break Hook
1Ch	Timer Hook
1Dh	Pointer to Video Parameters
1Eh	Pointer to Diskette Parameters
1Fh	Pointer to Extended Graphics Font

The eight hardware-IRQ services, Interrupts 08h through 0Fh, are omitted from the listings in this chapter because they should never be called directly by any of your applications. Some applications may have a need to hook these procedures to perform either pre- or post-processing, but the only calls to these services should be those initiated by hardware interrupt requests.

The two hook vectors, for Interrupts 1Bh and 1Ch, normally point only to an `iret` instruction unless some application hooks into them. Interrupt 1Bh is invoked from within the service routine for Interrupt 09h. Interrupt 1Ch is invoked from within the service routine for Interrupt 08h.

The three pointer vectors, for Interrupts 1Dh, 1Eh, and 1Fh, don't point to executable code at all. The first two point to tables of parameters that are used by normal BIOS services, and the last contains the address of the font patterns to be used to display extended ASCII characters in 8 by 8 graphics modes.

Video Services: Interrupt 10h

Interrupt 10h provides basic video services. In addition to the 23 functions described in the following pages, a number of private functions have been grafted into this area for enhanced operation with various types of super VGA systems. Because such private extensions vary widely from one brand of video card to the next, they are omitted from these pages.

Function 00h sets the video display mode. This clears the screen automatically unless the high bit of the AL register is set; if the automatic clear is not done, the screen content may be meaningless after the mode change, especially when switching between graphics and text modes.

Entry Conditions:	AH = 00h, AL = mode as listed in Table 15.1
Exit Conditions:	Not significant
Results:	Video system is placed in specified operating mode and all internal values adjusted as necessary. Video RAM will be cleared unless automatic clearing is disabled.

Table 15.1. Commonly available video modes.

Mode	Type	Size	Colors	Systems on which available
0	Text	40x25	2	All except MDA and Hercules
1	Text	40x25	16	All except MDA and Hercules
3	Text	80x25	16	All except MDA and Hercules
4	Graphics	320x200	4	All except MDA and Hercules
5	Graphics	320x200	4	All except MDA and Hercules
6	Graphics	640x200	2	All except MDA and Hercules
7	Text	80x25	None	MDA and Hercules
0Dh	Graphics	320x200	16	EGA, VGA, and above only
0Fh	Graphics	640x350	2	EGA, VGA, and above only
10h	Graphics	640x350	16	EGA, VGA, and above only
11h	Graphics	640x480	2	EGA, VGA, and above only
12h	Graphics	640x480	16	VGA and above only
13h	Graphics	320x200	256	MCGA, VGA, and above only

Function 01h sets the height of the cursor when in text mode (graphics modes do not display a cursor).

Entry Conditions:	AH = 01h, CH = top scanline number in range 0-32 decimal (set bit 5=1 to hide cursor), CL = bottom scanline number in same range.
Exit Conditions:	Not significant
Results:	Cursor immediately assumes specified shape, or disappears if Bit 5 of CH was set.
Related to:	Function 03h

Function 02h establishes the cursor location for the specified video page.

Entry Conditions:	AH = 02h, BH = page number (0=first page), DH = row (0 for top row), DL = column (0 for leftmost).
Exit Conditions:	Not significant
Results:	Cursor for specified page immediately moves to specified location.
Related to:	Function 03h

Function 03h returns the cursor location for the specified page, and the cursor size (which applies to all pages).

Entry Conditions:	AH = 03h, BH = page number (0=first page).
Exit Conditions:	CH = cursor size (top scanline), CL = cursor size (bottom scanline), DH = row of cursor location, DL = column of cursor location. Bit 5 of CH will be set if cursor is presently hidden.
Related to:	Functions 01h and 02h

Function 04h reads the light pen location. Not all systems support this function.

Entry Conditions:	AH = 04h
Exit Conditions:	If AH = 0, neither function is supported or light pen is not in operation, and BX, CX, DX remain unchanged. If AH = 1, status is valid and BX = pixel column, CX = scanline number, DH = text row, and DL = text column of light pen location.

Function 05h makes a specified video page active.

Entry Conditions:	AH = 05h, AL = video page to make active (0=first page).

Exit Conditions: Not significant
Results: Specified video page is displayed.
Related to: Function h

Function 06h scrolls the text screen up (toward the top).

Entry Conditions: AH = 06h, AL = number of lines to clear at bottom (0=clear all), BH = attribute to use when filling cleared lines with blanks, CH = top row of area to scroll, CL = left column of area to scroll, DH = bottom row of area to scroll, DL = right column of area to scroll.
Exit Conditions: Not significant
Results: All data on-screen scrolls upward the specified number of lines (or vanishes if AL was zero) and blanks of the specified color fill the new space at the bottom.
Related to: Function 07h

Function 07h scrolls the text screen down (toward the bottom).

Entry Conditions: AH = 07h, AL = number of lines to clear at top (0=clear all), BH = attribute to use when filling cleared lines with blanks, CH = top row of area to scroll, CL = left column of area to scroll, DH = bottom row of area to scroll, DL = right column of area to scroll.
Exit Conditions: Not significant
Results: All data on-screen scrolls downward the specified number of lines (or vanishes if AL was zero) and blanks of the specified color fill the new space at the top.
Related to: Function 06h

Function 08h returns the character and attribute at the cursor position.

Entry Conditions: AH = 08h, BH = page number (0=first page).
Exit Conditions: AH = attribute, AL = character.
Related to: Function 09h

Function 09h writes to the screen at the cursor location a single character and attribute. It can write multiple copies, however.

Entry Conditions: AH = 09h, AL = character, BH = page number (0=first page), BL = attribute (bit 7=1 to XOR with existing color), CX = Number of identical characters to write.
Exit Conditions: Not significant
Results: Specified number of copies of character in specified attribute appear on-screen, starting at present cursor location. Cursor position remains unchanged.
Related to: Function 0Ah

Function 0Ah writes to the screen at the cursor location a single character using the existing attribute. It can write multiple copies, however.

Entry Conditions: AH = 0Ah, AL = character, BH = page number (0=first page), CX = Number of same characters to write.
Exit Conditions: Not significant
Results: Specified number of copies of character appear on-screen, starting at present cursor location, with attributes unchanged from values already present on-screen. Cursor position remains unchanged.
Related to: Function 09h

Function 0Bh sets the color palette for low-resolution graphics mode and, on CGA systems, sets the overscan (border) color for text modes. To set the low resolution background and border colors, call this function as follows.

Entry Conditions: AH = 0Bh, BH = 0, BL = color for background and border use.
Exit Conditions: Not significant
Related to: Function 10h

To specify a low resolution color group this function is called as follows.

Entry Conditions: AH = 0Bh, BH = 1, BL = color group (0=green/red/brown or 1=cyan/magenta/white).
Exit Conditions: Not significant
Related to: Function 10h

Function 0Ch writes a single graphics dot to the screen at the specified location.

Entry Conditions: AH = 0Ch, AL = color (bit 7=1 to XOR with existing color), CX = pixel row, and DX = pixel column.
Exit Conditions: Not significant
Related to: Function 0Dh

Function 0Dh reads a single graphics dot from the screen at the specified location.

Entry Conditions: AH = 0Dh, CX = pixel row, and DX = pixel column.
Exit Conditions: AL = color of dot at that location.
Related to: Function 0Ch

Function 0Eh writes a single character to the screen at the current cursor location and advances the cursor afterwards. The CR, LF, BEL, and BkSp characters are executed as commands rather than being displayed.

Entry Conditions: AH = 0Eh, AL = character, and BL = color.
Exit Conditions: Not significant
Related to: Interrupt 29

Function 0Fh obtains the current video mode, screen width in text columns, and active video page.

Entry Conditions: AH = 0Fh
Exit Conditions: AH = number of columns, AL = current video mode, and BH = current active page (0=first page).
Related to: Functions 00h and 05h

Function 10h controls many aspects of EGA and VGA operation. Subfunction 00h sets a specific palette or attribute register.

Entry Conditions: AX = 1000h, BL = color register (0-15), and BH = color to set.
Exit Conditions: Not significant
Related to: Subfunctions 01h, 02h, 07h, 08h, and 09h

Subfunction 01h sets the border or overscan color.

Entry Conditions: AX = 1001h, BL = color register (0-15), and BH = color to set.
Exit Conditions: Not significant
Related to: Subfunctions 00h, 02h, 07h, 08h, and 09h

Subfunction 02h sets all 16 palette registers plus overscan from a user-supplied buffer.

Entry Conditions: AX = 1002h, ES:DX point to buffer that specifies 17 consecutive bytes which are the color values to set for colors 0 through 15, followed by one holding the color to be used for overscan.
Exit Conditions: Not significant
Related to: Subfunctions 00h, 01h, 07h, 08h, and 09h

Subfunction 03h controls background blinking in text mode (on VGA equipped systems only).

Entry Conditions: AX = 1003h, BL = blink mode (0=bright, 1=blink).
Exit Conditions: Not significant
Note: Present state of this mode is indicated by Bit 5 of the byte at 0040:0065.

Subfunction 07h reads a specific palette register.

Entry Conditions: AX = 1007h, BL = palette register to read.
Exit Conditions: BH = color in specified register.
Related to: Subfunctions 00h, 01h, 02h, 08h, and 09h

Subfunction 08h reads the overscan color.

Entry Conditions: AX = 1008h
Exit Conditions: BH = overscan value.
Related to: Subfunctions 00h, 01h, 02h, 07h, and 09h

Subfunction 09h reads all 16 palette registers plus overscan into a user supplied buffer.

Entry Conditions: AX = 1009h, ES:DX point-to buffer which receives 17 byte sequence of color values for all 16 colors and overscan.
Exit Conditions: Not significant
Related to: Subfunctions 00h, 01h, 02h, 07h, and 08h

Subfunction 10h sets the RGB values of a single DAC register.

Entry Conditions: AX = 1010h, BX = DAC register to set, CH = green value (0-63 decimal), CL= blue value (0-63 decimal), and DH = red value (0-63 decimal).

Exit Conditions: Not significant
Related to: Subfunctions 12h, 15h, and 17h

Subfunction 12h sets the RGB values of a block of consecutive DAC registers.

Entry Conditions: AX = 1012h, BX = first DAC register to set, CX = number of registers, ES:DX point to buffer containing RGB byte triplets for new values for registers.
Exit Conditions: Not significant
Related to: Subfunctions 10h, 15h, and 17h

Subfunction 13h sets DAC color page mode or selects the color page. To set the mode:

Entry Conditions: AX = 1013h, BL = 0, and BH = mode (0=4 blocks of 64 colors, 1=16 blocks of 16 colors).
Exit Conditions: Not significant
Related to: Subfunction 1Ah

To select the color page:

Entry Conditions: AX = 1013h, BL = 1, and BH = page number.
Exit Conditions: Not significant
Related to: Subfunction 1Ah

Subfunction 15h reads the RGB values of a single.

Entry Conditions: AX = 1015h, BX = DAC register to read.
Exit Conditions: CH = green value (0-63 decimal), CL= blue value (0-63 decimal), and DL = red value (0-63 decimal).
Related to: Subfunctions 10h, 12h, and 17h

Subfunction 17h copies the RGB values of a block of consecutive DAC registers into a user supplied buffer.

Entry Conditions: AX = 1017h, BX = first DAC register to get, CX = number of registers, ES:DX point to buffer to receive DAC register values.
Exit Conditions: Not significant
Related to: Subfunctions 10h, 12h, and 15h

Subfunction 1Ah gets information about the DAC color page mode and the current color page.

Entry Conditions:	AX = 101Ah
Exit Conditions:	BL = mode (0=4 blocks of 64 colors, 1=16 blocks of 16 colors), BH = page number.
Related to:	Subfunction 13h

Subfunction 1Bh converts the RGB values of a block of consecutive DAC registers to the corresponding shades of gray.

Entry Conditions:	AX = 101Bh, BX = first DAC register to get, CX = number of registers to convert.
Exit Conditions:	Not significant

Function 11h modifies fonts and display sizes for text, in both text and graphics modes, for EGA, MCGA, or VGA video systems. Subfunctions 00h through 14h work in text modes while 20h through 24h work in graphics modes. Subfunction 30h provides a pointer to a specified font table regardless of mode.

Subfunction 00h loads a user-specified font, and then initiates a video mode set for the current mode in order to recalculate internal variables for the new font.

Entry Conditions:	AX = 1100h, BH = bytes per char, BL = block in map 2 to load, CX = characters to load, DX = character offset into block for start, ES:BP point to table of font patterns.
Exit Conditions:	Not significant
Related to:	Subfunction 10h

Subfunction 01h loads the monochrome (8 by 14) character set, and then initiates a video mode set for the current mode in order to recalculate internal variables for the new font.

Entry Conditions:	AX = 1101h, BL = block to load, CX = characters to load, DX = character offset into block for start.
Exit Conditions:	Not significant
Related to:	Subfunction 11h

Subfunction 02h loads the ROM double wide (8 × 8) character set, and then initiates a video mode set for the current mode in order to recalculate internal variables for the new font.

Entry Conditions:	AX = 1102h, BL = block to load, CX = characters to load, DX = character offset into block for start.
Exit Conditions:	Not significant
Related to:	Subfunction 12h

Subfunction 03h sets a specifier that selects the block to load, and then initiates a video mode set for the current mode in order to recalculate internal variables for the new font.

Entry Conditions:	AX = 1103h, BL = block specifier (bits 0, 1, 4 = block selected by characters with attribute bit 3 clear to 0, bits 2, 3, 5 = block selected by characters with attribute bit 3 set to 1, bits 4 and 5 active only if VGA), CX = number to load, DX = character offset into block for start.
Exit Conditions:	Not significant
Related to:	Subfunction 13h

Subfunction 04h loads the 8×16 character set (VGA only), and then initiates a video mode set for the current mode in order to recalculate internal variables for the new font.

Entry Conditions:	AX = 1104h, BL = block to load, CX = characters to load, DX = character offset into block for start.
Exit Conditions:	Not significant
Related to:	Subfunction 14h

Subfunction 10h does the same as 00h, but must occur immediately after a mode set operation takes place.

Subfunction 11h does the same as 01h, but must occur immediately after a mode set operation takes place.

Subfunction 12h does the same as 02h, but must occur immediately after a mode set operation takes place.

Subfunction 13h does the same as 03h, but must occur immediately after a mode set operation takes place.

Subfunction 14h does the same as 04h, but must occur immediately after a mode set operation takes place.

Subfunction 20h sets user-defined 8x8 graphics characters into the vector for Interrupt 1Fh.

Entry Conditions: AX = 1120h, ES:BP = point to user's font patterns.
Exit Conditions: Not significant

Subfunction 21h loads user-defined graphics characters.

Entry Conditions: AX = 1121h, BL = row specifier (0=user set in DL, 1=14 rows, 2=25 rows, 3=43 rows), CX = bytes per character, DL = number of text rows if BL=0, ES:BP point to user's font patterns.
Exit Conditions: Not significant

Subfunction 22h loads the ROM 8 by 14 character set.

Entry Conditions: AX = 1122h, BL = row specifier (0=user set in DL, 1=14 rows, 2=25 rows, 3=43 rows), DL = number of text rows if BL = 0.
Exit Conditions: Not significant

Subfunction 23h loads the ROM 8×8 double wide character set.

Entry Conditions: AX = 1123h, BL = row specifier (0=user set in DL, 1=14 rows, 2=25 rows, 3=43 rows), DL = number of text rows if BL = 0.
Exit Conditions: Not significant

Subfunction 24h loads the ROM 8 by 6 character set.

Entry Conditions: AX = 1124h, BL = row specifier (0=user set in DL, 1=14 rows, 2=25 rows, 3=43 rows), DL = number of text rows if BL = 0.

Exit Conditions: Not significant

Subfunction 30h returns a far pointer to the specified font table.

Entry Conditions: AX = 1130h, BH = table specifier (0=Interrupt 1Fh, 1=Interrupt 43h, 2=8 by 14, 3=double wide, 4=double wide (top half), 5=mono 9 by 14, 6=VGA 8 by 16, 7=VGA 9 by 16).
Exit Conditions: CX = bytes per character, DL = number of text rows, and ES:BP point to specified font table.

Function 12h deals with miscellaneous video functions, using subfunctions specified in the BL register. Subfunctions 30h through 36h are for VGA only.

Subfunction 10h determines current video system characteristics.

Entry Conditions: AH = 12h, BL = 10h
Exit Conditions: BH = color mode in effect (0=color, 1=mono), BL = video RAM present (0-64K, 1=128K, 2=192K, 3=256K). CH = feature bits, CL = switch settings.

Subfunction 20h installs a print screen routine from video card's BIOS to work with EGA/VGA screen heights greater than 25 rows.

Entry Conditions: AH = 12h, BL = 20h
Exit Conditions: Not significant

Subfunction 30h sets the number of scanlines, indirectly setting the number of text rows displayed, and has no effect until the next subsequent mode change.

Entry Conditions: AH = 12h, BL = 30h, AL = number of scanlines (0=200, 1=350, 2=400).
Exit Conditions: AL = 12h if function supported.

Subfunction 31h controls loading of the default palette.

Entry Conditions: AH = 12h, BL = 31h, AL = palette load switch (0=allow loading, 1=disable loading).
Exit Conditions: AL = 12h if function supported.

Subfunction 32h controls processor access to video RAM.

Entry Conditions: AH = 12h, BL = 32h, AL = access switch (0=enable, 1=disable).
Exit Conditions: AL = 12h if function supported.

Subfunction 33h controls gray scale summing.

Entry Conditions: AH = 12h, BL = 33h, AL = summing switch (0=enable, 1=disable).
Exit Conditions: AL = 12h if function supported.

Subfunction 34h controls cursor emulation.

Entry Conditions: AH = 12h, BL = 34h, AL = emulation switch (0=enable, 1=disable).
Exit Conditions: AL = 12h if function supported.

Subfunction 35h switches between dual video displays.

Entry Conditions: AH = 12h, BL = 35h, AL = switch (0=adapter off, ES:DX point to 128-byte save state area, 1=motherboard on, 2=active video off, ES:DX point to save area, 3=inactive video on, ES:DX point to save area).
Exit Conditions: AL = 12h if function supported.

Subfunction 36h controls video refresh action.

Entry Conditions: AH = 12h, BL = 34h, AL = video refresh switch (0=enable, 1=disable).
Exit Conditions: AL = 12h if function supported.

Function 13h displays a character string on-screen, treating the CR, LF, BELL, and BS characters as operators that are acted upon rather than displayed. The four subfunctions differ only in the manner in which attributes are determined for each character in the string, and whether the cursor position is updated to be on the first character after the string at the end of the operation.

Subfunction 0 writes the string using a single attribute for all characters, and does not update the cursor position.

Entry Conditions: AX = 1300h, BH = video page (0=first), BL = attribute to be used for all, CX = number of characters, DH = starting row, DL = starting column, ES:BP point to first character of string.
Exit Conditions: Not significant

Subfunction 1 writes the string using a single attribute for all characters, and updates the cursor position.

Entry Conditions: AX = 1301h, BH = video page (0=first), BL = attribute to be used for all, CX = number of characters, DH = starting row, DL = starting column, ES:BP point to first character of string.
Exit Conditions: Not significant

Subfunction 2 writes the string using attributes embedded in the string (as alternating character and attribute bytes), and does not update the cursor position.

Entry Conditions: AX = 1302h, BH = video page (0=first), BL = attribute to be used for all, CX = number of characters, DH = starting row, DL = starting column, ES:BP point to first character of string.

Exit Conditions: Not significant

Subfunction 3 writes the string using attributes embedded in the string (as alternating character and attribute bytes), and updates the cursor position.

Entry Conditions: AX = 1303h, BH = video page (0=first), BL = attribute to be used for all, CX = number of characters, DH = starting row, DL = starting column, ES:BP point to first character of string.

Exit Conditions: Not significant

Function 1Ah, available with VGA cards only, gets or sets type codes that indicate the types of displays which are operating in the system.

Subfunction 0 gets the current display type codes.

Entry Conditions: AH = 1Ah, AL = 0.

Exit Conditions: AL = 1Ah if supported, BL = display code (Table 15.2) currently in use, BH = alternate display code.

Subfunction 1 sets the display type codes.

Entry Conditions: AH = 1Ah, AL = 1, BL = in use display code, BH = alternate display code.

Exit Conditions: AL = 1Ah if supported.

Table 15.2. Video display type codes.

Code	Display Type
0	No display
1	Monochrome adapter, monochrome display
2	CGA adapter, color display
4	EGA adapter, color display
5	EGA adapter, monochrome display
6	PGA adapter, color display
7	VGA adapter, monochrome display
8	VGA adapter, color display
0Bh	MCGA adapter, monochrome display
0Ch	MCGA adapter, color display
FFh	Display type not known

Function 1Bh provides access to additional details about the current video state for VGA-equipped systems.

Entry Conditions: AH = 00h, BX = 0, ES:DI point to 64-byte buffer to receive state information.
Exit Conditions: AL = 1Bh if function supported.
Results: Buffer filled with information.

Function 1Ch saves or restores the video state. Subfunction 0 obtains the size of buffer required to hold all state information.

Entry Conditions: AX = 1C00h
Exit Conditions: AL = 1Ch if function supported, BX = number of 64-byte blocks required to save state information.

Subfunction 1 saves the state information in a user-supplied buffer.

Entry Conditions: AX = 1C01h, ES:BX point to buffer to receive state information.
Exit Conditions: AL = 1Ch if function supported.

Subfunction 2 restores the state from the information saved earlier.

Entry Conditions: AX = 1C02h, ES:BX point to buffer containing saved state information, CX = state identifier bitmap (bit 0=video hardware, bit 1=BIOS data areas, bit 2=color registers and DAC, bits 3-15 reserved).
Exit Conditions: AL = 1Ch if function supported.

Hardware Information: Interrupt 11h

Interrupt 11h returns a bitmap indicating the system's hardware configuration, as determined during the most recent Power On Self Test (POST) operation. The POST is performed each time the system is cold-booted.

Entry Conditions: Not significant
Exit Conditions: AX = Equipment List Word (Table 15.3).

Table 15.3. Bits of equipment list word.

Bits	Meaning
0	At least one floppy disk installed (see bits 6-7)
1	80x87 coprocessor installed
2-3	Number of 16K banks of RAM on motherboard (PC only) Number of 64K banks of RAM on motherboard (XT only)
2	Pointing device installed (PS)
3	Unused (PS)
4-5	Initial video mode 00 EGA, VGA, or PGA 01 40x25 color 10 80x25 color 11 80x25 monochrome
6-7	Number of floppies installed less 1 (if bit 0 set)
8	DMA support installed (PCjr, some Tandy 1000s, 1400LT)
9-11	Number of serial ports installed
12	Game port installed
13	Serial printer attached (PCjr) Internal modem installed (PC/Convertible)
14-15	Number of parallel ports installed

Memory Size: Interrupt 12h

Interrupt 12h returns the amount of contiguous low memory available in the system, in kilobytes. It actually reports the value stored at 0040h:0013h; this value, in PC and XT models, is set from switches on the motherboard and may be incorrect. In later models, the value is counted up during POST operations and is more reliable.

Entry Conditions: Not significant

Exit Conditions: AX = kilobytes of contiguous memory starting at absolute address 00000h.

Disk Services: Interrupt 13h

The functions provided by this BIOS service apply to both floppy and fixed (hard) disks. Many of them can be achieved equally well by using the Generic IOCTL I/O commands for block devices that are discussed in Chapter 9. However, the Interrupt 13h services are still widely used and many programs continue to rely on them simply because of familiarity.

Function 00h initiates a reset of the disk controller for the specified drive, but the disk system does not react immediately. Rather, a flag is set. The next time the drive is used, the disk controller recalibrates it. That is, the controller forces the drive to pull the heads out to track 0, and to start the next I/O operation from track 0. This action causes the grinding sound sometimes heard after a disk error.

Entry Conditions: AH = 00h, DL = zero-based drive number (bit 7=0 for diskette, 1 for hard disk).

Exit Conditions: CY set if error, else CY clear. AH = result code as listed in Table 15.4.

Table 15.4. Interrupt 13h error codes.

Code	Meaning
0	Function OK
1	Invalid value passed or unsupported function
2	Cannot locate address mark
3	Floppy write protected
4	Sector not found
6	Floppy changed line on (1.2 Mb drives)
8	DMA overrun occurred
9	DMA attempted across 64K byte boundary
0Ch	Media type not found
10h	CRC read error
20h	Floppy controller failure
40h	Seek operation failed
80h	Floppy drive not ready

Function 01h reads and returns the Disk System Status from the most recent operation that used Interrupt 13h. Although this status is returned in the AH register after most other functions, Function 01h can be used to reread it if desired. It also can be used to retrieve the low-level status after any high-level disk operation has been done. You can use this function, for example, to detect a write-protected disk in the drive by testing AH for a return value of 3.

Entry Conditions: AH = 01h, DL = zero-based drive number (bit 7=0 for diskette, 1 for hard disk).

Exit Conditions: CY set if error, else CY clear. AH = result code as listed in Table 15.4.

Function 02h reads one or more sectors from the disk into memory. You must verify all input parameters, however, before you issue this call, because it performs virtually no testing for validity of the values received, and passing an invalid value to the controller can lead to unpredictable results.

When you use this function, error code 9 (DMA Boundary Error) can result if the DMA operation crosses a physical memory offset address that is (in its full 20-bit form) an exact multiple of 4096. This type of memory boundary must always correspond to a sector boundary in the disk read. If it does not, a DMA error will occur. When that happens, the program that experiences the error must move its buffers to a different memory address and try again.

Entry Conditions: AH = 02h, AL = number of sectors to read, ES:BX point to buffer to receive data, CH = starting track, CL = starting sector, DH = head number (0=head 0), DL = zero-based drive number (bit 7=0 for diskette, 1 for hard disk).

Exit Conditions: CY set if error, else CY clear. AH = result code as listed in Table 15.4.

Function 03h writes one or more sectors from memory to the disk. Like its read sectors counterpart, this function checks only the disk drive number for validity. You must check all parameters carefully before you issue this call, because an invalid value may result in serious damage to the user's file system.

Just as when reading, the DMA error code 9 (DMA Boundary Error) can result if the buffer crosses a 20-bit memory address that is a multiple of 4096.

Entry Conditions: AH = 03h, AL = number of sectors to write, ES:BX point to buffer containing data, CH = starting track, CL = starting sector, DH = head number

	(0=head 0), DL = zero-based drive number (bit 7=0 for diskette, 1 for hard disk).
Exit Conditions:	CY set if error, else CY clear. AH = result code as listed in Table 15.4.

Function 04h verifies the address fields of the specified disk sectors. No data is transferred either to or from the disk during this operation, which does not involve bit-for-bit verification of the data on the disk against the data in memory. The system reads the data in the buffer, computes its CRC (Cyclic Redundancy Check) value, and compares the computed value to that stored on the disk. If the comparison fails, the data definitely does not match what is on the disk, but a match does not guarantee that the data also matches.

This function can check the disk drive for presence of a readable disk. If the drive does not contain a disk that can be read, the function will return an error.

Entry Conditions:	AH = 04h, AL = number of sectors to compare, ES:BX = point to buffer where to compare data, CH = starting track, CL = starting sector, DH = head number (0=head 0), DL = zero-based drive number (bit 7=0 for diskette, 1 for hard disk).
Exit Conditions:	CY set if error, else CY clear. AH = result code as listed in Table 15.4, AL = number of sectors checked.

Function 05h formats an entire track for either a floppy diskette or a fixed disk, but the two kinds of format require different sets of parameters. In both cases, this function initializes the disk address fields and data sectors.

For a floppy disk track, the number of sectors per track is taken from the table pointed to by the vector for Interrupt 1Eh, which must be properly set up before this function is called.

Entry Conditions:	AH = 05h, AL = number of sectors to format, ES:BX = point to table of address fields, CH = starting track, DH = head number (0=head 0), DL = zero-based drive number (bit 7=0 for diskette, 1 for hard disk).
Exit Conditions:	CY set if error, else CY clear. AH = result code as listed in Table 15.4.
Related to:	Interrupt 1E

For a fixed disk track, Function 0Fh should be called first to initialize the sector buffer properly. Be sure to use this function with great care because it can cause permanent loss of all or any part of the disk storage on your machine.

Entry Conditions:	AH = 05h, AL = interleave value, ES:BX = point to table of address fields, CH = starting cylinder (low 8 bits, high 2 are in bits 7 and 6 of CL), DH = head number (0=head 0), DL = zero-based drive number (bit 7=0 for diskette, 1 for hard disk).
Exit Conditions:	CY set if error, else CY clear. AH = result code as listed in Table 15.4.
Related to:	Function 0Fh

Functions 06h and 07h format a single track or the entire drive, respectively, for the IBM Model XT and Portable systems only. These functions are not used with (or available on) more current machines.

Function 08h (which is not supported by all systems) allows you to obtain the characteristics of the disk in the designated drive, whether it is a floppy or a fixed disk.

Entry Conditions:	AH = 08h, DL = zero-based drive number (bit 7=0 for diskette, 1 for hard disk).
Exit Conditions:	CY set if error and status (Table 15.4) in AH, else CY clear, AX = 0, BH = 0, BL = drive type (1=360K 5.25, 2=1.2M 5.25, 3=720K 3.5, 4=1.4M 3.5), CX bits 7-6, 15-8 = number of tracks (0=1 track), CX bits 5-0 = number of sectors per track, DH = number of heads, DL = number of drives, ES:DI point to parameter table (floppies only).
Results:	May fail to indicate error even if drive specified does not exist. Value in DL at return should be checked to verify that drive number is valid.

Function 09h, which works only on fixed disks, sets the physical parameters.

Entry Conditions:	AH = 09h, DL = drive number (81h=fixed disk 1, 82h=fixed disk 2).
Exit Conditions:	CY set if error and AH = result code as listed in Table 15.4, else CY clear and AH = 0.

Results: Initialization information for the drive is taken from fixed disk parameter tables. Interrupt vector 41h points to the table for disk 1; vector 46h points to the table for disk 2. For any other disk, the function returns an `invalid command` result code in AH.

Function 0Ah reads a specified number of long sectors (standard sectors that contain four bytes of error-correcting code in addition to regular data) from a hard disk. This function, like other read/write functions, is susceptible to the DMA boundary error (AH=9).

Entry Conditions: AH = 0Ah, AL = number of sectors to read, ES:BX point to buffer to receive data, CH = track, CL = sector, DH = head, DL = drive (80h=hard disk 1, 81h=hard disk 2, and so on).

Exit Conditions: CY set if error and AH = result code as listed in Table 15.4, else CY clear and AH = 0.

Function 0Bh writes a specified number of long sectors to the hard disk. This function too is susceptible to the DMA boundary error (AH=9).

Entry Conditions: AH = 0Bh, AL = number of sectors to write, ES:BX point to buffer to receive data, CH = track, CL = sector, DH = head, DL = drive (80h=hard disk 1, 81h=hard disk 2, and so on).

Exit Conditions: CY set if error and AH = result code as listed in Table 15.4, else CY clear and AH = 0.

Function 0Ch moves the read/write heads (of a hard disk only) to a specified cylinder.

Entry Conditions: AH = 0Ch, CH = low-order cylinder number, CL = high-order cylinder number (bits 7 and 6), DH = head, DL = drive (80h=hard disk 1, 81h=hard disk 2, and so on).

Exit Conditions: CY set if error and AH = result code as listed in Table 15.4, else CY clear and AH = 0.

Function 0Dh, which works only on hard disks, resets the disk controller. It is identical to Function 00h.

Entry Conditions: AH = 0Dh, DL = drive (80h=hard disk 1, 81h=hard disk 2, and so on).

Exit Conditions: CY set if error and AH = result code as listed in Table 15.4, else CY clear and AH = 0.

Function 10h verifies that the specified hard drive is ready for use.

Entry Conditions: AH = 10h, DL = drive (80h=hard disk 1, 81h=hard disk 2, and so on).

Exit Conditions: CY set if error, else CY clear. AH = result code as listed in Table 15.4.

Function 11h recalibrates the specified hard drive, causing it to seek to cylinder 0.

Entry Conditions: AH = 11h, DL = drive (80h=hard disk 1, 81h=hard disk 2, and so on).

Exit Conditions: CY set if error, else CY clear. AH = result code as listed in Table 15.4.

Function 12h (available only on XT and PS models) performs a controller RAM diagnostic test.

Entry Conditions: AH = 12h, DL = drive (80h=hard disk 1, 81h=hard disk 2, and so on).

Exit Conditions: CY set if error, else CY clear. AH = result code as listed in Table 15.4.

Function 13h (available only on XT and PS models) performs a drive diagnostic test.

Entry Conditions: AH = 13h, DL = drive (80h=hard disk 1, 81h=hard disk 2, and so on).

Exit Conditions: CY set if error, else CY clear. AH = result code as listed in Table 15.4.

Function 14h performs controller internal diagnostics.

Entry Conditions: AH = 14h, DL = drive (80h=hard disk 1, 81h=hard disk 2, and so on).

Exit Conditions: CY set if error, else CY clear. AH = result code as listed in Table 15.4.

Function 15h (not supported by all systems) determines the DASD (Direct Access Storage Device) type. For hard disks it also reports disk capacity in sectors, and for floppies can determine whether Function 16h can be used to tell if the diskette has been changed since the last access.

Entry Conditions: AH = 15h, DL = zero-based drive number (bit 7=0 for diskette, 1 for hard disk).

Exit Conditions: CY set if error and AH = result code as listed in Table 15.4, else CY clear and AH = drive type (0=specified drive does not exist, 1=floppy disk, change line not available, 2=floppy disk, change line available, 3=hard disk). If hard disk, CX = high word of number of sectors and DX = low word of number of sectors.

Function 16h (not supported by all systems) checks a floppy drive for disk-changed status. Before calling this function, Function 15h should be used to verify that the disk-change status line is supported by the specified drive.

Entry Conditions: AH = 16h, DL = zero-based drive number (bit 7=0 for diskette, 1 for hard disk).

Exit Conditions: CY set if error or diskette changed and AH = result code as listed in Table 15.4 (code 6 indicates disk change), else CY clear and AH = 0.

Function 17h specifies the media type to use when formatting a floppy diskette.

Entry Conditions: AH = 17h, AL = format type (1=320/360K in 360K drive, 2=360K in 1.2M drive, 3=1.2M in 1.2M drive, 4=720K in 720K drive), DL = zero-based drive number (bit 7 must be 0 since this applies only to floppy diskettes).

Exit Conditions: CY set if error, else CY clear. AH = result code as listed in Table 15.4.

Function 18h (not supported by all systems) prepares for formatting a disk.

Entry Conditions: AH = 18h, CX bits 7-6, 15-8=number of tracks (0=1 track), CL bits 5-0=number of sectors per track, DL = zero-based drive number (bit 7=0 for diskette, 1 for hard disk).

Exit Conditions: CY set if error, else CY clear. AH = result code as listed in Table 15.4. ES:DI point to drive parameter table.

Serial Communications: Interrupt 14h

Most practical applications that need serial communications provide their own interrupt-driven I/O rather than using the primitive polled interface that is built into the BIOS, but the BIOS functions are still useful for initializing the port.

Only the first four functions were available in BIOS with the original systems; the remainder were added with the advent of the 80286 processor designs and the 101-key enhanced keyboard that accompanied it to market.

Function 00h initializes the addressed serial port, establishing its bit rate, parity, number of stop bits, and data word length.

Entry Conditions:	AH = 00h, AL = port parameters (see Table 15.5), DX = port number (00h-03h).
Exit Conditions:	AH = port status (Table 15.6), AL = modem status (Table 15.7).
Results:	Specified serial port is initialized to parameters supplied.

Parameters for the port are passed as a bitmap in the AL register. Significance of these bits is listed in Table 15.5.

Table 15.5. Communications Port Initialization parameters.

Bits	Meaning
7-5	Data rate in bits per second 000 = 110 001 = 150 010 = 300 011 = 600 100 = 1200 101 = 2400 110 = 4800 111 = 9600
4-3	Parity (00 or 10=none, 01=odd, 11=even)
2	Stop bits (set=2, clear=1)
1-0	Data bits (00=5, 01=6, 10=7, 11=8)

Port status is returned as a bitmap. Significance of each bit is listed in Table 15.6. Note that some bits indicate a "normal" condition while others indicate detection of errors or exception conditions.

Table 15.6. Communications Port Status.

Bit	Meaning
7	Timeout detected
6	Transmit shift register is empty
5	Transmit holding register is empty
4	Break detected
3	Framing error detected
2	Parity error detected
1	Overrun error detected
0	Receive data is ready

Like the Port status, Modem status also is returned as a bitmap. The upper four bits of this 8-bit return indicate the level of the associated signal line, while the lower four bits indicate that a change in level of the associated line has occurred since the previous report. Table 15.7 lists the lines associated with each bit.

Table 15.7. Communications Modem Status.

Bit	Meaning
7	Carrier detected
6	Ring Indicator
5	Data Set Ready
4	Clear To Send
3	Carrier change detected
2	Trailing edge of Ring Indicator
1	Data Set Ready change detected
0	Clear To Send change detected

Function 01h places a character into the transmitter holding register of the addressed port, from where it will be transferred automatically to the transmitter shift register and sent as soon as the character presently going out is finished. If no character is being sent, the transfer occurs immediately.

Entry Conditions:	AH = 01h, AL = character to write, DX = port number (00h-03h).
Exit Conditions:	AH bit 7 set on error or clear if successful, bits 6-0 = port status (Table 15.6).
Related to:	Function 02h

Function 02h waits for a character to become available in the receive data register of the addressed port, and then returns that character. In many BIOSs, this function times out if the Data Set Ready (Modem status register bit 5) condition is false, even when Function 03h shows data in the receive register.

Because of this, and also because Function 02h does not permit the system to do other processing in the relatively long intervals between receipt of incoming serial characters, most network and serial-port drivers replace this function with interrupt-driven routines that automatically buffer incoming characters while the system performs other tasks.

Entry Conditions:	AH = 02h, DX = port number (00h-03h).
Exit Conditions:	AH = port status (Table 15.6), AL = received character if AH bit 7 clear.
Related to:	Function 01h

Function 03h returns both the Port status and the Modem status of the addressed serial port.

Entry Conditions:	AH = 03h, DX = port number (00h-03h).
Exit Conditions:	AH = port status (Table 15.6), AL = modem status (Table 15.7).

Function 04h, first made available on the short-lived IBM Convertible line and subsequently on all later models, extends the initialization capability provided by Function 00h to allow control of response to BREAK signals, and to permit a higher maximum bit rate.

Entry Conditions:	AH = 04h, AL = break status (0=break, 1=no break), BH = parity (0=no parity, 1=odd parity, 2=even parity, 3=stick parity odd, 4=stick parity even), BL = number of stop bits (0=one stop bit, 1=two stop bits or 1.5 if 5-bit word length), CH = word length (0=5 bits, 1=6 bits, 2=7 bits, 3=8 bits), CL = rate in BPS (0=110, 1=150, 2=300, 3=600, 4=1200, 5=2400, 6=4800, 7=9600, 8=19200), DX = port number.

Exit Conditions:	AX = Port status (see Table 15.6)
Related to:	Function 00h

Function 05h, first made available on the short-lived IBM Convertible line and subsequently on all later models, allows control of the Modem Control Register within the addressed serial port. Subfunction 00h reads the port's modem control register.

Entry Conditions:	AH = 0500h, DX = port number (00h-03h).
Exit Conditions:	AH = port status (Table 15.6), BL = modem control register (bit 0=data terminal ready, bit 1=request to send, bit 2=OUT1, bit 3=OUT2, bit 4=LOOP, bits 5-7 reserved).
Related to:	Function 00h

Subfunction 01h writes the port's modem control register.

Entry Conditions:	AX = 0501h, BL = modem control register (bit 0=data terminal ready, bit 1=request to send, bit 2=OUT1, bit 3=OUT2, bit 4=LOOP, bits 5-7 reserved), DX = port number (00h-03h).
Exit Conditions:	AH = port status (Table 15.6), AL = modem status (see Table 15.7).
Results:	MCR's content is changed, which may greatly impact port's capability to communicate.
Related to:	Function 00h

System Interfaces: Interrupt 15h

Interrupt 15h was originally assigned to the cassette tape interface supplied with the original IBM PC in 1981. This feature was never widely-used, and as diskette storage grew in popularity became virtually completely obsolete. (Although the original tape functions remain in the newest BIOS chips for full capability, they remain ignored.)

Consequently, when it became necessary to find vectors for use by many new features not anticipated in the original PC design, this one was a logical choice. Today, nearly all the possible function numbers associated with this interrupt are in use, either by official system functions or by third-party extensions.

One of the first official functions added was the support of TopView, IBM's original effort at providing multi-tasking capability for the PC line. While TopView never became popular, third-party equivalents of it (notably DesqView from Quarterdeck Office Systems) are widely used, and they have kept the TopView assignments (Functions 10h, 11h, and 12h, together with several others) alive.

The next major official functions added came with the introduction of the PC-AT model 339 and its successors. Function 4Fh provides a method for programs to hook into BIOS code for Keyboard Interrupt 09h, and to prevent the normal code from processing any undesired keystrokes.

Interrupt 09h calls this function before examining any scan code read from the keyboard. Therefore, Function 4Fh can rearrange the keyboard, swapping the CapsLock and Control keys, for example. It also can cause any keystroke, or combination of them, to be ignored, thus removing the user's ability to warm-boot the system.

Entry Conditions:	AH = 4Fh, AL = hardware scan code, CY flag is set.
Exit Conditions:	AL = scancode for Interrupt 09h to process and CY still set, if keystroke is to be passed to Interrupt 09h. If CY flag cleared, Interrupt 09h ignores the keystroke.
Related to:	Interrupt 09h and Interrupt 15h Function C0h

Function 85h provides a hook to monitor SysReq Key activity. This function is called by the keyboard decode routine within Interrupt 09h.

Entry Conditions:	AH = 85h, AL = SysReq key state (0=pressed, 1=released), CY flag clear.
Exit Conditions:	CY flag clear if successful and AH = 00h; CY flag set on error.
Results:	The default handler returns successfully after doing nothing; programs which monitor the SysReq key must hook this call and may return status to indicate their actions.
Related to:	Interrupt 09h

Function C0h returns a far pointer to a configuration table provided by most recent systems, or else indicates that the call failed.

Entry Conditions: AH = C0h
Exit Conditions: CY set if error, else CY clear. AH = status (00h=success, 86h=unsupported function), ES:BX point to ROM table (see Table 15.8).

Table 15.8. Format of ROM configuration table.

Offset	Description
00h	Number of bytes which follow
02h	Model of system
03h	Submodel
04h	BIOS revision: 0 for first release, 1 for 2nd, and so on
05h	Feature byte 1.
	Bit 7 = DMA channel 3 is used by hard disk BIOS
	Bit 6 = 2nd 8259 is installed
	Bit 5 = Real-Time Clock is installed
	Bit 4 = Interrupt 15 Function 4Fh is called by Interrupt 09h
	Bit 3 = wait for external event is supported
	Bit 2 = extended BIOS area is supported
	Bit 1 = bus is Micro Channel rather than ISA
	Bit 0 reserved
06h	Feature byte 2.
	Bit 6 = Interrupt 16 Function 09h is supported
07h	Feature byte 3: reserved
08h	Feature byte 4: reserved
09h	Feature byte 5: reserved

Function C1h returns the segment address of the extended-BIOS data area.

Entry Conditions: AH = C1h
Exit Conditions: CY set if error, else CY clear. ES = segment of data area.

Function C2h interfaces to the pointing device (usually a mouse) on later model systems. Seven subfunctions find frequent use. All, however, are called automatically by the mouse driver (Interrupt 33h) when necessary and never need be called by your applications.

Subfunction 00h enables or disables the interface.

Entry Conditions: AX = C200h, BH = switch (0=disable, 1=enable).
Exit Conditions: CY set if error, else CY clear. AH = status (0=successful, 1=invalid function, 2=invalid input, 3=interface error, 4=need to resend, 5=no device handler installed).

Subfunction 01h resets the interface.

Entry Conditions: AH = C201h
Exit Conditions: CY set if error and AH = status (0=successful, 1=invalid function, 2=invalid input, 3=interface error, 4=need to resend, 5=no device handler installed), else CY clear and BH = device ID.
Related to: Interrupt 33h Function 0000h

Subfunction 02h establishes the sampling rate for the interface.

Entry Conditions: AX = C202h, BH = sampling rate (0=10 times per second, 1=20/second, 2=40/second, 3=60/second, 4=80/second, 5=100/second, 6=200/second).
Exit Conditions: CY set if error, else CY clear. AH = status (0=successful, 1=invalid function, 2=invalid input, 3=interface error, 4=need to resend, 5=no device handler installed).
Related to: Interrupt 33, Function 001Ch

Subfunction 03h establishes the count resolution for the interface.

Entry Conditions: AX = C203h, BH = resolution (0=one count per mm, 1=two counts per mm, 2=four counts per mm, 3=eight counts per mm).

Exit Conditions: CY set if error, else CY clear. AH = status (0=successful, 1=invalid function, 2=invalid input, 3=interface error, 4=need to resend, 5=no device handler installed).

Subfunction 04h determines what type of pointing device is present.

Entry Conditions: AX = C204h
Exit Conditions: CY set if error and AH = status (0=successful, 1=invalid function, 2=invalid input, 3=interface error, 4=need to resend, 5=no device handler installed), else CY clear and BH = device ID.

Subfunction 05h initializes the BIOS interface.

Entry Conditions: AX = C205h, BH = data package size (1-8 bytes).
Exit Conditions: CY set if error, else CY clear. AH = status (0=successful, 1=invalid function, 2=invalid input, 3=interface error, 4=need to resend, 5=no device handler installed).
Related to: Subfunction 01h

Subfunction 06h obtains status for, and controls the scaling factor used by, the device. Setting BH to 00h causes this subfunction to return device status.

Entry Conditions: AX = C206h, BH = 00h
Exit Conditions: CY set if error and AH = error status (0=successful, 1=invalid function, 2=invalid input, 3=interface error, 4=need to resend, 5=no device handler installed), else CY clear and BL = device status (bit 0=right button pressed, bit 1=reserved, bit 2=left button pressed, bit 3=reserved, bit 4=0 if 1:1 scaling, 1 if 2:1 scaling, bit 5=device enabled, bit 6=0 if stream mode, 1 if remote mode, bit 7=reserved), CL = resolution (0=one count per mm, 1=two counts per mm, 2=four counts per mm, 3=eight counts per mm), DL = sample rate, reports per second.

If BH is set to 1, the scaling factor is set to 1:1.

Entry Conditions: AX = C206h, BH = 01h

Exit Conditions: CY set if error and AH = status (0=successful, 1=invalid function, 2=invalid input, 3=interface error, 4=need to resend, 5=no device handler installed), else CY clear.

If BH is set to 2, the scaling factor is set to 2:1.

Entry Conditions: AX = C206h, BH = 02h
Exit Conditions: CY set if error and AH = status (0=successful, 1=invalid function, 2=invalid input, 3=interface error, 4=need to resend, 5=no device handler installed), else CY clear.

Subfunction 07h establishes the address of a user supplied handler routine for the device.

Entry Conditions: AX = C207h, ES:BX point to user device handler.
Exit Conditions: CY set if error and AH = status (0=successful, 1=invalid function, 2=invalid input, 3=interface error, 4=need to resend, 5=no device handler installed), else CY clear.

Keyboard Services: Interrupt 16h

The BIOS services for the keyboard provided by Interrupt 16h are widely used although MS-DOS makes similar services available (see Chapter 7, "Console I/O," and Chapter 13, "Interrupt 21h: The DOS Interface"). Not all of those listed here are available in all systems; BIOS chips created before the introduction of the 101-key enhanced keyboard often fail to provide support for any functions other than the first three.

Function 00h is the normal BIOS keyboard interface; it waits for a keystroke to become available, and then returns it in both BIOS scancode and ASCII form. The scancode is usually, but not always, the same as the hardware scancode; it is the same for ASCII keystrokes and most unshifted special keys (such as function keys, arrow keys, and so on), but differs for shifted special keys. If an extended keyboard is being used, this function discards any of the extended keystrokes, returning only when a nonextended keystroke is available.

Entry Conditions:	AH = 00h
Exit Conditions:	AH = BIOS scancode, AL = ASCII character (0 if no ASCII character exists, as for function and cursor keys).
Related to:	Functions 01h, 05h, and 10h

Function 01h checks for the availability of a keystroke.

Entry Conditions:	AH = 01h
Exit Conditions:	Z flag is clear if keystroke available, and AH = BIOS scancode, AL = ASCII character, else Z flag is set.
Results:	If a keystroke is present, it is not removed from the keyboard buffer; however, any extended keystrokes (those which are not compatible with 83/84-key keyboards) are removed from the buffer and thus discarded in the process of checking whether a non-extended keystroke is available.
Related to:	Functions 00h and 11h

Function 02h returns the standard shift flags status as a bitmap.

Entry Conditions:	AH = 02h
Exit Conditions:	AL = shift flags (Table 15.9).
Related to:	Function 12h

Table 15.9. Shift Flag Status.

Bit	Meaning
7	Insert active
6	CapsLock active
5	NumLock active
4	ScrollLock active
3	Alt key pressed (either Alt on 101/102-key keyboards)
2	Ctrl key pressed (either Ctrl on 101/102-key keyboards)
1	Left shift key pressed
0	Right shift key pressed

Function 03h (not present on all systems) sets typematic rate and delay values. Use Function 09h to determine whether its subfunctions are available on your system. Subfunction 05h sets the repeat rate and delay.

Entry Conditions: AH = 03h, AL = 05h, BH = delay value (0=250ms, 1=500ms, 2=750ms, 3=1sec), and BL = repeat rate (0=30 per second (fastest), 12=10 per second (default), 31=2 per second(slowest)).
Exit Conditions: Not significant

Subfunction 06h (available only on newer PS/2s) gets the repeat rate and delay.

Entry Conditions: AH = 03h, AL = 06h
Exit Conditions: BH = delay value (0=250ms, 1=500ms, 2=750ms, 3=1sec) and BL = repeat rate (0=30 per second (fastest), 12=10 per second (default), 31=2 per second(slowest)).

Function 05h (available only in BIOS code that supports the 101-key enhanced keyboard fully) stores a keystroke in the keyboard buffer.

Entry Conditions: AH = 05h, CH = scancode, CL = ASCII character.
Exit Conditions: AL = 00h if successful or 01h if keyboard buffer is full.
Results: Character and scancode are stored in buffer. This function often is used to test whether extended keyboard support is available, by placing an "impossible" combination such as 0FFFFh in the buffer, and then checking to see if it arrived.
Related to: Function 00h

Function 09h returns keyboard functionality as a bitmap. This information is available only if bit 6 of the second feature byte returned by Interrupt 15h Function C0h is set.

Entry Conditions: AH = 09h
Exit Conditions: AL = keyboard functions bitmap (bit 4=Function 0Ah is supported, bit 3=Function 0306h is supported, bit 2=Function 0305h is supported, bit 1=Function 0304h is supported, bit 0=Function 0300h is supported).
Related to: Functions 03h and 0Ah

Function 0Ah can be used, if supported, to obtain the keyboard ID value. Use Function 09h first, to determine whether this function is supported.

Entry Conditions:	0Ah
Exit Conditions:	BX = keyboard ID
Related to:	Function 09h

Function 10h (available only in BIOS code that supports the 101-key enhanced keyboard fully) is identical to Function 00h except that it responds to all enhanced keystrokes in addition to those available via Function 00h

Entry Conditions:	AH = 10h
Exit Conditions:	AH = scancode, AL = ASCII character.
Results:	If no keystroke is available, this function waits until one is placed in the keyboard buffer. Unlike Function 01h, extended keystrokes are not discarded.
Related to:	Functions 00h and 11h

Function 11h (available only in BIOS code that supports the 101-key enhanced keyboard fully) is identical to Function 01h except that it responds to all enhanced keystrokes in addition to those available via Function 01h.

Entry Conditions:	AH = 11h
Exit Conditions:	Z flag set if no keystroke available, else Z flag clear and AH = scancode, AL = ASCII character.
Results:	If keystroke is available, it is not removed from the keyboard buffer. Unlike Function 01h, extended keystrokes are not discarded.
Related to:	Functions 01h and 10h

Function 12h (available only in BIOS code that supports the 101-key enhanced keyboard fully) obtains both the normal shift flags bitmap (as does Function 02h) and the extended shift flags bitmap.

Entry Conditions:	AH = 12h
Exit Conditions:	AL = shift flags (Table 15.9), AH = extended shift flags (Table 15.10).
Related to:	Function 02h

Table 15.10. Extended Shift Flags Status.

Bit	Meaning
7	SysReq key pressed
6	CapsLock pressed
5	NumLock pressed
4	ScrollLock pressed
3	Right Alt key pressed
2	Right Ctrl key pressed
1	Left Alt key pressed
0	Left Ctrl key pressed

Printer Service: Interrupt 17h

The three functions of Interrupt 17h often are used to send output to the printer. Note, however, that they bypass many of the printer control features made available by MS-DOS (although PRINT.COM is aware of, and traps into, this interrupt service).

Function 00h writes a single character to the specified printer port.

Entry Conditions: AH = 00h, AL = character to write, DX = printer number (00h-02h).

Exit Conditions: AH = printer status (Table 15.11).

Table 15.11. Printer Status.

Bit	Meaning
7	Not busy
6	Acknowledge
5	Out of paper
4	Selected
3	I/O error
2	Used
1	Unused
0	Timeout

Function 01h initializes the specified printer port.

Entry Conditions: AH = 01h, DX = printer number (00h-02h).
Exit Conditions: AH = printer status (see Table 15.11).
Related to: Function 02h

Function 03h returns the status for the specified printer port. Not all printers return correct status information to the port, so this information cannot always be considered trustworthy.

Entry Conditions: AH = 02h, DX = printer number (00h-02h).
Exit Conditions: AH = printer status (Table 15.11).
Related to: Function 01h

ROM-BASIC Interface: Interrupt 18h

Only genuine IBM PCs contain BASIC in ROM, so the action of this interrupt is unpredictable for non-IBM equipment. It sometimes reboots the system, but frequently has no effect at all.

Entry Conditions: Not significant
Exit Conditions: Not significant

System Reboot: Interrupt 19h

Interrupt 19h is intended to reboot the system without clearing memory or restoring interrupt vectors. Because interrupt vectors are left unchanged and may point into RAM that is no longer valid, this interrupt usually causes a system hang if any TSRs have hooked vectors, particularly Interrupt 08h.

Entry Conditions: Not significant
Exit Conditions: Never returns

Time Services: Interrupt 1Ah

Interrupt 1Ah provides time and date services, both from the BIOS-maintained real-time clock counter that is derived from the CPU's clock signal, and from the hardware-maintained clock-calendar provided in 80286 and later systems.

Function 00h gets the system time from the real-time clock, in clock ticks since midnight. Clock ticks occur at approximately 18.2 per second, 1800B0h in 24 hours.

Entry Conditions: AH = 00h
Exit Conditions: AL = midnight flag (nonzero if midnight passed since time last read), CX:DX = number of clock ticks since midnight.
Results: IBM and many clone BIOSs set the flag for AL rather than incrementing it, leading to loss of a day if two consecutive midnights pass without a request for the time.
Related to: Functions 01h and 02h

Function 01h sets the system time for the real-time clock, in clock ticks since midnight. Clock ticks occur at approximately 18.2 per second, 1800B0h in 24 hours.

Entry Conditions: AH = 01h, CX:DX = number of clock ticks since midnight.
Exit Conditions: Not significant
Related to: Functions 00h and 03h

Function 02h (not available on all systems) gets the time in BCD from the hardware clock-calendar.

Entry Conditions: AH = 02h, CH = hour (BCD), CL = minutes (BCD), DH = seconds (BCD), DL = daylight savings flag (00h standard time, 01h daylight time).
Exit Conditions: CY set if error (clock stopped or in midst of updating), else CY clear.
Related to: Function 00h

Function 03h (not available on all systems) sets the time for the hardware clock-calendar in BCD.

Entry Conditions:	AH = 03h, CH = hour (BCD), CL = minutes (BCD), DH = seconds (BCD), DL = daylight savings flag (00h standard time, 01h daylight time).
Exit Conditions:	CY set if error (clock stopped or in midst of updating), else CY clear.
Related to:	Function 01h

Function 04h (not available on all systems) gets the time in BCD from the hardware clock-calendar.

Entry Conditions:	AH = 04h
Exit Conditions:	CY set if error, else CY clear, CH = century (BCD), CL = year (BCD), DH = month (BCD), and DL = day (BCD).
Related to:	Functions 02h and 05h

Function 05h (not available on all systems) sets the time for the hardware clock-calendar in BCD.

Entry Conditions:	AH = 05h, CH = century (BCD), CL = year (BCD), DH = month (BCD), and DL = day (BCD)
Exit Conditions:	Not significant
Related to:	Function 04h

Function 06h (not available on all systems) sets the time for the hardware clock-calendar's alarm feature. The alarm, when set and enabled, occurs every 24 hours until turned off, invoking Interrupt 4Ah each time it fires.

Entry Conditions:	AH = 06h, CH = hour (BCD), CL = minutes (BCD), DH = seconds (BCD).
Exit Conditions:	CY set if error (alarm already set or clock stopped for update), else CY clear.
Related to:	Function 07h

Function 07h (not available on all systems) sets the time for the hardware clock-calendar's alarm feature. This function does not disable the real-time clock's IRQ, only the alarm action.

Entry Conditions:	AH = 07h
Exit Conditions:	Not significant
Results:	Alarm action is disabled
Related to:	Function 06h

Function 08h (available only on some IBM models) sets the time for RTC-activated Power ON mode.

Entry Conditions: AH = 08h, CH = hours in BCD, CL = minutes in BCD, DH = seconds in BCD.
Exit Conditions: Not significant
Related to: Function 09h

Function 09h (available only on some IBM models) reads the time and status for RTC-activated Power ON mode.

Entry Conditions: AH = 09h
Exit Conditions: CH = hours in BCD, CL = minutes in BCD, DH = seconds in BCD, and DL = alarm status (00h alarm not enabled, 01h alarm enabled but will not power up system, 02h alarm will power up system).
Related to: Function 08h

Function 0Ah reads the count of days since January 1, 1980 from the real-time clock counters.

Entry Conditions: AH = 0Ah
Exit Conditions: CY set if error, else CY clear and CX = count of days since January 1, 1980.
Related to: Functions 04h and 0Bh

Function 0Bh sets the count of days since January 1, 1980 into the real-time clock counters.

Entry Conditions: AH = 0Bh, CX = count of days since January 1, 1980.
Exit Conditions: CY set if error, else CY clear.
Related to: Functions 05h and 0Ah

Index

Symbols

A

B

C

D

E

F

G

H

I

J-K

L

M

N

O

P

Q-R

S

T

U

V

W

X

Book ISBN 0-672-30291-8

What's on the Disk

- Complete source code for the author's example programs
- The latest shareware version of *4DOS* from JP Software, updated for DOS 6
- Turbo Power Software's *TRS Utilities*

Installing the Floppy Disk

The software included with this book is stored in a compressed form. You need to run the installation program to install the disk to your hard drive.

> **Note:** To install the files on the disk, you'll need at least 2.5Mb of free space on you hard drive.

1. From the DOS prompt, type <*drive*>**INSTALL** and press Enter (<*drive*> is the letter of the drive that contains the installation disk). For example, if the disk is in drive B:, type **B:INSTALL** and press Enter. Follow the on-screen directions in the install program.
2. You'll be given the option to change to the drive in which the programs will be installed. If you want to change to a drive other than C:, press Enter and select from the list of available drives.
3. Choose the Start Installation selection. The program will begin installing the files to the /DOS6DG directory of your hard drive.

   When the files have been installed, the file README will appear. It contains information on the files and programs that were installed. When you finish reading the file, press the Escape key.
4. Press any key to exit the install program.

> **Note:** You'll find information on 4DOS and the TRS Utilities in the section located behind this page. To install 4DOS, you must run the special 4DOS install program on the floppy disk. From the DOS prompt, type <*drive*>**4DOSINST** and press Enter (<*drive*> is the letter of the drive that contains the installation disk). For example, if the disk is in drive B:, type **B:INSTALL** and press Enter.
>
> Follow the on-screen directions in the install program. It will guide you through the installation of 4DOS.

Disk information

This section contains information on the bonus programs included on the disk—4DOS and the TSR Utilities.

- The TRS Utilities are © 1986, 1991 by Kim Kokkonen of Turbo Power Software. Although these programs are copyrighted, you may distribute them freely as long as you do not sell them or include them with other software that you sell.
- 4DOS is © 1988-1993 by JP Software, Inc. It is distributed as shareware. This means that you can use 4DOS on an evaluation basis, but you need to register the program if you wish to continue using the program.

Shareware is software distributed on a "try before you buy" basis. This method of distributing software works, because enough people have been honorable and have paid the registration fees for the shareware programs they use regularly. Please join their ranks by registering 4DOS if you find it to be useful.

As long as shareware works, shareware authors will continue to create and update their products. And the users of those programs will continue to have first-rate software available with the option of trying it before committing to buying it.

4DOS

Author: JP Software
P.O. Box 1470
E. Arlington, MA 02174
(617) 646-3975

Manual: 4DOS.DOC

4DOS is a command interpreter or "DOS Shell," and it is a complete replacement for COMMAND.COM.4DOS was designed so that you don't have to change your computing habits or unlearn anything to use it. It also offers dozens of features that DOS alone doesn't have. This version of 4DOS has been updated to work with DOS 6.

> **Note:** To get started quickly with 4DOS, read the file README.DOC. The file ORDERINF.DOC contains information on ordering the registered version of 4DOS.

4DOS understands all of the commands from MS-DOS and adds to them. Its purpose is to make DOS easier to use and much more powerful and versatile, without requiring you to use or learn a new program, a new set of commands, or a new style of work.

Memory usage with 4DOS is improved compared to MS-DOS because 4DOS can take advantage of extended memory, expanded memory, and memory managers. If you load both 4DOS and the environment "high," 4DOS will use only 256 bytes of base memory, less than any version of the traditional DOS command processor, COMMAND.COM.

Full-screen, context-sensitive help is available for all 4DOS commands and all DOS utilities. The F1 key accesses the help system from the 4DOS prompt. This help system is cross-referenced and includes examples.

If you want to take 4DOS for a spin without performing a complete installation, see the Guided Tour beginning on page 18 of the manual.

TSR Utilities

Author: Kim Kokkonen
TurboPower Software
P.O. Box 49009
Colorado Springs, CO 80949-9009
(719) 260-6641

Manual: TSR.DOC

The TSR Utilities are a collection of programs useful for managing DOS memory, particularly for managing memory-resident programs. The most popular use of these utilities is for removing TSRs from memory without rebooting the PC.

The TSR Utilities include the following 11 programs:

- MARK marks a position in memory above which TSR's can be released.
- RELEASE removes TSR's from memory.
- FMARK performs the same function as MARK but uses less memory by keeping its data in a disk file.
- MARKNET works like MARK, but saves a more complete picture of system status (for use with networks, primarily).

- RELNET removes TSR's marked with MARKNET.
- WATCH is a TSR itself that keeps records of other TSRs.
- DISABLE disables or reactivates TSRs, leaving them in memory.
- RAMFREE shows how much RAM memory is available.
- MAPMEM shows loaded memory resident programs.
- DEVICE shows loaded device drivers.
- EATMEM uses up memory for controlled program testing.